Claudia Maienborn, Klaus von Heusinger and Paul Portner (Eds.)
Semantics – Interfaces

This volume is part of a larger set of handbooks to Semantics

1   **Semantics: Foundations, History and Methods**
    Klaus von Heusinger, Claudia Maienborn, Paul Portner (eds.)

2   **Semantics: Lexical Structures and Adjectives**
    Claudia Maienborn, Klaus von Heusinger, Paul Portner (eds.)

3   **Semantics: Theories**
    Claudia Maienborn, Klaus von Heusinger, Paul Portner (eds.)

4   **Semantics: Noun Phrases and Verb Phrases**
    Paul Portner, Klaus von Heusinger, Claudia Maienborn (eds.)

5   **Semantics: Sentence and Information Structure**
    Paul Portner, Claudia Maienborn, Klaus von Heusinger (eds.)

6   **Semantics: Interfaces**
    Claudia Maienborn, Klaus von Heusinger, Paul Portner (eds.)

7   **Semantics: Typology, Diachrony and Processing**
    Klaus von Heusinger, Claudia Maienborn, Paul Portner (eds.)

Semantics
Interfaces

Edited by
Claudia Maienborn
Klaus von Heusinger
Paul Portner

DE GRUYTER
MOUTON

ISBN 978-3-11-058723-4
e-ISBN (PDF) 978-3-11-058984-9
e-ISBN (EPUB) 978-3-11-058729-6

Library of Congress Cataloging-in-Publication Data
Names: Maienborn, Claudia, editor. | Heusinger, Klaus von, editor. | Portner,
  Paul, editor.
Title: Semantics : interfaces / edited by Claudia Maienborn,
  Klaus von Heusinger, Paul Portner.
Description: Berlin ; Boston : De Gruyter, [2019] | Series: Mouton reader |
  Includes bibliographical references and index.
Identifiers: LCCN 2018031291 (print) | LCCN 2018057957 (ebook) | ISBN
  9783110589849 (electronic Portable Document Format (pdf) | ISBN
  9783110587234 (paperback) | ISBN 9783110589849 (e-book pdf) | ISBN
  9783110587296 (e-book epub)
Subjects: LCSH: Semantics. | BISAC: LANGUAGE ARTS & DISCIPLINES / Linguistics
  / Semantics.
Classification: LCC P325 (ebook) | LCC P325 .S37995 2019 (print) | DDC
  401/.43--dc23
LC record available at https://lccn.loc.gov/2018031291

Bibliographic information published by the Deutsche Nationalbibliothek
The Deutsche Nationalbibliothek lists this publication in the Deutsche Nationalbibliografie;
detailed bibliographic data are available in the Internet at http://dnb.dnb.de.

© 2019 Walter de Gruyter GmbH, Berlin/Boston
Cover image: tonymax/iStock / Getty Images Plus
Typesetting: Integra Software Services Pvt. Ltd.
Printing and Binding: CPI books GmbH, Leck

www.degruyter.com

Contents

Hubert Truckenbrodt
1 **Semantics of intonation** —— 1

Paul Kiparsky and Judith Tonhauser
2 **Semantics of inflection** —— 41

Rochelle Lieber
3 **Semantics of derivational morphology** —— 75

Susan Olsen
4 **Semantics of compounds** —— 103

Heidi Harley
5 **Semantics in Distributed Morphology** —— 143

Arnim von Stechow
6 **Syntax and semantics: An overview** —— 169

Dieter Wunderlich
7 **Operations on argument structure** —— 233

Helen de Hoop
8 **Type shifting** —— 277

Paul Kay and Laura A. Michaelis
9 **Constructional meaning and compositionality** —— 293

Gennaro Chierchia, Danny Fox, and Benjamin Spector
10 **Scalar implicature as a grammatical phenomenon** —— 325

Katarzyna M. Jaszczolt
11 **Semantics/pragmatics boundary disputes** —— 368

Thomas Ede Zimmermann
12 **Context dependence** —— 403

Holger Diessel
13 **Deixis and demonstratives** —— 463

David Beaver and Bart Geurts
14 **Presupposition** —— 494

Mandy Simons
15 **Implicature** —— 529

Gerhard Jäger
16 **Game theory in semantics and pragmatics** —— 563

Christopher Potts
17 **Conventional implicature and expressive content** —— 598

Index —— 623

Hubert Truckenbrodt
1 Semantics of intonation

1   Introduction: between prosody/intonation and meaning —— 1
2   Intonation in declaratives —— 6
3   Intonation in interrogatives —— 14
4   Other tune meanings and related issues —— 33
5   Summary —— 36
6   References —— 37

Abstract: This article concentrates on the meaning of intonation contours in English. It presents and combines results of Pierrehumbert and Hirschberg (1990) and Bartels (1999), among others, and adds new suggestions to issues that are unresolved there. In the resulting account, the H* tone (often found in a falling contour) requires a salient proposition that the speaker is adding to the common ground; the H- tone (often found in a rising contour) requires a salient proposition that the speaker is putting up for question. The speaker- and addressee parameters employed by the intonation are shared with the interpretation of pronouns. The discussion concentrates on intonation in declaratives and in a range of interrogatives. It includes the role of intonation in vocatives and in echo questions.

1 Introduction: between prosody/intonation and meaning

Section 1.1. introduces to the mediating role of syntax between prosody and meaning. Section 1.2. places intonation in this picture and introduces to the analysis of intonation. The remainder of the article concentrates on the meaning of intonation contours in English.

1.1 Prosody and meaning

When we parse a sentence, prosody and intonation seem to have a variety of effects on the interpretation of the sentence. Consider the prosodic divisions '|' in the example (1) from Hirschberg (2004). (1a) has a compound reading of *rice wine*, i.e. a total of two ingredients are to be stirred in. In (1b), three ingredients, i.e. rice and wine and seasonings, are to be stirred in.

(1) a. Stir in rice wine | and seasonings.
    b. Stir in rice | wine | and seasonings.

Yet in the classical conception of generative grammar in (2) (e.g. Chomsky 1981, 1995) there is no direct connection between prosody/intonation and semantics. Instead, the syntactic (surface) structure is mapped, on the one hand, to LF and semantic interpretation, on the other hand, to PF, a phonetic form, which is standardly taken to be preceded by a component of postlexical phonology. The PF-side of grammar includes, at the sentence level, phrasal stress and prosodic divisions of the sentence (Truckenbrodt 2007, Selkirk 2011) as well as a sentence melody (intonation, see below).

(2) semantics ← LF ← s-structure/spellout → prosody/tones (phonology) → phonetics

In this conception (to which this article adheres) any effect of intonation on the interpretation is indirect and mediated by the syntactic structure. For the distinction in (1) this is illustrated in (3). Different syntactic structures in (3b) are separately mapped to different prosodic structures in (3a), and to different schematic semantic structures in (3c). For the mapping to prosody, we may invoke the constraint that *the right edge of each lexical XP introduces a prosodic division* (Selkirk 1986, 2000). (3b) shows the relevant NPs of the two syntactic structures, (3a) shows the prosodic divisions derived from them. In the compound case on the left, the first right edge of an NP follows the compound *rice wine*, and introduces a prosodic boundary. In the case on the right, there are right edges of NPs after *rice* and after *wine*, which each introduce a prosodic division.

(3) a. PF   rice wine | and seasonings | rice | wine | and seasonings |
    b. syn   [[rice wine]$_N$$_{NP}$ and [seasonings]$_{NP}$ [rice]$_{NP}$ [wine]$_{NP}$ and [seasonings]$_{NP}$
    c. sem   1   2   1   2   3

Syntax thus feeds prosody (3b-to-3a), but it independently also feeds semantics (3b-to-3c). The syntactic structure on the left is interpreted by the semantic rules as a list of two elements in (3c), the first of which is a compound. The syntactic structure on the right is semantically interpreted as a three-member list in (3c). As long as semanticists and phonologists agree on the syntactic structure that feeds both components, they can each work out their side of the issue.

This is not a parsing model, but a model of tacit knowledge of grammar. It nevertheless makes detailed predictions for parsing. For example, a prosodic boundary between *rice* and *wine* can only be derived from the right edge of an NP there; it therefore disambiguates in favor of the syntactic structure on the right in (3), with semantic interpretation accordingly.

In another class of cases, this model has led to specific analytic choices. Consider the phenomenon of focus (see Rooth 1992, article 10 [Semantics: Sentence and Information Structure] (Hinterwimmer) *Information structure*). (4) shows standard assignment of sentence stress on the right in English (Chomsky & Halle 1968) in a neutral context. (5) shows how the semantic/pragmatic presence of a particular context forces sentence stress retraction to the sentence subject.

(4) A: What happened?
    B: Mary invited JOHN

(5) A: Who invited John?
    B: [MARY]$_F$ invited John

As suggested by Jackendoff (1972), the phenomenon is modeled by postulating a syntactic feature F, which is interpreted both in the prosody and in the semantics. F is marked in (5). The prosodic consequence, according to Jackendoff, is attraction of sentence stress, as in (5). The semantic interpretation has later been developed in the influential work of Rooth (1992). F requires the contextual presence of one or more alternatives that semantically share the background of the focus (in the cases discussed here: the non-focused parts of the sentence). In (5), they must share the background [x invited John] and be alternatives insofar they differ in x from the focus. These alternatives are in (5) alternative possible answers to the question: *Jane invited John, Sue invited John*, etc. Given Jackendoff's analysis in terms of the syntactic feature F, the analysis fits into the architecture of grammar in (2) in the same way as the analysis of (1) in (3): Syntactic elements (XPs, F) have consequences for prosody and have consequences for semantics. Different prosody ((1a)/(1b)), ((4)/(5)) reflects different syntax, which feeds into different semantic interpretations. Next to F(ocus), other information structure related features that have been argued to mediate between prosody and semantics are C(ontrastive) T(opic) (Büring 2003) and G(ivenness) (Féry & Samek-Lodovici 2006). Independent evidence for the syntactic nature of these features comes from their interaction with syntactic phenomena. For example, a natural class of focus movement and wh-movement to the same position is often analyzed in terms of the feature F (Haida 2007; see Truckenbrodt 2012, 2013 for the prosodic consequences of such a generalized F).

These information structure categories can show complex interactions with the semantic interpretation. Büring (1995: 109ff) accounts for the example (6) from Jacobs (1984) (the additions on the right are added here). With stress-placement as shown, the sentence only has a scope reconstruction reading (not all politicians are corrupt), while other stress-patterns also allow surface scope (e.g. *alle Politiker sind NICHT korrupt*, 'all politicians are NOT corrupt').

(6) ALLE$_F$ Politiker sind NICHT$_F$ korrupt   [aber MANCHE...SCHON...]   (German)
     ALL$_F$ politicians are NOT$_F$ corrupt   [but SOME...ARE....]

For the purpose at hand, the insight of Büring's account is rendered in a simplified form that employs only F (as marked in (6)), not the topics of Jacobs' and Büring's discussion. The reconstructed reading leads to an implicature that provides the required alternatives to the focused elements: *Not all . . .* implicates that *some . . . are . . . .* In this implicature, the complex focus <all, not> finds the required contextual alternative <some, VERUM/are> with pairwise contrast (*all* vs. *some*, *not* vs. *verum*/ARE). The surface scope reading does not lead to a comparable implicature that would provide alternatives to the focus <all, not>. It is therefore ruled out by the alternative semantics of focus, which requires that the focus have contextual alternatives.

Pronoun interpretation also interacts with stress assignment, as in the classical example (7) from Lakoff (1971).

(7) a. JOHN$_i$ called BILL$_k$ a REPUBLICAN and then he$_i$ INSULTED him$_k$.
     b. JOHN$_i$ called BILL$_k$ a REPUBLICAN and then HE$_k$ insulted HIM$_i$.

Lakoff's idea was that (7a) shows the unmarked construal, parallel between second and first clause, while stress on the pronouns leads to a marked interpretation, here the choice of inverse antecedents (see also Hirschberg & Ward 1991). The alternative semantics of focus leads to a more comprehensive account of the marked case (7b). A complex focus <HE, HIM> is formed with the background [x insulted y]. The context must provide this background [x insulted y] with an instantiation of <x, y> different from the focus, i.e. an alternative to the focus. The context provides [x insulted y] on the assumption that John's calling Bill a republican constitutes an insult, with <x, y> = <John, Bill>. Under parallel binding of the pronouns, the alternative <John$_i$, Bill$_k$> would be referentially identical to the focus <HE$_i$, HIM$_k$>. Under inverse binding, the alternative <John$_i$, Bill$_k$> differs in reference from the focus <HE$_k$, HIM$_i$> as required by the alternative semantics of focus.

For semantic stress-effects of this kind, we do not seem to require additional connections between prosody/intonation and semantics in the grammar. It seems that the correct way of analyzing them is in terms of a modular account that relies on the indirect prosody-semantics connection given to us in the theory of F and CT and G. See also Baltazani (2002) and Ishihara (2010) for investigations in this domain.

1.2 Intonation and meaning

The remainder of this article is about the meanings of intonation contours, largely concentrating on English. I primarily draw on Pierrehumbert & Hirschberg (1990) and Bartels (1999), who (building on Gussenhoven 1984) treat intonational meaning at a level of abstraction that is high and interesting enough for a semantics handbook. They show a number of differences in their conclusions and a range of open issues. I discuss what I think are the best parts of both and add some new elements, including a more detailed formalization in terms of presuppositions. I concentrate on H*/L* and H-/L-, central elements of the English intonation system for which a formal semantic account is within reach.

To begin with, consider (8), which shows that rising intonation [/] turns an elliptical utterance into a question and falling intonation leads to an interpretation as an assertion.

(8) John and Mary are taking a break from work. John is getting up and looks at Mary.
    a. John: Coffee [/]   (expressing: 'Do you want coffee?')
    b. Mary: Coffee [\]   (expressing: 'I want coffee.')

I assume the intonation analysis of English in Pierrehumbert (1980), Beckman & Pierrehumbert (1986). It has become the starting point for many investigations across languages, see Gussenhoven (2004), Ladd (2008). In this approach intonation contours are analyzed in terms of discrete H(igh) and L(ow) tones. The rise as in (8a) will stand for the sequence of tones L*H-H%, the fall in (8b) for the sequence H*L-L%. English contours from the nuclear stress to the right edge of an intonation phrase are composed of three tonal elements: First, a *pitch accent* on the nuclear stress; I concentrate on H* and L* in this article (see section 4.3 for other pitch accents). The same pitch accent often also occurs on preceding stressed elements as in (9) in section 2 below. The nuclear pitch accent is followed by a sequence of two edge tones. The first edge tone, H- or L-, is found in the area in between the nuclear stress and the end of the intonation phrase. The second edge tone, H% or L% is found at the right edge of the intonation phrase. The high and low regions defined by these tones can be seen separated in time in (10) and (12) below. H-/L- are analyzed as edge tones of the intermediate phrase, a smaller prosodic unit. They can also occur without the following H%/L% as in (13).

These tonal elements are conceived of as abstract morphemes (Gussenhoven 1984: ch. 6, Pierrehumbert & Hirschberg 1990, Bartels 1999, see also Bolinger 1957, 1989). The phonological side of these are the H or L tones that define high and low areas of the sentence melody. The semantic side is the semantic impact they bring to the utterance. What we want to get out of the semantic side is that (8a) constitutes a question and (8b) an assertion. I believe that these intonational morphemes need to be attached to the syntactic structure to fit into the architecture described here: As part of the syntactic structure, their semantic and phonological specifications are fed into the LF and PF components for interpretation. A specific suggestion for syntactic attachment is formulated in section 3.2.

There is a large array of descriptive observations in the literature about tunes that can be used on English example sentences and the nuances they seem to convey. The work of Bolinger (1957, 1986, 1989) in particular shows the great flexibility of tune choices. There are interactions with the syntactic sentence type, but the intonation often follows what the speaker wants to express. Gussenhoven (1984: ch. 6) initiated a search for more abstract meanings of elements of intonation contours in terms of the *common ground* (see Stalnaker 1978, 2002 and Clark 1996 on the notion common ground, though Gussenhoven employed a somewhat more narrow concept). The more specific suggestions of this search that I employ as a starting point are developed by Pierrehumbert & Hirschberg (1990), in the following *PH90*, and by Bartels (1999), in the following *B99*. We will see that B99 provides an approach to the flexibility of tune assignment. I often focus on cornerstone observations that seem to be promising for inferences about the tune meanings.

The intonation of declaratives is discussed in section 2, and the intonation of interrogatives in section 3. Related issues of tune meanings are addressed in section 4. The terms *declarative* and *interrogative* are here employed for syntactic sentence forms. The term *question* will sometimes also refer to the speech act.

2 Intonation in declaratives

In this section the intonation of declaratives is discussed. Section 2.1. is about falling (H*L-) and rising (L*H-) intonation in declaratives. Section 2.2. is about low intonation (L*L-) and section 2.4. about high intonation (H*H-) in declaratives.

These latter two sections are separated by section 2.3. on the nature of intonational meanings, which will be crucial at that point.

2.1 H*L- as assertive, L*H- as non-assertive

Bolinger (1957) distinguishes three pitch accents. His A accent, which he calls 'assertive', has two versions that would be analyzed as H*L-L% and H*L-H% in Pierrehumbert's analysis. PH90: 290 also see these two as "neutral declarative intonation", "appropriate when S's goal is to convey information". H*L-L% marks the standard assertion, as in (9) (PH90: 286).

(9)

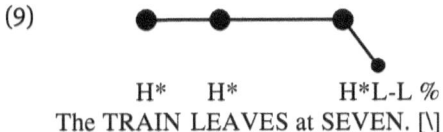

H*   H*   H*L-L %
The TRAIN LEAVES at SEVEN. [\]

H*L-H% conveys assertion plus something else. The 'something else' may be plain continuation as in (10) (Beckman & Ayers 1993). The contour is also called *continuation rise*. However, it may also occur at the end of an utterance and add a note of uncertainty to what is asserted, as in (11) (B99: 34).

(10)

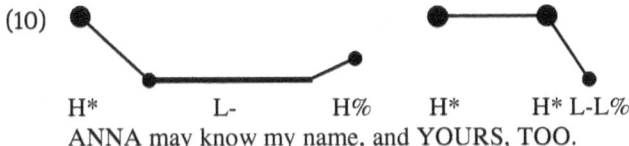

H*   L-   H%   H*   H* L-L%
ANNA may know my name, and YOURS, TOO.

(11) A: What's your opinion—can we leave the car parked here?
  H*   L-   H%
  B: I THINK it's alright.

The inverse contour, the rise, has its prototypical instantiation in L*H-(H%). L*H- is close to the C accent of Bolinger (1957), which he calls "anti-assertive". L*H- is possible in declarative questions like (12) (Beckman & Ayers 1993, see also Bartels 1999: 228ff). The example (13) (PH90: 292) shows particularly clearly how the speaker can distance himself from the content with L*H-(H%) by turning declaratives into questions. (In this example, intermediate phrases are marked by round brackets, intonation phrases by square brackets.)

(12)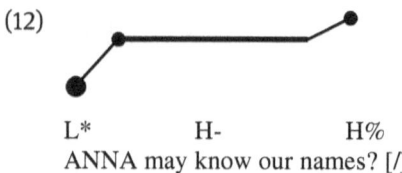
L*   H-   H%
ANNA may know our names? [/]

(13) Russian émigré joke; a staunch old Bolshevik is forced to confess publicly and reads:

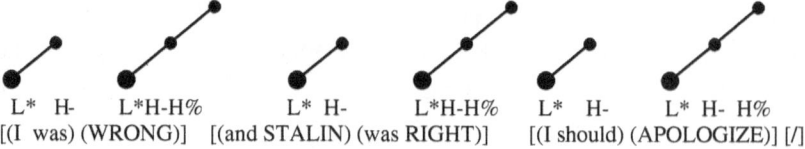

L* H-   L*H-H%   L* H-   L*H-H%   L* H-   L* H- H%
[(I was) (WRONG)]   [(and STALIN) (was RIGHT)]   [(I should) (APOLOGIZE)] [/]

The assertiveness of the fall resides in the H*L- combination according to Gussenhoven (1984), in the H* according to PH90, and in the L- according to B99. I find the position of PH90 convincing and review their motivation in connection with the additional combinations L*L- and H*H- on declaratives in the following sections. In addition, I develop a modification of the suggestion of B99. In the modification, H- has a question-related meaning. To begin with, (12) and (13) are questions and are marked by H-, while (9)–(11) are not questions and are marked by L-.

2.2 L*L- on declaratives: not new and not questioning

The examples with L*L- in (14) and (15) differ from both groups H*L- and L*H- above.

(14) [Question about wishes for birthday presents, where the desire for a Pavoni espresso machine is already mutually believed]
L*   L*   L* L-H%
WELL, I'd LIKE a PAVONI ... [__/]

(15) A: Let's order Chateaubriand for two.

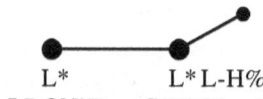

L*   L* L-H%
B: I DON'T eat BEEF [__/]   [conveys that A should have had this in mind]

These examples from PH90: 292f share with the H*L- cases in (9)–(11), with which they share the L-, that they are not question-like utterances. This separates them from the H- cases in (12) and (13), which have a clearly questioning flavor.

The L*L- cases also differ from the H*L- cases in (9)–(11). As pointed out by PH90, the H* in regular assertions like (9)–(11) correlates with the newness of the propositions presented there. The L* in (14) and (15), on the other hand, signals that the proposition is already given in the common ground. Thus, (14) is the repetition of an already jointly known wish. The reply in (15) could be said with H*L-L% in which case it would present this information as new. The realization with L* in (15) has an insulting effect according to PH90, because it suggests that the addressee should have had this in mind.

Adapting the suggestion that Gussenhoven (1984: ch. 6) makes for the fall, PH90 make the notion of newness conveyed by H* more precise in suggesting that the speaker seeks to add this information to the common ground, the shared beliefs or shared knowledge of speaker and addressee. This means that it must be new relative to the common ground. For example, in (16), (PH90: 290), the speaker may assume that the information is not new to the addressee. The speaker may still suggest to add this to the common ground in the sense that it is then also mutually believed. For this to work, the information must be new in the common ground, i.e. not already mutually believed.

(16)

H*   L-L%   H*   H*   H* L-L%
You TURKEY [\]   You DELIBERATELY DELETED my FILES [\]

There are then two reasons not to mark something as new in that sense and to choose L* instead: it may not be believed by the speaker at the time of the utterance, as in (12) and (13), or it may be believed by the speaker but taken to be in the common ground already, as in (14) and (15). In both cases it makes sense that the speaker does not want to instruct the addressee to add the proposition to the common ground.

2.3 Greetings and vocatives: relevance of salient propositions

This section makes a digression concerning the domain on which intonational meanings operate, by way of preparation for the discussion of H*H- on declaratives in the following section. What do intonational meanings operate on? PH90: 289 illustrate their idea with the example [George(H*) likes pie(H*)]. Here an open expression [x likes y] is formed into which x = George(H*) and y = pie(H*) are instantiated. The meaning of H* operates on the instantiation of the elements carrying H*. It is not easy to distinguish this suggestion from that of Hobbs (1990), who simply assumes that intonational meanings operate on the propositional content.

An important innovation was argued for by B99. She postulated it for the assertive meaning she assigns to L-. This assertive meaning, she argued, operates on a salient proposition (rather than on the compositional at-issue content). While her assertive meaning for L- is not adopted here, her discovery that intonational meaning can operate on salient propositions is generally assumed for all intonational meaning here. Many of Bartels' arguments carry over to the current account, as will be seen in section 3. In the current section initial motivation for it is shown in connection with vocatives and greetings. For these the deployment of salient propositions leads to an arguably better fit of these cases with the meaning of H* in PH90 than the discussion by PH90 (with different propositions to modify) was able to provide.

According to PH90, the contour involving L* in (17) is chosen because there is no content of the greeting that could be added to the common ground. They call these elements 'extrapropositional'.

(17)   L*   L*   L-H%
         GOOD MORNING [__/]

Notice, however, that greetings with H* as in (18) are entirely possible. A talk show host would greet his audience with the intonation in (18b). This would be excluded by PH90's treatment, where there is no propositional content to be added to the common ground.

(18) a. H*   H*   L-L%   b. H*   H*   L-L%
         GOOD MORNING [\]   GOOD EVENING [\] ladies and gentlemen!

Employing salient proposition, we can say that the intonational meanings operate on the salient propositions 'I wish you a good morning' and 'I wish you a good evening' in these cases. This is marked as to be added to the common ground in (18). In (17), we could adopt PH90's original explanation, assuming the presence of content is optional. However, it is also possible that the speaker presents his wishing a good morning as given in the sense of predictable from the context: 'We both knew that I would wish you a good morning'. It might be taken to be predictable from the time of day and the fact of the encounter, or from similar greetings on earlier days. This may lead to the conventionalized flavor of the intonation pattern in (17).

I turn to vocatives. PH90: 293f point out that *Anna* is spoken with H* as in (19a) in case the speaker does not yet have Anna's attention, and with L* as in (19b) if the speaker already has Anna's attention. When the vocative follows the clause as in (19c), L* is the only choice.

(19) a. H*   L-   H*   L-L%   b.   L* H-   H*   L-L%
        ANNA [\] your LUNCH is ready   ANNA [/] your LUNCH is ready
     c.   H*   L-   L*L-L%
        Your LUNCH is ready, ANNA [__]

PH90's analysis of this is preliminary: The frequent use of L* harmonizes with their understanding that L* here marks an extrapropositional element. However, the use of H* in (19a) is not compatible with a more precise analysis. An extrapropositional element would not provide propositional content that the addressee could be instructed to add to the common ground.

A more complete account can be given in terms of salient propositions. The salient proposition is the one that underlies the interpretation of the vocative: 'Anna is the addressee of the utterance', or, more informally, 'I am talking to you, Anna'. Where this is common ground, the speaker has Anna's attention. Where the speaker does not have Anna's attention, it is not common ground that Anna is the addressee: Anna may not be aware of being the addressee, or the speaker may not realize that Anna is aware of being the addressee. In (19a), then, Anna's being the addressee is not common ground initially. H* is used as an instruction to add this proposition to the common ground. Notice that the addition of this to the common ground is typically equivalent to getting Anna's attention in two ways: (a) by way of H* marking 'I am talking to you' as to be added to the common ground, and (b) by making her listen (i.e. getting her to add something to the common ground in the first place). If the proposition is already in the common ground, i.e. if the speaker already has Anna's attention as in (19b), L* is used. (We may take the medial H- in (19b) to convey continuation, see section 4.2.) For the analysis of (19c), a context in the sense of Kaplan (1989) for the interpretation of the sentence is assumed. It is taken to include the parameters S(peaker) and A(ddressee). This context is relevant (a) to the interpretation of pronouns, for example 2nd person is [+A, -S], (b) for the identification of the addressee of the utterance in the meaning of the vocative and (c) for the identification of S and A in the intonational meanings (more on this in section 3.2). In (19c) the sentence that precedes the vocative is addressed to Anna. Anna is the addressee A of that sentence. We know this because addressee-reference to Anna is possible with second-person pronouns in that sentence. This happens to be illustrated with the pronoun 'your' in (19c). Therefore, by the end of the sentence, Anna's being the addressee can not be presented as new information any more. L* is therefore the only choice on the final vocative.

Portner (2007) assigns to vocatives expressive meaning in the sense of Potts (2005) (see also article 17 [this volume] (Potts) *Conventional implicature and expressive content*): either a request for attention ('calls') or a reiteration of addresseehood ('tags' and 'addresses', the latter with an additional expressive element). He assumes that the classification rests on the intonation. In current terms the requests for attention are the vocatives marked H*. The current discussion is compatible with Portner's basing the distinction on the intonation. It seems that the intonation can derive the request for attention and the reiteration of addresseehood from a single underlying vocative meaning, as shown above. See Portner (2007) for other aspects of vocatives.

In summary, the pitch accents on simple greetings and vocatives fit with the analysis of H* in PH90, if the analysis is cast in terms of salient propositions. Since they are still assertion-like and not questions (cf. also the L- in (17)), the motivation for choosing L* is that the relevant proposition is already in the common ground, or presented that way.

Equipped with a notion of what intonational meanings operate on, we now return to the discussion of declaratives. After H*L-, L*H- and L*L- we will now address H*H- on declaratives. We apply our understanding of what intonational meanings operate on to declaratives as follows. In declaratives, the most salient proposition is the content of the declarative. It is therefore the first choice for intonational meanings to operate on. However, other choices are not excluded, in particular where the first choice is blocked, as we will see.

2.4 H*H-: news and a question

Consider then the sequence H*H- on declaratives. H* asserts the content of the declarative and H- adds a separate question. In (20), the impact of the utterance is paraphrased by PH90: 290 as 'My name is Mark Liberman, and are you expecting me, or, am I in the right place?'. Similarly, (21) is an utterance by a young woman who was asked after a movie whether she liked it. It conveys, according to PH90: 290, 'I thought it was good, but do you agree with me?'

(20) M. L. approaches a receptionist to find out
whether he is in the right place for his appointment:

         H*   H* H- H%
My name is MARK LIBERMAN [–/]

(21)   H*   H* H-H%
       I THOUGHT it was GOOD [–/]

PH90 point out that the impact is different from L*H-H% (lacking the assertive H*). Use of L*H-H% in (20) would suggest that Mark Liberman has forgotten his name, and in (21) that the speaker has forgotten her impression of the movie. This supports the assertive role of H* in (20) and (21).

Hirschberg & Ward (1995) discuss similar cases of H*H-H% on declaratives, including the contrast in (22). In (22a) the caller, in addition to asserting her whereabouts, asks the DJ something along the lines of whether the DJ has heard of Skokie. A similar question is not possible in (22), since everyone has heard of Chicago.

(22)   Chicago radio station DJ: Good morning Susan. Where are you calling from?
       a.   H*H-H%
            Caller: I'm calling from SKOKIE? [–/]
       b. #   H*H-H%
            Caller: I'm calling from CHICAGO? [–/]

Hirschberg & Ward (1995) suggest that H*H-H% is employed (in addition to the assertion) "to elicit information about whether the hearer can relate this propositional content to the hearer's own private belief space" (Hirschberg & Ward 1995: 410). They suggest that this component (though not the assertive part) is also present in the L*H-H% contour. I adopt the suggestion that the rise (here: H-) seeks to "elicit information", i.e. generates a question. I also agree in regard to the content of the question that arises in the examples at hand. I differ from Hirschberg & Ward (1995) only in that I think that we need to leave the choice of what is asked partly to the pragmatics. In (12) and in (13), the question that is posed is not about the connection to the addressee's knowledge. Rather, the content of the proposition is put up for question there. I suggest that H- puts up a salient proposition for question. In (12) and (13), this is the content of the declarative. In (20)–(22), the content of the declarative is marked as to be added to the common ground by H*, and so cannot be simultaneously put up for question. Another salient proposition is therefore marked as put up for question. It is contextually chosen. Since utterances generally call on the addressee to connect what is being said to their beliefs, and since questions generally elicit addressee beliefs or knowledge, it seems reasonable that the most salient proposition that might be recoverably asked about is typically one in the connection between what is being asserted and the addressee's relation to it, as in (20)–(22a). In the absence of such a salient proposition, as in (22b), it is not recoverable what proposition H- might mark, and infelicity results. I will return to this infelicity below.

Notice that (20)–(22) add striking support for Bartels' discovery of intonational meaning in terms of salient propositions. The propositions on which the meaning of H- operates are very clearly not the literal meanings of these utterances, and are very clearly contextually chosen in these cases.

In comparison with other contours, H*H- in (20)–(22) shares with H*L- in (9)–(11) the newness of the asserted proposition, in contrast to the L* cases in (12) and (13) (not believed) and in (14), (15), and (19b) (given). Thus H* plausibly marks a proposition as new in the sense of 'to be added to the common ground'.

H*H- in (20)–(22) shares with L*H- in (12) and (13) the questioning impact. This is here attributed to the H- that these cases share. The L- examples in (9)–(11) and in (14), (15), and (19c) do not show the questioning impact.

2.5 Summary: intonation in declaratives

The preceding cases motivate an assignment of meanings to the H tones as in (23). The L tones may be meaningless.

(23) a. H* marks a salient proposition as new in the sense of an instruction by the speaker to add the proposition to the common ground of speaker and addressee.
b. H- marks a salient proposition as put up for question by the speaker.

(23) applies as follows to the four classes we saw. The H*L- assertions in (9)–(11) are marked as to be added to the common ground by H* (and are not put up for question). The L*H- questioning utterances in (12) and (13) are put up for question by H- (and not marked as to be added to the common ground). The L*L- weak assertions in (14), (15) and (19c) are not put up for question (and thus remain statements, perhaps due to the declarative form); they are not marked as to be added to the common ground because their content is assumed to be given. The H*H- cases in (20)–(22) are marked as to be added to the common ground by H*, and a second salient proposition in the context is marked as put up for question by H-.

3 Intonation in interrogatives

The intonation of interrogatives is a complex area. The following sections navigate it by going back and forth between observations from the literature that give the account empirical support and formal semantic suggestions that make the analysis more precise.

Section 3.1. introduces to an elementary puzzle concerning the intonation in interrogatives. It shows how the suggestion about H- developed above approaches this. Section 3.2. offers an implementation of the meanings of H- and H* in terms of presuppositions. Section 3.3. applies the presuppositional analysis to the cases in 3.1. in detail and to other instances of yes/no-questions. Section 3.4. shows how the implicature that there is a true answer to a question is often crucial for an understanding of intonation in interrogatives. Section 3.5. discusses the high-rise in yes/no-questions. Section 3.6. addresses the accommodation of the presuppositional question meanings. Sections 3.7. and 3.8. treat the rise in echo-wh-questions and the friendly rise in wh-questions.

3.1 First interrogative intonation and the relevance of salient propositions

Let us begin the discussion of interrogative intonation with an old puzzle. Yes/no-questions are felt to be typical with rising intonation as in (24a). Wegener (1885) called German rising intonation "Verwunderungston", 'tone of wondering', which we may read as a suggestion that the rise is inherently related to a question. I partly agree. In examples like the elliptical (8a) and the declaratives (12), (13), and (20)–(22), the intonation that includes H- seems to add questioning impact. There is no other source of the questioning impact in sight. However, as pointed out by Kretschmer (1938) in Vienna with comparable German examples, questions are of course not generally marked with a rise. Wh-questions as in (24b) are often felt to be typical with a fall, and alternative questions as in (24c) require the final fall. Thus it would be wrong to tie rising intonation too closely to the questioning speech act. Notice that the interpretation of the alternative question in (24c) has the possible answers {you went to Berlin, you went to Potsdam}. 'Yes' and 'no' are not possible answers. Rising intonation as in (24d) turns this into a yes/no-question with the possible answers {you went to Berlin or to Potsdam ("yes"), you didn't go to Berlin or to Potsdam ("no")}. The use of rising intonation in (24d) is parallel to (24a), except that the proposition that is put up for question in (24d) happens to contain a disjunction.

(24) a. Did you go to BERLIN [/] L*H-(H%)
b. Where did you GO [\] H*L-(L%)
c. Did you go to BERLIN or to POTSDAM [\] H*L-(L%)
d. Did you go to BERLIN or to POTSDAM [/] L*H-(H%)

Deviating from most previous literature (apart from Wegener 1885) I suggest that H- carries questioning meaning after all. My suggestion draws on Bartels' analysis of the contours in (24) to which I return, and on Bartels' insight of the relevance of salient propositions. Implementing the questioning meaning in terms of salient proposition, H- does not mark questions more generally. It only marks a salient proposition as put up for question. It is a primitive question indicating and question generating device that does not have the complexity to keep up with the semantics of interrogatives, which employs sets of propositions (see e.g. Karttunen 1977). Nor does it always come into play when there is a questioning speech act. In (24a) then, the salient proposition 'you went to Berlin' is put up for question, and can be marked as such by H-. Similarly in the yes/no-question (24d), where the salient proposition 'you are going to Berlin or to Potsdam' is put up for question. In (24b) and (24c), no salient proposition is put up for question in a similar fashion. In a first approximation, there is therefore no motivation for employing H- in these cases. The move to assign the stronger questioning meaning (rather than absence of assertion) to H- is motivated by cases like the elliptical (8a) and the declaratives (12), (13), and (20)–(22), all of which are turned into questions by the intonation, without another source of the questioning impact in sight.

For further developing this picture below, I employ a more formal implementation of the relevance of salient propositions. This is developed in the following section.

3.2 A formal implementation of intonational meanings

The relevance of salient propositions in intonational meanings is reminiscent of the relevance of salient individuals to the interpretation of definite descriptions. In the formalization of Heim (1982), this arises for definite descriptions from a presupposition over the referent of a syntactic index. The presupposition can only be satisfied if the index has an antecedent for which the presupposition is true (unless it is accommodated). A salient and unique index is required (Heim 1982: 165, 233–236 for uniqueness). In such an account, the meaning of definite descriptions is stated as in (25). Here g is a variable assignment and i is a syntactic index. Using this as a point of orientation, we may define the meanings of H* and H- in English in (26). S and A stand for speaker and addressee.

(25) $[\![[\text{the NP}]_i]\!]^g$ is defined as $g(i)$ iff $g(i) \in [\![\text{NP}]\!]^g$

(26) Let English have the intonational morphemes <H*, new_j> and <H-, $question_j$>, where j is an index of type proposition. Let these morphemes right-adjoin to a syntactic constituent α. Then (ignoring the phonology in the semantic interpretation):

a. $[\![[\alpha <new_j>]]\!]^{g,S,A}$ is defined as $[\![\alpha]\!]^{g,S,A}$ iff S is adding g(j) to the common ground of S and A.
b. $[\![[\alpha <question_j>]]\!]^{g,S,A}$ is defined as $[\![\alpha]\!]^{g,S,A}$ iff S is putting up g(j) for question.

The interpretations are presuppositions on the interpretation of α. In the typical case, α is an unembedded sentence, the intonational morphemes are taken to be syntactically attached to it, and to contribute a presupposition to its interpretation by (26). The content that the intonational meanings modify is not the meaning of α, but a salient proposition, g(j) in (26). Just as the definite description 'the book' will look for a unique salient antecedent that is a book in the context, so <H*, new_j> will now look for a unique salient antecedent proposition in the context that S adds to the common ground of S and A. The presupposition is satisfied, and the meaning of its sister α defined, if <H*, new_j> finds such an antecedent. (I return to accommodation in section 3.6.) Similarly, <H-, $question_j$> will look for a unique salient antecedent proposition that S puts up for question. We must assume that α is linearly ordered before the intonational morphemes and is interpreted first, so that the salient propositional antecedents for p are those that are salient *after* the interpretation of α. The linear order of course corresponds to the fact that the edge tone H- is a tone of the right, rather than the left edge.

Notice that the logic of search for an antecedent proposition comes out in a more specific way in (26) than in Bartel's more general suggestion that salient propositions are relevant. Consider first our comparison case. In the interpretation of *the book*, the antecedent must be a uniquely salient book. It need not be a uniquely salient individual as such, nor the most salient individual of all. Similarly, the consequence of (26) is that an antecedent proposition for H* is a uniquely salient *speaker-asserted* proposition, not a uniquely salient proposition as such, nor the most salient proposition of all. Similarly, an antecedent proposition for H- is a uniquely salient *proposition put up for question by the speaker*. It need not be the most salient of all salient propositions. This seems to be very reasonable. For example, in *I'm calling from SKOKIE?* in (22a), H* finds a uniquely salient proposition that can be taken to be asserted by the speaker, namely the content of the declarative. H- finds a uniquely salient proposition that can be taken to be put up for question by the speaker, namely something along the lines of *You know Skokie*.

This suggestion is applied to the cases of section 3.1. in the following section and is further pursued after that. Notice for now that there is good evidence that the parameters S and A in (26) are shared between the intonational interpretation and the interpretation of α. This aspect of (26) adequately restricts the interaction of intonation with embedded clauses. I take S and A to be the part of a context in the sense of Kaplan (1989), which also serves for the interpretation of personal pronouns. This correctly restricts intonational meanings to be interpreted relative to the actual speaker and addressee of an utterance, unless S and A shift in case of quotations. Thus in (27a) the final rise cannot be triggered by the embedded question, because its proposition is put up for question by John, not by the speaker. (The parameters S and A have not shifted here: John is still referred to in the third person in the embedded clause.) This is different in (27b), where the quotation can be marked by intonation (Bolinger 1946, Bolinger 1989: 40f). Here the rise is triggered by the embedded yes/no-question "Should I bring a present". With quotational embedding, the parameters S and A shift to those of the quote, as can be seen by the use of a first person pronoun for John in the quote. Thus, the intonational meaning can here be adjoined to the quote (the quote is then α in (26)). The shifted speaker-parameters in the quote (with S = John) then license H-, since the shifted speaker John is putting this proposition up for question. Consider then also (27c). In the first person present, a rise is marginally licensed by such an embedded question, even though the most unmarked intonation would employ a fall that corresponds to the assertive character of the entire utterance. Where the marginal rise is used, the embedded proposition 'I should bring a present' is an antecedent that can be taken to be put up for question by the speaker. The speaker shows by the rising intonation that s/he is not just reporting about her wondering, but putting this proposition up for question in the context of the utterance.

(27) a. John wondered if/whether he should bring a present [\] #[/]
b. John wondered: "Should I bring a present" [/]
c. I wonder if I should bring a present [\] (#)[/]

In short, (26) correctly captures that intonational meanings are interpreted relative to the referents of 'I' and 'you'.

Are the presuppositions in (26) normally satisfied by independent speech act components or do we need to assume that they are typically accommodated? The answer depends on ones favorite assumptions about such independently established speech act components. There are suggestions about them since at least Ross (1970). More recent work includes Gunlogson (2001), Krifka (2001, 2011) and, for German, Gärtner (2000, 2002), Schwabe (2007a,b) and Truckenbrodt (2006a,b). Since there is no established consensus, the issue is largely left open here. I will advance on the following assumptions: Declaratives carry the seeds of assertions in them. Syntactic interrogatives carry the seeds of question speech acts in them. Furthermore, I will argue below that accommodation of the presuppositions in (26) is fairly straightforward. Where it occurs, it will be seen to *establish* a speech act. I will often ignore the issue of presupposition satisfaction vs. accommodation. The presuppositional analysis is primarily motivated indirectly in the parallel to definite descriptions that allows us to make sense of the relevance of salient propositions. An alternative implementation might pursue conventional implicatures in the sense of Potts (2005).

I nevertheless think that there are cases that are suggestive of a search for unique and recoverable antecedents, in the way familiar from definite descriptions. For one thing, we can now analyze (22b) as a failed search for an antecedent that results in presupposition failure. It is infelicitous in its context in the same way in which a definite description without an identifiable referent/antecedent is infelicitous in a given context ('Hi Susan, where are you calling from? I am calling from Skokie. # I like the cat.'). For another thing, consider again alternative questions. Why isn't a rise permitted in (24c), given that two propositions are put up for question, 'you went to Berlin' and 'you went to Potsdam'? A plausible answer is that they are parallel and both put up for question, and thus neither of them is uniquely recoverable. This is comparable to definite descriptions. *The raven* in (28) has no unique salient antecedent, since the two antecedents in question are parallel.

(28) A small raven and a large raven were sitting on a fence. # *The raven* opened its wings and . . . .

In summary, a formal implementation of intonational meanings was given in which Bartels' relevance of salient propositions finds its place. H* presupposes that the speaker is adding a proposition to the common ground. H- presupposes that the speaker is putting up a proposition for question. The context parameters S and A are shared with the interpretation of personal pronouns. The relation to these propositions is comparable to the relation between a definite description and its antecedent.

3.3 Applications to the three 'standard' cases and to further yes/no-questions

Let us then account for (24a–c) in the presuppositional analysis. The examples are repeated here as (29a-c).

(29) a. Did you go to BERLIN [/] L*H-(H%)
　　 b. Where did you GO [\] H*L-(L%)
　　 c. Did you go to BERLIN or to POTSDAM [\] H*L-(L%)

H- in (29a) now looks for a proposition put up for question by the speaker. It finds 'you went to Berlin', which can be taken to be put up for question due to the sentence form. The presupposition of H- is then satisfied for this proposition as its antecedent.

The absence of H- in (29b) corresponds to the absence of an obvious proposition put up for question here. However, what is asserted by H* here? According to Bartels, the intonation of (29b) (for her: the L- tone) asserts the existential implicature of the wh-question, here: 'you went somewhere'. In the current account: By (26a), H* looks for a speaker-asserted proposition. It finds the implicature that 'you went somewhere' is true. (The difference in strength of commitment between the actual implicature and the assertion that is required by the presupposition of H* may well be accommodated; see section 3.6. on accommodation.)

What is asserted by H* in (29c)? According to Bartels, the intonation here asserts the uninverted interrogative 'you went to Berlin or to Potsdam'. In the current account: H* in (26c) looks for a speaker-asserted proposition, and finds the speaker assumption 'you went to Berlin or to Potsdam'. (I return to the nature of this assumption.)

There are also uses of the syntactic yes/no-question form in which the salient proposition is asserted by H*. An example from Bartels:

(30) A: Let's start the meeting. John called to say he'd be late because he had trouble getting his car started.
                            H* L-L%
B: Does John have a CAR now [\] I didn't know that. (Bartels 1999: 128)

Here the speaker deploying H* seems to add to the common ground 'John has a car now'.

In a different use of [\] in yes/no-questions, it contributes a sense of "cross-examination" or of "keeping someone to the point" (Schubiger 1958: 63f) as in the examples (31a) and (32a) (B99: 127). Bartels relates this to a salient disjunction of the two possible answers 'yes' and 'no' which she calls *alternative-proposition*. [\] here marks the endorsement of this alternative-proposition, as shown in (31b) and (32b). Bartels (1999: 135) points out that the falling intonation in (33b) has a similar effect of insistence as the addition in (33c), where the disjunction is overt in an alternative question. The salient propositions operated on by the intonation are shown on the right.

(31) a. Prosecutor to witness in court:
                H*   L-L%
    Do you KNOW the defendant? [\]
  b. B99: Due to L-, S asserts: 'A knows the defendant or A doesn't know the defendant'

(32) a. A: I'm sure of it. I have heard it said many times.
$$H^*L\text{-}L\%$$
B: Yes, but did you see it YOURSELF? [\]
b. B99: Due to L-, B asserts: 'A saw it himself or A didn't see it himself'

(33) a. Did you buy it? [/]   (p = A bought it)
b. Did you buy it [\]   (p = A bought it or A didn't buy it)
c. Did you buy it or didn't you [\]   (p = A bought it or A didn't buy it)

When does the alternative-proposition come into play? The classical analysis of yes/no-questions [q?] is that they are hidden alternative questions, i.e. their possible answers are {q, not q}, see e.g. Karttunen (1977). Bolinger (1978b) presented interesting arguments against this. His suggestion, put in these terms, is that their set of possible answers is the singleton set {q}. For embedded questions, he distinguishes whether-questions {q, ¬q} from if-questions {q}. Bartels suggests that unembedded yes/no-questions can similarly have either the meaning {q} or the meaning {q, ¬q}. In the former case, q is particularly salient, in the latter case, 'q ∨ ¬q' is particularly salient. Bartels suggests that (31), (32) and (33b) are of the latter kind. The intonation here endorses the alternative proposition, with a sense of "keeping the addressee to the point." These suggestions are adopted here.

Is there some way of adding stability to the assumptions about salient propositions with interrogatives? I believe there is. Showing this in the following section will require another formal excursion.

3.4 The implicature that there is a true answer

A question is a request for the truth among the possible answers defined by the question (Karttunen 1977, Groenendijk & Stokhof 1997). In posing a question, the speaker will normally assume that there is a truth to the matter, i.e. that there is a true answer. In wh-questions, the existential implicature that we saw above is exactly this assumption. In (34a), for example, Mary can be taken to implicate that there is a true answer, i.e. that Bill brought something to the party. This assumption is attributed to the person asking the question, i.e. to Mary in (34a). In (34b), it is still attributed to Mary. It seems that the speaker of the utterance (34b), who here reports Mary's question, need not share that assumption.

(34) a. Mary to John: What did Bill bring to the party?
b. Mary asked John what Bill brought to the party.

The implicature is formulated in a general form in (35), due to Sigrid Beck (p.c.).

(35) If T is the set of true answers of a question Q (i.e. T is the meaning of Q according to Karttunen 1977), then a person asking Q implicates T ≠ ∅.

(35) is applied to a wh-question meaning following Karttunen in (36). It derives the existential implicature that we saw.

(36) Q in w: Who does John like?
T = {p | p(w) ∧ ∃x p = λw' likes'(w')(j,x)}
Implicature: {p | p(w) ∧ ∃x p = λw' likes'(w')(j,x)} ≠ ∅
⇔ ∃p, p(w) ∧ ∃x p = λw' likes'(w')(j,x)
⇔ ∃x ∃p, p(w) ∧ p = λw' likes'(w')(j,x)
⇔ ∃x likes'(w)(j,x)
'John likes someone in w.'

(37) shows the application of (35) to the meaning of an alternative question, again following Karttunen. It derives that the disjunction of the alternatives is implicated.

(37) Q in w: Did you go to Berlin or to Potsdam?
T = {p | p(w) ∧ (p = λw' went'(w')(A,Ber) ∨ p = λw' went'(w')(A,Pots))}
Implicature: {p | p(w) ∧ (p = λw' went'(w')(A,Ber) ∨ p = λw' went'(w') (A,Pots))} ≠ ∅
⇔ ∃p, p(w) ∧ (p = λw' went'(w')(A,Ber) ∨ p = λw' went'(w') (A,Pots))
⇔ went'(w)(A,Ber) ∨ went'(w)(A,Pots)
"You went to Berlin or you went to Potsdam."

For yes/no-questions I follow Bartels and assume that they are ambiguous between singleton question meaning (Bolinger 1978b) and hidden alternative question meaning (e.g. Karttunen 1977). For the singleton case {q}, (35) leads to the implicature that q is true. For the hidden alternative question meaning {q, ¬q}, the implicature that follows from (35) is 'q ∨ ¬q'. This is derived in a parallel fashion to the alternative question in (37) and is not shown for reasons of space.

The implicatures are summed up in (38).

(38) *Implicature that there is a true answer*
 a. Did you go to B? i. (singleton) You went to B.
  ii. (hidden alternative) You went to B or you didn't.

  b. Where did you go? You went somewhere.
  c. Did you go to B or to P? You went to B or to P. (alternative question)

We now see that for all falling interrogatives discussed up to here, in particular those in (29)–(33), the proposition marked by the intonational meanings is identical to the implicature that there is a true answer. The singleton proposition 'you went to Berlin' that is asserted by H* in (30) is the implicature that there is a true answer by (38a.i). In the hidden alternative cases (31), (32) and (33b), Bartels 'alternative-proposition' turns out to also be an implicature that there is a true answer as in (38a.ii). 'You went somewhere' is asserted in the wh-question (29b) and is implicated by (38b). 'You went to Berlin or to Potsdam' is asserted in the alternative question (29c) and is implicated by (38c).

We can therefore add stability to the assumptions about salient propositions by hypothesizing:

(39) In the interpretation of a standard interrogative the implicature that there is a true answer is a particularly salient speaker-endorsed proposition.

The implicature that there is a true answer is thus a likely and salient proposition for intonational marking by H* in an unembedded question.

  Notice that this implicature is not the only salient proposition that we want to assume even for the core cases discussed up to here. However, it so happens that the other salient propositions in the interrogatives discussed up to here are identical to the implicatures that there is a true answer. First, it is sometimes suggested that the disjunction of the alternatives in alternative questions, which is identical to the implicature in (38c), is independently a presupposition of the alternative question (Karttunen 1977: 176 "in the intuitive sense of the term 'presuppose' ", Bartels 1999, Truckenbrodt 2013). Thus, there may be a second source for the same proposition here. However, this is not detrimental to the current account.

  The second case involves the singleton yes/no-questions, which we now need to review with our assumptions further evolved. *Did you go to Berlin?* in (29a), for example, puts up for question 'you went to Berlin'. At the same time, 'you went to Berlin' is the implicature of this question by (38a) on a singleton meaning. How might this be reconciled? The assignment of H-, which additionally puts up for question 'you went to Berlin', may be taken as a way of backgrounding, suppressing or weakening this implicature, by foregrounding the questioning aspect. By contrast, in the singleton question (30), the implicature 'John has a car now' is not put up for question by the intonation. It is endorsed by H* which we may here take to be an endorsement of the implicature that John has a car now. In this case the seeds of the questioning speech act that come from the interrogative sentence form seem to be overridden.

For the questions in (31), (32), and (33b), we follow Bartels in treating them as hidden alternative questions. Deriving Bartels 'alternative-proposition' from (35) not only gives this proposition a non-arbitrary source. It also seems to complete Bartels' analysis. The question that did not receive a full answer there is why the presence of the alternative-proposition (overtly or covertly) brings with it the impact of 'keeping the addressee to the point'. Deriving it from (35) seems to fill this gap: The alternative-proposition is the existence of a true answer. It can also be paraphrased 'there is a true answer'. Where the speaker highlights this element, s/he highlights that s/he is out for the truth. This is plausibly the source of the effect of 'keeping the addressee to the point'.

We have now made Bartels' discovery of the relevance of salient propositions precise in two respects. For one thing, we have a presuppositional account (with a formal parallel in definite descriptions) that calls salient propositions on the plan to begin with. For another, we were able to identify a recurrent source of salient propositions in connection with falling interrogatives, namely their implicatures that there is a true answer. With this, let us turn to additional empirical observations.

3.5 High-rise in yes/no-questions

Yes/no-questions also allow a H*H-H% rising pattern. PH90: 291 give the example in (40). They note that the H*H-H% is more likely when the expected answer is 'yes', while a choice of L*H-H%, according to them, transports more of a sense that the issue is really open to S.

(40)   H*   H- H%
     May I INTERRUPT you? [–/]

Two examples from B99: 126 are shown in (41) and (42).

(41)   H*   H-H%
     You're BACK already? [–/]

(42)   A: (Showing B how to make a blouse) This is the left sleeve; and here is the right one.
      B: H*   H-H%
     Is there any DIFFERENCE between them? [–/]

The remarks by PH90: 290f about this case are tentative. The assumed contribution of H* goes in the expected direction, insofar a weakly assertive impact is added by H*. However, it would seem to be too strong to assume that the speaker of these questions instructs the addressee to add a full yes-answer to the common ground. This would seem to be in conflict with the questioning impact. The current extensions allows us to develop a more detailed understanding of the weak effect at hand.

Recall first from the discussion of H*H-H% on declaratives in section 2.4. that H* and H- cannot operate on the same proposition because they would require incompatible speech-acts of this proposition. In declaratives, the primary speech act is that of an assertion, and the context supports an assertion interpretation in (20)–(22). It is plausible that H* identifies this as a salient speaker-asserted proposition and takes it as its antecedent, so that H- then has to look for another proposition, one put up for question by the speaker, to mark. That is what we saw. In the interrogative sentences in (40)–(42), a question-interpretation is supported by the context (and in (40) and (42) by the sentence form). Here it is plausible that H- finds the proposition put up for question as its antecedent. In this case, then, H* is left to look for a (different) speaker-asserted proposition to modify. We look for this proposition in the neighborhood of the implicature of a true answer. We assume that (40)–(42) are singleton yes/no-questions, i.e. the content of their implicature is identical to the proposition put up for question. We must independently assume that this implicature can at best survive the questioning impact in a weaker form. It is compatible with the questioning impact, for example, that the speaker assumes, or supposes, that the answer is 'yes'. Let us assume that this is what remains of the implicature. In (42), then, the *content* of the implicature is 'there is a difference between them', but the *fact* of the implicature would be 'I suppose that there is a difference between them'. Since endorsing the content of the implicature by H* would lead to an interpretation that conflicts with the questioning intention, it is reasonable to maintain that H* instead operates on the proposition that corresponds to the *fact* of the implicature, i.e. 'I suppose that there is a difference between them'. This would correctly represent the weak effect of H* in yes/no-questions.

3.6 Accommodation

The suggestion that H- has a meaning connected to simple question speech acts is motivated by the way this separates the declarative examples with H- (questioning) from those without (not questioning). It is also motivated by examples like (8), repeated here as (43) with additions. In both kind of cases, it seems likely that the question-meaning comes directly from the intonation, since there is no other source for it in sight. In the current account, intonational meaning can induce a question meaning with the help of presupposition accommodation. In (43) the meanings presupposed by the intonation are shown on the right. We get the correct results if the intonational presuppositions are accommodated here. I make the standard assumption that unembedded presuppositions are requirements over the common ground, and that their accommodation is addition to this common ground (Stalnaker 1978, 2002). The result of accommodation in (43a) is then that it is part of the common ground of John and Mary that (as presupposed) John is putting up for question whether Mary wants coffee. In other words, it is then established in the common ground that John is asking this question. Similarly in (43b).

(43) John and Mary are taking a break from work. John is getting up and looks at Mary.
    a. John: Coffee [/] L*H-H%   H-: John presupposes:
                                             John is putting up for question whether Mary wants coffee
    b. Mary: Coffee [\] H*L-L%   H*: Mary presupposes:
                                             Mary is adding to the common ground: Mary wants coffee

Lewis (1979) argues that for presuppositions not otherwise satisfied, accommodation is the normal case. Here I discuss the two possible obstacles to accommodation that I am aware of and where they might intervene with accommodation in (43). (i) Accommodation may be refused for reasons of plausibility. *My brother* or *my cat* may be accommodated, but *my palace* or *my elephant* are more likely to prompt questioning. Similarly, *my desire to ask you a question* is likely to be accommodated, but *my desire to live on the moon* is not. This criterion does not seem to interfere with accommodation in (43), since putting up something for question or asserting something are harmless, expected actions in a conversation. (ii) Accommodation generally works well where the speaker is the expert on the matter to be accommodated. In the standard example of accommodation of *my brother*, the speaker is the expert on the existence of such a brother. The addressee will typically be trusting enough to go along. The addressee will, on the other hand, not normally accommodate something s/he is the expert on and didn't know about, such as the referent of *your brother*. Similarly, in 'Did I tell you about my satisfaction with the outcome of the case?', the satisfaction is easily accommodated, since it is in the realm of the speaker's thoughts, of which the speaker alone is an expert. On the other hand, *your satisfaction with the outcome of the case* cannot normally be accommodated since the addressee's feelings are in the expertise of the addressee. For this criterion, the questioning meaning of H- is unproblematic: It is in the realm of the speaker's thoughts what he may intend to put up for question. No addressee-contribution beyond listening seems to be required for this speech act to succeed. Matters are more complex for the presupposition of H* that the speaker is adding a specific proposition to the common ground. While the speaker's intention of doing so is straightforward to accommodate, satisfaction of this presupposition also requires the addressee's accepting the relevant proposition into the common ground. The supposition that the addressee will do so is embedded in the mutual knowledge about the relation between the two, on the basis of which the speaker also offers his information. This will typically include assumptions about the accepted expertise of the speaker in the issue he talks about. It therefore does not seems to be out of place in most cases. Notice in support of this that 'your trust in me' or 'your learning this from me' are not unreasonable presuppositions to offer for accommodation in many contexts. At the same time, the presupposition is a strong one. If such presuppositions occur, addressee objection to them is certainly a possibility and does of course occur.

It may be interesting in a more general way that the assertive impact that is attributed to H* in (26a) can derive the notion of assertion of Stalnaker (1978). Stalnaker's notion of assertion is that the content of the assertion is added to the common ground, unless the addressee objects. This is what results if the presuppositional meaning of H* is accommodated. First, the accommodation of (26a) requires the addition of the content to the common ground. Second, accommodation is more generally subject to the possibility of addressee objection (Lewis 1979), but does not require explicit addressee approval. If I talk to a stranger about my brother, I do not require a sign of approval for accommodation, but I do require absence of objection to the existence of my brother. Thus, if it is accommodated that the speaker adds a proposition to the common ground by (26a), addressee objection can prevent accommodation, but a sign of addressee approval is not required for accommodation that includes the addition of the proposition to the common ground.

The exact formulation in PB90 is that H* marks the relevant proposition as 'to be added to' the common ground (e.g. PB90: 290). The formulation in (26a) is slightly stronger: H* *presupposes* that the relevant proposition is *being* added to the common ground. We don't have enough evidence to choose between the formulations, but it is perhaps worth knowing that the stronger formulation is also coherent and that its effect amounts to Stalnaker's notion of assertion.

3.7 The rise in echo wh-questions

Echo wh-questions show the interesting intonational contrast in (44) (Bolinger 1978a: 108, Rando 1980: 250, Bartels 1999: 211). The obligatory rising intonation in (44a) is found in two readings: the speaker of the echo question may not have understood the object of the preceding utterance or may be in surprised disbelief about the object referent. The clear preference for a fall in (44b) occurs with definite pronouns in the echoed utterance.

(44) a. A: Where did John go?
           L*H-H%
       B: Where did WHO go [/]

   b. A: Where did he go?
           H*L-L%
       B: Where did WHO go [\]

I adduce some remarks about the interpretation of echo questions before proceeding. Reis (1991) noted that they do not have the expected existential implicature. I show this with (45). Here I am not committed to 'I visited someone.' I proceed on the suggestion of Jacobs (1991) in which the echo-question in (45) is interpreted along the lines of 'Who *are you saying* that I visited?'. (This is critically discussed in Reis 1991; Jacobs 1991 answers the criticism.) On this analysis, the implicature of a true answer in (45) is 'you said that I visited someone', which is reasonable. Similarly, the true answer is then not the truth about who I visited, but the truth about who you said that I visited, i.e. it is identical or near-identical to the echoed speech act. This also is reasonable.

(45) you: When you visited John ...
     me: I visited WHO? [/]

With this, I now return to (44). Rando (1980: 256) notes that cases like (44a) ask for a repetition of the preceding information while cases like (44b) ask for new information. Let us pursue the difference in these terms. Asking for new information is the normal case. Here we find the fall of wh-questions, as in (44b). I return to this case below. For now, let us pursue (44a). How do you ask for a repetition of preceding information? Consider (46), without rising intonation. Why is it odd for B to ask this question? What seems to be at work is a default assumption that the preceding utterance has become part of the common ground after it occurred, in the absence of an objection. Furthermore, that B's question with a fall in (46) does not count as an objection, i.e. it is not enough of a sign that the preceding utterance was not understood. Therefore, B's question is infelicitous because the answer to it is already in the common ground, and no sensible intention of the question can be inferred.

(46)   A: Rita married Jim Montague.
       B: # WHO did Rita marry? [\]

This would mean that asking for a repetition of a preceding utterance requires a clear sign that the default assumption (that the preceding utterance has been added to the common ground) does not apply. It seems plausible that the rise somehow generates this sign. How might this work? My answer is tentative and leaves some issues unresolved. For the reading of (44a) in which the echoed utterance is understood but not believed, a plausible antecedent proposition for H- is 'You asked where John went'. Put up for question by H-, this amounts to 'Are you asking where John went?'. This is the clearest possible sign that the echoed utterance has not become part of the common ground. We must leave open where exactly this antecedent proposition comes from: It might be the echoed speech act (a non-local antecedent of H-) or it might be the true answer of the echo question (a local antecedent of H-). For the reading of (44a) in which the echoed utterance was not completely understood, a plausible antecedent proposition for H- is 'You asked where someone went'. Put up for question by H-, this amounts to 'Are you asking where someone went?'. This is still a very clear sign that the preceding utterance was not understood. The source is again not uniquely clear: The antecedent proposition might be the echoed speech act, perhaps with existential closure for the non-understood part. Or it might be the implicature of the existence of a true answer to the echo question, which would be derived from the echo question interpretation 'Of which x are you asking where x went?'. In all these interpretations, it seems that the presupposition of H- must be accommodated.

We will not settle what distinguishes signs of objection to the preceding utterance from non-signs. A reasonable hypothesis is that challenges to the preceding utterance becoming common ground must in some sense be 'direct attacks'. Choosing H- to signal 'Are you asking where John/someone went?' is a direct challenge to the preceding speech act. In (46), on the other hand, the relation is more indirect: B's question would make sense if it was assumed that A's utterance has not become common ground. This is not a 'direct attack'. It may also play a role in (46) that the H* of the fall most likely endorses the implicature of a true answer, 'Rita married someone'. Thus part of the preceding utterance is acknowledged. In addition, the chance to signal with the use of H- that the preceding utterance was not understood was not taken.

Notice that there is independent support for the notion that the true answer to a question can be marked by the intonation. This seems to be the case in rhetorical questions like (47) (B99: 128). In rhetorical yes/no-questions the answer that is recognizably assumed to be true is typically the negation of the uninverted interrogative. Here the use of H* can be seen as endorsement of that negated (and indirectly asserted) proposition.

(47)   H*L-L%
   Why should I pay for that? Am I my brother's KEEPER? [\]
   (H* operates on the salient true answer 'I am not my brother's keeper')

Let us then complete the analysis of (44b). We now assume that the preceding speech act is becoming part of the common ground, despite the inability of B to resolve the reference of the pronoun. We may assume for concreteness that this is possible with a temporary e-type interpretation of the pronoun (Evans 1980, Heim 1990), here: 'the one Rita married'. No sign is therefore required that the preceding speech act has not become part of the common ground. H* might endorse 'you asked where someone went'. Thus, the difference between (44a) and (44b) can be made sense of in the current account: In (44a), but not in (44b), the rising intonation with H- is required to generate a sign that the preceding utterance has not become part of the common ground.

B99: chs. 5, 6 pursues a different idea about the rise in echo-questions. She suggests that in cases like (48) the rise has the motivation and effect of not asserting the existential implicature because the addressee knows it already. However, this would wrongly predict that the rise is also obligatory in (49), where the addressee also already knows the existential implicature. Examples like (16) also support the suggestion of PH90 that assertive addition to the common ground is possible where the addressee already knows the proposition.

(48) A: Rita married Jim Montague on Sunday
                         L*   H-H%
     B: Rita married WHO on Sunday [/]

(49) A: Rita married someone.
     B: Who did Rita marry [\] (or [/])

In summary, it seems that the function of the rise in echo-questions is to generate a sign that the echoed utterance has not become part of the common ground, and thus to clarify that the echo-question asks for a repetition or clarification of that utterance.

3.8 The friendly rise in wh-questions

We took the fall to be the default intonation in wh-questions. However, a friendly rise is optionally also possible as in (49) and many other cases. The variation between fall and friendly rise contrasts with the obligatory echo-question rise in (44a) and (48). It also contrasts with a strong preference for a fall in sentences in which the echo-question seeks to clarify the reference of a pronoun as in (44b) and in (50), which does not have echo-question syntax.

(50) A: Rita married him.
      H*   L-L%
   B: WHO did Rita marry [\]

This friendly rise is also seen in the examples (51) and (52) from Schubiger (1958: 59). She describes the connotation as "regardful; interested request for information" (Schubiger 1958: 58).

(51) a. A: I was on holiday last month.
                          L*H-H%
        B: Where did you GO [/]

   b. A: Ireland.
                    L*H-H%
      B: How did you LIKE it [/]

(52) To somebody showing a new purchase:
                L* H-H%
     How much did it COST you [/]

Let us develop an analysis. Notice first that something similar to 'keeping the addressee to the point' with a [\] also occurs with wh-questions, as in (53). Here 'keeping the addressee to the point' blocks the option of the friendly rise.

(53) a. Tell me the truth. Who left? [\] #[/]
     b. Well, SOMEONE left. Who is it [\] #[/]

I suggest the following understanding of these choices. First, since the typical fall in wh-questions presupposes a speaker-assertion of the existential implicature, it presupposes a speaker-assertion that there is a true answer (see section 3.4). In (53), this point is in the foreground. In other falling wh-questions and in alternative questions, where the fall similarly signals the existence of a true answer, the pragmatic effect of the fall is not as strong as with yes/no-questions: Only yes/no-questions have a standard alternative choice, namely highlighting by H- that a salient proposition is put up for question. The pragmatic effect of insisting on the existence of a true answer is here more striking, because an alternative without it would have been among the standard choices.

Second, we need to add a further source of salient propositions for the friendly rise. We obtain a plausible result if we take the speech act of the question into account. Following Hintikka (1975) the interpretation of 'Where did you go?' would be 'Bring it about that I know where you went'. Putting a propositional form of this up for question results in 'Will you bring it about that I know where you went?'. This would seem to add friendliness. It would show that it is up to the addressee to answer. (The addressee might prefer not to share the answer or might not know it.) I suggest that the source of the friendly rise in (51) and (52) is to be sought along these lines. We may assume that this is not a 'standard' choice in the sense of the preceding paragraph, because it accesses the speech act, unlike the two choices available for yes/no-questions.

An indication that it's up to the addressee to answer would not be appropriate in (53), where the speaker of the question is clearly out for the truth, and thus also for an answer that makes the truth known.

In (49), then, the friendly rise also signals that it's up to the addressee whether s/he wants to answer, i.e. whether s/he wants to share this information. Here the addressee used an indefinite object in the preceding utterance. Revealing the individual behind it would be a further step in sharing information. It now correctly follows that the friendly rise is a less likely intonation pattern in (50) and (44b), where the referent of a personal pronoun is asked for. Here the addressee of the question has already tried to share the relevant information in the use of the personal pronoun (even though unsuccessfully, since the referent of the pronoun was not recovered). There is no point then in signaling with the friendly rise that the addressee may prefer to keep this information to herself.

I sum up the discussion of the intonation in interrogatives. It seems that the meanings for H* and for H- that were first motivated with declaratives also fare well in the analysis of interrogative meanings. In the course of developing this point, a range of formal aspects were addressed: Presuppositional meanings for H* and H- were suggested, their accommodation was discussed, and it was motivated that the implicature that there is a true answer is a particularly salient proposition with interrogatives.

4 Other tune meanings and related issues

This section briefly raises a number of issues not addressed above: Do English L* and L- carry meaning (section 4.1.)? What about continuation rises (section 4.2.)? What meanings do English complex pitch accents carry (section 4.3.)? Can the intonation encode the distinction between declaratives and interrogatives (section 4.4.)?

4.1 Do English L* and L- carry meaning?

L* does not seem to carry any discernible meaning in English. However, there is no harm in assigning it meaning that is the negation of the meaning of H*, as in PH90. If no meaning is assigned to L*, we must ensure that L* is only chosen where H* is not appropriate. This would follow if the choice between L* and H* is subject to presupposition maximization (Heim 1991), so that H* with its presupposition is chosen for modification of the most salient available proposition where the context allows it.

The issue is more complex with L-, for which B99 postulates assertive meaning. The examples discussed here are compatible with adding a weakly assertive meaning to L-. However, the account above also leaves no clear motivation for such a move. Consider first declaratives. In many cases, H*, the standard choice, will contribute an assertive impact independently. Where it does not and where we still want some assertive impact in a weaker sense (speaker endorsement), as in (14) and (15), L- might in principle provide it. However, it is not clear whether it could not also come from morphosyntactic elements of the declarative sentence form or from the pragmatics, given the propositional meaning of the declarative. In various interrogatives, Bartels suggests that L- corresponds to an endorsement of different salient propositions by the speaker. Given the revisions above, however, (a) these salient propositions are all independently implicatures that there is a true answer, and thus, as implicatures, independently endorsed by the speaker and (b) they are often endorsed by the speaker with the H* that accompanies the L- in these cases and that signals assertion of the implicature in the current analysis. At this point, there is no clear motivation for additional speaker-endorsement of these propositions by L-.

In summary, the current account is compatible with assigning L* a meaning that is the negation of H* and with assigning L- a meaning of speaker endorsement, but there is no clear evidence for either of these moves.

4.2 Continuation

High right edges are also known to signal continuation. PH90: 302ff show that this applies to both H- and H% in English. They suggest that H- "indicates that the current phrase is to be taken as forming a part of a larger composite interpretative unit with the following phrase" (PH90: 302) and that H% indicates that the utterance is to be interpreted "with particular attention to subsequent utterances" (PH90: 305). The direction pursued here is that there is an H- morpheme with questioning meaning and a separate H- morpheme with continuation meaning. This is compatible with the discussion in Gussenhoven (2004: ch. 5) where different paralinguistic motivation is suggested for the H/L-contrast in its relation to questions vs. statements ('size code') and in relation to continuation ('production code'). In English, the typical continuation rise in statements is the H*L-H% (without H-) seen in (10) while the yes/no-question contour is L*H-H% (with H-). The continuation-marking function of H- is seen on H- tones at the end of intermediate phrases that are not also intonation phrase boundaries (PH90: 302ff). There are some open issues in regard to the H*H-L% contour as in (54) from PH90: 291. In this particular occurrence, H- is not questioning or non-assertive, but its final occurrence also does not indicate continuation.

(54) Mostly they just sat around and knocked stuff. You know.
      H*H-L%   H*H-L%
     The SCHOOL [——]   Other PEOPLE [——]

One might explore a definition of the 'continuation' H- in which the relevant proposition *forms part of a larger interpretative unit*, though not necessarily with following material. It might be typically used for indicating such a unit with following material. On the other hand, its occurrence in (54) could highlight that 'they talked about the school' and 'they talked about other people' also form part of a larger interpretative unit, 'they knocked stuff', regardless of whether this includes following material.

4.3 English complex pitch accents

In addition to H* and L*, English also has the complex pitch accents L*+H, L+H*, H*+L and H+L*. The starred tone is more narrowly associated with the stressed syllable, and the other tone precedes or follows it, not necessarily on the same syllable. These differences carry pragmatic meaning in English. For example, the L+H* seems to be more often used when the new (H*) element is also contrasted. The L*+H L-H% contour can be used to express uncertainty or incredulity (Hirschberg & Ward 1992). A range of observations and hypotheses can be found in PH90. In their account, the meanings of H* (new) and L* (not new) are retained in the complex pitch accents. In addition, the L+H accents (L*+H and L+H*) invoke a semantic scale on which the accented element is located. The H+L accents (H*+L, H+L*) indicate that support for what is expressed should be inferable in the common ground. See also Hobbs (1990) for suggested revisions. Parallels to German modal particles are explored in Schubiger (1965, 1980).

4.4 Declarative/interrogative

In many languages yes/no-questions are not distinguished from declaratives by morphosyntactic means. The distinction rests on the intonation. One such case, Brazilian Portuguese (BP) is investigated in Truckenbrodt, Sandalo & Abaurre (2009). The Campinas variety investigated shows H+L* L- on assertions, L+H* L- on yes/no-questions and L*+H L- on *surprise questions* which seem to be functionally equivalent to English declarative questions (Gunlogson 2001):

BP H+L*	is like English declarative+[H*]	(declarative with assertion: It was raining[\])
BP L+H*	is like English interrogative+[H-]	(yes/no-question: Was it raining[/])
BP L*+H	is like English declarative+[H-]	(declarative question: It was raining[/])

The paper offers a decomposition of the Brazilian Portuguese tunes in which the L*+H surprise/declarative question contour of BP shares the L* with the BP declarative (with assertion) and shares the L+H with the BP yes/no-question. The analysis thus identifies the star on the BP L* as the contribution that is provided by the English sentence form declarative, and the BP sequence L+H as the contribution that is provided by the English yes/no-question intonation (with a meaningful English H- in the current analysis). The study is limited in scope, and other question types were not investigated.

Aboh & Pfau (2011) present a final floating L tone that distinguishes unembedded yes/no-questions from declaratives in Gungbe. They show that the floating L also appears in embedded yes/no-questions and not in embedded declaratives. In embedded position the two clause types are additionally distinguished by different conjunctions.

5 Summary

The connection between intonational meaning and semantics is partly provided by the notion of an intonational morpheme. If this is attached to the syntactic structure as in (26), it can be interpreted in phonology and in semantics. The element shared with the semantic interpretation is the context in the sense of Kaplan (1989), which includes the parameters speaker and addressee. The intonational interpretation arguably shares these with the interpretation of personal pronouns.

According to (26), the intonational meanings do not operate on the meaning of the constituent they attach to, but on a salient proposition. The relevance of salient propositions, discovered by Bartels (1999), is here implemented in terms of presuppositional meanings of intonational elements.

The English H* is hypothesized to presuppose that the salient proposition is being added to the common ground by the speaker. This is a minimally strengthened version of the suggestion for H* in Pierrehumbert & Hirschberg (1990) and the suggestion of Gussenhoven (1984) for the fall. In its strengthened form, its accommodation (which is assumed to be allowed up to addressee objection) generates an assertion in the sense of Stalnaker (1978).

The English H- is hypothesized here to presuppose that the salient proposition is being put up for question by the speaker. This is a suggested revision of earlier accounts that treat (L*)H- as non-assertive. The strengthened version generates (by presupposition accommodation) a questioning speech act. This is seen as an advantage in particular with rising elliptical utterances and with declaratives marked with H-. These show no other source for a questioning impact. It also correctly accounts for the typical deployment of H- in yes/no-questions as opposed to wh- and alternative questions. This specific suggestion for H- necessitates the assumption of a second H- morpheme with 'continuation' meaning.

Throughout a case was made that these meanings are adequate insofar they account for a range of renditions of declaratives and interrogatives with their pragmatic impact. The salient propositions employed in the discussion were: the content of a declarative, the connection of what is asserted to the addressee's knowledge, the propositional interpretation of vocatives and of greetings, the implicature that there is a true answer of an interrogative, the true answer, and contextually salient propositions (you want *coffee*). It was also hypothesized that the fact of a weakened implicature (the speaker supposes that there is a true answer) and question speech acts can serve as salient propositions.

This research was funded in part by the Federal Ministry of Education and Research (BMBF) of Germany (Grant Nr. 01UG0711).

6 References

Aboh, Enoch O. & Roland Pfau 2011. What's a wh-word got to do with it? In: P. Beninca & N. Munaro (eds.). *Mapping the Left Periphery. The Cartography of Syntactic Structures, Vol. 5.* Oxford: Oxford University Press, 91–124.
Baltazani, Mary 2002. *Quantifier Scope and the Role of Intonation in Greek.* Ph.D. dissertation. University of California, Los Angeles, CA.
Bartels, Christine 1999. *The Intonation of English Statements and Questions. A Compositional Interpretation.* New York: Garland.
Beckman, Mary E. & Janet B. Pierrehumbert 1986. Intonational structure in Japanese and English. *Phonology Yearbook* 3, 255–309.
Bolinger, Dwight L. 1946. The intonation of quoted questions. *Quarterly Journal of Speech* 32, 197–202.
Bolinger, Dwight L. 1957. *Interrogative Structures of American English* (Publications of the American Dialect Society 28). Tuscaloosa, AL: University of Alabama Press.
Bolinger, Dwight L. 1978a. Asking more than one thing at a time. In: H. Hiz (ed.). *Questions.* Dordrecht: Reidel, 107–150.
Bolinger, Dwight L. 1978b. Yes-no questions are not alternative questions. In: H. Hiz (ed.). *Questions.* Dordrecht: Reidel, 87–105.
Bolinger, Dwight L. 1986. *Intonation and its Parts: Melody in Spoken English.* Palo Alto, CA: Stanford University Press.
Bolinger, Dwight L. 1989. *Intonation and its Uses.* Stanford, CA: Stanford University Press.
Büring, Daniel 1995. *The 59th Street Bridge Accent.* Doctoral dissertation. University of Tübingen.
Büring, Daniel 2003. On D-trees, beans, and B-accents. *Linguistics & Philosophy* 26, 511–545.
Chomsky, Noam 1981. *Lectures on Government and Binding.* Dordrecht: Foris.
Chomsky, Noam 1995. *The Minimalist Program.* Cambridge, MA: The MIT Press.
Chomsky, Noam & Morris Halle 1968. *The Sound Pattern of English.* New York: Harper & Row.
Clark, Herbert H. 1996. *Using Language.* Cambridge: Cambridge University Press.
Evans, Gareth 1980. Pronouns. *Linguistic Inquiry* 11, 337–362.
Féry, Caroline & Vieri Samek-Lodovici 2006. Focus projection and prosodic prominence in nested foci. *Language* 82, 131–150.

Gärtner, Hans-Martin 2000. Are there V2 relative clauses in German? *Journal of Comparative Germanic Linguistics* 3, 97–141.
Gärtner, Hans-Martin 2002. On the force of V2 declaratives. *Theoretical Linguistics* 28, 33–42.
Groenendijk, Jeroen & Martin Stokhof 1997. Questions. In: J. van Benthem & A. ter Meulen (eds.). *Handbook of Logic and Language*. Amsterdam: Elsevier, 1055–1124.
Gunlogson, Christine 2001. *True to Form: Rising and Falling Declaratives as Questions in English*. Ph.D. dissertation. University of California, Santa Cruz, CA.
Gussenhoven, Carlos 1984. *On the Grammar and Semantics of Sentence Accents*. Dordrecht: Foris.
Gussenhoven, Carlos 2004. *The Phonology of Tone and Intonation*. Cambridge: Cambridge University Press.
Haida, Andreas 2007. *The Indefiniteness and Focusing of wh-Words*. Doctoral dissertation. Humboldt-Universität zu Berlin.
Heim, Irene 1982. *The Semantics of Definite and Indefinite Noun Phrases*. Ph.D. dissertation. University of Massachusetts, Amherst, MA. Reprinted: Ann Arbor, MI: University Microfilms.
Heim, Irene 1990. E-type pronouns and donkey anaphora. *Linguistics & Philosophy* 13, 137–177.
Heim, Irene 1991. Artikel und Definitheit. In: A. v. Stechow & D. Wunderlich (eds.). *Semantik—Semantics. Ein internationales Handbuch der zeitgenössischen Forschung—An International Handbook of Contemorary Research* (HSK 6). Berlin: de Gruyter, 487–536.
Hintikka, Jaakko 1975. Answers to questions. In: H. Hiz (ed.). *Questions*. Dordrecht: Reidel, 279–300.
Hirschberg, Julia 2004. Pragmatics and intonation. In: L. Horn & G. Ward (eds.). *The Handbook of Pragmatics*. Oxford: Blackwell, 515–537.
Hirschberg, Julia & Gregory Ward 1991. Accent and bound anaphora. *Cognitive Linguistics* 2, 101–121.
Hirschberg, Julia & Gregory Ward 1992. The influence of pitch range, duration, amplitude and spectral features on the interpretation of the rise-fall-rise intonation contour in English. *Journal of Phonetics* 20, 241–251.
Hirschberg, Julia & Gregory Ward 1995. The interpretation of the high-rise question contour in English. *Journal of Pragmatics* 24, 407–412.
Hobbs, Jerry R. 1990. The Pierrehumbert-Hirschberg theory of intonational meaning made simple: Comments on Pierrehumbert and Hirschberg. In: P. R. Cohen, J. Morgan & M. E. Pollack (eds.). *Intentions in Communication*. Cambridge, MA: The MIT Press, 313–323.
Ishihara, Shin 2010. Negative polarity item and focus intonation in Japanese. In: S. Iwasaki (ed.). *Japanese/Korean Linguistics, Vol. 17*. Stanford, CA: CSLI Publications, 311–325.
Jackendoff, Ray S. 1972. *Semantic Interpretation in Generative Grammar*. Cambridge, MA: The MIT Press.
Jacobs, Joachim 1984. Funktionale Satzperspektive und Illokutionssemantik. *Linguistische Berichte* 91, 25–58.
Jacobs, Joachim 1991. Implikaturen und "alte Information" in w-Fragen. In: M. Reis & I. Rosengren (eds.). *Fragesätze und Fragen*. Tübingen: Niemeyer, 201–222.
Kaplan, David 1989. Demonstratives: An essay on the semantics, logic, metaphysics, and epistemology of demonstratives and other indexicals. In: J. Almog, J. Perry & H. Wettstein (eds.). *Themes from Kaplan*. Oxford: Oxford University Press, 481–563.
Karttunen, Lauri 1977. Syntax and semantics of questions. In: H. Hiz (ed.). *Questions*. Dordrecht: Reidel, 156–210.

Kretschmer, Paul 1938. Der Ursprung des Fragetons & Fragesatzes. In: A. Ballini et al. (eds.). *Scritti in onore di Alfredo Trombetti*. Milano: Ulrico Hoepli, 27–50.
Krifka, Manfred 2001. Quantifying into question acts. *Natural Language Semantics* 9, 1–40.
Krifka, Manfred 2011. *Embedding Speech Acts*. Ms. Berlin, Humboldt-Universität zu Berlin. http://amor.cms.hu-berlin.de/~h2816i3x/Publications/Krifka_EmbeddingSpeechActs.pdf, February 23, 2012.
Ladd, D. Robert 2008. *Intonational Phonology*. 2nd edn. Cambridge: Cambridge University Press.
Lakoff, George 1971. Presupposition and relative well-formedness. In: D. D. Steinberg & L. A. Jakobovits (eds.). *Semantics: An Interdisciplinary Reader in Philosophy, Linguistics, and Psychology*. Cambridge: Cambridge University Press, 329–340.
Lewis, David 1979. Scorekeeping in a language game. *Journal of Philosophical Logic* 8, 339–359.
Pierrehumbert, Janet B. 1980. *The Phonology and Phonetics of English Intonation*. Ph.D. dissertation. MIT, Cambridge, MA.
Pierrehumbert, Janet B. & Julia Hirschberg 1990. The meaning of intonational contours in the interpretation of discourse. In: P. R. Cohen, J. Morgan & M. E. Pollack (eds.). *Intentions in Communication*. Cambridge, MA: The MIT Press, 271–311.
Portner, Paul 2007. Instructions for interpretation as separate performatives. In: K. Schwabe & S. Winkler (eds.). *On Information Structure, Meaning and Form*. Amsterdam: Benjamins, 407–426.
Potts, Christopher 2005. *The Logic of Conventional Implicatures*. Oxford: Oxford University Press.
Rando, Emily 1980. Intonation in discourse. In: L. R. Waugh & C. H. van Schooneveld (eds.). *The Melody of Language*. Baltimore, MD: University Park Press, 243–277.
Reis, Marga 1991. Echo-w-Sätze und Echo-w-Fragen. In: M. Reis & I. Rosengren (eds.). *Fragesätze und Fragen*. Tübingen: Niemeyer, 49–76.
Rooth, Mats 1992. A theory of focus interpretation. *Natural Language Semantics* 1, 75–116.
Ross, John Robert 1970. On declarative sentences. In: R. A. Jacobs & P. S. Rosenbaum (eds.). *Readings in English Transformational Grammar*. Washington, DC: Georgetown University Press, 222–277.
Schubiger, Maria 1958. *English Intonation: Its Form and Function*. Tübingen: Niemeyer.
Schubiger, Maria 1965. English intonation and German modal particles. *Phonetica* 12, 65–84. Reprinted in: D.L. Bolinger (ed.). *Intonation—Selected Readings*. Harmondsworth: Penguin, 1972, 175–193.
Schubiger, Maria 1980. English intonation and German modal particles II: A comparative study. In: L. R. Waugh & C. H. van Schooneveld (eds.). *The Melody of Language*. Baltimore, MD: University Park Press, 279–298.
Schwabe, Kerstin 2007a. Old and new propositions. In: A. Späth (ed.). *Interface and Interface Conditions. Language, Context and Cognition*. Berlin: Mouton de Gruyter, 97–114.
Schwabe, Kerstin 2007b. Semantic properties of German solitaires. *Journal of Germanic Linguistics and Semiotic Analysis* 12, 233–254.
Selkirk, Elisabeth 1986. On derived domains in sentence phonology. In: C. Ewan & J. Anderson (eds.). *Phonology Yearbook 3*. Cambridge: Cambridge University Press, 371–405.
Selkirk, Elisabeth 2000. The interaction of constraints on prosodic phrasing. In: M. Horne (ed.). *Prosody: Theory and Experiment*. Dordrecht: Kluwer, 231–261.
Selkirk, Elisabeth 2011. The syntax-phonology interface. In: J. Goldsmith, J. Riggle & A. Yu (eds.). *The Handbook of Phonological Theory*. 2nd edn. Oxford: Blackwell, 435–484.

Stalnaker, Robert 1978. Assertion. In: P. Cole (ed.). *Syntax and Semantics 9: Pragmatics*. New York: Academic Press, 315–332.
Stalnaker, Robert 2002. Common ground. *Linguistics & Philosophy* 25, 701–721.
Truckenbrodt, Hubert 2006a. On the semantic motivation of syntactic verb movement to C in German. *Theoretical Linguistics* 32, 257–306.
Truckenbrodt, Hubert 2006b. Replies to the comments by Gärtner, Plunze and Zimmermann, Portner, Potts, Reis, and Zaefferer. *Theoretical Linguistics* 32, 387–410.
Truckenbrodt, Hubert 2007. The syntax-phonology interface. In: P. de Lacy (ed.). *The Cambridge Handbook of Phonology*. Cambridge: Cambridge University Press, 435–456.
Truckenbrodt, Hubert 2012. On the prosody of German wh-questions. In: G. Elordieta & P. Barbosa (eds.). *Prosody and Meaning*. Berlin: de Gruyter, 73–118.
Truckenbrodt, Hubert 2013. An analysis of prosodic F-effects in interrogatives: prosody, syntax and semantics *Lingua* 124 (special issue, ed. by S. Tomioka & Y. Kitagawa) 131–175.
Truckenbrodt, Hubert, Filomena Sandalo & Bernadett Abaurre 2009. Elements of Brazilian Portuguese intonation. *Journal of Portuguese Linguistics* 8, 75–114.
Wegener, Philipp 1885. *Untersuchungen über die Grundfragen des Sprachlebens*. Halle: Niemeyer.

Paul Kiparsky and Judith Tonhauser
2 Semantics of inflection

1 Inflectional categories —— 41
2 Person, number and gender —— 44
3 Case —— 61
4 Evidentiality —— 67
5 References —— 68

Abstract: This article presents a typology of inflection and discusses recent work on the semantics of number, person, gender, case, and evidentiality. Cross-linguistic evidence is brought to bear on the relationship between inflections and lexical classes and the typology of semantic case, and motivates an analysis of number inflections as expressing associative meanings. The article addresses semantic markedness in number, person and case paradigms, and analyses of inflections at the syntax-semantics interface.

1 Inflectional categories

This article presents a typology of inflection and discusses recent work on the semantics of number, person, gender, case, and evidentiality. Separate articles in the handbook cover the semantics of other inflections, including tense (articles 13 [Semantics: Noun Phrases and Verb Phrases] (Ogihara) *Tense* and 4 [Semantics: Typology, Diachrony and Processing] (Smith) *Tense and aspect*), mood (article 11 [Semantics: Noun Phrases and Verb Phrases] (Portner) *Verbal mood*), aspect (articles 9 [Semantics: Noun Phrases and Verb Phrases] (Filip) *Aspectual class and Aktionsart,* 10 [Semantics: Noun Phrases and Verb Phrases] (Portner) *Perfect and progressive* and 4 [Semantics: Typology, Diachrony and Processing] (Smith) *Tense and aspect*), and definiteness (article 2 [Semantics: Noun Phrases and Verb Phrases] (Heim) *Definiteness and indefiniteness*).

Inflectional morphemes assign values of functional features, whereas derivational morphemes form new lexical items. Thus, inflectional morphemes are bound functional heads (or their morphological equivalents, in lexicalist

Paul Kiparsky, Stanford, CA, USA
Judith Tonhauser, Columbus, OH, USA

Tab. 2.1: Inflection versus derivation

Inflection	Derivation
Specifies functional features	Forms new lexical items
Endocentric (non-category-changing)	May be exocentric
Typically outside derivation	Closer to stem
Typically paradigmatic	Often non-paradigmatic
Non-recursive	May be recursive
Portmanteau morphemes occur	No portmanteau morphemes
Assigned by government and agreement	Not assigned syntactically

theories), while derivational morphemes are bound lexical heads. This basic distinction accounts for a characteristic cluster of properties given in Tab. 2.1 that distinguish derivation and inflection (see also article 3 [this volume] (Lieber) *Semantics of derivational morphology).*

From a semantic perspective, inflections are a heterogeneous set. Jakobson (1985) noted that inflectional categories are intrinsically related to specific word classes (see section 2.4. below). He proposed a set of semantically defined features into which inflectional categories are decomposed. Each feature is binary and privative, i.e. has a positively characterized MARKED value and a negatively characterized UNMARKED (default) value, forming a two-point Horn (1989) scale. Jakobson (1957/1971: 136) puts semantic markedness this way:

> The general meaning of a marked category states the presence of a certain property A; the general meaning of the corresponding unmarked category states nothing about the presence of A and is used chiefly but not exclusively to indicate the absence of A.

On this view, morphological markedness is grounded in semantics, but has consequences in syntax, morphological form, and even in phonology. The most important formal reflex of markedness is that exponents of marked categories tend to be more complex and have a more restricted distribution. The convergence of semantic and formal markedness is widely assumed in grammatical theories (cf. the Monotonicity Hypothesis, Koontz-Garboden 2007).

Jakobson's analysis has four primitives: the speech event (E^s), the speech participants (P^s), the narrated eventuality (E^n, i.e. the eventuality denoted by an utterance) and the participants of the narrated eventuality (P^n); see Emonds (1985): ch. 5 for an alternative approach. These primitives combine to define three binary features:

(1) a. PARTICIPANT-ORIENTED (involves P^n) vs. NOT PARTICIPANT-ORIENTED.
 b. CONNECTOR (connects two narrated items, e.g. E^nE^n) vs. DESIGNATOR.
 c. SHIFTER (or DEICTIC, P^s or E^s, refers to the speech event) vs. NON-SHIFTER.

The three features cross-classify to specify the eight verbal categories in Tab. 2.2.

Tab. 2.2: Jakobson's (1957/1971: 136) classification of Russian verbal inflections

	P involved		P not involved	
	Designator	**Connector**	**Designator**	**Connector**
Non-shifter	P^n (gender, number)	$P^n E^n$ (voice)	E^n (status, aspect)	$E^n E^n$ (taxis)
Shifter	P^n/P^s (person)	$P^n E^n/P^s$ (mood)	E^n/E^s (tense)	$E^n E^{ns}/E^s$ (evidential)

According to this classification, gender and number characterize an eventuality participant P^n, and person characterizes an eventuality participant P^n with respect to a speech participant P^s. Status (affirmative, presumptive, negative, interrogative, ...) and aspect characterize an eventuality E^n, while tense characterizes an eventuality E^n with respect to the speech event E^s. Voice characterizes the relation between the eventuality E^n and its participants P^n, irrespective of E^s or P^s, while mood characterizes the relation between the eventuality E^n and its participants P^n with reference to the speech participants P^s. Taxis characterizes the relation between two eventualities E^n (dependent/relative tense, causality) and evidentiality characterizes the relation between two eventualities E^n (one a narrated speech event E^{ns}) with reference to the speech event E^s.

Not surprisingly, Jakobson's analysis requires revisions in the light of more recent findings of formal semantics, and the study of typologically diverse languages. Aspect is now often treated as a relation between the narrated event and the (contextually given) reference time (Reichenbach 1947; Kamp & Reyle 1993; Klein 1994) and evidentials encode "a speaker's (type of) *grounds* for making a speech act" (Faller 2002: 2). Inflections thought to pertain to a particular word class have been observed for others, such as tense/aspect for nouns, and number for verbs (section 2.4.). Still, every one of the basic questions addressed by Jakobson remains on the agenda: Are inflectional categories universal? Which meanings do they express? How do these meanings combine, and how can they be categorized? Which inflectional categories are relevant to which word classes, and why?

Many of his answers remain appealing as well. Regarding the universality of inflectional categories, although Jakobson's structuralism privileges the obligatory inflections of a language, he recognized that unexpressed categories may play a covert role in the grammar (as evidentiality does in Russian, or definiteness in Finnish case assignment, see section 3.2.). A more recent view holds that all languages specify the same functional categories, whether they are detectable in the grammar or not. Matthewson (2006), for instance, argues that tense meanings are observable in languages without overt tenses (but see e.g. Bohnemeyer 2002; Bittner 2005; Bittner 2008). This view has to be reconciled with the commonplace observation that adult language learners have considerable difficulty mastering inflectional distinctions that are not relevant in the grammar of their native language.

An attractive feature of Jakobson's theory of inflectional meanings is that it takes into account conventional meaning, the contribution made by contextual factors, and the relation between the two. Further, it makes predictions about the kinds of meanings realized by inflections. For instance, it excludes (correctly, it seems) inflections that denote a property of the speech event or a speech participant, inflections that denote a relation between two speech events, and "anti-shifters", i.e. inflections whose meaning is to characterize the speech event or a speech participant in relation to a narrated event or a participant of a narrated event.

Jakobson's approach to the classification and combinatorics of inflectional categories has also proved fruitful. For example, his natural classes predict relationship between gender and number, and in turn between these and person, a correct result as shown below. Finally, Jakobson's core formal proposal that all categories, including those usually treated as having three or more values, are built on binary features, and that these binary features are privative, has received increasing support in recent research, as outlined in section 2.2. below.

2 Person, number and gender

2.1 Semantic and structural features

The inflectional categories *person, number* and *gender* typically but not invariably encode semantic information about the speech act participants, the cardinality of the referent and the (biological) sex of the referent, respectively (cf. article 1 [Semantics: Lexical Structures and Adjectives] (Bierwisch) *Semantic features and primes*). In addition to semantic properties, phonological, morphological, and lexical factors also play a role in determining the inflectional class of nouns and pronouns. We therefore distinguish between semantic (or natural) and grammatical (or formal or syntactic) person, number and gender.

All gender systems are based wholly or in part on semantic categories (Aksenov 1984; Corbett 1991): the main semantic categories that determine gender are sex, animacy, humanness, and (ir)rationality. The grammatical genders of the German feminine noun *Frau* 'woman' and the masculine noun *Mann* 'man' correspond to their respective semantic gender, i.e. to the sex of their referents, but grammatical and semantic gender do not always accord: e.g. the grammatically neuter noun *Kind* 'child' can refer to a female or male individual, and the masculine noun *Tisch* 'table' has an inanimate referent. The distribution of semantic versus grammatical agreement follows the following hierarchy (Corbett 1991: 237):

(2) attributive > predicate > relative pronoun > personal pronoun

In German, an attributive adjective agrees with its head in grammatical gender, but anaphoric reference to a grammatically neuter noun that refers to a female can be with the neuter pronoun *es* 'it' or with the feminine pronoun *sie* 'she'.

(3) Ich sah das Mädchen. Es/Sie lief zur Schule.
I see.PAST the.NEUT girl.NEUT It/She went to school
'I saw the girl. She went to school.'

Number can also be either grammatical or semantic. Pluralia tantum nouns like *scissors* and *pants* trigger plural agreement even if they refer to singular entities. Grammatically singular group designations such as *team* or names referred to teams can trigger plural agreement in British English.

(4) a. The scissors are pretty. / My pants are on fire.
b. India is/are leading by 316 runs.

Likewise, grammatical and semantic person do not always match. French *on* is grammatically third person but can refer to a first person group:

(5) On a été loyaux
pron.3 have.3 be.PART loyal
'We have been loyal.'

2.2 Semantic features and markedness

2.2.1 Number and person

Traditional grammar treats number and person as orthogonal three-valued categories (singular/dual/plural number, first/second/third person), referring respectively to cardinality and speech act participation (Lyons 1968:276; Cysouw 2003; Cysouw 2005). The following (somewhat naive) formulations capture this plausible idea up to a point.

(6) a. Singular number denotes atomic entities.
b. Dual number denotes a pair of entities.
c. Plural number denotes a groups of two or more entities (three or more if there is a dual).

(7) a. First person refers to a group which includes the speaker.
  b. Second person refers to a group which includes the addressee but does not include the speaker.
  c. Third person refers to a group which does not include a speech act participant.

It has long been understood that dual and plural number in pronouns have an associative interpretation (Jespersen 1924:192; Benveniste 1966; Lyons 1968; Harley & Ritter 2002; Cysouw 2003; Cysouw 2005): First person dual and plural pronouns do not usually refer to a pair or chorus of speakers, but to a group that contains the speaker and some associates, i.e. one or more non-speakers. For example, *we* means 'I and the other people in some group' (which may be either implicit, or explicitly specified). Likewise, second person duals and plurals do not refer only to pairs or groups of addressees (regular plural) but also to groups containing at least one addressee plus other non-speaker individuals (associative plural). This much is captured by the formulations in (6) and (7), on the understanding that the cardinality of the group is determined by the number feature. Thus, first person singular *I* refers to the singleton group which includes the speaker, second person plural *you* refers to a group of more than one which includes at least one addressee but not the speaker; the associative reading is obtained when individuals other than addressees are included.

Two pieces of evidence show that this is not sufficient, that (6) and (7) are incorrect, and that a special semantics is required for the associative plural. The first piece of evidence is that the associative meaning is not restricted to pronouns. It also occurs in some languages in certain nominal duals and plurals, which denote not a set of two or more entities of the type denoted by the noun like the ordinary dual and plural, but a group containing one such referent and something else which forms a natural or conventional pair or group with it (Cysouw 2003; Moravcsik 2003): Spanish *los reyes*, for example, means either 'the kings' or 'the king and the queen'.

(8) Hungarian associative plural *-ék* versus regular plural *-ok* (Moravcsik 2003)
  a. *János-ék* 'János and associates'
  b. *János-ok* 'the Jánoses' = 'people called János'

(9) Dyirbal associative dual *-gara* (Dixon 1972: 230f.).
  a. burbula-gara   banijiu
     burbula-AssocDu come.PREs
     'Burbula and another person are coming'
  b. burbula-gara   badibadi-gara   banijiu
     burbula-AssocDu badibadi-AssocDu come.PREs
     'Burbula, being one of a pair, and Badibadi, being the other of the pair, are coming'

Even when the associative is not marked by a special morpheme, it may be available as an interpretation, e.g. for the Japanese plural morpheme *tati*:

(10) *sensei-tati* 'teacher-PL: (i) 'the teacher and his group', (ii) '(the) teachers'

The associative plural in nominals cannot be derived from the meaning of person in (7).

Still, associative duals/plurals occur only in nouns which are pronoun-like in that they without exception have a definite referent, and belong to a semantically restricted subclass, nearly always humans, and particularly often proper names, kin terms, or titles (Moravcsik 2003). The generalization is that the associative plural is available in a continuous segment from the top of the well-known "animacy" hierarchy (a better term would be INDIVIDUATION HIERARCHY) given in Fig. 2.1 down to some point which varies within narrow limits from language to language.

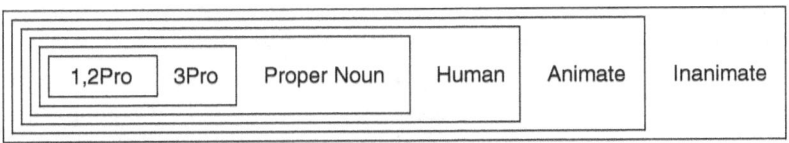

Fig. 2.1: Individuation hierarchy

A number of other pronominal phenomena are known to spill over into high-animacy nouns in just this way. Kiparsky (2011) argues that nouns behave this way in virtue of N-to-D raising (or its lexicalist equivalent), which syntactically assigns them to the category Pronoun and semantically converts them from property-denoting to individual-denoting. A corollary is that languages in which the plural is marked *only* in pronouns (Corbett 2000: 61–66) can be characterized simply as languages that allow only an associative plural. On this assumption, the associative plural and dual apply to an expression P to yield maximal individuals that include the individual denoted by P as a part:

(11) a. $[\![plural_{assoc}(P)]\!]$ presupposes that P denotes a (possibly complex) individual. If defined, $[\![plural_{assoc}(P)]\!] = \iota y \, (y = \{[\![P]\!]\} \cup \{x \mid x \in [\![Q]\!] \wedge [\![Q]\!] \sqsupset [\![P]\!]\})$ for some contextually given super-property Q of P
b. $[\![dual_{assoc}(P)]\!]$ presupposes that P denotes a (possibly complex) individual. If defined, $[\![dual_{assoc}(P)]\!] = \iota y \, (y = \{[\![P]\!] + z \wedge [\![Q]\!] \sqsupset [\![P]\!] \wedge z \in Atom \, ([\![Q]\!] \setminus [\![P]\!]))\}$ for some contextually given super-property P of Q

(11a), when applied to a noun like *teacher* (which functions as a title when used with the associative dual/plural) denotes a group consisting of the teacher and a contextually relevant group. An expression of the form 'father-dual' denotes, according to (1ib), a complex individual consisting of the father and an individual that is a member of an (immediate, contextually given) super-property Q, e.g. 'parent', resulting in the denotation 'the parents'.

Regular duals and plurals apply to *predicates* —in morphosyntactic terms to Ns rather than to DPs. One way of specifying the semantics of the plural and the dual is given in (12): the plural subtracts the atomic elements from the denotation of the (singular) predicate (which denotes a set consisting of atomic elements and all possible (non-empty) sets of atomic elements) and the dual denotes the set of sets of cardinality 2 in the denotation of P.

(12) a. $[\![plural]\!]([\![P]\!]) = [\![P]\!] \setminus Atom([\![P]\!])$
 b. $[\![dual]\!]([\![P]\!]) = \{X | X \in [\![P]\!] \wedge |X| = 2\}$

The second piece of evidence for associative number comes from languages that distinguish inclusive and exclusive 'we', i.e. that have separate forms for 'I and you (and possibly others)' and 'I and a (possibly singleton) group that does not contain you', respectively. In languages that additionally have a dual/plural number contrast, the form denoting 'I and you' does not behave as an "inclusive dual" as (6) would have it, rather the form denoting 'I and you and one other' does (despite the fact that its cardinality is 3). In Weri, which is such a language, basing number on cardinality, as in Tab. 2.3, would yield no unified semantics for the ending *-ip* and would require positing a Trial number instantiated only in the inclusive:

Tab. 2.3: Weri person/number paradigm (Daniel 2005: 15)

	Singular	Dual	Trial	Plural
Inclusive	—	tepir	tëar-ip	tëar
Exclusive	ne	ten-ip	—	ten
Second	në	ar-ip	—	ar
Third	pë	pëar-ip	—	pëar

Clearly *tepir* 'I and you' morphologically patterns with the *singular* pronouns, and *tëarip* 'I and you and one other' patterns with the *dual* pronouns. Since this alignment cannot be reconciled with the cardinality-based semantics of the number categories in (6), it has been proposed that these languages have a different set of number categories: minimal, unit-augmented, and augmented, instead of singular, dual, trial, and plural. Minimal number denotes a set of minimum cardinality (two for the dual inclusive); unit-augmented number denotes a set minimally greater than that, and the augmented number denotes a set greater than unit-augmented (Greenberg 1988; Corbett 2000: 166; Daniel 2005). The resulting analysis of Weri is shown in Tab. 2.4. The ending *-ip* now has the homogeneous function of deriving unit-augmented number from augmented number.

Tab. 2.4: Revised Weri person/number paradigm

	Minimal	Unit-augmented	Augmented
Inclusive	tepir	tĕar-ip	tĕar
Exclusive	ne	ten-ip	ten
Second	në	ar-ip	ar
Third	pë	pĕar-ip	pĕar

The new number categories are unnecessary since the definitions of associative dual and plural in (11) already give the right semantics: minimal is singular (a possibly complex individual), unit-augmented is associative dual, and augmented is associative plural. The suffix *-ip* restricts the "augmentation" to a single individual. This reduction does more than just simplify the set of number categories. It also explains why the applicability of unit-augmented and augmented number is restricted to pronouns. See Wechsler (2004) for a radical reanalysis of the customary person/number paradigm as a pure person paradigm with singular and augmented categories.

To fit the inclusive/exclusive distinction into the person inventory we assume that the inclusive is a fourth person category, defined as reference to both the speaker and to the addressee (Noyer 1992). Because it bears two feature specifications, it is the most marked person. The exclusive is just first person, defined as reference to the speaker.

The revised features form a Horn scale (inclusive > first > second > third), which determines priority in pronominal reference and agreement, a desirable result because the hierarchy appears to be universal (Cysouw 2003; Cysouw 2005).

Tab. 2.5: Feature analysis of person

Person	feature specification
Inclusive	[+speaker, +addressee]
First	[+speaker]
Second	[+participant]
Third	[ ]

Being the most marked person, the inclusive blocks all other persons in the shared domain. First person blocks second person, and second person blocks third.

(13) a. Inclusive person refers to a group which includes the speaker and the addressee.
  b. First person refers to a group which includes the speaker (and, when there is an inclusive person, excludes the addressee).
  c. Second person refers to a group which includes a speech participant (and, when there is a first person, excludes the speaker).
  d. Third person refers to any group (and, when there is a second person, excludes a speech participant).

It also follows that the inclusive is the person that is missing in reduced (three-person) systems such as that of English. Further, we get the right semantics for first person pronouns in such systems, or in those subparadigms of four-person systems that neutralize the inclusive/exclusive distinction.

2.2.2 The meanings of plural predicates

Plural expressions participate in a variety of meanings besides those illustrated above. English bare plurals receive interpretations with seemingly different quantificational forces: generic (14a), 'most' (14b) and existential (14c); cf. e.g. Carlson (1977); Chierchia (1998b); Krifka (2003) and articles 5 [Semantics: Noun Phrases and Verb Phrases] (Dayal) *Bare noun phrases* and 8 [Semantics: Noun Phrases and Verb Phrases] (Carlson) *Genericity*.

(14) a. Dogs are widespread.
  b. Dogs are smart.
  c. Dogs are barking.

According to Carlson, bare plurals uniformly denote names of kinds, e.g. *dogs* denotes the name of the dog-kind, and the verbal predicate that the bare plural combines with is responsible for its interpretation: Kind-level predicates such as *be widespread* apply directly to the kind denoted by the bare plural, resulting in a generic interpretation, whereas predicates such as *be smart* and *be barking* apply to (stages of) individuals that instantiate the kind. The denotation of the bare plural is semantically singular, but stage-level interpretations involve semantic plurality.

Bare plurals in the scope of a plural noun phrase may receive a 'dependent' plural interpretation (Chomsky 1975; de Mey 1981; Roberts 1991). Such interpretations are characterized by two properties: (i) the bare plural argument contributes an narrow-scope existential quantifier, and (ii) the truth of the sentence requires at least two distinct entities in the denotation of the bare plural (Zweig 2008).

Thus, (15) has a dependent plural reading since (i) each unicycle has a wheel, and (ii) the truth of (15) requires there to be at least two wheels (of unicycles).

(15) Unicycles have wheels.

Dependent plurals have been analyzed as a case of cumulative readings (e.g. de Mey 1981; Roberts 1991; Beck 2000), related to the cumulative reading of examples like *Three women gave birth to five babies*, according to which the group of three women together gave birth to five babies. Since bare plurals in downward-entailing contexts do not entail semantic plurality, other authors propose that singulars entail singular reference and that plurality arises from higher-order scalar implicatures (e.g. Spector 2003; Zweig 2008).

Plural nouns also participate in collective and distributive interpretations. In (16a), the individuals denoted by *the fathers* collectively participate in the gathering, while each individual in the denotation of *the fathers* in (16b) individually has the property denoted by the verb *laughed*. See e.g. Landman (1989) and Schwarzschild (1996) for other, e.g. group and bunch, readings.

(16) a. The fathers gathered.
b. The fathers laughed.

Such plural nouns are generally analyzed as semantically plural; the two interpretations are attributed to semantic differences between the verbs: for example, in contrast to *laugh*, *gather* requires the subject to denote a semantically plural entity.

(17) a. The father laughed,
b. #The father gathered.

The two main proposals for capturing the semantic plurality of noun phrases employ sets (e.g. Hoeksema 1983; Winter 2001) and sums (e.g. Link 1983). In e.g. Winter's (2001) set-based analysis of plurals, a plural predicate denotes (the characteristic function of) the set of sets of atomic individuals in the denotation of the singular. In Link's (1983) lattice-theoretic approach, the denotation of a plural predicate is the complete join-semilattice in the universe generated by the atomic individuals in the denotation of the singular. In both proposals, the denotation of the plural includes that of the singular, in contrast to the semantics given in (12); see section 2.2.3. for discussion.

(18) In a universe consisting of two boys a and b, the denotation of *boys* is
a. $[\![boys']\!] = \{\{a\}, \{b\}, \{a, b\}\}$ in Winter's (2001) set-based approach, and
b. $[\![BOYS']\!] = [\![*BOY']\!] = \{a, b, a \sqcup b\}$ in Link's (1983) sum-based approach.

Link (1983) rejects the use of sets for representing the denotation of nouns since "inherent in the notion of a set is atomicity which is not present in the behavior of mass terms" (305). Other authors argue that a representation of plurals as sets can still capture the parallels between plurals and mass; see Lasersohn (1988): ch. 4; Landman (1989: 568–571); Schwarzschild (1996): ch. 2; Zweig (2008): ch. 4 and article 7 [Semantics: Noun Phrases and Verb Phrases] (Lasersohn) *Mass nouns and plurals*.

The semantics of the plural in (12a), together with standard Montague Grammar assumptions about interpretation, accounts for the collective interpretation of a sentence like (19), according to which a group of three students collectively carries a single piano (19a). The distributive interpretation in (19b) is derived with a distributive operator or a distinct meaning for the verbal predicate (e.g. Landman 1989; Lasersohn 1995; Winter 2001). Schwarzschild (1996) shows that context also plays a role.

(19) Three students carried a piano.
 a. Collective: $\exists X \exists y (piano'(y) \wedge |X| = 3 \wedge X \subseteq students' \wedge carry'(X,y))$
 b. Distributive: $\exists X (|X| = 3 \wedge X \subseteq students' \wedge \forall x(x \in X \rightarrow \exists y(carry'(x,y)))$

The traditional distinction between collective predicates *(meet, gather, be a good team)*, distributive predicates *(laugh, enter, have a baby)* and mixed predicates that allow both interpretations *(carry a piano, build a house)* is based on whether a predicate distributes over individuals denoted by the subject (e.g. *Ali and Baba entered the gate* entails *Ali entered the gate and Baba entered the gate*) and whether a predicate can occur with a singular subject (cf. (17)). Refinements and alternative clasifications have been suggested in e.g. Dowty (1987) and Winter (2001).

Cross-linguistic research points to variation in the semantics of number. Kwon & Zribi-Hertz (2004) show that Korean mass nouns can be pluralized (cf. also Spathas 2007 for Greek) and they argue that Korean plural nouns *X-deul* means 'the various X's' (rather than 'who/whatever is X') and derive from this semantics their lack of certain readings: open kind readings, inalienable binding (e.g. body part plurals), quantificational binding, and narrow-scope readings. Similarly, Mizuguchi (2001: 532) proposes that "Japanese plurals are functions that individuate a set into atoms, while English plurals are functions that form a set from atoms". Finally, in contrast to e.g. English where the default number assigned to a noun in the absence of number morphology is singular, the default number in other languages in such cases is unpredictable and must be lexically specified for the noun. In Kiowa (Athapaskan, USA), for example, default number and number agreement divides nouns into nine classes (Watkins 1984; Harbour 2007). Depending on the class, the number assigned to a noun that bears no number marking may be non-plural (all animates, most body parts, tools), dual (many plants and artifacts), or nonsingular. The INVERSE or REVERSATIVE number morpheme -*do* assigns nouns the complement of their default number, as illustrated in Tab. 2.6.

Tab. 2.6: Kiowa inverse number

class	default number	inverse number
nonplural	*tógúl* 'one or two young men'	*tógúú-dɔ* 'three or more young men'
dual	*kɩ́ɔ̃n* 'two tomatoes'	*kɩ́ɔ̃ɔ̃-dɔ* 'one tomato or three or more tomatoes'
nonsingular	*áá* 'two or more sticks'	*áá-dɔ* 'one stick'

Similarly, Arabic has a class of "collective" nouns from which count nouns are derived by the "singulative" or "unit" suffix -*a* (Cowell 1964: 215, 297; Erwin 1963: 165): e.g. *bá'ar* 'cattle', *bá'r-a* 'a cow', *laḥam* 'meat', *laḥm-a* 'a piece of meat', *dafur* 'kicking', *dafr-a* 'a kick'.

2.2.3 Unmarked number

Theories of markedness maintain that semantic and formal markedness converge: the denotation of a formally more complex expression results in a more restricted (more marked) distribution than that of the formally less complex expression. The convergence of semantic and formal markedness is widely assumed in grammatical theories (cf. Koontz-Garboden 2007 for discussion) and has its roots in Roman Jakobson's (1957) proposal that inflectional categories are decomposed into a set of semantically defined features, each of which is binary and privative, as discussed in section 1. Evidence for this position is provided e.g. by the Korean number system, where the plural marker -*tul* contributes the meaning "more than one", while singular nouns lack such a specification, i.e. are semantically unmarked, and "may be either specifically singular, or on occasion be used when more than one object is involved" (Greenberg 1963: 73f.); see Ebert (1997) for psycholinguistic evidence for the markedness of the plural.

The claim that the singular is the semantically unmarked member of the singular/plural opposition has been challenged on the basis of data from English and a variety of other languages in e.g. McCawley (1968), Krifka (1987), Roberts (1991), Ojeda (1995), Sauerland, Anderssen & Yatsushiro (2005) and Farkas (2006). According to these proposals, the denotation of a singular (pro)noun conveys semantic singularity whereas the corresponding plural form is less specific, i.e. subsumes the denotation of the singular.

Both types of analysis need to account for the conditions under which the semantically less marked expression can be used: while proponents of the first position need to account for why a singular form is not typically used to express semantic plurality, proponents of the second position need to account for why plural forms are not typically used with singular meaning, e.g. why *I saw cows* is not used when the speaker saw a single cow. Blocking is appealed to in e.g. Krifka (1987) and Roberts (1991), while Sauerland (2003) and Sauerland, Anderssen & Yatsushiro (2005), who assume that the plural is unmarked since only the singular introduces a presupposition (that the denotation is an atom), appeal to Heim's (1991) *Maximize Presuppositions*. Farkas (2006) assumes that the singular is the default interpretation; the plural is used to override the default and hence receives plural interpretation; cf. Spector (2007) for an account using higher-order implicatures.

If there was a perfect correlation between formal and semantic plurality, examples where a singular (pro)noun does not have singular semantic reference would be evidence for the first position, while examples with plural (pro)nouns that do not have plural semantic reference would be evidence for the second position. Since such a correlation does not, however, exist (cf. section 2.1.), formally plural (pro)nouns that can be used with singular reference, such as German *Sie* or French *vous*, can not be taken as evidence that the denotation of the plural is unmarked with respect to the singular (contrary to e.g. Sauerland, Anderssen & Yatsushiro 2005, henceforth SAY05) but rather only shows that these grammatically plural forms can be used with singular reference, similar to pluralia tantum nouns. Wechsler (2004) shows that assuming that plural forms like *vous* are lexically unspecified for semantic plurality makes correct predictions about of the French pronoun system and also fits with the cross-linguistic semantics of person/number systems. Likewise, even if *their* in (20) can be used "even though it was just one umbrella owned by a single person that was left behind" (SAY05: 415), this only shows that the pronoun in question is only formally but not semantically plural, not that the denotation of semantically plural expressions includes singular entities.

(20) Someone left their umbrella.   (SAY05)

Rullmann's (2003) example in (21) shows that it is not tenable to assume that the plural form is used when "the gender marked singular pronouns *he/she/it* must be avoided" because "the gender of the referent is unknown" (SAY05: 416).

(21) Someone left their jockstrap in the locker room.   (Rullmann 2003: 253)

Rather, *their* seems to have emerged as a gender- and number-neutral variant of the singular pronouns *he* and *she*.

Another type of evidence provided in favor of the second position involves plural noun forms that are semantically plural, and whose denotation has been argued to include atomic entities, such as (22):

(22) Every boy should invite his friends.

Since (22) can be used felicitously in a context where some of the contextually salient boys only have one or no friend, one could assume that the denotation of the plural noun phrase *his friends* includes atomic friends (cf. e.g. SAY05). An alternative analysis of (22) that allows one to maintain traditional assumptions about the relationship between formal and semantic markedness is that *his friends* in (22) is a dependent plural (cf. section 2.2.2.), i.e. does not distribute below the subject universal quantifier, but rather denotes the collective group of friends of all of the contextually salient boys; a plural noun phrase is used since the group of boys invite more than one friend.

Noun phrases with the quantifier *no* such as *no chairs* in (23) are another semantically plural noun phrase whose denotation has been argued to include singular entities. Winter's (2001) contrast been *No teachers are similar* and **No teacher is similar* shows that the number distinction with *no* is not merely a grammatical reflex but semantically meaningful.

(23) No chairs are available.   (SAY05: 409)

SAY05 argue that the plural form does not mean 'two or more' by pointing out that (23) is not equivalent to *Two or more chairs aren't available,* which unlike (23) "implicates the availability of one chair" (410). While this shows that the two utterances have different sets of implications, it does not conclusively show that the denotation of *chairs* must include the atomic entities. Cf. also Schwarzschild's (1996: 5) example in (24), which he argues should be felicitous if the denotation of *men* only includes plural entities.

(24) #No men lifted the piano but John did.   (Chierchia 1998a: 10)

Contrary to Schwarzschild (1996) and SAY05, Chierchia (1998a: 75) argues that such examples do not warrant the conclusion that the plural is semantically less marked that the singular: a modification of the meaning of *no* so that it adds the atomic elements to the denotation of the plural common noun ensures the infelicity of (24). A similar analysis can be given to other determiners that trigger plural agreement but result in noun phrases whose denotation is not (necessarily) plural, e.g. *1.0 cows, zero cows* (Krifka 1987) or *fewer than four cows;* in fact, Krifka (1987) cautions against using such examples as evidence for the position that the plural is semantically unmarked.

Negation also features in examples like (25), which is claimed to be infelicitous in a context where John saw a single bear and hence taken to provide evidence that the denotation of the plural includes singular entities (Krifka 2003; SAY05; Spector 2007).

(25)   John didn't see bears.

There was, however, no consensus among the native speakers of English we consulted that (25) is infelicitous in this context. This fits with the observation that (25) can be felicitously followed with . . . *he only saw ONE bear*. That this reading of (25) is not a case of metalinguistic negation is shown by the acceptability of the negative polarity item *ever* in *John didn't ever see bears, but he often saw single ones.*

A final set of examples provided in favor of the position that the plural is semantically unmarked involves semantically plural forms in form headings (e.g. *schools attended, children,* cf. McCawley 1968), invitations *(You're welcome to bring your children)* and questions *(Do you have children?)* (e.g. Krifka 2003; SAY05; Spector 2007; Zweig 2008). Such plurals are felicitously used even if the person filling out the form or being asked the question only has one child (i.e. can answer with *Yes, one*), which is taken as evidence that the denotation of the plural includes that of the singular. But such examples are unproblematic for the other position, too, if one takes into consideration the role of context. Shared by these examples is the contextual requirement that the speaker (or writer) be maximally inclusive: form headings and invitations need to take into consideration that some people have more than one child, disregarding the fact that a particular person filling out the form or being addressed might only have one (or no) child. According to the position where the singular is semantically unmarked, use of the singular implicates the absence of a plural meaning, such that e.g. *You're welcome to bring your child* implicates that the addressee has (at most) one child, which is not acceptable in such contexts. Further evidence for this context-dependency is presented by examples like (26) and (27) which show that the plural is felicitous only in those contexts where it is plausible that the cardinality could be larger than one (cf. also Farkas 2006). If this condition is not met, as in (26a) and (27a), the singular form is used:

(26)   Context: Addressing a single person.
     a. Will you bring your spouse/#spouses?
     b. Will you bring your child/children?

(27)   a. (to a friend you are helping with a cleaning task) #Do you have brooms?
     b. (to a shop keeper) Do you have brooms?   (Zweig 2008: 24)

In sum, the currently available evidence does not warrant abandoning the traditional correlation between formal and semantic markedness in the singular/plural paradigm.

2.2.4 Gender

The inflectional category 'gender' classifies (pro)nouns. The semantic notion most commonly associated with the semantic exponents of this inflectional category is sex, although there are many conceivable ways of classifying entities, especially humans, such as animacy, humanness, and (ir)rationality (Corbett 1991). While every gender system has some (pro)nouns whose gender assignment depends on semantic gender (Corbett 1991: 63; Dahl 2000: 101), languages differ in the location of the cut-off point for the assignment of semantic gender on the animacy hierarchy in Fig. 2.1.

In Tamil (Dravidian, India), there are separate genders for male humans and female humans, while everything else is assigned to a third gender (Corbett 1991: 9), i.e. the cut-off point is between HUMAN and ANIMAL. In many Indo-European languages, humans and some higher animals are assigned masculine and feminine gender on the basis of their sex (e.g. German *die Kuh* 'the.FEM cow'), while inanimates and lower animals get their genders by lexeme-specific or formal criteria. Thus, the ANIMAL class does not always behave homogenously (Dahl 2000). Gender in Ket (isolate, Russia) distinguishes between male animates, female animates, and a residue class that includes mainly inanimates (Corbett 1991: 19). Since neither of the two sex categories is more or less marked than the other, establishing semantic markedness for the inflectional category 'gender' is inconclusive.

2.3 Person, number and gender at the syntax-semantics interface

Person, number and gender are formal categories that are semantically interpreted, but also have consequences for syntax, in the form of agreement. A key question in the formal treatment of these categories is the extent to which agreement is to be treated semantically; cf. also article 6 [this volume] (von Stechow) *Syntax and semantics*. Cooper (1983) proposes a semantic account according to which agreement markers trigger presuppositions. In *A neighbor$_i$ thinks that she$_i$ saw John*, for example, the pronoun *she$_i$* triggers the presupposition that the neighbor is female; the value of **The man washes herself* is undefined since the denotation of the subject is not in the domain of the partial function denoted by the reflexive pronoun (cf. also Dowty & Jacobson 1988). For arguments that number agreement is a semantic phenomenon see e.g. Bartsch (1973), Scha (1981), Link (1983), Hoek-sema (1983) and Lasersohn (1988). While some semantic analyses are restricted to non-local agreement (e.g. agreement of subjects with predicative adjectives, of pronominal anaphora with their antecedents), other analyses (e.g. Hoeksema 1983; Winter 2001) also treat local agreement semantically (e.g. subject-verb agreement, noun-adjective agreement). Winter (2001: ch. 5), for example, develops an analysis of collective and distributive readings of plurals that assigns different semantic types to singular and plural predicates and thereby also accounts for local agreement. In a departure from more classical treatments of inflection (e.g. Bennett 1974; Chierchia 1998a; Schwarzschild 1996), which assume that only inflectional morphology on nouns is semantically interpreted while that on verbs simply functions as markers of agreement, Winter (2001) assumes that every overt exponent of (number) inflection is semantically interpreted (be it on nouns, verbs or adjectives). Sauerland (2003) takes a leap in the opposite direction and proposes that none of the overt exponents of inflectional morphology (in a DP) are semantically interpreted, and instead analyzes them as (uninterpreted) markers of agreement with the (interpreted) number feature that is realized (covertly) in the head of the ø-phrase (øP), a syntactic head over D.

Examples like (28), attributed to Irene Heim, illustrate the need for distinguishing between the semantic and the grammatical reflexes of person, number and gender agreement. The two interpretations of (28), given as LF1 and LF2, differ in whether *my* receives a bound variable interpretation (LF1) or not (LF2). In the former case, (28) means that nobody but me is an x such that x did x's homework.

(28) Only I did my homework.
 LF1: [only I] $\lambda x\, x$ did x's homework.
 LF2: [only I] $\lambda x\, x$ did my homework.

Kratzer (1998) proposes that the first person features of the pronoun *my* are mere agreement reflexes, which need to be present at the level of phonological form (PF) but are absent at logical form (LF). Since pronouns can start out as zero pronouns, in which case they do not bear inflectional information, they do not contribute a presupposition at LF. Such pronouns receive features at PF under agreement with a suitable nominal antecedent (cf. also Rullmann 2004). An alternative proposal, von Stechow (2003), suggests that all pronouns start out with φ-features but that features of bound pronouns are deleted at LF.

In contrast to the above proposals, which assume that agreement involves checking features on targets that are specified on a trigger, Pollard & Sag (1988, 1994) motivate treatments of agreement as constraint satisfaction: for example, even through a ship can be referred to both as *she* and *it*, utterances such as *The ship lurched and then she rightened itself* are ruled out by requiring that the reflexive pronoun and its antecedent share the same features. Wechsler (2004) shows that it is not sufficient to treat agreement as the systematic co-variation in form. For example, Pollard and Sag's (1994: 97) claim that predicative adjectives show semantic agreement while finite verbs show grammatical agreement is satisfied for e.g. the formal use of *vous* (grammatically plural, semantically singular) as in (29a,b) but fails for pluralia tantum nouns like *ciseaux* 'scissors' in (29c), which can be semantically singular but nevertheless trigger plural agreement with predicative adjectives.

(29) a. Vous   êtes   loyal.
        you.PL/FORMAL be.2PL loyal.SG
        'You (one formal addressee) are loyal.'   (Wechsler 2004: 255)

   b. Vous   êtes   loyaux.
        you.PL/FORMAL be.2PL loyal.PL
        'You (multiple addressees) are loyal.'   (Wechsler 2004: 255)

   c. Ces   ciseaux   sont   idéaux   / *idéal   pour couper le velour
        this.PL SCISSORS(PL) are.PL ideal.M.PL / ideal.M.SG for CUT.INF the velour.
        'These scissors are ideal for cutting hair.'   (Wechsler 2004: 256)

Wechsler argues that assuming two plural features for French (one for grammatical number, the other for semantic number) is not empirically motivated since the language only has one plural inflection. His analysis instead holds that a plural agreement target is not semantically potent when the noun phrase it agrees with is plural-marked; otherwise, it may introduce semantic plurality. Thus, (30a) with *are* is grammatical since the subject noun phrase *these books* is semantically and grammatically plural; *are* in (30b) introduces optionally introduces semantic plurality since the subject noun phrase is only grammatically plural. The version with *is* is ungrammatical in (30a,b) since *is* requires grammatical and semantic singularity. In (30c), both *is* and *are* are acceptable: with *is* the subject noun phrase denotes a single entity, with *are*, it is required to denote two separate entities.

(30) a. These books are / *is interesting.
     b. These scissors are / *is dull.
     c. His lifelong friend and the editor of his autobiography is / are at his bedside.

The need for recognizing the semantic as well as the grammatical side of person, number and gender is also apparent in coordination resolution. In many languages, the inflectional properties of a coordinate noun phrase are determined on the basis of the semantic person, number or gender values of the individual noun phrase conjuncts (see Corbett 1991; Johannessen 1998 for other resolution strategies). The Fula (Niger-Congo) verb in (31a) is marked for first person inclusive since the coordinated noun phrase subject denotes a group that includes the speaker. The French verb in (31b) is marked for masculine gender since only semantically feminine noun phrases trigger feminine agreement and the grammatically feminine conjunct *la sentinelle* 'the sentry' denotes a man. Thus, number but not person is a non-distributive feature since none of the conjuncts in (31a) bears the value of the coordinate noun phrase (Dalrymple & Kaplan 2000).

(31) a. Fula (adapted from Dalrymple & Kaplan 2000: 782)
 an e Bill e min kö Afriki djodu-dèn.
 you and Bill and I in Afrika live.1INCL
 'You and Bill and I, we live in Afrika.'

 b. French (adapted from Wechsler 2009: 572)
 La sentinelle et sa femme ont été pris / *prises
 the.FEM sentry.FEM and POSS wife were taken.MASC taken.FEM
 en otage.
 hostage
 'The sentry and his wife were taken hostage.'

While Corbett's (1991) resolution rules can account for the person, number and gender of coordination constructions, their limitation to coordination constructions is problematic since plural anaphoric pronouns follow the same constraints, as pointed out in Farkas & Zee (1995): for example, the French utterance *Ils/*elles sont malheureux/*-malheureuse* (they.MASC/they.FEM are unhappy.MASC/unhappy.FEM) is a felicitous continuation of (31b). Formal analyses of resolution characterize the features of individual conjuncts as sets; the feature value of the coordinate noun phrase is the intersection or union of these sets (e.g. Hoeksema 1983; Sag et al. 1985; Dalrymple & Kaplan 2000; Sadler 2006; Wechsler 2009). In contrast to person and number resolution, which are purely semantic, both grammatical and semantic gender affect gender resolution (see Farkas & Zee 1995; Sadler 2006; Wechsler 2009 for discussion).

2.4 Inflectional meanings and lexical classes

Cross-linguistically, co-occurrence with particular inflectional morphemes determines lexical categoryhood. Expressions that occur with the same set of inflections are also assumed to form a natural class semantically, under the view that the meaning of a particular inflectional category is compatible with the inherent semantic type of the core members of a given word class (e.g. Bybee 1985: 13–19; Croft 1991: 79, 86). Tense, for instance, occurs with verbs since they denote temporally less stable entities (compared to nouns) that need to be temporally anchored, and definiteness is a category of nouns since these denote individualized, time-stable entities (Givón 1979; Givón 1984). These assumption have been challenged on the basis of descriptions of languages where markers of plurality and markes of tense, aspect or modality are morphologically realized and interpreted on verbs and nouns, respectively. Verbal plural markers, also called 'pluractional' markers, indicate the plurality of events and are found in a wide variety of languages (Mithun 1988; Lasersohn 1995: ch. 13, and references therein). The plurality of events can manifest itself as multiple event participants, multiple occurrences of the event over time, or occurrences of the event in different locations (Lasersohn 1995:240). In some languages, e.g. ǂHoan (Khoisan, Botswana) as described in Collins (2001), the same plural marker is used for nouns and verbs. Formal analyses have related pluractionality to the semantics of collectivity and distributivity (e.g. Ojeda 1998 for Papago (Uto-Aztecan, USA)), verbal aspect (e.g. van Geenhoven 2005 for Greenlandic (Eskimo-Aleut, Greenland) and reciprocity (e.g. Faller 2007 for Cuzco Quechua (Quechua, Peru)). Nordlinger & Sadler (2004) present cross-linguistic evidence that tense, aspect and mood can be cross-linguistically marked and interpreted on nouns (see also Tonhauser 2006: ch. 9 for discussion), but their claim of the existence of nominal tenses has been challenged in Tonhauser (2006, 2007, 2008) on the basis of a detailed analysis of such markers in Paraguayan Guaraní (Tupí-Guaraní, Paraguay), which are instead analyzed as aspect/modal markers. While these findings suggest that inflectional categories cannot be assumed to universally pertain to either nouns or verbs, they also demonstrate the need for rigorous formal semantic definitions of the meaning of (inflectional) categories for cross-linguistic and cross-category comparison (see Nordlinger & Sadler 2004; Nordlinger & Sadler 2008; Tonhauser 2008 for discussion).

3 Case

3.1 Semantic case features

Grammatical analysis of richly inflected languages shows that morphological cases fall into intersecting natural classes, revealed by neutralization patterns

(syncretism), shared syntactic properties, and other grammatical diagnostics. Traditional grammar holds that cases have meanings and fall into natural classes on the basis of shared meanings. Formal grammar provides three main ways to model such case groupings:
1. A linear ordering, such that any set of adjacent cases is a potential natural class (Plank 1991).
2. Cross-classifying privative semantically defined features (Jakobson 1936; Jakobson 1958; Neidle 1988).
3. An inheritance hierarchy (Przepiórkowski 1999: ch. 3) or a lattice (Grimm 2011) where cases in their syntactic function refer to coherent regions in this space.

The linear ordering method served Pāṇini well in his Sanskrit grammar, but does not generalize well to some other case systems. Jakobson's approach of decomposing cases into semantically defined features has been mainly applied to Slavic languages (but see Bierwisch 1967); it is undermined by the imprecise semantic definitions of his case features.

3.2 Structural and inherent case

Recent work distinguishes two types of case, GRAMMATICAL case and SEMANTIC case (Kuryłowicz 1964), or STRUCTURAL and INHERENT (or LEXICAL) case (Chomsky 1981), where the former have no meaning. Chomsky proposes that grammatical relations (ABSTRACT CASES) are determined by the syntactic configuration at S-structure, and SPELLOUT RULES assign morphological case to arguments that bear them. In minimalist terms, structural case is an UNINTERPRETABLE FEATURE. Inherent cases do have a meaning; they are assigned at deep (D-)structure, in some cases depending on the governing predicate's lexical semantic properties, or in some cases idiosyncrat-ically (QUIRKY CASE). A semantic decomposition seems more promising for them.

The richer the case system, the more compelling the case for semantic decomposition; it is inevitable for the elaborate local case systems of many richly inflected languages. Although the local cases are not necessarily morphologically complex, their semantics is like that of compound pre/prepositions, as illustrated by the subsystem of local cases in Lezgian (Haspelmath 1993) in Tab. 2.7.

In Jackendoff's (1983, 1990, 1996) analysis, locative cases are built from Path functions and Place functions:

Tab. 2.7: Lezgian local cases

	'at'	'in'	'behind'	'under'	'on'
location	adessive	inessive	postessive	subessive	superessive
source	adelative	inelative	postelative	subelative	superelative
goal	addirective	(indirective)	postdirective	subdirective	superdirective

(32) a. Path functions: at, to, from, toward, away-from, via
 b. Place functions: under, in, behind, on...

Path functions are applied to local relations, which are formed by applying a Place function to a Thing:

(33) Lezgian Postelative
 sew-re-qʰ-aj
 bear-ERG-POSTESSIVE-INELATIVE
 'from behind the bear'
 [Path FROM [Place BEHIND [Thing BEAR]]]

The same structure extends to non-local relations, though usually less transparently. Finnish treats States like Places, so cases denoting state and change-of-state pattern with the locative cases, as in Tab. 2.8.

Tab. 2.8: Finnish cases

	'at', accidental location	'in', inherent location		'as', state
state/location	adessive *-lla*	inessive *-ssa*		essive *-na*
source	ablative *-lta*		elative *-sta*	
goal	allative *-lle*	illative *-seen, -hen*		translative *-ksi*

The relation between essive (predication of state) and translative (predication of change-of-state) is quite parallel to that between inessive 'in' and illative 'into'.

(34) Se tuli iso-ksi ongelma-ksi
 It (be)came big-Transl problem-Transl
 'It became a big problem' ('came to as a big problem')

 [Path TO [State AS [Thing BIG PROBLEM]]]

Important non-local semantic cases include the instrumental 'with', 'by means of' (Strigin 1995; McKercher 2002), and the comitative (sociative, associative) 'with, accompanied by' (which are often syncretic; Croft 1991; McGregor 1989; Stolz 2001a; Stolz 2001b; Stolz & Stroh 2001), and the abessive (caritive) 'without'.

Localist theories of case (Hjelmslev 1935; Anderson 1971) and of Th-roles (Gruber 1965; Jackendoff 1987) hold that various abstract domains such as possession, emotion, desire, cognition etc. are organized in a way that is parallel to the domain of spatial relations.

An apparently hybrid intermediate class of cases pattern syntactically with the structural cases, but are semantically conditioned. These cases however depend on different semantic conditions than inherent cases do: instead of being sensitive to the thematic relation that the NP bears to the verbal predicate, they are sensitive to a subclass of functional categories, especially definiteness, animacy, quantificational properties, the aspectual or modal character of the VP, or some combination of these factors—pretheoretically characterized in the literature in terms of "affectedness" or "degree of transitivity". Examples include the Finnish accusative, which is assigned to complements of bounded (non-gradable) verbal predicates, while other complements are assigned partitive case (Kiparsky 1998); and the Hindi accusative case, which is assigned to specific complements.

Minimalist analyses have tried to accommodate these cases to the normal type of structural case by positing case assignment or checking in various higher functional projections. For example, it has been suggested that Finnish accusative is checked in AspP, a functional projection which induces telicity, while partitive is checked in a lower projection (Borer 2005; Megerdoomian 2000; van Hout 2000; Ritter & Rosen 2000; Csirmaz 2005; Kratzer 2004; Svenonius 2002; Thomas 2003).

A further challenge for theories that separate structural and inherent case is the substantial overlap between them. All structural cases except nominative function also as inherent case. In some Indo-European languages, accusative case marks not only objects, but direction and extent of time. Ergative case is commonly identical to instrumental case down to the last allomorphic detail, as in many Australian languages. The dative often doubles as a semantic case (typically syncretic with directional locative 'to' case) in quite systematic ways (e.g. Japanese *ni*, Romance *a*). While this does not invalidate the distinction between structural and inherent case, it does invite a search for a unification of them. One such approach is outlined in the next section.

3.3 The relational semantics of structural case

Grammatical relations reflect the semantic relations between predicates and their arguments. Nearly all linguistic theories are designed to capture this relationship, usually by some notion of Theta-roles. A weakness of all traditional case theories (including Jakobson's and Chomsky's) is that they provide no principled intrinsic relationship between grammatical relations and the morphosyntactic cases that mark them. Government & Binding Theory merely masks the stipulative character of the association by a terminological and typographical artifice. The lower-case morphosyntactic category "accusative", for example, *sounds* like the capitalized abstract Case "Accusative", but the relation between them is no less arbitrary within this theory.

Kiparsky (2001) has suggested that structural cases do have a semantic basis, but it is relational rather than material. Once this is recognized, morphosyntactic case and abstract case (grammatical relations) can be unified. He proposes two relational case features, [±H(ighest) R(ole)] and [±L(owest) R(ole)] (see also Wunderlich 2003). Their fully specified feature combinations define the four known grammatical relations A, S, O, D, and their underspecified negative feature values define the four morphosyntactic structural cases nominative, accusative, dative, ergative. These relations can be modeled equally well by a lattice. Either way, they yield the markedness scale nominative < accusative, ergative < dative. This correctly predicts that if a language has a dative it has either an accusative or an ergative, and that if it has case at all, it has nominative.

Tab. 2.9: Kiparsky's analysis of case

	Grammatical relations		Structural cases	
a.	[+HR,+LR]	S (intransitive subject)	[ ]	nominative
b.	[−HR,+LR]	O (direct object)	[−HR]	accusative
c.	[+HR,−LR]	A (transitive subject)	[−LR]	ergative
d.	[−HR,−LR]	D (indirect object)	[−HR,−LR]	dative

Structural case assignment is formal unification of feature matrices subject to the same principles that govern the distribution of all morphosyntactic elements. In particular, each Th-role is associated with argument bearing the most specific (most highly marked) morphosyntactic case that is compatible with (unifies with) the Th-role's abstract Case. Arbitrary spellout rules (correspondence rules, mapping rules) have no place in this approach.

Following Bierwisch (1967, 1983, 1986, 1997) and Bierwisch & Schreuder (1992), Kiparsky assumes a level of Semantic Form, an interface between conceptual knowledge and syntactic structure (see article 5 [Semantics: Theories] (Lang & Maienborn) *Two-level Semantics*). A predicate is represented at Semantic Form by a function, and the predicate's Th-roles correspond to λ-abstractors over the function's variables. The semantic role of the variable over which a λ-operator abstracts determines the semantic content of the resulting Th-role, and the variable's depth of embedding in Semantic Form (the inverse of the order of λ-abstractors) determines the Th-role's rank in the structural ordering known as the hierarchy of thematic roles. For example, *show* has three Th-roles, of which the highest, the Agent, is saturated last.

(35) *show:* λzλyλx [*x* CAUSE [CAN [*y* SEE *z*]]]

Abstract case and morphosyntactic case are assigned as follows:

(36)

$$\begin{bmatrix} \lambda x \\ [+HR] \end{bmatrix} \quad \begin{bmatrix} \lambda y \\ [\ ] \end{bmatrix} \quad \begin{bmatrix} \lambda z \\ [+LR] \end{bmatrix} \quad \text{Th-roles with abstract Case assigned}$$

$$\begin{bmatrix} \ \ \end{bmatrix} \quad \begin{bmatrix} -LR \\ -HR \end{bmatrix} \quad \begin{bmatrix} -HR \end{bmatrix} \quad \text{morphosyntactic case selected}$$

(NOM) (DAT) (ACC)

The case features define classes of grammatical relations which play a role in syntactic constraints, such as binding, control, and parallelism in coordination. For example, the feature [+HR] picks out "A" and "S" in any language, irrespective of its case system, and thus universally defines the relation of grammatical subject. They also provide the appropriate representation on which valency-changing operations are defined (see also article 7 [this volume] (Wunderlich) *Operations on argument structure*).

The compositional analysis brings out analogies between structural and semantic cases (Ostler 1979). The spatial domain corresponds to the four basic structural case categories.

Tab. 2.10: Structural and semantic case

		Structural	Spatial	Examples of locative cases
a.	[ ]	nominative	location ('at', 'in')	locative, inessive, adessive
b.	[–HR]	accusative	end point ('to', 'into')	illative, allative, terminative
c.	[–LR]	ergative	source ('from', 'out of')	elative, ablative, exessive
d.	[–HR,–LR]	dative	goal ('towards')	lative, directive

These correspondences are borne out by synchronic syncretism patterns and historical change.

4 Evidentiality

Evidentiality is "the grammatical encoding of the speaker's (type of) *grounds* for making a speech act [...]. For assertions, the speaker's grounds can be identified with the speaker's source for the information conveyed by the utterance" (Faller 2002: 2, emphasis in original). Crosslinguistically, three main types of source of information are encoded by evidentials (Willett 1988): information obtained from visual, auditory or other sensory sources, information that is based on reports from others or tales, and information attained through reasoning on the basis of logic, intuition, mental constructs or previous experience. Cuzco Quechua has separate morphemes (*-mi, -si* and *-chá*) for these three evidential meanings: while the examples in (37) all convey a similar content (p = 'It is/might be/must be raining'), they differ in the speaker's source of evidence (EV).

(37) Cuzco Quechua evidentials (data adapted from Faller 2002: 3)

   a. Para-sha-n-mi.
      rain-PROG-3-mi
      p = 'It is raining.', EV = speaker sees that p

   b. Para-sha-n-si.
      rain-PROG-3-si
      p = 'It is raining.', EV = speaker was told that p

   c. Para-sha-n-chá.
      rain-PROG-3-chá
      p = 'It might/must be raining.', EV = speaker conjectures that p

Evidential systems of other languages code more evidential distinctions than Cuzco Quechua (cf. e.g. Morse & Maxwell 1999 on Cubeo (Tucanoan, Columbia)) or less; see Aikhenvald (2004) for a typology of evidential systems.

Faller (2002) formally analyzes the Cuzco Quechua evidentials as illocutionary operators (Austin 1962) which modify the sincerity conditions of the proposition that is their argument and express an evidential relation between the speaker and the proposition expressed. Evidentials of other languages, including Bulgarian (Izvorski 1997) and St'át'imcets (Salish, Canada; Matthewson, Rullmann & Davis 2008), have been analyzed as epistemic modals (see also Palmer 1986; Kiefer 1994), i.e. as quantifiers over possible worlds: an utterance containing an evidential denotes the proposition that, in every world in the modal base (which contains e.g. worlds in which the perceived or reported evidence holds), the proposition the evidential applies to is true. While evidentials are a type of epistemic modal on this view, Faller (2002) argues that the two are separate but overlapping categories; see Chafe (1986) for the position that evidentiality subsumes modality. A set of empirical criteria for distinguishing the two types of evidentials is presented in Matthewson, Rullmann & Davis (2008). Murray's (2010) dynamic semantic analysis of evidentials in Cheyenne (Algonquian, USA) as contributing both an evidential restriction and an illocutionary relation reconciles the two types of analysis.

While the St'át'imcets evidentials are part of the modal paradigm of the language, the Cuzco Quechua evidentials in (37) are traditionally analyzed as part of the focus enclitics (Faller 2002). The language also has a past tense marker that gives rise to a non-visual evidential meaning by locating the eventuality outside the speaker's perceptual field at topic time (Faller 2004). A different type of interaction between evidentials and tense is observed in Korean, where the evidentials are part of the mood system (as in Cheyenne): while distinct evidential meanings are often expressed in other languages by different evidential markers, the two Korean evidentials give rise to different evidential meanings in interaction with the tenses (Lee 2010). An interaction between evidentiality and aspect has been found in Bulgarian and Turkish, which express evidentiality in the form of the present perfect (Izvorski 1997; Slobin & Akşu 1982).

5 References

Aikhenvald, Alexandra Y. 2004. *Evidentiality*. Oxford: Oxford University Press.
Aksenov, A. T. 1984. K probleme ekstralingvisticeskoj grammaticeskoj roda [On the extralinguistic motivation of the grammatical category of gender]. *Voprosy jazykoznanija* 3, 14–25.
Anderson, John 1971. *The Grammar of Case. Towards a Localist Theory*. Cambridge: Cambridge University Press.
Austin, John L. 1962. *How to Do Things with Words*. Cambridge, MA: Harvard University Press.
Bartsch, Renate 1973. The semantics and syntax of number and numerals. In: J. P. Kimball (ed.). *Syntax and Semantics 2*. New York: Seminar Press, 51–93.
Beck, Sigrid 2000. Star operators. Episode 1: Defense of the double star. In: K. Kusumoto & E. Villalta (eds.). *Issues in Semantics* (UMass Occasional Papers in Linguistics 23). Amherst, MA: GLSA, 1–23.
Bennett, Michael R. 1974. *Some Extensions of a Montague Fragment of English*. Ph.D. dissertation. University of California, Los Angeles, CA.
Benveniste, Emile 1966. Relationships of person in the verb. In: E. Benveniste. *Problems in General Linguistics*. Coral Gables, FL: University of Miami Press, 195–204. English translation of: E. Benveniste. *Problemès de linguistique générale*. Paris: Gallimard, 1966.

Bierwisch, Manfred 1967. Syntactic features in morphology. General problems of so-called pronominal inflection in German. In: *To Honor Roman Jakobson. Essays on the Occasion of his Seventieth Birthday, Vol. I*. The Hague: Mouton, 239–270.

Bierwisch, Manfred 1983. Semantische und konzeptuelle Repräsentationen lexikalischer Einheiten. In: W. Motsch & R. Ruzicka (eds.). *Untersuchungen zur Semantik*. Berlin: Akademie Verlag, 125–175.

Bierwisch, Manfred 1986. On the nature of semantic form in natural language. In: F. Klix & H. Hangendorf (eds.). *Human Memory and Cognitive Capabilities, Part B*. Amsterdam: Elsevier, 765–783.

Bierwisch, Manfred 1997. Lexical information from a minimalist point of view. In: Ch. Wilder, H.-M. Gärtner & M. Bierwisch (eds.). *The Role of Economy Principles in Linguistic Theory*. Berlin: Akademie Verlag, 227–266.

Bierwisch, Manfred & Robert Schreuder 1992. From concepts to lexical items. *Cognition* 42, 23–60.

Bittner, Maria 2005. Future discourse in a tenseless language. *Journal of Semantics* 22, 339–387.

Bittner, Maria 2008. Aspectual universals of temporal anaphora. In: S. Rothstein (ed.). *Theoretical and Crosslinguistic Approaches to the Semantics of Aspect*. Amsterdam: Benjamins, 349–385.

Bohnemeyer, Jürgen 2002. *The Grammar of Time Reference in Yukatek Maya*. Munich: Lincom.

Borer, Hagit 2005. *Structuring Sense*. Oxford: Oxford University Press.

Bybee, Joan 1985. *Morphology*. Amsterdam: Benjamins.

Carlson, Gregory 1977. *Reference to Kinds in English*. Ph.D. dissertation. University of Massachusetts, Amherst, MA.

Chafe, Wallace 1986. Evidentiality in English conversation and academic writing. In: W. Chafe & J. Nichols (eds.). *Evidentiality. The Linguistic Coding of Epistemology*. Norwood, NJ: Ablex Publishing Corporation, 203–213.

Chierchia, Gennaro 1998a. Plurality of mass nouns and the notion of "semantic parameter". In: S. Rothstein (ed.). *Events and Grammar*. Dordrecht: Kluwer, 53–103.

Chierchia, Gennaro 1998b. Reference to kinds across languages. *Natural Language Semantics* 6, 339–405.

Chomsky, Noam 1975. Questions of form and interpretation. *Linguistic Analysis* 1, 75–109.

Chomsky, Noam 1981. *Lectures on Government and Binding*. Dordrecht: Foris.

Collins, Chris 2001. Aspects of plurality in ǂHoan. *Language* 11, 457–476.

Cooper, Robin 1983. *Quantification and Syntactic Theory*. Dordrecht: Reidel.

Corbett, Greville 1991. *Gender*. Cambridge: Cambridge University Press.

Corbett, Greville 2000. *Number*. Cambridge: Cambridge University Press.

Cowell, Mark 1964. *A Reference Grammar of Syrian Arabic*. Washington, DC: Georgetown University Press.

Croft, William 1991. *Syntactic Categories and Grammatical Relations*. Chicago, IL: The University of Chicago Press.

Csirmaz, Aniko 2005. *Semantics and Phonology in Syntax*. Ph.D. dissertation. MIT, Cambridge, MA.

Cysouw, Michael 2003. *The Paradigmatic Structure of Person Marking*. Oxford: Oxford University Press.

Cysouw, Michael 2005. What it means to be rare. The case of person marking. In: Z. Frajzyngier & D. Rood (eds.). *Linguistic Diversity and Language Theories*. Amsterdam: Benjamins, 235–258.

Dahl, Östen 2000. Animacy and the notion of semantic gender. In: B. Unterbeck & M. Rissanen (eds.). *Gender in Grammar and Cognition, Vol. 1: Approaches to Gender*. Berlin: de Gruyter, 99–115.

Dalrymple, Mary & Ron Kaplan 2000. Feature indeterminacy and feature resolution. *Language* 76, 759–798.
Daniel, Michael 2005. Understanding inclusives. In: E. Filimonova (ed.). *Clusivity. Typology and Case Studies of the Inclusive-Exclusive Distinction*. Amsterdam: Benjamins, 3—48.
Dixon, Robert M. W. 1972. *The Dyirbal Language of North Queensland*. Cambridge: Cambridge University Press.
Dowty, David 1987. Collective predicates, distributive predicates and all. In: F. Marshall (ed.). *Proceedings of the Eastern States Conference on Linguistics (= ESCOL) 3*. Columbus, OH: Ohio State University, 97–115.
Dowty, David & Pauline Jacobson 1988. Agreement as a semantic phenomenon. In: J. Powers & K. de Jong (eds.). *Proceedings of the Eastern States Conference on Linguistics (= ESCOL) 4*. Columbus, OH: Ohio State University, 95–108.
Ebert, Kathleen 1997. The marked effect of number on subject-verb agreement. *Journal of Memory and Language* 36, 147–164.
Emonds, Joseph 1985. *A Unified Theory of Syntactic Categories*. Dordrecht: Foris.
Erwin, Wallace 1963. *A Short Reference Grammar of Iraqi Arabic*. Washington, DC: Georgetown University Press.
Faller, Martina 2002. *Semantics and Pragmatics of Evidentials in Cuzco Quechua*. Ph.D. dissertation. Stanford University, Stanford, CA.
Faller, Martina 2004. The deictic core of "non-experienced past" in Cuzco Quechua. *Journal of Semantics* 21, 45–85.
Faller, Martina 2007. The ingredients of reciprocity in Cuzco Quechua. *Journal of Semantics* 24, 255–288.
Farkas, Donka 2006. The unmarked determiner. In: S. Vogeleer & L. Tasmowski (eds.). *Non-Definiteness and Plurality*. Amsterdam: Benjamins, 81–106.
Farkas, Donka & Draga Zee 1995. Agreement and pronominal reference. In: G. Cinque & G. Giusti (eds.). *Advances in Roumanian Linguistics*. Amsterdam: Benjamins, 83–101.
van Geenhoven, Veerle 2005. Aspect, pluractionality and adverb quantification. In: H. Verkuyl, H. de Swart & A. van Hout (eds.). *Perspectives on Aspect*. Dordrecht: Springer, 107–124.
Givón, Talmy 1979. *On Understanding Grammar*. New York: Academic Press.
Givón, Talmy 1984. *Syntax. A Functional/Typological Introduction. Vol. I*. Amsterdam: Benjamins.
Greenberg, Joseph H. 1963. Some universals of grammar with particular reference to the order of meaningful elements. In: J. H. Greenberg (ed.). *Universals of Language*. Cambridge, MA: The MIT Press, 73–113.
Greenberg, Joseph H. 1988. The first person inclusive dual as an ambiguous category. *Studies in Language* 12, 1–18.
Grimm, Scott 2011. Semantics of case. *Morphology* 21, 515–544.
Gruber, Jeffrey 1965. *Studies in Lexical Relations*. Ph.D. dissertation. MIT, Cambridge, MA.
Harbour, Daniel 2007. *Morphosemantic Number. From Kiowa Noun Classes to UG Number Features*. Dordrecht: Springer.
Harley, Heidi & Elizabeth Ritter 2002. Person and number in pronouns. A feature-geometric analysis. *Language* 78, 482–526.
Haspelmath, Martin 1993. *A Grammar of Lezgian*. Berlin: Mouton de Gruyter.
Heim, Irene 1991. Artikel und Definitheit (Article and definiteness). In: A. von Stechow & D. Wunderlich (eds.). *Semantik—Semantics. Ein internationales Handbuch der zeitgenössischen Forschung—An International Handbook of Contemporary Research* (HSK 6). Berlin: de Gruyter, 487–535.

Hjelmslev, Louis 1935. *La catégorie des cas*. Aarhus: Universitetsforlaget.
Hoeksema, Jack 1983. Plurality and conjunction. In: A. ter Meulen (ed.). *Studies in Modeltheoretic Semantics*. Dordrecht: Foris, 63–83.
Horn, Laurence 1989. *A Natural History of Negation*. Chicago, IL: The University of Chicago Press.
van Hout, Angeliek 2000. Event semantics in the lexicon-syntax interface. In: C. Tenny & J. Pustejovsky (eds.). *Events as Grammatical Objects*. Stanford, CA: CSLI Publications, 239–282.
Izvorski, Roumyana 1997. The present perfect as an epistemic modal. In: A. Lawson & E. Cho (eds.). *Proceedings of Semantics and Linguistic Theory (= SALT) VII*. Ithaca, NY: Cornell University, 222–239.
Jackendoff, Ray 1983. *Semantics and Cognition*. Cambridge, MA: The MIT Press.
Jackendoff, Ray 1987. The status of thematic relations in linguistic theory. *Linguistic Inquiry* 18, 369–411.
Jackendoff, Ray 1990. *Semantic Structures*. Cambridge, MA: The MIT Press.
Jackendoff, Ray 1996. The architecture of the linguistic-spatial interface. In: P. Bloom et al. (eds.). *Language and Space*. Cambridge, MA: The MIT Press, 1–30.
Jakobson, Roman 1936. Beitrag zur allgemeinen Kasuslehre. *Travaux du Cercle Linguistique de Prague* 6, 240–288.
Jakobson, Roman 1957/1971. Shifters, verbal categories, and the Russian verb. In: R. Jakobson. *Selected Writings, Vol. 2: Word and Language*. The Hague: Mouton, 386–392.
Jakobson, Roman 1958. Morphological observations on Slavic declension. The structure of Russian case forms. Reprinted in: L. Waugh & M. Halle (eds.). *Russian and Slavic Grammar: Studies, 1931–1981*. The Hague: Mouton, 1984, 105–133.
Jakobson, Roman 1985. The primary syntactic split and its corollary. In: R. Jakobson. *Selected Writings, Vol. 7*. The Hague: Mouton, 66–67.
Jespersen, Otto 1924. *The Philosophy of Grammar*. London: Allen & Unwin.
Johannessen, Janne Bondi 1998. *Coordination*. Oxford: Oxford University Press.
Kamp, Hans & Uwe Reyle 1993. *From Discourse to Logic*. Dordrecht: Kluwer.
Kiefer, Ferenc 1994. Modality. In: R.E. Asher (ed.). *The Encyclopedia of Language and Linguistics*. Oxford: Pergamon Press, 2515–2520.
Kiparsky, Paul 1998. Partitive case and aspect. In: M. Butt & W. Geuder (eds.). *Projecting from the Lexicon*. Stanford, CA: CSLI Publications, 265–307.
Kiparsky, Paul 2001. Structural case in Finnish. *Lingua* 11, 315–376.
Kiparsky, Paul 2011. Grammaticalization as optimization. In: D. Jonas, J. Whitman & A. Garrett (eds.). *Grammatical Change. Origins, Nature, Outcomes*. Oxford: Oxford University Press, 15–50.
Klein, Wolfgang 1994. *Time in Language*. New York: Routledge.
Koontz-Garboden, Andrew 2007. *States, Changes of State, and the Monotonicity Hypothesis*. Ph.D. dissertation. Stanford University, Stanford, CA.
Kratzer, Angelika 1998. More structural analogies between pronouns and tenses. In: D. Strolovitch & A. Lawson (eds.). *Proceedings of Semantics and Linguistic Theory (= SALT) VIII*. Ithaca, NY: Cornell University, 92–110.
Kratzer, Angelika 2004. Telicity and the meaning of objective case. In: J. Guéron & J. Lecarme (eds.). *The Syntax of Time*. Cambridge, MA: The MIT Press, 389–424.
Krifka, Manfred 1987. Nominal reference and temporal constitution. Towards a semantics of quantity. In: J. Groenendijk, M. Stokhof & F. Veltman (eds.). *Proceedings of the Sixth Amsterdam Colloquium*. Amsterdam: ILLC, 153–173.

Krifka, Manfred 2003. Bare NPs. Kind-referring, indefinites, both, or neither? In: R. Young & Y. Zhou (eds.). *Proceedings of Semantics and Linguistic Theory (= SALT) XIII*. Ithaca, NY: Cornell University, 111–132.

Kurylowicz, Jercy 1964. *The Inflectional Categories of Indo-European*. Heidelberg: Winter.

Kwon, Song-Nim & Anne Zribi-Hertz 2004. Number from a syntactic perspective. Why plural marking looks 'truer' in French than in Korean. In: O. Bonami & P. Cabredo Hofherr (eds.). *Empirical Issues in Formal Syntax and Semantics* 5. Paris: CSSP, 133–158.

Landman, Fred 1989. Groups, I. *Linguistics & Philosophy* 12, 559–605.

Lasersohn, Peter 1988. *A Semantics for Groups and Events*. Ph.D. dissertation. Ohio State University, Columbus, OH.

Lasersohn, Peter 1995. *Plurality, Conjunction, and Events*. Dordrecht: Kluwer.

Lee, Jungmee 2010. The Korean evidential -*te*: A modal analysis. In: O. Bonami & P. Cabredo Hofherr (eds.). *Empirical Issues in Formal Syntax and Semantics* 8. Paris: CSSP, 287–312.

Link, Godehard 1983. The logical analysis of plural and mass nouns. A lattice theoretic approach. In: R. Bäuerle, Ch. Schwarze & A. von Stechow (eds.). *Meaning, Use, and Interpretation of Language*. Berlin: de Gruyter, 303–323.

Lyons, John 1968. *Introduction to Theoretical Linguistics*. Cambridge: Cambridge University Press.

Matthewson, Lisa 2006. Temporal semantics in a supposedly tenseless language. *Linguistics & Philosophy* 29, 673–713.

Matthewson, Lisa, Hotze Rullmann & Henry Davis 2008. Evidentials as epistemic modals. Evidence from St'át'imcets. In: J. van Craenenbroeck & J. Rooryck (eds.). *The Linguistic Variation Yearbook* 7, 201–254.

McCawley, James D. 1968. Review of "Current Trends in Linguistics, vol. 3: Theoretical Foundations", edited by Thomas A. Sebeok. *Language* 44, 556–593.

McGregor, William B. 1989. Greenberg on the first person inclusive dual. Evidence from some Australian languages. *Studies in Language* 13, 437–454.

McKercher, David 2002. Kim kissed Sandy with enthusiasm. With-phrases in event semantics. In: D. Beaver et al. (eds.). *The Construction of Meaning*. Stanford, CA: CSLI Publications, 137–162.

Megerdoomian, Karine 2000. Aspect and partitive objects in Finnish. In: R. Billerey Brook & D. Lillehaugen (eds.). *Proceedings of the West Coast Conference on Formal Linguistics (= WCCFL) 19*. Somerville, MA: Cascadilla Press, 316–328.

de Mey, Sjaak 1981. The dependent plural and the analysis of tense. In: V. A. Burke & J. Pustejovsky (eds.). *Proceedings of the North Eastern Linguistic Society (= NELS) 11*. Amherst, MA: GLSA, 58–78.

Mithun, Marianne 1988. The evolution of number marking. In: M. Hammond & M. Noonan (eds.). *Theoretical Morphology*. New York: Academic Press, 211–234.

Mizuguchi, Shinobu 2001. Plurality in classifier languages. In: S. Takeda et al. (eds.). *The Interface between Meaning and Form. A Festschrift for Dr. Minoru Nakau on the Occasion of his Sixtieth Birthday*. Tokyo: Kuroshio Shuppan, 525–535.

Moravcsik, Edith 2003. A semantic analysis of associative plurals. *Studies in Language* 27, 469–503.

Morse, Nancy L. & Michael B. Maxwell 1999. *Cubeo Grammar, Studies in the Languages of Colombia 5*. Arlington, TX: Summer Institute of Linguistics.

Murray, Sarah E. 2010. *Evidentiality and the Structure of Speech Acts*. Ph.D. dissertation. Rutgers University, New Brunswick, NJ.

Neidle, Carol 1988. *The Role of Case in Russian Syntax*. Dordrecht: Kluwer.

Nordlinger, Rachel & Louisa Sadler 2004. Nominal tense in cross-linguistic perspective. *Language* 80, 776–806.

Nordlinger, Rachel & Louisa Sadler 2008. When is a temporal marker not a tense? Reply to Tonhauser 2007. *Language* 84, 325–331.
Noyer, Robert Rolf 1992. *Features, Positions, and Affixes in Autonomous Morphological Structure*. Ph.D. dissertation. MIT, Cambridge, MA. Reprinted: New York: Garland, 1997.
Ojeda, Almerindo 1995. The semantics of the Italian double plural. *Journal of Semantics* 12, 213–237.
Ojeda, Almerindo 1998. The semantics of collectives and distributives in Papago. *Natural Language Semantics* 6, 245–270.
Ostler, Nicholas 1979. *A Theory of Case and Verb Diathesis, Applied to Classical Sanskrit*. Ph.D. dissertation. MIT, Cambridge, MA.
Palmer, Frank R. 1986. *Mood and Modality*. Cambridge: Cambridge University Press.
Plank, Frans 1991. Rasmus Rask's dilemma. In: F. Plank (ed.). *Paradigms. The Economy of Inflection*. Berlin: Mouton de Gruyter, 161–196.
Pollard, Carl & Ivan Sag 1988. An information-based theory of agreement. In: D. Brentari, G. N. Larson & A. MacLeod (eds.). *Papers from the 24th Regional Meeting of the Chicago Linguistic Society (= CLS): Part II: Parasession on Agreement in Grammatical Theory*. Chicago, IL: Chicago Linguistic Society, 236–257.
Pollard, Carl & Ivan Sag 1994. *Head-Driven Phrase Structure Grammar*. Chicago, IL: The University of Chicago Press.
Przepiórkowski, Adam 1999. *Case Assignment and the Complement-Adjunct Dichotomy. A Non-Configurational Constraint-Based Approach*. Doctoral dissertation. University of Tübingen.
Reichenbach, Hans 1947. *Elements of Symbolic Logic*. Berkeley, CA: University of California Press.
Ritter, Elizabeth & Sara Rosen 2000. Event structure and ergativity. In: C. Tenny & J. Pustejovsky (eds.). *Events as Grammatical Objects*. Stanford, CA: CSLI Publications, 187–238.
Roberts, Craige 1991. *Modal Subordination, Anaphora, and Distributivity*. New York: Garland.
Rullmann, Hotze 2003. Bound-variable pronouns and the semantics of number. In: B. Agbayani, P. Koskinen & V. Samiian (eds.). *Proceedings of the Western Conference on Linguistics (= WECOL) 2002*. Fresno, CA: California State University, 243–254.
Rullmann, Hotze 2004. First and second person pronouns as bound variables. *Linguistic Inquiry* 35, 159–168.
Sadler, Louisa 2006. Gender resolution in Rumanian. In: M. Butt, M. Dalrymple & T. Holloway King (eds.). *Intelligent Linguistic Architectures. Variations on Themes by Ron Kaplan*. Stanford, CA: CSLI Publications, 437–454.
Sag, Ivan A., Gerald Gazdar, Thomas Wasow & Steven Weisler 1985. Coordination and how to distinguish categories. *Natural Language and Linguistic Theory* 3, 117–171.
Sauerland, Uli 2003. A new semantics for number. In: R. Young & Y. Zhou (eds.). *Proceedings of Semantics and Linguistic Theory (= SALT) XIII*. Ithaca, NY: Cornell University, 258–275.
Sauerland, Uli, Jan Anderssen & Kazuko Yatsushiro 2005. The plural is semantically unmarked. In: S. Kepser & Marga Reis (eds.). *Linguistic Evidence. Empirical, Theoretical and Computational Perspectives*. Berlin: Mouton de Gruyter, 409–430.
Scha, Remko 1981. Distributive, collective and cumulative quantification. In: J. Groenendijk, T. Janssen & M. Stokhof (eds.). *Formal Methods in the Study of Language*. Amsterdam: Mathematical Centre, 483–512.
Schwarzschild, Roger 1996. *Pluralities*. Dordrecht: Kluwer.
Slobin, Dan & Ayhan Akşu 1982. Tense, aspect and modality in the use of the Turkish evidential. In: P. Hopper (ed.). *Tense-Aspect. Between Semantics and Pragmatics*. Amsterdam: Benjamins, 185–200.

Spathas, Giorgos 2007. On the interpretation of gender on nouns and pronouns. Paper presented at the *Workshop on Greek Syntax and Semantics at MIT.*

Spector, Benjamin 2003. Plural indefinite DPs as PLURAL-polarity items. In: J. Quer et al. (eds.). *Romance Languages and Linguistic Theory 2001. Selected papers from 'Going Romance'.* Amsterdam: Benjamins, 295–313.

Spector, Benjamin 2007. Aspects of the pragmatics of plural morphology. On higher-order implicatures. In: U. Sauerland & P. Stateva (eds.). *Presuppositions and Implicatures in Compositional Semantics.* Houndsmills: Palgrave Macmillan, 243–281.

von Stechow, Arnim 2003. Feature deletion under semantic binding. Tense, person, and mood under verbal quantifiers. In: M. Kadowaki & S. Kawahara (eds.). *Proceedings of the North Eastern Linguistic Society (= NELS) 34.* Amherst, MA: GLSA, 379–404.

Stolz, Thomas 2001a. Comitatives vs. instruments vs. agents. In: W. Bisang (ed.). *Aspects of Typology and Universals.* Berlin: Akademie Verlag, 153–174.

Stolz, Thomas 2001b. To be with X is to have X. Comitatives, instrumentals, locative, and predicative possession. *Linguistics* 39, 321–350.

Stolz, Thomas & Cornelia Stroh 2001. Wenn Komitative Instrumentale sind und umgekehrt. In: W. Boeder & G. Hentschel (eds.). *Variierende Markierung von Nominalgruppen in Sprachen unterschiedlichen Typs.* Oldenburg: University of Oldenburg, 387–411.

Strigin, Anatoli 1995. The semantic form of *mit*. In: M. Bierwisch & P. Bosch (eds.). *Semantics and Conceptual Knowledge.* Stuttgart: IMS, University of Stuttgart, 223–236.

Svenonius, Peter 2002. Case is uninterpretable aspect. In: H. Verkuyl, A. van Hout & H. de Swart (eds.). *Proceedings of the Conference on Perspectives on Aspect.* http://www.hum.uit. n0/a/svenonius/paperspage.html, May 5, 2011.

Thomas, Rose 2003. *The Partitive in Finnish and its Relation to the Weak Quantifiers.* Ph.D. dissertation. University of Westminster.

Tonhauser, Judith 2006. *The Temporal Semantics of Noun Phrases. Evidence from Guaraní.* Ph.D. dissertation. Stanford University, Stanford, CA.

Tonhauser, Judith 2007. Nominal tense? The meaning of Guaraní nominal temporal markers. *Language* 83, 831–869.

Tonhauser, Judith 2008. Defining cross-linguistic categories. The case of nominal tense. A reply to Nordlinger & Sadler 2008. *Language* 84, 332–342.

Watkins, Laurel 1984. *A Grammar of Kiowa.* Lincoln, NE: University of Nebraska Press.

Wechsler, Stephen 2004. Number as person. In: O. Bonami & P. Cabredo Hofherr (eds.). *Empirical Issues in Formal Syntax and Semantics* 5. Paris: CSSP, 255–274.

Wechsler, Stephen 2009. "Elsewhere" in gender resolution. In: K. Hanson & S. Inkelas (eds.). *The Nature of the Word. Essays in Honor of Paul Kiparsky.* Cambridge, MA: The MIT Press, 567–586.

Willett, Thomas 1988. A cross-linguistic survey of the grammaticalization of evidentiality. *Studies in Language* 12, 51–97.

Winter, Yoad 2001. *Flexibility Principles in Boolean Semantics.* Cambridge, MA: The MIT Press.

Wunderlich, Dieter 2003. Optimal case patterns. German and Icelandic compared. In: E. Brandner & H. Zinsmeister (eds.). *New Perspectives on Case Theory.* Stanford, CA: CSLI Publications, 331–367.

Zweig, Eytan 2008. *Dependent Plurals and Plural Meaning.* Ph.D. dissertation. New York University, New York.

Rochelle Lieber
3 Semantics of derivational morphology

1 The scope of data to be covered —— 75
2 Frequently found derivational types —— 78
3 Theoretical issues in the semantics of derivation —— 88
4 Conclusions —— 101
5 References —— 101

Abstract: This article discusses issues concerning the semantic analysis of derivational morphology. We discuss difficulties in distinguishing the semantic scope of derivation from that of roots and bound bases on the one hand and from inflection on the other. After a review of the semantic consequences of so-called transposition and of various other semantic categories of derivation in the languages of the world, we address theoretical approaches to the semantics of derivation. We end with a discussion of such issues as the analysis of affixal polysemy, and of mismatches between form and content in derivation.

1 The scope of data to be covered

1.1 Formal types included under derivation

We will examine here the semantics of those aspects of morphology usually referred to as word formation, that is, those that are used for formation of new lexemes, including affixation, conversion, reduplication, ablaut, and templatic (root and pattern) morphology. In effect, a wide range of formal mechanisms can be used to create new lexemes, so although we will generally make reference to affixation in what follows, the reader should understand that the semantic categories we identify and the issues that we review pertain to these other formal mechanisms as well as to affixation. On the other hand, we will not consider here the semantics of compounding, of concatenation of bound roots, or of complex stem formation.

Rochelle Lieber, Durham, NH, USA

https://doi.org/10.1515/9783110589849-003

1.2 Difficulties distinguishing affixation from compounding of bound roots

It is important to point out at the outset that it is sometimes not easy to decide whether a particular bound form is an affix or a bound root. We find this issue to some extent in familiar languages like English, where the distinction between affixes and elements of neo-classical compounds is problematic: are items like *bio-* and *eco-* to be considered bound stems or prefixes? (See Bauer 1998 for an insightful discussion of this problem.)

Similarly, in English even though the second element of items like *mailman* sometimes contains a reduced vowel, it is not yet quite bleached enough of its lexical content to qualify as a suffix. In other words, it is often implicit in the distinction between roots and affixes that the latter carry meanings that are general and abstract, whereas the former can have more robust semantics along the lines of simplex lexemes. But the dividing line is unclear.

The problem is especially vexed in languages that have so-called lexical affixes, that is, affixes with the sort of lexical content that in Indo-European languages at least tends to be confined to roots. The discussion of this problem in Mithun (1999) is instructive. So-called lexical affixes occur in many Native American languages, across many language families. A simple example comes from the Native American language Koasati (Musk-ogean family). According to Kimball (1991), Koasati has verbal prefixes that have meanings like 'action on the ground or in fire' or 'action in water' (1991: 117–118). Even more prolific in affixes of this kind is Yup'ik (Eskimo-Aleut), which according to Mithun (1999: 49) has over 450 derivational suffixes that bear meanings such as 'catch game', 'gather', 'hit', and 'hurt', among many others. Spokane (Salishan) has upwards of 100 noun-like affixes that bear meanings like 'knob', 'stomach', and 'floor covering' (Mithun 1999: 48).

According to Kimball, the Koasati affixes are either bleached forms of historically independent nouns, or related to existing noun forms synchronically, and Mithun concurs that this is often the case (1999: 54–55). Nevertheless, she gives cogent arguments that they are indeed affixes and not bound roots. Real roots are potentially unlimited in number, but the so-called lexical affixes constitute closed, although sometimes surprisingly large classes. In Spokane and Yup'ik roots can stand alone (although they may need inflections), but these affixes cannot. In terms of their position in the word, the affixes differ from roots; roots in Yup'ik, for example, come first, followed by derivational suffixes. The so-called lexical affixes cannot occur in first position. And in spite of having substantial lexical content, they are less specific in content than roots, and more prone to metaphorical extension; for example, the affix *-cin* in Spokane can cover a range of meanings from 'mouth' and 'lips' through 'edge', 'speech', and 'food' (Mithun

1999: 50). Further, such lexical affixes are often lexicalized in specific forms. Finally, in discourse such affixes often serve to designate old information. On first mention, an independent noun root will be used, but in subsequent mentions the suffix can be used to background the already mentioned item. Mithun argues further that although lexical affixes might have developed historically from compounding forms, the above factors suggest that they are no longer compounding forms, but constitute bona fide affixes.

It should be noted that even Indo-European languages occasionally have affixes that seem to have robust lexical content. For example, French has an affix *-ier* that attaches to roots denoting types of fruit to derive the corresponding type of fruit tree: *poire* 'pear' ~ *poirier* 'pear tree'.

The conclusion we are forced to is that lexical affixes indeed present a challenge to the notion that derivation covers a rather abstract, fixed set of categories. We will see that this issue arises again in connection with the theoretical treatment of derivational semantics in section 3.

1.3 Difficulties in distinguishing derivation from inflection

Just as it is difficult in some cases to delimit the semantics of derivation with respect to compounding of bound roots, it is also sometimes difficult to circumscribe those semantic categories that belong to derivation from those that belong to inflection (cf. also article 2 [this volume] (Kiparsky & Tonhauser) *Semantics of inflection*). The distinction between inflection and derivation is frequently made on the basis of formal criteria: inflection, according to Anderson (1982) is what is relevant to the syntax. In other words, markings that induce or participate in syntactic dependencies such as agreement are said to be inflectional.

Similarly, distinctions that are reflected paradigmatically are often said to be inflectional. The English comparative might be relevant here. It can certainly be presented paradigmatically (*red* ~ *redder* ~ *reddest; pure* ~ *purer* ~ *purest*), but it does not trigger agreement, and is syntactically relevant only insofar as the comparative, for example, may license certain sorts of clauses. But it is not clear why comparative semantics should be considered inflectional rather than derivational.

Indeed some distinctions that can figure in syntax are nevertheless every bit as robust semantically as distinctions that are usually said to be derivational. For example, if one of the hallmarks of derivation is a substantial addition of meaning (even without category change), aspectual categories such as the imperfective or the inchoative could arguably be seen as derivational. Another borderline category might be affixation which changes the diathesis of a verb— for example, formation of causatives and applicatives. Certainly the addition of arguments has substantial effects in the syntax, but it also effects a significant semantic change on a verbal base. In what follows, I will discuss not only clear cases of derivation, but also some cases which might be considered inflectional. Such cases often fall into the category of what Booij (1996) has called 'inherent inflection', that is, inflectional markings that can induce dependencies in the syntax (for example, triggering agreement), but are not themselves the result of agreement with other elements in a sentence. These include number marking on nouns, and aspectual marking on verbs.

2 Frequently found derivational types

This section will survey a range of semantic categories that are frequently signaled by derivation in the languages of the world.

2.1 Transposition

Transposition is said to be word formation that changes the lexical category of an item without making any semantic changes other than those that are necessitated by the change of category. According to Beard (1995: 166), transposition involves "asemantic reclassification." Adams (2001) implicitly disagrees with this definition, as she refers to any derivation that involves change of lexical category as a 'transposition' regardless of its semantic content; in contrast, Beard considers only those cases of derivation to be transposition that involve change of lexical class without concomitant change in 'grammatical function', for example, change from verb to nominalization (*accuse ~ accusation*) as opposed to change of verb to agent or patient noun (*accuse ~ accuser ~ accusee*). I will tentatively follow Beard's narrower usage here.

Having accepted this definition, it must nevertheless be acknowledged that even the least contentful of category-changing derivation has semantic consequences. It is worth contemplating, then, whether transposition is in fact a distinct semantic category in derivation, or whether there is a cline from less contentful to more contentful category-changing morphology, without a clear division between transpositional and non-transpositional derivation.

2.1.1 Transposition to noun

Perhaps the most straightforward and least contentful type of transposition is from adjective to noun, but even here, there are several semantic categories that seem to be formed. Transpositions from adjective to noun create nouns denoting either 'the abstract quality of x' or 'thing which has quality x', in other words, either abstract or concrete nouns: *hard ~ hardness; pure ~ purity*; Slovak *stribrny* 'silver' ~ *stribrnak* 'silver coin' (Pavol Štekauer, p.c.). Abstract derivations seem to be more frequent in the languages of the world.

Transpositions of verbs to nouns are more complex, and arguably even less 'asemantic' than transpositions from adjectives. Nominalizations from verbs like *construction* or *refusal* are often ambiguous between two readings, what Grimshaw (1990: 45) calls the 'complex event' and 'result' readings (cf. also article 12 [Semantics: Noun Phrases and Verb Phrases] (Grimshaw) *Deverbal nominalization*). We get the former reading when the transposed verb maintains its complete argument structure; in a noun phrase such as *the doctor's examination of the patient* the noun *examination* is perhaps as close in meaning to that of its base verb *examine* as is possible with a change of lexical category. The same nominalization, however, also admits of another reading which is less dynamic and more referential in nature; this is what Grimshaw calls the 'result' reading, although it is not clear that all such non-eventive nominalizations actually denote results. Referential nominalizations are decidedly less 'verby' in flavor than their eventive correlates; for example, *the examination* can refer to the end-product of examining in a sentence like *the examination was successful*, or even to a concrete object in a sentence like *the examination was four pages long*. Concrete interpretations are frequently the result of lexicalization of individual items. Especially prone to concrete interpretations are the nominalizations of verbs of creation, for example, items like *construction* or *invention*.

In addition to nominalizations of adjectives and nouns, which are typically considered transpositional, we might consider word formation that does not change syntactic category, but does change semantic category. For example, English has several ways of creating abstract nouns from concrete nouns (*child ~ childhood, king ~ kingship*), although the reverse does not seem to happen in English at least. New concrete nouns in English seem, rather, to be created most often by compounding, rather than derivation.

2.1.2 Adjectival

When verbs or nouns are transposed to adjectives, the result is an adjective conveying 'the property or quality of X' where X is a noun (*history ~ historic*) or 'the property or quality of Xing' where X is a verb (*describe ~ descriptive*). Such derivations can have two slightly different interpretations, however: the relational or the qualitative interpretation. Relational adjectives are not gradable and do not permit modification by an adverb: for example, *more congressional, *very congressional*. Qualitative adjectives, in contrast, are gradable and can be modified: *impressive, more impressive, very impressive*. In English at least, particular adjective-forming affixes do not seem to be specialized for one meaning or the other: *-al*, as noted above, can form adjectives that are clearly relational (*congressional, janitorial*), but also adjectives that have a qualitative interpretation; *professorial*, for example, can describe a kind of behavior or demeanor that can be graded (*more professorial*) or modified (*not very professorial*). However, Chukchee is reported to have two distinct affixes that create relational and qualitative adjectives; qualitative affixes are derived by prefixing *nə-* and suffixing *-qIn*, and relational affixes are derived by suffixing *-kIn* (Beard 1995; Muravyova 1998).

2.1.3 Verbal

Of all so-called transpositions, the least 'asemantic' or most contentful is transposition to verbs. By its very nature transposition to the category of verb involves the addition of arguments or participants, and therefore necessarily the addition of some semantic content (this point is noted by Beard (1995: 179) as well). Depending upon the number of arguments added, verbs may have different nuances. In English, a suffix like *-ize* can induce a variety of argument structures on its base, and therefore a variety of interpretations. The verb *philosophize* has a single argument, and a performative interpretation: *to philosophize* is to act as a philosopher does. Verbs like *hospitalize* and *apologize* require two arguments, but have slightly different readings. The former is locative in interpretation: to *hospitalize* is to cause something to go into the hospital, whereas *apologize* has what Plag (1999) terms an 'ornative' meaning: to *apologize* is to cause an apology to go to someone. See Plag (1999) and Lieber (2004) for further discussion of the polysemy of verb-forming affixes. It is likely that the semantics of the base predisposes the affixed form in *-ize* to have one or the other interpretation. Bases like *hospital* that denote places or bases like *container* that denote receptacles are likelier to give rise to locative interpretations. Bases like *philosophy* or *theory* which denote abstract systems are likelier to deliver performative readings.

Languages other than English of course have affixes that are more specific in their semantic (or argument structural) contributions to their bases. Bantu languages, for example, are well-known for having affixation processes that add and delete arguments from verb stems. For example, in Chichewa, the causative suffix *-its/-ets* (1) and the applicative suffix *-ir/-er* (2) (the choice between the two allomorphs is a matter of vowel harmony)each add an argument to the diathesis of the verb, the former an agent argument and the latter a benefactive, locative, or instrumental argument (Mchombo 1998). The suffix -*ik/-ek* has the effect of deleting an agent argument, creating a stative (not passive) sentence (3):

(1) Causative (Mchombo 1998: 505)
 Kalúlú a-ku-sék-éts-a chigawênga
 3-lion 1SM-pres.-laugh-caus.-fv 7-terrorist
 'The hare is making the terrorist laugh'

(2) Applicative (Mchombo 1998: 506)
 Kalúlú a-ku-phík-ír-a mkángó maûngu
 1a-hare 1SM-pres.-cook-appl-fv 3-lion 6-pumpkins
 'The hare is cooking (for) the lion some pumpkins.'

(3) Stative (Mchombo 1998: 509)
 maûngu a-ku-phík-ík-a
 6-pumpkins 6SM-pres.-cook-stat.-fv
 'The pumpkins are getting cooked.'

2.1.4 General remarks

As I have implied in the sections above, the notion that some derivations are asemantic, and therefore that there is a special category of 'transpositional' derivation is quite problematic. Changing category necessitates some quite specific semantic effects: choice of argument structure in verbs, of gradability in adjectives, and of concrete or abstract, and eventive or noneventive semantics in nouns. The issue is that the interpretation of items derived by 'transposition' is underdetermined by syntactic category-change; a single syntactic category does not correspond neatly to a single semantic category. My conclusion is that derivations that have been called transpositional are in fact not fundamentally different from the non-transpositional derivations, to which we turn next.

2.2 Participant oriented

Languages frequently have derivational processes that create nouns corresponding to particular sorts of participants in an event: agent, patient, location, manner, and so on. In English, it is possible to derive nouns that refer to agents (*writer, accountant, attendee*), experiencers (*hearer, dependent*) instruments (*printer, irritant*), stimuli (*pleaser*), location (*diner, orphanage, cattery*), measure (*six-footer*), and patient (*employee, loaner*). We will return in section 3 to the question of why the same affixes that convey these participants can overlap in meaning in some languages.

A related group of affixes that might be called participant-oriented are those like *-ite* and *-ian* that derive names for people who originate in certain places (*New Hampshireite, Bostonian*), or are followers or disciples of particular people (*Darwinite*). Although they attach to nouns, rather than to verbs, they nevertheless imply an eventive meaning (x comes from or follows y).

Yet another common derivational category that might at least indirectly be considered participant-oriented is what Haspelmath (2002: 71) calls 'facilitative'. Facilitatives do not directly denote participants in an event, but facilitative affixes modify the argument structure of their base verbs such that one participant, the theme, is eliminated. An example is the suffix *-able* in English, which requires a transitive verb as its base (*drinkable, *arrivable, *yawnable*); this suffix has the effect of binding the theme argument from the verbal diathesis, in effect preventing it from being satisfied syntactically. Interestingly, in English *-able* occasionally attaches to nouns as well as to verbs, in which case the affix 'binds' an argument of the event implied by the base noun (e.g., *marriageable*).

2.3 Negative

Languages also frequently have affixes expressing various nuances of meaning that can be roughly classed together as 'negative'. Most straightforward are what logicians have termed 'contradictory' and 'contrary' negation. The former is a sort of negation that follows the Law of the Excluded Middle; that is, contradictory negations are those in which P (some property) and not P cannot both be true at the same time, but cannot both be false at the same time. Contrary negations do not adhere to the Law of Excluded Middles; while P and not P cannot both be true at the same time, they can both be false at the same time. Negative prefixation in English can give rise to either interpretation, depending on the base carrying the prefix. For example, *discourteous, ineffectual,* and *unreliable* all have contrary interpretations for me (someone can be neither *discourteous* nor *courteous* at the same time), whereas *disengaged, incalculable,* and *undeniable* all have contradictory readings.

Clearly, whether a given negative adjective has a contrary or a contradictory reading has something to do with whether or not we can conceive of the base adjective as being gradable in meaning: the more likely that a given base admits of gradation, the more likely the negation is to have a contrary rather than a contradictory reading. In fact, particular adjectives can be either gradable or nongradable, and therefore contrary or contradictory in reading when prefixally negated, depending on nuances of meanings. For example, in *nonAmerican,* the adjective *American* refers exclusively to nationality, a property which does not admit of gradation; one is either American or not, depend-ing upon one's citizenship. The negated form *nonAmerican* therefore has the contradictory reading. On another reading, however, *American* can refer to all the various properties that make up 'American behavior', whatever those might be. With this reading, the negated form *unAmerican* does admit of gradation, and therefore has a contrary reading; someone can be neither American nor unAmerican in the sense of bearing those specific properties. Indeed, different speakers may have different judgments on the gradability of specific adjectives, and therefore on whether the negative prefixed forms of those affixes express either a contradictory or a contrary reading.

Also clearly related to the notion of negation is privation, a notion which is frequently signaled by a derivational affix. In English, the suffix *-less* is very productive, deriving privative adjectives from nouns (*shoeless, hopeless*). It is also possible to form privative verbs in English from both nouns and verbs. The prefix *de-*performs this function in English (*debug, demilitarize, dehumidify*).

A final relation that might be classed under negation is reversativity in verbs (*untie, unwind*). While it might at first seem that this relationship is somewhat different—to *untie* is to reverse the action of tieing—it has nevertheless been argued in the literature (Maynor 1979; Andrews 1986; Horn 2002; Lieber 2004) that negativity is at the bottom of reversativity: assuming that a verb *tie* can be interpreted as something like 'cause to be tied', the reversative reading results when a negative takes scope over the predicate *tied* (so *to untie* is 'to cause to be not tied').

2.4 Prepositional/Relational

Affixes may also express a wide range of spatial or temporal relations that can in some languages be expressed by adpositions (prepositions or postpositions). Indeed, in many Romance and Germanic languages, the affixes and the adpositions are the same items. In English, for example, the prepositions *over-, after-, up-, down-, under-, out-, through-, back-,* and *by-*double as prefixes with varying degrees of productivity. In Dutch (Booij 2002: 116) prepositions like *aan-, achter-, door-, om-, onder-, over-* and *voor-*have prefixal counterparts.

The question might again arise whether these items are to be treated as true prefixes, or rather should be considered the first elements of compounds. In some cases, there are good arguments in favor of treating them as prefixes. For example, in English *out-* and *over-*may have an effect on the argument structure of verbal bases they attach to:

(4) a. Letitia ran.
    b. *Letitia ran Prunella.
    c. Letitia outran Prunella.

(5) a. The plane flew over the field.
    b. *The plane flew the field.
    c. The plane overflew the field.

The case can therefore be made that at least these items behave differently from their corresponding prepositions, and therefore might be considered prefixes rather than compounding elements. In other cases it is perhaps less clear what to call these items.

Some of the Native American languages present an abundance of affixes that convey spatial concepts. Mohawk (Iroquoian), for example has prefixes that are glossed as Cislocative (denoting the direction towards the speaker) and Translocative (denoting the direction away from the speaker (Mithun 1999: 139):

(6) a. Cislocative
       ta-s-at-awei-a't
       CISLOC-2AGT-MIDDLE-be.in-CAUS
       'Come in'
    b. Translocative
       ia'-s-at-awei-a't
       TRANSLOC-2AGT-MIDDLE-be.in-CAUS
       'Go in'

Mithun also reports the language Chumash (Chumashan family) to have a variety of directional affixes expressing such relations as 'on', 'around', 'across', 'back', 'penetrating', among others (1999: 140). The language Karok (isolate) has a range of spatial affixes expressing such concepts as 'blocking', 'at rest', 'into a container', 'around in a circle', and 'downriver' (Mithun 1999: 142).

Temporal relations are also expressed affixally in some languages. English, for example, has the prefix *ex-*, meaning 'former'. Yup'ik not only has an affix with the meaning 'former', but also one which attaches to nouns to mean 'future x' (Mithun 1999: 154).

The prefix *ex-*in English has interesting scopal properties: although it takes a noun as its base, it may actually take scope over a specifier of the noun (*my ex-car* is still a car, but it's no longer mine), or an adjunct of the noun (*an ex-shortstop for the Red Sox* may still be a shortstop, only not for the Red Sox).

2.5 Quantitative/Aspectual

Quantitative derivation covers such concepts as number and collectivity in nouns, as well as aspectual distinctions such as duration, punctuality, iterativity, and distributiveness in verbs. Aspect is one of the categories that hovers on the edge between inflection and derivation. Still, there are clear cases of languages that express aspectual distinctions derivationally and in any case, whether derivational or inflectional the semantic distinctions are sufficiently robust that they merit discussion. I will, however explain in more detail below why quantity in nouns and aspect in verbs have come to be treated as the same semantic category.

Although number marking in English and other Indo-European languages is clearly inflectional, there are languages that do mark number derivationally: in these languages number marking is optional, and it does not trigger syntactic effects like agreement. One such language is Koasati, which optionally marks plural or paucal number on nouns (paucal is used for 2–6 kinsmen or children): *athómma* 'Indian' ~ *athómma-ha* 'Indians'; *tá:tasi* 'paternal uncle' ~ *tá:tasi-ki* '2–6 paternal uncles') (Mithun 1999: 83–84). An interesting case of derivational number is represented by Jemez (Kiowa-Tanoan), which has what Mithun calls 'Inverse' number. A single affix *-sh* is used for singular or plural; its semantic effect is to deliver the reverse of what the expected number of an item is. For items that usually come in pairs or groups (e.g. *lips, weeds*), the affix delivers a singular meaning; on items that usually come in singles, like human beings, it delivers a plural reading (1999: 81). Blackfoot (Algonkian) also allows collective marking on nouns (e.g. *otáákii-ʔsin-ʔa* 'womenfolk', where *–ʔsin* is the collective suffix) (Mithun 1999: 91).

It has long been argued in the philosophical literature that concepts of quantity apply to verbs as well as to nouns (Carlson 1981; Bach 1986, among others). Various sorts of aspectual marking on verbs conceptualize actions or states as being bounded or unbounded, composed of one or more parts, or as being internally undifferentiated. Morphology designating repeated actions, for example, might be seen as analogous to morphology forming plurals of count nouns. Looked at in this way, the prefix *re-*, usually glossed as 'again', in English might be considered a quantitative affix, as it designates a distinct but identical event corresponding to its base. Semelfactive affixes, that is, affixes which denote a single, punctual action, are arguably the correlate of singular number on count nouns; they denote temporally bounded unitary events, just as singular count nouns denote spatially bounded, unitary entities. Distributives of various sorts might be correlated with collectives. For example, Mohawk has an affix *-nion'* which distributes an action over space (Mithun 1999: 89):

(7) te-w-anine'kara'wa-nion'-s
DUALIC-NEUTER.AGENT-lightning.strike-
DISTRIB-IMPRF
'Lightning was striking all over'

In a distributive of this sort, we think of a series of identical events which nevertheless together constitute a whole event, in the same way that a collective noun (e.g. *herd*) consists of multiple identical entities conceived of as a whole. Similarly, duratives might be considered analogous to mass nouns in that they designate unbounded actions that persist in the same way over a period of time without internal differentiation of parts.

Another aspectual distinction that might be mentioned here is telicity. A telic situation is, according to Comrie (1976: 4) "one that involves a process that leads up to a well-defined terminal point." Lieber (2004) has argued that there is no specific morphology in English that makes a verb telic, telicity instead being built at the level of the proposition with contributions from the lexical meaning of the verb, and quantificational characteristics of its arguments and adjuncts. Other languages, however, may well have derivational morphology that makes verbs telic. Levin & Rappaport Hovav (1998: 260) report that the prefix *vy*-in Russian has the effect of turning an atelic verb (e.g., *pit'* 'drink') into a telic one (*vypit'* 'drink up'). Other candidates might be affixes that are glossed 'completive' in the literature.

Some Native American languages have especially rich systems of aspectual markers, and no one, to my knowledge, has as yet tried to broaden the analogy between number in nouns and aspect in verbs to all of these categories. Mithun (1999: 168) reports, for example, that Koyukon (Athapaskan) marks a broad range of aspectual distinctions. Given the verb root *-tlaatl* 'chop', one can derive the forms in Tab. 3.1:

Tab. 3.1: Aspectual categories in Koyukon

Semelfactive	yeetletł	'she chopped it once/ gave a chop'
Consecutive (= repetitive)	yegheetletł	'she chopped it repeatedly'
Dir-repetitive	yootlaał	'she chops at it repeatedly'
Bisective	yenaaltletł	'she chopped it in two'
Momentaneous	neeyeneetlaatl	'she chopped it all up'
Conclusive	yeghedaaltlaatl	'she hewed it into a shape'
Durative	yegheetlaatl	'she was chopping it for a while'

Still, it doesn't seem out of the question that all of these might correlate in some way with categories of quantity in nouns. Aside from the repetitive, durative, and semelfactive meanings we have mentioned above, what Mithun calls Momentaneous seems to convey a notion of boundedness or completion that is perhaps related to telicity, and the Bisective seems clearly quantitative as well.

2.6 Evaluative derivation

The most frequently discussed types of evaluative morphology are diminutives and augmentatives, but this is a semantic category that extends as well to derivation conveying intensive ('very') and approximative ('sort of') meanings; or creating feminine, ameliorative ('nice, good X'), honorific, and pejorative ('nasty, bad X') forms; or morphology expressing childishness or childlikeness, familiarity (as in hypocoristics), or intimacy. A variety of examples is given in Tab. 3.2 (examples from Jurafsky (1996: 536); Haspelmath (2002: 68–69)(Russian); Bauer (1997: 545)):

Tab. 3.2: Types of evaluative morphology

Language	Type of evaluative derivation	example	gloss
Yiddish	diminutive	mil ~ milexl	mill ~ little mill
Russian	augmentative	borod-a ~ borod-išča	beard ~ huge beard
Latin	intensive	parvus ~ parvulus	small ~ very small
Greek	approximative	ksinos~ ksinutsikos	sour ~ sourish
English	female ameliorative	steward ~stewardess	male ~ female
Fula	pejorative (diminutive)	loo-nde ~ loo-ŋgum	storage pot ~ worthless little pot
Tibetan	child	dom ~ dom-bu	bear ~ bear cub
Big Nambas	honorific	dui ~ dui-et	man ~ sacred man
English	familiarity, intimacy	sweetie, various nicknames	

Indeed, as Jurafsky (1996) and others have pointed out, these concepts are often expressed in languages by precisely the same set of affixes or other derivational devices, something we will return to in section 3.2.

Some theorists have argued that expressive morphology is formally akin to neither inflectional nor derivational morphology (e.g., Scalise 1984), but rather constitutes a special category of word formation in its own right. Bauer (1997), however, disputes this claim, arguing that in some languages evaluative morphology seems to be purely inflectional, for example, in the Bantu languages, where certain noun classes are specifically diminutive or augmentative, and in other languages more clearly like derivational morphology. Either way, from the point of view of their robust semantic contribution to words, evaluative derivation deserves to be treated here.

2.7 Summary

This survey of semantic types frequently expressed by derivation is inevitably incomplete. There are no doubt derivational affixes in some languages that convey semantic nuances not discussed here, or that don't fall into one of the above categories easily. Nevertheless, it seems safe to say that the vast majority of non-lexical derivational affixes in the languages of the world will fall into these major categories.

Before we go on to survey theoretical treatments of derivational semantics, a word might be said about reduplication. In the sections above, I have not distinguished reduplication from other forms of derivation (affixation, root and pattern or templatic derivation, etc.) Generally any of the semantic categories discussed above is compatible with any of the formal means of deriving new lexemes. It might be expected that reduplication would be used for some semantic categories more frequently than for others, for example, plurality, intensiveness, repetition, frequency, and iteration. In other words, we might expect reduplication to be semantically iconic: phonological full or partial doubling ought to lend itself to semantic categories that signal multiplicity in various forms. But as Inkelas & Zoll (2005: 12) point out, "Iconic semantics is not, however, the general rule. Reduplication, especially partial reduplication, is associated cross-linguistically with all sorts of meanings, both inflectional and derivational, whose degree of iconicity is often negligible."

3 Theoretical issues in the semantics of derivation

It seems safe to say that the most neglected area of morphological theory in the last three decades has been derivational semantics. Following a brief treatment in Dowty (1979) in the framework of model theoretic semantics, only a few theorists have offered extended treatments of this topic, among them Beard (1990, 1995) in the framework of Lexeme Morpheme Base Morphology, Jurafsky (1996) in the framework of Cognitive Linguistics, and Lieber (2004) in the framework of

Conceptual Semantics. Several key issues are addressed in these works: whether there are limitations on the range of meaning that can be conveyed by derivation; why individual affixes tend to be polysemous; why there are often several affixes in a given language that convey the same meaning; and generally why there are mismatches between form and meaning in derivation. We will consider each of these issues in turn.

3.1 Limitations in the range of meaning conveyed by derivation

The catalogue in section 2 of semantic categories that are frequently manifested in derivation raises a question: is it purely accidental that such categories are repeated over and over in derivation in the languages of the world, or is there a reason for this circumscription? To the extent that this issue has been addressed in the literature, the consensus is that this cannot be an accident, but several different explanations for the semantic circumscription of derivation have been proposed.

Beard (1990, 1995) argues that derivation parallels inflection, and therefore that any semantic category that can be expressed in the inflection of some language can be used in derivation. In fact, his position seems to be even stronger. He proposes what he calls the Universal Grammatical Function Hypothesis (UGF) which "limits the number of categories available for this type of derivation [i.e., derivation of adjectives and nouns R.L.] to those of the inflectional paradigm" (1990: 125). Starting from the case-marking system in Indo-European languages, Beard (1995), following Szymanek (1988), proposes 44 grammatical categories into which derived nouns and adjectives can fall. Included are Agent and Patient, of course, but also Measure, Means, Manner, Location, Purpose, and a variety of others that are listed in Tab. 3.3.

Beard's claim is that any of the inflectional categories into which nouns and adjectives can fall in Indo-European languages can also form the basis of a derivational category. For example, corresponding to the inflectional category of Subject (nominative), languages can have subjective derivations, that is, affixes that derive subject nouns (generally agentives). A given inflectional relation does not, of course, have to exist in a particular language for that language to express one of the 44 possible relationships derivationally. Languages like English and Dutch that lack overt case marking can nevertheless have derivational affixes that form 'subjective nominals'.

One immediate difficulty with Beard's hypothesis is that it pertains only to the derivation of nouns and adjectives. Beard is forced to categorize a fairly wide range of derivation as asemantic, that is, as transpositions. But as we have seen

Tab. 3.3: Beard's derivational categories (1995: 391–395)

Inflectional functions	Corresponding derivational categories
*Agent	
*Patient	
Subject	Subjective nominal
Object	Objective nominal
Possessivity	Possessive adjective
Possession	Possessional adjective
Measure	Mensurative nominal
Material	Material nominal
Partitivity	Partitive nominal
Distinction	
Absolute	
Means	Modalic nominal
Route	Vialic adjective
Manner	Similitudinal adjective
Ession	Essive adjective
Duration	Durative adjective
Iteration	Iterative adjective
Accordance	Accordant nominal
Purpose	Purposive nominal
Exchange	Permutative
Cause	
Sociation	Sociative noun
Location	Locative noun
Goal	Goal nominal
Origin	Originative nominal
Inession	Locative noun
Adession	Locative noun
Anteriority	Anterior nominal
Posteriority	Posterior nominal
Superession	Superessive nominal
Subession	Subessive nominal
Transession	Transessive nominal
Intermediacy	Intermediative nominal
Prolation	Prolative nominal
Proximity	Proximate nominal
Opposition	Oppositive adjective
Perlation	Perlative nominal
Circumession	Circumessive
Termination	Terminative
Concession	Concessive
Distribution	Distributive
Exception	Exceptive

inflectional functions	Corresponding derivational categories
Privation	Privative adjective
Thematicity	

*In ergative/absolutive languages

in section 2.1, transposition is rarely truly asemantic: the so-called transpositions still have specific readings that are underdetermined by simple change of syntactic category. Beard's theory also has nothing to say about derivation of verbs, which again is relegated to the realm of transposition and deemed asemantic. But to relegate so many derivational categories to transposition is to beg the question of semantic limits.

A second difficulty that Beard's proposal encounters concerns the so-called lexical affixes that are found in polysynthetic languages. As Mithun argues, these cannot be dismissed as bound roots. But their semantic robustness precludes treating them as variations on case relations that appear in Indo-European languages. In other words, although lexical affixes are probably atypical in the larger scheme of things, a semantic framework that is based on inflectional categories in effect predicts that they should not exist at all.

Lieber (2004) develops another framework that can be used to circumscribe the typical semantic range of derivation, without however, ruling out the existence of lexical affixes. Lieber claims that the circumscription in the semantic range of derivation follows not from the semantics of inflection, but rather from the semantic categories that distinguish classes and subclasses of simplex lexical items from one another. A brief discussion of her framework is necessary to make sense of this claim.

According to Lieber (2004), the lexical semantic representation of a simplex item has two parts. The skeleton is that part of the lexical semantic representation that is of significance to the syntax. Formal and tightly constrained, it consists of functions and arguments arranged hierarchically, similar to the LCSs of Jackendoff (1990) (cf. article 4 [Semantics: Lexical Structures and Adjectives] (Levin & Rappaport Hovav) *Lexical Conceptual Structure*, and article 4 [Semantics: Theories] (Jackendoff) *Conceptual Semantics*). The body is that part of the lexical semantic representation that is encyclopedic, consisting of those aspects of perceptual and cultural knowledge that form the bulk of lexical meaning, but are of no consequence with respect to syntax.

Skeletal functions in Lieber's system consist of features that can be used crosscategorially, and in either a binary or privative fashion. For example, simplex nouns are either [+material] (concrete: *dog, hand*) or [−material] (abstract: *truth, minute*), and may also bear the feature [dynamic] if they have an eventive or processual flavor (*author, sunset*). Basic verbal classes can be distinguished on the basis of two features. The feature [+/−dynamic] distinguishes events from states, where [+dynamic] items are eventive (*eat, yawn*) and [–dynamic] stative (*own, love*). Eventive ([+dynamic]) lexical items can also bear the feature [+/–IEPS] ("Inferable Eventual Position or State"), which essentially distinguishes those verbs for which a path is relevant (*fall, grow, walk*) from those for which no path is relevant (*eat, yawn*). [+IEPS] items have directed paths as part of their meaning (*fall*), whereas [–IEPS] items imply a non-directed or random path (*walk*). Lieber (2004) develops a number of other semantic features which apply cross-categorially and delimit various locational and quantitative classes.

Derivation, Lieber argues, can create new lexemes that fall into any of the classes to which simplex lexical items belong. Typical derivational affixes have skeletons that are added to the skeletons of their bases, but they have little or nothing in the way of semantic body: they are devoid of encyclopedic content. This does not preclude, however, that some affixes in some languages might have encyclopedic content; this leaves the way open for the lexical affixes that we find in polysynthetic languages.

Given that there are a limited number of lexical classes into which simplex items can fall, the range of affixes (or derivational processes of other sorts) is predicted to be equally limited. Tab. 3.4 gives an idea of basic lexical semantic categories in Lieber's system, and some of the affixes that can contribute those meanings in English.

Tab. 3.4: Lieber's lexical semantic classes

Class	Simplex example	Derivational affix
[+material]	chair, leg	
[–material]	time, fact	-ness, -ity, -hood, -ship
[+material, dynamic]	author, chef	-er, -ee, -ant, -ist
[–material, dynamic]	habit, war	-ation, -al, -ment, -ure
[+dynamic]	eat, kiss	
[–dynamic]	know, fond	-ic, -ive, -ary, -al,
[+dynamic, +IEPS]	fall, go, grow	
[+dynamic, –IEPS]	walk, run, vary	
causative*	kill	-ize, -ify

* Following Dowty (1979) and Rappaport & Levin (1992), Lieber (2004) uses a bipartite skeleton to capture the semantics of causative verbs. See Lieber (2004) for details of this analysis.

Where there seem to be categories in which English lacks affixes, there are other (non-affixational) word formation devices that create new lexemes in those classes. For example, new material (concrete) nouns are frequently created by compounding, and new eventive verbs by conversion from nouns. Other languages, of course, can use derivational means to create items of those categories. Czech, for example, appears to have an affix -*ivo* which attaches to verbs to create mass nouns: *rezat*' ~ *rezivo* 'cut' ~ 'timber'; *tkat*' ~ *tkanivo* 'weave' ~ 'fiber' (Pavol Štekauer, p.c.).

The framework that Lieber develops avoids two of the pitfalls of Beard's proposal mentioned above. First, it is not confined to derivation of nouns and adjectives, but covers all sorts of derivation, including those that Beard is forced to call asemantic. Second, it can account for lexical affixes: although typical derivational affixes bear skeletons but have little or nothing in the way of semantic body (that is, encyclopedic meaning), nothing prevents them from having semantic bodies. Lexical affixes are simply affixes that have the type of encyclopedic content that is more typical of simplex roots.

The two formal stances also give rise to different predictions that can be tested by looking at the various mappings of form to meaning that can be found in derivation cross-linguistically. We turn to these in the following sections.

3.2 Polysemy vs. homophony

One of the important questions that arises with respect to the semantics of derivation is why a single affix can often cover a range of meanings. For example a single affix is used in many languages to cover both agentive and instrumental meanings. This happens in English, of course, with the suffix -*er* (*writer*, *printer*), and in other Indo-European languages as well, (e.g., Dutch, Czech). But it happens as well in such genetically unrelated languages as Kannada (Dravidian) (Sridhar 1993) and Yoruba (Niger-Congo) (Pulleyblank 1987). Similarly, in many languages diminutive affixes also cover a whole range of meanings including 'small', 'child', 'affection', 'good', 'nasty'. They may double as intensive or attentuative affixes as well.

One conceivable answer to this question is that it is simply an accident that these meanings are frequently clustered together under a single affix. This answer claims in effect that there are several homophonous -*er* suffixes in English (and Dutch, etc.), and that there is no more relation between the agentive and instrumental -*er* suffixes than between the agentive and the comparative, which is also signaled by -*er* in English. After all, this clustering of meanings is not necessary; Bauer (1993: 514) reports that Maori has a prefix that derives agentives but not instrumentals. Nevertheless, the two meanings fall together frequently enough to call into question an analysis of accidental homophony and to make it worth asking the question why these particular meanings should cluster together so often.

Several theorists have addressed the issue of affixal polysemy. There is a substantial literature on the polysemy of the affixes -*er* and -ee in English and other Germanic languages. The former affix is treated by Booij (1988), Rappaport Hovav & Levin (1992), Beard (1990, 1995), and Lieber (2004), and the affix -*ee* by Barker (1998) and Lieber (2004), all treatments that fall roughly within the tradition of generative morphology. Jurafsky (1996) discusses the polysemy of diminutive morphology from the perspective of Cognitive Grammar. These approaches are quite different, as we will see.

Beard's treatment of polysemy follows from the principle of Uniform Grammatical Function (see section 3.1 above). He argues that since derivational affixes display the semantic categories made available by the inflectional system, where two or more inflectional categories are marked by the same case, we might expect those categories to fall together under the same derivational affix (1990: 125). For example, in Russian both passive agent and instrument are marked with the Instrumental case. Beard therefore predicts (1990: 121) that agent and instrument should both be derived with the same derivational suffix, as indeed is the case in Russian.

The difficulty with Beard's proposal is in defining just what counts as the same "case" marking in a particular language. For example, Beard counts the passive agent in German as being marked Ablative because it requires the preposition *von*, which is also the directional preposition 'from'. Beard predicts from this that both agentives and nouns designating place of origin should use the same suffix in German: *Lehrer* 'teacher'; *Amerikaner* 'American'. However, the nominal object of *von* is in fact marked with the Dative case. If we take Dative as the relevant category that gives rise to derivational polysemy, we ought to expect the existence of derivational affixes which put together any combination of the relationships that are expressed by the Dative. But this does not happen in German. It is only when we count a particular preposition plus the case it governs as a "case" that Beard's prediction follows.

The notion of "case" is even more vexed in English: Beard considers the passive agent in English to be marked with the Instrumental case, because it is signaled by the preposition *by*. Because *by* also marks instruments (*by candlelight*), Beard argues that we would then expect some derivational morpheme to be polysemous between an agent and an instrument reading, which -*er* certainly is. English, of course, has virtually nothing left in the way of case marking, but as with German, Beard treats prepositional choice as the equivalent.

The problem with this idea is that a preposition like *by* can signal many relations in English, not only passive agent and instrument (*by candlelight*), but also locative (*by the river*), quantity (*by the minute*), and a variety of other relations. Instrument is in fact more often signaled in English by the preposition *with*. The fact that agent and instrument fall together in English is explained only if we accept Beard's characterization of the "case" function of one particular preposition.

Booij (1988) and Rappaport Hovav & Levin (1992) explain the polysemy of *-er* on the basis of argument structure. They show that any thematic relation that can be expressed by the external argument (the subject) can be expressed by nominalizations in *-er*, since this suffix essentially binds or saturates the external argument. Since the external argument can express such roles as agent, instrument, stimulant, experiencer, and even patient/theme (with unaccusatives and middles), all of these relations can occur in *-er* nominalizations:

(8) agent: writer, driver
 instrument: opener, printer
 experiencer: hearer
 stimulus: pleaser, thriller
 patient/theme: fryer
 denominal noun: Londoner, freighter
 measure: fiver
 location: diner

This analysis covers a great deal of ground, but does not cover all cases of polysemy with *-er*. Specifically, it does not account for the interpretation of *-er* forms that have nouns, rather than verbs as bases, for example, *Londoner, freighter*. Since the base nouns do not have argument structure in the classic sense, the Booij/Rappaport Hovav & Levin analysis fails to explain why these are interpreted as personal nouns and instruments, just as the deverbal nouns are.

Barker (1998) argues that the polysemy of the suffix *-ee* in English cannot be explained on the basis of argument structure, but must take semantics into account. Like *-er*, suffix *-ee* can express a number of semantic relations:

(9) patient/theme: employee, nominee
 agent/subject: escapee, standee
 ind. obj.: addressee, dedicatee
 prepositional: experimentee
 no argument: amputee
 denominal person noun: biographee

But it is impossible to say that *-ee* saturates or binds any particular syntactic argument of its base verb: the saturated argument is sometime the direct object, sometimes the indirect object, sometimes the object of a governed preposition, and sometimes even the subject. Rather, he argues that the suffix *-ee* must satisfy a number of semantic needs in choosing the semantic argument it binds: the argument must be a (direct or implied) participant in an event, it must be sentient, and it must be non-volitional. For a verb like *employ*, the direct object is the argument that fulfills these requirements; the object of employ is generally human, and therefore sentient, but not under direct control of getting the job. But for *address*, which has a non-sentient direct object (i.e., one addresses a letter), the indirect object is the argument that satisfies the semantic needs of the suffix. If none of the arguments of a verb (e.g., *amputate*) fulfills the requirements, it can even be an implied argument that the *-ee* form expresses: an *amputee* is the person whose limb has been removed. The reader is referred to Barker's (1998) article for the full details of the analysis.

Lieber (2004) provides an analysis of affixal polysemy that builds on the insights of Booij, Rappaport Hovav & Levin, and Barker. The formalism of her framework provides a tightly constrained set of features that can constitute the skeletons of various affixes. Noun-forming affixes must have some value of the feature [material] (that is, they must be concrete or abstract), and they may bear the feature [dynamic] (that is, they may be processual or eventive in some way). Given the two values of [material] and the presence or absence of [dynamic], four categories are defined:

(10) [+material]
[−material]
[+material, dynamic]
[−material, dynamic]

As affixes bear skeletal features, but typically have no encyclopedic information as part of their semantics, there are in effect only a few meanings that affixes can bear. Some noun-forming affixes form purely abstract nouns (*-hood, -ship, -ism*), some form abstract processual nouns (*-ation, -ment, -al*) and others concrete processual nouns: this is the category into which *-er* and *-ee* in English fall. The polysemy of the affixes stems from the abstractness of their semantic content; since they only supply a concrete processual meaning, they are equally amenable to agent, patient, instrument, or locational meanings. The differences between the affixes stem from constraints on the way in which the affixal skeleton is integrated with the skeleton of its base. All other things being equal, affixes typically bind the highest argument of their base. This is the case with *-er*. But affixes may also place particular semantic requirements on the base argument which they bind. As Barker has argued, *-ee* requires that that argument be both sentient and non-volitional. It therefore typically skips over the agent argument (although it need not), and binds the patient/theme, the goal, or some other argument that is more in tune with its requirements. The sort of polysemy that Lieber attributes to -*er* and -*ee* has been termed 'logical polysemy' (Pustejovsky & Boguraev 1996).

Neither Beard (1995) nor Lieber (2004) treats the issue of polysemy in evaluative morphology, and it appears that neither theory is currently equipped to account for it. The range of meanings found in evaluative affixes (e.g., diminutive, childlike, pejorative, intensive, attenuative, etc.) clearly cannot be derived from inflectional categories, as in Beard's analysis. Nor does Lieber (2004) provide semantic features that cover this range of meanings (although nothing precludes her from adding such features). In contrast, Cognitive Grammar gives an interesting way of explaining this range of polysemy: Jurafsky (1996) considers 'diminutive' to be a radial category, with prototypical meanings such as 'child' and 'small' at its center, and links from these prototypical senses that "represent metaphorical extensions, image-schematic transfer, transfers to different domains, or inferences" (1996: 542). In other words, Jurafsky classes the polysemy of evaluative affixes as 'sense extension' rather than as logical polysemy (Pustejovsky & Boguraev 1996).

The use of diminutives for pets, for example, results from a metaphorical extension: pets are conceived of as children. The extension of diminutives to affection and intimacy results inferentially from the prototypical meaning of child: we usually feel affection for and intimacy with our children, so over time this inferred affection and intimacy becomes conventionalized in the meaning of the diminutive.

Jurafsky argues that the radial category not only represents the synchronic net of meaning relations borne by this category, but also its historical development; morphology dealing with affection, intimacy, and the like is predicted to have developed at one time or another from central senses of 'child' or 'small' even if it no longer conveys those central meanings in a particular language. Jurafsky's treatment of evaluative morphology is convincing, but it is not clear whether the cognitive approach can be extended to other polysemous derivational categories as well.

3.3 Multiple affixes with the same function

A second issue that arises in the treatment of the semantics of derivation in many languages is why there are frequently several different affixes that have the same function or semantic effect on their bases. In English, for example, there are several cohorts of affixes that seem to cover the same territory: -*ity* and -*ness* form abstract nouns from adjectives; -*ation*, -*ment*, and -*al* form nouns from verbs; and -*ize* and -*ify* form verbs from nouns and adjectives. It might be thought that the existence of these cohorts can be explained merely as historical accident; English, for example, has both native and borrowed affixes that do the same work. But this cannot be the whole story. With respect to simplex lexemes, we know that a foreign term can be borrowed even where a native equivalent exists, but the usual course of events is for one of the two to die out eventually, or for the meanings of the two to diverge. Such is not the case with affixes, where native and borrowed can exist side by side with no semantic drift. Why should this be the case?

Beard (1995) argues that the existence of multiple affixes follows from the general architecture of Lexeme Morpheme Base Morphology. Part of this theory is what Beard calls the Separation Hypothesis. The Separation Hypothesis bifurcates the morphology into a morphosyntactic part in which morpho-syntactic features are added to lexemes, and a morpho-phonological part in which the affixes themselves (that is, their phonological content) are added. Several different phonological affixes (e.g., *-er, -ant*) can correspond to the same set of morphosyntactic features (e.g., [+agentive]). Given that there are limitations on the range of morpho-syntactic features, affixes are likely to overlap in meanings.

Note that the Separation Hypothesis is not unique to Lexeme Morpheme Base morphology. It is also embraced by Distributed Morphology (Halle & Marantz 1993; Harley & Noyer 1999; cf. also article 5 [this volume] (Harley) *Semantics in Distributed Morphology*), within a rather different architecture of inflection and word formation.

Lieber (2004) also explains the multiple affix issue on the basis of the limited number of lexical semantic classes into which affixes can fall. If featural representations are highly circumscribed (see above), and if derivational affixes normally consist of skeletal features without body (that is, encyclopedic material), there is limited semantic space that affixes can cover. If a language—like English—has many derivational affixes, some of them are bound to fall into the same categories, thus giving rise to the multiple affix phenomenon.

3.4 Other mismatches between form and meaning

Affixal polysemy and the existence of multiple affixes are two instances of a mismatch between form and meaning: polysemy pairs several meanings with one form, and multiple affixes represent different forms corresponding to a single meaning. There are other potential mismatches between form and meaning as well, which we will consider here.

The first case concerns so-called conversion or zero derivation, in which new lexemes are derived with no overt formal morphology. In such cases a change in meaning corresponds to no change in form. Both Beard (1995) and Lieber (2004) argue that this form/meaning mismatch is theoretically unproblematic.

Beard's reason for dismissing this form/meaning mismatch derives from his Separation Hypothesis. Since the Separation Hypothesis bifurcates the morpho-syntactic part of derivation from the phonological part, with morpho-syntactic features being paired with various phonological forms, on the one hand, and various phonological forms being paired with different sets of morpho-syntactic features, on the other, nothing precludes his theory from pairing some set of morpho-syntactic features with no phonological form at all. In other words, in such cases derivation consists only of addition of morpho-syntactic features.

Lieber's solution to this form/meaning mismatch is to say that conversion is in fact not a form of derivation at all, but rather is a form of lexical relisting of items. While derivation is expected to be constrained to one of the major lexical semantic categories (with of course room for logical polysemy, and in some cases additional encyclopedic content), conversion should be unconstrained in meaning, with converted forms having the ability to be relisted in any of the semantic categories into which new lexemes might be coined. With respect to conversion of nouns to verbs, Lieber (2004) shows that this is indeed the case. As shown in (11)-(12), noun-to-verb conversions in English fall into a far broader range of semantic categories than verbs derived with such affixes as *-ize* and *-ify* that take nouns as their bases:

(11) Range of meanings exhibited by *-ize*, *-ify*
 make x: standardize, acidify
 make x go to/in/on sthg.: apologize, glorify
 make sthg. go to/in/on x: hospitalize, codify
 do x: theorize, speechify
 do in the manner of x: despotize
 become x: oxidize, calcify

(12) Range of meanings exhibited by noun-to-verb conversion in English
 make x: yellow, bundle
 make x go to/in/on sthg.: jail
 make sthg. go to/in/on x: leaflet
 do x: hostess
 do in the manner of x: buffalo
 become x: cool
 use x: hammer
 remove x: peel
 be x: landmark

move using x: jet
move on x: quarterdeck
move in x manner: cartwheel

The wider range of semantic categories exhibited by noun-to-verb conversion in English suggests that it is correct to distinguish the semantic effects of conversion from those of affixational derivation. It remains to be seen if this conclusion holds for languages other than English.

The final semantic mismatch we will consider here is the case in which derivational form corresponds to no meaning at all. What we have in mind here is so-called 'empty affixation', that is, phonological material that appears to be meaningless. For Beard, again, this sort of derivation poses no problem: the Separation Hypothesis allows him to say that just as there can be meaning without form (as in the case of conversion), there can be form without meaning.

But Lieber's theory is more constrained: derivation requires both form and meaning. She argues that apparently meaningless derivation is actually a by-product of allomorphy. For example, in the English examples in (13), it might be thought that -*at,* -*et,* -*ut,* -*in,* -*t,* and -*n* are empty morphs:

(13) orient-at-ion
retard-at-ive
them-at-ic
observ-at-ory
theor-et-ic
revol-ut-ion
absol-ut-ory
longitude-in-al
schema-t-ic
Messia-n-ic

Lieber points out (2004: 173) that the choice of empty morph is arbitrary; there is no phonological motivation for the choice of one empty morph over another with a particular stem. For example, *schema* and *Messiah,* the bases of *schematic* and *Messianic,* both end in schwa, and yet take different empty morphs. She also points out that the choice of empty morph seems to take place once per stem: given the stem *invite,* the empty morph is always -*at* (*invitation, invitatory*). She therefore argues that what appear to be empty morphemes are actually stem allomorphs that occur with Latinate morphology. In other words, there is no semantically empty morpheme -*at* or -*it,* only stem allomorphs like *themat*-alongside of *theme.* The former is selected by derivational affixes, the latter occurs as a free form.

4 Conclusions

It has been remarked several times that the semantics of word formation is one of the most understudied areas of morphology (Carstairs-McCarthy 1992; Levin & Rappaport Hovav 1998). This brief survey gives further proof that the semantics of derivation is a rich area that deserves far wider attention than it has previously enjoyed. From a cross-linguistic perspective, it would be worth looking more closely at the so-called lexical affixes to explore further the range of meaning that is exhibited from one language to another. The question of polysemy also deserves more work: besides agent/instrument nouns and evaluative morphology what other areas of derivation are prone to polysemy? It should also be considered whether all cases of so-called empty morphs can be explained as cases of stem allomorphy. Especially important will be to test current theoretical proposals against data from a wide range of languages.

5 References

Adams, Valerie 2001. *Complex Words in English*. Essex: Pearson Education.
Anderson, Stephen 1982. Where's morphology? *Linguistic Inquiry* 13, 571–612.
Andrews, Edna 1986. A synchronic analysis of *de-* and *un-* in American English. *American Speech* 61, 221–232.
Bach, Emmon 1986. The algebra of events. *Linguistics & Philosophy* 9, 5–16.
Barker, Chris 1998. Episodic *-ee* in English: A thematic role constraint on new word formation. *Language* 74, 695–727.
Bauer, Laurie 1997. Evaluative morphology: In search of universals. *Studies in Language* 21, 533–575.
Bauer, Laurie 1998. Is there a class of neoclassical compounds in English and if so is it productive? *Linguistics* 36, 403–422.
Bauer, Winifred 1993. *Maori*. London: Routledge.
Beard, Robert 1990. The nature and origins of derivational polysemy. *Lingua* 81, 101–140.
Beard, Robert 1995. *Lexeme Morpheme Base Morphology*. New York: SUNY Press.
Booij, Geert 1988. The relation between inheritance and argument-linking: Deverbal nouns in Dutch. In: M. Everaert et al. (eds.). *Morphology and Modularity*. Dordrecht: Foris, 57–74.
Booij, Geert 1996. Inherent versus contextual inflection and the split morphology hypothesis. In: G. Booij & J. van Marle (eds.). *Yearbook of Morphology 1995*. Dordrecht: Kluwer, 1–16.
Booij, Geert 2002. *The Morphology of Dutch*. Oxford: Oxford University Press.
Carlson, Lauri 1981. Aspect and quantification. In: P. Tedeschi & A. Zaenen (eds.). *Syntax and Semantics 14: Tense and Aspect*. New York: Academic Press, 31–64.
Carstairs-McCarthy, Andrew 1992. *Current Morphology*. London: Routledge.
Comrie, Bernard 1976. *Aspect*. Cambridge: Cambridge University Press.
Dowty, David 1979. *Word Meaning and Montague Grammar: The Semantics of Verbs and Times in Generative Semantics and Montague's PTQ*. Dordrecht: Reidel.
Grimshaw, Jane 1990. *Argument Structure*. Cambridge, MA: The MIT Press.

Halle, Morris & Alec Marantz 1993. Distributed morphology and the pieces of inflection. In: K. Hale & S.J. Keyser (eds.). *The View from Building 20: Essays in Linguistics in Honor of Sylvain Bromberger*. Cambridge, MA: The MIT Press, 111–176.
Harley, Heidi & Rolf Noyer 1999. Distributed morphology. *Glot International* 4, 3–9.
Haspelmath, Martin 2002. *Understanding Morphology*. London: Arnold.
Horn, Laurence 2002. Uncovering the un-word: A study in lexical pragmatics. *Sophia Linguistica* 49, 1–64.
Inkelas, Sharon & Cheryl Zoll 2005. *Reduplication: Doubling in Morphology*. Cambridge: Cambridge University Press.
Jackendoff, Ray 1990. *Semantic Structures*. Cambridge, MA: The MIT Press.
Jurafsky, Daniel 1996. Universal tendencies in the semantics of the diminutive. *Language* 72, 533–578.
Kimball, Geoffrey 1991. *Koasati Grammar*. Lincoln, NE: University of Nebraska Press.
Levin, Beth & Malka Rappaport Hovav 1998. Morphology and lexical semantics. In: A. Spencer & A. Zwicky (eds). *The Handbook of Morphology*. Oxford: Blackwell, 248–271.
Lieber, Rochelle 2004. *Morphology and Lexical Semantics*. Cambridge: Cambridge University Press.
Maynor, Natalie 1979. The morpheme un. *American Speech* 54, 310–311.
Mchombo, Sam 1998. Chichewa (Bantu). In: A. Spencer & A. Zwicky (eds.). *The Handbook of Morphology*. Oxford: Blackwell, 500–520.
Mithun, Marianne 1999. *The Languages of Native North America*. Cambridge: Cambridge University Press.
Muravyova, Irina 1998. Chukchee (Paleo-Siberian). In: A. Spencer & A. Zwicky (eds.). *The Handbook of Morphology*. Oxford: Blackwell, 521–538.
Plag, Ingo 1999. *Morphological Productivity: Structural Constraints in English Derivation*. Berlin: de Gruyter.
Pulleyblank, Douglas 1987. Yoruba. In: B. Comrie (ed.). *The World's Major Languages*. Oxford: Oxford University Press, 971–990.
Pustejovsky, James & Brad Boguraev 1996. Introduction: Lexical semantics in context. In: J. Pustejovsky & B. Boguraev (eds.). *Lexical Semantics: The Problem of Polysemy*. Oxford: Clarendon Press, 1–14.
Rappaport Hovav, Malka & Beth Levin 1992. -er nominals: Implications for the theory of argument structure. In: T. Stowell & E. Wehrli (eds.). *Syntax and Semantics 26: Syntax and the Lexicon*. New York: Academic Press, 127–153.
Scalise, Sergio 1984. *Generative Morphology*. Dordrecht: Foris.
Sridhar, S.N. 1993. *Kannada*. London: Routledge.
Szymanek, Bogdan 1988. *Categories and Categorization in Morphology*. Lublin: Catholic University Press.

Susan Olsen
4 Semantics of compounds

1 Introduction —— 103
2 Early treatments of compound meaning —— 105
3 Semantic approaches to compound meaning —— 110
4 Cognitive psychological approaches to compound meaning —— 116
5 Origin of compounds in a protolanguage? —— 121
6 Compounds in the lexical system of grammar —— 123
7 Left-headed compounds —— 128
8 Constraints on the productive compounding process —— 134
9 Conclusion —— 139
10 References —— 139

Abstract: Compounds, at least on the surface, seem to exemplify a baffling array of different types and patterns. This contribution concentrates on the characterization of the regular, productive, determinative pattern of noun-noun combinations in its search for a theoretical analysis able to unite the different constructions in a coherent way into a single pattern of interpretation that is to be expected of such a simple juxtaposition of lexemes. It proceeds chronologically through several different analytical perspectives to arrive at a simple analysis in terms of a template that conjoins two predicates mediated by an open conceptual inference. The success of the compound template provides the basis for the consideration of such further questions as the different function of compounds vis-à-vis seemingly equivalent syntactic phrases (computer screen—screen of a computer, table top—top of a table). It then broaches the questions of how less regular patterns can be subsumed under the general analysis and what restrictions apply to the inference process of a conceptual relation underlying compound meaning.

1 Introduction

Compounding is a process of word formation in which two lexemes are combined to form a complex lexeme, cf. *trumpet blast*. It is a highly productive process in many languages which results in a binary grouping of constituents in which one

Susan Olsen, Berlin, Germany

of the constituents functions as the head. For example, *smart phone* is a noun because *phone*, the head, is a noun. A certain amount of recursion is permitted, cf. [[*bumper-sticker*] *slogan*], [[*Sunday morning*][*news program*]], [*home* [[*health care*] *worker*]], but basically compounds represent simple structures that are made up exclusively of lexical categories that combine freely with one another. The combination is not restricted by the categorial or selectional properties of the head as is generally the case in derivational and syntactic configurations. Because of their lack of functional categories, compounds do not overtly express the logical or grammatical relations that exist between their constituents. Therefore, they are inherently ambiguous. Within the class of compounds, different types of formal and semantic structures can be identified. The traditional classes of determinative, possessive, and copulative compounds stemming from the early study of Sanskrit grammar can be broken down into further subtypes and cross-classified with respect to their endocentric (headed) and exocentric (non-headed) nature. However, by considering the conjunction of predicates as one possible strategy open to determinative compounds and by recognizing the possessive interpretation as an instantiation of a more general metonymic strategy of interpretation, modern theories of word formation are able to reduce the classes of copulative (*architect-sculptor* 'both an architect and sculptor') and possessive (*airhead* 'someone with a head of air') compounds to the determinative pattern and, hence, speak more generally of a single class of modifier-head structures that have become known as root or primary compounds, cf. *adrenaline junkie* 'junkie dependent on (thrill induced) adrenaline'. In addition, synchronic approaches recognize further types of compound structures, the most important of these being synthetic or verbal compounds in which the first constituent satisfies a (basic or inherited) argument position of the head, cf. *town mayor* and *window installer*.

In contrast to the relatively simple structural properties of compounds, their interpretative possibilities give rise to a surprising number of complex, far-reaching and intriguing problems which are the focus of this article. In order to provide a systematic discussion of the substance and development of these issues, concentration will be placed first and foremost on the class of regular determinative compounds consisting of two nouns which represents the most productive pattern of compounding in most languages. After gaining insight into this area, the results of the discussion will be applied in conclusion to a number of less frequent and more peripheral compound types.

Since compounding is a productive process of word formation, novel compounds enter the language continuously. In order for communication to be successful, these new complex expressions must be understood in the sense in which they are intended. A central question to be asked in this context, therefore, concerns their meaning constitution: what semantic components enter the interpretation besides those explicitly given in the component parts? Compounds, as morphological units, strongly tend to take on a categorizing and naming function in contrast to the descriptive function of syntactic expressions. Furthermore, as names of categories, compounds tend to take over a permanent need in the vocabulary and are therefore prone to idiosyncratic and other specializations of meaning. Such drifts of meaning, including non-transparent (e.g., *lord* from OE *hlaf* 'loaf' + *weard* 'warden') and lexicalized compounds (*cupboard* 'cabinet'), will be left out of consideration here because their idiosyncratic features are not predictable and, hence, must be explicitly recorded in the lexicon.

2 Early treatments of compound meaning

2.1 Descriptive approaches

Within the framework of traditional descriptive linguistics, there has been a strong tendency to study compounding via the general semantic patterns instantiated by established compounds and to use this fixed set of patterns as a prediction for the types of meanings that are possible in compounding. Jespersen (1909), for example, discerns eight categories, partly syntactic but mostly semantic in nature. He acknowledges, however, that such an analysis can never be "exhaustive" (Jespersen 1909: 138). His categories are: 'apposition' (*woman doctor*), 'subject or object of an action' (*sunrise, sun-worship*), 'location' (*garden-party*), time (*evening-star*), 'purpose' (*wineglass*), 'instrument' (*gunshot*), 'contained-in' (*feather-bed*), and 'material content' (*gold ring*). Criticizing Jespersen's method of classification as employing "a random group of criteria" (Hatcher 1960: 359), Hatcher (1960) attempts an "exhaustive" account of compound meaning by setting up a classification scheme based on what she considers to be "logically consistent criteria" (Hatcher 1960: 356) consisting of four abstract symmetrical categories that are, in her view, general enough to accommodate all compound types. These are 'A is contained in B' (*sand paper*), 'B is contained in A' (*broomstick*), 'A is source of B' (*cane sugar*), 'A is goal of B' (*sugar cane*). She claims that 'location', 'time' and Jespersen's two verbal types are subsumed by this scheme as well. Admitting that these four categories are extremely "vague and elastic" (Hatcher 1960: 366), Hatcher goes on to predict more specific relations within each general category by taking into consideration the semantic features of the constituent nouns in each group. This idea, however, is only briefly illustrated by means of a table of classified examples, cf. Hatcher (1960: 368).

Marchand's (1969) analysis focuses on the idea that nominal compounds are based on the same relations that underlie sentences and consequently he uses syntactic terms to structure his categorization: "Morphologic composites (= compounds, suffixal derivatives, prefixal derivates) are 'reduced' sentences in substantival, adjectival, or verbal form and as such explainable from 'full' sentences:" (Marchand 1969: 31). His subgroups, however, include reference to semantic notions yielding the following classes: 'subject type' including attributive (*girl friend*), resemblance (*eggplant*) and possession (*picture book*), matter (*bread crumb*), production (*disease germ*); 'predication type' including affected object (*air-brake*), effected object (*candlelight*), production (*corn whisky*); and 'adverbial complement' including place (*corn belt*), time (*tea time*), and instrument (*writing pen*), cf. (Marchand 1969: 39–53). The influence of syntactic relations on the study of compounding found in Marchand may have had two different sources: the earlier Bloomfieldian (1933) and Brugmannian (1900) tradition as well as the generative tradition of the 1960's to be discussed in the next section. Bloomfield's view of compounding was that it depended on the syntactic features of the language. 'Syntactic' compounds are made up of constituents that stand in the same grammatical relation as in a syntactic phrase (*blackbird*), while 'asyntactic' compounds do not reflect syntactic constructions of the language (*door-knob*). An intermediate type of 'semi-syntactic' compounds reflects syntactic relations but in a deviant form (cf. *housekeep* vs. *to keep house*). Bloomfield's analysis is complemented by a second classification into endocentric and exocentric compounds (Bloomfield 1933: 233–235).

Influenced by Jesperson's and Marchand's analyses, Adams (1973) uses eleven categories (i.e., subject-verb, verb-object, appositional, associative, instrumental, locative, resemblance, composition, adjective-noun, names) to arrive at an extensive typology of compound meaning. Her approach subdivides each general category according to a mixture of syntactic, morphological and more specific semantic notions.

The general criticism leveled against these analyses has focused on the problem that the categories are so broad that it is often not clear to which class a compound belongs; indeed, it is often possible to place a compound in more than one class. Hence, a great deal of artificial ambiguity results. Furthermore, the extremely general categories used are unnecessarily vague in that they disguise the more specific meanings that compounds actually have. *Gold ring*, for instance, belongs in the class of 'material content' for Jespersen but instantiates the category 'A contained in B' for Hatcher. So whereas *gold ring* and *sandpaper* are distinguishable via the contrast between 'material content' and 'contained-in' for Jespersen, these two compounds exemplify the same relation for Hatcher. From a more sophisticated semantic vantage point, it is easy to recognize that the progress-inhibiting mistake of these early taxonomic approaches is one of elevating frequently occurring relations to the level of linguistic primitives rather than having the meaning of compounds follow from an interaction among the semantic properties of the participating constituents.

Warren's (1978) treatment of noun-noun compounding rises to a certain extent above this criticism in that, although basically taxonomic in its approach, it nevertheless is based on a large corpus of data which are first grouped under a set of general relations (constitute and resemblance, belonging to, location and purpose) and then each relation is analyzed into reversible semantic roles. The purpose relation represents, for example, the semantic classes of place-object (*tablecloth*), object-place (*water bucket*), time-object (*nightdress*), object time (*dinnertime*), object-causer (*ball bat*) and causer-object (*football*). The systematicity of the discussion substantiates on the one hand the more sketchy analyses of previous works, while transcending them on the other in its principled attempt to ground the productivity and restrictiveness of the individual patterns in a detailed discussion of the finer semantic properties of each subclass.

2.2 Early generative approaches to compound formation

In the early stages of transformational generative grammar, the lexicon was limited to monomorphemic forms. All complex expressions were a product of the phrase structure rules generating an underlying deep structure and a set of generalized transformations operating on the deep structure. In the first study of nominalizations within this framework, Lees (1963) derived nominal compounds from underlying sentence structures in which the relationship between the two nouns was given by an explicit predicate. Lees' 'NPN-transformation' deleted the overt predicate (often prepositional, therefore 'P') and reversed the two flanking 'N' categories in their order (Lees 1963: 174). The semantic ambiguity found in compounds, e.g., German *Holzschuppen* from 'shed for storing wood' or 'shed made out of wood', could be explained according to Motsch (1970: 208) by tracing the compound structure back to different underlying phrasal representations for the compound.

This proposal immediately triggered a discussion of the problem of ambiguity resulting from the irrecoverability of the deleted material. In the standard theory of generative grammar, deep structure was the sole basis for semantic interpretation. Therefore, transformations operating on deep structures had to preserve meaning; i.e., they were not permitted to delete material whose content could not be recovered from the surface structure. A solution for the irrecoverability of deletion that his earlier analysis had engendered was sought by Lees himself in Lees (1970). In this paper, Lees attempted to establish a small number of compound types in which the participating nouns were assigned a Fillmore-type case role and associated via grammatical rule with a small number of generalized verbs. For instance, the representation of *steam boat* would be formalized as 'Verb-Object-Instrument', where the generalized 'Verb' for this class contained the minimal set of semantic features that are shared by the variants: *impel, propel, energize, activate, power, drive, actuate*, etc. By assigning each compound to a specific semantic pattern by a grammatical rule "the compounds in question need not be described by the grammar in such a way as to imply that they are indefinitely ambiguous." (Lees 1970: 182). In a similar vein, Brekle (1970) postulated underlying semantic representations in symbolic logic (so-called 'Satzbegriffe') that contained only a limited set of predicates that were deleted after the topicalization operation applied to yield a surface compound structure. Kürschner (1974), as well, adopted an analysis very similar to Lees (1970) for German compounds based on underlying case roles, abstract verbs and permutation transformations.

Most notably however, it was Levi (1978) who pressed the idea of a 'recoverably deletable predicate' the furthest. Her approach assumed that the predicate in the underlying form of a noun-noun compound was limited to one of nine recoverably deletable predicates that were later removed by a predicate deletion rule. These predicates were: *cause, have, make, be, use, for, in, about, from*, whereby the first three allowed subject and object reversal. Thus, her system predicted a twelve-way ambiguity for each noun-noun combination. However, in line with the criticism at the end of section 2.1, the notion of a recoverably deletable predicate yielding such extremely abstract classes makes little headway into an understanding of compound meaning.

2.3 The naming function of words and the notion 'appropriately classificatory predicate'

Zimmer (1971, 1972) suggested abandoning the attempt at an exhaustive positive characterization of compound types undertaken by his predecessors. He argued that, in producing a new compound, speakers do not "check its underlying structure against a list of possible compounding rules to see if it matches the input to one of them." (Zimmer 1971: C10). Instead, he proposed that any relation that is 'appropriately classificatory' can underlie compound formation. A noun has an appropriately classificatory relationship to a noun B "if this relationship is regarded by a speaker as significant for his classification—rather than description—of

B." (Zimmer 1972: 4). It is mistaken in his view to define nominal compounds in terms of sentence structures without consideration of the basic function of words vis à-vis sentences, namely that of categorizing experience and naming the resulting categories rather than describing facts or events. Zimmer's view was influenced by a similar line of thought expressed much earlier in Bradley (1906). In discussing the semantic openness of nominal compounds like *house-boat* which, in addition to its conventionalized meaning 'both a house and boat', can also mean 'boat kept in a house', 'boat belonging to a house' or 'boat supplying the needs of a house', Bradley (1906: 81) states: "The general meaning of this class of compounds might be expressed by saying that the noun which is formed of the two nouns A and B means 'a B which has some sort of relation to an A or to A's in general'."

Other linguists have since independently converged upon this insight. Describing the meaning of compounds, Selkirk (1982: 23) states "it would seem that virtually any relation between head and non-head is possible—within pragmatic limits ...." And Bauer (1978: 122) suggests adopting a covert PRO-verb that would underlie all compound structures and carry the meaning "stands in such a relationship as one might expect, given all contextual factors, to."

Zimmer's idea of an appropriately classificatory relationship is given further weight in Downing (1977) who stresses that the compounding relationship differs noticeably with the various classes of head nouns. In her view, different types of relationships have different classificatory value, depending on the nature of the entity being referred to. Humans are most often characterized in terms of occupation or sexual or racial identity (*police woman*), animals and plants according to their appearance or habitat (*giraffe bird, prairie dog*), natural objects in terms of their composition or location (*salt flats, mountain stream*) and synthetic objects in terms of their purpose (*banana fork*), cf. Downing (1977: 35) Drawing on Zimmer's and Downing's insights, Dowty (1979: 316) formalized the idea of an open, yet classificatory relation between the constituents of a compound by relating the external arguments of the predicates involved in the compound to one another via an unspecified relation variable 'R' that was qualified by the higher-order predicate 'appropriately classificatory'. Allen (1978: 93) attempted to characterize the range of possible meanings of a compound in terms of a Variable R Condition that ensured a matching of semantic feature content between the two constituents.

The major insight achieved by this line of argumentation is that the semantics of compounding is seen as being anchored in both the psychological act of categorizing experience with the real world as well as in the linguistic need for the efficient naming of the resulting categories.

3 Semantic approaches to compound meaning

3.1 Inferred stereotypic and basic relations

In the early 1980s, the content and orientation of the linguistic debate reviewed in the previous section began to shift as linguists started to reconsider the theoretical relevance of the implicit relation that completes the meaning of a noun-noun compound. The question coming into focus was not whether the missing relation could be seen as a covert instantiation of one of a fixed set of general semantic relations such as 'purpose', 'location', etc., or even as the deletion of a generalized verb, the realization of a PRO-predicate or a silent, appropriately classificatory relation inferable from the linguistic or situative context. Rather, the true linguistic task was to discover what meaningful units enter into the interpretation of a compound in addition to those that are actually represented by its overt constituents and what parameters restrict the process of inferring this implicit information. It had become clear that the answer to this question could not be anchored in the formal structure of the compound; hence, it must be sought in a theory of linguistic meaning. One of the first attempts to do so was Fanselow (1981a). Working within the framework of Montague Grammar, Fanselow (1981a) formalized approximately 23 different rules that combine two nouns A and B into a compound AB and assign the newly formed compound a semantic interpretation. The application of a particular rule is triggered by the subcategorizational properties of the nouns involved (i.e., whether they denote a relation or an individual, group, mass, proper name, etc.). The compound *street corner* 'corner of a street', for example, would be interpreted by the rule given in (1)

(1) Let B be a relational noun and A a non-relational noun. Then AB is a non-relational noun. If a' is the meaning of A and b' is the meaning of B, then the meaning of AB is:
{x | There is a y, y from a', so that (x, y) from b'}

and the compound *Time-Warner* by the rule in (2):

(2) Let A, B be proper names. Then AB is a proper name. If the meaning of A is a' and that of B is b', then the meaning of AB is: the smallest thing that has a' and b' as parts.

These rules are taken from Fanselow (1981b: 49–50) in order to avoid the complex formal detail of the Montague account in Fanselow (1981a).

The need for an extensive set of 23 rules arose from the basic assumption of Montague Grammar that each semantic interpretation is tied to a distinct formal rule. But precisely this inflation of rules engendered quite a bit of criticism. Handwerker (1985) and Meyer (1993: 24), for example, both note that it is highly implausible that a battery of 23 different rules is necessary to account for a phenomenon that entails one very simple binary branching structure. Consequently, Fanselow's analysis merely describes a number of compound types without offering an explanation for why these particular types occur and whether other types are possible. In answer to this criticism, Fanselow (1981b) simplified his (1981a) position by working in a less technical framework that enabled him to formulate the idea that all nouns are relational in an extended sense in that they invoke extra-linguistic associations from which a stereotypic relation can be inferred and applied to the semantics of the second constituent to complete the meaning of the compound. So, for instance, a *car motor* is a motor that drives a car because speakers know that that 'driving' is what motors are stereotypically built for. In the same vein, a *knife wound* is a wound inflicted by a knife because speakers associate 'cutting' stereotypically with knives. In addition to inferring a relation in this manner, it is also possible to extract a salient property from the non-head constituent and use it to modify the head, cf. *snail mail*, where a prominent property of 'snail' is its slow motion, or *snake dance*, where the form of a snake gives a characteristic property of the dance. Furthermore, there are a set of basic relations including 'and', 'part-of', and 'location' that also may underlie the interpretation of compounds, cf., e.g., *astronomer-geologist*, *piano keys*, and *country road*.

3.2 Knowledge structures and discourse

Meyer (1993) criticizes Fanselow's (1981a) analysis of compound interpretation for being based on underlying relations that do not result directly from the meaning of the constituent nouns but have to be induced by special processes of finding stereotypes and identifying basic relations. Meyer attempts to show that compound interpretation results directly from the lexical and conceptual knowledge associated with the constituent nouns. He bases his theory on a framework that incorporates the two-level semantic approach to meaning (Bierwisch 1983; Bierwisch & Lang 1989; cf. also article 5 [Semantics: Theories] (Lang & Maienborn) *Two-level Semantics*) into discourse representation theory (Kamp 1981; Kamp & Reyle 1993; cf. also article 11 [Semantics: Theories] (Kamp & Reyle) *Discourse Representation Theory*) and also makes use of knowledge structures and scripts such as those developed in the field of artificial intelligence. The formalities of his approach will not be delved into here, since the insightful ideas he develops that are relevant in this context can be illustrated without them. The two-level theory of semantics distinguishes the context invariant aspects of lexical meaning from the variable aspects of conceptual structure that arise in the context of use. A noun like *museum*, for example, denotes in its invariant lexical-semantic sense a family of related concepts (= (3)) that may be fixed in a particular discourse to a specific concept: 'institution' (= (4a)), building' (= (4b)), or 'staff' (= (4c)). This type of disambiguation is termed conceptual shift (cf. Bierwisch 1983):

(3)   The museum is interesting.

(4)   a. The museum plays an important role in the cultural life of the city.
      b. The museum is being repainted.
      c. The museum is on strike.

On the basis of this insight, Meyer (1993) identifies four levels of knowledge that play a role in the interpretation of isolated compounds: first, the grammatical level of argument satisfaction; second, the level of lexical-semantic knowledge consisting of the context-independent information contained in the lexical entries of the individual nouns; and third, the level of conceptual knowledge including context-dependent information and information about prototypical properties associated with a concept. An additional level, the level of discourse, takes background knowledge in the form of scripts into account and allows the hearer to identify antecedents for the compound's constituents as well as relations that exist between them in an actual discourse. This fourth level, therefore, is concerned not with the potential meanings a compound can have in isolation, but with the actual utterance meaning assigned to a compound on the basis of its position in a discourse. These four levels of knowledge form a network that is ordered with respect to the salience of the relation they produce.

When considering the potential meanings of isolated compounds, the most salient interpretations result from the grammatical process of argument satisfaction. *Opera fan* has such a strong tendency to be interpreted on the basis of the 'fan' relation (i.e., 'fan of opera') that no other meaning seems even remotely plausible. And German speakers will reject the compound *Patientenbesitzer* 'patient owner' as incoherent until they are made aware of a context that allows a legitimate argument-head relation to hold between the constituents (e.g., words on a sign in the parking lot of a veterinarian's office). If the head noun is not relational but sortal, the first level of grammatical knowledge cannot apply and an attempt will be made to find an appropriate lexical relation at the second level of lexical knowledge. Artifacts have as a prominent relation in their lexical structures the purpose for which they are created, hence *wine glass* has the reading 'glass for holding wine' and *cement factory* 'factory producing cement'. If no plausible relation can be found at the lexical level, or if for other reasons an alternative interpretation is necessary, the search moves on to the conceptual level where a larger number of interpretative possiblities suggest themselves due to the richness of conceptual knowledge: things can be related to one another in a variety of ways, e.g., via location (*sand crab*), the material of which they are made (*cement factory*), whether they are composed substances (*flour dough*), and so on. Even more complex chains of relations are possible as in *commuter city* 'city consisting of a suburban area where people live and an urban area where they work' (Meyer 1993: 102–141).

Interestingly, the level at which the relation arises influences the compound's ability to undergo conceptual shifts. At the level of argument satisfaction, the selectional restrictions of the head noun fix the concept-specific meaning of the non-head. Therefore, *Museumseite* is interpreted as the side of a museum building (and not a museum as an institution) and *book cover* is the cover of the physical object 'book' (and not its informational content). Once the head noun assigns its internal role to the non-head, no further contextual variation is found (Meyer 1993: 109–110). At the level of lexical knowledge however, the lexical relation chosen is part of the context-independent meaning of the head noun and, hence, need not invoke access to a specific concept for either itself or the non-head noun. For example, the lexical entry for 'museum' will specify its purpose as one of 'exhibiting things'. This relation will not fix the conceptual domain of its internal argument. Consequently, the meaning of 'book' in *book museum* is not fixed to a specific concept. Even after satisfying the internal role of the relation 'exhibit', the 'book' concept is still open in both the examples (5) a) and (5) b) below. And as the different readings of the sentences in (5)(a) and (5)(b) also show, the head concept 'museum'—which is open initially—shifts to a more specific concept when the further sentential context is taken into account to be understood an institution in (5a) but as a building in (5b), cf. Meyer (1993: 114, 150–151):

(5) The *book museum* is closing
    a) for lack of funds.
    a. museum (institution) exhibiting books (complete concept or physical object)
    b) at 7 p.m.
    b. museum (building) where books (complete concept or physical object) are exhibited

Some purpose relations, on the other hand, require their internal argument to belong to a specific ontological domain and when such a relation is invoked the non-head will be fixed to the requisite domain. By way of example, the lexical entry for 'cup' has the purpose relation 'containing a liquid'. Therefore, the concept 'coffee' in *coffee cup* is limited to 'beverage', thus eliminating the 'bean', 'powder' and 'plant' variants of 'coffee' (Meyer 1993: 112, 150–151).

When a conceptual relation is involved, it relates specific concepts to one another, so no further conceptual shifts, for either the head or the non-head, are possible. The readings of *museum book* based—not on the lexical relation 'exhibit', but—on the conceptual relations 'written-by', sold-by', 'published-by' or 'located-in' can only make reference to a specific concept in both the denotation of 'museum' and in the denotation of 'book'. This yields the disambiguated readings shown in (6), cf. Meyer (1993: 153–154).

(6) museum book
    a. book (information mediator) written by a museum (institution)
    b. book (physical object) sold by a museum (institution)
    c. book (physical object) sold in a museum (building)
    d. book (physical object) located in a museum (building)
    e. book (complete concept) published by a museum (institution)

Thus, conceptual shifts and relation selection are independent processes. Conceptual shifts are general processes of meaning constitution and, as such, are also free to occur in compounds, but they do not occur in the non-head of a compound when the subcategorization restrictions of (the grammatically or lexically recruited) relation limit its denotation to a specific conceptual domain. At the conceptual level, where a conceptual relation holds between two specific concepts, they do not occur at all because the conceptual relation arises on the basis of specific concepts. In interpreting isolated compounds, the saliency of a relation is predicted by the hierarchy of knowledge structures; grammatical relations take precedence over lexical relations and lexical relations take precedence over conceptual relations. If one level is not applicable, the search for a plausible relation moves on to the next. Within the complex domain of conceptual knowledge, object-specific properties will take precedence over more general relations like 'part-of', 'made-of' and 'has-part', which in turn take precedence over completely general relations like 'location' which can apply to almost any object (Meyer 1993: 148).

Discourse knowledge differs from the other knowledge types in yielding a specific utterance meaning rather than a potential meaning or meanings assigned to a compound in isolation of context. The information presented in a discourse may allow one to find an anaphoric referent for one or both of the compound's constituents, especially if the compound occurs in a definite noun phrase, and may also supply a specific relation between the two antecedents (Meyer 1993: 189), cf. also Boase-Beier & Toman (1984):

(7) In der Sahara gibt es eine Schlange, die sich von Skorpionen ernährt. Die Skorpionsschlange ist sehr giftig.
'In the Sahara there exists a snake that feeds on scorpions. The scorpion snake is very poisonous.'

Discourse relations, being explicit, are the most salient relations of all and can even override a relation based on argument satisfaction. Independent of context, the compound *Dichterfreund* would be interpreted via argument satisfaction as, friend of a poet'. However, in the discourse in (8), its meaning is clearly 'friend and poet'.

(8) Der Dichter Heiner Müller hatte Geburtstag. Der Regisseur Hans Neuenfels schenkte dem Dichterfreund einen Blumenstrauß.
'It is the poet Heiner Müller's birthday. The director Hans Neuenfels gave his poet-friend a bouquet of flowers.'

The discourse has absorbed the internal argument of 'friend' (it is assigned to Hans Neuenfels). Consequently, the compound contains two nouns from the same ontological domain with compatible functions whose external arguments can be linked to a common discourse referent, Heiner Müller, yielding a conjunctive interpretation (Meyer 1993: 171).

Scripts activated by a discourse also supply the source of an utterance meaning. The mentioning of *Bahnhofscafe* in a discourse will open up a script about coffee houses enabling the interpretation of *Bahnhofskaffee* as 'coffee (beverage) purchased at the train station' (Meyer 1993: 183). It is even possible for a discourse to provide a highly unusual interpretation, one that would never occur in isolation, such as 'museum that gives away books' for *book museum*:

(9) In Hamburg gibt es ein Museum, das Bücher an seine Besucher verschenkt. Das Büchermuseum...
'In Hamburg there is a museum that gives books to its visitors. The book museum...'

This process, however, is not without limitations; a discourse relation cannot successfully contradict the lexical meaning of the constituents, (Meyer 1993: 190):

(10) In Hamburg gibt es ein Museum, das alte Bücher vernichtet. ?Das Büchermuseum...
'In Hamburg there is a museum that destroys books. The book museum...'

Meyer (1994) takes up the topic of compounds in context again and shows how dynamic processes of abduction play a role in the interpretation process.

4 Cognitive psychological approaches to compound meaning

4.1 Analogy and linguistic templates

Although Ryder (1994) does not achieve the same degree of coverage and insight into the complex semantic properties of compounds as the approaches reviewed in section 3, her approach nevertheless brings to light an important aspect of compound interpretation that has not yet been touched upon, namely the role played by analogy. Working within the theory of cognitive grammar developed by Langacker (1987), Ryder assumes that conventionalized expressions determine the interpretation of novel forms by functioning as patterns or 'linguistic templates'. A single conventionalized compound can function in this sense as an analogical base for a new formation (e.g., *blackmail* > *whitemail* 'obtaining results via promises rather than threats'), as can more general patterns centered around a common first or second constituent, or 'core word', cf. *cigar box, shoe box, matchbox, gift box* > X + *box* 'box intended to hold X' (Ryder 1994: 80). The latter phenomenon is known in psycholinguistic studies as the 'positional family size' of a constituent, cf., e.g., Baayen (2010) and Plag & Kunter (2010). At an even more abstract level, a cluster of semantically similar cases such as *suitcase, ice bag, wastebasket, wine glass, dustbin*, etc., will give rise to the abstract pattern: *Y + Container* = 'X that holds Y' (Ryder 1994: 99). By generalizing from groups of semantically similar established expressions to patterns of different degrees of abstraction, a speaker builds up a repertoire of linguistic templates in his grammar that function as models for the creation and interpretation of new words. When the listener is confronted with a novel compound, a salient template is identified and a search begins in the semantic information schemas associated with the compound's constituents to find a common schema that can be used to justify the template. The hearer then uses a plausible relation in the schema to fill in the meaning of the compound. Upon hearing *giraffe cage*, for example, the template *Y + Container* will be called up and can be justified, licensing the meaning 'cage that holds a giraffe'. In integrating the meanings of the nouns into a common semantic information schema, it will sometimes to be necessary to accommodate one or both of the meanings. The meaning of 'dog' in *doghouse* is not altered, but the meaning of 'house' has been accommodated to fit the combination since this is not a prototypical use of 'house'. If no interpretation can be constructed on the basis of a common semantic information schema, a similarity relation may be used, i.e., a compound XY will be interpreted as a 'Y that is like X in shape, size, color, activity, etc.' (Ryder 1994: 91). Ryder considers the similarity relation a strong default interpretation, but her data show that it is often possible to obtain this reading along with a reading based on a linguistic template. So, on the one hand, the novel compound *fire-spider* elicited a response by her informants on the basis of the low-level template *fire-ant* yielding 'spider whose bite stings', but interpretations based on similarity were actually in the majority, i.e., 'spider that is red/that glows like fire', cf. (Ryder 1994: 161).

4.2 Concept combination

In recent years psycholinguists, psychologists and cognitive scientists have joined theoretical linguists in their interest in the interpretation of compounds. This increasing interest can be attributed to the fact that compounds represent combinations of concepts in the purest sense. Concept combination is the process whereby two independent concepts are integrated into an innovative combination. By nature, combinations of concepts are not restricted to compounds but underlie all types of phrases. However, in a compound, in contadistinction to a phrase, the concepts are often conjoined with the intention of creating at least a temporary name for a new complex concept and without additional information as to how they are interrelated. The primary reason for the interest in the nature of concept combination on the part of psychologists and cognitive scientists is the light this process sheds on both the structure of simple concepts and the flexibility of the categorization process, cf. also article 12 [Semantics: Typology, Diachrony and Processing] (Kelter & Kaup) *Conceptual knowledge, categorization, and meaning*. When two concepts are combined, the combination often invokes more information than is present in the union of the simple concepts (this phenomenon is referred to as 'emergent attributes', cf. Hampton 1987; Murphy 1988, 1990). For example, a 'wooden spoon' is typically understood as a larger object than a 'metal spoon' and an 'empty store' as one that is not only empty, but also loosing money. Consequently, the area of concept combination is a good testing ground for theories that attempt to answer the question of how concepts are structured and represented in the human mind. Often the empirical data considered are adjective-noun combinations as, for instance, in Smith & Osherson's (1984) feature weighting model. Here adjectives, construed as denoting a single feature, pick out a slot in the schema of the head noun and add weight to it: a 'red table' is a 'table' with additional weight added to the feature COLOR via the property 'red'. Murphy (1988) is concerned with the inadequacy of this model in accounting for noun-noun combinations. Nouns represent more complex concepts than adjectives. In *apartment dog*, for example, the concept 'apartment' picks out the HABITAT slot in the head concept 'dog' and replaces all other possible fillers for this slot. The process of specifying the concept of the head via the modifier (known as 'concept specialization') is highly dependent on world knowledge in at least two senses: world knowledge is needed to pick out the correct slot (speakers know that it is more likely that a dog *lives* in an apartment than *bites* one or *looks like* one), and once the appropriate slot is filled, the combination undergoes a second process of elaboration to "clean up" the complex concept, making it more complete and coherent. An apartment dog is likely to be smaller, quieter and friendlier than, e.g., a farm dog (Murphy 1988: 532–533).

For Wisniewski (1996), as well, the study of concept combination is important because it offers insight into how concepts are represented in the mind. When the individual concepts are accessed, a fit between them must be determined. Wisniewski distinguishes three basic strategies for achieving this fit: linking the concepts via a relation, mapping properties from one concept onto the other, and combining the concepts into a hybrid. Relation linking yields two whole concepts connected by means of a relevant relation, cf. *car squirrel* with the meaning 'squirrel that *chases* cars' or *snake robin*, meaning 'robin that *eats* snakes'. Property mapping yields a single concept modified by a feature from the modifier concept as in 'thin rake' for *pencil rake* or 'pony with stripes' for *zebra pony*. The strategy of property mapping clearly shows that concepts are not represented in the mind as impermeable wholes but must be structured in terms of relevant properties that can be accessed individually when the concept is activated. Hybridization, finally, yields a combination in which both objects are represented, cf. *moose elephant* 'creature with properties of both a moose and an elephant'. In addition to property mapping, Wisniewski (1996) found that the informants in his experiments were using another type of 'noun construal' where a concept is not accessed in its entirety. When employing the strategy of relation linking, often a representation of one of the objects was chosen instead of the object itself to complete the relation, cf. *stone squirrel* 'figure of a squirrel made of stone' and *clay elephant* 'figure of an elephant made of clay', or a part of the object was selected instead of the whole object as in *tiger chair* 'chair covered with tiger skin'. Again, the phenomenon of noun construal shows that world knowledge plays a role in interpretation of complex concepts. When it is recognized that a constituent does not plausibly fit a relation, the concept will be construed to obtain a sensible combination. Wisniewski (1996), as well as Murphy (1988, 1990), recognizes the need for a second stage of processing beyond slot filling, i.e., 'concept elaboration'. Once a slot is filled, world knowledge is used to refine the resulting combination. For example, upon hearing the compound *elephant box*, it could be postulated that the box has air holes in it. What Wisniewski's notion of construal suggests is that the process of elaboration sometimes goes beyond mere refinement and involves altering the typical referent of a constituent by picking out a depiction of it or a particularly salient feature or a relevant part of it.

Concept combinations often display an ambiguity in interpretation with readings resulting from more than one of the strategies. For instance, *snake vase* can be interpreted via relation linking as 'vase in which snakes are kept' or via property mapping yielding 'vase in the form of a snake'. Likewise, *cow horse* can be understood as a 'horse that herds cows' via relation linking or an 'animal that is both a cow and a horse' via hybridization. Relation linking and property mapping are conceptually different processes for Wisniewski. His experiments show that concepts that are highly similar to one another lend themselves to an interpretation via property mapping or even hybridization rather than relation linking, cf. *zebra horse* 'horse with stripes' and *newspaper magazine* 'newspaper and magazine in one'. In these cases, a property (or several properties) of the modifier concept are relevant to the head concept. Relation linking, however, doesn't depend on shared properties but holds when a concept expressed by the modifier fits the preconditions for filling a slot in the head concept (Wisniewski 1996: 448–449).

Gagné & Shoben (1997), Gagné (2000) and Gagné & Spalding (2006) take issue with the previously mentioned studies and suggest an alternative approach which they term the CARIN ('competition among relations in nominals') theory. Murphy (1988), Wisniewski (1996) and others view concept combination as a process whereby the head provides a schema in which the modifier selects a particular slot and fills it with its own concept. The more prominent the slot is in the concept, the easier it is to interpret the combination (e.g., *cold beer*). Deviant complex concepts arise when the dimension expressed by the modifier is not relevant to or incongruent with the head concept as in *cold garbage* and *sliced typewriter* respectively, cf. (Murphy 1990). The CARIN theory, however, views the interpretative process the other way around: The interpretation of a complex concept is determined primarily by the modifying constituent of the combination and not the head. A relation previously used with a modifier becomes associated with the lexical representation of that modifier and strongly influences the interpretation of a novel combination when the same modifier is used again. In cases where several relations are associated with a modifier, the different relations compete with one another in the interpretation process. For example, the 'made-of' relation is more strongly associated with the constituent *chocolate* than the 'derived-from' relation, hence *chocolate bee* will be interpreted as a 'bee *made of* chocolate'. And since 80% of combinations with *mountain* as a first constituent are interpreted via the 'location' relation (cf. *mountain stream, mountain path, mountain cabin*), *mountain bird* will be more easily interpreted than *mountain magazine*, where the latter requires the infrequent 'about' relation. In order to justify the idea that the relation comes from the modifier and not the head constituent, the authors appeal to the functional difference between the two: The head provides the category name for the new concept, while the modifier names the 'contrast set' belonging to the category. Hence, 'mountain' in *mountain bird* sets up a contrast with other types of birds and, in so doing, actually alters the concept of the head. Thus, in opposition to the assumptions of the concept specialization approach to compound interpretation, the authors of the CARIN theory propose that the interpretative relation stems from the modifier and is evaluated for its goodness of fit by the head, thus altering the concept expressed by the head alone.

New experimental evidence has lead the authors of the earlier CARIN theory to revise their initial assumptions in a modified approach now termed the RICE ('relational interpretation competitive evaluation') theory, cf. Spalding et al. (2010). Experiments based on a different experimental task indicate that when the meaning of the head is active in a context, it is also able to suggest possible relations for the interpretation of the compound. Hence, the relational meaning used in interpreting a compound is not limited to the modifier but can also be associated with the head. The earlier claims of the CARIN theory were derived from sense/nonsense tasks in which the participants saw a prime in which one of the constituents was identical to its counterpart in the target and the prime had either the same or a different relation from the target. After viewing the prime, participants were asked to judge whether the target compound made sense. A priming effect for the relation was found only when the modifier was the same in prime and target; the head constituent did not exert a similar influence. Furthermore, it took more time to judge the target when the modifier was associated with a number of relations than when it had only one strong relation. This was the source of the claim that the different relations associated with the modifier compete with one another as they are being evaluated as to their compatibility with the meaning of the head. The stronger the competition is between the relations, the harder it is to make a sense judgment, which is reflected in elevated reaction times by the participants. The so-called relational strength of the modifier was a better predictor of reaction time than the frequency of the relation chosen. However, the use of a relation verification task in which the relation is already provided and hence available to the participant who must simply affirm its plausibility, has shown that relations associated with the head constituent are also available during the interpretation of a compound. In the verification tasks, the largest amount of relational priming occurred when the head was the repeated constituent. Modified to accommodate these new findings, the RICE theory now assumes that both constituents, modifier and head, store and activate relational information. Multiple relations compete and are evaluated in a parallel process that rules out implausible fits. This step is followed by a process of elaboration in which the relational interpretation is enriched with further conceptual information that is not literally part of either the constituent concepts or the relation connecting them, but is necessary for understanding the complex concept. Importantly, however, the RICE theory, as the

CARIN theory before it, holds to its criticism of theories of concept combination in terms of 'concept specialization' in which new complex concepts are derived from the schema of the head via modification of one of its inherent features by the modifier constituent. Spalding et al. (2010) argue that such theories cannot account for the modifier-based effects they find in their experiments. The idea of competition among relations plays a key role as well in Štekauer's (2005) theory of compound interpretation, cf. Štekauer's notion of 'objectified predictability rate'.

5 Origin of compounds in a protolanguage?

How exactly do the simple structures of compounds with their semantic openness, their pragmatic flexibility, and their conceptual motivation fit into the architecture of grammar? Fanselow (1985) considers this question and proposes a novel view-point concerning the theoretical status of compounding. Differentiating compounding from other types of morphology, he argues that compounding is not part of formal grammar and, thus, differs in status from both derivation (cf. article 3 [this volume] (Lieber) *Semantics of derivational morphology*) and inflection which do obey grammatical principles. Compounds are composed exclusively of lexical categories; functional categories that form the foundation of syntax are absent from their structures. Moreover, compounds actually violate central principles of grammar like X-bar theory, theta theory, case theory, binding theory, etc. Since central semantic categories like tense, modality, definiteness and quantification are also absent from compound structures, compounds cannot be explained by the principles of semantics either. Fanselow adduces further grammatical, neurocognitive and evolutionary evidence to strengthen his argument that compounds originate from a rudimentary language code that was a precursor to grammar. The rudimentary code is a symbolic system in the right hemisphere that contains an inventory of meaningful symbols denoting objects and events. It allows a certain amount of manipulation and inference on the content of these symbols which results in the production and comprehension of simple messages that lack the characteristic elements of formal syntax. Actually this symbolic ability is common to both cerebral hemispheres, but is consistently overridden in the left hemisphere by the superiority of the task-specific language centers. Products of the primitive code may be found in certain other peripheral areas of modern grammar besides compounds such as in the non-configurational structures of syntax, elliptical discourse structures, telegraphic speech, headlines, etc. It surfaces furthermore as a means of primitive communication when linguistic ability is absent or impaired as in the earliest stages of child grammar, the language of apes taught to sign, the language of linguistically deprived children like Genie, as well as in aphasic speech.

Normal language learners begin the acquisition process with the null hypothesis that compounds and other products of the primitive code are not part of grammar. This initial assumption is modified according to the strength of the presence of these structures in the input. To the extent that a child is exposed to compounds in the primary linguistic data, he will accommodate the relevant patterns into his grammar. Their formal structure is simple enough to be learned without the help of Universal Grammar. Nevertheless, their accommodation into grammar enforces certain restrictions on their structure. In order for a complex lexical expression to be introduced into a phrase structural position, one of its parts must correspond to a lexical category that can function as the head of the word. As a head, it will express the morphosyntactic features which are overtly encoded in the grammar of the language.

Fanselow draws a parallel between the structural properties of compounds and the combinations of the earliest stage of language acquisition before the development of grammar takes effect. The earliest two-word stage of child language acquisition is universally characterized by an overabundance of nominal elements whose combinations instantiate conceptual patterns like agent + action, action + patient, object + location, etc., and whose interpretations are dependent on inferential processes rooted in general knowledge about how different types of objects relate to one another. In the first stage of language acquisition before the child has an awareness of grammar, nominal combinations stand on their own and can have sentence character, cf. *Mommy sock* 'I see Mommy's sock', 'Mommy is wearing a sock', 'Mommy should put my sock on me', etc. After the grammar begins to develop, such a combination must fit into a nominal position in phrase structure and hence will be limited in its denotation to a nominal meaning. Thus, a compound structure like *Merkel biographer* must denote a one-place predicate, i.e., 'x = biographer of Merkel' and can no longer express a proposition, i.e., 'Merkel is a biographer'. Where such expressions are not bound to grammar, this constraint on meaning type does not hold even in the adult grammar. And, indeed, non-nominal, sentential meaning can be found for such combinations in certain situations as, for instance, in the telegraphic style of headlines, cf. *MERKEL CHANCELLOR!* (cf. Fanselow 1985: 117).

Recently, Jackendoff (1999, 2002, 2009) in his deliberations on language evolution has also expressed doubts as to whether compounding involves grammatical competence. Bickerton (1990) proposed that human language evolved in two stages: our modern language ability developed as a refinement of an earlier 'protolanguage' that was structured into a vocabulary and pragmatics. Jackendoff scrutinizes our modern language for remnants of the earlier protolanguage postulated by Bickerton and concludes, like Fanselow, that elements of the protolanguage can still be observed in situations where modern language is incapacitated. Such cases include for Bickerton the two-word stage of language acquisition, pidgins, late language learning as in the case of Genie, the language of apes and agrammatical aphasia. Jackendoff adds to Bickerton's cases four further examples: the language of the right hemisphere, the so-called 'home sign' of deaf children of non-signing parents, the steady state of second language by immigrant learners (termed 'The Basic Variety' by Klein & Perdue 1997) and compounding. These, too, are all cases where derivational and inflectional morphology, function words and the complex configurations of syntax are absent. In Jackendoff's terms, phonology in these simple structures interfaces directly with conceptual semantics and meaning results from the inferences hearers make as to what the words can take on.

6 Compounds in the lexical system of grammar

6.1 Compounds as lexical items in grammar

Fanselow's and Jackendoff's insights into the origin of compounds vis-à-vis grammar shed light on the nature of the compounding process and help us to make sense of the properties of compounds as entities in the lexical systems of modern-day languages. Fanselow's analysis of compounds was reviewed in section 3.1. Jackendoff's current work assumes that the interpretation of a compound is the realization of one of two general configurations. First, a non-head constituent can fill an argument position of the head as exemplified in (11) for *helicopter attack* yielding the interpretation 'attack on something by a helicopter' (Jackendoff 2009: 123):

(11) helicopter$_1$ attack$_2$ = (ATTACK$_2$ (HELICOPTER$_1$, INDEF))

Otherwise the non-head constituent serves as a modifier to the head and, hence, is bound by an inferred function that also binds the head (Jackendoff 2009: 124). The function can have one of two origins. First, it may belong to a set of basic functions (SAME, LOC, CAUSE, PART, etc.) that form part of a generative system yielding an unlimited number of possibilities. This is illustrated in (12) for *window seat* that requires the basic function LOC yielding the meaning 'seat located at a window' (Jackendoff 2009: 124):

(12) window$_1$ seat$_2$ = SEAT$_2^\alpha$; [LOC [α, AT WINDOW$_1$]]

Secondly, the function relating the head and non-head can be coerced in Pustejovsky's (1995) sense from the semantic structure of the head. Coercion will, in most cases, supply a proper function (= PF) anchored in the qualia structure of the head, cf. (13) where the proper function of 'cup' is that of 'holding' a liquid. The PF is then cocomposed in Pustejovsky's sense with the meaning of the head yielding the interpretation 'cup for holding coffee' (Jackendoff 2009: 125):

(13)   coffee$_1$ cup$_2$ = CUP$_2^\alpha$; [PF [HOLD (COFFEE$_1$, IN α)]]

Jackendoff (2009: 125ff.) goes on to provide the formal interpretation of more complex cases requiring a concatenation of functions. Examples are *coattail* 'something similar to a tail that is part of a coat' and *piano bench* 'a bench for **sitting on while playing** a piano' (where I have underlined the basic functions and placed the coerced functions in boldface type, S.O.).

So it would appear that, even if compounds can be traced back to a protolanguage in an attempt to explain their simple, non-formal, open and ambiguous character, basic compound patterns have been adopted into the lexical system of many modern languages.

6.2 Complex words vs syntactic phrases

The insights gained from section 5, however, justify a closer consideration of precisely this question. Have compounds become fully integrated into the lexical system and grammar of the individual languages that allow them or does a principled divide perhaps still remain between the simple, concatenative structure of compounds and the complex formal configurations of modern syntax?

Bücking (2009, 2010) argues that compounds and phrases typically fulfill complementary functions: Compounds name concepts and are closely associated with the denotation of 'kinds'; they specify a link between a linguistic expression and a complex concept. Phrases, on the other hand, describe objects and are compositional in a way that compounds are not. Furthermore, they are less closely related to kind terms. Working within the two-level theory of semantics (cf. article 5 [Semantics: Theories] (Lang & Maienborn) *Two-level Semantics*), Bücking assumes that compounds exemplify an abstract version of the general modification template that holds for modifier-head structures in general, as discussed by Higginbotham (1985), Zimmermann (1992) and Maienborn (2003) (cf. also article 8 [Semantics: Theories] (Maienborn) *Event semantics* and article 14 [Semantics: Lexical Structures and Adjectives] (Maienborn & Schäfer) *Adverbs and adverbials*). Intersective modification has generally been analyzed as the conjunction of predicates provided by a modifier and head. This process was termed "theta identification" by Higginbotham (1985: 564). The somewhat extended version of the modification template adopted by Bücking is shown in (14). This template conjoins two predicates in such a way that their external variables are related via an unspecified relation R. The use of the unspecified relation variable R allows Bücking to capture both what the modification structures of phrasal grammar and of compounds have in common as well as how they differ. When the modification template applies to phrases, the relation R is instantiated as the identity function. When applying at the lexical level, R will be instantiated as a relation that is associated in an integral way with one of the predicates of the construction. The specific relation that is chosen to complete the variable R is inferred from extra-linguistic knowledge and is instantiated during the mapping of the semantic form of the complex expression onto its conceptual structure, cf. Bücking (2010: 256).

(14) Modification template: $\lambda Q\, \lambda P\, \lambda x\, [P(x) \wedge R(x, v) \wedge Q(v)]$

The result is that, for instance, the German noun phrase *blauer Tee* 'blue tea' receives the interpretation in (15) as 'the set of x which are tea and blue'

(15) [blauer Tee]
= $\lambda x.\ \text{TEA}(x) \wedge \text{IDENTITY}\,(x,v) \wedge \text{BLUE}(v)$
= $\lambda x.\ \text{TEA}(x) \wedge \text{BLUE}(x)$

while the corresponding compound *Blautee* carries the interpretation via the open integral relation as 'the set of x which are tea which stand in an integral relation to v which is blue', cf. Bücking (2010: 257)

(16) [Blautee]
=$\lambda x.\ \text{TEA}(x) \wedge R_{\text{integral}}\,(x,v) \wedge \text{BLUE}(v)$

The compositional meaning of the noun phrase thus contrasts with the more flexible meaning of the compound. Bücking shows how a compound based on this template will allow incompatible attribution (cf. (17a)) that is strictly prohibited in a phrase (= (17b)).

(17) a. Dies ist ein roter Blautee.   'This is a red [blue tea]'
     b. *Dies ist ein roter blauer Tee.   'This is a red blue tea'

The compound [blue tea] with the attribute 'red' will have the interpretation in (18), in which the incompatible predicates 'red' and 'blue' are predicated of different variables by virtue of the relation R:

(18) [roter Blautee]
= $\lambda x. \text{RED}(x) \wedge \text{TEA}(x) \wedge R_{integral}(x,v) \wedge \text{BLUE}(v)$

In the case of an incompatible attribution with a phrasal adjective-noun combination, however, a contradiction arises by virtue of the fact that the two incompatible predicates are predicated of the same entity:

(19) [roter blauer Tee]
= $\lambda x. \text{RED}(x) \wedge \text{TEA}(x) \wedge \text{BLUE}(x)$

The assumption that compound meaning arises by means of an abstract version of the modification template thus predicts the more flexible meanings of compounds vs. their phrasal counterparts. The most plausible candidate for the relation R in the interpretation of compounds is found by means of abductive reasoning which searches for the simplest explanation for the semantic form of a linguistic expression that is compatible with the given knowledge.

6.3 The compound template

Bücking's studies concentrate on the contrast between adjective-noun combinations at the lexical and the phrasal level. Olsen's (2004) and (2010) investigations of noun-noun compounds make use of a similar template and come to the conclusion that, if compound interpretation is based on the modification template, there is no need for a principled division between the so-called primary and verbal interpretations of compounds. All interpretations can be traced back to the conjunction of predicates mediated by the relational variable R in the compound template in (14), repeated here as (20). This includes the copulative reading of noun-noun compounds as well. So, *pasta chef* would receive the "primary" interpretation 'chef that cooks pasta' if the 'cook' relation is inferred on the basis of knowledge related to the predicate 'chef' and is used to instantiate the variable R of the template, cf. (21). I assume that at this stage of the interpretation a free variable such as y will be existentially bound if not otherwise specified. *Ophthalmogist-politician* would receive the copulative reading 'ophthalmologist and politician' in (22) if the identity relation (IDENT) is chosen to specify the variable R on the basis of the recognition that the two predicates can both characterize a single individual in accordance with the Principle of Ontological Coherence that applies to the conjunction of predicates at the lexical level as discussed in Olsen (2004).

(20) Compound template
$\lambda Q \, \lambda P \, \lambda x \, [P(x) \wedge R(x,y) \wedge Q(y)]$

(21) pasta chef:
 $\lambda x \exists y \ [\text{CHEF}(x) \wedge \text{COOK}(x,y) \wedge \text{PASTA}(y)]$

(22) ophthalmologist-politician:
 $\lambda x \ [\text{POLITICIAN}(x) \wedge \text{IDENT}(x,y) \wedge \text{OPHTHALMOGIST}(y)]$
 $\equiv \lambda x \ [\text{POLITICIAN}(x) \wedge \text{OPHTHALMOGIST}(x)]$

Furthermore, the interpretation of the compound *street corner* with a relational head arises via the same assumption that the modifier predicate *street* stands in a relevant relation to another predicate P, the head of the construction, mediated by the relational variable R. The modifier and head constituent are introduced into the template and the free variable R is replaced by the most salient information available, i.e. the relation denoted by the lexical head *corner* and the free variable y is identified with u, the internal argument of the CORNER relation. The meaning of *street corner* becomes 'the set of x such that x is a corner of a street'.

(23) a. $\lambda Q \lambda P \lambda x \ [P(x) \wedge R(x,y) \wedge Q(y)] \ (\lambda z \ [\text{STREET}(z)])$
 $\equiv \lambda P \lambda x \ [P(x) \wedge R(x,y) \wedge \text{STREET}(y)]$
 b. $\lambda P \lambda x \ [P(x) \wedge R(x,y) \wedge \text{STREET}(y)] \ (\lambda u \lambda o \ [\text{CORNER}(o,u)])$
 $\equiv \lambda x \ [\lambda u \ \text{CORNER}(x,u) \wedge R(x,y) \wedge \text{STREET}(y)]$
 c. $\lambda x \exists y \ [\text{CORNER}(x,y) \wedge \text{STREET}(y)]$

Consequently, compounds in all their potential interpretations make use of the same combinatorial mechanism as modification. The difference is that modification in the unmarked case instantiates the variable R as the identity relation and any deviant cases are structurally marked (Maienborn 2003). In the case of compounds, the opposite holds. The unmarked case is the abduction of a salient relation via conceptual knowledge (or lexical knowledge if the head is a relational item), while the choice of the identity relation results in the special case of the copulative reading.

The same strategy seen in (23) applies to *horse rescuer* and other 'synthetic' compounds in which the agentive head noun has inherited the arguments of its verbal base (skipping over the event argument). In contrast to the relational interpretation of the compound *street corner* and *horse rescuer*, the interpretation of the syntactic phrases *corner of the street* and *rescues the horse* results when *corner* and *rescue* head a noun phrase and verb phrase, respectively, in which they can assign their internal theta role to their complement directly. This process is referred to in Higginbotham (1985) as theta-marking which has as its semantic counterpart the functional application of the head to its complement. In order for functional application to apply, the referential argument of the complement must be bound (Higginbotham's theta binding) so that the complement represents an individual. One choice of binder is the iota operator yielding a definite determiner phrase of (24). But in principle the referential argument of the complement is open to other operators such as the existential operator (*corner of a street*) or a quantifier (*rescued two/ many horses*).

(24) a. *corner* $\lambda y \lambda x.$ CORNER(x, y)
　　 b. *corner of the street* $\lambda x.$ CORNER(x, [ιy. STREET(y)])

Thus, the difference between the phrases on the one hand and the nominal compounds on the other is one of direct theta assignment from the head position in a phrase as opposed to the mediation in the compound of an inferred relation between two conjoined predicates that function as a head and modifier. The relation chosen in the two cases is similar—both interpretations are based on the relation inherent to the relational lexeme functioning as head of the construction. Nevertheless, the relationality of the compound template is indirect, arising via abductive reasoning to instantiate the open parameter R in the general modification template. First, it is merely one of several other possible options, cf. *street corner—shop corner; news reporter—newspaper reporter; taxi driver—Sunday driver*, etc. Secondly, similar relations can be inferred from non-relational heads as in *car thief* 'steal' *snow gun* 'shoot', *speech synthesis* 'produce'. The relationality of the syntactic head on the other hand results from the grammatically specified argument structure associated with the head in its lexical entry that triggers obligatory theta assignment. Thus, *to drive a Sunday* and *to report a newspaper* are not well-formed VPs.

It would seem, therefore, that the original (in Jackendoff's terms:) "pragmatic" aspect of compound interpretation stemming from the origin of compounds in a pre-modern 'protolanguage' has apparently been retained as a characteristic feature of compound interpretation in modern language even after such simple and free combinations have been reanalyzed as complex words. Compound structures have been accommodated into the lexical system insofar as the predicates that are involved are actual lexemes of the grammar. Their role in a compound structure, however, does not derive from the grammatical information encoded in their lexical entry but rather stems from a contextual or conceptual inference based on general reasoning strategies that is captured in the compound template.

7 Left-headed compounds

The analysis just sketched holds for languages that allow genuine compound structures in their lexical systems. In their discussion of compounds in the Romance languages, Rainer & Varela (1992) and Kornfeld (2009) for Spanish,

Bauer (1978), Zwanenburg (1992) and Fradin (2009) for French as well as Scalise (1992) for Italian draw attention to the fact that the determinative pattern of noun-noun compounds, so prevalent in Germanic, is highly restricted in the Romance languages. The formations that do appear have the atypical property for words that they are left headed:

(25) a. Sp.: *tren mercancías* 'train goods' = "freight train"
 b. Fr.: *timbre-poste* 'stamp postage' = "postage stamp"
 c. It.: *capostazione* 'master station' = "station master"

The plural forms of these examples are *tren<u>es</u> mercancías, timbr<u>es</u>-poste,* and *cap<u>i</u>stazione* where the underlined plural morpheme attaches to the left constituent in defiance of the definition of a word as an indivisible morphological unit. As the head of the word, the left constituent determines the gender of these complex words as well, as the masculine nouns Sp. *año luz* 'year light', Fr. *timbre-poste* and It. *capostazione* attest in which the second constituent is feminine and the first masculine. The left-headedness of the noun-noun combinations in Romance renders them highly marked word structures.

Two further features characteristic of Germanic compounds are absent from their Romance counterparts, namely their productivity and their openness in interpretation. The productive noun-noun formations that occur in Romance are restricted to a few fixed semantic patterns such as the 'resemble' formations of (26), cf. Rainer & Varela (1992: 126), Fradin (2009: 430) and Scalise (1992: 177),

(26) a. Sp.: *ciudad dormitorio* 'town dormitory' = "bedroom community",
  empresa fantasma 'company ghost' = "ghost company"
 b. Fr.: *poisson-chat* 'fish cat' = "catfish", *requin-marteau* 'shark hammer" = "hammerhead shark"
 c. It.: *pescecane* 'fish dog' = "shark"

and the coordinative constructions in (27), cf. Kornfeld (2009: 441), Fradin (2009: 430) and Scalise (1992: 183):

(27) a. Sp.: *poeta-pintor* 'poet-painter', *casaquinta* 'house-villa', *panadería-pastelería* 'bakery pastry', *pollera pantalón* 'skirt-trousers', *cantante autor* 'singer author'
 b. Fr.: *chanteur-compositeur* 'singer-composer', *enseignant-chercheu* 'teacher-researcher', *boulanger-pâtissier* 'baker-confectioner" *physique-chimie* 'physics-chemistry', *guide-interprète* 'guide interpreter'
 c. It.: *caffelatte* 'coffee milk', *cassapanca* 'box seat'

Noun-noun constructions that show an open relation similar to the compounds of Germanic are either borrowings from the other languages, mostly Germanic, (Bauer 1978: 84; Rainer 1993) or are reduced versions of the more typical native N+P+N structures, cf. Sp. *tren de mercancías* > *tren mercancías* (Rainer & Varela 1992: 120) and Fr. *stylo à bille* > *stylo-bille* 'ballpoint pen' (Fradin 2009: 433).

The N+P+N construction of Romance (cf. Fr. *pomme de terre* 'apple of ground' = "potato"), on the other hand, is not as restricted semantically as the N+N construction. Despite first appearances, these structures are not merely lexicalized noun phrases consisting of a head noun on the left followed by a prepositional phrase modifier. Several facts speak against such an analysis. First, in a syntactic construction, the governed N inside the adjunct PP must have an article if it is a count noun while such functional categories are absent in the lexical N+P+N pattern, cf. *estrella de mar* 'starfish' with the corresponding NP *una estrella del mar* 'a star of the sea' (Kornfeld 2009: 445). Secondly, the combinations in (28) do not describe objects but denote fixed conceptual units and hence function as names of categories. Finally, the prepositions involved are the most neutral prepositions of the languages (e.g., *de*, and *a*) and are syntactically opaque in the N+P+N constructions (Bauer 1978: 191 and Kornfeld 2009: 442):

(28) a. Sp.: *agente de seguridad* "security officer", *bicicleta de montaña* "mountain bike", *botas de lluvia* "rain boots", *casa de campo* "country house", *diente de leche* "milk tooth", *patas de rana* 'legs of frog' = "fins"
b. Fr.: *carte de visite* "calling card", *sortie de secours* "emergency exit", *chemin de fer* "railroad", *chambre d'hôtes* "guest room", *avion à réaction* "jet plane", *serpent à sonnettes* "rattlesnake", *poêle à frire* "frying pan"
c. It.: *mulino a vento* "windmill", *film a colori* "color movie"

It appears, then, that the productive nominal patterns in Romance are the coordinative N+N combinations and the N+P+N pattern whose status as a proper compound is unclear. Rainer & Varela (1992: 120) and Kornfeld (2009: 441) report that the latter formations are termed "improper compounds" in traditional treatments of Spanish word formation and Fradin (2009: 415–420) surveys their controversial status in the handbooks of French.

Interestingly, a highly productive pattern found in Romance is the so-called exocentric V+N pattern which derives agentive and instrumental nouns by combining a verb form of the third person singular with a noun that is understood as its direct object. Thus, Fr. *coupe-légumes* 'cut vegetables' and Sp. *cuentachistes* 'tell jokes' are interpreted similarly to their endocentric Germanic counterparts, which display an overt agentive suffix on their deverbal head, as *vegetable cutter* and *joke teller*. Again, these combination cannot simply be seen as a VP that has been reanalyzed as an N, as Di Sciullo & Williams (1987: 81) claim, because the formations systematically lack the article that must accompany count nouns in phrasal structure, cf. Sp. *girasol* 'turn sun' "sunflower" and Fr. *essuie-mains* 'wipe hands' = "hand towel" which cannot be used as well-formed VPs. The phrasal equivalent of the latter would be *Ce tissu essuie les mains* 'This cloth wipes the hands", not **Ce tissu essuie mains*, (Fradin 2009: 423). This makes it clear that the V+N structures—just as the N+P+N constructions in (28)—are correctly situated in the lexical system although, due to their left-headedness, neither can be considered genuine "morphological objects" in Di Sciullo & William's (1987) sense. If the noun is a count noun it occurs with plural inflection (Sp. *espantapájaros* 'scare birds' = "scare crow", It. *spazzacamini* 'sweep chimneys' = "chimney sweep). If it is a mass noun, it appears in the singular (Sp. *quitaesmalte* 'remove polish' = "polish remover", Il. *portacenere* 'hold ash' = "ashtray"), cf. Kornfeld (2009: 445) and Scalise (1992: 189–190).

(29) a. Sp.: *cuidacoches* 'care cars' = "car watcher", *tocadiscos* 'toss records' = "record player", *friegaplatos* 'wash dishes' = "dish washer", *sacacorcos* 'pull corks' = "cork screw", *abrepuertas* 'open doors' = "door opener"
b. Fr.: *essui-glace* 'wipe windshield', *tire-bouchon* 'pull cork', *abat-joir* 'weaken light' = "lampshade", *brise-glace* 'break ice' = "ice breaker"
c. It.: *stuzzica-denti* 'pick teeth' = "tooth pick", *portalettere* 'carry letters' = "postman", *lavapiatti* 'wash dishes', *scolapasta* 'drain pasta' = "colander"

Although there are analyses that consider the constructions of (29) left-headed endocentric structures by postulating the conversion of the verbal element to a noun, this question is under debate in the literature and most linguists consider them formally exocentric constructions in which neither the V nor the N is the head. Such exocentric formations are a frequent feature of Romance, one further example being the nominal P+N combinations in (30), which—again—cannot simply be considered as reanalyzed PPs because the article that must accompany the N in a phrasal structure is lacking in the complex word, cf. Sp. *sintecho* 'without roof' = "homeless person".

(30) a. Sp.: *sinvergüenza* '(person) without shame', *sin papeles* '(person) without documents'
b. Fr.: *sans-coeur* '(person) without heart', *sans papier* '(person) without papers'
c. It.: *senzatetto* '(person) without roof'

This peculiar arrangement of data found in Romance begins to make sense when considered on the basis of the semantic analysis of compounds presented in the previous section.

In section 6.3 it was proposed that the simple juxtaposition of two nouns is interpretable by means of a general reasoning strategy. The compound template is a formalization of this strategy. When two nouns are juxtaposed, it is normal to assume that their cooccurrence has some relevance and the mind begins to search for an appropriate connection between them. This covert interpretative step, captured by the relational variable R in the compound template, is not triggered by an overt signal in Germanic, hence the hypothesis that the interpretation of compounds has its origin in general reasoning strategies that are independent of grammatical processes (although such reasoning may also be employed in the interpretation of grammatical constructions, cf. article 14 [Semantics: Lexical Structures and Adjectives] (Maienborn & Schäfer) *Adverbs and adverbials*).

Whatever the origin of the Romance compounds may be, synchronically it is evident that they carry certain features of the grammatical systems of the individual languages. The influence of the grammar on these complex words reveals itself in several ways. First of all, they are consistently left-headed in accordance with the position of the syntactic head in the phrasal structures of Modern Romance, rendering the resulting structures highly atypical words and at variance with the other morphologically complex constructions of the lexical system, in particular the well-behaved right-headed derived words. Secondly, Romance compounds do not generally allow a simple juxtaposition of lexemes, but display a functional element as an overt signal of the subordinative relation between the head and modifier that is necessary in syntax when a nominal adjunct follows a head. The functional elements that mediate between a head and modifier in syntax are case morphemes (e.g., genitive markings) or equivalent functional prepositions. As seen in the examples in (28) above, the compounds of Romance make use of the latter, i.e., the prepositional elements *de* and *a*. (Case and agreement morphemes are not interpretable by the lexical system.) These relational elements signal the subordination of the N they govern and trigger an interpretative inference that relates the subordinate N to its head.

In Germanic, there is no overt signal present in the compound itself of the relation needed to complete the compound meaning; the relation is implicit and inferred via general reasoning strategies. The small caps in the column under the variable R in (31a) are intended to indicate its covert status. The situation is different in Romance. Here, the subordinative (or determinative) relation is explicitly encoded in the structure via a functional preposition, (31b). This type of functional marking which would break up the unity of a genuine word is possible because the head noun precedes the modifier.

(31) λQ λR λP λx   [P(x)   ∧   R(x,y)   ∧   Q(y)]
   a. righthand head: chef   COOK   pasta   pasta chef
                       novelist   =   lawyer   lawyer-novelist
                       corner   CORNER   street   street corner

   b. lefthand head: botas   de   lluvia   botas de lluvia
                       poeta   =   pintor   poeta-pintor

The need in Romance to overtly signal a subordinate relation also explains the nature of the data in (29) and (30). The relational meanings of the V+N and P+N nouns are triggered by the use of the specific relational lexeme that instantiates the variable R of the compound template while leaving the head constituent implicit. This yields formations such as Sp. *rompecabezas* 'break heads' = "puzzel" and *sintecho* 'without roof' = "homeless" in which the head noun is not expressed, but the relation between the head and modifier is. The absence of the head is the source of the exocentric reading; the predicate variable P functions as an open parameter to be instantiated via a conceptual inference. It is understood as the entity that carries out the action expressed by V+N or that is characterized by P+N. The exocentric compounds of Germanic are of a different nature (although English does display a few remnants of the V+N pattern, cf. *pickpocket, telltale, scofflaw, scarecrow*). Typically the exocentric Germanic compounds are A+N or N+N combinations that conform to the compound template, as for instance *flatfoot, loudmouth, fathead, low life, heavy weight, longhorn*. Their exocentricity lies in the metonymic shift from a literal A+N (*redhead*) to an individual (person, animal or thing) characterized by the relevant property, i.e., 'a person with red hair'.

(32) λQ λR λP λx   [P(x)   ∧   R(x,y)   ∧   Q(y)]
   c. lefthand head: —   rompe   cabezas   rompecabezas
                       —   sin   techo   sintecho

   d. righthand head: head   HAS(x,HAIR)   red   redhead

Finally, the logic of this analysis provides an explanation for the regularity and productivity of the coordinative N+N pattern. Simple coordinative N+N combinations (Engl. *lawyer-novelist* and Sp. *poeta-pintor*) are to be expected since they instantiate a pure coordination of predicates as the default case of modification that carries no requirement for an overt relational element, even at the syntactic level, cf. Engl. *small dog* or Sp. *perro pequeño*.

So, whereas the Germanic compounds appear to have retained the original pre-grammatical "pragmatic" strategy that lacks an overt signal of the subordinative relation needed to complete the meaning of a combination of two predicates, the Romance languages have not adopted this strategy into their lexical systems. Predicates are combined in the lexical system but the subordinative relation that holds between them is signaled by an overt element—either a functional category (i.e., a semantically reduced preposition) or a relational lexeme.

8 Constraints on the productive compounding process

8.1 Conceptual restrictions

The discussion up to now has made it clear that the meaning of a regular, productively formed compound is a function of the meaning of its constituents together with implicit information about how they relate to one another. The implicit relation is variable, and hence open in one sense, but it is restricted in another sense, in that it is anchored in the lexical and conceptual meaning of the compound's constituents. The question to be taken up in this section is whether there are further constraints on the meanings that compounds can express—constraints that restrict the type of conceptual or contextual inference made to instantiate the variable R of the template. The answer to this question is affirmative; there are constraints of a general nature on the compounding process and, in addition to these, language-specific constraints can be found as well that serve to limit the productivity of certain compound patterns in a particular language.

The most general restriction of all guarantees that the interpretation given to a compound must be inferable from the information present. Consequently, relations based on negation (Zimmer 1971: C11; Downing 1977: 825; Dowty 1979: 316) including dissimilarity and privation (Warren 1978: 247), do not occur. An *earthquake school* cannot be construed as a 'school that is not located near a region prone to earthquakes' just as a *cousin-chair* cannot be a 'chair reserved for non-cousins' or *snake dish* a 'dish not similar to a snake'. The notions 'non-location', 'not for', 'non-similar', etc., leave open such a vast number of possibilities that such a designation provides no basis for a classification.

It has been pointed out by Zimmer (1971: C16), Downing (1977: 823), Warren (1978: 257) and Bücking (2009, 2010), among others, that compounds serve as names for relevant categories of a speaker's experience. First and foremost, then, a compound must denote a category that conforms in a relevant manner to human experience. These categories will pick out an individual from one of the domains of individuals in human ontology. *Fisherman-logician* is a possible compound picking out an individual that is both a fisherman and a logician, but the combination *diplomat-boat can never induce the 'and' relation because human ontology does not entertain the assumption that an individual can be both animate and inanimate (cf. Olsen 2004: 23).

A further general restriction derives from the asymmetrical nature of compound structure: the modifier restricts the denotation of the head. Hence, all regular compounds denote hyponyms of the head concept. A compound violating this endocentric structure because the modifier denotes a superset—rather than a subset—of the head is therefore deviant, cf. *book novel, *building house (Meyer 1993: 102) and *animal horse (Bauer 1978: 86). Further, in order to pick out a subcategory that is relevant to the speakers' cognitive organization in a coherent manner, the modifier must make reference to a property that is not necessarily shared by the class as a whole. The choice of a default property as in *whisker-cat* (Ryder 1994: 90) or German *Seitenbuch* 'page book' (Meyer 1993: 103) does not result in hyponymy because all cats have whiskers and all books have pages. *Water fish (Warren 1978: 72), *wind-flag (Downing 1977: 824) and *waist-belt (Ryder 1994: 101) fail in the same manner to denote a relevant subset of the head, since they do not name anything more specific than what is already in the denotation of the head and, hence, are—again—simply redundant.

Meyer (1993: 123) points to other violations of the condition that the compound must denote a specialization of the head. Since 'flour' is a powder, it can be formed into heaps. But since there are no other options for the formation of uncontained powder, *Haufenmehl 'heap flour' is odd. Furthermore, the conceptual relation 'part-of' has several variants. The patterns 'area–place' (*Campuswiese* 'campus lawn') is possible as are the patterns 'activity–phase' (*Einkaufsbezahlung* 'purchase payment') and 'mass–portion' (*Zuckerkörnchen* 'sugar grain', *Wassertropfen* 'water drop', *Kuchenstück* 'cake piece', *Wurstscheibe* 'sausage slice'). 'Collective-element' concatenations, however, are ruled out because their heads denote necessary parts of the modifier and hence the compounds do not express a specialization of the head, cf. *Waldbaum 'forest tree', *Herdenantilope 'herd antelope', *Geflügelfasan 'poultry pheasant'. If the constituents are interchanged to the order 'element-collective' however, the construction no longer violates the specialization constraint: *Antilopenherde* 'antelope herd' denotes one of many possible types of 'herd'. Similarly, the 'has-part' relation is restricted in certain general ways. When the modifier represents a necessary part of the head, it does not specify the head concept. For instance, *Blütenblume 'blossom flower', *Dachhaus 'roof house', and *Gestellbrille 'frame glasses' are odd, but Schnurtelefon 'cord telephone' on the other hand is fine because there are now other options, i.e., cordless telephones and cell phones. Again, this is an example of a violation of specialization: the 'has-part' relation can be used for compounding only if the modifier expresses a "disjunction of elements standing in that relation to the head", cf. Meyer (1993: 136–138).

It is difficult to know where exactly to draw the line between general and language-specific constraints. Warren (1978: 85–87) notes that the 'mass-portion' pattern that Meyer just illustrated as possible for German (cf. *Wurstscheibe, Kuchenstück*) must be differentiated in English. English allows *raindrop, teardrop* but not **winedrop*, **sweat drop*. It allows *raincloud, dustcloud* but not **powdercloud*, **flourcloud*; furthermore *airwave* is possible but not **people wave*, and *rainstorm* but not **applause storm*. Warren suggests that when 'shape' actually indicates 'quantity', English must employ a phrasal construction, cf. **sausage slice* vs. *slice of sausage*; **cake piece* vs. *piece of cake* as well as *drop of wine, cloud of flour, wave of people, storm of applause* etc. This restriction is not active in German where *Wassertropfen, Mehlwolke, Butterberg, Applaussturm* are all possible; hence, it appears to be language-specific.

What about the restrictions applying to the use of human nouns? Are they general (i.e., founded in human cognition) or language-specific? Warren notes that human nouns cannot denote the 'part' in a 'part-whole' relation, cf. **girl crowd, *women group, *people queue, *child gang*; the equivalent phrasal constructions show that the concept itself is not deviant: *crowd of girls, group of women, queue of people, gang of children*. Since inanimate nouns are possible in this position (cf., *tree clump, apartment block, car line*), she debates whether this has to do with the randomness with which humans enter a group relation and, thus, the inability of these combinations to form a stabile class (Warren 1978: 89–90). German, however, allows this pattern. cf. *Menschenmenge, Frauengruppe, Menschenschlange, Kinderschar*. Furthermore, human nouns are disallowed in English as the modifier to a kinship relation, but permitted in German: **doctor widow, *professor son, *artist aunt* vs. *Arztwitwe, Professorensohn, Künstlertante*. So perhaps the restrictions on the use of human nouns in compounds are particular to English.

Ryder (1994: 148) notes that English does not use a compound to refer to a part of an animal's body in relation to the body as a whole: *chicken-wing* refers to a part of the animal that has been removed; an intact part is referred to phrasally as *a chicken's wing*. *Calf skin, chicken fat, turkey leg,* and *horsehair* substantiate this assessment and show that this type of compound implies that the part has not only been removed, but has also been processed. Here, the German data seem to coincide, *Rindernase* 'steer nose', *Kuhhaut* 'cow skin', *Hühnerbrust* 'chickenbreast', *Froschschenkel* 'frog leg', *Schweineohr* 'pig ear'. Furthermore, when parts of living bodies (human or animal) occur in the head position, the compound does not denote the part itself, but shifts its meaning out of the realm of regular, endocentric compounds into an exocentric interpretation in the meaning 'someone/ something having the part' (Ryder 1994: 149), cf. animals: *longhorn, cotton tail, diamondback*; person: *tenderfoot, airhead, butterfingers, loudmouth, paleface*. Since German data fit this pattern as well, it seems to be a general restriction on the pattern, cf. animal: *Plattnase* 'flat nose', plant: *Rotdorn* 'red thorn', person: *Krauskopf* 'curl head', *Dickbauch* 'fat belly', *Langbein* 'long leg'. If, in addition, the modifier denotes an animal of which the head is a part, the compound takes on a metaphoric interpretation (what Ryder 1994: 149 terms a 'whole-compound metaphor'): *dogleg* 'bend in fairway', *rabbit ears* 'dipole antenna', *ponytail* 'hairdo'. German *Löwenzahn* 'dandelion', *Fuchsschwanz* 'pad saw', etc. confirm this. So, in this case, the shift in meaning seems to be principled. Human nouns acts differently in head position from animal nouns with the modifier *house*; an animal will live in the house and be domesticated (*house cat*), while a person will work there (*houseboy*). The 'living' relation is redundant for people and therefore avoided, cf. *house-woman, where other location modifiers are possible with head nouns denoting humans: *caveman, country girl, seaman* (Ryder 1994: 156). So again, we are back to a violation of the general constraint requiring a specification of the head.

It is also most likely a general cognitive constraint that dictates when and to what extent accommodations and metaphors are used. Ryder notices that the head noun in *sea* + N constructions is almost always metaphorical when referring to a plant or animal, cf. *sea horse, sea lion, sea cucumber, sea fan, seaweed*. Its metaphorical nature is attributed to the original need to find a name for the large amount of unfamiliar flora and fauna found at sea and the ability of humans to find similarities with objects already known from land (Ryder 1994: 165). The reason *sea* almost never occurs in head position is that it does not lend itself to specialization; the normal person has no need to differentiate the individual seas (Ryder 1994: 165). Tacit knowledge of established patterns may have an influence on compound interpretation leading to the extension of a group of compounds that share a common component, cf. *newspaper mogul, cinema mogul, media mogul, oil mogul*, etc., 'powerful person with respect to X' or *smart key, smart card, smart phone* 'X with electronic access'. Ryder (1994) claims such patterns arise via analogy, while Olsen (2012) assigns the relevant constituents a derived relational entry of their own in the mental lexicon.

8.2 Categorial restrictions

Compounds can be realized by constituents from the other lexical categories besides nouns. Verbs and prepositions, however, are not found as heads of compounds for principled reasons: The category preposition is not an open category and, hence, not extendable by word formation processes, cf. Fanselow (1988). But most importantly, verbs and prepositions have internal arguments that must be expressed syntactically in non-polysynthetic languages, cf. Wunderlich (1986). All lexical categories are found in the non-head position, however, and exemplify there the basic interpretation strategy outlined above. In adjective-noun and verb-noun combinations the property expressed by the non-head modifies the head (*sweet corn; search party* 'party that searches', *drawbridge* 'bridge that is drawn', *wash cloth* 'cloth for washing', *payday* 'day on which one is paid'). Prepositional-noun combinations construe the prepositional relation as a region modifying the head (*overcoat* 'coat worn over sth.'). In noun-adjective combinations the nominal first constituent often expresses a norm of comparison (*paper thin, sky blue*), or it satisfies the relational meaning inferred from the head (*fat free* 'free of fat', *power hungry* 'hungry for power'). The adjective-adjective combinations the modifier may modify the head (*greenish blue*) or yield a coordinative interpretation (*sweet-sour*). A verb as first constituent can satisfy the relation gleaned from the relational head as in *fail safe* 'safe from failure' or *trustworthy* 'worthy of trust'. Adjectival participles occur in constructions with nominal first constituents that express local, instrumental and temporal adjunct relations such as *farm-grown, hand-picked, home-made*.

Neoclassical compounds made up of combining forms stemming from the classical languages also display both a relational and non-relational meaning depending of the semantic structure of the head constituent, cf. *suicide* 'killing one's self', *xenophobia* 'fear of foreigners', *biology* 'study of life forms' in relational readings and *telescope* 'instrument for viewing at a distance', *xenobiotic* 'foreign compound', *homophone* 'same sound' in non-relational interpretations. Adjectival combining forms can also be coordinated, cf. Sp. *hispano-franco*, but interestingly equivalent nominal constructions don't seem to occur. And finally, even the recent tendency to used a phrase as the non-head (so-called 'phrasal compounds') conforms to the expected array of interpretations found in regular determinative compounds. A non-relational head encourages the inference of an open relation: *present-is-the-key-to-the-past approach, please-smoke-all-you-like policy* while a relational head yields a relational interpretation: *cost-of-living increase, right-to-life campaigner, thousand-words-a-day contributor*. Coordinative combinations are not possible due to the absence of categorial equivalence between the components.

9 Conclusion

The aim of this contribution has been to characterize the meaning of regular, productively formed, compounds. It has been proposed that their interpretation centers around the question of what relation(s) speakers can conceptualize to relate the component parts. The relevant interpretation strategy was formalized as a compound template in example (20) of section 6.3 which is an abstract version of the general modification template developed to model the interpretative process of predicate conjunction in the intersective modifier-head configurations in syntax. The compound template obviates the need for distinguishing different types of compound meaning such as the primary (root or non-verbal-nexus), verbal (relational, synthetic, verbal-nexus) and copulative (coordinative, appositive) readings. All interpretations go back to the simple conjunction of predicates mediated by an unspecified relation between them. Compounds differ from the modificational structures of syntax in that the later instantiate the default identity relation. Furthermore, the verbal interpretation of compounds also differs from theta assignment in syntax. It is merely a special case of conceptual inference, i.e., one in which the relation inherent to a relational head is chosen to instantiate the variable R of the template. The nature of the inferred relation in the meaning of a compound predisposes compounds as names rather than descriptions, cf. Bücking (2009, 2010). Finally it was shown how untypical word structures such as the left-headed compounds of Romance comply with this analysis as well.

10 References

Adams, Valerie 1973. *An Introduction to Modern English Word Formation*. London: Longman.
Allen, Margaret 1978. *Morphological Investigations*. Ph.D. dissertation. University of Connecticut, Storrs, CT.
Baayen, R. Harald 2010. The directed compound graph of English—an exploration of lexical connectivity and its processing consequences. In: S. Olsen (ed.). *New Impulses in Word-Formation*. Hamburg: Buske, 383–402.
Bauer, Laurie 1978. *The Grammar of Nominal Compounding with Special Reference to Danish, English and French*. Odense: Odense University Press.
Bickerton, Derek 1990. *Language and Species*. Chicago, IL: The University of Chicago Press.
Bierwisch, Manfred 1983. Semantische und konzeptuelle Repräsentation lexikalischer Einheiten. In: R. Růžička & W. Motsch (eds.). *Untersuchungen zur Semantik*. Berlin: Akademie Verlag, 61–99.
Bierwisch, Manfred & Ewald Lang 1989 (eds.). *Dimensional Adjectives: Grammatical Structure and Conceptual Interpretation*. Berlin: Springer.
Bloomfield, Leonard 1933. *Language*. Chicago, IL: The University of Chicago Press.

Boase-Beier, Joan & Jindrich Toman 1984. *Komposita und Kontext* (Regensburg Arbeitsbericht 29, DFG-Projekt 'Nominalkomposita'). Regensburg: University of Regensburg.
Bradley, Henry 1906. *The Making of English*. London: Macmillan.
Brekle, Herbert E. 1970. *Generative Satzsemantik und transformationelle Syntax im System der englischen Nominalkomposition*. The Hague: Mouton.
Brugmann, Karl 1900. Über das Wesen der sogenannten Wortzusammensetzung. Eine sprachpsychologische Studie. *Berichte über die Verhandlungen der Königlich Sächsischen Gesellschaft der Wissenschaften. Philologisch-historische Classe* 52, 359–401.
Bücking, Sebastian 2009. How do phrasal and lexical modification differ: Contrasting adjective-noun combinations in German. *Word Structure* 2, 184–204.
Bücking, Sebastian 2010. German nominal compounds as underspecified names for kinds. In: S. Olsen (ed.). *New Impulses in Word-Formation*. Hamburg: Buske, 253–281.
Di Sciullo, Anna Maria & Edwin Williams 1987. *On the Definition of Word*. Cambridge, MA: The MIT Press.
Downing, Pamela 1977. On the creation and use of English compounds. *Language* 53, 810–842.
Dowty, David 1979. *Word Meaning and Montague Grammar*. Dordrecht: Kluwer.
Fanselow, Gisbert 1981a. *Zur Syntax und Semantik der Nominalkomposition*. Tübingen: Niemeyer.
Fanselow, Gisbert 1981b. Neues von der Kompositafront oder zu drei Paradigmata in der Kompositagrammatik. *Studium Linguistik* 11, 43–57.
Fanselow, Gisbert 1985. Die Stellung der Wortbildung im System kognitiver Module. *Linguistische Berichte* 96, 91–126.
Fanselow, Gisbert 1988. 'Wort Syntax' and semantic principles. In: G. Booij & J. van Marle (eds.). *Yearbook of Morphology 1987*. Dordrecht: Kluwer, 95–122.
Fradin, Bernard 2009. IE, Romance: French. In: R. Lieber & P. Štekauer (eds.). *The Oxford Handbook of Compounding*. Oxford: Oxford University Press, 417–435.
Gagné, Christina 2000. Relation-based combinations versus property-based combinations. *Journal of Memory and Language* 42, 365–389.
Gagné, Christina & Edward Shoben 1997. Influence of thematic relations on the comprehension of modifier-noun combinations. *Journal of Experimental Psychology: Learning, Memory, and Cognition* 23, 71–87.
Gagné, Christina & Thomas Spalding 2006. Conceptual combination: Implications for the mental lexicon. In: G. Libben & G. Garema (eds.). *The Representation and Processing of Compound Words*. Oxford: Oxford University Press, 145–168.
Hampton, James 1987. Inheritance of attributes in natural concept conjunctions. *Memory & Cognition* 15, 55–71.
Handwerker, Brigitte 1985. Rezension von Fanselow (1981). *Beiträge zur Geschichte der deutschen Sprache und Literatur (PBB)* 107, 114–117.
Hatcher, Anna 1960. An introduction to the analysis of English noun compounds. *Word* 16, 356–373.
Higginbotham, James 1985. On semantics. *Linguistic Inquiry* 16, 547–593.
Jackendoff, Ray 1999. Possible states in the evolution of the language capacity. *Trends in Cognitive Sciences* 3, 272–279.
Jackendoff, Ray 2002. *Foundations of Language*. Oxford: Oxford University Press.
Jackendoff, Ray 2009. Compounding in the parallel architecture and conceptual semantics. In: R. Lieber & P. Štekauer (eds.). *The Oxford Handbook of Compounding*. Oxford: Oxford University Press, 105–128.

Jespersen, Otto 1909. *A Modern English Grammar on Historical Principles*. Part I: *Sounds and Spelling*. London: George Allen & Unwin.
Kamp, Hans 1981. A theory of truth and semantic representation. In: J. Groenendijk, T. Janssen & M. Stokhof (eds.). *Formal Methods in the Study of Language, vol. I*. Amsterdam: Mathematical Centre, 277–322.
Kamp, Hans & Uwe Reyle 1993. *From Discourse to Logic*. Dordrecht: Kluwer.
Klein, Wolfgang & Clive Perdue 1997. The basic variety (or: Couldn't natural languages be much simpler?). *Second Language Research* 13, 301–347.
Kornfeld, Laura M. 2009. IE, Romance: Spanish. In: R. Lieber & P. Štekauer (eds.). *The Oxford Handbook of Compounding*. Oxford: Oxford University Press, 436–452.
Kürschner, Wilfred 1974. *Zur syntaktischen Beschreibung deutscher Nominalkomposita*. Tübingen: Niemeyer.
Langacker, Ronald 1987. *Foundations of Cognitive Grammar, vol. I: Theoretical Prerequisites*. Stanford, CA: Stanford University Press.
Lees, Robert D. 1963. *The Grammar of English Nominalizations*. Bloomington, IN: Indiana University Press.
Lees, Robert 1970. Problems in the grammatical analysis of English nominal compounds. In: M. Bierwisch & K.-E. Heidolph (eds.). *Progress in Linguistics*. The Hague: Mouton, 174–186.
Levi, Judith 1978. *The Syntax and Semantics of Complex Nominals*. New York: Academic Press.
Maienborn, Claudia 2003. Event-internal modifiers: Semantic underspecification and conceptual interpretation. In: E. Lang, C. Maienborn & C. Fabricius-Hansen (eds.). *Modifying Adjuncts*. Berlin: de Gruyter, 475–509.
Meyer, Ralf 1993. *Compound Comprehension in Isolation and in Context*. Tübingen: Niemeyer.
Meyer, Ralf 1994. Komposita-Interpretation durch Abduktion. In: E. Wiegand & F. Hundsnurscher (eds.). *Lexical Structures and Language Use*. Tübingen: Niemeyer, 225–235.
Motsch, Wolfgang 1970. Analyse von Komposita mit zwei nominalen Elementen. In: M. Bierwisch & K.-E. Heidolph (eds.). *Progress in Linguistics*. The Hague: Mouton, 208–223.
Murphy, Gregory 1988. Comprehending complex concepts. *Cognitive Science* 12, 529–562.
Murphy, Gregory 1990. Noun phrase interpretation and conceptual combination. *Journal of Memory and Language* 29, 259–288.
Olsen, Susan 2004. The case of copulative compounds. In: A. ter Meulen & W. Abraham (eds.). *The Composition of Meaning. From Lexeme to Discourse*. Amsterdam: Benjamins, 17–37.
Olsen, Susan 2012. Der Einfluss des mentalen Lexikons auf die Interpretation von Komposita. In: L. Gaeta & B. Schlücker (eds.), *Das Deutsche als kompositionsfreudige Sprache*. Berlin: Walter de Gruyter, 135–170.
Plag, Ingo & Gero Kunter 2010. Constituent family size and compound stress assignment in English. In: S. Olsen (ed.). *New Impulses in Word-Formation*. Hamburg: Buske, 349–382.
Pustejovsky, James 1995. *The Generative Lexicon*. Cambridge, MA: The MIT Press.
Rainer, Franz 1993. Spanische Wortbildungslehre. Tübingen: Niemeyer.
Rainer, Franz & Soledad Varela 1992. Compounding in Spanish. *Rivista di Linguistica* 4, 117–142.
Ryder, Mary Ellen 1994. *Ordered Chaos. The Interpretation of English Noun-Noun Compounds*. Berkeley, CA: University of California Press.
Scalise, Sergio 1992. Compounding in Italian. *Rivista di Linguistica* 4, 175–199.
Selkirk, Elisabeth 1982. *The Syntax of Words*. Cambridge, MA: The MIT Press.
Smith, Edward & Daniel Osherson 1984. Conceptual combination with prototype concepts. *Cognitive Science* 8, 337–361.

Spalding, Thomas, Christina Gagné, Allison Mullaly & Hongbo Ji 2010. Relation-based interpretation of noun-noun phrases: A new theoretical approach. In: S. Olsen (ed.). *New Impulses in Word-Formation*. Hamburg: Buske, 283–315.

Štekauer, Pavol 2005. *Meaning Predictability in Word Formation*. Amsterdam: Benjamins.

Warren, Beatrice 1978. *Semantic Patterns of Noun-Noun Compounds* (Gothenburg Studies in English 41). Lund: Acta Universitatis Gothoburgensis.

Wisniewski, Edward 1996. Construal and similarity in conceptual combination. *Journal of Memory and Language* 35, 434–453.

Wunderlich, Dieter 1986. Probleme der Wortstruktur. *Zeitschrift für Sprachwissenschaft* 2, 209–252.

Zimmer, Karl 1971. Some general observations about nominal compounds. *Working Papers on Linguistic Universals* 5, C1–C21.

Zimmer, Karl 1972. Appropriateness conditions for nominal compounds. *Working Papers on Linguistic Universals* 8, 3–20.

Zimmermann, Ilse 1992. Der Skopus von Modifikatoren. In: I. Zimmermann & A. Strigin (eds.). *Fügungspotenzen*. Berlin: Akademie Verlag, 251–279.

Zwanenburg, Wiecher 1992. Compounding in French. *Rivista di Linguistica* 4, 221–240.

Heidi Harley
5 Semantics in Distributed Morphology

1 Introduction —— 143
2 Distributed Morphology: The framework —— 144
3 Differences with lexicalist approaches —— 152
4 Morphosemantics in Distributed Morphology —— 155
5 Conclusion —— 165
6 References —— 165

Abstract: This article introduces the grammatical framework of Distributed Morphology, with special attention to the implications of the framework for semantic interpretation. The derivation of a sample sentence is given, illustrating the dissociation between the semantically contentful abstract units which are the input to syntactic and semantic composition, and the phonologically contentful Vocabulary Items which compete to realize them. The central assumptions of the framework are contrasted with those of more established Lexicalist approaches, particularly with respect to the predictions for bracketing paradoxes, the Mirror Principle and the status of lexical roots. Areas in which Distributed Morphology has produced developed semantic proposals are described, including argument structure operations, idiomatic interpretation, the interpretation of nominal features, and the nature of on-line speech errors.

1 Introduction

Distributed Morphology (DM) is a morphosyntactic framework which employs the same combinatoric and interpretive mechanisms for both word-formation and phrase-formation. Viewed in this way, morphology just *is* syntax, and vice versa. The locus classicus for the framework is Halle & Marantz (1993).

Given the assumption that morphology is syntax, and given that in modern Minimalist syntactic theory, syntactic representations are deterministically mapped to semantic representations, many DM analyses make significant semantic predications, and semantic evidence is often brought to bear in the DM literature. Many practitioners have employed the term 'morphosemantics' to describe their research.

Heidi Harley, Tucson, AZ, USA

https://doi.org/10.1515/9783110589849-005

This article attempts first to give the reader a feel for the structure of the framework, providing an introductory overview and a toy example of a derivation within the theory. Then certain differences between DM and more traditional Lexicalist approaches are remarked upon, touching on issues such as bracketing paradoxes and the question of whether word-formation has any special semantic effects or status. Then the paper provides a brief tour of some particularly significant issues within the theory, including argument structure, lexical decomposition, idiomatic interpretation, underspecification, zero morphology, nominal ('phi') feature interpretation and semantically-motivated speech errors.

2 Distributed Morphology: The framework

As noted above, DM is a framework for morphological, syntactic and semantic analysis in which word-formation is primarily a syntactic operation, in the usual sense of 'syntactic'. That is, the same mechanism that generates complex phrasal structure also generates complex morphological structure. There is only one 'generative engine' in the theory. In that sense, the theory does without a conventional generative lexicon. There are no lexicon-internal operations which create or operate on complex word-forms prior to their being fed into the syntactic computation. One consequence is the prediction that there can be no morphological operations that implement non-monotonic semantic changes. This is because semantic content can be added to a complex structure but not deleted from it by the introduction of a new terminal node with new semantic content. Hence morphology, like syntax, is predicted to obey the Monotonicity Hypothesis (Koontz-Garboden 2007).

In DM, the primitive elements which the combinatoric system operates on are abstract bundles of syntacticosemantic features, for example [PL] ('plural') or [√CAT] ('cat'). These feature bundles have denotations which are the input to semantic composition and interpretation after syntactic computation is complete, at the level of Logical Form (LF). There are two broad categories of items in this first list. Roots, or l-morphemes, like [√CAT], whose final interpretation includes Encyclopedic information, will determine the idiosyncratic aspects of the final semantic representation. Abstract Morphemes, or f-morphemes, like [PL], provide the functional structure and make deterministic semantic contributions. (In Chomsky's famous *Colorless green ideas* sentence, the 'semantic ill-formedness' which the sentence was intended to illustrate results from incompatibilities in the Encyclopedic content of the Root morphemes in the sentence. The functional elements are both syntactically and semantically coherent—in other words, the sentence has a well-formed LF.)

The mental storehouse of these feature bundles is termed List 1 (see the diagram in Fig. 5.1), and provides the raw material from which the syntactic computation begins. The contents of List 1 vary from language to language, both the particular Roots on the list and the particular content of the abstract grammatical feature bundles being determined during acquisition, subject to constraints imposed by Universal Grammar and the acquisition mechanism.

The operations which combine these bundles of features into larger hierarchical structures are essentially those of Minimalist syntactic theory. A subset of feature bundles is selected as input for combination (the Numeration). These feature bundles undergo the Merge, Agree, and Move operations, subject to relevant syntactic requirements, such as the Minimal Link Condition (Chomsky 1995), which constrains the potential targets of the Agree and Move operations.

As in garden-variety Minimalism, the derivation reaches a point at which it must be interpreted by the phonological and semantic interfaces, called Spell-Out. Here, the derivation branches. On the way to the interface with phonology, the syntactic representation is subject to some purely morphological operations, then morphophonological ones, before the final PF form is reached. Similarly, on the way to the semantic interface, it could be the case that some specialized operations apply to the syntactic representation to achieve an interpretable Logical Form. Most crucially, the phonological realization of the terminal nodes of the syntactic structure is determined on the way to PF, by an operation called 'Late Insertion'. The elements of List 1 have no phonological content. Purely phonological information about the realization of lexical items is therefore not present at the LF interface. For example, the LF representation does not 'see' the morphological difference between the realization of the [PL] feature as -*en* in *children* and as -*s* in *cats*; the LF representations of both words contain just the same [PL] feature, and are interpreted accordingly.

The Late Insertion operation, on the PF branch, accesses a second list of information, specifying phonological realizations associated with particular feature bundles. The elements of this List 2 are termed "Vocabulary Items" (VIs). Importantly, VIs may be underspecified—the VI which is inserted to realize a particular feature bundle may be listed with only a subset of the features contained in the bundle. Insertion of Vocabulary Items proceeds according to a 'best fit' principle: the VI which wins insertion is the VI whose feature specification comes the closest to matching the features of the terminal node without containing any clashing features. Consider a pronominal terminal node specified for [+1, +SG, +NOM] (a first person singular subject), and three hypothetical VIs with different feature specifications, as illustrated below:

Terminal node   Vocabulary items

$D_{[+1, +sg, +Nom]}$ 'ba' ⇔ [+1]
　　　　　　　　'da' ⇔ [+1, +Nom]
　　　　　　　　'ga' ⇔ [+2, +sg, +Nom]

The *ga* VI is not eligible to realize the terminal node, because it refers to the clashing feature [+2]. Both *ba* and *da* are eligible for insertion, as their features are a subset of the terminal node's, but *da* wins out over *ba* because *da* refers to more compatible features than *ba* does. This best-fit competition for insertion thus obeys Kiparsky (1973)'s *Elsewhere Principle*. (VIs may also be conditioned by features on other terminal nodes in the surrounding syntactic context; the same Elsewhere Principle applies.)

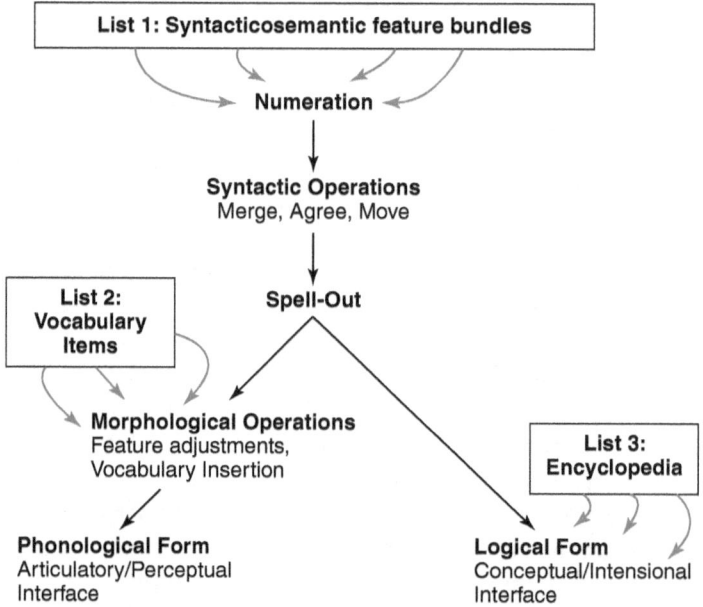

Fig. 5.1: The Distributed Morphology Model

Over at the LF interface, besides the normal semantic composition which computes the denotation of the syntactic representation, special information is accessed concerning the interpretation of particular Root items in the syntacticosemantic context in which they now appear. Both idiomatic and conventional interpretations of Roots are represented in this third list of idiosyncratic information, called the Encyclopedia or List 3. This special information composes with the denotations of the f-morphemes to produce the final interpretation of the structure. Standard model-theoretic semantic mechanisms of composition, those adopted by semanticists working in a broadly Minimalist context (e.g. like those in Heim & Kratzer 1998), are employed.

A schematic of the overall model is presented in Fig. 5.1.

2.1 Sample derivation

As an illustration of the kind of mechanisms at play, a toy derivation of the sentence *John slept*, with very basic assumptions concerning the denotations of the feature bundles involved, is illustrated below. Overall, the type of syntax-semantics interface outlined in article 6 [this volume] (von Stechow) *Syntax and semantics* is assumed to apply.

Step 1: Selection of syntacticosemantic features from List 1. (I follow Demirdache & Uribe-Etxebarria (2007) in using 'i' to represent a variable over time intervals.)

Feature(s)	Denotation
$[JOHN]_{D, \alpha Nom}$	The relevant individual named 'John'
$[PAST]_{T, +Nom}$	$\lambda i.[BEFORE(\text{utterance-time}, i)]$
$[SLEEP]_V$	$\lambda x.\lambda e.[SLEEP(e, x)]$

Step 2: Syntactic derivation. (I am assuming the VP-Internal Subject Hypothesis. I also silently include projection of the determiner $[JOHN]_D$ to a DP as well as projection of the verb $[SLEEP]_V$ to a V'. In fact, under Bare Phrase Structure assumptions (Chomsky 1995), $[JOHN]_D$ in this configuration is simultaneously a head and a phrase, and non-branching projection does not occur.)

(i) $[JOHN]_{D, \alpha Nom}$ undergoes Merge with $[SLEEP]_V$, producing a VP:

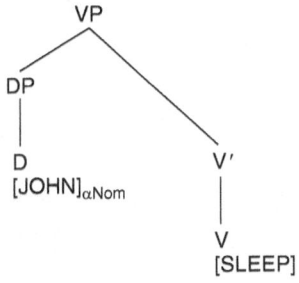

(ii) [PAST]$_{T, +Nom}$ undergoes Merge with the VP, producing a T' constituent:

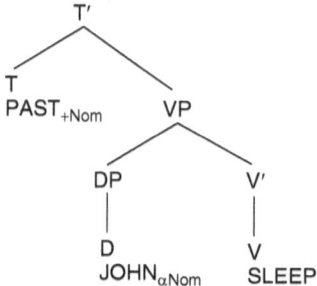

(iii) The active [+Nom] Case feature within the [PAST]$_T$ feature bundle Probes its c-command domain for a Case feature with which it can Agree, finding [JOHN]$_{D, \alpha Nom}$. The DP headed by [JOHN]$_{D, \alpha Nom}$ undergoes Move to Spec-TP, where it enters into Spec-Head Agreement with [PAST]$_{T, +Nom}$. This results in a fully convergent syntactic structure with no unchecked features:

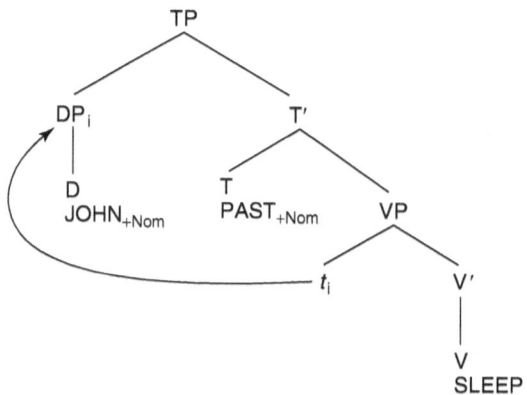

Step 3: Spell-Out

The representation in (iii) above is sent for interpretation to the LF and PF interfaces. I first present a sketch of the derivation of the LF interpretation, then that of the PF interpretation.

Step 3.1: LF Interpretation

(i) The denotation of VP is computed by composing the denotation of the V with the denotation of the chain {DP$_i$, t$_i$}, which (especially under the 'Copy' theory of movement) is identical to the denotation of the DP.

$[[VP]] = \lambda e[SLEEP(e, \text{'John'})]$

Standardly, the VP [JOHN SLEEP] denotes a function from events to truth values such that f(e) = 1 iff e is an event of John sleeping. The identity criteria with which the speaker identifies sleeping events as such are contained in the List 3 entry for the l-morpheme [SLEEP]—they are part of the content of the Encyclopedia, accessed once the final LF is determined.

(ii) Existential closure at the VP binds the event variable, asserting the existence of a John-sleeping event.

$[[VP]] = \exists e[SLEEP(e, \text{'John'})]$

(iii) Type mismatch resolution: The $[PAST]_T$ feature is a function from time intervals to truth values, but at this point the VP's denotation is not a time interval. For the purposes of this illustration, I assume that before the VP is composed with T°, some operation applies that maps the event denoted by the VP to the time interval during which it takes place—something like the Temporal Trace Function τ proposed in Krifka (1998) (see article 13 [Semantics: Noun Phrases and Verb Phrases] (Ogihara) *Tense* for discussion). This function could conceivably enter the derivation as the denotation of some feature bundle occupying an intermediate head position between VP and TP (e.g. an Asp° head), but I will treat it here as an LF-specific compositional operation which applies just when this type mismatch is detected. This would be an example of a kind of special semantic operation which the PF computation could never be sensitive to, as it applies after the split at Spell-Out—a semantic analogue of the special morphological operations that can apply to adjust the representation on the way to PF. Following the application of this operation, very roughly speaking, the VP denotes the unique time interval during which the sleeping event took place:

$[[VP]] = (\iota i)\lambda i[\exists e[SLEEP(e, \text{'John'}))] \& DURING(e,i)]]$

(iv) The denotation of T' is computed by composing the denotation of T with that of the VP:

$[[T']] = BEFORE(\text{utterance-time}, (\iota i)\lambda i[\exists e[SLEEP(e, \text{'John'})] \& DURING(e,i)])$

i.e. The unique time during which there was an event of John sleeping was before utterance time.

(v) For present purposes, let us assume the denotation of TP is the same as that of T', since the DP-chain has already been interpreted within the VP—i.e., reconstruction has applied.

Step 3.2: PF Interpretation

Each terminal node in the syntactic structure is associated with a morphophonological Position-of-Exponence which must be filled by a phonological exponent—a Vocabulary Item—in order for the structure to be pronounced. Terminal nodes filled by traces or other empty categories explicitly marked as lacking a PF representation are excluded.

(i) Linearization: The hierarchical structure of the syntactic tree is linearized according to the Head Parameter setting for the language. In the case of English, specifiers are on the left and complements on the right of their heads, as in the tree diagrams above. By hypothesis, however, the linear order among terminal nodes is not relevant until PF; the hierarchical structure is all that matters for the computation of syntactic relations and for LF.

(ii) At this point, some operation is necessary to ensure that the PAST suffix is realized attached to the V within the VP, rather than above it in the T position. Following Bobaljik (1994), I'll assume that Morphological Merger applies to the $[PAST]_T$ terminal node and the $[SLEEP]_V$ terminal node, essentially lowering the T° head to form a complex segment with the V° head. This English-specific example of Morphological Merger is essentially a technical implementation of affix-hopping within the DM framework. It is also an example of the kind of PF-specific operation whose effects are never seen in the LF representation.

(iii) Now Late Insertion begins, by hypothesis from the Root morpheme upwards (though nothing in the framework would preclude top-down insertion of VIs; see section 4.6 below for discussion). The Vocabulary Items which compete for the l-morpheme SLEEP are accessed from List 2. I will assume that two such items are present in English, since SLEEP is an irregular verb (alternatively there could be just one, [slijp], which is subject to a special vowel-shortening morphophonological readjustment rule later in the derivation, as Halle & Marantz (1993) originally proposed). The first of our two VIs for SLEEP is specified for insertion in the environment of a +PAST Tense node, and the second is available for all other contexts—i.e. it's the 'elsewhere' item.

SLEEP ⇔ /slɛp/ / $[[PAST]_T$ ___]
SLEEP ⇔ /slijp/ elsewhere

The first VI wins insertion at the terminal node for SLEEP since it is a better fit in the current context than the second.

(iv) The Vocabulary Items specified for the f-morpheme [PAST]$_T$ are accessed. Again, there are several such VIs in English. Each of the irregular PAST VIs is specified for input in the context of particular l-morphemes:

PAST ⇔ ∅ / [___ { [HIT] [RUN] [SIT] ... }]

⇔ /t/ / [___ { [FEEL] [MEAN] [LEAN] ... }]

⇔ /d/ elsewhere

In this case, the elsewhere morpheme /d/ wins insertion, since [SLEEP] is not on any of the lists conditioning the insertion of the irregular suffixes ∅ or /t/.

(v) The Vocabulary Items specified for the individual-denoting [JOHN]$_D$ (in fact, probably better represented in List 1 as a simple index which receives an interpretation under an assignment at LF) are accessed. There's only one:

[JOHN] ⇔ /dʒɑn/

(vi) Phonological constraint satisfaction: The terminal nodes all having been realized with VIs, the structural representation is now something like this, with the vacuous T' brackets eliminated for clarity:

[[/dʒɑn/]$_{DP}$[/slɛpd/]$_{VP}$]$_{TP}$

The string of phonemes is then subject to English-specific phonological allomorphy, adjusting the voicing in the word-final consonant cluster /pd/ in /slɛpd/. The past-tense suffix surfaces as [t] in the environment of the stem-final voiceless consonant [p] to its left. The string is then phonetically interpreted, with the correct intonational contours, stress, allophonic selection, etc, surfacing as [ˈdʒɑn ˈslɛpt].

With this impression of the details of a DM derivation in mind, let us explore some of the semantic ramifications of the framework.

3 Differences with lexicalist approaches

3.1 Absence of bracketing paradoxes

In DM the same interpretive mechanisms are employed to compute the meaning of complex syntactic phrases and complex word-forms; such computations are often interleaved. For example, assuming bottom-up composition, the denotation of the VP [$_{VP}$ love [$_{DP}$ Mary]] in the sentence *John loved Mary* will be computed before the contribution of the T° node is composed with the denotation of the VP; there is no need to compute a meaning for the phonological word *loved* before composition of the verb with the direct object. In a strongly Lexicalist model, *loved Mary* is a kind of bracketing paradox, since the interpretation of Tense scopes over the whole VP, while the morphological realization of Tense is within the domain of the verb only—inside the word *loved* that occupies the V° node in the tree. No such puzzles arise in DM. The fact that the past tense morpheme *-ed* is affixal and the future tense morpheme *will* is an independent word is an epiphenomenon of the particular Vocabulary Items which are inserted to realize the Tense node; it has no effect on the relative order of semantic composition. Tense and the VP in *John loved Mary* are composed in the same order that they are in *John will love Mary*. Similarly, the classic example *transformational grammarian* can be analyzed in the syntax and at LF as having the structure [[*transformational grammar*]-*ian*]; the fact that the element *-ian* is affixal becomes relevant only at PF.

3.2 Mirror Principle is entailed

The architecture entails that a scopally-motivated order of affixation should be the norm, as in the analysis of Athapaskan morphology presented in Rice (2000). The observation that morpheme order generally reflects syntactic hierarchies—and hence the order of semantic composition—has been implemented in some form or other in Chomskyan grammar since Baker (1985) proposed the Mirror Principle. In DM, the Mirror Principle effect falls out of the architecture of the theory; deviations from it must be explained, but the general existence of the effect is entailed.

3.3 The special status of Roots

A consequence of treating syntactic and morphological composition with the same mechanism is that morphological phenomena must be taken seriously by those interested in clausal semantics. In DM, there is a guiding assumption that all overt morphological exponents represent the realization of some syntactic terminal node. This extends to derivational morphology, which has further consequences for syntactic structure and semantic interpretation. For example, it becomes important to characterize the syntactic and semantic role of the terminal nodes realized by derivational morphemes like *-ize* and *-ify* (verbal), *-tion* and *-ness* (nominal), and *-al* and *-y* (adjectival).

Such categorizing nodes have the special property of being able to compose directly with Root morphemes. DM suggests that Roots are a-categorial, and must Merge with a categorizing f-morpheme (or more than one, in cases like *[[[[nomin]$_v$al]$_a$iz]$_v$ation]$_n$)*. This categorizing morpheme provides the Root to which it attaches with a syntactic category. Further, since all Roots must occur with at least one such categorizer, the Encyclopedia provides the Root with a fixed interpretation in the context of particular categorizers. The hypothesis that Roots are acategorial, achieving interpretable status only through composition with v°, n° and a° heads, is a key component of the framework, allowing a characterization of the different but related contribution of, for example, the root √ELECTR-in *electr-on* (Noun) and *electr-ic* (Adjctive) and *electr-ify* (Verb). This theoretical feature has been particularly exploited in the DM analysis of Semitic root-and-pattern morphology proposed in Arad (2003, 2005).

(Note that the toy derivation provided in section 2.1 above does not include a separate √ projection for √SLEEP embedded under verbalizing v° morpheme. Rather, it started with the result of the combination of v° and √SLEEP, the verb SLEEP, although such decomposition is standardly assumed in the framework. The usual interpretation assumed for the individual terminal nodes of unergative verbs is based on Hale & Keyser (1993)'s proposal, [DO [SLEEP]$_V$]$_{vP}$. See Harley (2005, 2014) for further discussion of the type-theoretic denotations of roots.)

3.4 The phonological word has no special status in semantic interpretation

Erasing the borders between morphological and syntactic composition in this way allows the resolution of several empirical conundrums. One positive consequence is that the typological differences between polysynthetic and isolating languages do not require the postulation of radically different combinatoric and compositional mechanisms in UG. For example, true noun incorporation constructions (Baker 1988), in which the incorporated nominal object forms part of the complex verb, can be structurally and semantically identical to pseudo-noun-incorporation constructions like those in Niuean (Massam 2001) and Hindi (Dayal 2003). In pseudo-noun-incorporation, a bare nominal acts semantically as if it's incorporated—it is interpreted in the same way as in cases of genuine morphological incorporation like those documented by Mithun, Baker, and others—even though it retains its morphophonological autonomy as a separate word. (See article 5 [Semantics: Noun Phrases and Verb Phrases] (Dayal) *Bare noun phrases* for relevant discussion.) In DM, at LF, status as a word or multiple words is irrelevant. In a more familiar example, the LF structure and interpretation of English comparatives can be treated as uniform regardless of the variable affixal status of the comparative morpheme (*-er* vs. *more*, Embick 2007), without causing any major theory-internal upset at the morphology/syntax interface. What is more, semantic proposals about the LF operations required to interpret comparatives, for example QR of the Degree Phrase headed by *-er* after Spell-Out, need not necessarily be concerned with the question of whether the QR operation will dissociate a suffix and its host, since at the point at which QR applies, the issue of whether the actual phonological realization of the Deg head is an affix or not is irrelevant. (Thanks to Ora Matushansky for this point. Interesting questions still arise, however, concerning the realization of comparative adjectives, particularly with respect to suppletion in the realizations of certain Roots; e.g. the Root √BAD is realized alternatively as *bad, worse,* or *worst* depending on the content of the Deg feature bundle in its immediate context. See Bobaljik (2007) and article 13 [Semantics: Lexical Structures and Adjectives] (Beck) *Comparison constructions* for relevant discussion.)

The same point holds cross-linguistically. Both affixal and non-affixal complex forms can both be purely compositionally interpreted or idiosyncratically, idiomatically interpreted. A good example is the equivalent interpretations of the morphologically complex English *awaken* and the syntactically complex Persian complex predicate *bîdar shodan*, 'awake become' (Folli, Harley & Karimi 2005). More trivially, it is clear that phrases can have both literal (compositional) and idiomatic interpretations, as in *kick the bucket*. Similarly, morphologically complex words can also have both literal and idiomatic interpretations. The famous example case *transmission* can refer idiomatically to the relevant car part, or literally, compositionally, to the event or result of transmitting. There is no principled reason that morphophonological unification within a single phonological word should necessarily trigger a special semantic interpretation (Marantz 1997). Multimorphemic and multi-word expressions can in principle represent the same structure and receive the same interpretations. Wordhood confers no privileged semantic status.

However, as noted above, although there is no morphophonologically motivated semantic domain, the acategorial Root hypothesis entails that there is at least one such morphosyntactic dividing line, at the point at which the categorizing head is composed with the Root (Marantz 2001, Arad 2003).

4 Morphosemantics in Distributed Morphology

4.1 Argument structure

In many, perhaps most, languages, diathesis alternations are realized by the addition or alternation of overt verbal morphology. In DM, this entails that argument structure alternations are effected syntactically. The notion that external arguments are introduced by a separate verbal projection, for example, first proposed by Hale & Keyser (1993), provided DM approaches with a natural first hypothesis concerning the locus of causative and inchoative verbal morphology, which is cross-linguistically common (indeed, such morphology was part of the original motivation for the proposal.) For example, the unaccusative Japanese verb *hie-*, 'cool, intr.' is made up of a root *hi*-plus an inchoative morpheme -*e*-. Its causative counterpart, *hiyas*, is the same root *hi*-plus the causative morpheme -*as*-. The additional external argument correlates with the change in suffixal morphology; it is natural to ascribe the addition of the former to the semantic contribution of the latter:

a.
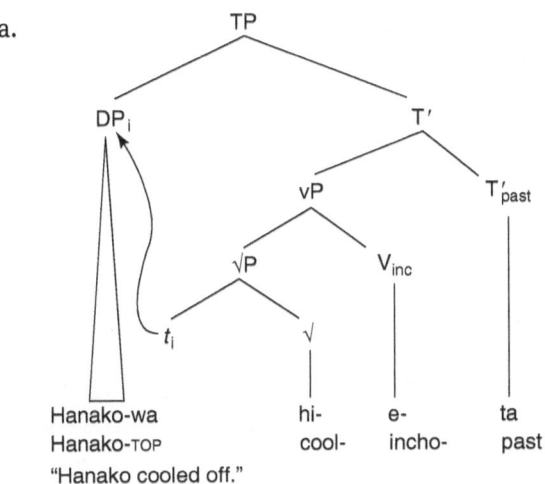
"Hanako cooled off."

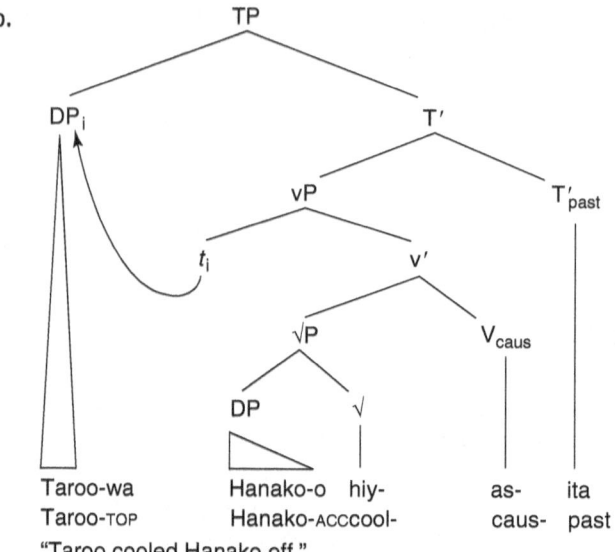

"Taroo cooled Hanako off."

Given such complex syntactic structures for the causative and inchoative forms in Japanese, the source of apparently word-internal scope ambiguities with adverbials like *again* ('repetitive' vs 'restitutive' scope) should be clear: such scope ambiguities are syntactic ambiguities, resulting from the decomposition of the form into a constituent denoting 'cool' and another phrasal element meaning 'cause'. Such analyses thus represent the re-introduction of many of the key ideas of the Generative Semantics work in the late 60s and early 70s. (See article 2 [Semantics: Lexical Structures and Adjectives] (Engelberg) *Frameworks of decomposition* for relevant discussion.)

Given this kind of approach to argument structure, it is a short step to recognize that similar analyses are necessary for other argument-structure introducing morphology. For example, applicative morphemes, which add an internal argument to the argument structure of agentive verbs, can occupy a position between the upper, externalargument-introducing head and the lower verb Root, which selects for the verb's usual internal arguments. This accounts for the syntactic prominence of the applied argument compared to other internal arguments (McGinnis 2003). Semantically, the Applicative head expresses a relationship between an individual (the applied argument) and an event (Pylkkänen 2002). The Applicative head composes with the lower VP and the higher vP via Kratzer (1996)'s Event Identification operation. It simply adds an event-modifying predicate and expresses the relationship between its new argument and the event. Nothing special needs to be said about the semantics of the VP or the vP; they have just the (Davidsonian) interpretation which they normally would. Pylkkänen's syntactic structure and semantic interpretation for a straightforward benefactive applicative sentence from Chaga is given below:

a. N-"a-"1-**lyì**-í-à   m-kà   k-élyá
    FOC-1s-PR-**eat**-**APPL**-FV   1-wife   7-food
    '*He is eating food for his **wife***'
    (Bresnan & Moshi 1993:49)

b. *Syntactic constituent structure*   *Denotation of constituents*

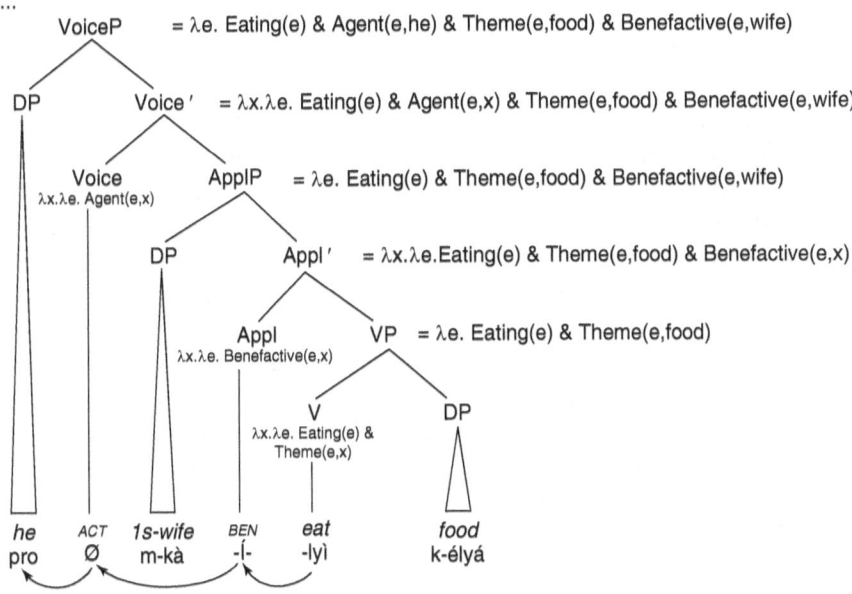

As indicated by the arrows in the diagram, head movement of V through Appl, Voice and the higher functional projections (not shown) assembles the complex constellation of feature bundles that will be realized as the final verb form and derives its sentence-initial position. (Kratzer and Pylkkänen use the term 'Voice' for the external-argument introducing position, rather than vP; Pylkkänen reserves the label 'vP' for a purely verbalizing head lower in the structure. For our purposes here, the difference is not crucial, however.)

4.2 Zero morphemes

In DM, it is frequently necessary to posit the existence of zero morphology. For example, the diathesis alternation between English *melt* (intr.) and *melt* (tr.) is accomplished without any overt change in morphology. The semantic and syntactic changes that are observed, however, require that a syntactic projection is present but not overtly morphologically realized. By hypothesis, this syntactic projection is realized by a zero morpheme. (The deployment of zero morphemes means that DM analyses are not literally engaging in lexical decomposition when the verb 'melt' is represented in a structure as $[[\text{cause}]_v \, [\text{melt}]_{\sqrt{}}]_{vP}$; the 'cause' content is contributed by a separate head realized by a zero morpheme, not by the verb 'melt' itself.)

Similarly, a zero morpheme is needed to block the insertion of default *-s* into the PL terminal node which is necessarily present on the noun in the DP *These sheep*—without a zero morpheme, the form *These sheeps* would surface, given the mechanisms of the theory.

Above we saw that it is axiomatic in DM that a surface realization must correspond to some kind of structure in the morphosyntactic system, and hence can often be taken as evidence for the presence of some element in the semantic representation as well. The reverse is emphatically not the case: syntactic and semantic evidence can point to the existence of structure that receives no realization in the phonological representation. This is not a surprise—the existence of syntactically and semantically motivated empty elements has been a cornerstone of modern generative syntax—but it is a controversial point within morphological theory. Indeed, within DM, the nature of a 'zero' morpheme is a matter of some disagreement. Considering VIs to be sketches of instructions for the articulatory system, one possibility is that a zero morpheme could be considered an instruction to 'do nothing'. However, no consensus has emerged on the correct way to model a 'zero' realization.

4.3 Underspecification

As we have seen above, in DM, the relationship between a terminal node's feature content and the Vocabulary Item which realizes that terminal node is subject to underspecification: The Vocabulary Item which best fits the content of the terminal node realizes it phonologically, but the featural match between the two need not be exact. The DM framework thus helps break the assumption that a given piece of morphophonology should in principle correspond to only one meaning.

This has proven helpful in understanding the syntacticosemantic structure involved in several puzzling cases where the same morphological formative appears to be behaving semantically in two or more distinct ways, as in for example, the analysis of the interaction of causative and reflexive morphology in Kannada in Lidz (2003).

One particularly fruitful line of analysis along these lines has considered the composition of apparently identical morphological items with distinct levels of syntactic structure, dubbed in Harley (2008) the *High/Low Attachment Hypothesis*. Participial morphology in many languages seems to have the option of attaching to an event-denoting constituent in the verbal projection and receiving an eventive passive interpretation, or attaching to a lower constituent and receiving a stative interpretation (Marantz 1997, Embick 2004, Kratzer 2001, Jackson 2005, Alexiadou & Agnastopoulou 2008, *inter alia*). The point is made in great detail in von Stechow (1998), in which the distinct semantics of no less than four constructions in German, all employing Participle II morphology, are analyzed and given distinct model-theoretic interpretations. The 'Transparent Logical Form' von Stechow argues for is very much in line with the elaborate vP syntax proposed in the related Distributed Morphology work. The puzzle of how such distinct interpretations can be realized by identical morphology is resolved when it is realized that the morphology may be sensitive just to a subset of the syntacticosemantic features involved—even a very minimal subset, such as category information. Below, I illustrate Embick (2004)'s distinct structures for English resultative participles and eventive passive participles. The key feature of the analysis is that both involve an Asp(ect) head (though see Maienborn 2009 for an opposing view). The default 'elsewhere' morpheme for spelling out this Asp head is the *-ed* suffix, which is why the same morphology can appear in structures with such very different kinds of interpretations:

a. Resultative participle

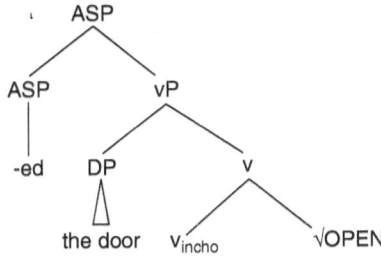

The door is opened.

b. Eventive passive participle

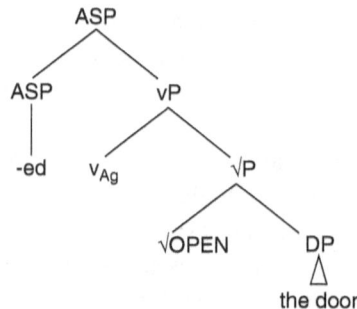

The door was opened by John

Similar effects have been observed cross-linguistically in causative morphology (Miyagawa 1998, Travis 2000, Svenonius 2005, *inter alia*.) Harley (2008) provides a detailed discussion of the Japanese case.

4.4 Nominal features and their interpretation

The relationship between the morphological realization and the semantic interpretations of certain syntacticosemantic feature distinctions (for example, the various values of person, number and gender features) has been a key question in DM and related research, e.g. Rullman (2004), Cowper (2005), McGinnis (2005a), Harbour (2007), Sauerland (2008), Acquiviva (2008), inter alia. It is axiomatic that the same alphabet of features constitutes the input to the semantics and the morphological component, and there has been a great deal of work on understanding the relationship between the features and the morphological exponents that realize them. The morphologist's traditional 'feature bundle' has usually been syntactically decomposed, as in Ritter (1992), but the semantic contributions and compositional reintegration of the various features, however, is less well understood. Several very interesting results have emerged, however.

Harbour (2006) reports the remarkable observation that the semantic content of the feature [±augmented] (a cardinality-neutral alternative to the [Plural] feature) has essentially the same semantics as Krifka (1992)'s crucial definition of cumulativity.

Harbour gives the following definition of augmented:
A predicate, P, is *augmented* iff

$$\exists x \exists y [P(x) \wedge P(y) \wedge x \supset y]$$

i.e. iff it is satisfied by two individuals, one containing the other, an individual being an atom or a set of atoms.

The notion of augmentation was first proposed as the correct way to characterize number systems like that of Ilocano, which has a 1st person inclusive plural form, referring to speaker, hearer and at least one other. This plural form contrasts with another first person inclusive form referring just to the speaker and the hearer. The cardinality of the non-plural inclusive form is not 1, so it is inappropriate to use the feature [singular] (or [-plural]) to describe it. Since the form is of cardinality 2, the traditional terminology calls it a 'dual', but this results in positing the Dual category just for the first person inclusive non-plural, within such languages:

Person	Singular	Dual	Plural
1 incl		-ta	-tayo
1 excl	-ko		-mi
2	-mo		-yo
3	-na		-da

Using the feature [+augmented], with the semantics given above, results in a much more satisfactory cross-classification:

Person	-Augmented	+Augmented
1 incl	-ta	-tayo
1 excl	-ko	-mi
2	-mo	-yo
3	-na	-da

Harbour treats the person specification as the basic predicate of the pronominal which the [+augmented] feature modifies, so, for example, a '1 incl' pronoun has as its denotation the predicate 'includes Speaker and Addressee'. '1 excl' is the predicate 'includes Speaker and excludes Addressee'. Given the semantics for 'augmented' above, consider the denotation of the [1incl, +aug] pronoun *tayo*. The [+aug] feature asserts that $\exists x \exists y [INCLUDESSp\&Ad(x) \land INCLUDESSp\&Ad(y) \land x \supset y]$—that is, it says that the model must contain two individuals, both containing 'Speaker' and 'Addressee', the one individual contained in the other. Minimally, then, the model contains {Speaker, Addressee, Other}, since this model contains the individual {Speaker, Addressee} and the individual {Speaker, Addressee, Other}, and the former is contained in the latter.

Applied to 2nd person, on the other hand, [+augmented] just requires that the model contain minimally {Addressee, Other}. 2nd person is the predicate 'includes Addressee'. Applied to this predicate, the {+aug} feature asserts $\exists x \exists y [INCLUDESAd$

(x) ∧ INCLUDESAd(y) ∧ x ⊃ y]—that, the model must contain two individuals, both containing Addressee, such that one individual contains another. The minimal model {Addressee, Other} can accomplish this, since it contains {Addressee} and {Addressee, Other}, the former contained in the latter. Of course, models with more than one 'Other' entity will also satisfy a [+aug] form. The potential referents for, e.g., the [+2, +aug] pronouns, then, will be exactly "Addressee and one or more others"—precisely the denotation necessary for a second person plural form. [+Augmented], then, allows for the expression of plurality without reference to specific cardinality.

Harbour goes on to show that augmentation entails additivity for non-cardinality predicates, and that augmentation and additivity together entail Krifka's notion of strict cumulativity, and vice versa. Krifka could thus have characterized the event-object homomorphism in terms of [+augmented], rather than [+cumulative].

Acquaviva (2006, 2008) develops a related characterization of the contribution of the Num and Classifier heads within DP, in which Classifier Ns behave like Numberless measure terms, essentially taking the place of the Number head (*pound, liter, inch*, etc.) and are characterized by abnormal number morphology, adducing evidence from the semantic characteristics of nominals with irregular number morphology in the complex number systems of the Goidelic languages.

(See also articles 1 [Semantics: Noun Phrases and Verb Phrases] (Büring) *Pronouns* and 2 [this volume] (Kiparsky & Tonhauser) *Semantics of inflection* for more developed discussion of nominal features and related issues.)

4.5 Interpretation of idioms

The characterization of idiomatic expressions has been a recurrent theme in the Distributed Morphology and related literature (Kratzer 1996; Marantz 1996, 1997, 2001; Richards 2002; Arad 2005, *inter alia*.) As noted above, one issue has concerned the semantic contribution of the Root element, which necessarily has an arbitrary, Encyclopedic interpretation (see Harley 2005 for some discussion of the semantic ontology for Root elements). Recall that while Root elements have Encyclopedia entries, while functional morphemes do not; consequently Roots can be specified for idiomatic interpretation, sometimes restricted to very elaborate interdependent syntactic and semantic contexts, while functional morphemes cannot. Functional morphemes must contribute their standard denotation to any structure which they find themselves in. So, for example, the expression *Put a sock in it!* does not literally instruct the addressee to do anything with a sock. Nonetheless, it is still formally and effectively an imperative, and it does consequently instruct the addressee to do *something*. The semantic contribution of the functional elements in the clause is inescapable.

McGinnis (2002) puts these assumptions together with the results of recent work showing a deterministic relationship between a predicate's event structure and the functional superstructure of the clause, including the definiteness, plurality, etc. of the object or other verbal complement. She argues that, while idiomatic interpretations of particular phrases can vary dramatically from their literal counterparts, they should *not* be able to vary from them in their event structure characteristics. So, for example, the idiom *She was the cat's pyjamas* is stative, as shown by standard tests such as the (in)ability to occur in the progressive (*#She was being the cat's pyjamas*); similarly, the (nonsensical) literal interpretation of the same sentence is also a state. The idiom *Harry jumped through hoops* is an atelic activity predicate, as diagnosed by its ability to co-occur with *for an hour* adverbials; similarly, the literal interpretation of the same sentence is also an atelic activity predicate (with an iterative atelicity contributed by the plural DP *hoops*).

Importantly, roughly synonymous non-idiomatic expressions need *not* have the same Aktionsart properties as their idiomatic synonyms. So, for example, while the phrase *kick the bucket* is commonly glossed as *die*, *die* and *kick the bucket* behave differently with respect to certain event structure tests. The well-formedness of the progressive in *He was dying for weeks*, which exhibits the pre-event focus typical for Achievement predicates in the progressive, is not paralleled in *kick the bucket*: *#He was kicking the bucket for weeks* is impossible, or at best gives the impression that he was dying, coming back to life, and dying again for weeks. That is, *kick the bucket*, in its idiomatic interpretation, behaves exactly like its literal interpretation, a punctual semelfactive predicate which is coerced to an iterative reading in the environment of *for-an-hour* adverbials. McGinnis's observation, then, provides important confirmation of the fundamental DM distinction between the deterministic semantics of functional elements and the Encyclopedic content of Roots. (Glasbey (2003) objects to McGinnis' generalization, adducing a class of putative counterexamples; McGinnis (2005b) responds. See articles 5 [Semantics: Lexical Structures and Adjectives] (Fellbaum) *Idioms and collocations*, 8 [Semantics: Theories] (Maienborn) *Event semantics* and 9 [Semantics: Noun Phrases and Verb Phrases] (Filip) *Aspectual class and Aktionsart* for relevant discussion of idiomaticity, event semantics, and Aktionsart.)

4.6 Psycholinguistic semantics, speech errors and Distributed Morphology

Finally, it is worth noting that the DM model has been shown to be isomorphic in many ways to the most broadly adopted psycholinguistic model of speech production. In a study of a large corpus of German speech errors, Pfau (2000, 2009) notes that a key feature of DM—Late Insertion of phonological material—is also a key feature of the two-stage speech production model first proposed in Garrett (1975) and developed further in Levelt (1989) et seq. Further, many DM mechanisms, understood in the context of a model of on-line production, can be useful in capturing certain patterns of behavior.

In the two-stage models, the message to be articulated, once conceptualized, is first syntactically organized, requiring access only to grammatical and semantic information. Only after this process is complete are the phonological exponents of the lemmas retrieved. That is, a two-stage model is essentially a Late Insertion model.

One of the crucial features of such frameworks is their ability to model the intriguing differences between "semantically-motivated" and "phonologically-motivated" speech errors. In semantically-motivated speech errors, an Encyclopedically-related word is substituted for the intended production (e.g. *magazine* for *newspaper*). The model locates this error in the first, conceptually-driven, stage of lexical access—in DM terms, the point of access of List 1, the syntacticosemantic primitives that are the input to the syntactic derivation. This error consists of extracting a related but incorrect Root element from List 1 for inclusion in the derivation.

Semantically-driven errors occur prior to insertion of phonological material. Consequently, the realization of associated functional morphemes may be adjusted depending on the identity of the incorrect Root, if the morphemes happen to be conditioned by the Roots in their environment. Consider, for example, the speech error reported by Fromkin (1973), *I think it's **careful** to measure with reason*, an error for the intended production, *I think it's **reasonable** to measure with **care***. In this error, two noun stems in the intended production are correctly selected, but are inserted into each other's places in the syntactic structure. The key thing to note is that this affects the adjective-forming suffix which appears. Rather than produce the result that would obtain from a straight swap—***careable***—the adjective-forming suffix is instead realized as *-ful*. In a non-Late-Insertion model, this would have to be modelled as a deletion and replacement of an already-present *-able* suffix. In DM, however, the adjective-forming morpheme has no phonological content at the point of exchange. When the phonological exponents are inserted at the end of the derivation, everything proceeds normally: $[[\sqrt{CARE}]_v \, adj]_{aP}$ triggers insertion of the root 'care', and then the appropriate adjective-forming suffix conditioned by that root, *-ful* (not *-able*).

Pfau illustrates this basic point with a wealth of additional examples from German, showing, for example, that semantically-motivated noun-exchange errors in which the erroneous noun is of a different gender than the intended noun result in accommodation for gender agreement on determiners and adjectives in the DP—exactly as predicted if the derivation proceeds normally in the DM fashion, following the erroneous insertion of the nominal. The syntax will copy the nominal's gender features in agreement operations and consequently spell them out with the appropriate Vocabulary Items at Late Insertion. In a model in which the phonological form of the various feature bundles is present from the beginning, the selection of the erroneous nominal would result in feature clash between the nominal and the intended determiners, adjectives, etc, and an abnormal derivation would result. The production of the accommodated gender agreement would involve either rewriting the items and their features during the course of the derivation, or else a flat-out crash in the derivation; either way, speech errors of this kind would represent a major dysfunction in the production mechanism. With a Late Insertion, two-stage model, however, the whole derivation proceeds smoothly after the initial error is made—a scenario which appears to be much more consistent with the behavioral data.

5 Conclusion

For many semantic purposes, the issue of which particular syntactic framework is adopted can seem moot. However, in sincere attempts to determine the semantic contributions of specific morphological formatives, the choice of framework can push an analysis in widely differing directions. If the past tense formative composes with the verb, rather than the verb phrase, while the future tense formative composes with the verb phrase, they will have to have quite different types, for example. I hope to have shown that by adopting a Distributed Morphology view of the morphology/syntax connection, several issues in semantic analysis can receive insightful analyses, carving the linguistic data at their joints, rather than at word boundaries.

Acknowledgement: I would like to gratefully acknowledge the helpful suggestions of Paolo Acquaviva, Andrew Koontz-Garboden, Jeff Lidz, Ora Matushansky, Andrew Nevins, Milan Rezac and especially Andrew Mcintyre. Any shortcomings in this discussion do not, of course, reflect in any way on them, and remain entirely my fault and responsibility.

6 References

Acquaviva, Paolo 2006. Goidelic inherent plurals and the morphosemantics of number. *Lingua* 116, 1860–1887.

Acquaviva, Paolo 2008. *Lexical Plurals: A Morphosemantic Approach*. Oxford: Oxford University Press.

Alexiadou, Artemis & Elena Anagnostopoulou 2008. Structuring participles. In: Ch. B. Chang & H. J. Haynie (eds.). *Proceedings of the West Coast Conference on Formal Linguistics (= WCCFL) 26*. Somerville, MA: Cascadilla Press, 33–41.
Arad, Maya 2003. Locality constraints on the interpretation of roots: The case of Hebrew denominal verbs. *Natural Language and Linguistic Theory* 21, 737–778.
Arad, Maya 2005. *Roots and Patterns: Hebrew Morpho-Syntax*. Dordrecht: Springer.
Baker, Mark 1985. The mirror principle and morphosyntactic explanation. *Linguistic Inquiry* 16, 373–415.
Baker, Mark 1988. *Incorporation*. Chicago, IL: The University of Chicago Press.
Bobaljik, Jonathan D. 1994. What does adjacency do? In: H. Harley & C. Phillips (eds.). *The Morphology-Syntax Connection* (MIT Working Papers in Linguistics 22). Cambridge, MA: MIT, 1–32.
Bobaljik, Jonathan D. 2007. *On Comparative Suppletion*. Ms. Storrs, CT, University of Connecticut.
Bresnan, Joan & Lioba Moshi 1993. Object asymmetries in comparative Bantu syntax. In: S. A. Mchombo (ed.). *Theoretical Aspects of Bantu Grammar 1*. Stanford, CA: CSLI Publications, 50–93.
Chomsky, Noam 1995. *The Minimalist Program*. Cambridge, MA: The MIT Press.
Cowper, Elizabeth 2005. A note on number. *Linguistic Inquiry* 36, 441–455.
Dayal, Veneeta 2003. *A Semantics for Pseudo-Incorporation*. Ms. New Brunswick, NJ, Rutgers University.
Demirdache, Hamida & Myriam Uribe-Etxebarria 2007. The syntax of time arguments. *Lingua* 117, 330–366.
Embick, David 2004. On the structure of resultative participles in English. *Linguistic Inquiry* 35, 355–392.
Embick, David 2007. Blocking effects and analytic/synthetic alternations. *Natural Language and Linguistic Theory* 25, 1–37.
Folli, Raffaella, Heidi Harley & Simin Karimi 2005. Determinants of event type in Persian complex predicates. *Lingua* 115, 1365–1401.
Fromkin, Victoria (ed.) 1973. *Speech Errors as Linguistic Evidence*. The Hague: Mouton.
Garrett, Merrill F. 1975. The analysis of sentence production. In: G. Bower (ed.). *Psychology of Learning and Motivation*. New York: Academic Press, 33–177.
Glasbey, Sheila R. 2003. Let's paint the town red for a few hours: Composition of aspect in idioms. In: A.M. Wallington (ed.). *Proceedings of the ACL Workshop on the Lexicon and Figurative Language (= ACL) 2003*. Sapporo: ACL, 42–48.
Halle, Morris & Alec Marantz 1993. Distributed Morphology and the pieces of inflection. In: K. Hale & S. J. Keyser (eds.). *The View from Building 20: Essays in Linguistics in Honor of Sylvain Bromberger*. Cambridge, MA: The MIT Press, 111–176.
Harbour, Daniel 2006. On the unity of 'number' in morphology and semantics. In: R. Otoguro, G. Popova & A. Spencer (eds.). *Proceedings of the York-Essex Morphology Meeting 2* (Essex Research Reports in Linguistics 47). Colchester: University of Essex, 21–30.
Harbour, Daniel 2007. *Morphosemantic Number: From Kiowa Noun Classes to UG Number Features*. Dordrecht: Springer.
Harley, Heidi 2005. How do verbs get their names? Denominal verbs, manner incorporation and the ontology of verb roots in English. In: N. Erteschik-Shir & T. R. Rapoport (eds.). *The Syntax of Aspect*. Oxford: Oxford University Press, 42–64.

Harley, Heidi 2008. On the causative construction. In: S. Miyagawa & M. Saito (eds.). *Handbook of Japanese Linguistics*. Oxford: Oxford University Press, 20–53.
Harley, Heidi 2014. On the identity of roots. *Theoretical Linguistics*, 40(3–4), 225–276.
Heim, Irene & Angelika Kratzer 1998. *Semantics in Generative Grammar*. Oxford: Blackwell.
Jackson, Eric 2005. Derived statives in Pima. Paper presented at the *Annual Meeting of the Society for the Study of Indigenous Languages of the Americas (= SSILA)*, January 6–9, 2005, San Francisco, CA, http://linguistics.ucla.edu/people/grads/ejackson/SSILAS05PimaDerivedStatives.pdf, February 24, 2012.
Kiparsky, Paul 1973. 'Elsewhere' in phonology. In: S. R. Anderson & P. Kiparsky (eds.). *A Festschrift for Morris Halle*. New York: Holt, Rinehart & Winston, 93–106.
Koontz-Garboden, Andrew 2007. *States, Changes of State, and the Monotonicity Hypothesis*. Ph.D. dissertation. Stanford University, Stanford, CA.
Kratzer, Angelika 1996. Severing the external argument from the verb. In: J. Rooryck & L. Zaring (eds.). *Phrase Structure and the Lexicon*. Dordrecht: Kluwer, 109–137.
Kratzer, Angelika 2001. Building statives. In: L. J. Conathan et al. (eds.). *Proceedings of the Annual Meeting of the Berkeley Linguistics Society (= BLS) 26*. Berkeley, CA: Berkeley Linguistics Society, 385–399.
Krifka, Manfred 1992. Thematic relations as links between nominal reference and temporal constitution. In: I. Sag & A. Szabolcsi (eds.). *Lexical Matters*. Stanford, CA: CSLI Publications, 29–53.
Krifka, Manfred 1998. The origins of telicity. In: S. Rothstein (ed.). *Events and Grammar*. Dordrecht: Kluwer, 197–235.
Levelt, Willem J. M. 1989. *Speaking: From Intention to Articulation*. Cambridge, MA: The MIT Press.
Lidz, Jeff 2003. Causation and reflexivity in Kannada. In: V. Dayal & A. Mahajan (eds.). *Clause Structure in South Asian Languages*. Dordrecht: Springer, 93–130.
Maienborn, Claudia 2009. Building event-based ad hoc properties: On the interpretation of adjectival passives. In: A. Riester & T. Solstad (eds.). *Proceedings of Sinn und Bedeutung (= SuB) 13*. Stuttgart: University of Stuttgart, 31–46.
Marantz, Alec 1996. *'Cat' as a Phrasal Idiom: Consequences of Late Insertion in Distributed Morphology*. Ms. Cambridge, MA, MIT.
Marantz, Alec 1997. No escape from syntax: Don't try morphological analysis in the privacy of your own lexicon. In: A. Dimitriadis et al. (eds.). *Proceedings of the 21st Annual Penn Linguistics Colloquium* (University of Pennsylvania Working Papers in Linguistics 4.2). Philadelphia, PA: Penn Linguistics Club, 201–225.
Marantz, Alec 2001. Words. Paper presented at the *West Coast Conference on Formal Linguistics (= WCCFL) 20*, February 23–25, 2001, University of Southern California, Los Angeles, CA. http://homepages.nyu.edu/~ma988/Phase_in_Words_Final.pdf, February 24, 2012.
Massam, Diane 2001. Pseudo noun incorporation in Niuean. *Natural Language and Linguistic Theory* 19, 153–197.
McGinnis, Martha 2002. On the systematic aspect of idioms. *Linguistic Inquiry* 33, 665–672.
McGinnis, Martha 2003. Variation in the phase structure of applicatives. In: P. Pica (ed.). *Linguistic Variation Yearbook 2001*. Amsterdam: Benjamins, 105–146.
McGinnis, Martha 2005a. On markedness asymmetries in person and number. *Language* 81, 699–718.
McGinnis, Martha 2005b. Painting the wall red for a few hours: A reply to Glasbey 2003. *Snippets* 10, 9–10.

Miyagawa, Shigeru 1998. (S)ase as an elsewhere causative and the syntactic nature of words. *Journal of Japanese Linguistics* 16, 67–110.

Pfau, Roland 2000. *Features and Categories in Language Production*. Doctoral dissertation. University of Frankfurt/Main.

Pfau, Roland 2009. *Features and Categories in Language Production: A Distributed Morphology Account of Spontaneous Speech Errors*. Amsterdam: Benjamins.

Pylkkänen, Liina 2002. *Introducing Arguments*. Ph.D. dissertation. MIT, Cambridge, MA.

Rice, Keren 2000. *Morpheme Order and Semantic Scope: Word Formation in the Athapaskan Verb*. Cambridge: Cambridge University Press.

Ritter, Elizabeth 1995. On the syntactic category of pronouns and agreement. *Natural Language and Linguistic Theory* 13, 405–443.

Richards, Norvin 2001. An idiomatic argument for lexical decomposition. *Linguistic Inquiry* 32, 183–192.

Rullman, Hotze 2004. First and second person pronouns as bound variables. *Linguistic Inquiry* 35, 159–168.

Sauerland, Uli 2008. On the semantic markedness of phi-features. In: D. Harbour, D. Adger & S. Bejar (eds.). *Phi-Theory: Phi-Features across Modules and Interfaces*. Oxford: Oxford University Press.

von Stechow, Arnim 1998. German participles II in Distributed Morphology. Paper presented at the *Conference on the Syntax and Semantics of Tense and Mood Selection*, July 2–4, 1998, University of Bergamo, Italy, http://www2.sfs.uni-tuebingen.de/~arnim10/ Aufsaetze/ German-Participles-II.pdf, February 24, 2012.

Svenonius, Peter 2005. Two domains of causatives. Paper presented at CASTL, University of Tromsø, March 10, 2005, http://www.hum.uit.no/a/svenonius/papers/Svenonius05TwoDomains.pdf, February 24, 2012.

Travis, Lisa 2000. Event structure in syntax. In: C. Tenny & J. Pustejovsky (eds.). *Events as Grammatical Objects: The Converging Perspectives of Lexical Semantics and Syntax*. Stanford, CA: CSLI Publications, 145–185.

Arnim von Stechow
6 Syntax and semantics: An overview

1   Introduction —— 169
2   A Fregean conception of syntax/semantics —— 170
3   The syntax/semantics interface in Generative Grammar —— 173
4   A λ-language and the interpretation of external and internal merge —— 178
5   The two most important rules of construal: FI and QR —— 183
6   Intensionality —— 190
7   The interpretation of traces —— 200
8   Abstract operators in syntax and the PF/LF-branches —— 205
9   Getting rid of abstract syntax? —— 218
10 The big picture —— 227
11 References —— 229

Abstract: Semanticists working in the tradition of Chomsky's GB-theory assume that there is a branching point (SS, more recently Spell-Out) where syntactic structures split into phonetic forms (PFs) and logical forms (LF). LFs are disambiguated structures that have a compositional semantic interpretation, which is introduced in the article. The most important rule for the creation of an LF is Quantifier Raising (QR), which creates λ-abstracts that serve as arguments for a moved phrase. The article illustrates the most important applications of the rule (problem of the object, scope ambiguities, pronoun binding). Compositional semantics is illustrated by the analysis of some non-trivial extensional and intensional constructions. We also discuss the integration of abstract semantic operators into the syntax (question, comparative, tense, negation, plural) and their interaction with morphology. The syntax of an LF is occasionally rather abstract and distant from its correspondent PF. The article contains a brief outlook to other approaches to semantics (type shifting, variable free semantics, dynamic semantics) and asks whether their LFs might be nearer to the surface.

1 Introduction

Syntax is a device for generating the expressions of language. Semantics is the device that interprets the expressions by assigning them meanings. This article

---
Arnim von Stechow, Tübingen, Germany

https://doi.org/10.1515/9783110589849-006

presents the syntax/semantics interface for a generative grammar in the style of the GB-theory and later developments (PPT, MP). It does so in developing syntactic and semantic structures for a range of interesting constructions of English (and occasionally other languages). And it shows how the semantic structures are obtained from the syntactic ones by rules of construal. The semantic structures have a precise interpretation, which is indicated. The constructions considered are in most cases extremely simple and neglect complicated issues that have been discussed in the literature. But they are complicated enough to see what is needed for the syntax/semantics interface. And they give a concrete idea what the rules/principles of construal might look like. If we looked at other languages, different principles might be needed. I have confined myself to a sort of toy box English, because this is the language that most linguists understand and use for theoretical investigations. The sketch of a theory of interpretation is appropriate for GB-theory and perhaps the Minimalist Program. Later architectures like Phases have not yet been explored by formal semanticists and are therefore ignored in this article. The picture I am drawing is certainly too simple (and occasionally wrong). But it is complicated enough. In particular, it makes an essential use of all sorts of LF-movements. There are theories like variable free categorial or combinatory grammars that try to do everything without movement. I am not seriously discussing these alternatives. They would be the topic for a different article. I have said something about these issues in von Stechow (1991), but the theory has developed since.

2 A Fregean conception of syntax/semantics

Most theoreticians doing formal semantics of natural language take the following principles attributed to the German philosopher Gottlob Frege as guiding lines:
1. *Compositionality* ("Frege Principle"): The meaning of complex expression is a function of the meaning of its parts and their syntactic composition.
2. *Context principle*: Make the meaning of words (and parts) so that the sentence meanings come out correctly by compositionality.
3. *Sentence meanings*: The meaning of an unembedded sentence is a truth-value (an *extension*). The meaning of an embedded sentence is a proposition (an *intension*).

The precise spell-out of the principles is under debate. We will see that sentence meanings can be more complicated depending on the range of semantic phenomena to be considered. In some theories, sentence meanings are context change potentials (functions from propositions to propositions), in other theories sentence meanings are (Kaplanian) characters (functions from contexts to propositions) and so on. We will touch upon these issues in the development of the article.

Note that this is a narrow concept of semantics. All pragmatic aspects are ignored such as illocutionary force, implicatures of different kind, social constraints for use and so on. Similarly, presuppositions are not treated, though one might count these as belonging to the domain of semantics proper. Thus semantics is understood as truth-conditional semantics.

Here is a first illustration of Frege's guide-lines.
Consider the sentences:

(1) a. Bill likes Mary.
    b. Mary likes Bill.

The sentences are made of the same material, but they obviously mean something different. Thus it is not enough to know the meanings of the words **Bill**, **likes** and **Mary** to determine the sentence meaning. The computation must take into account the syntactic structure. To calculate the meaning of (1a), we first compute the meaning of the VP **likes Mary** from the meaning of **likes** and **Mary** by an appropriate semantic function/operation. Then we go on and compute the meaning of the sentence by combining the meaning of the subject **Bill** with that of the VP by means of another (or perhaps the same) semantic operation. The calculation of the meaning of (1b) uses the same semantic operations for the calculation, but the input is different, and therefore it doesn't come as a surprise that the result reached for the sentence might be different. Suppose Bill likes Mary, but she doesn't like him. In that case, the first sentence is true but the second one is false.

The meanings of expressions are conventionally represented by the use of double square brackets $[\![.]\!]$. For the truth-value "true" we use the number 1, for the truth-value "false" we use the number 0. The meaning of the two sentences can then be described as:

(2) a. $[\![$**Bill likes Mary**$]\!]$ = 1 iff Bill likes Mary.
    b. $[\![$**Mary likes Bill**$]\!]$ = 1 iff Mary likes Bill.

An inspection of the example shows the usefulness of the context principle. We have a clear intuition of what the sentences mean. But what do the words mean? Everyone would say that **Bill** and **Mary** denote particular persons known to the user in the context of use. But what does **likes** denote? We may say "the attitude/state of liking". But this description would give us no idea of how we could combine this meaning first with the object and than with the subject, following the syntax of the sentences, i.e. the structure [$_S$NP [$_{VP}$ V NP]]. According to the context principle the following function is a useful meaning for **likes**:

(3) ⟦[$_V$ **likes**]⟧ = that function f from individuals such that for any individual x, f(x) is that function g from individuals such that for any individual y, g(y) = 1 if y likes x and g(y) = 0 if y doesn't like x.
Short: ⟦[$_V$ **likes**]⟧ = $\lambda x.\lambda y.y$ likes x

We assume that the meaning of the VP is obtained by applying the meaning of the verb to the meaning of the object via *functional application* (**FA**). Similarly the meaning of S is computed by combining the meaning of the VP with the meaning of the subject via FA. Here is the calculation of (2b):

⟦ [$_{VP}$ [$_V$ **likes**] [$_{NP}$ **Bill**]] ⟧	= ⟦ [$_{VP}$ [$_V$ **likes**] ⟧ (⟦ [$_{NP}$ **Bill**]] ⟧)	by FA
= [$\lambda x.\lambda y.y$ likes x] (⟦ [$_{NP}$ **Bill**]] ⟧)	meaning of **likes**	
= [$\lambda x.\lambda y.y$ likes x] (Bill)	meaning of **Bill**	
= $\lambda y.y$ likes Bill	function conversion ("λ-conversion")	
⟦ [$_S$ [$_{NP}$ **Mary**] [$_{VP}$ [$_V$ **likes**] [$_{NP}$ **Bill**]]] ⟧ =		
= ⟦ [$_{VP}$ [$_V$ **likes**] [$_{NP}$ **Bill**]] ⟧ (⟦[$_{NP}$ **Mary**]⟧)	FA	
= [$\lambda y.y$ likes Bill](Mary)	former calculation and lexicon	
= Mary likes Bill	FA	
= 0	by assumption	

An even more dramatic illustration of the context principle would involve functional words like **not, or, and, if...then, every, some** or modals like **must** or **can**. No rational person would claim that he has a pre-theoretical intuition of their meanings.

Let us illustrate the third principle of Frege's: embedded sentences don't express truth-values but propositions (*senses* in Frege's terminology). It is easy to convince oneself that embedded sentences cannot express truth-values in the general case. Consider the following two examples:

(4) a. Bill believes that he, Bill, likes Mary.
  b. Bill doesn't believe that Mary likes him.

The complement clauses are synonymous with (1a) and (1b) respectively. Suppose that both sentences are true, i.e., their meaning is 1. Then Bill would be an irrational person because he would believe and not believe the same meaning. But the scenario does not imply any irrationality of the subject. Possible world semantics solves this problem by providing propositions as meanings. The propositions for the complements in question are the sets of worlds [λw.Bill likes Mary in w] and [λw.Mary likes Bill in w]. The two propositions are different though they are both true in the actual world. So Bill might believe the first and disbelieve the second without being irrational. The semantics has to say, of course, how it is possible that sentences have different meanings in different contexts. The interpretation principle that achieves that will be introduced below. For the beginner the idea that (unembedded) sentences should denote truth-values is puzzling. In order to understand that we have to think of sentences as presenting facts or non-facts of the real world: if a sentence presents a fact, it is true and if it represents a non-fact, it is false.

A note on the literature. Frege's Principle is never stated explicitly in the above form by Frege himself. The passage that is mostly quoted is Frege (1923: 23). The Context Principle is stated in Frege (1884). The sense/meaning dichotomy is introduced in Frege (1892). The method of splitting an n-place function into a sequence of one-place functions is due to Schönfinkel (1924). I write functions in the λ-notation with the conventions of Heim & Kratzer (1998: ch. 3). Metalinguistic sentences such as *y likes x* stand for truth-values.

For the varieties of meaning in linguistics, see article 1 [Semantics: Foundations, History and Methods] (Maienborn, von Heusinger & Portner) *Meaning in linguistics*; for an extensive discussion of Fregean semantics, see article 3 [Semantics: Foundations, History an Methods] (Textor) *Sense and reference*.

3 The syntax/semantics interface in Generative Grammar

3.1 Generative conceptions of grammar

The toy grammar underlying the examples of the last section is so to speak an ideal realisation of Frege's theory of language. The syntax of a language generates trees and each node has a semantic interpretation. The interpretations of the terminal trees are taken from the lexicon. The interpretation of a branching node is obtained by the semantic values of its daughters via functional application (FA). Grammars of this kind exhibit *surface compositionality*: each constituent has exactly one semantic interpretation that is obtained from the meaning of its direct components by an appropriate semantic operation. There are grammars that try to realise this conception, e.g. variable free categorial grammars (see Szabolcsi 1989, Jacobson 1999, Steedman 2000, among others).

The widely accepted architecture among linguists working in the Chomsky tradition is that of GB-theory and more recent developments building upon it; cf. Chomsky (1981, 1992). In this theory syntax generates structures, which may be called *Syntactic Structures (proper)* (SSs). These structures are transformed into semantic representations called *Logical Forms* (LFs) on the one hand and *Phonetic Forms/Representations* (PFs) on the other hand. The rules that translate SSs into LFs are called *rules of construal*, those that transform SSs into PFs are called *PF-rules*. The LFs are interpreted by semantic operations in the style of the previous sections. Thus the LFs form a language that has a Fregean interpretation. The PFs are the input for phonological rules.

It is important to note that SSs might be quite far away both from PFs and from LFs though for some simple constructions, like the examples discussed, the three structures might coincide. Chomskyan syntax is therefore an abstract system that typically does *not* meet the slogan WYSIWYG ("What you see is what you get"). The article will provide some examples that speak for the soundness of this conception. Here is the organisation of the GB-model:

(5) The GB-model

$$\begin{array}{c} \text{GEN} \\ \Downarrow \\ \text{DS} \\ \Downarrow \\ \text{PF} \Leftarrow \text{SS} \Rightarrow \text{LF} \end{array}$$

The syntax proper (GEN) generates a *deep structure* (DS), which encodes grammatical functions: everything is in 'its' position, i.e. movement hasn't occurred yet. After application of movement rules (e.g. A-movement as in passives, A-bar-movement as in relative clause or interrogatives, head movement like the movement of the finite verb to COMP in German) we reach the level of *surface structure* (SS). SSs are translated into LFs by rules like *Quantifier Raising* (QR) (see below) and by deletion of uninterpretable material (*Full Interpretation*). They are translated into PFs by rules like clitization, Focus Interpretation and perhaps others. The model of the Minimalist Program is alike with the difference that DS is eliminated and SS is called *Spell-Out* (SO).

(6) The MP-model

$$\begin{array}{c} \text{GEN} \\ \Downarrow \\ \text{PF} \Leftarrow \text{SO} \Rightarrow \text{LF} \end{array}$$

The innovation of the Phase-model (Chomsky 1995) is cyclic branching: there is not only one branching point SS or SO but one at every "phase", vP or CP, substructures that occur in the recursive generation of a syntactic structure.

(7) The Phase-model

$$
\begin{array}{c}
\text{GEN} \\
\Downarrow \\
PF_1 \Leftarrow phase_1 \Rightarrow LF_1 \\
\Downarrow \quad\quad \Downarrow \quad\quad \Downarrow \\
\cdots\cdots\cdots\cdots\cdots\cdots \\
\Downarrow \quad\quad \Downarrow \quad\quad \Downarrow \\
PF_n \Leftarrow phase_n \Rightarrow LF_n
\end{array}
$$

Different architectures of grammar may differ by:
- The type of grammar used for generating syntactic structures (Context-Free Grammars, Categorial Grammars, Tree Adjunction Grammars, Montague-Grammar, Transformational Grammars and many others)
- The type of grammars used for the LF generation (typed languages with abstraction and possibly other syncategorematic rules, categorial grammars with type shifters, context change semantics, DRT and so on)
- The PF rules and phonological rules in general
- The interface organisation

Linguists working in the Chomskyan tradition usually assume that LFs are made of the same material as SSs, i.e. they are trees. An important difference between syntactic trees and semantic trees is that the nodes of the former carry syntactic categories (N, A, P, V, and possibly others) but the latter carry semantic categories, called logical types such as e, t, et, and so on. In what follows I will use the term *surface structure* (SS) and *spell-out* (SO) synonymously. This might be confusing because one might think that surface structure is "what we see". But recall that we have syntactic rules that operate on the way from SS/SO to PF. The PFs are what we see, and a PF may be very different from its SS/SO and *a forteriori* from its LF.

The heart of the syntax/semantics interface consists of the *rules of construal*, which convert SSs into LFs. The most restrictive interface theory is one that does it without such rules. Syntactic and semantic structures coincide and each node is directly interpreted. Some categorial grammars try to realise this ideal. A less restrictive (but more realistic) framework derives LFs from SSs by rules of construal. The GB-theory assumes that we first generate a complete SS, which we then transform into an LF. The LF is interpreted semantically. A phase model is more restricted. It translates each phase into an LF. These LFs may not undergo any essential change in later steps of the generation. The interpretation should use the meaning of the previous phase plus some syntactic information stemming from the current LF.

3.2 Building structures: External and internal merge

In this article we stick to the GB/MP-model. We assume that SS/SOs can be generated by a lexicon, phrase structure rules (nowadays called *External Merge*), and movement rules (called *Internal Merge*). The LFs will be trees with logical types as categories. The language has variables for each type and certain syncategorematic symbols like the λ-operator.

The SOs of a language are generated by the rules External and Internal Merge on the basis of a *lexicon* consisting of *lexical trees*, i.e. words dominated by a *syntactic category* and a *logical type*. We will represent lexical trees by labelled brackets or by terminating context-free phrase structure rules. Phrase structure rules have the advantage that they can be used for writing many trees at once. For instance, the rules (8a) stand for the trees [$_{Ne}$ **Bill**] and [$_{Ne}$ **Mary**].

(8) Some lexical entries
    a. N_e → **Bill, Mary**
    b. N_{et} → **boy, child, student**
    b. V_{et} → **sleeps, snores**
    c. $V_{e(et)}$ → **likes, hates**
    d. $Det_{(et)((et)t)}$ → **every, a, no**
    e. A_{et} → **nice, obnoxious**

The rule *External Merge* (EM) takes two trees α and β and combines them to the new tree [$_X$ α β], where X is either the syntactic category of α or that of β. The daughter that projects its category to the new tree is called *head*. Here is a derivation of a SS for the sentence **Bill hates every obnoxious child**. For the time being, we ignore the types for the generation.

1.	[$_A$ **obnoxious**]	Lexicon
2.	[$_N$ **child**]	Lexicon
3.	[$_N$ [$_A$ **obnoxious**] [$_N$ **child**]]	EM(1,2)
4.	[$_{Det}$ **every**]	Lexicon
5.	[$_{Det}$ [$_{Det}$ **every**] [$_N$ [$_A$ **obnoxious**] [$_N$ **child**]]]	EM(4,3)
6.	[$_V$ **hates**]	Lexicon
7.	[$_V$ [$_V$ **hates**] [$_{Det}$ [$_{Det}$ **every**] [$_N$ [$_A$ **obnoxious**] [$_N$ **child**]]]]	EM(6,5)
8.	[$_N$ **Bill**]	Lexicon
9.	[$_V$ [$_N$ **Bill**] [$_V$ [$_V$ **hates**] [$_{Det}$ [$_{Det}$ **every**] [$_N$ [$_A$ **obnoxious**] [$_N$ **child**]]]]]	EM(8,7)

Following common practice, we will write X' for intermediate projections, XP for complete phrases. A complete V projection is also written as S, and a V with one or two objects is written as VP. In other words, the last line will also be written as:

(9) [$_S$ [$_{NP}$ **Bill**] [$_{VP}$ [$_V$ **hates**] [$_{DP}$ [$_{Det}$ **every**] [$_{NP}$ [$_{AP}$ **obnoxious**] [$_N$ **child**]]]]]

Internal Merge (IM) is used to generate structures that involve movement. Consider, e.g. the complement clause in **Bill wonders who Mary likes**. It has the following structure:

(10) [[$_{NP}$ **who**]$_1$ [$_{C'}$ C [$_S$ **Mary** [$_{VP}$ **likes** t$_1$]]]]

Suppose we have already generated the structure [$_{C'}$ C [$_S$ Mary [$_{VP}$ likes [$_{NP}$ who]]]] using the lexicon and **EM**. (The generation involves the lexicon entry C, i.e. a lexical tree dominating the empty string and the NP **who**.)

n.   [$_{C'}$ C [$_S$ **Mary** [$_{VP}$ **likes** [$_{NP}$ **who**]]]]   generated via Lexicon and EM

The next step of the generation is this:

n+1.   [[$_{NP}$ **who**]$_1$ [$_{C'}$ C [$_S$ **Mary** [$_{VP}$ **likes** [$_{NP}$ **who**]$_1$]]]]   by Internal Merge

Internal Merge takes a subtree from a tree and adjoins it to the tree. As the name indicates, the material adjoined is not taken from outside but from inside of the structure. The lower copy in the movement chain is called *trace* of the moved constituent, here **who**. The moved constituent is called *antecedent* (of the trace). The Minimalist Program assumes that both constituents **who** are fully present in the structure. The lower is deleted at PF, i.e. not pronounced. Most semanticists assume that the lower copy is empty in the syntax already. Furthermore they assume co-indexing between the higher copy, the antecedent, and the trace. (The latter assumption is not shared by minimalism either, but it is important for the interpretation.) So a more convenient representation of step n+1 for semantic purposes is therefore:

n+1.   [[$_{NP}$ **who**]$_1$ [$_{C'}$ C [$_S$ **Mary** [$_{VP}$ **likes** [$_{NP}$ t$_1$]]]]

where t$_i$ is the empty string with an index. Another instance of the movement rule is *head movement*, e.g. the movement of the finite verb to COMP in German matrix clauses. As an instance, consider the sentence:

(11) **Der Fritz mag jedes Kind**
      the Fritz likes every child

A standard assumption in German syntax is that the sentence is generated by moving **mag** to C and subsequently moving **der Fritz** to [Spec, CP]:

n.   [$_{CP}$ C [[**der Fritz**] [[**jedes Kind**] **mag**]]]|
n+1.   [$_{CP}$ [**mag**$_1$ C] [[**der Fritz**] [[**jedes Kind**] t$_1$]]]   IM
n+2.   [$_{CP}$[**der Fritz**]$_2$ [$_{C'}$[**mag**$_1$C][t$_2$[[**jedes Kind**] t$_1$]]]]   IM

It is obvious that the two rules Merge heavily overgenerate. We have to build in constraints that rule out undesirable ("ungrammatical") structures. This is the real work to be achieved by syntax, which however is not the concern of this article. It is sufficient to have an idea of how syntactic structures of language come into life by simple principles. I should add that the SSs in recent generative syntax are more complicated than the ones assumed in this article. There are many additional functional projections used for case checking and other purposes.

In the next section we will see how this kind of syntax can be combined with semantic interpretation.

A note on the literature. The different interface organisations of Generative Grammars are outlined in Chomsky (1981, 1995, 2001). The claim that the following analyses belong to these frameworks is to be taken *cum grano salis*. Many details, even important ones, will differ from current syntactic research. The overall picture of the syntax/semantics interface is however consistent with the architecture of Generative Grammar, I believe. The first clear conception of the syntax/semantics interface is presumably due to R. Montague. Montague said that syntactic rules have meanings. Each syntactic rule is associated with a particular semantic operation (typically FA), which puts the meanings of the arguments of the rule together. This is a direct implementation of the Frege Principle; see Montague (1970a, 1970b, 1970c). We will see that Montague's conception can be applied in a straightforward way to the Minimalist Program: The standard interpretation of External Merge will be FA, and that of Internal Merge will be FA plus λ-abstraction.

4 A λ-language and the interpretation of external and internal merge

4.1 Logical Form

The majority of semanticists use a typed language for the representation of LFs. The structures of these languages are rather close to SSs and they have a simple

and transparent interpretation. A typed language consists of trees whose nodes are labelled with *logical types*. A type represents the type of meaning a node denotes. LF languages may differ in the following way:
1. The types are different. Apart from the basic types e,t mentioned in the first section we may have types like s (world), i (time), l (place), v (event). Accordingly, the complex types might be different from language to language as well.
2. The types may encode different kinds of meaning.
    a. In an extensional language, types encode extensions unambiguously.
    b. In an intensional language, types ambiguously encode extensions and intensions.
    c. In a character language, types ambiguously encode extensions, intensions and characters.
    d. In a dynamic language, types encode context-change potentials.
    e. There are typed languages that don't make the distinction between extension and intension at all, e.g. Cresswell's λ-categorial languages.
3. The trees of LF-languages may differ with respect to the types admitted at the branching nodes. Every language admits the splitting of a type into a functor type and an argument type. But other splits are possible depending on the semantic operations available for the interpretation.
4. A language may differ with respect to the syncategorematic rules and symbols they admit. Most LF languages have variables and λ-abstraction.

4.2 Syntax and semantics of EL

We start with an extensional λ-categorial language. It is the system used in the first twelve chapters of Heim & Kratzer (1998) [henceforth H&K]. We call this language *EL* ("Extensional Language"). The categories of the language are the following types.

(12) The *type system for EL*
    The basic types are e ("entities") and t ("truth-values"). The complex types are generated by the rule: if a and b are types, then (ab) is a type.

Types of form (ab) are called *functional types*. We will mostly omit the outermost brackets. There are other notational conventions for functional types: H&K use <a,b>, Montague uses b/a, b//a or b///a, Kratzer (1977) uses b:a, and Ajdukiewicz (1935) uses $\frac{b}{a}$; there are still more variants. The basic types are written in different ways as well. Most categorial grammarians follow Ajdukiewicz and write n ("name") for e and s ("sentence") for t. Cresswell (1973) uses 1 for e and 0 for a propositional type. He writes our functional types (ab) as <b,a>. So there is no uniformity in the literature and the reader has to be aware of the particular notation used by different authors. Our type system is a simplified version of the H&K-notation.

The *semantic domains* for these types are the following ones.

(13) a. $D_e = E$ = the set of individuals
 b. $D_t = \{1,0\}$ = the set of truth-values
 c. $D_{ab} = D_b^{D_a}$ = the set of (partial) functions from D_a into D_b.

The LF-language EL consists of a *lexicon*, *variables* for any type and the following structures:

(14) *Syntax of EL*
 1. If α is a lexical tree of type a, α is a tree of type a. (L)
 2. If x is a variable and a is a type, then $[_a \, x]$ is a tree of type a. (Var)
 3. If α is a tree of type ab and β is a tree of type a, then $[_b \, \alpha\beta]$ is a tree of type b. (FA)
 4. If α and β are trees of type et, then $[_{et} \, \alpha\beta]$ is a tree of type et. (PM)
 5. If α is a tree of type b and x is a variable of type a, $[_{ab} \, \lambda x \alpha]$ is a tree of type ab. (λ)

The syntactic rules have names reminding of their semantic interpretation (L = lexicon, Var = variable rule, FA = functional application, PM = predicate modification, λ = λ-abstraction). H&K use the notation $[_{ab} \, x\alpha]$ for our tree $[_{ab} \, \lambda x \alpha]$.

The *lexicon* consists of lexical trees that are labelled with types. We have entries such as $[_e \,$ **Mary**$]$ or $[_{et} \,$ **snores**$]$. To simplify the notation, we write these as **Mary**$_e$ and **snores**$_{et}$ respectively. The LF for the sentence **Mary snores** is the following tree:

(15) $[_t \, [_e \,$ **Mary**$] \, [_{et} \,$ **snores**$]]$

The interpretation of the language is given by interpreting the lexicon and by stating recursive interpretation principles for the syntactic structures. The lexicon is interpreted by a function F that maps each word α of type a to a meaning in D_a. Here is the interpretation for some lexical trees.

(16) Some entries of the *semantic lexicon*
 F(**Mary**$_e$) = Mary

$F(\textbf{snores}_{et}) = \lambda x.\ x \in D_e.x$ snores.
$F(\textbf{child}_{et}) = \lambda x.x \in D_e.x$ is a child.
$F(\textbf{hates}_{e(et)}) = \lambda x.x \in D_e.\lambda y.y \in D_e.y$ hates x.
$F(\textbf{obnoxious}_{et}) = \lambda x.x \in D_e.x$ is obnoxious.
$F(\textbf{every}_{(et)((et)t)}) = \lambda P.P \in D_{et}.\lambda Q.Q \in D_{et}.(\forall x)(P(x) \rightarrow Q(x))$
$F(\textbf{some}_{(et)((et)t)}) = \lambda P.P \in D_{et}.\lambda Q.Q \in D_{et}.(\exists x)(P(x)\ \&\ Q(x))$
$F(\textbf{no}_{(et)((et)t)}) = \lambda P.P \in D_{et}.\lambda Q.Q \in D_{et}.(\neg\exists x)(P(x)\ \&\ Q(x))$

The semantic meta-language uses obvious abbreviations. In particular, I am using H&K's convention that meta-linguistic sentences stand for the truth-value 1 if they are true, for the value 0 otherwise. In what follows I will even use a shorter notation and write λf_a for $\lambda f.f \in D_a$.

Given the semantic lexicon, we are in a position to state a recursive interpretation $[\![.]\!]$ for the entire language. This function depends on the structure $M = (E, \{0,1\}, F)$ and a variable assignment g. M is called a *model*.

(17) The *interpretation* $[\![.]\!]^{M,g}$ *for EL*
 1. Let α be a lexical tree of type a. Then $[\![\alpha]\!]^{M,g} = F(\alpha)$. (L)
 2. Let x be a variable of type a. Then $[\![x]\!]^{M,g} = g(x)$. (Var)
 3. Let γ be a branching tree of type b with daughters α of type ab and β of type a. Then $[\![\gamma]\!]^{M,g} = [\![\alpha]\!]^{M,g}([\![\beta]\!]^{M,g})$. (FA)
 4. Let γ be a branching tree of type ab with daughters α and β both of type ab. Then $[\![\gamma]\!]^{M,g} = \lambda x \in D_a.[[\![\alpha]\!]^{M,g}(x)\ \&\ [\![\beta]\!]^{M,g}(x)]$. (PM)
 5. Let α be a tree of type ab of the form $[_{ab} \lambda x\beta]$, x a variable of type a and β a tree of type b. Then $[\![[_{ab} \lambda x\beta]]\!]^{M,g} = \lambda u \in D_a.[\![\beta]\!]^{M,g[x/u]}$ (λ)

The most complicated interpretation principle is the abstraction rule λ. We will illustrate it below. g[x/u] is a variable assignment that is defined like g with the possible exception that g[x/u](x) = u. (There are other notations: H&K use g[x → u], sometimes we find g[x\u] and so on.) The relativisation of the interpretation function to a model is omitted if the model is self-understood from the context. Similarly, reference to the assignment function g is ignored if we don't need it. The LF in (15) can now be interpreted along the lines indicated in section 2.

4.3 Interpretations of external merge

Here is a first overview of the relation of languages of the EL-type and those of the MP-type. This comparison reveals which kind of interpretation rules (rules of construal) we have to expect.

The rule *External Merge (EM)* combines two expressions $\alpha + \beta$ to a new expression γ. The following cases may arise.

(a) One of the two expresses a function and the other expresses an argument of the right type. In this case the Interpretation is Functional Application. This is the case if **Mary** + **snores** combine to a sentence by EM.
(b) The two expressions are of the same type, say et. In this case EM is interpreted as Predicate Modification. An example will be the combination of an NP with a relative clause, e.g. **woman** + **that snores**.
(c) One of the two expressions is semantically empty. In this case, we delete the semantically void expression at LF. An example is the preposition **of** in **the mother of Mary**. **mother** expresses a function of type e(et). **Mary** has the type e and is a good argument. The preposition **of** doesn't add anything to the content and is therefore deleted at LF.
(d) The two expressions have types that fall neither under (a) nor (b). In this case we need a special interpretation rule. We won't be concerned with such cases in this article. Cases like this are the domain of generalized categorial grammar.

These are the simplest standard interpretations. More fancy interpretation rules are possible and in fact used in categorial grammar. See section 6.2 ("IFA") and 9.2 ("Geach's rule") to get an idea.

4.4 Interpretation of internal merge

The interpretation of *Internal Merge (IM)* will deal with the following cases.
1. A head is moved, e.g. a verb. In this case the meaning of the expression is not affected and the head is *reconstructed* to its base position at LF.
2. An argument expression is moved. If the argument is of the logical type required by the argument position, the moved expression might be reconstructed at LF.
3. The argument position is of type e and the expression located there is of type (et)t. In this case, the argument is moved for type reasons. This movement will create a trace of type e and an abstract of type et. The interpretation of this kind of movement will be the rule QR (*Quantifier Raising*). QR will typically be a covert movement and apply at the LF branch. QR will play a central rule in this survey.
4. An argument position is occupied by a semantically empty pronoun. This is an expression without meaning and without logical type, often called PRO. This expression is moved at the left periphery and creates a λ-abstract. We will call this kind of movement *PRO-movement*. It can be used to create any kind of λ-abstract. PRO movement plays an important role for the treatment

of quantifiers in DPs or PPs. It is also used for question formation and plays a central role for the interpretation of tense and aspect. At LF, PRO is deleted. PRO originates in a case-less position. Semantically empty pronouns that are base-generated at a case position are called WH(-operators). The movement of WH is called WH-movement. A typical instance of WH is the relative pronoun. Semantically, there is no difference between PRO and WH. Both are semantically void.

A note on the literature. There are many versions of typed languages. The versions used in linguistics, especially the semantics for λ-abstraction, go perhaps back to different writings of Montague, e.g. Montague (1970c). The tradition of these languages is, however much older and goes back to Frege's abstraction of the graph of a function, Russell's type theory and so on. Montague uses an intensional system (see below). An influential extensional system is the Ty2 language by Gallin (1975).

5 The two most important rules of construal: FI and QR

This section introduces two important interface principles: the *Principle of Full Interpretation* (FI) and the rule *Quantifier Raising* (QR). We will discuss three tasks performed by QR: (a) resolution of type conflicts, (b) spelling out scope ambiguities of a quantifier, and (c) variable binding.

5.1 Full Interpretation

Let us see first how the LF for **Mary snores** is obtained from the syntax. Recall that lexical trees come from the syntax with both a syntactic category and a logical type. (More accurately, the lexicon contains for each word a pair of lexical trees $<\alpha, \beta>$, where α is for the syntax and β is for the LF.)

(18)　SS: [$_S$ [$_{N,e}$ **Mary**] [$_{V,et}$ **snores**]]

The syntactic categories S, V and N are not relevant for the LF-language. Therefore we delete them and obtain the intermediate sequence of lexical trees:

[[$_e$ **Mary**] [$_{et}$ **snores**]]

The rule FA tells us that these combine to a tree of type t, i.e., the derived LF is the tree

(19) LF: [$_t$ [$_e$ **Mary**] [$_{et}$ **snores**]]

The personal ending **-s** is not important for the interpretation and may be deleted as well (but we ignore this possibility). We call the principle that is responsible for the deletion of semantically inert material the *Principle of Full Interpretation* (**FI**). A version of this principle is stated in Chomsky (1986).

(20) **FI:** An LF tree contains only material that is important for the semantic interpretation. (Similarly a PF tree only contains material that is important for phonetic interpretation.)

FI is the first important interface principle.

5.2 QR resolves type-clashes

Let us construct next an LF for the SS in (9), here repeated as:

(21) [$_S$ [$_{NP}$ **Bill**] [$_{VP}$ [$_V$ **hates**] [$_{DP}$ [$_{Det}$ **every**] [$_{NP}$ [$_{AP}$ **obnoxious**] [$_N$ **child**]]]]]

We assume the following lexical rules for the generation with EM.

(22) Some lexical entries
    N_e → **Bill, Mary**
    N_{et} → **boy, child, student**
    V_{et} → **sleeps, snores**
    $V_{e(et)}$ → **likes, hates**
    $Det_{(et)((et)t)}$ → **every, a, no**
    A_{et} → **nice, obnoxious**

If we proceed according to the principle FI, i.e., we delete the syntactic categories and try to project the logical types according to the rules of the LF-syntax, we get as far as this:

(23) A type clash

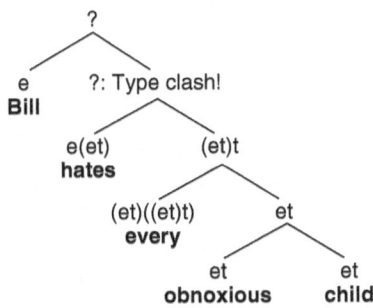

There is no way to assign a type to the VP-node in our system. The daughters of that node can neither be combined by FA nor by PM. This is due to the fact that the object is a *generalised quantifier*, i.e., a function that assigns truth-values to sets of individuals. H&K call this the *problem of the object*. Before we solve this problem, we calculate the meaning of the object because the calculation illustrates the usefulness of the rule PM.

$[\![[_{(et)t} \textbf{every}_{(et)((et)t)} [_{et} \textbf{obnoxious}_{et} \textbf{child}_{et}]]]\!]$

$= [\![\textbf{every}_{(et)((et)t)}]\!] ([\![[_{et} \textbf{obnoxious}_{et} \textbf{child}_{et}]]\!])$ FA

$= [\lambda P_{et}.\lambda Q_{et}.(\forall x)(P(x) \rightarrow Q(x))] ([\![[_{et} \textbf{obnoxious}_{et} \textbf{child}_{et}]]\!])$ L

$= [\lambda Q_{et}.(\forall x)([\![[_{et} \textbf{obnoxious}_{et} \textbf{child}_{et}]]\!] (x) \rightarrow Q(x))]$ λ-conversion

$= [\lambda Q_{et}.(\forall x)(\lambda y[[\![\textbf{obnoxious}_{et}]\!] (y) \& [\![\textbf{child}_{et}]\!] (y)](x) \rightarrow Q(x))]$ PM

$= [\lambda Q_{et}.(\forall x)([\![\textbf{obnoxious}_{et}]\!] (x) \& [\![\textbf{child}_{et}]\!] (x) \rightarrow Q(x))]$ λ-conversion

$= [\lambda Q_{et}.(\forall x)([\lambda y_e.y \text{ is obnoxious}](x) \& [\lambda y_e.y \text{ is a child}] (x) \rightarrow Q(x))]$ L: 2×

$= \lambda Q_{et}.(\forall x)(x \text{ is obnoxious} \& x \text{ is a child} \rightarrow Q(x))$ λ-conversion: 2×

This is the correct meaning, viz. the property that is true of a set if every obnoxious child is a member of that set. The derivation illustrates what the rule Predicate Modification (PM) achieves: it is set-theoretical intersection.

Since we know that there is a compositional interpretation for the object in (23), we can simplify the structure by letting the general quantifier unanalysed, i.e., we assume that we have a lexical entry $[_{(et)t}$ **every obnoxious child**], which has the meaning just calculated.

The type clash is resolved by May's rule *Quantifier Raising* (**QR**); cf. May (1977, 1985), which creates a λ-abstract by movement.

(24) *The rule QR*

Move an NP or DP out of an XP and adjoin it to XP. Leave a co-indexed trace. If i is the index created by the rule, the trace t_i is interpreted as a variable of type e, the movement index i, i.e., the index of the moved NP/DP, is spelled out as λi at LF.

QR may be regarded as an instance of Internal Merge. We apply the rule before we delete uninterpretable stuff by FI. Here is a picture that illustrates the solution of the problem of the object by means of QR:

(25)

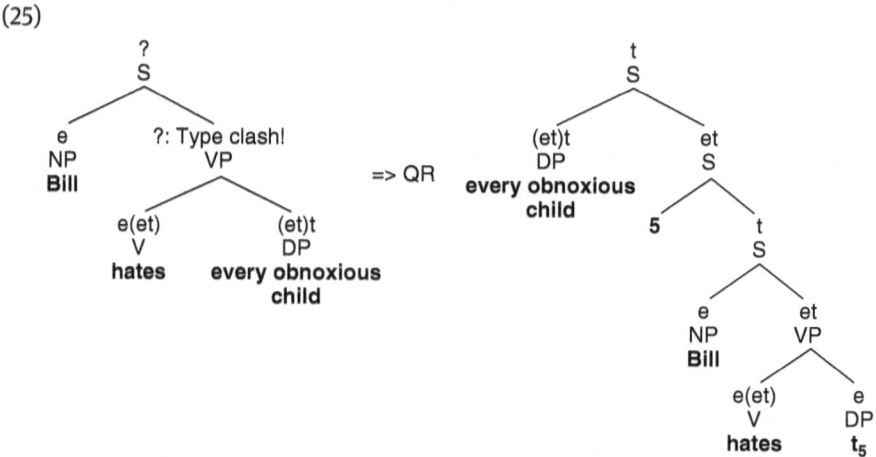

We see that the types project according to the syntactic rules of the LF-language. We delete the syntactic categories, interpret the movement index **5** as λ_5 and the trace t_5 as a variable of type e. Thus we derive the LF-tree:

(26) $[_t [_{(et)t}$ **every obnoxious child**$] [_{et} \lambda_5 [_t [_t $ **Bill**$_e [_{et}$ **hates**$_{e(et)} t_5]]]]$

To see how the abstraction rule (λ) works, let us calculate the meaning of the λ-abstract.
Let g be any variable assignment.

$[\![[_{et} \lambda_5 [_t $ **Bill**$_e [_{et}$ **hates**$_{e(et)} t_5]]]]\!]^g$
$= \lambda u_e[[\![[_t $ **Bill**$_e [_{et}$ **hates**$_{e(et)} t_5]]]]\!]^{g[t5/u]}]$ λ-rule: Variable binding!
$= \lambda u_e[[\![[_{et} $ **hates**$_{e(et)} t_5]]\!]^{g[t5/u]}([\![$ **Bill**$_e]\!]^{g[t5/u]})]$ FA
$= \lambda u_e[[\![[_{et} $ **hates**$_{e(et)} t_5]]\!]^{g[t5/u]}(\text{Bill})]$ L
$= \lambda u_e[[\![$ **hates**$_{e(et)}]\!]^{g[t5/u]} ([\![t_5]\!]^{g[t5/u]})(\text{Bill})]$ FA
$= \lambda u_e[[\![$ **hates**$_{e(et)}]\!]^{g[t5/u]} (g[t_5/u](t_5))(\text{Bill})]$ Var
$= \lambda u_e[[\![$ **hates**$_{e(et)}]\!]^{g[t5/u]} (u)(\text{Bill})]$ Def. of $g[t_5/u](t_5)$
$= \lambda u_e[[\lambda x_e.\lambda y_e.y \text{ hates } x] (u)(\text{Bill})]$ L
$= \lambda u_e[\text{Bill hates } u]$ λ-conversion: 2 ×

The essential step in the computation, i.e. the binding of the variable t_5 is achieved by the λ-rule. The rest of the computation is straightforward.

Now we combine the two immediate constituents of the LF in (26) by means of FA. In other words, we have for an arbitrary assignment g:

$[\![\,[_t [_{(et)t} \textbf{every obnoxious child}] \,[_{et} \lambda_5 \,[_t \textbf{Bill}_e \,[_{et} \textbf{hates}_{e(et)} \textbf{t}_5]]] \,]\!]^g$
$= [\![\,[_{(et)t} \textbf{every obnoxious child}] \,]\!]^g \,([\![\,[_{et} \lambda_5 \,[_t \textbf{Bill}_e \,[_{et} \textbf{hates}_{e(et)} \textbf{t}_5]]] \,]\!]^g)$ FA

We substitute the two meanings computed before and obtain:

$= [\lambda Q_{et}.(\forall x)(x \text{ is obnoxious} \& x \text{ is a child} \to$
  $Q(x))](\lambda u_e[\text{Bill hates u}])$ previous calculation
$= (\forall x)(x \text{ is obnoxious} \& x \text{ is a child} \to \text{Bill hates x})$ λ-conversion 2×

Thus the rule QR solves the problem of the object. More generally, the rule QR helps to overcome many type clashes arising with DPs that express generalised quantifiers. QR is therefore a further very important interface principle mediating between SS and LF.

5.3 QR resolves scope ambiguities

The best-known job done by QR is the spelling out of quantifier scope. Consider Cresswell's (1973) favourite sentence:

(27) Everyone loves someone.

It has two readings:

(28) a. $(\forall x)[x \text{ is a person} \to (\exists y)[y \text{ is a person} \& x \text{ loves y}]]$
      b. $(\exists y)[y \text{ is a person} \& (\forall x)[x \text{ is a person} \to x \text{ loves y}]]$

The two quantifiers involved have the type (et)t. Therefore the SS exhibits the same type clash as before. We resolve the conflict by QR. QR-ing the object gives us the following structure:

(29) $[[_{DP} \textbf{someone}_{(et)t}]_1 \,[_S [_{DP} \textbf{everyone}_{(et)t}] \,[_{VP} [_v \textbf{loves}_{(e(et))}] \,t_1]]]$ (from SS by QR)
      => (FI) $[_t[\textbf{someone}_{(et)t}] \,[_{et} \lambda_1 \,[_t [\textbf{everyone}_{(et)t}] \,[_{et} [\textbf{loves}_{(e(et))} \,t_1]]]]$

The deletion of the syntactic categories by FI and the projection of the types according to the LF-syntax gives us an LF with the reading in (28b). Note that we did not have to QR the subject because we can apply the subject to the VP.

If, however, we QR the subject in a second step and adjoin it to the entire structure, we obtain an LF that expresses the reading in (28a):

(30) $[[_{DP}\textbf{everyone}_{(et)t}]_2 [[_{DP} \textbf{someone}_{(et)t}]_1 [_S t_2 [_{VP} [_V \textbf{loves}_{(e(et))}] t_1]]]]$
(from SS by QR: 2×)
=> (FI) $[_t[\textbf{everyone}_{(et)t}] [_{et} \lambda_2[_t[\textbf{someone}_{(et)t}] [_{et} \lambda_1 [_t t_2 [_{et} [\textbf{loves}_{e(et))}] t_1]]]]]]$

The somewhat tedious computation of the meanings of the LFs is left to the reader. We presuppose obvious interpretations for the words **everyone**, **someone** and **loves**.

A note to the terminology *scope*: The scope of a phrase is its c-command domain. A quantifier α has wide scope with respect to a quantifier β ("α outscopes β") if α c-commands β. At SS, **everyone** has wide scope with respect to **someone**. The LF in (30) preserves the scope relation. But the LF in (29) reverses the relative scope: **someone** out-scopes **everyone**.

5.4 QR binds pronouns

To illustrate *pronoun binding* by QR, consider the following sentences with their intended interpretations:

(31) **Every actor₁ admires himself₁**
 $(\forall x)$[if x is an actor, x admires x]

(32) **Every student₁ owns the computer in front of him₁**
 $(\forall x)$[x is a student → x owns the unique y[y is a computer & y is in front of x]]

The co-indexing represents binding. A notation like this is used in the GB-theory and its followers, but it is not explained there. Let us interpret it. The pronouns **himself₁** and **him₁** both represent the variable 1 of type e and hence have the same meaning, viz. they denote the individual g(1), where g is the relevant variable assignment. The difference in use come from different binding conditions, to which we will return in due time.

Here is the SS of the first sentence:

(33) $[_S [_{DP(et)t} \textbf{every actor}]_1 [_{VPet} [_{Ve(et)} \textbf{admires}] [_{NPe} \textbf{himself}_1]]]$

Up to the VP, there is no type conflict. If we ignored the index of the subject, we could combine the subject with the VP by means of FA. That would yield the wrong reading, viz. $(\forall x)[x$ is an actor $\to x$ admires g(1)]. Suppose g(1) = Bill, then the LF would be true if every actor admires Bill. The sentence cannot have this meaning.

Recall H&K's interpretation of movement indices: they are regarded as λ-operators. Let us adopt the convention, that an index is interpreted as a λ-operator if it cannot be a "referential" index of a variable, i.e. a diacritic that distinguishes the variable from others of the same type. The indices of non-pronominals (e.g. quantifiers or names) are interpreted as λ-operators.

Returning to (33) it appears that we haven't gained anything by this move. Suppose, the index 1 of **every actor** were λ1. Then the λ-abstract $[_{e(et)}\lambda_1$ $[_{VPet}$ $[_{Ve(et)}$ **admires**] $[_{NPe}$ **himself**$_1]]]$ would have the type of a transitive verb. This generates our familiar type clash. So this is not an option. Suppose therefore, we adopt the convention that the index of **every actor** is regarded as a movement index: it tells us that the DP has to be QR-ed and has that index after movement. In other words, the λ-operator is already there, but the DP has not yet been moved. According to this recipe the SS in (33) is transformed into the following structure by **QR**:

(34) $[[_{DP(et)t}$ **every actor**$]_1$ $[_S$ t_1 $[_{VPet}$ $[_{Ve(et)}$ **admires**] $[_{NPe}$ **himself**$_1]]]]$

Applying FI and projecting the types, we obtain the desired LF:

(35) $[[_{(et)t}$ **every actor**$][_{et}$ λ_1 $[_t$ t_1 $[_{et}$ $[_{e(et)}$ **admires**] $[_e$**himself**$_1]]]]]$

The reader may compute for himself that the LF is true if the condition in (31) holds. In particular, he should check that the λ-abstract expresses the property $[\lambda u_e. u$ admires u]. If we apply the meaning of the generalised quantifier expressed by the subject to this, the claim follows immediately.

The SS in (32) is construed along the same lines. The LF is something like this:

(36) $[_t[_{(et)t}$ **every student**] $[_{et}$ λ_1 $[_t$ t_1 **owns** $[_e$ **the** $[_{et}$ **computer** $[_{et}$ **in_front** of **him**$_1]]]]]$

We QR the subject and thereby bind the variable **him**$_1$. The rule for the definite article is this:

(37) The *definite article*
    the has the type (et)e. F(**the**)(P$_{et}$) is only defined if P is a singleton. If defined, F(**the**)(P) = the unique element of P.

The modifier $[_{et}$ **in_front** of **him**$_1$] is combined with the head noun **computer** by PM. I am assuming the preposition **of** is semantically empty and therefore deleted at LF. The semantic lexicon entry of the complex preposition **in_front** is this:

(38) [$_{P,e(et)}$ **in_front**] selects a PP with head *of*. *of* has no type and no meaning. (That's why it doesn't deserve a bold face print.)

F([$_{P,e(et)}$ **in_front**]) = $\lambda x_e.\lambda y_e.y$ is in front of x.

The SS [$_{P,e(et)}$ **in_front**] [$_{PP}$ of$_P$ [$_{NPe}$ **him**$_1$]] is transformed into [$_{e(et)}$ **in_front**] [$_e$ **him**$_1$]] by **FI**. The reader may convince himself that the LF in (36) expresses indeed the truth-condition stated in (32). Again, a full computation is tedious.

QR applies on the way to LF. At SS we have the DPs in argument positions, where they might cause a type conflict. QR solves the type conflict. After the application of QR we delete semantically vacuous material according to FI and project the types according to the rules of the logical syntax.

Summary: In this section we have shown that QR serves three purposes: (a) it solves (certain) type clashes; (b) it spells out scope ambiguities arising with more than one quantifier; (c) it performs pronoun/variable binding. In section 9 we will ask whether we really need the rule QR. The problem of the object can be solved by type-lifted lexical entries. Pronoun binding can be done by special rules of composition. Ambiguities can be resolved by certain type shifting rules. Still, the rule QR is the most transparent method for solving the three problems and all the alternative methods hide the rule somewhere else in the rules of composition.

A note on the literature. QR has been introduced into the literature in May (1977). May doesn't give a semantics for the rule, however. The only use he makes of QR is the spell out of quantifier ambiguities. The present semantics has been developed by Irene Heim in lecture notes. Montague has a rule of *Quantifying-in*, which does the same job with a different syntax and precise semantics (cf. the Rule S14$_n$ in Montague 1970c). The term *Generalised Quantifier* has become popular through Barwise & Cooper (1981). Ajdukiewicz (1935: last page) is presumably the inventor of the Generalised Quantifier. For a detailed discussion of quantifiers, see article 4 [Semantics: Noun Phrases and Verb Phrases] (Keenan) *Quantifiers*. For the semantics of definiteness, see article 2 [Semantics: Noun Phrases and Verb Phrases] (Heim) *Definiteness and indefiniteness*. The three tasks of QR are addressed in article 1 [Semantics: Sentence and Information Structure] (Szabolcsi) *Scope and binding*, too.

6 Intensionality

6.1 Intension and extension

The language EL correctly describes whether a declarative sentence is true or false in our world, but it cannot grasp sentence meanings in general. The reason is very simple: there are only two truth-values but infinitely many sentence meanings. As said in the beginning, sentence meanings must be more complicated entities, at least propositions. Most semanticists are adherents of possible world semantics according to which a sentence expresses a set of possible worlds (or the characteristic function of such a set). Consider the following sentences:

(39) a. **Bill believes** that **Mary** is **obnoxious**.
     b. **Bill** does**n't believe** that **Mary snores**.

Suppose both sentences are true. Suppose further that both complement clauses are true. In the language EL the two complement clauses would then have the same meaning and Bill would be an irrational person because he would believe and not believe the same thing at the same time. But the scenario is perfectly possible without Bill being irrational. We have indicated Frege's solution for this problem: in certain embedded contexts a sentence doesn't express a truth-value ("Bedeutung") but a proposition ("Sinn"). Here are the propositions expressed by the two complements:

(40) a. 〚**Mary** is **obnoxious**〛 = $\lambda w.$Mary is obnoxious in w.
     b. 〚**Mary snores**〛 = $\lambda w.$Mary snores in w.

A proposition reconstructs what Wittgenstein called the *truth-condition* of a sentence: We know the meaning of a sentence when we know under which conditions it is true. Think of possible worlds as scenes presented on a TV screen. We want to find out of some person whether he knows the meaning of **Mary snores**. We show him scenes in which Mary snores and others in which she doesn't. The test person has to answer the question: Is the sentence **Mary snores** true in this scene or not? If he gives the correct answer for each scene, we conclude that he has understood the sentence. In fact, the function in (40b) assigns 1 to every scene in which Mary snores and 0 to every scene in which she doesn't. So this notion of proposition is a reasonable approximation to the truth-condition of a sentence.

Sentence meanings like those in (40) are called *intensions*. Not only sentences have intensions but also every expression of the language has one, be it basic or complex. The language IL is designed to reconstruct that idea. The name IL reminds of Montague's *Intensional Logic*; cf. Montague (1970a, 1970c, 1973). The system used here has, however, a slightly different syntax from Montague's IL. It is the system sketched in chapter 12 of H&K. For a systematic discussion of intensional semantics and related issues, see article 7 [Semantics: Theories] (Zimmermann) *Model-theoretic semantics*.

6.2 Syntax and semantics of IL

The initially rather confusing feature of the language IL is that the types are largely as before but they encode something different, namely *intensions*. For instance the meaning of **snores**$_{et}$ will be the intension [λw ∈ W.λx.x snores in w], where W is the set of *possible worlds*. Only when we apply the verb meaning to a particular world w, we obtain an *extension*, viz. the set [λx.x snores in w]. I will say something more about this in a moment. Let us introduce the syntax first.

The type system for the language is slightly richer. There are the types of EL plus a new type *s* ("sense") that can be prefixed to any EL-type producing an IL-type. The type grammar is therefore this:

(41) The type system for IL
 The basic types are e and t. The complex types are generated by two rules:
 (a) If a and b are types, then (ab) is a type.
 (b) If a is a type, (sa) is a type.

The system of semantic domains belonging to IL is the following one:

(42) a. $D_e = E$ = the set of individuals
 b. $D_{(ab)} = D_b^{D_a}$
 c. $D_{(sa)} = D_a^W$, where W is the set of possible worlds.

The functions in D_{sa} are called *a-intensions*. If f is an a-intension and w is a possible word, f(w) is the *extension of f in w*.

The syntax of IL is more or less the same as that of EL. The only innovation is the rule IFA, which is due to H&K.

(43) *The syntax of IL*
 consists of the same rules as the syntax of EL with the addition of the following rule:
 If α is an IL-tree of type (sa)b and β is an IL-tree of type a, then [$_b$ αβ] is an IL-tree of type b. (IFA)

The rule is called *Intensional Functional Application*.

The interpretation of IL depends on a semantic lexicon, i.e. a function F that interprets the lexical trees.

At this step we have to be aware of the main characteristics of IL: *the meanings of expressions of type a are a-intensions*. In other words, if α is of type a, then ⟦α⟧ will not be in D_a but in D_{sa}. Here are some entries of our EL-lexicon in (16) adapted to this IL-requirement. (Instead of "λw ∈ W" I will write "λw".)

(44) Some entries of the semantic lexicon
$F(\mathbf{Mary}_e) = \lambda w.\text{Mary}$
$F(\mathbf{snores}_{et}) = \lambda w.\lambda x_e.x \text{ snores in } w.$
$F(\mathbf{child}_{et}) = \lambda w.\lambda x_e.x \text{ is a child in } w.$
$F(\mathbf{hates}_{e(et)}) = \lambda w.\lambda x_e.\lambda y_e.y \text{ hates } x \text{ in } w.$
$F(\mathbf{obnoxious}_{et}) = \lambda w.\lambda x_e.x \text{ is obnoxious in } w.$
$F(\mathbf{every}_{(et)((et)t)}) = \lambda w.\lambda P_{et}.\lambda Q_{et}.(\forall x)(P(x) \to Q(x))$

In order to be able to interpret the sentences in (39), we add the entries for **not** and **believes**.

(45) $F(\mathbf{not}_{tt}) = \lambda w.\lambda x_t.x = 0.$
$F(\mathbf{believes}_{(st)(et)}) = \lambda w.\lambda p_{st}.\lambda x_e.x \text{ believes } p \text{ in } w.$

The interpretation for **believes** looks rather trivial because it does not analyse what it means to believe something. Following Hintikka (1969), the standard analysis for **believe** is that of a verbal quantifier: "x believes p in world w" is true if p is true in every world w' compatible with what x believes in w. For our purposes this analysis is not relevant. The important point is that the object of **believe** has to be a proposition and not a truth-value. If we look at the types of our lexical entries we see that the entry of **believes** is the only one that has an intensional type as an argument. Functors with such a type are called *intensional*. Functors that only have extensional types as arguments are *extensional*. The intensions expressed by extensional functors are constant functions.

Given the semantic lexicon, we are in a position to state a recursive interpretation $[\![.]\!]$ for the language IL. This function depends on the model $M = (E, \{0,1\}, W, F)$ and a variable assignment g.

(46) The *interpretation* $[\![.]\!]^{M,g}$ *for IL*
1. Let α be a lexical tree of type a. Then $[\![\alpha]\!]^{M,g} = F(\alpha)$. (L)
2. Let x be a variable of type a. Then $[\![x]\!]^{M,g} = \lambda w.g(x)$. (Var)
3. Let γ be a branching tree of type b with daughters α of type ab and β of type a. Then $[\![\gamma]\!]^{M,g} = \lambda w[[\![\alpha]\!]^{M,g}(w)([\![\beta]\!]^{M,g}(w))]$. (FA)
4. Let γ be a branching tree of type b with daughters α of type (sa)b and β of type a. Then $[\![\gamma]\!]^{M,g} = \lambda w[[\![\alpha]\!]^{M,g}(w)([\![\beta]\!]^{M,g})]$. (IFA)
5. Let γ be a branching tree of type at with daughters α and β both of type at. Then $[\![\gamma]\!]^{M,g} = \lambda w.\lambda x_a.[\ [\![\alpha]\!]^{M,g}(w)(x) \ \& \ [\![\beta]\!]^{M,g}(w)(x)\ ]$. (PM)
6. Let α be a tree of type ab of the form $[_{ab} \lambda x\beta]$, x a variable of type a and β a tree of type b. Then $[\![[_{ab} \lambda x\beta]]\!]^{M,g} = \lambda w.\lambda u \in D_a.[\![\beta]\!]^{M,g[x/u]}(w)$ (λ)

6.3 Complement clauses: IFA or FA + ^

There are two methods to compose a complement clause with the embedding verb: either we need H&K's new rule IFA or we insert a covert operator in front of the complement, viz. Montague's operator ^. In the latter case we can work with FA. ^ is a type shifter. It shifts any type a to the type sa. This is the first example that we have to insert covert operators in the syntax for reasons of interpretation, or we have to enrich the semantic composition rules. We will be faced with this alternative many more times.

We are now in a position to analyse the sentences in (39). The SS of (39a) is this:

(47) $[_S$ **Bill**$_e$ [**believes**$_{(st)(et)}$ $[_{CP}$ that $[_S$ **Mary**$_e$ $[_{VP}$ is $[_{AP}$ **obnoxious**$_{et}$]]]]]

I am assuming that "that" and "is" are semantically empty and hence deleted by **FI**. After type projection we obtain the following IL-tree:

(48) $[_t$ **Bill**$_e$ $[_{et}$ **believes**$_{(st)(et)}$ $[_t$ **Mary**$_e$ $[_{et}$ **obnoxious**$_{et}$]]]]

At first sight it looks as if we had a type clash between the types of the daughters of the matrix VP-node, because its daughters are of type (st)(et) and t respectively. These cannot be put together by the rule FA, but the rule IFA takes care of them. Let us see how this works. I leave it to the reader to convince herself that $[_t$ **Mary**$_e$ $[_{et}$ **obnoxious**$_{et}$]] expresses indeed the proposition in (40a), i.e. we assume:

$[\![[_t$ **Mary**$_e$ $[_{et}$ **obnoxious**$_{et}$]$]\!] = \lambda w'$.Mary is obnoxious in w'.

We calculate the meaning of the matrix VP:
$[\![[_{et}$ **believes**$_{(st)(et)}$ $[_t$ **Mary**$_e$ $[_{et}$ **obnoxious**$_{et}$]]]$]\!]$
$= \lambda w[[\![$**believes**$_{(st)(et)}]\!](w)(\lambda w'$.Mary is obnoxious in w')]   **(IFA)** and assumption
$= \lambda w[\lambda w.\lambda p_{st}.\lambda x_e.x$ believes p in w] (w)($\lambda w'$.Mary is obnoxious in w')]   (L)
$= \lambda w[\lambda x_e.x$ believes [$\lambda w'$.Mary is obnoxious in w'] in w] λ-conversion: 2×

Next we calculate the meaning of the entire sentence:
$[\![$ $[_t$ **Bill**$_e$ $[_{et}$ **believes**$_{(st)(et)}$ $[_t$ **Mary**$_e$ $[_{et}$ **obnoxious**$_{et}$]]]] $]\!]$
$= \lambda w[$ $[\![$ $[_{et}$ **believes**$_{(st)(et)}$ $[_t$ **Mary**$_e$ $[_{et}$ **obnoxious**$_{et}$]]] $]\!](w)([\![$**Bill**$_e$ $]\!]$ (w))]   (FA)
$= \lambda w[\lambda w[\lambda x_e.x$ believes [$\lambda w'$.Mary is obnoxious in w'] in w](w)(λw.Bill(w))]

(L, FA, previous calculation)
= $\lambda w[[\lambda x_e.x$ believes $[\lambda w'.$Mary is obnoxious in w'$]$ in w$]$(Bill)] λ-conversion: 2×
= $\lambda w[$Bill believes $[\lambda w'.$Mary is obnoxious in w'$]$ in w$]$ λ-conversion

It is revealing to compare the rule IFA with Richard Montague's method to deal with intensional operators. Montague's IL contains a logical operator ^, which may be called *up*-operator. It converts an expression of type *a* into one of type *sa*. Here is the syntax and semantics.

(49) *Montague's ^-operator*
 If $[_a \alpha]$ is a tree of type a, then $[_{sa} {}^\wedge[_a\alpha]]$ is a tree of type sa.
 $[\![[_{sa}{}^\wedge[_a\alpha]]\,]\!]^{M,g} = \lambda w[\lambda w'[\![[_a\alpha]\,]\!]^{M,g}(w')] = \lambda w.[\![[_a\alpha]\,]\!]^{M,g}$

Thus the intension of $^\wedge\alpha$ is a function that assigns to any world w the intension of α. In other words, the extension of $^\wedge\alpha$ in world w is the intension of α. Montague assumes that *that*-clauses are translated into IL-trees prefixed with ^. If we do that, we don't need the rule IFA, FA suffices. Let us see how this works. Let us assume that the LF of (39a) is not (48) but the following tree instead:

(50) $[_t$ **Bill**$_e$ $[_{et}$ **believes**$_{(st)(et)}$ $[_{st}$ ^$[_t$ **Mary**$_e$ $[_{et}$ **obnoxious**$_{et}]]]]]$

The matrix VP doesn't exhibit a type conflict, and we can use FA for the evaluation. The reader may compute for herself that the complement now expresses the following intension:

(51) $[\![\,[_{st}$ ^$[_t$ **Mary**$_e$ $[_{et}$ **obnoxious**$_{et}]]]\,]\!] = \lambda w[\lambda w'.$Mary is obnoxious in w'$]$

Note that this is *not* the proposition that Mary is obnoxious. It is the intension that assigns any world the proposition that Mary is obnoxious. This is the correct meaning for the computation of the VP-meaning via FA. The reader may check that the following evaluation is true:

$[_{et}$ **believes**$_{(st)(et)}$ $[_{st}$ ^$[_t$ **Mary**$_e$ $[_{et}$ **obnoxious**$_{et}]]]]$
= $\lambda w\,[[\![$**believes**$_{(st)(et)}]\!]\,(w)([\![[_{st}$ ^$[_t$ **Mary**$_e$ $[_{et}$ **obnoxious**$_{et}]]]]\!]\,(w))]$ FA
= $\lambda w[\lambda x_e.x$ believes $[\lambda w'.$Mary is obnoxious in w'$]$ in w$]$

This is the same intension we had computed using the H&K strategy, i.e. IFA and no ^-operator. The answer is that both methods are equivalent. We may regard the ^-operator as a logical operation that helps to eliminate the type conflict between an operator of type *(sa)b* and an argument of type a. We prefix the argument with ^ and the conflict is solved. H&K's IFA put the information that the functor does not apply to the extension of the argument but to the intension into the composition rule. The lesson to be drawn from this is that type conflicts do not exist as such. Whether the types of the daughters of a branching node are in conflict or not is a matter of the composition rules that determine the interpretation of the language. Montague's system doesn't have IFA, but it has the ^-operator instead. In what follows, we will stick to H&K's rule IFA.

Here is the summary of this section. The meaning of complement clauses cannot be truth-values. They must be something more fine-grained, viz. propositions. This motivates the notion of intensions as functions from worlds to extensions. The expressions of intensional languages denote intensions. We obtain an extension if the expression is evaluated at some world. We have two methods to treat intensional functors. The first is the introduction of an additional interpretation of EM, viz. IFA. The second method is the insertion of a covert type shifter, Montague's ^-operator. Both methods do the same work. I know of no empirical argument that favours one method over the other.

6.4 Modality

The section makes the following points. We motivate the need of *Reconstruction*: a DP is interpreted at the position of its trace. Modals are raising verbs: the subject of a VP embedded under a modal is raised at SS to the subject position of the modal. If the subject is a generalised quantifier and it is interpreted at its SS-position, we obtain the so-called *de re* interpretation. But modal constructions have a second reading, the so-called *de dicto* interpretation. We obtain it, if we interpret the quantifier in the position of its trace.

The second point concerns the status of the world parameter. An intensional interpretation depends on the world of evaluation. World variables do not appear in the syntax, they are implicit parameters. But quantifiers in modal constructions do not only have *de re* and *de dicto* readings. For indefinites we have a third reading, the so-called *non-specific de re* reading. This reading cannot be expressed in an intensional framework but requires world variables in the syntax. World variables are pronouns that are never pronounced.

6.4.1 de re/de dicto

Modals are quantifiers over possible worlds that are restricted by a contextually given set of worlds called *conversational background* (Kratzer) or *accessibility relation* (Kripke). They are raising verbs. If the subject of the modified VP ("the prejacent") is a quantifier, we observe the so-called *de re/de dicto* ambiguity. The latter reading requires *reconstruction* of the quantifier on the way from SS to LF. *Reconstruction* therefore is a rule of construal.

Here is a modalised sentence with its SS and LF:

(52) You may/must be infected.

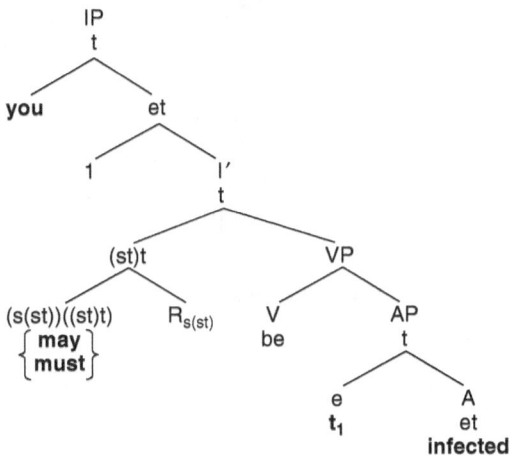

The meanings of the two modals are these:

(53) a. Possibility: $F(\mathbf{may}) = \lambda w.\lambda R_{s(st)}.\lambda p_{st}.(\exists w')[R(w)(w') \& p(w')]$
b. Necessity: $F(\mathbf{must}) = \lambda w.\lambda R_{s(st)}.\lambda p_{st}.(\forall w')[R(w)(w') \to p(w')]$

I am assuming that the subject originates as the subject of the adjective (or participle) **infected**. It is raised to [Spec, IP] by IM ("A-movement"). The interpretation of this movement is the same as that of **QR**. **FI** makes these structures fully interpretable. (We have to use **IFA** when we apply the modal to the prejacent.) With respect to a variable assignment g, the two LFs mean:

(54) a. $\lambda w.(\exists w')[g(R)(w)(w') \& \text{you are infected in } w']$
b. $\lambda w.(\forall w')[g(R)(w)(w') \to \text{you are infected in } w']$

Think of g(R) as the function that assigns to each world w the symptoms you have in w plus the proposition that you are infected if you have symptom x and you are infected or drunk if you have symptom y. Consider a world w_1 in which you have symptom x. In this world both propositions are true. Next consider a world w_2 in which you have symptom y. In this world the proposition in (54a) is true but that in (54b) is false.

Next consider a sentence with a quantifier in subject position. It has the two readings indicated in (55a) and (b).

(55) Everyone may be infected.
 a. $\lambda w.(\forall x)[x$ is a person in $w \to (\exists w')[g(R)(w)(w')$ & x is infected in $w']]$
 b. $\lambda w.(\exists w')[g(R)(w)(w')$ & $(\forall x)[x$ is a person in $w' \to x$ is infected in $w']]$

The first reading is called *de re*: the quantifier ranges over persons in the evaluation world, the "actual" world. The second reading is called *de dicto*: the quantifier speaks about persons in the accessible worlds.

We obtain the *de re* reading immediately from the surface by **FI**:

(56) [everyone [λ_1 [[may $R_{s(st)}$] [t_1 infected]]]]

To obtain the *de dicto* reading, two methods are available for this example: (a) We could abstract over a variable of type (et)t. Then the quantifier would be *semantically reconstructed* by λ-conversion. (b) We move the quantifier to the position of its trace (*syntactic reconstruction* **(Rec)**). Here is the derivation of a reconstructed LF:

(57) a. [everyone [λ_1 [[may $R_{s(st)}$] [t_1 infected]]]]
 b. => (Rec) [[may $R_{s(st)}$] [everyone infected]]

In Chomsky's MP, Rec is a rather natural process. Recall that the SS/SO obtained by Internal Merge has not exactly the form in (57a) but rather the following one:

(58) [everyone$_1$ [[may $R_{s(st)}$] be [everyone$_1$ infected]]]]

FI says that we have to delete uninterpretable stuff. One way of doing that is to delete the copy in base position leaving the index, which is interpreted as a variable. This gives us (57a). The other possibility is to delete the moved DP with its index. The index at the copy in base position doesn't make sense semantically anymore, and it is therefore deleted. This gives us the *de dicto* LF in (57b).

6.4.2 Non-specific de re

There is a reading in modal constructions that cannot be obtained by means of the methods outlined. Consider the following sentence:

(59) A friend of mine must win.

The scenario is this: My three friends Anna, Bertha and Cecile participate in a competition and I want one of them to win no matter which one, I like them with equal love. If I give the DP **a friend of mine** wide scope with respect to the modal, I have a wish about a particular friend. This is not the case. If I give it narrow scope, I seem to refer to the friends in the bouletic accessible worlds. There my friends might be very different from those in the actual world. The reading in question has been discovered by Fodor (1970), who gives the example "Mary wanted to buy a hat just like mine", and has been called *non-specific de re*. Von Fintel & Heim (2000: ch. 6.1) point out that the reading is best analysed by assuming a world pronoun **w-pro** as an argument of **a friend of mine**. **w-pro** has to be bound by stipulation. In other words, we must be able to refer to the hitherto implicit world argument in the syntax, i.e., we replace our intensional language by a purely extensional one. By convention we assume that the world argument is the first argument of a predicate. In order to form a proposition, von Fintel & Heim assume that these are formed by PRO-movement. The authors assume a **W-PRO** is generated at an s-position, where s is the type of worlds. **W-PRO** (but not **w-pro**!) is semantically empty and must be moved for type reasons generating a λ-operator. Here are some analyses:

(60) SS: [$_t$ a friend of mine w-pro$_1$ [$_{et}$ wins W-PRO]]
 => PRO-movement (**QR**)
 LF: W-PRO λ$_1$[$_t$ a friend of mine w-pro$_1$ [$_{et}$ wins t$_1$]]
 = λw.(∃x)[x is a friend of mine in w & x wins in w]

The representation of the *de dicto* reading is this:

(61) W-PRO λ$_2$ **must(t$_2$)(R)** W-PRO λ$_1$[$_t$ a friend of mine w-pro$_1$ [$_{et}$ win t$_1$]]

Here, **w-pro$_1$** is bound by λ$_1$ (and therefore indirectly by the modal). The *de re* reading is generated by giving the indefinite term wide scope with respect to the modal:

(62) W-PRO λ$_2$ a friend of mine w-pro$_2$ λ$_3$ **must(t$_2$)(R)** W-PRO λ$_1$[$_t$ t$_3$ [$_{et}$ win t$_1$]]

This time the **w-pro** of the indefinite is bound by the matrix **W-PRO** and hence will refer to the actual world, if the proposition is applied to it.

We now see what the method buys: we can represent Fodor's *non-specific de re* reading by leaving the indefinite in the scope of the modal but binding its **w-pro** by the matrix **W-PRO**:

(63) The non-specific *de re* reading
W-PRO λ_2 **must(t_2)(R)** W-PRO $\lambda_1 [_t$ **a friend of mine w-pro$_2$** $[_{et}$ **win t_1**]]

Note that our lexical entries haven't changed, but the types have changed. The first argument of a predicate will always be a world. For instance, the rule for **wins** will be

(64) $F(\textbf{wins}_{s(et)}) = \lambda w.\lambda x.x$ wins in w.

Fodor's observation shows that something like this is the correct approach and the switch to an extensional language with world arguments is ultimately mandatory. We will however stick to our intensional language IL because most semanticists assume something like this.

A note on the literature. The key idea for intensional semantics is that the meaning of a sentence can be identified with its truth-condition; it is due to Wittgenstein (1922/1984: 4.024). Cresswell (1991) takes difference in truth-conditions as the most certain principle for the non-identity of meaning. The semantics for modality was invented by Kripke (1959). The unification of Kripke's semantics for an application to natural language is due to different publications by A. Kratzer, e.g. Kratzer (1977, 1978, 1981). The intension/extension dichotomy is due to the Frege tradition in the philosophy of language. Important systems that do it with a unified system of meanings (basically intensions without extensions) are Lewis (1972) and Cresswell (1973). The detailed development of intensional logical languages and their application to the semantic interpretation is due to the work of Richard Montague; the milestones for the syntax/semantics interface are Montague (1970b, 1970a, 1973). The need for reconstruction in modal constructions is presumably first addressed in May (1985). The examples of section 6.4.2 are taken from von Fintel & Heim (2000). The theory of **w-pro/W-PRO** is due to these authors. Evidence that something like this is necessary is much older; see e.g. Heim (1991). The typed language needed for the implementation of the theory is Gallin's ty2-language; cf. Gallin (1975). For a more extensive discussion of modality, see article 14 [Semantics: Noun Phrases and Verb Phrases] (Hacquard) *Modality*.

7 The interpretation of traces

Chomskyan Generative Grammar assumes the existence of traces, which are generated by movement. Ignoring reconstruction and complications stemming from the copy theory of movement, the simplest assumption is that all DP-traces are λ-bound variables. Recall that QR leaves a co-indexed trace and interprets the movement index as a λ-operator. Here we review different kinds of DP-movement and what they mean for the organization of the syntax/semantics interface. Another trace is generated by the semantically empty pronoun PRO that must be moved for type reasons, thereby creating a λ-abstract.

7.1 A-movement

Here are two typical raising constructions in the GB-style; see Chomsky (1981):

(65) a. John$_1$ AGR [was arrested t$_1$]
    +Case   −Case
b. John$_1$ AGR [may [t$_1$ win]]
    +Case   −Case

These traces are what Chomsky calls NP-traces (or anaphors) and the movement that generates the trace is called A-Movement (movement to an argument position). The verb meaning is generated by a passive operator, which applies to the participle. A passivized verb doesn't assign a case to its argument in the GB-theory. Therefore the DP **John** has to be moved to a case position, viz. the subject position of the finite sentence. Assuming that A-movement is interpreted like QR, the LFs of the two constructions are these:

(66) a. **John** λ$_1$ was_arrested t$_1$
b. **John** λ$_1$ may t$_1$ win

In these cases, Raising is semantically inert because names are semantically scope-less. In other words, we can reconstruct the subject to its D-position and obtain the same interpretation. But when the subject is a quantifier, A-movement may affect the interpretation.

Suppose **was_arrested** means $\lambda w.\lambda x.(\exists y)[person(y) \& arrest(y,x,w)]$, where tense is ignored. Consider the following constructions:

(67) a. Everyone$_1$ AGR [was arrested t$_1$]
    +Case   −Case
b. Everyone$_1$ AGR [may [t$_1$ win]]
    +Case   −Case

The LF for (67a) is the following:

(68) **everyone** λ_1 **was_arrested**(t_1)
= $\lambda w(\forall x)[person(x, w) \to (\exists y)[arrest(y,x,w)]]$

Since **was-arrested** is of type et, the quantifier cannot be interpreted at the position of its trace; it has wide scope with respect to the invisible logical subject of the passivized verb, viz. "someone".

On the other hand, (67b) can have two LFs because the subject can be interpreted at the position of its trace:

(69) a. **everyone** λ_1 **may$_R$ t_1 win**
= $\lambda w.(\forall x)[person(x,w) \to (\exists w')[wRw' \& win(x,w')]]$
b. **may$_R$ everyone win**
$\lambda w. (\exists w')[wRw' \& (\forall x)[person(x,w') \to win(x,w')]]$

So in this case, a morpho-syntactically motivated movement has an impact on possible interpretations.

Since case checking is a morphological thing, A-movement must be done at SS and not at the LF-branch. This is an important difference with respect to applications of QR motivated for type reasons, for disambiguation or for variable binding. In these cases there is no morphological motivation for movement and the movement is done on the LF-branch. This is the reason why QR may be covert. Raising may be regarded as overt QR. As we have seen, Raising doesn't exclude Reconstruction, where the latter is done on the LF-branch and is therefore covert.

7.2 A-bar movement

In this section we consider the interpretation of relative pronouns. There is a long tradition among semanticists to interpret moved relative pronouns as λ-operators that bind a variable in the base position of the pronoun. English relative pronouns are either overt (*who, whose, whom*) or covert, i.e. unpronounced, represented as WH.

(70) a. Bill is a boy who(m)$_4$ C Mary likes t_4
b. Bill is a boy WH$_4$ that Mary likes t_4

Relative pronouns occur in an argument position, so there is no morpho-syntactic reason such as case checking to move them. But they have to be moved for type reasons.

Assume that relative pronouns are semantically vacuous, i.e. they have no meaning and no type. When we move a relative pronoun, it leaves a co-indexed trace of type *e*. By FI we delete the pronoun at LF and are left with the adjoined index, the wanted λ-operator. This gives us the LF for the relative clause in (70b):

(71) [$_{et}$ λ$_4$ [$_t$ **Mary**$_e$ [$_{et}$ **likes**$_{e(et)}$ t$_4$]]]

Chomsky calls the kind of movement involved here A-bar as opposed to A-movement presented in the previous section. There is no semantic difference with respect to the interpretation of the trace. The difference is that in the previous case the moved DP had meaning whereas here it doesn't have meaning. Thus WH-movement in relative clauses amounts to λ-abstraction.

7.3 PRO-movement

In the GB-theory PRO is the subject of an infinitive clause and it is not moved at all:

(72) a. Bill wants [$_{CP}$ PRO to win]
      b. [$_{CP}$ PRO to win] is pleasant

With Chierchia (1989) many semanticists assume that non-finite CPs express properties, i.e., objects of type s(et). It seems to be plausible then that these are generated in analogy to the relative clauses studied in the last section. H & K propose that PRO is a semantically empty pronoun without type and meaning. It follows that PRO must be QR-ed for type reasons. Somehow the theory has to make sure that this movement is local, i.e. PRO is adjoined to its CP. This theory would generate the LF [λ$_n$. t$_n$ win] for the infinitival in the examples. **Want** and **pleasant** then have to select a property of type s(et).

H&K launch the natural generalisation that PRO may be the subject of all the other lexical projections as well (NP, AP, PP). This theory easily explains the occurrence of quantifiers within such phrases, i.e. *Quantifying into NP*.

(73) **Every owner of a Macintosh hates Windows.** (Quantifying into NP)

Note first that the N-object **a Macintosh** must have narrow scope with respect to the determiner **every**. If QR gave the quantifier wide scope with respect to **every**, we would obtain a reading that is at best marginal, viz.

(74) ? (∃x)[Mac(x) & (∀y)[y is an owner of x → y hates Windows]]

The reading we are after is:

(75) $(\forall y)[(\exists x)[\text{Mac}(x) \;\&\; y \text{ is an owner of } x] \to y \text{ hates Windows}]$

Here is the SS of the subject DP with **PRO** as the NP subject.

(76) [$_{DP}$ **every** [$_{NP}$ **PRO** [$_{N'}$ **owner**$_{e(et)}$ [$_{PP}$ **of** [$_{DP((et)t)}$ **a Mac**]]]]] (SS)

Ignoring the intervening preposition **of**, we encounter the familiar type clash between the head noun **owner** and the object **a Mac**. The clash is resolved by QR. First we QR **a Mac** and then we QR PRO over **a Mac**. This gives us the following LF:

(77) [**every** [~~PRO~~ λ_1[**a Mac** [λ_2 [t_1 [**owner** t_2]]]]]]

We interpret **owner** exactly as if it were the transitive verb **own**. The reader may convince himself that this structure expresses the generalised quantifier $\lambda P_{et}.(\forall y)[(\exists x)[\text{Mac}(x) \;\&\; y \text{ is an owner of } x] \to P(y)]$.

An example requiring *Quantifying into PP* is analysed in H&K, p. 221 ff.:

(78) Every student from a foreign country is admitted.

We analyse it exactly as before, i.e., the input for the rules of construal is the following SS for the subject:

(79) **every student** [$_{PP}$ PRO **from**$_{e(et)}$ **a foreign country**]

An example involving an adjective might be the following:

(80) **No guest** [$_{AP}$ PRO **dissatisfied**$_{e(et)}$ [$_{PP}$ with **something**]] **complained**
 = $\neg(\exists x)[x \text{ is a guest } \& (\exists y)[y \text{ is a thing } \& x \text{ is dissatisfied with } y] \& x \text{ complained}]$

Here *with* is a semantically empty preposition.

All these movements are covert. Hence they take place on the LF branch.

To summarise this section: the grammar has to assume semantically empty pronouns, which may be overt (the relative pronoun **WH**) or covert (**PRO**). These must be QR-ed for type reasons. Semantically empty elements thus provide a close link between the grammar of natural languages and that of λ-abstraction. The method helps to understand a large array of constructions.

Notes on the literature. Relative pronouns have always been interpreted as λ-operators by semanticists. The tradition goes back at least to Quine (1960b: 121). It remained, however, quite mysterious how the λ-operator was connected with WH-movement. The puzzle was solved by H&K's theory of semantically empty pronouns. In Heim & Kratzer (1998), the authors develop such a theory for **PRO** only, but the extension to relative pronouns is obvious. For a detailed discussion of questions, see article 5 [Semantics: Sentence and Information Structure] (Krifka) *Questions*.

8 Abstract operators in syntax and the PF/LF-branches

Compositional semantics requires the assumption of many abstract (covert) operators, i.e. material that is not pronounced. For the syntax the problem arises how these operators are made visible. One method is that the operator carries a feature F that has a reflex somewhere in the morphology. The feature of the operator is usually called interpretable (prefix i) and its morphological reflex is called un-interpretable (prefix u). The implementation of the agreement relation between the features is one of the central topics of Minimalism. Most current syntactic approaches assume movement somewhere: the material carrying one feature is moved to a local environment of the other feature and there the features agree. Or there is abstract movement of one feature and the material stays in situ. Another method is long distance agreement (e.g. "Multiple Agree") or feature transmission under binding. For the syntax/semantics interface the important question is where features are checked. The discovery of the correct LF of an expression hosting an abstract operator may be obscured by PF rules such as Head Movement, Topicalization, Deletion (ellipsis) and others. PF rules don't influence semantic interpretation but they may prevent the analyst from finding the correct LF because he confuses PF with SS or even LF.

8.1 The question operator

Questions involve both overt and covert WH-movement and are therefore interesting constructions for understanding the interface rules. In Karttunen's (1977) theory of questions, the sentence in (81a) expresses the intension in (81b):

(81) a. Which boy snores?
 b. $\lambda w.\lambda p_{st}.(\exists x)[x$ is a boy in w & p = [$\lambda w'.x$ snores in w'] & p(w)]

Suppose that Bill and John are the boys in w that snore in w. Then the question assigns to w the set of propositions {that Bill snores, that John snores}. The SS/SO of the question is this:

(82) [$_{CP}$ [**which boy**]$_1$ [$_{C'}$[$_C$ Q$_{(st)((st)t)}$ WH] [$_S$ t$_1$ **snores**]]]

The determiner **which** has the same meaning as the indefinite article, in other words **which boy** means the same as **a boy**. The movement rule that places the wh-phrase to the position [Spec, CP] is called WH-movement. It has the same semantic characteristics as QR. To obtain the correct meaning for the question the covert interrogative operator Q in C is a crucial ingredient:

(83) The *question operator*
$F(Q_{(st)((st)t)}) = \lambda w.\lambda p_{st}.\lambda q_{st}.p = q$

The pronoun WH is semantically void. It may be thought of as a relative pronoun of type st. In order to obtain an LF, we apply WH-movement and delete the uninterpretable material by FI. The result is this:

(84) A *constituent question*
[$_{(st)t}$ ~~WH-PRO~~$_{2,st}$ [$_t$ [**which boy**] [$_{et}$ λ$_1$[$_t$[$_{(st)t}$ Q$_{(st)((st)t)}$ t$_{2,st}$] [$_t$ t$_{1,e}$ **snores**]]]]]

The interpretation of the C'-node requires IFA. The reader may check that the LF gives us precisely the intension in (81b).

Apart from the movement of the empty pronoun WH, the LF is almost the same as the SS/SO. Multiple questions, however, require covert WH-movement of wh-phrases, i.e. the rule belongs to the rules of construal as well. Consider the following question:

(85) **Which girl likes which boy?**

The SS is as before with the object left in base position. The LF is generated by WH-moving the object to [Spec,CP]:

(86) A *multiple question*
[$_{(st)t}$ ~~WH-PRO~~$_{2,st}$ [$_t$[**which boy**] [$_{et}$ λ$_3$[$_t$ [**which girl**] [$_{et}$ λ$_1$[$_t$[$_{(st)t}$ Q$_{(st)((st)t)}$ t$_{2,st}$] [$_t$ t$_{1,e}$ **likes** t$_{3,e}$]]]]]]]
= $\lambda w.\lambda p_{st}.(\exists x)[x$ is a boy in w & $(\exists y)[y$ is a girl in w & $p = [\lambda w'.y$ likes x in w'] & p(w)]]

The analysis of **whether**-questions is still under debate. The simplest analysis is presumably due to Guerzoni (2004). It treats **whether** as an existential quantifier over one-place truth-functions. The question **whether it is raining** is then interpreted as [λwλp.[p = λw'.rain(w') or p = λw'.¬rain(w')] and p(w)]. The details are a bit complicated, therefore I will not introduce them. To make the question operator Q visible, it is assumed that it has the feature [iWH], which agrees with the feature [uWH] of the wh-phrase. In the Karttunen semantics of questions the wh-phrase must move to [Spec,C] to make the question interpretable. It is therefore plausible to assume that the agreement between Q and the wh-phrases is checked in this position. Given that WH-movement may be covert, the features are checked at LF. As to be expected, languages differ with respect to wh-movement: in some languages we have multiple wh-movement at SS (e.g. Bulgarian) in others wh-phrases stay in situ at SS (e.g. Chinese). In a framework that distinguishes between SS/SO and LF it is straightforward to account for the difference.

Questions motivate the existence of QR in surface syntax and LF.

8.2 The comparative operator

Most comparative constructions are elliptic, i.e. they lack material that is needed for the interpretation. We will see that there are two ways of treating the ellipsis. Either the SS/SO contains already empty phrases and the missing material is inserted at the LF-branch by a copy rule, or the material is present at SS/SO and deleted at the LF-branch. Another interesting feature of comparative constructions is that the comparative operator ER is best analysed as covert. It is made visible by the comparative morphology of the adjective. The semantics of the constructions will require the application of QR.

Our first example is:

(87) The table is longer than the drawer is wide.

The standard assumption is that the *than*-clause is the complement of a comparative operator ER. The comparative morpheme *-er* of the adjective signalizes the presence of the operator. The DS/SS of the sentence is the following:

(88) SS: The table is [ER than the drawer is wide]-long(er)

The analysis assumes that ER is the head of a Degree Phrase (DegP), which is generated as a degree argument of the adjective. Let us assume that (88) is the input for PF and LF. Thus we have an example for an SS that is quite different from what we say. We assume that the DegP is extraposed at the PF-branch. The covert ER operator is deleted at PF after checking the comparative features.

(89) PF: The table is _long(er) [ER than the drawer is wide]

Starting from the SS in (88), the DegP is QR-ed at LF and we roughly obtain the following structure:

(90) [ER than the drawer is wide] λ_1 the table is t_1 long(er)

More precisely, the analysis works as follows:

(91) Degree adjectives   type d(et)
$F(\textbf{wide/long}) = \lambda w.\lambda d.\lambda x.\text{WIDTH/LENGTH}(x,w) \geq d$

d is the type of degrees. LENGTH is a measure function that assigns lengths to objects.

(92) The *comparative operator ER*: category Deg, type (dt)((dt)t)
$F(ER) = \lambda w.\lambda P_{dt}.\lambda Q_{dt}.(\forall d)[P(d) \rightarrow Q(d)] \ \& \ (\exists d)[Q(d) \ \& \ \neg P(d)]$
$= \lambda w.P \subset Q$

ER is thus simply a strong universal quantifier over degrees, which says that its restriction is a proper subset of its nuclear scope.

We know that generalised quantifiers must be QR-ed when they occur in object position. After deletion of the uninterpretable stuff by FI, we therefore obtain the following LF:

(93) $[_{(dt)t}$ ER $[_{dt} \lambda_2$ **the drawer** t_2 **wide**$]] \lambda_3[_t$ **the table** $\lambda_1 [t_{1,e} \ t_{3,d}$ **long**$_{d(et)}]]]$
$= \lambda w.\lambda d[\text{the drawer in w is d-wide in w}] \subset \lambda d[\text{the table in w is d-long in w}]$

We have ignored tense and therefore deleted the auxiliary **is**.

Usually, the comparative operator is identified with the comparative morpheme **-er**, cf. e.g. Heim (2001). There is a problem for theories of this kind, however. The comparative morpheme **-er** is not pronounced at its SS-position. It is a part of the morphology of the adjective **long-er**. If *ER* were identical with the morpheme **-er**, it would be necessary to reconstruct it into the adjective at PF. Then the adjective must contain an **-er** trace. Recall, however, that *ER* is a sort of determiner. I don't know of any syntactic process that could move a part of the adjective to the quantifier position. Therefore, I will assume that *ER* is a phonetically empty operator that has the feature [iER], while an adjective with comparative morphology has the feature [uER]. The interpretable feature licenses the uninterpretable feature under binding. So the official representation is this:

(94) [$_S$**the table**$_1$ [$_{VP}$ is [$_{AP}$ t$_1$ [$_{DegP,(dt)t}$ ER$_{[iER]}$ [$_{CP}$WH$_2$ than **the drawer** is t$_2$ **wide**]] **long-**er$_{d(et)[u\text{-}ER]}$]]]

The agreement between the two features is presumably mediated via binding: the operator ER binds the degree variable of the adjective **longer**.

Comparative constructions show rather different manifestations on the different levels of syntax SS/SO, LF, and PF. The example discussed is one of the few cases where the complement clause is a full CP. But in most cases, the *than*-clause is reduced:

(95) a. Bill is taller than Mary ~~is tall~~
    b. Bill is taller than Mary is ~~tall~~

In (a) the VP is deleted ("Comparative Deletion") and in (b) only the AP is deleted ("Comparative Subdeletion"); cf. Bresnan (1973).

In fact, "deletion" is not the right term if we apply the method of ellipsis interpretation introduced in Williams (1977), where empty VPs are present at SS. Consider the following sentence:

(96) **Caroline observed more birds than Arnim did [$_{VP}$ Δ]**

The symbol Δ stands for a phonetically empty phrase. If we assume that DegP has been QR-ed at SS-structure already, the only thing that remains to do is to fill the VP-gap Δ via copying:
1. [ER than **Arnim** did [$_{VP}$ Δ]] λ$_1$[**Caroline** [$_{VP}$ **observe**d t$_1$ **more birds**]] SS + QR
2. [ER than **Arnim** did [$_{VP}$ **observe**d t$_1$ **more birds**]]
    λ$_1$[**Caroline** [$_{VP}$ **observe**d t$_1$ **more birds**]]   VP-copying

We have to QR the two DPs **[t more birds]** in object position and we have to apply **FI** and obtain a fully interpretable LF, which expresses the following proposition:

(97) λw.λd[Arnim observes d-many birds in w] ⊂ λd[Caroline observes d-many birds in w]

The comparative adjective **more** means the same as **many**. Recall that the comparative morphology means nothing, but it points to the semantic operator ER. We assume that the plural DP in object position has a covert indefinite article, which denotes the existential quantifier for pluralities.

(98) $F(\mathbf{more}_{d(et)}) = F(\mathbf{many}_{d(et)}) = \lambda w.\lambda d.\lambda x.|x| \geq d$, where $|x|$ denotes the cardinality of x

(99) $F(\exists_{(et)((et)t)}) = \lambda w.\lambda P_{et}.\lambda Q_{et}.P \cap Q \neq \emptyset$

The precise structure of the object DP in the example is therefore:

(100) $[_{DP,(et)t} [_D \exists] [_{NP,et} [_{AP,et} t_1 \mathbf{more}] [_{N,et} \mathbf{birds}]]]$
 $= \lambda w.\lambda P_{et}.(\exists x)[x \text{ are birds in } w \;\&\; |x| \geq d \;\&\; P(x)]$

(The trace t_1, i.e., the free variable d is bound by ER, which is located higher up in the LF.) We will say later how plural predication works. If we take it for granted, this is precisely the meaning we need for the construction.

Comparative deletion as exhibited by example (95a) is analysed exactly alike. The same holds for the subdeletion in (95b); the only difference is that this time the gap is an AP in the **than**-clause. I leave it to the reader to work out the ellipsis resolution for that example.

For the derivation of the LF, it is crucial that VP-copying applies after the application of QR because before the application of QR, the VP to be copied contains the $[_{VP} \Delta]$. Therefore an early copy process would lead us to an infinite loop. The phenomenon exhibited by the example is called *antecedent contained deletion*, where the term is motivated by a different treatment of ellipsis. Suppose that the SS/SO doesn't contain the empty VP but a full form. In order to find a matching VP that licenses the ellipsis, we first have to QR the DegP.

1. Caroline $[_{VP}$ observed [ER than Arnim did $[_{VP}$ observe many birds]]-many birds]
 SS/SO
2. [ER than Arnim did $[_{VP}$ ~~observe many birds~~]]$_i$ Caroline $[_{VP}$ observed t_i many birds]
 QR + VP-deletion

At SS/SO we don't find a second VP that matches the VP **observe many birds**, but after QR we find one provided we ignore the trace. This second method is used by Fiengo & May (1991) for other cases of VP-deletion. For both procedures the application of QR is essential. Both methods make an essential use of QR.

Note on the literature. Most approaches to the syntax of comparative constructions follow the seminal article Bresnan (1973). The semantics for *ER* and that of degree adjectives follows Heim (2001). Pioneer articles on the LF of comparatives are Cresswell (1976) and von Stechow (1984). For an extensive discussion of comparison constructions, see article 13 [Semantics: Lexical Structures and Adjectives] (Beck) *Comparison constructions*.

8.3 Tense operators

Tenses are abstract operators that are made visible by the tense morphology of the verb. In English, there are two semantic tenses Present and Past.

(101) a. $[\![N]\!] = \lambda w.\lambda P_{it}.P(s^*)$, where s* is the speech time
N has the feature [iN] "interpretable now"
b. $[\![PAST]\!] = \lambda w.\lambda t.\lambda P_{it}.\exists t'[t' < t \ \& \ P(t')]$
PAST has the feature [iP] "interpretable Past"

N reminds of "now". Verbs and other predicates have a temporal argument of type i. We assume that the argument is the first one. Up to now we have assumed that verbs like **called** have the type et. If we include tense, the verb has type i(et). (If we included Aspect, the verb would have an event argument instead of a time argument. Semantic aspects like Perfective or Imperfective would then link the events with times. We are ignoring these complications.) The entry of the verb is this:

(102) *Past tense morphology*
$F(\textbf{arrived}_{i(et)}) = \lambda w.\lambda t.\ \lambda x.x$ arrives in w at time t.
The verb has the feature [uP] "uninterpretable Past"

It is important to keep in mind that **arrives** has a tenseless meaning. It means precisely the same as the infinitive form **arrive**. This is so because the tense morphology has no semantic interpretation. But the morphology points, of course, to a semantic tense located elsewhere in the clause. That semantic tenses must be separated from their verb is obvious by looking at the interaction with time adverbs: time adverbs like **yesterday** or **tomorrow** must have narrow scope with respect to a semantic tense but wide scope with respect to the verb:

(103) John arrived yesterday
N λ_1 PAST(t_1) λ_2 [**yesterday**(t_2) **John arrived**(t_2)]
   iP   uP

Here **yesterday** means [λw.λt.t is on the day preceding the speech time s*]. The semantics of **tomorrow** is analogous. The adverb and the VP are composed by PM. In English, the semantic Future is expressed by the auxiliary **will**, which means [λw.λt.λP$_{it}$.(∃t' > t)P(t')]].

(104) John will arrive tomorrow
N λ$_1$ **will**(t$_1$) λ$_2$ [**John arrive**(t$_2$) **tomorrow**(t$_2$)]
iN   uN

Languages with a synthetic Future have an abstract tense operator FUT, which has the same meaning as **will**. For instance, the French counterpart of (104) is

(105) N λ$_1$ FUT(t$_1$) λ$_2$ [**Jean arrivera**(t$_2$) **demain**(t$_2$)]   (French)
         iF   uF

The two constructions are almost alike. The only difference is that we find a covert tense operator in French where English has an open one. The abstract operator has a reflex in the morphology of the verb. The split between semantic and morphological tense is best seen from long distance agreement phenomena as we see them in Sequence of Tense languages such as English. The following example is due to Abusch (1988), Ogihara (1996):

(106)   PAST John <u>decided</u> a week ago that in ten days at breakfast he <u>would</u> say to his
         [iP]   [uP]   [uP]

         mother that they <u>were</u> having their last meal together.
                           [uP]

The point is that we have three past forms but only one semantic PAST, which temporally locates **decides**. The verbs **would** and **were** are semantically tenseless and their tense morphology is licensed by the semantics PAST by a sort of multiple agreement.

There is a natural connection of these representations with QR: Semantic tenses like PAST(N) are quantifiers of type (it)t. They may be generated at the argument position of the verb and they must be QR-ed for type reasons. If a verb only has a temporal variable as argument, QR-ing of a higher tense could bind that variable as in the following example:

(107)   John saw(PAST(N)) a boy that was(t$_1$) crying like a baby   SS
        PAST(N) λ$_1$ John saw(t$_1$) a boy that was(t$_1$) crying like a baby   SS+QR

Thus QR makes it possible that two tensed verbs are bound by the same semantic tense. Another way to generate the structure is to generate PAST(N) at the surface position and to move a semantically empty pronoun TPRO from the temporal argument position of **saw** up to PAST(N). This method is used in von Stechow (2009) and Grønn & von Stechow (2011) and yields the same result. Both methods involve QR, perhaps even at SS/SO, because the binding of the temporal variable might be the vehicle for transmission of the temporal feature from the semantic tense to the verb.

A note on the literature. The idea that semantic tense has to be separated from morphological tense occurs in many places in the generative literature. For a recent motivation of an account along these lines, see Kusumoto (2005). The relation between semantic tense and verbs requires QR or something like temporal PRO movement; for the latter see von Stechow (2009). A general discussion of the issues of tense semantics is contained in article 13 [Semantics: Noun Phrases and Verb Phrases] (Ogihara) *Tense*.

8.4 Negation

Negation (NEG) is a simple operator. But the syntax can be very confusing if one has a wrong picture of it. NEG switches the truth-value of a sentence from truth to falsity and the other way round.

(108) $F(NEG) = \lambda w.\lambda t.T = 0.$

The simplest realisation in language would be an adverb like the German particle **nicht** ("not"). In German, adverbs have scope to the right. Hence we would expect that the adverb occurs in a sentence initial position. But already Jespersen (1917) was wondering why German has the negation at the end of a sentence in many cases. He thought that German was quite exceptional in this respect. As a simple example consider the following sentence:

(109) Das glaube ich nicht   (German)
       that believe I not

It looks as if the negation adverb **nicht** ("not") occurs at a sentence final position. A closer inspection, however, shows that this puzzle has an easy solution. Every syntactician of German would agree that the analysis of the sentence is something like this:

(110) DS: [$_{CP}$ C [$_{VP}$ nicht [$_{VP}$ ich das glaube]]]
SS: [$_{CP}$ das$_1$ [$_{C'}$ glaube$_2$ [$_{VP}$ ich$_3$ [$_{VP}$ nicht [$_{VP}$ t$_3$ t$_1$ t$_2$]]]]]

At SS the object is moved to [Spec, CP]. The finite verb is moved to C. The subject is moved to the subject position (or simply scrambled out of the VP; referential terms never occur in the scope of the negation **nicht** in German at s-structure). The negation particle **nicht** is not moved. If we disregard tense, it occupies a sentence initial position, exactly as Jespersen wants to have it. All these movements are *reconstructed* at LF and we are left with the configuration given by the DS. Another possible analysis is to say that Verb Movement and Topicalization are rules that apply at the PF-branch. In that case our DS would coincide with the SS and no reconstruction would be needed.

In Slavic languages (and Negative Concord languages in general), negation is expressed covertly as NEG and it is made visible at the verb and indefinites in the scope of NEG. In Russian the verb has the prefix **ne-** and the indefinites have the prefix **ni-**.

(111) Nikto   nichego ne videl.
n-person n-thing n-saw
'Nobody saw anything.'

The widely accepted analysis of the construction is due to Zeijlstra (2004). Negative indefinites mean the same as non-negative indefinites, i.e. n-person means **someone**, n-thing means **something**, and n-saw means **saw**. So we have no overt negation. But the n-words have an uninterpretable feature [uNEG], which must be checked by the negation operator NEG with feature [iNEG]. This checking process is called Multiple Agree. Disregarding QR, the LF for the construction is therefore the following:

(112) NEG [n-someone n-saw n-something]
= $\neg(\exists x)$[person(x) & $(\exists y)$[thing(y) & x saw y]]

Negative Concord has puzzled analysts for decades. Zeijlstra's analysis relies on the assumption that there may be covert semantic operators in the syntax, and these operators must be made visible by the morphology via an agreement relation.

Thus we have here a construction with three negative forms but only one semantic negation. Again the relation between the operator and the morphology is an agreement relation. The examples from German tell us that certain syntactic rules like V-movement, Topicalization and Scrambling should better apply at the

PF branch. The path to LF is before the application of these rules. The semantics of negation should be very simple.

A note on the literature. Negative Concord is not always such a clean phenomenon as in Slavic. There are mixed cases like Italian and French. Furthermore, some languages show the phenomenon of *scope splitting* (Germ. *Du (you) must (must) keine (no) Krawatte (tie) tragen (wear)* (= *It is not required that you wear a tie):* A negative indefinite is licensed by an abstract negation NEG across a modal. For a recent account of such and related phenomena see Penka (2010). See also article 2 [Semantics: Sentence and Information Structure] (Herburger) *Negation.*

8.5 Plural operators

The plural operator for nouns may perhaps be regarded as a lexical operation PL, but VPs can be pluralized in different ways: transitive verbs can be pluralized by a one-place or a two-place plural operator, di-transitive verbs can be pluralized as well by a two-place plural operator PL^2 and a three-place plural operator PL^3 respectively. The pluralization of verbs happens in the syntax, i.e., a plural operator applies to the VP. Generalized quantifiers may have scope interactions with the covert plural operators and we can derive readings that cannot be derived without such operators.

To understand these remarks we need some definitions. With Schwarzschild (1996) we identify individuals with their singletons. (The principle stems from Quine's set theory.)

(113) For any individual x: $x = \{x\} = \{\{x\}\} = ...$ ("Quine's innovation")

The sum of two individuals is their union (fusion):

(114) a. $x + y = x \cup y = \{x\} \cup \{y\} = \{x,y\}$
 b. $\Sigma M = \{x \mid (\exists y \in M)\, x \in y\}$, for any set of individuals.

x+y is the group consisting of the atoms x and y. This meaning is represented by non-Boolean **and**, a symbol of type e(ee). ΣM is the generalized sum/fusion, which forms groups of any size. The one-place plural operator PL^1 gives us the power set of M (perhaps minus the empty set and the singletons, possibilities we disregard).

(115) The 1-place plural operator PL:
 $[\![PL_{\langle et,et \rangle}]\!] = \lambda w.\lambda P_{et}.\{M \mid M \subseteq P\}$

This is the power set of M. We are ready for the first plural sentence:

(116) [**Anna and Bertha**] [PL **laugh**]

⟦**Anna and Bertha**⟧ = a+b. Suppose ⟦**laugh**⟧ = {a,b,c}. Then ⟦PL **laugh**⟧ = {∅, a, b, c, a+b, a+c, b+c, a+b+c}. Since a+b is in the extension of the plural predicate, the sentence is true.

One might think that one could get the same result by defining the subject as the generalized quantifier [λP.P(Anna) & P(Bertha)]. Cross-linguistic comparison shows that this would be a mistake. All languages that have overt plural morphology for verbs have the verb in the plural in this construction, e.g. Germ. **Anna und Berta lachen/*lach**t. Note that the denotation of the plural subject is not in the extension of the singular verb.

Next consider a sentence with a definite plural subject:

(117) [the [PL^1 girls]] [PL^1 laugh]

Here is a meaning for the *definite article* that works for singular and plural count nouns and for mass nouns likewise.

(118) $F(\textbf{the}_{(et)e}) = \lambda w.\lambda P_{et}:\exists x[P(x) \ \& \ \forall y[P(y) \to y \subseteq x].\iota x[P(x) \ \& \ \forall y[P(y) \to y \subseteq x]$

As an illustration we consider the LFs for **the girl** and **the** [PL **girls**]. Suppose, ⟦ **girl** ⟧ = {a}. So ⟦ **girl** ⟧ (a) is true. By Quine's innovation, a = {a} ⊆ {a}. This is the only girl. Therefore the presupposition is fulfilled and ⟦ **the girl** ⟧ = a. Suppose next, ⟦ **girl** ⟧ = {a,b}. Obviously, the presupposition is not fulfilled. So the article is undefined for this case. Now consider ⟦ **the** [PL **girls**] ⟧ for this scenario. ⟦ PL **girls** ⟧ = {∅, a, b, a+b}. Obviously a+b contains every group in the noun extension as a part. So the presupposition is fulfilled and ⟦ **the** [PL **girls**] ⟧ = a+b.

So far we had no argument for the claim that PL is a covert operator that applies in the syntax. It would be possible to have both singular and plural predicates in the lexicon. So we go to more complicated cases:

(119) a. Carl kissed the girls
    b. [**the** [PL **girls**]] PL[λ$_1$ **Carl kissed** t$_1$]

We assume that ⟦ **girl** ⟧ = {a,b}, ⟦ **Carl** ⟧ = c and ⟦ **kissed** ⟧ = {<c,a>, <c,b>}. Then ⟦PL[λ$_1$ **Carl kissed** t$_1$] ⟧ = {∅, a, b, a+b}. ⟦**the** [PL **girls**] ⟧ = a+b. Therefore the sentence is true in this scenario.

The construction of the LF is done as follows. First the object is QR-ed out of the *singular* VP. Then PL is inserted between the moved object and the λ-operator created by movement. This kind of insertion is called counter-cyclic in the recent literature.

The following example, which is due to Beck & Sauerland (2000), requires a two-place plural operator as we will see in a moment.

(120) The boys gave the girls a flower.

Here is a general definition of plural operators that modify n-place verbs. The definition is due to Sternefeld (1993):

(121) Let φ be a n-place predicate (of type $e^n t$). Then PL^n φ is of the same type. $[\![PL^n \varphi]\!]$ is the smallest relation R such that $[\![\varphi]\!] \subseteq R$
$(\forall x_1,...,x_n,y_1,...,y_n)[R(x_1)...(x_n) \& R(y_1)...(y_n) \rightarrow R(x_1+y_1)...(x_n+y_n)]$.

Sternefeld uses the notation ** for PL^2, *** for PL^3 and so on. These operators are also called cumulation operators. The LF for the sentence in (120) is now this:

(122) **The** PL **boys** [**the** PL **girls** [PL^2 $\lambda_2\lambda_1$ **a flower** λ_3 **gave**$(t_3)(t_2)(t_1)$]]
"Every boy gives a flower to some girl and every girl gets a flower from some boy"

The construction of the LF proceeds as follows: we start from a statement with a singular verb. We QR the subject and then we QR the object under the subject. We then insert the two-place plural operator countercyclically between the object and the double abstract. Suppose the girls are a+ b and the boys are c+d, $[\![\textbf{flower}]\!]$ = {f1, f2, f3}, $[\![\textbf{gave}]\!]$ = {<c,f1,a>, <d,f2,b>}. The relation $[\![\lambda_2\lambda_1$ **a flower** λ_3 **gave**$(t_3)(t_2)(t_1)]\!]$ is then {∅, <c,a>, <d,b>, <c+d, a+b>}. Clearly the sentence is true in the scenario. To obtain this reading, it is crucial that the plural operator is inserted in the syntax.

It is interesting to think about the relation between the plural operators and the morphology. For NPs the case seems clear: PL has the feature [iPL] and agrees with the feature [uPL] of the noun. DPs inherit the feature. But what about plural VPs? A plural VP is always modified by a semantic plural, but the morphology may be singular as example (119) shows. So [uPL] of the verb is not checked by the PL-operator that modifies the verb but by the feature [iP] of the subject, a case of subject-predicate agreement.

Notes on the literature. The plural operator for nouns has been introduced into semantics by Link (1983). Cumulation of verbs goes back at least to Krifka (1989). A classic is Schwarzschild (1996), who has a slightly different architecture. The exposition given here closely follows Sternefeld (1993) and Beck & Sauerland

(2000). The best survey of plural semantics is presumably Heim (1994). Issues arising with plural semantics are discussed in article 7 [Semantics: Noun Phrases and Verb Phrases] (Lasersohn) *Mass nouns and plurals*.

9 Getting rid of abstract syntax?

In the theory of LF outlined in this article, QR plays a central role. In most cases the rule is covert in the sense that it applies at the LF branch. As it stands, the rule is unconstrained and overgenerates in the sense that it produces LFs that have unattested readings. Much of the work done in Generative Grammar is devoted to constraints on overt movement, i.e. movement visible at SS. Since QR is a covert rule, the criterion for a correct restriction on movement must be that the rule doesn't produce unattested readings. The commonly accepted restriction is that QR is clause bound. This restriction would prevent to QR out of a relative clause. For instance, (123a) cannot mean (123b), which is derived by long QR.

(123) a. John knows a professor that every student likes.
　　　b. For every student x, John knows a professor that x likes.

But there are other examples with indefinite DPs that seem to support long QR. QR is a covert rule and the restrictions for its application are not clear. Reasons like these have motivated many semanticists, notably categorical grammarians, to look for a syntax without such covert rules. So let us ask whether we need QR at all.

9.1 Type shifting

QR was motivated by three tasks that had to be performed: (i) Quantifiers in object positions had to be QR-ed for type reasons; (ii) scope ambiguities must be resolved by QR; (iii) variable binding, i.e., the binding of pronouns requires QR.

Consider the problem of the object first. A quantifier in object position requires QR to solve a type conflict. An alternative solution would be introduce a type shifting operation in the syntax that applies to the transitive verb:

(124)　$[\![\text{SHIFT-1}_{(e(et))((et,t)(et))}]\!] = \lambda w.\lambda R_{e(et)}.\lambda Q_{(et,t)}.\lambda x.Q(\lambda y.R(y)(x))$

The analysis of **Barbara knows every linguist** would then be

(125) **Barbara** SHIFT-(**knows**) **every linguist**

The reader may check for herself that this would give us the same result we obtain if we QR the object over the subject. It is not a problem to formulate an operation SHIFT-2 that raises the type of the direct and the indirect object of di-transitive verbs as for instance in **John** (SHIFT-2 **gave**) **every child a present**. I have introduced the type shifters as covert operators. An equivalent formulation would be to introduce one-place syntax rules that have the interpretation of the corresponding type shifters. For instance, SHIFT-1 would be the syntax rule $V_{(et,t)(et)} \to V_{e(et)}$ with meaning $[\![V_{(et,t)(et)}]\!] = \lambda w.\lambda Q_{(et,t)}.\lambda x.Q(\lambda y.[\![V_{e(et)}]\!] (y)(x))$. The LF would then be

(126) Barbara [$_{V(et,t)(et)}$ [$_{Ve(et)}$ knows]] every linguist

The type lifting of the verb would then be done by the meaning of the syntax rule SHIFT-1.

A general recursive definition for this kind of lifting rules is given in Büring (2005). So we don't need QR for solving the problem of the object, but we need type shifters, and these apply in the syntax. A third alternative would be to assume multiple entries for each verb in the lexicon, i.e., lexemes with the lifted types and the corresponding lifted meanings.

So the problem of the object doesn't require QR, but we need a considerable number of type shifting devices. And a closer look at the meta-language in which these type shifters are formulated shows that QR is hidden in the formulation of the rules. It is not clear whether there are empirical reasons that favour one method over the other. One could argue that these rules are local and therefore more constrained. But there is no reason why type shifters should not apply to entire phrases. Given the present state of the art, the rule QR still seems to be the most transparent method of dealing with the problem of the object.

Next let us take up the question of whether we need QR for resolving scope ambiguities. Consider the ambiguous sentence:

(127) Everybody likes somebody.

The reading with wide scope of the subject with respect to the object can be obtained by applying SHIFT-1 to the verb. To generate the reading where the object has wide scope with respect to the subject, we need a further shifter:

(128) $F(\text{SHIFT-3}_{(e(et))((et,t)((et,t)t))}) = \lambda w.\lambda R_{(et)t}.\lambda P.\lambda Q_{(et)t}.P(\lambda x.Q(\lambda y.R(y)(x)))$

As the reader may check for himself, the following LF gives us the intended reading:

(129) [$_t$ **everybody** [SHIFT-3 (**likes**) [**somebody**]]]
λw.(∃x)[person(x,w) & (∀x)[person(y,w) → likes(y,x,w)]]

So QR is eliminated in favour of appropriate type shifters. The shifter (128) over-generates for it gives **everybody** wide scope over a negative quantifier in subject position:

(130) *[$_t$ **nobody** [SHIFT-3(**likes**) [**everybody**]]]
λw.(∀y)[person(x,w) → ¬(∃y)[person(y,w) & likes(y,x,w)]]

This reading ("Nobody likes anybody") is not possible for the sentence. So we have to block it somehow. Note, however, that a theory with QR faces the same problem. We have to forbid to QR over the negation. Thus QR is not necessary for disambiguation. Type shifters can do the same work.

Finally, let us ask whether we need QR for variable binding. If we look at the cases of legitimate pronoun binding by QR, we see that the movement is so local that we may ask whether we can get rid of QR for the purpose of binding. Büring (2005) offers a method. He proposes a surface interpretation of Chomsky's indexed structures. He first formalizes the binding indices n of NPs that are not operators (i.e. no *wh*-phrases, relative pronouns etc.) by a binding prefix β$_n$. The following LF-rule does this:

(131) *Binder rule* (Büring)
[NP$_n$ φ] ⇨ [NP [β$_n$ φ]]

This is almost identical to H&K's convention for QR, where the movement index is adjoined to the XP to be modified and interpreted as a λ-operator. The difference is that the binding index n is not created by movement. It might be thought to be present at SS as Chomsky assumed or it might be created by the Binder rule itself as Büring assumes. Our version of the Binder rule sticks closer to the GB-notation. Büring calls β$_n$ *binding prefix*.

(132) *Binder index evaluation*
Let φ be of type et. Then [β$_n$ φ] is of the same type.
⟦[β$_n$ φ]⟧^{g} = λx.(⟦φ⟧$^{g[n/x]}$(x))

Here is a simple example illustrating the rule:

(133) **everyone [β$_n$ shaved himself$_n$]**

The structure can be interpreted without QR, and it has the correct meaning. A closer inspection of the rule reveals that it is a lexicalised version of QR: β_n is not simply a λ-operator. It binds the variable **n** that occurs in the VP φ, it introduces the same variable as subject of the VP and identifies it with the interpretation of n. If we apply a generalised quantifier to that meaning, we get exactly the same result as if the quantifier had been QR-ed out of the subject position of the sentence.

Büring's method can be applied to objects that bind variables, but we need a more complicated composition principle for this case:

(134) a. **John gave everyone₁ a present that he₁ liked**
   b. **John [$_{et}$ everyone [$_{((et)t)(et)}$ β_1 [$_{e(et)}$ gave a present that he₁ liked]]]]**
   = $\lambda w.(\forall x)[\text{person}(x,w) \to$ John gave x a present in w that x liked in w]

The rule for binding prefixes that bind a dative position is this:

(135) Let γ be of type (e(et)). Then [β_n γ] is of type ((et)t)(et).
   $[\![[\beta_n \gamma]]\!]^g = \lambda Q_{(et)t}.\lambda x.Q(\lambda y.([\![\gamma]\!]^{g[n/y]}(y)(x)))$

Again the meta-linguistic notation shows that QR is hidden in this rule.

With techniques of this kind we can deal with all standard cases of variable binding without QR in the syntax. But we need these alternative binding rules.

Obviously, there is a general method behind the different binding rules. We may generalize the compositional principles to get some general scheme. See Büring (2005) for details. For binding purposes this method seems to work rather well and it provides a viable alternative to block over-generation.

9.2 Variable free syntax/semantics

The alternatives to QR all assumed that pronouns or traces are variables, and variables are bound by an appropriate abstraction. A more radical approach that eliminates QR for the task of variable binding is a variable free semantics. If there are no variables in the syntax, there is no variable binding and we don't have QR. Already Quine (1960a) has shown that we can have a variable free predicate logic.

The main ideas for a variable free semantics are the following. Pronouns are not variables but functions expressing identity, i.e. $\lambda x.x$. In the syntax the information that a pronoun has been used is passed upward as λx. This is done by Geach's type lifting rule G. We can identify two pronouns by Quine's reflexivization rule, which identifies two arguments of a relation. Here is an example.

(136) Everyone thinks he wins

We have in mind a reading where **everyone** binds **he** in traditional accounts. Here is a variable free analysis:

(137)

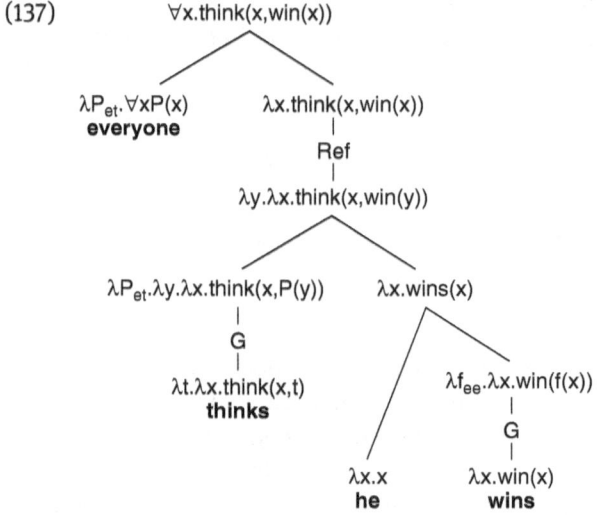

To simplify the exposition, I have made the (untenable) assumption that the complement of **think** is a truth-value. Geach's type lifting rule raises the type of an argument: it inserts a function f that applies to an argument of the original type. The argument is abstracted away and passed higher up. As you can see from the tree the information that the pronoun **he** has been used is passed to the higher node until it is identified with the subject of **think** by Quine's rule Ref, which has the meaning $\lambda R_{e(et)}.\lambda x.R(x)(x)$. Note that we have variables in the semantic meta-language, but they are always bound. So this framework needs no variable binding and therefore no QR.

Is this kind of syntax less abstract, i.e. nearer to the surface? This is questionable. We need all sort of type lifting rules, which are covert logical operations. Beside of the rules G and Ref illustrated here we need the shifters discussed previously and a couple of other operations.

9.3 Dynamic semantics

Geach (1962) has brought our attention to sentences that contain bound pronouns that cannot be analysed by means of QR:

(138) a. If *a farmer* owns *a donkey*, *he* beats *it*.
 b. Every farmer who owns *a donkey* beats *it*.

In (138a), the pronoun **he** seems to be anaphoric to **a farmer**, and in (138a/b), **it** seems to be anaphoric to **a donkey**. Let us try to bind the pronouns of the first sentence by means of QR. The only way to do this consists of giving **a farmer** and **a donkey** scope over the entire conditional, i.e., the LF has to be something like the following construction:

(139) **a farmer λ_1 a donkey λ_2 if t_1 owns t_2, he$_1$ beats it$_2$**
 = There is a farmer x_1 and a donkey x_2 such that if x_1 owns x_2, then x_1 beats x_2.

This LF speaks about a particular farmer and a particular donkey and says that the farmer beats this donkey in case he owns it. Even if there exists this reading, which is doubtful, it certainly isn't the prevailing interpretation. Sentence (138a) is synonymous with sentence (138b) and both seem to have a universal reading, something like:

(140) For every x and y, if x is a farmer and y is a donkey and x owns y, then x beats y.

The problem raised by these "donkey sentences" is then how we can obtain this reading in a compositional way from surface syntax.

The binding problem for donkey pronouns can be resumed like this. Semantic binding is only possible if the antecedent c-commands the pronoun to be bound at SS. Donkey pronouns seem to have antecedents binding them. But the antecedents don't c-command the pronouns at SS. The problem has triggered a different approach to binding viz. the *Context Change Semantics* of Heim (1982, 1983) and the DRT of Kamp (1981). We stick to the system of Heim, because it is more explicit about the SS-LF interface. The SS of the sentence is this:

(141) SS/SO

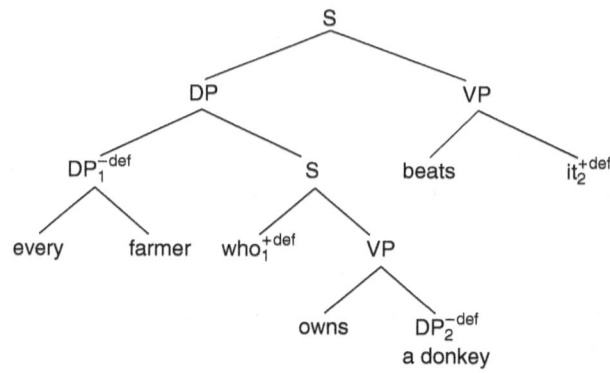

From this the LF is generated by two rules, which we introduce below.

(142) LF

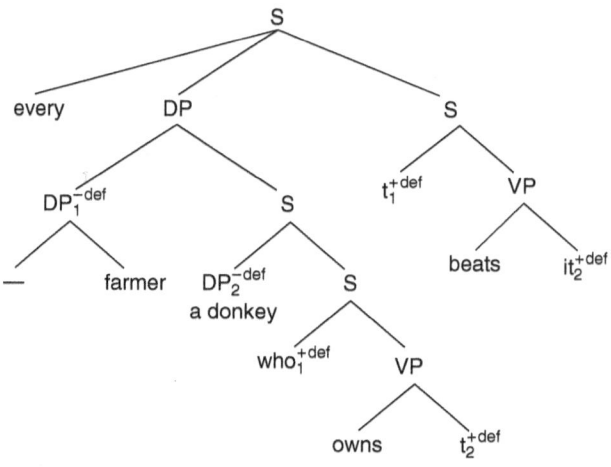

The system knows two kinds of variables, definite ones (feature [+def]) and indefinite ones (feature [-def]). Personal pronouns, relative pronouns and traces are definite. Non-pronominal DPs, i.e. those with an article are predicates that apply to their referential index, which is an indefinite variable. The indefinite article means nothing, but quantifiers like **every** or **most** are interpreted by a syncategorematic rule. In Heim's system DPs express truth-values (or propositions) and therefore they cannot be interpreted at the argument position of a VP. So we need an analogue of QR, which we call DR "DP-raising":

(143) **DR**: Adjoin DP to S and leave a co-indexed trace.

The other construction rule is:

(144) Quantifier Scope: [[$_{DP}$ every NP]$_i$ S] ▯ [every [– NP]$_I$ S]

The LF is constructed from the SS by two applications of the rule DR: the subject is scoped over its sentence and **a donkey** is scoped over its relative clause. Finally, the rule Quantifier Scope is applied and the tree is slightly restructured.

To make the analogy with the non-dynamic system clearer, consider the specific reading of the sentence **Every boy loves a girl**, i.e., the one where **a girl** has wide scope. The LF in Heim's system is:

(145) **a girl**$_2$ [**every** [_ **boy**]$_1$ [t$_1$ **loves** t$_2$]]

As before, the indefinite term must have wide scope over the quantified subject.

We now give a short sketch of the semantics for the system. Sentences don't have truth-values but a *context change potential* (CCP). A context c is a set of partial variable assignments. Dom(c) contains the variables used by the assignments in c. If p is a sentence and c is a context, ⟦p⟧(c) is the new context, written as c + p. The semantic language used consists of the following expressions: (a) Atomic formulae consisting of an n-place predicate P and n variables, where each is definite or indefinite; (b) molecular formulae of the form [p q], were p and q are formulae; (c) quantified formulae such as [**every** p q] or [**not** p].

As usual we assume that predicates P have extensions Ext(P). The recursive definition of the context change function + is given by the following rules, were c is an arbitrary context:

(146) Definition of +
  a. If p is an atomic formula of shape P(x$_1$,...,x$_n$), then c + p = {f ∪ g | f ∈ c & <g(x$_1$), ..., g(x$_1$)> ∈ Ext(P)}, were dom(g) = {x$_1$,...,x$_n$} and c + p is only defined if the definite variables in p are in dom(c) and the indefinite variables in p are not in dom(c) (*familiarity/novelty-condition*)
  b. If p is a molecular formula of the form [q r], then c + p = (c+q)+r
  c. If p = [**every** q r], then c + p = {f ∈ c |(∀g ⊃ f) If g ∈ c + q, then (∃h ⊃ g) h ∈ (c+q) + r}

It can now be calculated that c + (142) = {f ∈ c | (∀g ⊃ f) If g(1) ∈ Ext(**farmer**) & g(2) ∈ Ext(**donkey**) & <g(1), g(2)> ∈ Ext(**own**), then <g(1), g(2)> ∈ Ext(**beat**)}.

Since all the variables in this LF are new, the context is not changed if every farmer who owns a donkey beats it. If the latter is not the case, the new context will be empty.

A sentence p is true in c if there is at least one assignment in c + p.

In predicate logic, we can write the truth-condition of the donkey sentence as $(\forall x)(\forall y)[\text{farmer}(x) \& \text{donkey}(y) \& \text{own}(x,y) \rightarrow \text{beat}(x,y)]$. Similarly, the reader may convince himself that the LF in (145) amounts to the truth-condition $(\exists x)[\text{girl}(x) \& (\forall y)[\text{boy}(y) \rightarrow \text{like}(y,x)]]$.

It is interesting to think a moment about the consequences of dynamic semantic for the Binding Theory (= BT) of Chomsky (1981). Recall that an expression is A-bound if it is co-indexed with a c-commanding expression in argument position. BT says that A-elements (e.g. reflexive pronouns) are A-bound in their binding category, roughly the next finite clause (Principle A), that B-elements (e.g. personal pronouns) are A-free in their binding category (Principle B), and that C-elements (e.g. names and non-pronominal DPs) are free in their binding category (Principle C). The binding principles apply at SS. Among other things, the binding theory gives a distribution of definite and indefinite terms. Consider the SS of the donkey sentence, i.e. (141). Both the C-element **a donkey**$_2$ and the B-element **it**$_2$ are A-free as required by BT. The compatibility of the dynamic system with BT can also be seen from the behaviour of names. In dynamic semantics **John**$_i$ is a definite DP. The prediction is that

(147) Every girl that knows him$_1$ likes John$_1$

is a good sentence, because **John**$_1$ and **him**$_1$ are A-free. So one criterion for the correctness of a syntactic account is that Chomsky's BT can be implemented.

I know no really convincing alternative analysis of donkey sentences. Therefore a framework of this kind seems needed. Obviously the choice has repercussions to syntax. In particular, QR has to be replaced by the two rules discussed. As QR, the rule DR is needed for the problem of the object, for scope disambiguation and for binding. So a framework of this kind is not less abstract than the previous account.

A note on the literature. Heim's and Kamp's logical languages are first order. The syntax proposed by Heim is very elegant and there might come a time for its revival. Kamp's Discourse Representation Theory treats the same phenomena but it mostly gives only logical LFs in a box notation plus a comparable semantics. Kamp & Reyle (1993) give some rules that relate DRS's with syntactic structures; see also article 11 [Semantics: Theories] (Kamp & Reyle) *Discourse Representation Theory*. The architecture is rather different and we cannot give details here. Chierchia (1995) and Beaver (2001) embed Heim's dynamic semantics in a typed language, where Beaver is closer to Heim than Chierchia. There are a number of proposals for *Dynamic DRT,* e.g. Muskens (1996). For type shifting, see articles 10 [Semantics: Lexical Structures and Adjectives] (de Swart) *Mismatches and coercion* and 8 [Semantics: Interfaces] (de Hoop) *Type shifting*; for variable free semantics, see article 1 [Semantics: Sentence and Information Structure] (Szabolcsi) *Scope and binding*; for dynamic semantics, see article 12 [Semantics: Theories] (Dekker) *Dynamic semantics*.

10 The big picture

The plot of this article was to give an idea of the syntax/semantics interface by studying concrete examples. The approach is Fregean, i.e. we assume that the meaning of a sentence is determined by its syntactic structure and the meaning of its parts, where the smallest parts are phrases and words. This means that syntactic rules have meaning, i.e., the semantic operations associated with them. We tried to get along with very few principles of semantic composition, above all FA and PM. In addition we needed λ-abstraction and movement rules creating it, above all QR. We could achieve quite a lot with these ingredients. But the theory relied on the assumption that the simple principles of composition mostly apply on LF, where we took LF as that structure that determines the truth-conditions of a sentence. Some researchers have called this kind of LF *transparent LF*. Now, why should LF be different from SS/SO and PF?

I am not concerned with obvious differences caused by phonological rules that form phonological phrases and phonological words, thereby destroying a lot of constituent structure. The more interesting cases are rules that alter the structure that is best for semantic composition such as Verb Movement, Topicalization in German, Scrambling in German, Extraposition, VP deletion and so on. If these rules don't affect the truth-conditions we can assume that they apply at the PF-branch. In many cases we could give trivial interpretation to this kind of movement rules. Suppose, for example that verb movement never affects the truth-conditions in German. The movement rule could then leave a trace of the type of the verb and we would have semantic reconstruction via λ-conversion. The technique is not easily applicable when the moved material contains a bound variable. In these cases semantic reconstruction obviously needs more complicated methods like those used in variable free semantics. If the same result can be obtained by ignoring the movement (because it occurs at the PF branch), then this is a simpler and more attractive theory. But ultimately, this issue is an empirical one.

Suppose then that PF is different from SS/SO. Once we have made that step, there is nothing mysterious anymore in the assumption that LF is different from

SS and therefore also different from "what we see", i.e. PF. In particular there is no reason why we shouldn't have a covert rule like QR.

On the other hand, we need abstract operators in the syntax anyway. Let us recapitulate: For questions we needed the operator Q, we needed overt WH-movement and also covert WH-movement. The relevant rule is QR.

In order to interpret the comparative, we had to QR the DegP. There is no known way to deal with the data without such a movement. The construction raises interesting questions for the LF-PF-interface. Either we have empty VPs at SS and have a copy rule at the LF-branch, or we have a deletion rule at the PF-branch.

Tense is an example that motivates the split between semantic and morphological tense. The semantic tense is related with the verb by QR. Semantic and morphological tenses are related by agreement. In SOT constructions the agreement relation can relate very distant items. This raises interesting issues for the PF-LF interface. If tense agreement is mediated via variable binding, the relevant configurations should be the input for PF. So some types of covert QR presumably occur at SS/SO.

Negation motivated the assumption that Verb Movement, Topicalization and Scrambling either occur at the PF-branch or they must be reconstructed at the LF-branch. Negative Concord in the Slavic languages shows that negation can be an abstract operator that is made visible by negative prefixes on indefinites and the verb. At LF these prefixes are deleted by the Principle of Full interpretation. In the semantics something covert, viz. NEG does the relevant job. The presence of NEG is made visible by Multiple Agree that relates NEG with the said negative morphemes.

The study of the plural showed that we can modify VPs by a covert plural operator PL^n. This operator may scopally interact with a generalized quantifier that is an argument of the verb. A semantically pluralized VP is not always a morphological plural: the morphological plural requires a plural subject. To get the facts right, covert QR is necessary, furthermore countercyclic insertion of PL^n.

We asked whether we can get rid of covert rules like QR and studied techniques from categorical grammar and variable free semantics, notably some type-shifting operations and a version of Geach's type-lifting rule. We said that these principles sometimes hide QR in the semantic meta-language, and they are certainly not less abstract. (A personal remark to these techniques is that I understand variable free semantics only because I understand the meta-language that uses variables all the time.)

The semantic techniques discussed here are still too simple to deal with a broader range of phenomena of natural language. For instance, I haven't touched *Alternative Semantics* at all, i.e. theories that deal with focus-sensitive operators;

see e.g. Rooth (1996). The theory requires different techniques, but I am convinced that it is compatible with the big picture outlined here.

Another problem was raised by dynamic semantics. This theory can treat phenomena that classical frameworks in the Montague style cannot treat at all. We saw that the theory outlined is in no way less abstract than the classical framework. We need movement rules of the QR type all the time. We discussed the compatibility of this theory with Chomsky's binding principles. Any syntax of natural language should have a place where the BT can apply.

So we assume that the general architecture of the system is correct, i.e. Chomsky's T-model as outlined in the GB/MP-theory. In particular, LFs are syntactic structures made of the same material as surface structures and PFs but without material that is semantically not interpretable. And LFs are unambiguous, they fully determine the interpretation.

I have nothing to say about the issue whether the approach is compatible with newer versions of Minimalism, e.g. the Phase Model. One would have to go through the examples and check whether the analyses can be carried over.

I wish to thank Atle Grønn for correcting the many typos that were in the original version of this article.

11 References

Abusch, Dorit 1988. Sequence of tense, intensionality and scope. Paper presented at the *7th West Coast Conference on Formal Linguistics*, Stanford, CA.
Ajdukiewicz, Kazimierz 1935. Die syntaktische Konnexität. *Studia Philosophica* 1, 1–27.
Barwise, John & Robin Cooper 1981. Generalized quantifiers and natural language. *Linguistics & Philosophy* 4, 159–219.
Beaver, David I. 2001. *Presupposition and Assertion in Dynamic Semantics*. Stanford, CA: CSLI Publications.
Beck, Sigrid & Uli Sauerland 2000. Cumulation is needed. A reply to Winter (2000). *Natural Language Semantics* 8, 349–371.
Bresnan, Joan 1973. Syntax of the comparative clause in English. *Linguistic Inquiry* 4, 275–343.
Büring, Daniel 2005. *Binding Theory*. Cambridge: Cambridge University Press.
Chierchia, Gennaro 1989. Anaphora and attitudes de se. In: R. Bartsch, J. van Benthem & P. van Emde Boas (eds.). *Semantics and Contextual Expression*. Dordrecht: Foris, 1–31.
Chierchia, Gennaro 1995. *Dynamics of Meaning. Anaphora, Presupposition, and the Theory of Grammar*. Chicago, IL: The University of Chicago Press.
Chomsky, Noam 1981. *Lectures on Government and Binding*. Dordrecht: Foris.
Chomsky, Noam 1986. *Knowledge of Language. Its Nature, Origin and Use*. New York: Praeger.
Chomsky, Noam 1992. *A Minimalist Program for Linguistic Theory*. (MIT Occasional Papers in Linguistics 1). Cambridge, MA: The MIT Press.
Chomsky, Noam 1995. *The Minimalist Program*. Cambridge, MA: The MIT Press.

Chomsky, Noam 2001. Derivation by phase. In: M. Kenstowicz (ed.). *Ken Hale: A Life in Language*. Cambridge, MA: The MIT Press, 1–52.
Cresswell, Max J. 1973. *Logic and Languages*. London: Methuen.
Cresswell, Max J. 1976. The Semantics of degree. In: B. Partee (ed.). *Montague Grammar*. New York: Academic Press, 261–292.
Cresswell, Max J. 1991. Basic concepts of semantics. In: A. von Stechow & D. Wunderlich (eds.). *Semantik – Semantics. Ein internationales Handbuch der zeitgenössischen Forschung – An International Handbook of Contemporary Research* (HSK 6). Berlin: de Gruyter, 24–31.
Fiengo, Robert & Robert May 1991. *Indices and Identity*. Cambridge, MA: The MIT Press.
von Fintel, Kai & Irene Heim 2000. *Notes on Intensional Semantics*. Ms. Cambridge, MA, MIT.
Fodor, Janet D. 1970. *The Linguistic Description of Opaque Contexts*. Ph.D. dissertation. MIT, Cambridge, MA.
Frege, Gottlob 1884. *Die Grundlagen der Arithmetik*. Breslau: Koebner.
Frege, Gottlob 1892. Über Sinn und Bedeutung. *Zeitschrift für Philosophie und philosophische Kritik* 100, 25–50.
Frege, Gottlob 1923/1976. Das Gedankengefüge. Reprinted in: G. Patzig (ed.). *Gottlob Frege. Logische Untersuchungen*. Göttingen: Vandenhoek & Ruprecht, 1976, 72–91.
Gallin, Daniel 1975. *Intensional and Higher-order Modal Logic. With Applications to Montague Semantics*. Amsterdam: North-Holland.
Geach, Peter 1962. *Reference and Generality*. Ithaka, NY: Cornell University Press.
Grønn, Atle & Arnim von Stechow 2011. Tense in adjuncts. Paper presented at the *CAS Conference on Discourse Representation, Comprehension and Production on a Cross-Linguistic Perspective*, Oslo.
Guerzoni, Elena 2004. Even-NPIs in YES/NO questions. *Natural Language Semantics* 12, 319–343.
Heim, Irene 1982. *The Semantics of Definite and Indefinite Noun Phrases*. Ph.D. dissertation. University of Massachusetts, Amherst, MA. Reprinted: Ann Arbor, MI: University Microfilms.
Heim, Irene 1983. File change semantics and the familiarity theory of definitess. In: R. Bäuerle, Ch. Schwarze & A. von Stechow (eds.). *Meaning, Use and Interpretation of Language*. Berlin: Mouton de Gruyter, 164–189.
Heim, Irene 1991. Artikel und Definitheit. In: A. von Stechow & D. Wunderlich (eds.). *Semantik – Semantics. Ein internationales Handbuch der zeitgenössischen Forschung – An International Handbook of Contemporary Research* (HSK 6). Berlin: de Gruyter, 487–534.
Heim, Irene 1994. *Plurals*. Ms. Cambridge, MA, MIT.
Heim, Irene 2001. Degree operators and scope. In: C. Féry & W. Sternefeld (eds.). *Audiatur Vox Sapientiae. A Festschrift for Arnim von Stechow*. Berlin: Akademie Verlag, 214–239.
Heim, Irene & Angelika Kratzer 1998. *Semantics in Generative Grammar*. Oxford: Blackwell.
Hintikka, Jaakko 1969. Semantics for propositional attitudes. In: J.W. Davis et al. (eds.). *Philosophical Logic*. Dordrecht: Reidel, 21–45.
Jacobson, Pauline 1999. Towards a variable-free semantics. *Linguistics & Philosophy* 22, 117–184.
Jespersen, Otto 1917. *Negation in English and other Languages*. Copenhagen: Hœst.
Kamp, Hans 1981. A theory of truth and semantic representation. In: J. Groenendijk, T. Janssen & M. Stokhof (eds.). *Formal Methods in the Study of Language*. Amsterdam: Mathematical Centre, 277–322.

Kamp, Hans & Uwe Reyle 1993. *From Discourse to Logic*. Dordrecht: Kluwer.
Karttunen, Lauri 1977. Syntax and semantics of questions. *Linguistics & Philosophy* 1, 3–44.
Kratzer, Angelika 1977. What 'must' and 'can' must and can mean. *Linguistics & Philosophy* 1, 337–355.
Kratzer, Angelika 1978. *Semantik der Rede. Kontexttheorie, Modalwörter, Konditionalsätze*. Kronberg/Ts.: Scriptor.
Kratzer, Angelika 1981. The notional category of modality. In: H.J. Eikmeyer & H. Rieser (eds.). *Words, Worlds, and Contexts*. Berlin: de Gruyter, 38–74.
Krifka, Manfred 1989. Nominal reference, temporal constitution and quantification in event semantics. In: R. Bartsch, J. van Benthem & P. van Emde Boas (eds.). *Semantics and Contextual Expression*. Dordrecht: Foris, 75–115.
Kripke, Saul 1959. A completeness theorem in modal logic. *Journal of Symbolic Logic* 24, 1–14.
Kusumoto, Kiyomi 2005. On the quantification over times in natural language. *Natural Language Semantics* 13, 317–357.
Lewis, David 1972. General Semantics. *Synthese* 22, 18–67.
Link, Godehard 1983. The logical analysis of plurals and mass terms: A lattice-theoretical approach. In: R. Bäuerle, Ch. Schwarze & A. von Stechow (eds.). *Meaning, Use, and Interpretation of Language*. Berlin: Mouton de Gruyter, 302–323.
May, Robert 1977. *The Grammar of Quantification*. Ph.D. dissertation. MIT, Cambridge, MA.
May, Robert 1985. *Logical Form*. Cambridge, MA: The MIT Press.
Montague, Richard 1970a. Universal Grammar. *Theoria* 36, 373–398.
Montague, Richard 1970b. English as a formal language. In: B. Visentini (ed.). *Linguaggi nella Società e nella Tecnica*. Milano: Edizioni di Comunità, 189–224.
Montague, Richard 1970c. Pragmatics and intensional logic. *Synthese* 22, 68–94.
Montague, Richard 1973. The proper treatment of quantification in ordinary English. In: J. Hintikka, J. Moravcsik & P. Suppes (eds.). *Approaches to Natural Language. Proceedings of the 1970 Stanford Workshop on Grammar and Semantics*. Dordrecht: Reidel, 221–242.
Muskens, Reinhard 1996. Combining Montague semantics and Discourse Representation. *Linguistics & Philosophy* 19, 143–186.
Ogihara, Toshiyuki 1996. *Tense, Attitudes, and Scope*. Dordrecht: Kluwer.
Penka, Doris 2010. *Negative Indefinites*. Oxford: Oxford University Press.
Quine, Willard van Orman 1960a. Variables explained away. *Proceedings of the American Philosophical Society* 104, 343–347.
Quine, Willard van Orman 1960b. *Word and Object*. New York: Wiley.
Rooth, Mats 1996. Focus. In: S. Lappin (ed.). *The Handbook of Contemporary Semantic Theory*. London: Blackwell, 271–297.
Schönfinkel, Moses 1924. Über die Bausteine der mathematischen Logik. *Mathematische Annalen* 92, 305–316.
Schwarzschild, Roger 1996. *Pluralities*. Dordrecht: Kluwer.
von Stechow, Arnim 1984. Comparing semantic theories of comparison. *Journal of Semantics* 3, 1–77.
von Stechow, Arnim 1991. Syntax und Semantik. In: A. von Stechow & D. Wunderlich (eds.). *Semantik – Semantics. Ein internationales Handbuch der zeitgenössischen Forschung – An International Handbook of Contemporary Research* (HSK 6). Berlin: de Gruyter, 90–148.
von Stechow, Arnim 2009. Tenses in compositional semantics. In: W. Klein & P. Li (eds.). *The Expression of Time*. Berlin: de Gruyter, 129–168.

Steedman, Mark 2000. Does grammar make use of bound variables? In: M. Böttner & W. Thümmel (eds.). *Variable-free Semantics*. Osnabrück: secolo Verlag, 200–209.

Sternefeld, Wolfgang 1993. *Plurality, Reciprocity, and Scope* (SfS-Report 13-93). Tübingen: Seminar für Sprachwissenschaft, Universität Tübingen.

Szabolcsi, Anna 1989. Bound variables in Syntax (Are there any?). In: R. Bartsch, J. van Benthem & P. van Emde Boas (eds.). *Semantics and Contextual Expression*. Dordrecht: Foris, 294–318.

Williams, Edwin 1977. Discourse and Logical Form. *Linguistic Inquiry* 8, 101–139.

Wittgenstein, Ludwig 1922/1984. *Tractatus logico-philosophicus*. Frankfurt/M.: Suhrkamp, 7–86.

Zeijlstra, Hedde 2004. *Sentential Negation and Negative Concord*. Utrecht: LOT.

Dieter Wunderlich
7 Operations on argument structure

1 Introduction —— 233
2 Argument reduction: passive, antipassive, reflexive, and others —— 241
3 Argument extension: causative, applicative, resultative, and others —— 250
4 Functor vs. incorporation —— 257
5 Parsimony in the set of exponents: polyfunctional affixes —— 260
6 Multiple operations and the order of derivation —— 264
7 Argument alternation through lexical marking —— 269
8 Argument alternation: dative shift, and others —— 270
9 References —— 273

Abstract: In a framework with lexical decomposition, argument hierarchy is determined by the depth of embedding, and in turn determines the realization of structural arguments (1). Operations that reduce the number of arguments operate directly on the argument hierarchy (2), while operations that extend the number of arguments add semantic predicates, and thus themselves contribute to semantic composition (3). Causatives add a highest argument, while applicatives add a non-highest argument – what kind of machinery is necessary to represent this difference (4)? Certain affixes realize a whole bundle of possible operations, some of them even opposite ones (5). Multiple operations are possible; their order reflects steps of semantic composition (6). Lexical marking can override the argument hierarchy (7). Argument alternations such as the dative shift reflect lexical alternatives with different argument hierarchies that are not derived from each other (8). – Various kinds of evidence is given that morphological operations reflect semantic properties and relations rather than syntactic ones.

1 Introduction

Considering triplets such as those in (1), it is easy to see that *open* is an ambiguous lexical item, whose specifications belong to the same semantic classes as *dead*, *die*, and *kill*. That the main predicates of (1a), (1b), and (1c) belong to different semantic classes is attested by the different morphosyntactic contexts required by these predicates. The verbs in (1b) clearly differ in their argument structure from those in (1c), which is captured by the distinction between intransitives vs.

Dieter Wunderlich, Berlin, Germany

https://doi.org/10.1515/9783110589849-007

transitives, while it is less obvious whether adjectives and intransitives differ in their argument structure. Probably most linguists would say yes, they do.

(1) a. The bear is dead.   The door is open.   Die Tür ist offen.
    b. The bear died.   The door opened.   Die Tür öffnete sich.
    c. Mary killed the bear. Mary opened the door. Maria öffnete die Tür.

That *open* is threefold ambiguous raises the question of how these three meanings are related to each other. The answer provided in this article is that they are related by certain operations on argument structure. The adjective *open* denotes a relation between an object and a state holding at a certain time, while the intransitive *open* denotes a relation between an object and an event that ends in such a state; finally, the transitive *open* denotes a relation between an agent, an object, and an event in which the object ends in such a state. This semantic description suggests that the predicates in (1a) to (1c) are increasingly more complex, which implies the derivational chain (a) → (b) → (c).

In contrast, the German equivalents of *open* seem to indicate the derivational chain (a) → (c) → (b). The verb, showing umlaut, is derived from the adjective, not showing umlaut. However, (b) is a special case of (c); more precisely, (b) *sich öffnen* is the reflexive form of (c) *öffnen*, often called medium (an intransitivization operation that has several semantic interpretations, see section 5). Note that the same operation is active in many languages, see, e.g., Latin (c) *aper-ire* → (b) *se aper-ire*. Latin also shows the variant in which three different suffixes are attached to one and the same stem: (a) *aper-tus*, (b) *aper-iri*, (c) *aper-ire* – here, morphology does not show what derives from what, just as in English *dead, die, kill*.

There is some tension between morphological and semantic complexity. Insofar as one is concerned with particular languages, systematic morphological derivation leads one to assume underlying operations on argument structure – passive, causative, or medium being typical examples. There is no need of universality; certain operations may be active only in a small subset of languages. On the other hand, constellations such as English *dead/die/kill* vs. *open$_1$/open$_2$/open$_3$*, force us to assume semantic relations between the individual elements, even if they are not supported by morphological familiarity (as in *dead/die/kill*) or by morphological distinctness (as in *open$_1$/open$_2$/open$_3$*).

In the following, the notions 'argument structure' and 'operations on argument structure' will be made more precise.

Lexical items belonging to one of the major lexical categories (verb, noun, adjective, adposition) are generally considered to be predicates which have one, two, three, or even more arguments, represented by open slots or variables. An n-place predicate (of type $<e_n,<\ldots,<e_1,t>\ldots>>$ in the simplest case) together with n argument variables forms an open proposition (of type t), while λ-abstraction forms a more articulated predicate (of the same complex type) from it, for instance with n = 3:

(2) $\lambda z\, \lambda y\, \lambda x\, \text{PRED}(x,y,z)$ of type $<e,<e,<e,t>>>$

If such an expression is applied to a series of argument expressions, it gets converted into a saturated proposition, for instance

(3) $\lambda z\, \lambda y\, \lambda x\, \text{PRED}(x,y,z)\, (a)(b)(c)$ becomes $\text{PRED}(a,b,c)$.

Both λ-abstraction and λ-conversion are stepwise operations: stepwise λ-abstraction produces a λ-sequence, and stepwise λ-conversion works off this sequence backwards.

One can identify PRED with what an individual verbal, nominal, adjectival, or adpositional item contributes semantically, and the series of argument expressions with what the morphological or syntactic complements of that item contribute semantically.

There are some specific differences between the lexical categories. The maximal projections of nouns can be used predicatively (*this is John's house*) or referentially (*let us meet at John's house*), a fact that in some languages (e.g. the Semitic ones) is marked by a nominal vs. verbal clause type – all other categories only allow predicative use. The highest argument of a noun is said to be its referential argument R; in the referential use the noun functions as the complement of another predicate expression (e.g., *meet_at*), and R is identified with an argument of that predicate, while in the predicative use R is overtly expressed by a DP (e.g., *this*) the noun is predicating of. Although verbs can only be used predicatively, they still refer to some sort of temporal event and therefore can be said to have a referential argument E (cf. article 8 [Semantics: Theories] (Maienborn) *Event semantics*); E is specified (or bound) by functional elements such as aspect, tense, mood, but never by a complement. If the verb undergoes event nominalization (*our meeting at John's house*), E becomes R of the resulting noun (cf. Bierwisch 1989b, and article 12 [Semantics: Noun Phrases and Verb Phrases] (Grimshaw) *Deverbal nominalization*).

In view of these differences, the featural encoding of argument hierarchy (Wunderlich 1997a) disregards the event argument of a verb but pays regard to the referential argument of a noun. That is, for the working of grammar the highest argument of a transitive verb is usually taken to be the agent (rather than the event in which the agent is involved), while the highest argument of a relational noun must be R. Adjectives and adpositions are typically considered to lack a referential argument, so that no specific functional elements are found with them. To anchor the information of adjectives and adpositions, they must be construed together with some noun or verb as an attribute, adverbial, or secondary predicate.

The representations in (4) to (6) illustrate the predicate-argument structure of a few examples. The possessed noun is considered to be derived from the simple noun by possessivization, which operates on $\lambda x\ N(x)$, yielding $\lambda y\ \lambda x\ [N(x)\ \&\ \text{POSS}(y,x)]$ (Barker 1995). Similarly, the transitive variant of *cook* can be derived from the intransitive variant by causativization, which adds an agent argument ('one who causes that something cooks'). This result can undergo further operations: event nominalization, which only shifts the lexical category ('a process of cooking something by someone'), or agent nominalization, which binds the event argument existentially ('someone who cooks something'). Adjectives as well as adpositions can have one or two arguments.

(4) Nouns and possessed nouns
    a. *house*: $\quad\quad\quad\quad \lambda x\ \text{HOUSE}(x) \quad\quad\quad\quad\quad\quad\quad\quad\quad x = R$
    b. *someone's house*: $\quad \lambda y\ \lambda x\ [\text{HOUSE}(x)\ \&\ \text{POSS}(y,x)] \quad\quad x = R$

(5) Verbs and nominalizations
    a. *cook*, intransitive: $\quad \lambda y\ \lambda s\ \text{COOK}(y)(e) \quad\quad\quad\quad\quad\quad e = E$
    b. *cook*, transitive: $\quad\ \ \lambda y\ \lambda x\ \lambda e\ [\text{AGENT}(x)\ \&\ \text{COOK}(y)](e) \quad e = E$
    c. *cooking*, noun: $\quad\ \ \ \lambda y\ \lambda x\ \lambda e\ [\text{AGENT}(x)\ \&\ \text{COOK}(y)](e) \quad e = R$
    d. *cook*, noun: $\quad\quad\ \ \ \lambda y\ \lambda x\ \exists e\ [\text{AGENT}(x)\ \&\ \text{COOK}(y)](e) \quad x = R$

(6) Adjectives and adpositions/adverbs
    a. *proud*: $\quad \lambda y\ \lambda x\ \text{PROUD}(x,y), \quad$ *quick*: $\quad \lambda x\ \text{QUICK}(x)$
    b. *behind*: $\ \lambda y\ \lambda x\ \text{BEHIND}(x,y), \quad$ *quickly*: $\ \lambda x\ \text{QUICK}(x)$

Arguments other than R and E are sometimes called participants, they must be realized by some pronominal affix or syntactic complement – otherwise existential closure would have to take place in order to yield a saturated proposition. The sequence of λ-abstractors indicates that part of a lexical item which is morphosyntactically active.

Turning now to the concept of argument structure, three distinct but related notions come to mind.

(i)   Argument structure is identified with the list of semantic roles attributed to the participants x, y, z of the predication, for instance, x = agent(e), y = recipient(e), z = theme(e) for a ditransitive verb of the *give* type. This position is characteristic for Neo-Davidsonian approaches; although they mostly assume a flat structure (an unordered list of arguments), it is possible for them to

induce additional structure by assuming a thematic role hierarchy (cf. article 3 [Semantics: Lexical Structures and Adjectives] (Davis) *Thematic roles*).
(ii) Argument structure is identified with the morphosyntactic structure of complement expressions (a)(b)(c) that realize the argument requirements of a predicate. Of course, (a)(b)(c) can vary in various ways, including word order and morphological case. This position is characteristic for syntactic approaches, taking syntax as the generative source of language.
(iii) Argument structure is identified with the sequence of λ-abstractors, which models the need of complements. These λ-abstractors can be regarded as generalized θ-roles.

In any case, the notion of argument structure plays a role for all lexical categories. Verbs are in the center when one considers (operations on) argument structure only because they are particularly complex. Stiebels (2006) argues, however, that nouns can in principle show the same types of operations as verbs.

In this article, I will argue for position (iii) above, thereby restricting the discussion to verbs. Let us call λe VERB(x,y,z)(e) the semantic CORE of a verb (in this case, of a ditransitive verb), and λz λy λx CORE the respective θ-structure, representing an argument hierarchy with x as the highest and z as the lowest argument. For computational reasons, any list of arguments must be strictly ordered. Let us assume that the relative position of the λ-abstractors reflects the path in which the θ-structure is abstracted from CORE. Bierwisch (1989a) proposed an algorithm to perform this abstraction from a lexical decomposition structure, which shows how the meaning of a word is built up from a set of more atomic components (cf. article 2 [Semantics: Lexical Structures and Adjectives] (Engelberg) *Frameworks of decomposition*). Intuitively, this algorithm reflects the depth of embedding: the deeper an argument is embedded, the lower it is placed in the θ-structure, i.e. the respective λ-abstractor is positioned closer to the beginning of the sequence of λ-abstractors. (A similar account is found in Baker's (1997) relativized UTAH principle (Uniformity of Theta Assignment Hypothesis): the ordering of roles must correspond to their relative depth in D-structure.)

I take it for granted that for each individual predicate the arguments form a hierarchy. (If it appears that the arguments can be exchanged in their order, strictly spoken there exist two different, although similar predicates, see section 8.) It is often assumed that the argument hierarchy of an individual predicate is induced by a more general thematic hierarchy such as Agent > Instrument > Recipient > Theme > Goal (or similar ones). This requires that the typology of thematic roles be fine enough to capture all possible semantic roles of individual predicates, and that all these thematic roles can be ordered uniquely – which are probably just two unsolvable tasks (cf. article 3 [Semantics: Lexical Structures and Adjectives] (Davis) *Thematic roles*). Instead, the following tests can be used to determine the argument hierarchy of an individual predicate, without any reference to thematic roles.

(i) Binding properties: Among others, the higher argument can asymmetrically bind the lower argument (Barss & Lasnik 1986, Larson 1988).
(ii) Salience properties: According to harmonic alignment, the higher argument is more likely to be more salient (in terms of person, animacy, definiteness, topic, and so on) than the lower argument (Wunderlich 2006).

The θ-structure thus preserves structural properties of a lexical decomposition structure in terms of argument hierarchy, which in turn is mapped onto a morphosyntactic structure; in other words, it interfaces between semantic core and morphosyntactic structure. The θ-structure is the negative print of the hierarchy inherent to CORE and can produce various morphosyntactic positive copies of that hierarchy. For instance, the ordering $\lambda z\ \lambda y\ \lambda x$ (with x as the highest argument) is mapped onto the default ordering X Y Z in the syntax.

Linguists in the tradition of Grimshaw (1990), Jackendoff (1990), Dowty (1991) and others assume a direct mapping from semantic core properties onto morphosyntactic structure. The assumption of a separate θ-structure, however, is advantageous for a few reasons (Wunderlich 1997a).

Most importantly, the θ-structure allows us to formulate a very elegant mechanism of argument linking, first proposed by Kiparsky (1992) (cf. also Kiparsky 2001, and the section on case in article 2 [this volume] (Kiparsky & Tonhauser) *Semantics of inflection*). If both the argument hierarchy and the structural cases are encoded by the same set of relational features, argument linking can easily check which structural case pattern fits best with a given θ-structure. Lexical Decompositional Grammar (Wunderlich 1997a, 2000, 2006) uses the features +hr = 'there is a higher argument role' (= 'not the highest role'), and +lr = 'there is a lower argument role' (= 'not the lowest role'); for reasons of markedness, these features differ slightly from those proposed by Kiparsky. The structural cases are specified as follows: dative = [+hr,+lr] is compatible with the medial argument, accusative = [+hr] with a non-highest, ergative = [+lr] with a non-lowest, and nominative = [ ] (the unspecified case) with any argument. (Cf. section 7 in article 2 [Semantics: Lexical Structures and Adjectives] (Engelberg) *Frameworks of decomposition*.)

(7) Featural encoding of the argument hierarchy:
    a. Er kaufte ihr einen Ring. ('He bought her a ring'; NOM – DAT – ACC)
    b. λz λy λx PRED(x,y,z)
       +hr   +hr   –hr
       –lr   +lr   +lr

The actual case pattern (in this case NOM – DAT – ACC) follows as the optimal solution if a certain constraint ranking is observed. It should be clear that ergative appears under different circumstances than accusative, and that dative is present only in a subset of both the ergative- and the accusative-languages. Stiebels (2000, 2002) gives a full typology of structural case systems in terms of those constraint rankings. Wunderlich (2003) also includes lexical case marking, which interacts with structural case; he shows that all possible case patterns in German (11 different ones) as well as all possible case patterns in Icelandic (18 different ones), including those that appear in the passive, are determined by the same constraint ranking; the main difference is that Icelandic has more lexical case marking than German. Wunderlich (2006) points out that argument linking by case or pronominal affixation is not the only possible system; he presents a typology of argument linking that goes beyond case.

There are further advantages of introducing a separate θ-structure. First, expletive arguments can be represented by additional λ-elements that do not have a variable as semantic counterpart in CORE (so-called empty abstraction).

(8) Expletive arguments
   a. Es schneit. ('It snows.')
   b. λx GO(SNOW)

Second, lexical case can be represented by associating a feature that overrides what the actual hierarchy of arguments would predict. For instance, verbs with dative for the highest argument must be lexically marked, in particular if verbs with the same meaning exist that have nominative instead, consider German *gefallen* vs. *mögen*, expressing the same psychological state.

(9) Lexically marked vs. unmarked case.
   a. Er gefiel ihr.   Sie mochte ihn.   (both: 'She liked him.')
   b. λy λx LIKE(x,y)   λy λx LIKE(x,y)
       +hr

When lexical marking is lost historically, the DAT-NOM verb shifts into a NOM-ACC verb, compare Icelandic *líka*, a DAT-NOM verb, with English *like*.

Moreover, individual elements of a θ-structure can be associated with sortal restrictions such as animacy, or subcategorization information such as prepositional case or infinitive/participle for dependent verbs.

(10) Association with SUBCAT information
   a. Er wartete auf Diana. ('He waited for Diana.')
   b. λy λx WAIT(x,y)
           AUF

Third, the working of certain valency-decreasing operations can easily be represented by existential binding; in that case, the respective argument is invisible for argument linking.

(11) Valency-decreasing operations.
    a. Er wurde geliebt. ('He was loved.' = 'Someone loved him.')
    b. $\lambda y\ \exists x\ \text{LOVE}(x,y)$

Valency-decreasing operations such as passive and antipassive can be defined directly on the θ-structure (section 2). In contrast, valency-increasing operations such as causative and applicative do not only add an argument but also a licensing predicate, and thus enrich the semantic core (section 3). The question of how exactly these valency-increasing operations function is dealt with in section 4. Cross-linguistically there is often a certain parsimony in the set of exponents; thus the problem arises that one and the same affix may, e.g., signal causative in one context but anticausative in another context – which is the subject of section 5. The ordering of operations is considered in section 6. Two further types of argument alternations are only briefly touched upon: those that come about through lexical marking (section 7), and those that make a choice in a set of complementary core predicates (section 8).

Most operations on argument structure can be marked morphosyntactically (by derivational affixes or syntactic constructions), or be left unmarked and only visible by their effects in the morphosyntactic complement structure. Languages widely differ in the amount of marking, and, of course, in the specific means of realizing these operations. English, e.g., often leaves the causative unmarked but marks the passive (12), whereas Basque marks the causative and leaves the passive unmarked (13).

(12) a. The horse galloped.
    b. Someone galloped the horse.
    c. The horse was galloped.

(13) a. Mikel joan   da.   ('Mikel is gone.')
        Mikel GO.PERF   3.be
    b. Mikel joan-araz-i   du.   ('Someone made Mikel go.')
        Mikel go-CAUS-PERF 3E/3N.have
    c. Mikel joan-araz-i   da.   ('Mikel was made to go.')
        Mikel go-CAUS-PERF 3.be

With GALLOP, a typical intransitive predicate, the two-argument clause (12b) is only intelligible if a further predicate introducing the extra argument is assumed. Conversely, a causativized verb with only one argument, as in (13c), suggests some invisible argument reduction. Operations that have to be inferred by the listener can only apply in canonical instances, whereas a morphologically marked operation can also apply in more peripheral instances and may also lead to idiomatic lexicalization.

A still open question is why languages have all these operations. The most plausible answer is that every participant of an event should get the chance to be expressed as the most prominent argument (discourse anchor or topic, syntactic pivot or subject). For that reason, many operations can even apply in series. In languages that allow for at most two structural arguments, argument extension often has the effect that another participant is promoted to structural object, which in a way means that it is made more 'visible' and could become the topic or subject.

A last general remark concerns the relationship between semantic operations and their morphosyntactic counterparts. The Latin deponential verbs (such as *auxiliari* 'help', *minari* 'threaten', *partiri* 'divide') are semantically active, but nevertheless require passive morphology when they are inflected (*auxili-or tibi* 'help-1sg.PRES.PASS you', 'I help you'). One can assume that these verbs have the *lexical* feature +pass, which triggers passive morphology, and at the same time blocks the semantic operation of passive (which would have to use the same morphology). This shows that the morphological exponent of an operation and the operation itself must be distinguished. In this article, mismatches between lexical features and morphosemantic operations will not be considered any further.

2 Argument reduction: passive, antipassive, reflexive, and others

Valency-decreasing operations reduce the number of syntactically active arguments; they apply directly on the θ-structure. (14) shows the passive, which binds the highest argument existentially, so that it remains unexpressed. (The event argument is irrelevant here and therefore ignored.)

(14)   **PASS**[... $\lambda x \text{ VERB}(x, ...)$] = ... $\exists x \text{ VERB}(x, ...)$
           –hr

Some languages only allow passivization of transitive verbs, while other languages also include some subclasses of intransitive verbs. The class of verbs that can be passivized is often restricted to agentive verbs, but certain nonagentive verbs can be included as well (e.g., *The garden is surrounded by a fence*). Existential binding causes the passivized n-place verb to be realized with at most n-1 morphosyntactic complements; thus, a transitive verb is detransitivized, and an intransitive verb becomes impersonal. As a consequence, another argument is realized by nominative (the default case) and thus becomes morphosyntactic subject. (15) and (16) show that in the passive of ditransitive verbs there are different options regarding the choice of object that becomes nominative. In the two languages illustrated here (Yaqui and Georgian), both objects are marked by accusative in the active. If the recipient shifts to nominative in the passive (as in Yaqui) it is said to be the primary object, while if the theme shifts to nominative (as in Georgian) it is said to be the direct object (Dryer 1986).

(15) Double accusative and passive in Yaqui (van Valin 2006)
    a. Joan   Peo-ta   ?uka   vaci-ta   miika-k.
       Juan   Pedro-ACC   DET.ACC   corn-ACC   give-PERF
       'Juan gave Pedro the corn.'

    b. Peo   ?uka   vaci-ta   miik-wa-k.
       Pedro   DET.ACC   corn-ACC   give-PASS-PERF
       'Pedro was given the corn.'

    c. * U?u   vaci   Peo-ta   miik-wa-k.
       DET.NOM   corn   Pedro-ACC   give-pass-PERF
       'The corn was given to Pedro.'

(16) Double accusative and passive in the present series of Georgian (Joppen-Hellwig 2001: 50)
    a. Ketino   Eka-s   xalitša-s   s-čukni-s.
       Ketino   Eka-ACC   carpet-ACC   3D-present-PRES.3N
       'Ketino presents Eka with a carpet.'

    b. xalitša   e-čuk-eb-a   Eka-s.
       carpet   PASS-present-TH-PRES.3N   Eka-ACC
       'The carpet is presented to Eka.'

    c.* Eka   e-čuk-eb-a   xalitša-s.
       Eka   PASS-present-TH-PRES.3N   carpet-ACC
       'Eka is presented with a carpet.'

This shows that passivization is not only a test for subjecthood (answering the question of which argument is demoted in the passive) but also for objecthood, in that it makes a distinction between two types of double objects: primary vs. secondary object on the one hand, and direct vs. indirect object on the other (Dryer 1986, Wunderlich 2006: 136). Languages with symmetric objects (Bresnan & Moshi 1990) allow both alternatives: either the recipient or the theme becomes the syntactic subject in the passive. These differences clearly indicate that the promotion to nominative is not part of the passive operation, but a subsequent effect dependent on typological factors.

Passive is an operation found in nearly every language because it reflects a ubiquitous salience shift. If an argument other than the highest one is the actual topic, definite/specific, or a speech act participant, it might be more salient than the current highest argument; in that case, passive can shift it to a higher argument position, thus making its high salience also visible. (Aissen 1999 discusses subject choice in the framework of Optimality Theory.)

In most languages, the passive operation is marked by a verbal affix, a particle, or an auxiliary, but it can also be made visible by a shift in the complement pattern even if a separate marker of the passive is lacking. Some languages allow the so-called personal passive, in which the highest argument of a passivized verb is expressed by an oblique instrument, source, or agent phrase; such a phrase is best seen as an adjunct whose free argument is coindexed with the existentially bound argument. Assume that the sentence *John was kissed by Ann* is represented as $\lambda y \, \exists e \, \{\exists x \, \text{KISS}(x,y)(e) \, \& \, \text{AGENT}(\text{Ann},e)\}(\text{John})$, then $x = \text{Ann}$ is a contextual default for the value of x.

Various theories of the passive have been proposed, among them the voice hypothesis (Kratzer 1994), claiming that verbs have a basic form without agent, and only if they are integrated into a voice phrase, is an agent either added (in the active voice) or not (in the passive voice). This hypothesis suggests that active voice is the more marked variant of a transitive verb, which, however, is only rarely observed cross-linguistically (e.g., in languages of the Austronesian family). Moreover, it does not describe the semantic effect of passive as existential binding but rather as the absence of an argument.

In view of examples such as those in (17), Keenan (1980) and Dowty (1982) argued that English passive must operate on transitive verb phrases rather than verbs, e.g., on the VP *think cancer to be unlikely to be caused by hot dogs* in (17a). However, already Bresnan (1982) showed that a lexical rule of passive is able to handle these more complex instances, too.

(17) Passive of raising and control predicates (Bresnan 1982: 65)
    a. Cancer is now thought to be unlikely to be caused by hot dogs.
    b. Intruders are now forced to be prepared to be attacked by dogs.

Let us assume that (18a) represents the passive of *think* and (18b) the embedded complex (itself being passivized), then (18c) results through functional composition as the approximate representation of (17a). This clearly shows that the most internal argument is shifted to the subject of the whole complex by means of two passive operations. (Note that in a polysynthetic language such as Greenlandic all the higher predicates are affixes, thus the operations are necessarily word-internal rather than affecting VPs.)

(18) Analysis of raising + passive
    a. $\lambda p\ \exists x\ \text{THINK}(x,p)$
    b. $\lambda z\ \exists y\ \text{UNLIKELY}(\text{CAUSE}(y,z))$ Raising
    c. $\lambda z\ \exists x\ \text{THINK}(x,\ \exists y\ \text{UNLIKELY}(\text{CAUSE}(y,z)))$

Similarly, with the three pieces in (19a) one gets (19b) in the first step, and (19c) in the second step, representing (17b). Here, the most internal argument is stepwise identified with the subject of *be prepared* and the object of *force*; again, two passives are involved.

(19) Analysis of control + passive
    a. $\lambda z\ \exists u\ \text{ATTACK}(u,z)$
        $\lambda P\ \lambda y\ \text{PREPARED}(y,P(y))$ Subject control
        $\lambda Q\ \lambda x\ \exists v\ \text{FORCE}(v, x, Q(x))$ Object control

    b. $\lambda y\ \text{PREPARED}(y,\ \exists u\ \text{ATTACK}(u,y))$

    c. $\lambda x\ \exists v\ \text{FORCE}(v, x,\ \text{PREPARED}(x,\ \exists u\ \text{ATTACK}(u,x)))$

Antipassive is the counterpart to passive; it binds the lowest (rather than the highest) argument existentially, as shown in (20).

(20) **ANTIPASS**$[\lambda z \ldots \text{VERB}(\ldots, z)] = \exists z \ldots \text{VERB}(\ldots, z)$
          −lr

While the passive is induced by a particularly high salience status of the lower argument, the antipassive is induced by a particularly low status of that argument. It is therefore expected to be a less universal operation than passive. Whereas a canonical NOM-ACC verb turns into Ø-NOM by passivization, a canonical ERG-NOM verb turns into NOM-Ø by antipassivization; in both instances, a realization with a marked case is avoided. Although antipassive is particularly often found in ergative languages, it is not restricted to this type of language, the same way as passive is not restricted to accusative languages. A language can show both passive and antipassive by means of marked morphemes; an example is given in (21). One often finds a combination of causative with antipassive, as in (21c). Similarly, *he is cleaning* is derived from the causative verb *to clean* in English; 'object deletion' in languages such as English or German is just a form of antipassive without using a morpheme.

(21) Passive, antipassive, and causative+antipassive in Zoque (Johnson 2000)
    a. hu/c-/əm-wə   bi   wakaš.
       stab-PASS-COMPL   DEF   COW
       '(They) killed the cow.'
    b. behča   cəm-/oy-pa.
       horse   carry-ANTIP-INCOMPL
       'The horses will carry (it).'
    c. miš-yak-keš-/oy-wə-/am   dey.
       2>1-CAUS-eat-ANTIP-COMPL-NOW now
       'Now you have already fed me.'

What is known as antipassive (AP) in the Eskimo languages seems to be a more general construction. Several AP-markers are used with various imperfective, inceptive, frequentative or distributive readings; all of them lead to an intransitive verb morphologically, but preserve the original valency syntactically. The ERG-NOM pattern of a transitive verb gets shifted to a NOM-instrumental pattern. According to Beach (2003), there is an important difference between dative-marked agent phrases in the passive and instrumental-marked patient phrases in the antipassive. The latter can be associated with a floating quantifier (22c), and allows interclausal binding (23b), while the former resists those operations (22a,b, 23a). Beach concludes that the instrumental NP of the antipassive construction is a core argument, while the dative NP of the passive construction is a peripheral adjunct. (/-ja/ marks a simple passive, /-naq/ marks the combination of passive and causative, /-tit/ marks the simple causative, and /-si/ marks the antipassive.)

(22) Floating quantifiers in Inuktitut (Beach 2003)
    a. arnaq   anguti-nut   taku-ja-u -laur -tuq   (*atuniit)
       woman.ABS   man-DAT.pl   see-PASS.PRT-be-PAST-IND.3sg (*each)
       'The woman was seen by (*each of) the men.'
    b. anguti-nut   aannia -na-laur-tuq   (*atuniit)
       man-DAT.pl   be.sick-PASS.CAUSE-PAST-IND.3sg (*each)
       'It made (*each of) these men sick.'

c. anguti-nik   aannia -tit-si -laur -tuq   atuniit
      man-INS.pl   be.sick-CAUSE-AP-PAST-IND.3sg   each
      'It made each of the men sick.'

(23) Interclausal binding in Inuktitut (Beach 2003)
   a. (*immi-nit) [Jaani-mut   ulla-guma-na   -raluar -ti -lu-gu]
                                                              sukannisaqalaurtuq
      self -ABL   [John-DAT   run-want-PASS.CAUSE-indeed-OBV-APPL-3s]
                                                              there.was. someone.faster
      'Although it made John want to run, there was someone faster (*than self).'

   b. immi-nit   [Jaani-mik   ulla-guma-tit-si-galuar-ti-lu-gu]   sukan-
                                                              nisaqalaurtuq
      self -ABL   John-INS   run-want-CAUSE-AP-although-OBV-APPL -3s]
                                                              there. was. someone.faster
      'Although he/she/it made John$_i$ want to run, there was someone faster than him$_i$.'

Moreover, the Eskimo antipassive construction is associated with semantic readings that are not usually attributed to antipassive. As Bittner (1987) showed, the instrumental NP in the antipassive needs neither to be indefinite nor unspecific, on the contrary it can be realized with proper nouns as well as with demonstratives. On the other hand, the nominative subject could also be indefinite or unspecific, so that in this respect a contrast between the two arguments is not necessary. According to Bittner, the various semantic effects of the antipassive construction show up in the context of an operator such as negation, quantifier, tense, modality, or distributive plural. Unlike the nominative object-NP of the plain transitive clause, the corresponding instrumental NP of the antipassive may have narrow scope, and that reading is preferred if the construction is contrasted with the plain transitive; only in that case is the instrumental NP indefinite or unspecific. (24) to (26) show some of Bittner's examples. The a-sentences are transitive and only allow the wide scope reading A, whereas the b-sentences are antipassivized and allow the narrow scope reading B as well. The notation is Bittner's, except that '∀y∈{they}' is used for her distribution operator.

Narrow scope readings of Greenlandic antipassive (Bittner 1987)
(24) a. *arnaq   franskiq   angirlaat-tar-pa-a.*   = A,*B
         woman.NOM French.NOM   [come.home.with]-HAB-TR.INDIC-3sgE/3sgN

     b. *[arnaq-mik   franskiq-mik   angirlaat-(ss)i]-tar-pu-q.*   = A, B
         [woman-INS   French-INS   come.home.with-AP]-HAB-TR.INDIC-3sgN

'He often comes home with French woman.'
A. It's always the same woman.
B. Different women on different occasions.
A. ∃x[x is a French woman & *often* (he comes home with x)]
B. *often* (∃x[x is a French woman & he comes home with x])

(25) a. *ullut tamaasa*   *irinarsurtuq*   *tusar-pa-a.*   = A, *B
         days all   singer.NOM   [hear]-TR.INDIC-3sgE/3sgN

      b. *ullut tamaasa*   *irinarsurtuq-mik*   *tusar-si-pu-q.*   = A, B
         days all   [singer-INS   hear-AP]-INTR.INDIC-3sgN
         'Every day he hears singer.'
         A. Same singer every day.
         B. Different singers on different days.
      A. ∃x[x is a singer & *every day* (he hears x)]
      B. *every day* (∃x[x is a singer & he hears x])

(26) a. *cigaretti*   [*ikit*]-*pa-at*   = A, *B
         cigarette.NOM   [light]-TR.INDIC-3plE/3sgN
      b. [*cigaretti-mik ikit-si*]-*ppu-t*   = A, B
         [cigarette-INS light-AP]-INTR.INDIC-3plN
         'They lit cigarette.'
         A. What they lit was just one cigarette for the whole group.
         B. They lit a cigarette each.
      A. ∃x(x is a cigarette & ∀y∈{they}(lit(y, x)))
      B. ∀y∈{they}(∃x(x is a cigarette & lit(y, x)))

Inspired by these findings, Bittner detected similar effects of case alternations in Basque, Polish, Russian, and Finnish, where nominative has wide scope over negation, modals, etc., while genitive and partitive, triggered by these elements, can or must have narrow scope – this leads to the generalization in (27).

(27) *The Scope Generalization (Bittner 1987)*

If an argument can be expressed either by an NP in the case predicted by the parameter settings for the language [canonical argument structure] or by some other kind of phrase, then the parametric alternant [the NP] will obligatorily take wide scope with respect to sentential operators, such as negation, tense, aspect, modals, distributive operators, etc., while the nonparametric alternant [the other kind of phrase] will be permitted to take scope under these operators. It may in fact be restricted to take narrow scope.

This generalization suggests that argument structure alternations such as antipassive are motivated by the need to express different scope relations. Let us assume that a structural argument, in particular the nominative argument, is a good candidate for the topic, which usually has wide scope; then existential binding and/or a semantic case reduce the possibility of being the topic. Structurally, a semantic case typically indicates an adjunct rather than an argument; adjuncts belong to the VP predicating of the subject. The above-mentioned negation, modals, etc. are part of the VP, and therefore are able to take a semantic adjunct, but not the subject, into their scope.

Another argument reduction operation is the lexical reflexive. It establishes an anaphoric relationship by identifying a lower argument with the highest one. Such an operation is distinct from using a reflexive anaphora (such as *themselves*) in the syntax.

(28) **REFL**[$\lambda z \ldots \lambda x$ VERB(x, ..., z)] = λx VERB(x, ..., x)
     +lr   −lr   −lr

(29a) shows the canonical case, in which a transitive verb is detransitivized. In (29b) however, the verb remains transitive; in this case a possessor is added to the core arguments (which makes the verb ditransitive) and is then identified with the highest argument. In general, reciprocal functions similarly, but has a more complex semantics (Heim, Lasnik & May 1991, Williams 1991): the antecedent X must be plural and must receive a distributed interpretation, and any $x \in X$ is paired with some (or every) $y \in X$, where $y \neq x$. Interestingly, (29c) illustrates a case in which the reciprocal morpheme must be combined with the reflexive in order to unfold its full semantics.

(29) Reflexive and Reciprocal in Bolivian Quechua (van de Kerke 1996: 160, 146)
    a. Pedru   maylla-ku-n
       Pedru   wash-REFL-3sg
       'Pedro   washes himself.'
       REFL[$\lambda y \lambda x$ WASH(x,y)] = λx WASH(x,x)

    b. Pedru uya-n-ta   maylla-ku-n
       Pedru face-3sg-ACC wash-REFL-3sg
       'Pedro washes his (own) face.'
       REFL[$\lambda z \lambda y \lambda x$\{WASH(x,z) & POSS(y,z)\}}] = $\lambda z \lambda x$\{WASH(x,z) & POSS(x,z)\}

    c. maylla-na-ku-yku
       wash-REC-REFL-1pl
       'We wash each other.'

Incorporation is quite a different type of argument reduction; in this case, an argument is realized by a morphologically integrated nominal predicate. For instance, a noun can be prefixed to the verb stem, which indicates that this noun predicates of the lowest argument of the verb. Van Geenhoven (1998) analysed incorporated nouns as predicative indefinites. Formally, one can assume an operation that takes two elements in the input, a noun and a verb, and produces a coherent verb reading by argument identification, see (30).

(30) **INCORP** < λv NOUN(v), $\lambda z \ldots$ VERB($\ldots$, z)> = $\exists z \ldots$ {VERB($\ldots$, z) & NOUN(z)}
$$-lr$$

This analysis suggests that noun incorporation always leads to a general or unspecific reading; however, some languages also allow a specific reading of the incorporated noun, as in (31a), where a demonstrative is stranded. Its referent has to be identified with the entity the complex N-V predicate predicates of, see (31b).

(31) Noun incorporation with definite reading in Southern Tiwa (Baker 1988: 93)
    a. Yede a-seuan-mu-ban.
        that   2sg-man-see-PAST
        'You saw that man.'
    b. R('that') = ιz {SEE(you,z) & MAN(z)}.

Noun incorporation cannot be iterated, and only the lowest argument can be incorporated – probably because canonical λ-application takes place, affecting the lowest θ-role first. Noun incorporation creates a configuration where arguments other than the lowest one can function as structural object (or even as subject): a recipient (32a), an instrument (32b), a possessor (32c,d), or a goal (32e). A ditransitive verb is transitivized in (32a), and a transitive verb is detransitivized in (32b,c), but then either undergoes instrumental applicative (see next section) or inherits the possessor from the incorporated possessed noun, and thus again shows a transitive construction. Similarly, an intransitive verb again becomes intransitive when it undergoes applicative (32e) or inherits the possessor (32d). (The bracketing in the semantic representations shows the respective ordering of operations.)

(32) Noun incorporation (Baker 1988)
    a. Ka-'u'u-wia-ban.   *Southern Tiwa*
       1sg/2sg-baby-give-PAST
       'I gave you the baby.'
       $\lambda y \lambda x \exists z$ {(ACT(x) &$_{CAUS}$ BEC POSS(y,z)) & BABY(z)}

b. Kua ta fakatino   he tama   e malala.   *Niue (Polynesian)*
   PERF-draw-picture   ERG-child   NOM-charcoal
   'The child has been drawing pictures with a charcoal.'
   λz λx {∃y (DRAW(x,y) & PICTURE(y)) & INST(z)}

c. Wa-hi-nuhs-ahni:nu: John.   *Oneida*
   PAST-1sg/3m-house-buy   John
   'I bought John's house.'
   λz λx ∃y {BUY(x,y) & (HOUSE(y) & POSS(z,y))}

d. Hrao-nuhs-rakv   ne sawatis.   *Mohawk*
   3m-house-white   John
   'John's house is white.'
   λy ∃x {WHITE(x) & (HOUSE(x) & POSS(y,x))}

e. Am-seuan-wan-ban   liora-n.   *Southern Tiwa*
   3pl-man-come-PAST   lady-pl
   'The man came to the ladies.'
   λy {∃x (COME(x) & MAN(x)) & GOAL(y)}

3 Argument extension: causative, applicative, resultative, and others

The opposite of argument reduction is argument extension: valency-increasing operations extend the number of syntactically active arguments. Argument reduction always binds an existing argument, so the semantic core can remain unaffected. An additional argument, however, needs to be licensed by an additional predicate; therefore, argument extension always affects the semantic core itself. Either a higher predicate together with a higher argument is added, or a lower predicate together with a lower argument. A prototypical instance of the former type of operations is the causative, whereas different variants of the applicative are characteristic for the latter type of operations.

The causative adds a causer, who instigates the event expressed by the basic verb, either by direct coercion, or more indirectly by giving an order or admitting a certain course of affairs. Some version of causative is found in nearly every language, and many languages have more than one type of causative (differing morphosyntactically and often also in their finer semantic aspects). It is disputed in the literature whether the causative has to be represented explicitly by the predicate CAUSE (and whether this CAUSE is a relation between two events or between an entity and an event), or whether the causal relationship can be inferred from the lexical combination of an action predicate with another, simpler predicate (see, e.g., the different views advocated by Bierwisch 2002 vs. Wunderlich 2000, 2012). For the purposes of this article, I use the notion $\&_{CAUSE}$, taken as a contextually-induced reading of the connector AND. (Notice that $\&_{CAUSE}$ is asymmetric, just as &, when used in a lexical decomposition from which argument hierarchy is derived.) Moreover, the causative usually gets a factive reading, which is expressed by existential binding of the verb's original event variable.

(33) CAUS [λe' VERB(...)(e')] = ...λx λe {ACT(x) $\&_{CAUSE}$ ∃e'VERB(...)(e')}(e)

In a typical causative formed from a transitive verb the causee becomes the medial argument; it is marked dative in an accusative language such as Japanese (see below (39a)), as well as in an ergative language such as Basque (34).

(34) Causative in Basque
Ama-k   haurr-a-ri   zopa   jan-eraz-i   dio.
mother-ERG   child-DET-DAT   soup.NOM   eat-CAUS-PERF   have.3N.3sgD.3sgE
'Mother let the child eat the soup'
λz λy λx λe {ACT(x) $\&_{CAUSE}$ ∃e'EAT(y,z)(e')}(e)

In a double object construction the causee is realized as the primary object (which can become the subject under passive, can be co-indexed with an object affix, etc.). Besides this unmarked option, illustrated in (35a), there is also a marked option, in which the causee is obliquely realized and does not function as a structural object (35b). Such a marked option is found in various languages, even in those that otherwise have a dative; in Hungarian, for instance., it can be captured by the assumption that the causative morpheme lexically assigns instrumental case (36b) (Wunderlich 2002).

(35) Causative variation in Bantu: Chimwiini (a) vs. Chichewa-A (b) (Baker 1988: 183,163)
a. Mwa:limu   Ø-wa-andik-ish-ize   wa:na   xati.
   teacher   SU-OB-write-CAUS-ASP   children   letter
   'The teacher made the children write a letter.'

b. Anyani   a-na-wa-meny-ets-a   ana   kwa buluzi.
   baboons   SU-PAST-OB-hit-CAUS-ASP children   to lizard
   'The baboons made the lizard hit the children.'

(36) Medial arguments in Hungarian
    a. Anna   Péter-nek adott   egy   könyv-et.
       Anna   Peter-DAT gave   a   book-ACC
       'Anna gave a book to Peter.'

    b. Anna   könyv-et   olvas-tat   Péter-rel.
       Anna   book-ACC   read-CAUS   Peter-INST
       'Anna has Peter read a book.'

Another possible variant of the causative is a construction formed with an object control verb, such as *force, make,* or *let* (*force him to go, make him go, let him go*). Such a verb adds two arguments, whereby it identifies the object with the subject of a dependent (infinitive) clause (37a). However, that a single morphological operation produces an object control configuration would be unexpected if a simpler alternative is available (37b).

(37) Object control vs. causative
    a. $\lambda P\, \lambda y\, \lambda x\, \text{FORCE}(x,y,P(y))$
    b. $\lambda p\, \lambda x\, \{\text{ACT}(x)\, \&_{\text{CAUSE}}\, p\}$

A few languages have operations that add a highest argument in a function distinct from causer. One such operation is the assistive in Quechua. (38) shows that causative and assistive are structurally alike in Quechua: either a causer or a helper is added as the highest argument. Note that a helper does not necessarily contribute an additional event because she is involved in the same type of action as the helpee. (Quechua lacks a dative, therefore all objects are realized as accusative; object agreement on the verb refers to the highest object, which is the causee or helpee in these cases.)

(38) Causative and Assistive in Bolivian Quechua (van de Kerke 1996: 153, 157)
    a. mama-y   Maria-ta   maylla-chi-wa-rqa
       mother-1sg   Mary-ACC   wash-CAUS-1A-PAST
       'My mother made me wash Maria.'
       $\lambda z\, \lambda y\, \lambda x\, \lambda e\, \{\text{ACT}(x)\, \&_{\text{cause}}\, \text{WASH}(y,z)\}(e)$

    b. mama-y   Maria-ta   maylla-ysi-wa-rqa
       mother-1sg   Mary-ACC   wash-ASS-1A-PAST
       'My mother helped me to wash Maria.'
       $\lambda z\, \lambda y\, \lambda x\, \lambda e\, \{\text{HELPER}(x)\, \&\, \text{WASH}(y,z)\}(e)$

Another operation that adds a highest argument is the affective in Japanese. That causative and affective are structurally alike is shown in (39a,b). Although the affective is formed with the same suffix (*-are*) as the passive and is therefore traditionally called 'indirect passive', its argument structure is clearly distinct from that of a passive (39c). (Note that *-ni* functions both as dative and as adverbial postposition.)

(39) Causative, affective and passive in Japanese (Washio 1995: 6)
 a. John-ga   Mary-ni   tokei-o   nusum-ase-ta.
    John-NOM   Mary-DAT   watch-ACC   steal-CAUS-PAST
    'John let Mary steal a watch.'
    λy λx λu λe {ACT(u) &$_{CAUSE}$ STEAL(x,y)}(e)

 b. John-ga   Mary-ni   tokei-o   nusum-are-ta.
    John-NOM   Mary-DAT   watch-ACC   steal-AFF-PAST
    'John had a watch stolen by Mary.'
    = 'John was affected by Mary stealing (his) watch.'
    λy λx λu λe {AFF(u) & STEAL(x,y)} (e)

 c. Tokei-ga   Mary-ni   nusum-are-ta.
    watch-NOM   Mary-BY   steal-PASS-PAST
    'The watch was stolen by Mary.'
    λy λe ∃x STEAL(x,y) (e)

For operations that add a non-highest argument, the term 'applicative' is used as a collective name; the added argument can be a recipient/beneficiary, a possessor, a location, or an instrument. In some languages, a single morpheme encodes all these extensions, while other languages have several distinct morphemes. The general scheme of applicatives when applied to a transitive verb is given in (40). (Whether BECOME is present or not depends on further circumstances, especially on the dynamics of the verb.)

(40) **APPL**[VERB(x,y)] = VERB(x,y) & POSS(z,y)   'z is (or becomes) a possessor of y'
                                  & LOC(y AT z)   'y is (or becomes) located at z'
                                  & INST(z,y)   'z operates as an instrument on y'

In principle, the operation is possible with ditransitive verbs, too. Locative and instrumental applicatives mostly apply on intransitive verbs as well; they then characterize a relation to the intransitive subject, or just a further participant of the event. Applied objects can also stand in a manner, comitative or sociative relation. In any case, the subject remains the same, while an object is added and therefore the realization of objects is shifted. In that sense one can say that *enter* ('x goes-and-becomes-located-at y') is a local applicative of *go* ('x goes'), although the relation *enter-go* is formally a suppletion.

The most prototypical instance of applicative is the benefactive alternation, shown in (41); here, the transitive verb 'buy' becomes ditransitive by means of the applicative suffix in (41b). Following Baker (1988), one might say that the preposition 'for' is incorporated into the verb, so that the prepositional object becomes a direct argument of the verb. However, since *untuk* 'for' and the applicative *kan* are quite distinct morphemes, 'incorporation' would have to be understood in a rather abstract sense. Conceptually it is more convenient to consider the applicative as a way of expressing further participants, independently of whether corresponding prepositional means exist. Thus, the relationship between (41a) and (41b) is purely semantical, not generative; the applicative applies on the verb, not on a syntactic construction. The predicate variable 'P' in (41a) serves as a placeholder for the prepositional phrase, which could also be 'with', 'in', etc. Even if one concedes that the applicative could have a comitative rather than a benefactive meaning, the verb in (41b) is more specific than that in (41a) because it has a third structural argument.

(41) Benefactive alternation in Bahasa Indonesia (Chung 1976)
    a. Ali   memi   telefisi   untuk   ibu-nja.
       Ali   TR.buy   televison   for   mother-his
       'Ali bought a televison for his mother.'
       $\lambda P\ \lambda z\ \lambda x\ \lambda e\{\text{BUY}(x,z)\ \&\ P(z)\}(e)$

    b. Ali   mem-beli-kan   ibu-nja   telefisi.
       Ali   TR-buy-APPL   mother-his   televison
       'Ali bought his mother a televison.'
       $\lambda z\ \lambda y\ \lambda x\ \lambda e\{\text{BUY}(x,z)\ \&\ \text{BECOME POSS}(y,z)\}(e)$

A similar argumentation holds for the locative alternation as described for English, German, or Hungarian. The semantically related sentences in (42a,b) or (43a,b) can be assumed to be base-generated rather than derived from each other. (This does not exclude the possibility of preposition incorporation in instances like (44).) It has often been observed that there are finer semantic differences between the respective a- and b-sentences (Brinkmann 1995), which follow from the different status of the arguments involved. The a-sentences are preferred if one wants to communicate that all parts of the stuff (hay, paint) were located somewhere, whereas the b-sentences are preferred if all parts of a location were occupied by the stuff. The question why 'hay' in (42b) and 'paint' in (43b) cannot be expressed as structural arguments cannot be discussed here, but see Wunderlich (1997a,b).

(42) Locative alternation in Hungarian (Ackermann 1992)
    a. a paraszt (rá-)rakta a szénát a szekérre.
       the peasant (onto-)loaded.3sg.DEF the hay.ACC the wagon.SUBL
       'The peasant loaded the hay onto the wagon.'
       $\lambda P \lambda y \lambda x \lambda e \{\text{LOAD}(x,y) \& P(y)\}(e)$

    b. a paraszt meg-rakta a szekeret (szénával).
       the peasant PERF-loaded.3sg.DEF the wagon.ACC (hay.INSTR)
       'The peasant loaded the wagon (with hay).'
       $\lambda z \lambda x \lambda e \{\text{LOAD}(x,y) \& \text{BECOME LOC}(y, \text{AT}(z))\}(e)$

(43) Locative alternation in German (Brinkmann 1995)
    a. Die Vandalen spritzten Farbe auf das Auto.
       the vandals sprayed paint onto the car

    b. Die Vandalen be-spritzten das Auto (mit Farbe).
       the vandals BE-sprayed the car (with paint)

(44) Preposition incorporation in German
    a. Sie flogen über die Ostsee.
       they flew over the Baltic Sea.
       $\lambda P \lambda x \lambda e \{\text{FLY}(x) \& P(x)\}(e)$

    b. Sie über-flogen die Ostsee.
       they over-flew the Baltic Sea.
       $\lambda y \lambda x \lambda e \{\text{FLY}(x) \& \text{LOC}(x,\text{AT}(y))\}(e)$

The examples (45a–c) illustrate some applicative variants in the Bantu language Kinyarwanda; benefactive, possessor-raising, and instrumental applicative are marked by different suffixes. As one can see, *-iish* is ambiguous; it either marks instrumental applicative or causative (45c, d). The reading depends on the sortal properties of the complements: usually a child but not a piece of soap is washed, while soap but not a child can be an instrument of washing.

(45) Applicatives in Kinyarwanda (Polinsky & Kozinsky 1992)
    a. umugóre y-a-som-e-ye umwáana igitabo.
       woman 3sg-PAST-read-APPL-PERF child book
       'The woman read the book to the child.' (*benefactive applicative*)

    b. umugabo a-ra-kikir-ir-a umugóre umwáana.
       man 3sg-PRES-hold-APPL-IMPF woman child

'The man is holding the woman's child.' (*possessor-raising applicative*)

c. umugóre   y-Ø-uhag-iish-ije   umwáana   isábune.
   woman   3sg-PAST-wash-APPL-PERF   child   soap
   'The woman washed the child with soap.' (*instrumental applicative*)

d. umugóre   y-Ø-uhag-iish-ije   umukoóbwa umwáana.
   woman   3sg-PAST-wash-CAUS-PERF   girl   child
   'The woman made the girl wash the child.' (*causative*)

A further type of argument extension on the lower end of the argument hierarchy is the strong resultative, by which both an object and a predicate are added to the verb (Washio 1997, Wunderlich 1997b, Kaufmann & Wunderlich 1998, Wunderlich 2000). As the examples (46a,b) show, the object is only licensed by the result predicate, not by the verb itself. (46c) shows the general templatic operation.

(46) Strong resultatives
  a. Paul ran the lawn flat. (*Paul ran the lawn)
     $\lambda y\, \lambda x\, \lambda e \{\text{RUN}(x)\ \&_{\text{CAUSE}}\ \text{BECOME FLAT}(y)\}(e)$
  b. Paul drank the fridge empty. (*Paul drank the fridge)
     $\lambda y\, \lambda x\, \lambda e\, \exists z\, \{\text{DRINK}(x,z)\ \&_{\text{CAUSE}}\ \text{BECOME EMPTY}(y)\}(e)$
  c. **RES** [VERB(...)] = {VERB(...) $\&_{\text{CAUSE}}$ BECOME RESULT(z)}, where RESULT is a predicate variable.

Interestingly, unlike causatives, which are usually encoded by a generalized morpheme leaving the causing action unspecific, resultatives are rarely encoded by a generalized morpheme, but mostly by the presence of a predicate that specifies the result. This might be predicted by a general cognitive principle "A causal action can remain unspecific, but a result must be specified". In any case, although they add a lower argument as well, resultatives crucially differ from applicatives in that they always specify the result property. The only generalized resultative marker I am aware of is Chinese *de*, derived from the verb 'obtain', which is used in a verbal compound as in (47).

(47) Chinese *de*-construction
  a. Ta   ku-**de**   shoujuan   quan shi   le.
     he   cry-DE   handkerchief all wet   FIN
     lit. 'He cried such that the handkerchief got all wet.'
     'He cried the handkerchief all wet.'

b. Lisi   zhui-**de**   Zhangsan   hen lei.
   L   chase-DE   Z   very tired
   lit. 'Lisi chased somebody and [as a result] Zhangsan got very tired.'
   'Lisi chased Zhangsan very tired.'

More specific markers of resultativity are found as prefixes or particles in languages such as Hungarian, Russian, or German. In (48), the prefix *er-* contributes the result predicate POSS.

(48) German prefix verbs (Stiebels 1996)
    a. Sie er-schrieb   sich   den Pulitzer-Preis.
       She **er**-wrote   herself   the Pulitzer price.
       'She won the Pulitzer price by her writing'

    b. $\lambda v\, \lambda u\, \lambda x\, \lambda e\, \exists y\, \{\text{WRITE}(x,y)\, \&_{\text{CAUSE}}\, \text{BECOME POSS}(u,v)\}(e)$
       y becomes non-structural here and cannot be realized as a complement (Wunderlich 1997b).

4 Functor vs. incorporation

Derivational morphemes such as causative and applicative are usually considered to be morphological heads; they apply on a verb in order to form a more complex verb. Even if the Kinyarwanda suffix *-iish* is ambiguous between causative and applicative, there is certainly no difference in the headedness status between causatives and applicatives. However, as outlined above, the causative adds a new highest argument, while the applicative adds a non-highest argument; therefore, they must have a different status in functional composition. I take it for granted that the functor in a derivation contributes the highest argument. Thus, the causative morpheme is a functor that takes the verb, but, in virtue of the same logic, the applicative morpheme cannot be the functor. Hence, in that case the verb itself must be the functor, but has to undergo a templatic predicate extension in order to incorporate a further predicate.

(49a,b) repeats the pair of sentences (45d,c) from above, and adds a benefactive formed from the same verb. Let (50a) represent the causative reading of *-iish*, and (50b) the verb 'wash'. Then, (50c) derives via functional composition; a highest argument is added, and all original arguments of the verb are inherited.

(49) Causative, instrumental, and benefactive applicative in Kinyarwanda
    a. umugóre   y-Ø-uhag-iish-ije   umukoóbwa   umwáana.
       woman   3sg-PAST-wash-CAUS-PERF   girl   child
       'The woman made the girl wash the child.'
    b. umugóre   y-Ø-uhag-iish-ije   umwáana   isábune.
       woman   3sg-PAST-wash-APPL-PERF   child   soap
       'The woman washed the child with soap.'
    c. umugóre   y-Ø-uhag-e-ye   umukoóbwa   umwáana.
       woman   3sg-PAST-wash-APPL-PERF   girl   child
       'The woman washed the child for the girl.'

(50) The causative as a functor on the verb
    a. causative *-iish*: $\lambda V \lambda u \lambda e \{\text{ACT}(u) \&_{\text{CAUSE}} \exists e'\ V(e')\}(e)$
    b. *uhag*: $\underline{\lambda y \lambda x} \lambda e\ \text{WASH}(x,y)(s)$
    c. *uhag-iish*: $\underline{\lambda y \lambda x} \lambda u \lambda e \{\text{ACT}(u) \&_{\text{CAUSE}} \exists e'\ \underline{\text{wash}(x,y)}(e')\}(e)$

However, with applicatives preserving the original subject, the verb must function as functor. In order for that, the verb undergoes the templatic extension shown in (51), incorporating the predicate P, whatever it is.

(51) Predicate incorporation into a verb:
    P-INCORP$<P, \ldots \lambda e\ \text{VERB}(\ldots)(e)> = \lambda P \ldots \lambda e\{\text{VERB}(\ldots)(e)\ \&\ P(e)\}$,
                           which can be simplified as $\{\text{VERB}(\ldots)\ \&\ P\}(e)$

Let us assume that the verb 'wash' is augmented in this way (52a), and that P is instantiated by an instrumental predicate (52b), then (52c) is derived via functional composition. Here, the original arguments of the verb remain the highest ones, whereas those of the incorporated predicate become lower ones. For the complex event denoted by the derived verb to be coherent, incorporans and incorporandum should share an argument. In principle, v can be identified with either e or y (with slightly different readings: 'instrument of performing an action', 'instrument operating on an individual entity'), but certainly not with x. This yields one of the representations given in (52d); the difference is that the instrumental object is either the lowest or the medial argument of the complex verb. When combined with a transitive verb, the applied instrumental object (u) in the Bantu languages does in fact sometimes have properties of the lowest, and sometimes of a medial argument (Marantz 1993).

(52) The (extended) verb as functor on the applicative
    a. P-INCORP(*uhag*): $\lambda P \lambda y \lambda x \lambda e\ \{\text{WASH}(x,y)\ \&\ P\}(e)$

    b. applicative -*iish*: $\lambda v\, \lambda u$ INSTR(u,v)
    c. *uhag-iish*: $\lambda v\, \lambda u\, \lambda y\, \lambda x\, \lambda e$ {WASH(x,y) & INSTR(u,v)}(e)
    d. $\lambda u\, \lambda y\, \lambda x\, \lambda e$ {WASH(x,y) & INSTR(u)}(e)
       $\lambda y\, \lambda u\, \lambda x\, \lambda e$ {WASH(x,y) & INSTR(u,y)}(e)

In contrast, the applied beneficiary mostly shows properties of the medial argument, and the applied locative object shows properties of the lowest argument (Alsina & Mchombo 1990). This is expected, given that the predicate that integrates beneficiaries is assumed to be POSS(**u**,v), with u being the applied object, whereas the predicate in the case of locative application is LOC(v, AT **u**), again with u being the applied object. (McGinnis (2005) proposes a phase-theoretic analysis for the different behavior of these types of applicatives.)

Of course, one could think of representing the causative and applicative morphemes in a more uniform way, e.g. as {CAUSER(u) & VERB} vs. {VERB & INSTR(u)}, but in that case the actual hierarchy of arguments would not be determined by functional composition, and additional reasons would have to be found.

In the German prefix verbs, the verb is both the head and the functor. (53a) repeats (48a) from above. (53b) shows the verb extended by P-INCORP, and (53c) the semantic contribution of the prefix *er-*. Functional composition then yields the result in (53d). As a matter of fact, the document written (y) cannot be expressed because it neither is in the position of a structural argument (Wunderlich 1997b) nor can be identified with the thing to become possessed (v); therefore it must be bound existentially.

(53)   German prefix verbs (Stiebels 1996)
    a. Sie *er*-schrieb sich   den Pulitzer-Preis.
       She *er*-wrote   herself the Pulitzer price.
       'She won the Pulitzer price by her writing'

    b. **P-INCORP**(*schreib*): $\lambda P\, \lambda y\, \lambda x\, \lambda e$ {WRITE(x,y) & P}(s)

    c. resultative *er-*: $\lambda v\, \lambda u$ BECOME POSS(u,v)

    d. *er-schreib*: $\lambda v\, \lambda u\, \lambda y\, \lambda x\, \lambda e$ {WRITE(x,y) & BECOME POSS(u,v)} (e)
                         $\Rightarrow$. $\lambda v\, \lambda u\, \lambda x\, \lambda e\, \exists y$ {WRITE(x,y) & BECOME POSS(u,v)}(e)

The representation (53d) is still unsatisfactory because it doesn't make explicit the difference between a factual and an intended result. If I write a novel for Paul I intend Paul to become the possessor of the novel (WRITE(x,y) &$_{\text{INTEND}}$ BECOME POSS(u,y)), however, if Paul then wins the Pulitzer price with this novel (pretending to have written it himself) the sentence 'Ich erschrieb Paul den Pulitzer-Preis' becomes true. The minimal repair in (53d) would be '&$_{\text{CAUSE}}$' instead of '&', but this would require a slightly different incorporation template to start with.

5 Parsimony in the set of exponents: polyfunctional affixes

In the Pama-Nyungan languages of Australia a single affix often functions as a general transitivization marker. For instance, the Kalkatunga suffix *-nti* adds a causer if it is combined with an inchoative or stative verb (54a), but it adds a beneficiary, instrument, or location if it is combined with an agentive verb (54b). In a subgroup of these languages the same affix can be applied to transitive verbs as well, but usually only when they have first been detransitivized by antipassive, as in (54c), where the demoted object is realized by oblique dative marking.

(54) Transitivization in Kalkatunga (Austin 1997)
    a. iti 'return'   iti-nti 'send/bring back'
        nguyi 'fall'   nguyi-nti 'push over'

    b. nuu 'lie'   nu-nti 'lie on (something)'
        wani 'play'   wani-nti 'play with (something)'

    c. Nga-thu   kati-nti-mi   tharntu   kupangurru-u.
        1-ERG   bury-TR-FUT   hole.NOM   old.man-DAT
        'I will bury the old man in a hole.'

A canonical transitive verb can possibly be decomposed into an active (controller) and an affected predicate. Given that an intransitive verb is either active or affected, the function of the transitivizing affix then is to derive a canonical verb, i.e. to add the respective complementary predicate.

(55)   TR [VERB] results in a canonical transitive verb
        TR [$\lambda y\ \text{AFF}(y)$] = $\lambda y\ \lambda x\ \text{ACT}(x)\ \&\ \text{AFF}(y)$
        TR [$\lambda x\ \text{ACT}(x)$] = $\lambda y\ \lambda x\ \text{ACT}(x)\ \&\ \text{AFF}(y)$

A different type of affix such as *-e* in Japanese either transitivizes or detransivizes. Comrie (2006) lists 57 inchoative/causative pairs in which *-e* derives the causative verb (56a), and 36 pairs in which it functions as the opposite, namely derives the inchoative verb from the transitive one (56b). Even larger is the number of pairs where the two verbs are derived by different means (56c).

(56) Causatives vs. anticausatives in Japanese (Comrie 2006)
    a. ak-u 'open'   ak-e-ru 'open (tr.)'
        itam-u 'hurt'   tam-e-ru 'injure'
        tat-u 'stand'   tat-e-ru 'raise'

b. nuk-u 'remove'   nuk-e-ru 'come off'
   or-u 'break (tr.)'   or-e-ru 'break'
   tuka-u 'use'   tuka-e-ru (be usable)

c. kowa-s-u 'destroy'   kowa-re-ru 'be destroyed'.

A similar phenomenon has been observed in other languages as well (Haspelmath 1993). The majority of languages tend to use the causative operation more frequently than its opposite, called anticausative. Only the semitic languages exhibit more anticausatives, however, they use a number of different prefixes. Formally, one can describe the function of Japanese -e as in (57). It is important to note that, unlike passive, the anticausative does not imply the presence of an agent.

(57) VERB and -e[VERB] differ in their transitivity status
      -e [λy AFF(y)]   =   λy λx{ACT(x) &$_{CAUSE}$ AFF(y)}
      -e [λy λx{ACT(x) &$_{CAUSE}$ AFF(y)}]   =   λy AFF(y))

Obviously, the anticausative operation conflicts with the principle of monotonicity, which states that no semantic information is deleted in the course of derivation. Therefore it is hard to imagine that an affix could have emerged with a pure anticausative function; it would have been blocked by the monotonicity principle. What one indeed finds are morphemes with a broader function including the anticausative reading as a special case. One possibility is, within the inchoative/causative pairs, that a marker can choose either the more complex or the more basic item. Given a grammatical dimension in which pairs of lexical items derived from a common stem can be ordered, one member of the pair should have the semantic property X, while the other lacks it. Usually one expects pairs <σ,σ'> such that σ=<PF,SF> and σ'=<PF+pf, SF+sf>, where <pf,sf> is the contribution of an affix or some other morphophonological operation. However, if a form expressing SF+sf is more likely to be used than the alternative form expressing SF simpliciter it is conceivable that the more complex meaning is combined with the simpler PF, i.e., pairs <σ,σ'> such that σ=<PF,SF+sf> and σ'=<PF+pf, SF> might become possible as well. (Bidirectional optimality theory would be able to model such a situation, see Blutner & Zeevat 2004).

The other possibility is detransitivization as a multi-functional operation, which derives several kinds of intransitive readings, depending on the specific meaning of the verb. The middle voice is typically known for its multiple readings. Unlike passive and antipassive as special operations for deactivating the higher or the lower argument (the agent or patient) respectively, the middle seems to be a general operation that basically contrasts intransitives (of any kind) with transitives. According to the diagram (58) general transitivizers and general detransitivizers can be distinguished from more specific operations. Above I illustrated the specific pair causative/anticausative; it would be interesting to know whether other specific pairs such as antipassive/applicative exist as well, and if not, why not.

(58) Transitivity alternations

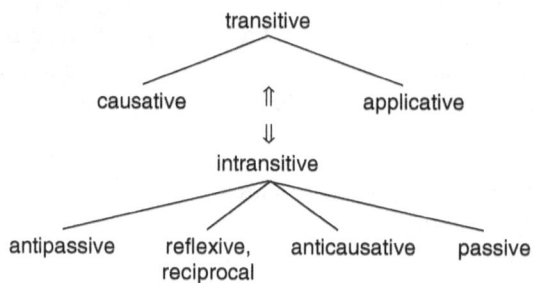

A fusion of detransitivizing operations in a single affix is much more common than the fusion of causative and applicative in a single affix (see (54)). An extreme example of polyfunctionality is attested in Chukchi, where the suffix -*tku*/-*tko* not only functions as a general detransitivizer comprising anticausative, antipassive, reflexive, and reciprocal (59), but also derives both paucer ('island' → 'a group of islands') and iterative ('bite' → 'bite several times') readings; moreover, this affix also derives verbs from instrumental nouns ('rifle' → 'to shoot'), and functions as 1pl object marker in the presence of a 2nd person subject (*pela-tko-tək* leave-1pl-2pl 'you left us'); of course, some of the latter functions should be considered accidental homonymy.

(59) Detransitivization in Chukchi (Nedjalkov 2006: 222)
 a. ejpə-nin 'he closed it' ejpə-*tku*-γʔi 'it closed' (*anticausative*)
 b. ʔattʔ-e juu-nin 'the dog bit him' ʔattʔ-ən nə-jγu-*tku*-qin 'the dog bites'
 (*antipassive*)
 c. tewla-nen 'he shook it off' tewla-*tko*-γʔe 'he shook himself'
 (*reflexive*)
 d. ommačajpə-nen 'he hugged him' ommačajpə-*tko*-γʔat 'they hugged each
 other' (*reciprocal*)

Thus, besides all its other functions, -*tku*/-*tko* provides a whole set of detransitivizing operations.

(60) **-tku/-tko** [λy λx(ACT(x) & AFF(y))]   =
    {λy AFF(y), λx ∃y (ACT(x) & AFF(y)), λx(ACT(x) & AFF(x)), . . .}

In Kharia, a South Munda language, every predicate must be voice-marked for either middle or active (where voice is always fused with tense-mood). Several verbs are middle-only or active-only, whereas the majority of verbs allow both options. The verb gets an inchoative reading in the middle, but a causative reading in the active (61a). Furthermore, verbs that are independently marked for passive/reflexive require the middle (61b), and those that are marked for causative require the active (61c).

(61) Middle/active pairs in Kharia (Peterson 2006)
   a. ayo   'become a mother'   'accept s.o. as a mother'
      khatam   'come to an end'   'finish' (TR)
      sebol   'become sweet'   'make sweet'
      tuta   'go down'   'put down'

   b. yo dom-ki-kiyar.
      see PASS/REFL-MIDDLE.PAST-DUAL
      'They two were seen (by someone else). / They two saw themselves.'

   c. yohan   beta   o-dam-e.
      John   boy   CAUS-arrive-ACT.IRR
      'John will bring the boy.'

Besides some sorts of intransitivity, the middle characterizes habitual, persistent, self-directed, attempted (but not successful), spontaneous or unexpected actions, as well as those in which the subject participates only indirectly. As Peterson (2006) argues, the middle appears to mark those events which differ somewhat from prototypical actions, in contrast to the active, which marks events that are closer to prototypical actions.

Similarly, the middle voice in Greek, and the reflexive in Spanish, Russian, and other Indo-European languages of Europe are notoriously known for their multifunctionality, including the anticausative reading.

(62) Spanish reflexives (Kaufmann 2004: 191)
      a. Juan se lava.   'Juan washes himself.'   (*reflexive*)
      b. La cuerda se rompe.   'The rope splits.'   (*anticausative*)
      c. El libro se publicó en 1952. 'The book was published in 1952.'
                                                                (*passive*)

d. Se vive bien aqui.   'People live well here.'   (*impersonal*)
e. Estas frutas se comen.   'These fruits are edible.'   (*modal*)

Kaufmann (2004) tried to find a general meaning of the middle affixes in Classical Greek and those in Fula from which the specific subreadings could follow as special contextual instances. Regardless of whether such a reconstruction succeeds for a number of readings, one might remain skeptical whether such an enterprise is on the right track in general. Could it be that the 'reflexive' *se* just marks intransitivity, contrasting with the transitive verb – whatever the preferred reading might be for the intransitive variant?

Watters et al. (2005) reports about Kusunda, a language isolate of Nepal, that a particular harmonic mutation on verbs marks the semantically more articulated category in a pair of categories, regardless of the particular dimension; it marks causative in the transitivity dimension, irrealis in the modality dimension, negation in the polarity dimension, and dependent in the dependency dimension. Thus, a single phonological feature (mutation) is paired with semantic markedness, whereas the concrete semantic operation has to be chosen from a set of alternatives.

In a language in which each verb has exactly one canonical semantic variant, in one of many possible dimensions, there would be no problem with maximal parsimony, marking all of the respective marked variants in the same way. Then, knowing the meaning of a marked item only requires knowing what the canonical semantic variant is. This does not exclude the possibility that non-canonical variants (differing in one of the other dimensions) are formed by more articulate means.

6 Multiple operations and the order of derivation

Operations on argument structure can be combined cyclically, so that the output of a first operation serves as the input for a further operation. In particular, argument reduction and argument extension often alternate. Yucatec Maya illustrates a type of language in which no more than two structural arguments are possible; in a certain state of affairs a verb can either be transitivized or detransitivized. More precisely, causative (suffixation with -s) or applicative (suffixation with -t) applies to verbs in an intransitive state, whereas passive, antipassive or noun incorporation applies to verbs in a transitive state. These operations can easily be combined. (63a) shows the ordering V-CAUS-PASS, (63b) V-APPL-PASS, (63c) V-PASS-CAUS-PASS, and finally (63d) V-INCORP-APPL. The last line in each example indicates the semantic representation of the complex verb.

(63) Alternation of transitivization and intransitivization in Yucatec Maya
(Krämer & Wunderlich 1999)
    a. kíin-s-áab-en   tumèen   leti
       die-CAUS-PASS.PERF-1   PREP   PRON.3.SG
       'I was killed by him.'
       $\lambda y\, \lambda e\, \exists x\, \{\text{ACT}(x)\, \&_{\text{CAUS}}\, \text{DIE}(y)\}(e)$
    b. k=a   kóoy-t-áal
       INCOMPL=2   dig -APPL-PASS.IMPF
       'It gets dug (up).'
       $\lambda y\, \lambda e\, \exists x\, \{\text{DIG}(x)\, \&\, \text{AFFECTED}(y)\}(e)$
    c. k=u   káan-s-áal
       INCOMPL=3   learn.PASS-CAUS-PASS.IMPF
       'It is being taught'
       $\lambda z\, \lambda e\, \exists x\, \{\text{ACT}(x)\, \&_{\text{CAUS}}\, \exists y\, \text{LEARN}(y,z)\}(e)$
    d. taan=u   kon-lol-t-ik-et
       INCOMPL=3   sell-flower-APPL-IMPF-2
       'He's selling you flowers.' (lit. 'he's flower-selling you')
       $\lambda y\, \lambda x\, \lambda e\, \{\exists z\, (\text{SELL}(x,z)\, \&\, \text{FLOWER}(z))\, \&\, \text{AFFECTED}(y)\}(e)$

Several other languages supply evidence that argument changing operations can be combined freely, though they may be subject to some sequential constraints. (64a) gives an example from Chichewa with the ordering V-APPL-REC-CAUS. (64b) shows the stepwise semantic derivation; the symbol ⊕ indicates a reciprocal relationship between the two occurrences of a variable.

(64) Interaction of argument changing operations in Chichewa (Bantu)
    a. M-lenje   a-na-mang-ir-an-its-a   a-tsikana   nkhuni.
       1-hunter   1-PAST-tie-APPL-REC-CAUS-FV   2-girl   firewood
       'The hunter caused the girls to tie firewood for each other'
    b. *mang:* $\lambda y\, \lambda x\, \lambda e\, \text{TIE}(x,y)(e)$
       mang-ir: $\lambda y\, \lambda z\, \lambda x\, \lambda e\, \{\text{TIE}(x,y)\, \&\, \text{BEC POSS}(z,y)\}(e)$ (*benefactive appl.*)
       mang-ir-an: $\lambda y\, \lambda x\oplus \lambda e\, \{\text{TIE}(x,y)\, \&\, \text{BEC POSS}(x,y)\}(e)$ (*reciprocal*)
       mang-ir-an-its: $\lambda y\, \lambda x\oplus \lambda u\, \lambda e\, \{\text{ACT}(u)\, \&_{\text{CAUSE}}\, \exists e'\{\text{TIE}(x,y)\, \&\, \text{BEC POSS}(x,y)\}(e')\}(e)$
                                                                                                                       (*causative*)

It is easy to imagine that any other order of affixes would yield a different interpretation:
- REC-CAUS-APPL: 'The hunter caused the girls to tie each other at the firewood';
- CAUS-REC-APPL: 'The hunters caused each other to tie firewood for the girls'.

However, some surface orders of suffixes are forbidden. According to Hyman & Mchombo (1992), the causative suffix-*its* may not appear after the applicative suffix -*ir* or the passive suffix -*idw*. In other words, the affix ordering is fixed, independently of semantic scope.

(65) Surface alignment constraints in Chichewa
    a. *-ir-its   (-APPL-CAUS)
    b. *-idw-its   (-PASS-CAUS)

That the first constraint leads to ambiguity, which, however, can be resolved in a normal context, is shown in (66). In (66a), the applied instrument 'sticks' clearly relates to 'making cry' and not 'cry', whereas in (66b) the applied instrument 'spoon' relates to the lower verb 'stir'. (Interestingly, the passive of (66a) requires 'sticks' as the subject, and the passive of (66b) requires 'woman' as the subject, thereby reflecting the different semantic scope.)

(66) Chichewa CAUS-APPL representing both scopes (Hyman 2003)
    a. alenjé   a-ku-líl-**íts-il**-a   waná   ndodo.
        hunters   3pl-PROG-cry-CAUS-APPL-FV   child   sticks
        'The hunters are making the child cry with sticks.'   (INST (CAUSE (CRY)))
    b. alenjé   a-ku-tákás-**íts-il**-a   mkází   mthíko.
        hunters   3pl-PROG-stir-CAUS-APPL-FV   woman   spoon
        'The hunters are making the woman stir with a spoon. (CAUSE (INST (STIR)))

A similar ambiguity is caused by the second constraint: TIE-PASS-CAUS 'u causes y to be tied' and TIE-CAUS-PASS 'x is caused to tie y' clearly mean different things, that is, two different semantic compositions are mapped onto the same surface string *mang-its-idw-a*. Unless there is a strong contextual bias to the contrary, the compositional reading in which the order of suffixes reflects the order of semantic operations should be assumed to be the default option for the hearer.

Another type of mismatch found in Chichewa is semantically empty suffix repetition. In (67), the second occurrence of the reciprocal suffix -*an* has to be ignored because the semantic reciprocal operation cannot be repeated in the same domain.

(67) Redundancy in Chichewa:
    A-tsikana   a-na-mang-an-**its-idw**-ir-*an*-a   m-nkhalango.
    2-girl   2-PAST-tie-REC-CAUS-PASS-APPL-(REC)-FV   LOC-forest
    'The girls were caused to tie each other in the forest.'

Similarly, double or triple causative found in languages of India often only means emphasized causative, e.g., Kashmiri *khy-aav-inaav* 'eat-CAUS-CAUS' and *khy-aav-inaav-inaav* 'eat-CAUS-CAUS-CAUS' both mean 'have someone feed someone'.

Several other studies (e.g., Muysken 1986 and van de Kerke 1996 on Quechua) have established the insight that the order of affixes reflects the order of semantic composition in most instances, though unfortunately not in all. Surface alignment constraints partially destroy the ideal picture. Hyman (2003) argues that Proto-Bantu started with a fixed template (verb-CAUS-APPL-REC-PASS) of which many residuals are still present; he also cites Abasheikh (1978), who found that Chimwiini (a Swahili dialect of Somalia) has a fixed affix ordering.

In order to see how constraints such as those in (65) work, parallel processing can be assumed: For each suffix (contributing a phonological form and a semantic operation), the phonological output PF and the semantic output SF are computed separately. Differences between the input and output in PF do not affect the output in SF. The derivation fails only if one of the parallel lines of processing yields a zero output.

(68) Input: PF   SF
     a   mang $\lambda y\, \lambda x\, \lambda s\, \text{TIE}(x,y)(s)$
     b   mang-idw $\lambda y\, \exists x\, \lambda s\, \text{TIE}(x,x)(s)$ (*passive*)
     c   mang-idw-its $\lambda y\, \exists x\, \lambda u\, \lambda s\, \{\text{ACT}(u)\ \&\ \exists s'\text{TIE}(x,x)(s')\}(s)$ (*causative*)
    ↓
    Output: *mang-its-idw*

According to (65b), the PF arrived at in line c is forbidden, so the second-to-best position of *-its* is chosen, that is, *-its* is in fact infixed.

Stiebels (2003) distinguishes between transparent, restricted and opaque affix orders. If both affix orders (-A-B and -B-A) occur and transparently reflect the underlying scope relations they are called transparent. If due to a language-specific constraint only one affix order occurs and receives a surface-true, i.e. compositional, interpretation it is called restricted. If a given affix order has both the compositional and the non-compositional interpretation – the latter violating the revised mirror principle – it is called opaque.

(69) Mirror Principle
    a. Morphological derivations must directly reflect syntactic derivations (and vice versa). (Baker 1985: 375)
    b. Revised: The affix order must mirror semantic composition. (Stiebels 2003: 292)

The revised mirror principle claims a correspondence between morphology and semantics rather than between morphology and syntax. Crucial for this claim are scope relations.

As the reader will have observed, the argument shifting operations presented in this article are realized by suffixes on the verb, except for the resultative prefixes, which are special. Thus, the linear ordering from left to right indicates the actual path of computing argument structure. Everything that precedes a certain suffix (operation) is in its scope: the underlying predicate together with all of the arguments as well as the result of preceding operations. Different suffix orders such as -CAUS-REC vs. -REC-CAUS generate different readings because they manipulate argument *variables*, which are scope-internal and therefore independent of the position of DPs that realize the arguments, hence, independent of any DP movement. If, in contrast, argument changing operations were phrasal, they would operate on VPs (rather than Vs), so that some arguments would already be saturated, and DP movement could easily extract the DP from the relevant scope.

(70) Morphologically determined scope relations are immune to DP movement, syntactically determined scope relations are not.

The following data from Wechsler (1989) show that only core arguments and not PPs are included in the scope of a bound morpheme. The participants of the repeated situation expressed in the Chichewa example (71a) include the writer and the essay, but not the instrument; in (71b), however, the instrument is included as well, because the (instrumental) applicative has applied.

(71) Chichewa repetitives (Wechsler 1989: 429)
    a. Mu-lembe=<u>nso</u>   chimangirizo   [ndi nthenga]$_{PP}$
        you-write=again   essay   with feather
        'you write the essay again, with a quill (this time)'
        AGAIN [λy λx λe WRITE(x,y)(e)] & INSTR(feather,e)

    b. Mu-lembe-*re*=<u>nso</u>   nthenga   chimangirizo.
        you-write-APPL=again   feather   essay
        'you write the essay with a quill again'
        AGAIN [{λy λz λx λe WRITE(x,y) & INSTR(z,y)}(e)]

Conversely, the English examples in (72) show that the repetitive adverb can include the locative PP in its scope (72a), but the repetitive prefix cannot (72b). Only if the location is incorporated into the verb is it in the scope of the prefix *re-* (72c); recall that *enter* is in fact a locative applicative in English.

(72) English repetitives
 a. John ran to the forest again.
  AGAIN (to the forest (run (John)))
 b. * John reran to the forest.
  § to the forest (AGAIN (run (John)))
 c. John reentered the forest. – This forest, John reentered several times.
  AGAIN (entered (John, the forest))

Note that *rerun* with the only possible reading λx λe AGAIN(RUN(x)(e)) is semantically deviant because running is an unbounded event, but *re-* only applies to bounded events. However, *reenter* is possible because entering something is a bounded event.

These examples clearly show that morphology is in a way immune to syntax. A bound morpheme such as 'again' – be it an affix or a clitic – takes in its scope all core arguments of the simple or derived verb to which it is attached, but nothing from outside, e.g., an adjunct. In the syntax it is possible to move argument-realizing DPs, thereby shifting scopal properties, which, however, has no influence on the scope of *re-* (which only sees the argument variables). Conversely, a PP or an adverb (syntactic adjuncts) can take the verb and some or all of the syntactically realized arguments into its scope. Von Stechow's (1996) idea was that 'again' can have scope over different parts of the lexical decomposition of a verb; in which sense that could be true is still a matter of dispute (Wunderlich 2001: 492ff).

In any way, there is strong evidence that morphology and syntax behave differently. Although both reflect semantic conditions, they are not derived from each other. Therefore, morphological theories that are couched in a syntactic framework, such as Distributed Morphology, seem to be on the wrong track. Similarly, when phase theory, a syntactic theory, is used to clarify the conditions that govern multiple applicatives in the Bantu languages (McGinnis 2005), primarily a morphological phenomenon, one has to assume either that phase theory is particularly semantically inspired or that it is the wrong tool for this subject matter.

7 Argument alternation through lexical marking

From the semantic point of view, lexical marking is a trivial operation on argument structure. In the history of the Germanic languages (English, German, Scandinavian, Icelandic), many verbs encoding dative-nominative (73a) shifted to nominative-accusative (73b) without any relevant semantic change.

(73) Lexical marking shift from Early New High German to Modern German
    a. Mir   ahnte   das.
        I.DAT   anticipated   that (NOM)
    b. Ich   ahnte   das.
        I.NOM   anticipated   that (ACC)

The case-pattern shown in (73b) represents canonical transitive verbs, while the pattern in (73a) is characteristic for a certain subclass, the experiencer verbs. In general, lexical marking serves to classify verbs according to their inherent meaning, nevertheless it is a pure surface operation, which only affects subcategorization and not the semantic core. These lexical features, whatever they are (Wunderlich 2003), are added or removed during historical development. Small meaning differences can only emerge if for a particular verb different states of lexical marking coexist. It is important to note that lexical marking on the highest argument usually excludes passivization – verbs of the type (73a) cannot be passivized. However, (73b) allows passivization, at least in principle; *das wurde von niemandem geahnt*, the passive of 'nobody anticipated that', is fine.

8 Argument alternation: dative shift, and others

Another type of argument alternation results from a choice between semantically similar core representations, and not from a particular operation. In the so-called dative shift of English a verb with a prepositional object (PO) is shifted to a verb with double object (DO).

(74) PO-DO alternation in English
    a. Anna gave a photo to Max.   (PO)
    b. Anna gave Max a photo.   (DO)

However, a more precise investigation, provides evidence that the two alternative constructions are connected with slightly different semantic representations, spelled out as 'change of location' vs. 'change of possession', so that there cannot be an operation between them (Pinker 1989, Krifka 2004).

(75) Semantic representation of the PO-DO alternation
    a. PO: $\lambda y\, \lambda z\, \lambda x\, \{\text{ACT}(x)\, \&_{\text{CAUSE}}\, \text{BECOME LOC}(z, \text{AT}y)\}$
    b. DO: $\lambda z\, \lambda y\, \lambda x\, \{\text{ACT}(x)\, \&_{\text{CAUSE}}\, \text{BECOME POSS}(y, z)\}$

These two representations crucially differ with respect to argument hierarchy: the recipient (= goal) is the medial argument in (75b), but the lowest one in (75a). This fact allows us to make some important predictions.

In the DO construction, the recipient (y) should consistently behave as the higher object: it should be able to bind a reflexive theme, license a negative polarity item (such as *any*), be moved in multiple questions, etc., which is indeed the case according to the several tests applied by Larson (1988). In contrast, in the PO construction the recipient (y, construed as a goal) should behave consistently as the lower argument: it should not allow binding by a theme, movement in multiple questions, etc. One of the possible tests is that a quantifier in the higher argument can bind the possessor of a lower argument, but not vice versa, as exemplified in (76),

(76) Argument hierarchy in the PO vs. DO construction
    a. He gave every baby$_i$ to its$_i$ mother.
       *He gave her$_i$ baby to every woman$_i$.
    b. He gave every woman$_i$ her$_i$ baby.
       *He gave its$_i$ mother every baby$_i$.

Another prediction concerns harmonic alignment. In general, the construction in which the higher argument outranks the lower one in terms of saliency should be favored. It is thus expected that PO is preferred if the theme is more salient than the recipient, e.g., first or second person, animate, a pronoun, definite, specific, or the topic. Conversely, DO should be preferred if the recipient (rather than the theme) has one of these properties. This is indeed the case, as shown by Bresnan & Nikitina (2003). (77) illustrates the distribution of pronominal vs. NP arguments.

(77) Salience in the PO vs. DO construction
    a. They gave him to an old woman.
       ?They gave a crying baby to him.
    b. They gave him a crying baby.
       *They gave an old woman him.

Similar observations have been made regarding the alternation between the serial verb (SV) construction and the DO construction in West African languages. In Fongbe, a Kwa language of Benin, the SV construction in (78) shows the ranking theme > recipient, while the DO construction in (79) shows the reverse ranking recipient > theme, indicated by the possibility of a quantifier binding a possessive pronoun.

(78) Serial verb construction in Fongbe (Lefebrve & Brousseau 2001: 463)
    a. Ùn sɛ́ fɔ̀tóò dòkpódòkpó xlɔ fɔ̀tóó'tɔ̀! tɔ̀n.
       1sg take picture every show picture.owner GEN
       'I showed every picture to its owner.'
    b. *Ùn xlɔ̀! fɔ̀tóò tɔ̀n xlɔ mɔ̀ dòkpódòkpó
       1sg take picture GEN give person every
       * 'I showed his picture to every person.'

(79) Double object construction in Fongbe (Lefebrve & Brousseau 2001: 455)
    a. Ùn xlɔ̀! mɔ dòkpódòkpó fɔ̀tóò tɔ̀n.
       (or: ... fɔ̀tóò tɔ̀n mɔ̀ dòkpódòkpó)
       1sg show person every picture GEN
       'I showed every person his picture.'
    b. *Ùn xlɔ̀! fɔ̀`tóò dòkpódòkpó fɔ̀tóó'tɔ tɔ̀n
       1sg show picture every picture.owner GEN
       * 'I showed its owner every picture.'

In Akan, a related Kwa-language of Ghana, pronominal or definite themes, which are high in salience, require the SV-construction.

(80) SV and DO construction in Akan (Campbell 1996: 101)
    a. Me-tOnn nwoma no maa Kofi.
       1sg-sold book that gave Kofi
       'I sold the book to Kofi.'
    b. Me-maa Kofi nwoma (*no).
       1sg-gave Kofi book (that)
       'I gave Kofi a/*the book.'

It has been argued that POSS(y, z) and LOC(z, AT y) are weakly equivalent because usually if one of them is true, the other is true as well. If z is located at y, then y is able to exert some ownership on z. Conversely, if y has possession of z, then z must be located in the vicinity of y for y to be able to exert his possessorship (Wunderlich 2006: 151). For that reason possession is often expressed by means of a locative construction (e.g., Russian *u menja kniga* 'at me.GEN book' means 'I have a book'). Note that POSS(y, z) and LOC(z, AT y) are not exactly converse to each other because AT y refers to some neighboring region of y rather than to y itself. However, this fact doesn't seem to have any influence on the capability of (80a,b) to represent alternative readings of one and the same verb; what counts here is the difference in argument hierarchy.

9 References

Abasheikh, Mohammad 1978. *The Grammar of Chimwi:ni Causatives*. Ph.D. dissertation. University of Illinois, Urbana-Champaign, IL.

Ackerman, Farrell 1992. Complex predicates and morphological relatedness: Locative alternation in Hungarian. In: I. Sag & A. Szabolcsi (eds.). *Lexical Matters*. Stanford, CA: CSLI Publications, 55–83.

Aissen, Judith 1999. Markedness and subject choice in Optimality Theory. *Natural Language and Linguistic Theory* 17, 673–711.

Alsina, Alex & Sam Mchombo 1990. The syntax of applicatives in Chichewa: Problems for a theta theoretic asymmetry. *Natural Language and Linguistic Theory* 8, 493–506.

Austin, Peter 1997. Causatives and applicatives in Australian Aboriginal languages. In: K. Matsumara & T. Hayasi (eds.). *The Dative and Related Phenomena*. Tokyo: Hituzi Syobo, 165–225.

Baker, Mark 1985. The mirror principle and morphosyntactic explanation. *Linguistic Inquiry* 16, 373–415.

Baker, Mark 1988. *Incorporation. A Theory of Grammatical Function Changing*. Chicago, IL: The University of Chicago Press.

Baker, Mark 1997. Thematic roles and syntactic structure. In: L. Haegeman (ed.). *Elements of Grammar*. Dordrecht: Kluwer, 73–137.

Barker, Chris 1995. *Possessive Descriptions*. Stanford, CA: CSLI Publications.

Barss, Andrew & Howard Lasnik 1986. A note on anaphora and double objects. *Linguistic Inquiry* 17, 347–354.

Beach, Matthew 2003. Asymmetries between passivization and antipassivization in the Taramiutut subdialect of Inuktikut. In: M. Butt & T. H. King (eds.). *Proceedings of the LFG '03 Conference*. Stanford, CA: CSLI Publications, 1–21.

Bierwisch, Manfred 1989a. *Thematische Rollen und Dekomposition*. Lecture notes for the *Third DGfS Summer School*, University of Hamburg, September 1989.

Bierwisch, Manfred 1989b. Event nominalization: Proposals and problems. In: W. Motsch (ed.). *Wortstruktur und Satzstruktur*. Berlin: Akademie Verlag, 1–73.

Bierwisch, Manfred 2002. A case for cause. In: I. Kaufmann & B. Stiebels (eds.). *More than Words*. Berlin: Akademie Verlag, 327–353.

Bittner, Maria 1987. On the semantics of the Greenlandic antipassive and related constructions. *International Journal of American Linguistics* 53, 194–231.

Blutner, Reinhard & Henk Zeevat (eds.) 2004. *Optimality Theory and Pragmatics*. Basingstoke: Palgrave Macmillan.

Bresnan, Joan 1982. The passive in lexical theory. In: J. Bresnan (ed.). *The Mental Representation of Grammatical Relations*. Cambridge, MA: The MIT Press, 3–86.

Bresnan, Joan & Lioba Moshi 1990. Object asymmetries in comparative Bantu syntax. *Linguistic Inquiry* 21, 147–185.

Bresnan, Joan & Tatiana Nikitina 2003. *On the Gradience of the Dative Alternation*. Ms. Palo Alto, CA, Stanford University.

Brinkmann, Ursula 1995. *The Locative Alternation. Its Structure and Acquisition*. Ph.D. dissertation. University of Nijmegen.

Campbell, Richard 1996. Serial verbs and shared arguments. *The Linguistic Review* 13, 83–118.

Chung, Sandra 1976. An object-creating rule in Bahasa Indonesia. *Linguistic Inquiry* 7, 41–87.

Comrie, Bernard 2006. Transitivity pairs, markedness, and diachronic stability. *Linguistics* 44, 303–318.
Dowty, David R. 1982. Grammatical relations and Montague grammar. In: P. Jacobson & G. K. Pullum (eds.). *The Nature of Syntactic Representations*. Dordrecht: Reidel, 79–130.
Dowty, David R. 1991. Thematic proto-roles and argument selection. *Language* 67, 547–619.
Dryer, Matthew S. 1986. Primary objects, secondary objects, and antidative. *Language* 62, 808–845.
van Geenhoven, Veerle 1998. *Semantic Incorporation and Indefinite Descriptions: Semantic and Syntactic Aspects of Noun Incorporation in West Greenlandic*. Stanford, CA: CSLI Publications.
Grimshaw, Jane 1990. *Argument Structure*. Cambridge, MA: The MIT Press.
Haspelmath, Martin 1993. More on the typology of inchoative/causative verb alternations. In: B. Comrie & M. Polinsky (eds.). *Causatives and Transitivity*. Amsterdam: Benjamins, 87–120.
Heim, Irene, Howard Lasnik & Robert May 1991. Reciprocity and plurality. *Linguistic Inquiry* 22, 63–101.
Hyman, Larry M. 2003. Suffix ordering in Bantu: A morphocentric approach. In: G. Booij & J. van Marle (eds.). *Yearbook of Morphology 2002*. Dordrecht: Kluwer, 245–281.
Hyman, Larry M. & Sam Mchombo 1992. Morphotactic constraints in the Chichewa verb stem. In: L. Buszard-Welcher, L. Wee & W. Weigel (eds). *Proceedings of the 18th Annual Meeting of the Berkeley Linguistics Society (= BLS)*. Berkeley, CA: Berkeley Linguistics Society, 350–364.
Jackendoff, Ray 1990. *Semantic Structures*. Cambridge, MA: The MIT Press.
Johnson, Heidi. 2000. *A Grammar of San Miguel Chimalapa Zoque*. Ph.D. dissertation. University of Texas, Austin, TX.
Joppen-Hellwig, Sandra 2001. *Verbklassen und Argumentlinking*. Tübingen: Niemeyer.
Kaufmann, Ingrid 2004. *Medium und Reflexiv. Eine Studie zur Verbsemantik*. Tübingen: Niemeyer.
Kaufmann, Ingrid & Dieter Wunderlich 1998. *Cross-linguistic Patterns of Resultatives* (Arbeitspapiere des Sonderforschungsbereichs 282 'Theorie des Lexikons', Bericht Nr. 109). Düsseldorf: University of Düsseldorf.
Keenan, Edward L. 1980. Passive is phrasal (not sentential or lexical). In: T. Hoekstra, H. van der Hulst & M. Moortgat (eds.). *Lexical Grammar*. Dordrecht: Foris, 181–213.
van de Kerke, Simon 1996. *Affix order and interpretation in Bolivian Quechua*. Ph.D. dissertation. University of Amsterdam.
Kiparsky, Paul 1992. *Structural Case*. Ms. Berlin, Institute for Advanced Studies.
Kiparsky, Paul 2001. Structural case in Finnish. *Lingua* 111, 315–376.
Krämer, Martin & Dieter Wunderlich 1999. Transitivity alternations in Yucatec, and the correlation between aspect and argument roles. *Linguistics* 37, 431–479.
Kratzer, Angelika 1994. *The Event Argument and the Semantics of Voice*. Ms. Amherst, MA, University of Massachusetts.
Krifka, Manfred 2004. Lexical representations and the nature of the dative alternation. *Korean Journal of English Language and Linguistics* 4, 1–32.
Larson, Richard K. 1988. On the double object construction. *Linguistic Inquiry* 19, 335–391.
Lefebrve, Claire & Anne-Marie Brousseau 2002. *The Structure of Fongbe*. Berlin: Mouton de Gruyter.
Marantz, Alec 1993. Implications of asymmetries in double object constructions. In: S. A. Mchombo (ed.). *Theoretical Aspects of Bantu Grammar*. Stanford, CA: CSLI Publications, 113–150.

McGinnis, Martha 2005. UTAH at Merge: Evidence from multiple applicatives. In: M. McGinnis & N. Richards (eds.). *Perspectives on Phases* (MIT Working Papers in Linguistics 49). Cambridge, MA: MIT, 183–200.

Muysken, Pieter 1986. Approaches to affix order. *Linguistics* 24, 629–643.

Nedjalkov, Vladimir P. 2006. Chukchi reciprocals. In: T. Tsunoda & T. Kageyama (eds.). *Voice and Grammatical Relations. In Honor to Masayoshi Shibatani*. Amsterdam: Benjamins, 217–246.

Peterson, John 2006 *Kharia. A South Munda Language*. Habilitation thesis. University of Osnabrück.

Pinker, Steven 1989. *Learnability and Cognition. The Acquisition of Argument Structure*. Cambridge, MA: The MIT Press.

Polinsky, Maria & Isaac Kozinsky 1992. Ditransitive constructions in Kinyarwanda: Coding conflict or syntactic doubling? In: C. P. Canakis, G. P. Chan & J. M. Denton (eds.). *Papers from the 28th Regional Meeting of the Chicago Linguistic Society (= CLS)*. Chicago, IL: Chicago Linguistic Society, 426–442.

von Stechow, Arnim 1996. The different readings of *wieder* 'again': A structural approach. *Journal of Semantics* 13, 87–138.

Stiebels, Barbara 1996. *Lexikalische Argumente und Adjunkte: Zum semantischen Beitrag von verbalen Präfixen und Partikeln*. Berlin: Akademie Verlag.

Stiebels, Barbara 2000. Linker inventories, linking splits and lexical economy. In: B. Stiebels & D. Wunderlich (eds.). *Lexicon in Focus*. Berlin: Akademie Verlag, 211–245.

Stiebels, Barbara 2002. *Typologie des Argumentlinkings: Ökonomie und Expressivität*. Berlin: Akademie Verlag.

Stiebels, Barbara 2003. Transparent, restricted and opaque affix orders. In: U. Junghanns & L. Szucsich (eds.). *Syntactic Structures and Morphological Information*. Berlin: Mouton de Gruyter, 283–315.

Stiebels, Barbara 2006. From rags to riches. Nominal linking in contrast to verbal linking. In: D. Wunderlich (ed.). *Advances in the Theory of the Lexicon*. Berlin: Mouton de Gruyter, 167–234.

van Valin, Robert D. 2007. The role and reference grammar analysis of three-place predicates. *Suvremena Lingvistika* 33, 31–64.

Washio, Ryuichi 1995. *Interpreting Voice. A Case Study in Lexical Semantics*. Tokyo: Kaitakusha.

Washio, Ryuichi 1997. Resulatives, compositionality and language variation. *Journal of East Asian Linguistics* 6, 1–49.

Watters, David E., Yogendra P. Yadava, Madhav P. Pokharel & Balaram Prasain 2005. *Notes on Kusunda Grammar (A Language Isolate of Nepal)*. Kathmandu: National Foundation for the Development of Indigenous Nationalities.

Wechsler, Stephen 1989. Accomplishments and the prefix *re-*. In: J. Carter & R.-M. Déchaine (eds.). *Proceedings of the 19th Annual Meeting of the North Eastern Linguistic Society (= NELS)*. Amherst, MA: GLSA, 419–438.

Williams, E. 1991. Reciprocal scope. *Linguistic Inquiry* 22, 159–173.

Wunderlich, Dieter 1997a. Cause and the structure of verbs. *Linguistic Inquiry* 28, 27–68.

Wunderlich, Dieter 1997b. Argument extension by lexical adjunction. *Journal of Semantics* 14, 95–142.

Wunderlich, Dieter 2000. Predicate composition and argument extension as general options. In: B. Stiebels & D. Wunderlich (eds.). *Lexicon in Focus*. Berlin: Akademie Verlag, 247–270.

Wunderlich, Dieter 2001. Prelexical syntax and the voice hypothesis. In: C. Féry & W. Sternefeld (eds.). *Audiatur vox sapientiae. A Festschrift for Arnim von Stechow*. Berlin: Akademie Verlag, 487–513.

Wunderlich, Dieter 2002. On the nature of dative in Hungarian. In: I. Kenesei & P. Siptár (eds.). *Approaches to Hungarian 8: Papers from the Budapest Conference*. Budapest: Akadémiai Kiadó, 161–184.

Wunderlich, Dieter 2003. Optimal case patterns: German and Icelandic compared. In: E. Brandner & H. Zinsmeister (eds.). *New Perspectives on Case Theory*. Stanford, CA: CSLI Publications, 331–367.

Wunderlich, Dieter 2006. Towards a structural typology of verb classes. In: D. Wunderlich (ed.). *Advances in the Theory of the Lexicon*. Berlin: Mouton de Gruyter, 58–166.

Wunderlich, Dieter 2012. Lexical decomposition in grammar. In: W. Hinzen, E. Machery, & M. Werning (eds.). *The Oxford Handbook of Compositionality*. Oxford: Oxford University Press, 307–327

Helen de Hoop
8 Type shifting

1   Introduction —— 277
2   Transitivity and case alternations —— 279
3   Word order variation —— 286
4   Conclusion —— 291
5   References —— 291

Abstract: Since the seminal paper of Barbara Partee in 1987, type shifting principles, which allow syntactic categories to correspond to more than one semantic type and to shift between them, have been proven invaluable for the analysis of crosslinguistic data at the syntax-semantics interface, involving various types of nominal denotations. This article reviews some of these analyses that make use of type shifting principles, in particular for the denotation of object noun phrases in transitivity, case, and word order alternations.

1 Introduction

In semantic type theory the two basic semantic types are e (for 'entity') and t (for 'truth value') and if a is a type and b is a type, then $<a,b>$ is a type as well. The type $<a,b>$ is a function that takes an argument of type a and yields an expression of type b. Montague (1974) assumed a homomorphism from syntactic categories to semantic types. Thus, an element belonging to a certain syntactic category is assigned the semantic type associated with that category. For example, a noun is always assigned the type of a predicate, $<e,t>$, and each noun phrase is assigned the type of a generalized quantifier, type $<<e,t>,t>$. Many linguists afterwards have argued that such a one-to-one mapping between syntax and semantics is not feasible and that several syntactic categories in fact correspond to a variety of semantic types. Type shifting refers to the shifting of one semantic type to another. A type shifting operation can for example map an expression of type a to the more complex type $<<a,b>,b>$. Partee (1987) distinguishes between very general type shifting principles and others which are not of any formal generality but which are commonly employed because of their cognitive naturalness. As an example, she provides the rule which turns proper names into common nouns denoting one characteristic

Helen de Hoop, Nijmegen, The Netherlands

https://doi.org/10.1515/9783110589849-008

property, as in 'He's a real Einstein'. Partee & Rooth (1983) propose that each basic expression is lexically assigned the simplest (basic) type needed to capture its meaning, while other types can be used when they are required in order to combine meanings by available compositional rules (see also Hendriks 1993, Steedman 1996, as well as article 10 [Semantics: Lexical Structures and Adjectives] (de Swart) *Mismatches and coercion*). While Partee & Rooth (1983) mainly focus on type assignments to verbs, Partee (1987) extends this idea to account for the different semantic types of noun phrases proposed in the literature. General type shifting principles are responsible for going from one interpretation to the other in a certain context, thus allowing for more flexibility in relating syntax and semantics than Montague's (1974) strict correspondence between syntactic category and semantic type. Partee (1987) provides some evidence for the claim that there are noun phrase interpretations of at least three types: the referential type *e*, the predicative type <*e,t*>, and the quantificational type <<*e,t*>,*t*>. The three types are related via type shifting devices, some of which are more 'natural' than others. For example, an operation of existential closure turns a predicate (type <*e,t*>) into an existential generalized quantifier. This operation can be conceived of as the meaning of an indefinite article, such as *a* in English. Chierchia (1998) argues that in some languages, a determiner is obligatory in order for such a type shift to occur (hence, a bare noun cannot be used in an argument position), whereas in other languages, such as Chinese, nouns refer to arguments and can therefore occur freely without a determiner in argument position. Chierchia (1998) assumes that non-lexicalized (free) type shifting in a certain language is only allowed if there is no lexical counterpart of the relevant type shifter available in that language, a principle that he dubs "Type Shifting as Last Resort". The reverse type shifter (from a referential or generalized quantifier type to the type of a predicate), called *BE*, is attested in natural language in the form of a copular verb, such as *be* in English. Again, languages differ in whether they have a lexicalized type shifter of this kind, i.e., a copular verb, or not.

In addition to the three types Partee (1987) proposes for noun phrase interpretations, de Hoop (1996) argues in favour of the predicate modifier type <<*e,t*>,<*e,t*>> for certain noun phrase interpretations, in particular for objects that bear partitive case in Finnish. Her idea is that syntactic case-marking alternations reflect the type shifting operations as proposed by Partee (1987). According to Partee, natural languages may show considerable diversity in the use of type shifting principles, encoding them via lexical items, syntactic rules, or not encoding them at all (cf. Chierchia 1998, see also article 13 [Semantics: Foundations, History and Methods] (Matthewson) *Methods in cross-linguistic semantics*). Matthewson (2001), like Chierchia (1998), argues that type shifting is highly restricted. She shows that in St'át'imcets (Salish, Canada), determiners are unable to take arguments of the predicative type <*e,t*>; instead they take arguments of type *e*, the referential type.

Another approach along these lines is found in de Hoop (1997), who argues that some 'upstairs' determiners in a partitive construction select type e noun phrases, while others select type $<e,t>$, and only a few are ambiguous in this respect and can take either type of noun phrase.

Also, Partee (1987) discusses several 'sort-shifting' operations within a single type, for converting count to mass reference and vice versa, or within the domain of entities, to be able allow for events as entities, or for plural individuals (Link 1983). One recent approach that proposes further additional structure within the domain of entities is de Swart, Winter & Zwarts (2007), who argue that bare nominals referring to capacities, e.g., *teacher* or *president*, denote in the domain of type e expressions, as a subtype e_C which is similar but sortally distinct from kind referring expressions, that are assumed to denote in subtype e_K. Although Partee does not say much about constraints on the mapping of syntax to semantics, her paper has opened up a new perspective on type shifting principles that seems very promising for the study of semantic universals and language typology. In this article I focus on type shifting and the correspondence between the syntax and semantics of noun phrases from a cross-linguistic perspective. In section 2 I will discuss different ways of how a transitive verb is combined with an object noun phrase, dependent among other things on the strength of the object. Section 3 explains a difference between definite and indefinite objects and their scrambling behaviour in Dutch, giving a new twist to the strategy of Partee & Rooth (1983) to assign noun phrases a preferred type – usually the simplest type possible – by using these preferences to phrase soft constraints. Thus it becomes possible to judge whether type shifting is optimal and the output accordingly grammatical in a certain context.

2 Transitivity and case alternations

As Keenan (1989) points out, in principle transitive sentences are underdetermined as to which noun phrase is interpreted as the subject and which as the object. Keenan provides a way of specifying this information without commitment as to how any particular language structures transitive sentences, or what case system is used, if any. He does so by expressing the argument structure of a sentence in terms of case extensions: 'nominative' (subject) and 'accusative' (object) case extensions are added to the basic denotations of the constituents. Given the denotation of a basic noun phrase, for instance *Robert*, and a binary relation *kiss*, the nominative extension of *Robert* sends the binary relation *kiss* to the set of entities which Robert kissed. Similarly, the accusative extension of *Robert* sends *kiss* to the set of entities which kissed Robert:

(1) For F basic, F_{nom} or the *nominative case extension* of F is that extension of F which sends each binary relation R to $\{b: F(R^b) = 1\}$ with $R^b =_{df} \{a: (a,b) \in R\}$

(2) For F basic, F_{acc} or the *accusative case extension* of F is that extension of F which sends each binary relation R to $\{b: F(R^b) = 1\}$ with $R^b =_{df} \{a: (b,a) \in R\}$

Keenan (1989) argues that in English, word order determines that the first noun phrase is interpreted 'nominatively' and the second one 'accusatively'. In Japanese, if there is a noun phrase with suffix -*o*, it must be interpreted accusatively, otherwise a -*ga* suffixed one is interpreted accusatively. This constraint accounts for the fact that (3) is not ambiguous, while (4) is (Japanese, Japan; Keenan 1989).

(3) Taroo-ga Hanako-o nagutta.
    Taroo   Hanako   hit
    'Taroo hits Hanako.'

(4) Taroo-ga Hanako-ga suki da.
    Taroo   Hanako   likes
    'Taro likes Hanako.' or 'Hanako likes Taroo.'

In Warlpiri (Australian, Australia), according to Keenan (1989), if there is an NP marked with (the ergative case-marker) -*ngku*, it is interpreted nominatively, and otherwise a zero marked NP is interpreted nominatively. Note that the only difference between Keenan's 'nominative' and 'accusative' case is the difference between the denotation of the first and the second NP argument of a transitive verb (normally the subject and the object).

In Keenan's approach, transitive verbs denote in type $<e,<e,t>>$, and they combine with deictic NPs (type e) or basic NPs (type $<<e,t>,t>$). The latter type is also called 'quantificational' but it is the type that is in principle available for all NPs, whence Keenan's term 'basic'. Since Keenan interprets transitive verbs (binary relations) invariably as functions from the set of individuals to functions from the set of individuals to the set of truth values (type $<e,<e,t>>$), the basic semantic types of 'nominative' and 'accusative' NPs do not change (both are either e or $<<e,t>,t>$); only their extension (being interpreted as the subject or the object) differs. However, in order to deal with case and voice alternations in a variety of languages, several semanticists have abandoned this strict view, and propose more flexibility in the semantic composition of transitive sentences.

Partee (1987) suggests that e is the unmarked type for subjects and for arguments of extensional verbs generally. Semantically, a transitive verb denotes a relation between two entities. Syntactically, however, such transitive 2-place relations are not always expressed as transitive constructions. Compare for example the following two sentences. The Mandarin Chinese example in (5) consists of a transitive verb *chi* 'eat' and two arguments, the subject *Zhang San* and the object *pingguo* 'apple' (Mandarin, Sino-Tibetan, China; Yang 2008).

(5) Zhang San chi pingguo le.
    Zhang San eat apple PARTICLE
    'Zhang San ate an apple/apples.'

However, in West Greenlandic (Eskimo-Aleut, Greenland; Van Geenhoven 1996), the same event is expressed by an intransitive construction in which the bare noun is morphologically incorporated in the verb which functions as a 1-place predicate:

(6) Arnajaraq ipili-tur-p-u-q.
    Arnajaraq apple-ate-IND-[-TR]-3SG
    'Arnajaraq ate an apple/apples.'

Other examples of syntactically intransitive constructions that express semantically transitive relations between two participants are easily found. One well-known case is the use of a passive construction in English, as in (7):

(7) The apple was eaten (by Peter).

Likewise, not all syntactically transitive sentences in natural language correspond to 2-place relations between two equal arguments. As pointed out in Bary & de Swart (2005) and de Swart (2007), the object in a cognate object construction behaves semantically as a predicate modifier rather than as a full-fledged argument.

(8) Peter smiled an angelic smile.

In English, clearly, the cognate object is realized as any other direct object in a transitive construction, that is, it does not show its deviant semantic status. Yet, in a relatively rich case marking language like Russian (Indo-European, Russia), the different semantic type of the cognate object is mirrored by the use of a different type of case, i.e., instrumental case in (9) (Bary & de Swart 2005; Pereltsvaig 1999).

(9) On   ulybnulsja ulybkoj   angela.
    he.NOM   smiled   smile.INSTR angel.GEN
    'He smiled an angelic smile.'

For an extensive discussion of different types and degrees of mismatches between syntactic and semantic transitivity, see de Swart (2007).

Thus, transitive verb phrases can be semantically composed in at least two different ways. Firstly, the verb can be straightforwardly transitive (type $<e,<e,t>>$), as in Keenan's (1989) approach, in the sense that it denotes a relation between two semantically equal or equally prominent arguments of either type e or type $<<e,t>,t>$. Secondly, the verb can be formally intransitive (type $<e,t>$) with its object functioning as a predicate modifier (type $<<e,t>,<e,t>>$), as argued in de Hoop (1996), and Bary & de Swart (2005).

Cross-linguistically, the semantic type of an object can influence its case-marking. Let me illustrate this with an example of differential object marking. In Finnish (Uralic, Finland), depending on the reading associated with it, the object of certain transitive verbs can be marked either with accusative or with partitive case:

(10) Ostin   leipää.
     I.bought bread.PART
     'I bought (some) bread.'

(11) Ostin   leivän
     I.bought bread.ACC
     'I bought the bread.'

The partitive case in (10) goes with a non-specific reading of the object, while the accusative case in (11) goes with a specific reading of the object. In traditional grammars (cf. Karlsson 1983), the alternation between a partitive object and an accusative object is not only attributed to the definiteness or specificity of the object, as exemplified in (10)–(11), but also and even more so to the resultatitivity of the verb phrase. The latter phenomenon is illustrated by the alternation in (12)–(13):

(12) Presidentti ampui lintua.
     President   shot bird.PART
     'The president shot at a/the bird.'

(13) Presidentti ampui linnun.
     President   shot bird.ACC
     'The president shot a/the bird.'

In (13) we get the resultative reading and the result of the shooting is clear (the bird was shot), but in (12) the result is not known. That is, (12) is about the shooting rather than about the bird.

De Hoop (1996) proposes to unify these two semantic distinctions (object related and verb phrase related) by the notion of 'predicate modification'. Her basic idea is that the object that bears partitive case can syntactically still be a 'full-fledged' argument, but semantically it functions as a predicate modifier of type $<<e,t>,<e,t>>$, both in a context such as in (10)–(11) above where the noun phrase differs in specificity or definiteness, as well as in the other type of context, illustrated by (12)–(13) above, where the verb phrase differs in resultativity. Note that even a quantificational object bearing partitive case would be interpreted as a predicate modifier of type $<<e,t>,<e,t>>$, as in the following example (de Hoop 1996):

(14) Presidentti   ampui   kaikkia   lintuja.
      president   shot   all.PART   birds.PART
      'The president shot at all birds.'

There is yet a third option of composing a transitive verb phrase. The third option is that the verb functions as a predicate modifier (type $<<e,t>,<e,t>>$) which semantically incorporates a weak (predicative) object of type $<e,t>$, as proposed by Van Geenhoven (1996). In West-Greenlandic, the incorporating verb is intransitive from a morpho-syntactic perspective. The Greenlandic example in (6) above clearly shows *syntactic* incorporation of the indefinite noun phrase into the predicate. Consider another example of object incorporation in West Greenlandic (Eskimo-Aleut, Greenland; Van Geenhoven 1996):

(15) Esta   nutaa-mik   aalisagar-si-v-u-q.
      Ester   fresh-INSTR.SG   fish-get-IND-[-TR]-3SG
      'Ester got (a) fresh fish.'

The object is incorporated in the verb and also receives its existential quantificational force from the verb (cf. Carlson 1977). Van Geenhoven (1996) assumes that in these cases the verb is of the 'incorporating' type $<<e,t>,<e,t>>$, looking for an indefinite noun phrase which is of the predicative type $<e,t>$. Note that in (15) the incorporated noun is modified by means of an adjective that bears instrumental case. In Van Geenhoven's approach, the full object is semantically incorporated, i.e. including the independently case-marked adjective (see also article 5 [Semantics: Noun Phrases and Verb Phrases] (Dayal) *Bare noun phrases*). Van Geenhoven (1996) assumes that whereas certain verbs are inherently incorporating and others can never semantically incorporate their object, there are also verbs that can type shift, from one semantic type to the other. Clearly, a type shift from a transitive verb type $<e,<e,t>>$ to the incorporating type of verb $<<e,t>,<e,t>>$ requires a concomitant shift from e to $<e,t>$ in the type of the object.

In fact, Van Geenhoven argues that not only the indefinite object in a West Greenlandic noun incorporation construction is of this predicative type, but so are the indefinite objects in the following Dutch, German and English transitive sentences. She claims that these indefinite noun phrases are of the predicative type <e,t> too, and they are *semantically* though apparently not syntactically incorporated into the predicate:

(16) dat Peter gisteren een televisie heeft gekocht.
(17) daß Peter gestern einen Fernseher gekauft hat.
(18) that Peter bought a TV yesterday.

According to Van Geenhoven (1996), the transitive sentences in (16)–(18) are semantically similar to the syntactically intransitive sentences in (6) and (15) above. That is, Van Geenhoven assumes that also in these examples the verb functions as a predicate modifier (type <<e,t>,<e,t>>) which incorporates a predicative object (type <e,t>) to build a verb phrase of type <e,t>.

Note that although the components of the derived transitive verb phrases may differ in their type complexity, the result of the semantic composition in all cases discussed above is a verb phrase of type <e,t>. That is, a regular transitive verb of type <e,<e,t>> combines with an object of type *e* or <<e,t>,t> to form a verb phrase of type <e,t>. An incorporating verb of type <<e,t>,<e,t>> that combines with a predicative object of type <e,t> forms a verb phrase of type <e,t> as well, and so does an intransitive verb of type <e,t> that combines with a predicate modifier object of type <<e,t>,<e,t>>. So, in the end the semantic result of the composition is the same.

If we now turn to syntactic composition, we find that cross-linguistically the variation in semantic composition in many languages is reflected in the syntax through a variety of voice and/or case alternations. A nominative-accusative or ergative-absolutive case frame most often corresponds to the standard transitive relation, that is, a verb of type <e,<e,t>> taking two arguments of type *e* or <<e,t>,t>.

Deviations from this transitive case frame, e.g. when the object is in an oblique case instead of in the accusative, as in the Finnish examples discussed above, correspond to changes in semantic structure. In languages with differential object marking on the basis of definiteness or specificity, for instance, it has been argued that noun phrases that are 'strong' (type *e* or <<e,t>,t>) are likely to be overtly case marked with accusative case, while 'weak' (indefinite or non-specific) objects either show up in a different case or they do not show overt case marking at all (cf. de Hoop 1996). Also, weak objects are typically the ones that can occur in antipassive and noun incorporation structures, as illustrated in the West-Greenlandic examples (20) and (21) respectively (West Greenlandic, Eskimo-Aleut, Greenland; Fortescue 1984).

(19) Tuttu   taku-aa.
     caribou see-3SG.3SG
     'He saw the caribou.'

(20) Tuttu-mik   taku-nnip-puq.
     caribou-INSTR   see-ANTIP-IND.3SG
     'He saw a caribou.'

(21) Tuttu-si-vuq.
     caribou-see-IND.3SG
     'He saw a caribou.'

Clearly, some languages closely mirror the differences in semantic composition whereas others do not (cf. de Swart 2007).

So far, I only discussed the different types of objects of extensional verbal predicates (such as *eat* and *see*). Van Geenhoven (1996) shows that an incorporated object of an intensional predicate (such as *look for*) only allows for a non-specific reading (also called a *de dicto* reading in intensional contexts), as illustrated by the following example (West Greenlandic, Eskimo-Aleut, Greenland; Van Geenhoven 1996):

(22) Vittu   cykili-ssar-siur-p-u-q.
     Vittu   bike-FUT-seek-IND-[-TR]-3SG
     a. 'Vittus is looking for an (arbitrary) bike.'
     b. * 'There is a specific bike that Vittus is looking for'.

Van Geenhoven argues that the property introduced by the noun *bike* is the object of the intensional predicate *look for* in the above example. Thus, "an intensional verb is semantically incorporating par excellence: it absorbs a property as its argument" (Van Geenhoven 1996: 202). Thus, the object of an intensional verb is of the predicative type <e,t>. Note that this not only holds for lexically intensional verbal predicates such as *look for* but also for predicates that are intensional because they are in the scope of a modal affix. Van Geenhoven claims that in the following sentence the instrumental partitive noun phrase is also interpreted as a predicative noun phrase of type <e,t>, denoting a property even though this is the property of being a member of a specific set of students:

(23) Atuartu-t   ila-an-nik   ikiu-i-sariaqar-p-u-nga.
     Student-ERG.PL PART-3PL.SG-INST.PL help-AP-must-IND-[-TR]-1SG
     'I must help one of the students (any one will do).'

Van Geenhoven (1996) claims that the basic denotation of intensional predicates are semantically incorporating, which means that they preferably combine with a property-denoting, i.e., predicative type of object.

Similarly, Partee & Borschev (2004) hypothesize that where we see nominative/genitive and accusative/genitive alternations in Russian (both under negation and under intensional verbs), the nominative or accusative object represents an ordinary *e* or *<<e,t>,t>* type, whereas a genitive noun phrase is always interpreted as a property of type *<e,t>*. In the case of intensional verbs like *ždat'* 'expect, wait for' they argue that there is a shift in verb sense correlated with the shift in the interpretation of the object (Russian, Indo-European, Russia; Neidle 1988):

(24) On ždet   podrugu.
     he waits girlfriend.ACC
     'He's waiting for his girlfriend.'

(25) On ždet   otveta   na vopros.
     he waits answer.GEN   to question
     'He's waiting for an answer to the question.'

The object in (24) is specific, but the intensional variant of the verb *wait for* in (25) selects a non-specific NP. This would be a semantically incorporating type of verb in Van Geenhoven's approach, and the genitive object gets the concomitant predicative or property-denoting type. Partee & Borschev put forward the hypothesis that genitive subjects are of type *<e,t>* as well.

3 Word order variation

Not only case and transitivity alternations may result in different types of noun phrases, also variation in word order may yield a shift in meaning. An important question with respect to type shifting is whether 'anything goes' or not? Clearly, if we allow arbitrary type shifting from one type to another, this would make the theory much too powerful (cf. Hendriks 1993, Chierchia 1998, Matthewson 2001 for relevant discussion). Chierchia (1998) assumes that type shifting is constrained by his principle "Type Shifting as a Last Resort", and notes that this principle, which blocks free type shifting when there is a lexical type shifter present in a language, might interact with a general principle of economy in language. In the recently developed framework of Optimality Theoretic semantics (Hendriks & de Hoop 2001), type shifts would only occur as the optimal result of the interaction of potentially conflicting violable constraints. A principle such as Chierchia's "Type Shifting as a Last Resort" is then simply translated in terms of the interaction between a faithfulness constraint that requires a syntactic category to be assigned its basic semantic type, and a markedness constraint (economy) that prohibits the use of a lexical type shifter. Van der Does & de Hoop (1998) account for the word order variation called 'scrambling' in terms of such an Optimality Theoretic type shifting perspective. They show how the interpretive tendencies that arise with different word orders (see also article 12 [Semantics: Sentence and Information Structure] (Ward & Birner) *Discourse and word order*) can be modelled using a notion of optimal derivations, phrased in terms of the preferred semantic types of different types of noun phrases and verbs. They argue that referential definites have a natural interpretation in type *e*, while the predicative meaning of an indefinite noun phrase is the denotation of its noun, i.e. type $<e,t>$ (see also article 2 [Semantics: Noun Phrases and Verb Phrases] (Heim) *Definiteness and indefiniteness* and article 5 [Semantics: Noun Phrases and Verb Phrases] (Dayal) *Bare noun phrases*). However, certain definite noun phrases look very similar to predicative indefinites, forming a semantic unity with a 'light' verb, verbs which do not have much semantic content of their own. Compare the pair of sentences below, which only differ in the (in)definiteness of the object. The meaning of these two sentences is basically the same, and in both sentences the object does not get a referential meaning:

(26) dat ik ook mazelen heb.
 that I also measles have
 'that I also have the measles.'

(27) dat ik ook de mazelen heb.
 that I also the measles have
 'that I also have the measles.'

But even though there does not seem to be a difference between the sentence with a bare plural object in (26) and the one with a definite plural in (27), when the word order is changed, there is. That is, the definite object in (27) can scramble to the left of the adverb, but the indefinite one cannot:

(28) dat   ik   *(de)   mazelen   ook   heb.
     that   I   the   measles   also   have
     'that I also have the measles.'

Van der Does & de Hoop (1998) argue that indefinites can scramble to a marked position to the left of the adverb, but only when they type shift from their basic predicative type to a generalized quantifier type $<<e,t>,t>$. However, when the indefinite noun phrase scrambles and shifts to an $<<e,t>,t>$ reading, then the verb with which it combines must be of the transitive type $<e,<e,t>>$. Light verbs, however, such as *hebben* 'have' in the examples above, have the incorporating verb type $<<e,t>,<e,t>>$ as their preferred type. That means that scrambling the indefinite object would induce type shifting of the object as well as of the light verb. This leads to a suboptimal derivation, yielding an ill-formed output. By contrast, definite noun phrases preferably denote in type *e*. Thus, when the definite object is semantically incorporated in the light verb, it has to shift to the predicative type $<e,t>$ in order to combine with the type $<<e,t>,<e,t>>$ light verb. Alternatively, when the definite object does not type shift to a predicative type, the light verb has to shift to the transitive verb type $<e,<e,t>>$. Van der Does & de Hoop (1998) leave both options open: either the definite object in (27) and (28) type shifts to the predicative type, or the light verb type shifts to the transitive type. Either way, one type shift has to take place in a construction like this, and both derivations are optimal, and the meanings are equivalent. To sum up, van der Does & de Hoop argue that whereas the predicative use of indefinites prefers to live in type $<e,t>$, definites have their basic denotation in type *e*. In the case of a light verb, with the preferred type $<<e,t>,<e,t>>$ interpretation of incorporating verbs, a predicative indefinite object gives one optimal derivation. Definite objects allow for two optimal derivations when combined with light verbs: either the definite or the verb denotes in its preferred type. This explains the free scrambling behaviour of definite objects as compared to indefinite objects. Merging an incorporating light verb and a predicative type of definite is synonymous with merging a shifted light verb and a referential type of definite. The result is the same, in the sense that both derivations are equally costly as they require one type shift each.

The different derivations for indefinite and definite objects can be illustrated by two Optimality Theoretic tableaux (van der Does & de Hoop 1998):

In Tab. 8.1, an OT semantic tableau is given that illustrates the process of optimization of a sentence that contains a light verb and an indefinite object. The first candidate output, which combines a light transitive verb of type $<<e,t>,<e,t>>$ (an incorporating type of verb) with an indefinite object of basic type $<e,t>$ is optimal as it does not violate either constraint. By contrast, the second candidate output combines a regular transitive verb type with a generalized quantifier type of

Tab. 8.1: OT semantic tableau of a light verb combined with an indefinite object (Dutch)

Light verb + indefinite object	Indefinite in type <e,t>	Light verb in type <<e,t>,<e,t>>
☐ <<e,t>,<e,t>> + <e,t>		
<e,<e,t>> + <<e,t>,t>	*	*

object. This output violates both the constraint that requires a light verb to denote in type <<e,t>,<e,t>> and the constraint that requires an indefinite noun phrase to denote in type <e,t>. Hence, the first candidate comes out as the winner of the competition, i.e., as the optimal candidate. For a definite object in combination, on the other hand, the two candidate outputs both violate one of the constraints, as shown in Tab. 8.2. Therefore, dependent on the ranking of the constraints (for Dutch, van der Does & de Hoop argue that they are not ranked with respect to each other, but of course this can be different for other languages), each candidate can win the competition. If we relate this to the position with respect to an adverbial in Dutch, we can account for the fact that definite objects of light verbs in Dutch scramble freely, while indefinite objects of light verbs have to stay in situ, adjacent to the verb (cf. van der Does & de Hoop 1998).

Tab. 8.2: OT semantic tableau of a light verb combined with an definite object (Dutch)

Light verb + definite object	Definite in type e	Light verb in type <<e,t>,<e,t>>
☐ <<e,t>,<e,t>> + <e,t>	*	
☐ <e,<e,t>> + e		*

Yang (2008) argues that in Chinese the semantic type of a noun phrase interacts with the interpretive characteristics of its word order position as well. The preverbal position in Chinese is typically associated with 'strong' (referential or quantificational) types of noun phrases. Therefore, an indefinite object in preverbal position as in (29) is subject to two conflicting constraints. Because the object is indefinite its preferred type is <e,t> but because it is in scrambled (preverbal) position, its preferred meaning is a (specific) type e reading.

(29) Ta   ba   yi-ge   pingguo chi   le.
     he   ACC   one-CL   apple   eat   PRT
     'He ate an apple.'

The question is how this conflict is resolved. Which type comes out as optimal, that is, is the resulting meaning non-specific (predicative) or specific (referential) for *yi-ge pingguo* 'one apple'? Yang (2008) argues that the non-specific predicative reading of the indefinite object comes out as the winner of the competition. Hence, the constraint that favours a predicative reading for an indefinite noun phrase is claimed to outrank the one that penalizes a non-specific reading in preverbal position (Mandarin Chinese, Sino-Tibetan, China; Yang 2008). This is illustrated by the following tableau:

Tab. 8.3: OT semantic tableau of an indefinite object in preverbal position (Mandarin Chinese)

Ta ba yi-ge pingguo chi le	Indefinite in type <e,t>	Avoid <e,t> in preverbal position
☐ <e,t> (He ate an apple)		*
e (He ate a specific apple)	*	

However, when the predicate is changed to a predicate that denotes a bounded event, the specific reading comes out as optimal:

(30) Ta   ba   yi-ge   pingguo   chi-wan   le.
     he   ACC   one-CL   apple   eat-finish PRT
     'He finished a (particular) apple.'

Unlike in (29), in (30) the specific reading becomes optimal and according to Yang (2008) this is due to the semantic type of the bounded predicate, which apparently does not shift to an incorporating type. The constraint that penalizes the combination of a non-specific indefinite object and a bounded predicate outranks the constraint that favours a type <e,t> reading of an indefinite object. However, this constraint itself is in competition with a constraint that favours the <e,t> reading of an object in an intensional context (Zimmermann 1993). The indefinite object in (31) is interpreted as either specific (type *e*) or non-specific (type <e,t>), according to Yang (2008), which means that the two highest ranked constraints are tied constraints, i.e., they are not ranked with respect to each other.

(31) Ta   neng   ba   yi-ge   pingguo   chi-wan   le.
     he   can   ACC   one-CL   apple   eat-finish PRT
     'He can finish a (particular) apple.'

Yang's (2008) Optimality Theoretic account of different violable constraints that influence the preferred types of indefinite objects thus nicely accounts for the possible semantic types of preverbal objects in Mandarin Chinese.

4 Conclusion

This article examined some of the syntactic factors that appear to influence type shifting of object noun phrases, namely case and transitivity alternations and word order. I hope to have shown that type shifting principles which allow for different denotations of noun phrases offer a nice approach to cross-linguistic phenomena where different readings occur in similar contexts.

I am grateful to my colleagues from the research group Optimal Communication, in particular Peter de Swart, for helpful discussions on semantic type shifting possibilities in natural language.

5 References

Bary, Corien & Peter de Swart 2005. Arguments against arguments: Additional accusatives in Latin and Ancient Greek. In: J. Gervain (ed.). *Proceedings of the Tenth ESSLLI Student Session*. Edinburgh: Heriot Watts University, 12–24.
Carlson, Gregory 1977. *Reference to Kinds in English*. Ph.D. dissertation. University of Massachusetts, Amherst, MA.
van der Does, Jaap & Helen de Hoop 1998. Type-shifting and scrambled definites. *Journal of Semantics* 15, 393–416.
Fortescue, Michael 1984. *West Greenlandic*. London: Croom Helm.
Van Geenhoven, Veerle 1996. *Semantic Incorporation and Indefinite Descriptions: Semantic and Syntactic Aspects of Noun Incorporation in West Greenlandic*. Doctoral dissertation. University of Tübingen.
Hendriks, Herman 1993. *Studied Flexibility*. Ph.D. dissertation. University of Amsterdam.
Hendriks, Petra & Helen de Hoop 2001. Optimality theoretic semantics. *Linguistics & Philosophy* 2, 1–32.
de Hoop, Helen 1996. *Case Configuration and Noun Phrase Interpretation*. New York: Garland.
de Hoop, Helen 1997. A semantic reanalysis of the partitive constraint. *Lingua* 103, 151–174.
Karlsson, Fred 1983. *Finnish Grammar*. Juva: Werner Söderström Osakeyhtiö (WSOY).
Keenan, Edward L. 1989. Semantic case theory. In: R. Bartsch, J. van Benthem & P. van Emde Boas (eds.). *Semantics and Contextual Expression*. Dordrecht: Foris, 33–56.
Link, Godehard 1983. The logical analysis of plurals and mass terms: A lattice-theoretical approach. In: R. Bäuerle, Ch. Schwarze & A. von Stechow (eds.). *Meaning, Use and Interpretation of Language*. Berlin: de Gruyter, 302–323.
Matthewson, Lisa 2001. Quantification and the nature of crosslinguistic variation. *Natural Language Semantics* 9, 145–189.
Montague, Richard 1974. *Formal Philosophy: Selected Papers of Richard Montague*. Edited and with an introduction by Richmond Thomason. New Haven, CT: Yale University Press.
Neidle, Carol 1988. *The Role of Case in Russian Syntax*. Dordrecht: Kluwer.

Partee, Barbara H. 1987. Noun phrase interpretation and type shifting principles.
    In: J. Groenendijk, D. de Jongh & M. Stokhof (eds.). *Studies in Discourse Representation Theory and the Theory of Generalized Quantifiers*. Dordrecht: Foris, 115–143.
Partee, Barbara H. & Vladimir Borschev 2004. The semantics of Russian genitive of negation: The nature and role of perspectival structure. In: K. Watanabe & R. B. Young (eds.). *Proceedings of Semantics and Linguistic Theory (= SALT) XIV*. Ithaca, NY: Cornell University, 212–234.
Partee, Barbara H. & Mats Rooth 1983. Generalized conjunction and type ambiguity. In: R. Bäuerle, Ch. Schwarze & A. von Stechow (eds.). *Meaning, Use and Interpretation of Language*. Berlin: de Gruyter, 361–383.
Pereltsvaig, Asya 1999. Cognate objects in Russian: Is the notion "cognate" relevant for syntax? *Canadian Journal of Linguistics* 44, 267–291.
Steedman, Mark 1996. *Surface Structure and Interpretation*. Cambridge, MA: The MIT Press.
de Swart, Peter 2007. *Cross-linguistic Variation in Object Marking*. Ph.D. dissertation. Radboud University Nijmegen.
de Swart, Henriëtte, Yoad Winter & Joost Zwarts 2007. Bare nominals and reference to capacities. *Natural Language and Linguistic Theory* 25, 195–222.
Yang, Ning 2008. *The Indefinite Object in Mandarin Chinese: Its Marking, Interpretation and Acquisition*. Ph.D. dissertation. Radboud University Nijmegen.
Zimmermann, Thomas E. 1993. On the proper treatment of opacity in certain verbs. *Natural Language Semantics* 1, 149–179.

Paul Kay and Laura A. Michaelis
9 Constructional meaning and compositionality

1 Constructions and compositionality —— 293
2 Continuum of idiomaticity —— 298
3 Kinds of constructional meanings —— 301
4 Model-theoretic and truth-conditional meaning —— 301
5 Argument structure —— 304
6 Conventional implicature, or pragmatic presupposition —— 308
7 Less commonly recognized illocutionary forces —— 312
8 Metalinguistic constructions —— 313
9 Information flow —— 316
10 Conclusion —— 321
11 References —— 322

Abstract: One of the major motivations for constructional approaches to grammar is that a given rule of syntactic formation can sometimes, in fact often, be associated with more than one semantic specification. For example, a pair of expressions like *purple plum* and *alleged thief* call on different rules of semantic combination. The first involves something closely related to intersection of sets: a purple plum is a member of the set of purple things and a member of the set of plums. But an alleged thief is not a member of the intersection of the set of thieves and the set of alleged things. Indeed, that intersection is empty, since only a proposition can be alleged and a thief, whether by deed or attribution, is never a proposition. This chapter describes the various ways meanings may be assembled in a construction-based grammar.

1 Constructions and compositionality

It is sometimes supposed that constructional approaches are opposed to compositional semantics. This happens to be an incorrect supposition, but it is instructive to consider why it exists. A foundation of construction-based syntax is the idea that rules of syntactic combination (descriptions of local trees) are directly

Paul Kay, Berkeley, CA, USA
Laura A. Michaelis, Boulder, CO, USA

associated with interpretive and use conditions, in the form of semantic and pragmatic features that attach to the mother or daughter nodes in these descriptions (Kay 2002; Sag 2010). This amounts to the claim that syntactic rules mean things. Meaning, of course, is generally viewed as the exclusive purview of words, and in the prevailing view of meaning composition, syntactic rules do no more than determine what symbol sequences function as units for syntactic purposes. So while syntactic rules assemble words and their dependent elements into phrases, and the phrases denote complex concepts like predicates and propositions, the rules cannot add conceptual content to that contributed by the words; nor can they alter the combinatoric properties of the words. On this view, which Jackendoff (1997: 48) describes as the "doctrine of syntactically transparent composition", "[a]ll elements of content in the meaning of a sentence are found in the lexical conceptual structures [. . .] of the lexical items composing the sentence" and "pragmatics plays no role in determining how [lexical conceptual structures] are combined". To embrace a construction-based model of semantic composition is not to reject the existence of syntactically transparent composition but instead to treat it, as per Jackendoff (1997: 49), as a "default in a wider array of options". That is, whenever a class of expressions can be viewed as licensed by a context-free phrase structure rule accompanied by a rule composing the semantics of the mother from the semantics of the daughter, a construction-based approach would propose a construction that is functionally equivalent to such a rule-to-rule pair. But constructional approaches also provide a revealing way to represent linguistic structures in which semantics of the mother does not follow entirely from the semantics of the daughters. A case in point is the pattern exemplified by the attested sentences in (1), retrieved from Google. We will call such sentences pseudo-conditionals, and we will refer to the *if*-clause and main clause as the pseudo-protasis and pseudo-apodosis, respectively.

(1) a. If you're 3Com right now, you're considering buying add space in next week's issue.
   b. If you're George Bush, you're now allowed to lie in the faces of trusting young voters.
   c. [I]f you're Betty Ford right now, you're probably thinking, you know, I hope everybody's OK.
   d. [More than one able program director thinks commercials, promos and features is not an all-news station,] but if you're new CBS President Dan Mason right now you're going to leave well enough alone.

Example (2) shows that the pseudo-apodosis, like a true apodosis, can be extended beyond the bounds of the initial sentence.

(2) If you are George W. Bush and this vending machine represents Iraq, you keep putting money into the machine. When you have none left and it is obvious to all rational persons that trying again is not going to result in a different outcome, you borrow more and keep going.

Syntactically the sentences in (1) and the first sentence in (2) appear to be ordinary conditional sentences like (3).

(3) If you're pleased with the outcome, you may feel like celebrating.

But the sincere speaker of the protasis of an ordinary conditional sentence does not hypothesize a patently impossible state of affairs, while the *if*-clauses of (1)–(2) appear to pose the manifest impossibility that the addressee is identical to Peter Angelos/Betty Ford/George Bush/Dan Mason/etc. Of course that is not what is being said in (1)–(2). Exactly what is being said is difficult to pin down with certitude. The syntactic form is roughly given by (4).

(4) If you are x, $p(x)$.

The semantics seems to assert the proposition expressed by $p(x)$, qualified in different examples by a number of different illocutionary forces or speaker attitudes. In any case, no hypothetical situation is posed; it appears that a categorical judgment is expressed (possibly hedged or epistemically qualified in some way) and the subject of that judgment is not the addressee but the person identified as x; e.g., example (2) is clearly about George Bush, not about the consequences of a hypothetical identity between George Bush and the addressee. Pseudo-conditionals have the same form as (one type of) familiar conditional but entirely distinct semantics.

If the grammar accords to a sentence a different interpretation from what could be built up piece by piece from its words and constituent phrases, syntactically transparent compositionality scores this as an instance of non-compositionality. As such, the pseudo-conditional pattern could appropriately be called an idiom, but, as numerous proponents of construction-based approaches have observed, idiomaticity is not the same thing as inflexibility (Fillmore, Kay & O'Connor 1988; Michaelis & Lambrecht 1996; Culicover 1997). The pseudo-conditional pattern is evidently a productive one, and an adequate grammar must describe the interpretive and combinatoric constraints that define it. In a construction-based grammar, the pseudo-conditional sits on a continuum of idiomaticity (or generality) of expressions, somewhere between tightly bound idioms and fully productive processes (cf. article 5 [Semantics: Lexical Structures and Adjectives] (Fellbaum) *Idioms and collocations*). A construction grammar models this continuum with an array of constructions of correspondingly graded generality (Kay & Fillmore 1999; Sag 2010). Doing so obviously requires many more rules of composition than are countenanced in most non-constructional approaches – roughly as many as there are constructions listed in an (ideal) traditional grammar. A construction-based grammar sees nothing special about any part of the syntactic structure of sentences like (1)–(2); the syntax of (1)–(2) is the same as the syntax of (3) – that of a common, garden-variety conditional sentence. But the meaning is different, and not obviously derivable by conversational implicature. So one posits a special construction with the syntax of a vanilla conditional, constrained as in (4), but with a semantic form unlike that of an ordinary conditional: a hedged categorical judgment is expressed – one whose subject is not denoted in the pseudo-protasis.

The pseudo-conditional is important for our purposes because the existence of this interpretive affordance appears to undermine one of the foundational assumptions of syntactically transparent composition, as expressed by the following quote (from the online *Stanford Encyclopedia of Philosophy*):

(5) "If a language is compositional, it cannot contain a pair of non-synonymous complex expressions with identical structure and pairwise synonymous constituents." (Szabó 2007)

If we use Szabó's diagnostic, the existence of pseudo-conditionals entails either that English is not compositional or that pseudo-conditionals are syntactically distinct from ordinary present-tense conditionals. A view of compositionality this narrow also presumably necessitates different syntactic analyses for any pair of readings attached to sentences in the large class illustrated by (6)–(7). Each such sentence yields both an idiomatic and a composed interpretation:

(6) My yoga instructor sometimes pulls my leg.

(7) I'm afraid he's going to spill the beans.

A constructional approach welcomes a single syntactic analysis in all of these cases and posits constructions in the case of the idiomatic readings that attach semantic interpretations directly to certain relatively complex syntactic objects. In short, constructional approaches recognize as instances of compositionality cases in which two different meanings for the same syntactic form are licensed by two different collections of form-meaning licensers, i.e., by two different collections of constructions. Construction-based grammars are nevertheless compositional in a quite usual sense: if you know the meanings of the words and you know *all* the rules that combine words and phrases into larger formal units, while simultaneously combining the meanings of the smaller units into the meanings of the larger ones, then you know the forms and meanings of all the larger units, including all the sentences. The 'bottom-up' procedural language used here is intended only heuristically: most constructional approaches are explicitly or implicitly declarative and constraint based, notwithstanding the tempting metaphorical interpretation of *construction* as denoting the building of big things out of little things.

Constructional approaches tend to pay special attention to the fact that there are many such rules, and especially to the rules that assign meanings to complex structures. And such approaches do not draw a theoretical distinction between those rules thought to be of the 'core' and those considered 'peripheral'. Proponents of construction-based syntax assume that accounting for *all* the facts of a language as precisely as possible is a major goal, if not the major goal, of scientific linguistics. One can in fact view construction-based theories of syntax as upholding standards of grammar coverage that the original proponents of generative grammar abandoned, as they sought to reduce the theory's dependence on linguistic facts. Chomsky (1995: 435) describes this shift in the goals of grammarians as follows: "A look at the earliest work from the mid-1950s will show that many phenomena that fell within the rich descriptive apparatus then postulated, often with accounts of no little interest and insight, lack any serious analysis within the much narrower theories motivated by the search for explanatory adequacy, and remain among the huge mass of constructions for which no principled explanation exists – again, not an unusual concomitant of progress". It seems safe to say that most proponents of construction-based syntax would not consider the loss of insightful and interesting accounts a mark of progress, and find the search for putatively narrower theories of explanatory adequacy unrequited. Whether *narrower* properly describes a relation between the Minimalist Program, for example, and, say, the construction-based version of Head Driven Phrase Structure Grammar of Ginzburg & Sag (2000) is itself open to question. It can be plausibly argued that a formal theory, such as that of Ginzburg & Sag, is *ipso facto* "narrower" than an informal one, such as the Minimalist Program, by virtue of the fact that formalism imposes a limit on potential predictions.

In the remainder of this article, we will examine how and what constructions mean. Section 2 focuses on the continuum of idiomaticity alluded to above. Section 3 surveys the range of constructional meanings. Section 4 outlines the constructional approach to model-theoretic and truth-conditional meaning. In section 5, we focus on argument-structure constructions of the kind proposed by Goldberg (1995, 2006). In section 6, we describe the relationship between constructional meaning and conventional implicature. Less commonly recognized illocutionary forces expressed by constructions are discussed in section 7. Section 8 discusses the relationship between constructions and metalinguistic operators, as discussed by Kay (1997), among others. In section 9 we will discuss constructional accounts of the discourse-syntax interface, with particular attention to the assignment of prosodic peaks. Section 10 contains brief concluding remarks.

2 Continuum of idiomaticity

Related to the less restrictive view of compositionality is the recognition that there exists a gradient of idiomaticity-to-productivity stretching from frozen idioms, like *the salt of the earth, in the doghouse,* and *under the weather* on the one hand to fully productive rules on the other, *e.g.,* the rules licensing *Kim blinked* (the Subject-Predicate Construction) or *ate oranges, ready to leave,* and *in the kitchen* (the Head-Complement Construction). Several examples discussed below occupy intermediate points on this scale.

At one end of the scale we find expressions like *right away, as of* [requiring a date or time expression as complement], *by and large, cheek by jowl,* which are not only entirely fixed as regards their lexical makeup but also exhibit idiosyncratic syntax. Somewhat less idiosyncratic are expressions with fixed lexical makeup that exhibit syntax found elsewhere in the language, such as *a red herring, carrying coals to Newcastle,* and *water under the bridge.* Fillmore, Kay & O'Connor (1988: 504) follow Makkai (1972) in pointing out that many idiomatic expressions are no less idiomatic for being merely 'encoding' idioms. That is, someone who knows everything about the language except a particular encoding idiom may be able to decode that idiom on a first hearing, while still not knowing that the expression is a standard way of expressing that meaning. Examples of encoding idioms that are not decoding idioms are expressions like *twist* NP's *arm, as for* [when preceding a topic-resuming NP], *rock the boat* or the French *de vive voix* ('orally in person', as against in writing; lit. 'of living voice'). In other words, idioms are defined not only as those expressions that are not interpretable by a naïve speaker but also as those expressions that a naïve speaker would not know to use in a given context. Close behind these come idioms that allow morphological inflection or minor syntactic alteration such as *kick/kicks/kicked/kicking the bucket*. More productive than these are idioms with partially fixed lexical membership. Examples include the [*Watch* NP[ACC] VP[bare-stem-infinitive]] pattern that occurs in a sentence like "I've taught you well, now *watch you/*yourself beat me.*" Many subtypes of idioms fit in this category: among others, VP idioms with fixed verb and controlled or uncontrolled pronominal argument (8), VP idioms with variable object (9), the rare subject idioms (10). Note in the case of (10c) that the idiom (construction) specifies interrogative form but does not specify main-clause syntax versus that of embedded question.

(8) a. blow one's nose
    b. blow someone's mind

(9) a. slip someone a Mickey
    b. give someone the slip

(10) a. The world has passed someone by.
     b. Someone's time is up.
     c. Where does someone get off?/I wonder where someone gets off.

Nunberg, Sag & Wasow (1994) demonstrate that VP idioms behave in ways that are explicable only if they have compositional properties – that is, if their parts map in a one-to-one way to the parts of their paraphrases. In particular, they argue, the rarity of subject idioms, exemplified in (10), follows from the fact that the arguments of verb-headed idioms, even when lexically animate, denote inanimate entities, as evidenced by the second arguments of the expressions *let the cat out of the bag*, *throw the baby out with the bath water*, *take the bull by the horns*. Since subject arguments tend to be interpreted as agents, and therefore as animates, it stands to reason that so few idiomatic expressions constrain the subject role. In addition, they argue, differences in the degree of syntactic flexibility exhibited by VP idioms can be attributed to differing degrees of (sometimes metaphorically based) semantic compositionality, where flexibility includes the availability of a passive paraphrase (e.g., *The beans were spilled*, as against **The bucket was kicked*) and the felicity of nominal modification, as in the attested example *Clinton and McCain both have much larger, more repugnant skeletons in their closet* (retrieved from Google), as against, e.g., **He blew some ludicrous smoke*. Crucially, the type of semantic transparency that Nunberg, Sag & Wasow (1994) see as driving syntactic flexibility cannot be equated with the existence of a general semantic motivation for the VP idiom, e.g., one involving metaphor or metonymy. For example, the expression *chew the fat* describes the jaw motions associated with talking, while the expression *drop the ball* presumably evokes the metaphor LIFE IS A GAME. Neither expression, however, maps in a one-to-one fashion to its literal paraphrase (which we presume to be 'converse' and 'fail', respectively). Accordingly, neither expression exhibits syntactic flexibility: **The fat was chewed*, **He dropped the important ball*. Because semantically transparent VP idioms must combine with constructions like passive and modification, they require a compositional representation, as verbs with partially lexically filled valence lists.

An example of an idiom, or construction, which is both defined largely syntactically and also contains a significant amount of specified lexical material is Nominal Extraposition, an exclamatory construction studied by Michaelis & Lambrecht (1996) and exemplified by attested cases in (11):

(11) a. It's amazing the people you see here. (Michaelis & Lambrecht 1996: 215, (1a))
b. It was terrible, really, the joy I took at the notion of skunking Pigeyes. (Michaelis & Lambrecht 1996: 215, (1e))
c. It's staggering the number of books that can pile up. (Michaelis & Lambrecht 1996: 215, (1g))

The syntax of the construction is roughly as summarized in (12):

(12) It BE AP [$_{NP}$ the CN].

Michaelis & Lambrecht argue that Nominal Extraposition, in contrast to the superficially similar pattern right-dislocation pattern, has a nonreferential subject (invariantly *it*) and a focal rather than topical post-predicate NP. The pattern qualifies as an idiomatic pattern on the basis of its syntax (adjectives do not otherwise license non-oblique complements) and its semantics: the post-predicate NP is metonymically construed as referring to a scalar parameter, e.g., the number or variety of people seen in (11a).

Moving onward toward purely formal idioms, we encounter the much discussed Correlative Conditional (or, equivalently, Comparative Correlative), exemplified in (13):

(13) The more I drink the better you look.

The only lexically specified elements in the Correlative Conditional are the two tokens of *the*, which only coincidentally have the form of the definite article: these forms are in fact reflexes of Old English instrumental-case demonstratives (Michaelis 1994a). With the exception of idiomatic comparative expressions like *the better to see you with* and *all the more reason to*, the word *the* serves as a degree marker only in the Correlative Conditional (Borsley 2004; Culicover & Jackendoff 1999; Fillmore, Kay & O'Connor 1988; Fillmore 1986). Finally, when no lexical material is encountered in an idiom, we have entered the realm of minor syntactic patterns. Well-known examples include the Incredulity Construction (Akmajian 1984; Lambrecht 1990), as exemplified in (14), and the conjunctional conditional. The latter construction, exemplified in (15), expresses a range of comissive speech acts (Culicover 1970; Cornulier 1986):

(14) Him get first prize?!

(15) a. One more beer and I'm leaving.
 b. Bouges pas ou je tire! ('Don't move or I'll shoot!')

The step from these relatively special-purpose syntactic patterns to those that license canonical statements, imperatives, questions of many different types (Ginzburg & Sag 2000), ordinary noun phrases, head-complement phrases, etc. is a small one. A close look at the variety of constructions in English – and presumably in many, if not all, other languages – reveals, not a dichotomy between core and peripheral constructions, but a gradient of fully fixed to fully productive patterns of phrase construction. The semantics of constructions is the semantics to be discovered along the full length of this gamut.

3 Kinds of constructional meanings

Probably any kind of meaning that occurs can be the semantic contribution of a construction. The classification implied in the following list is intended to be neither definitive nor exhaustive.

(i) Literal meaning in general, especially that concerned with the truth conditions of statements and the straightforward interpretations of questions and imperatives: the kind of meaning that formal semantics has traditionally been primarily concerned with.
(ii) Argument structure in particular.
(iii) Conventional implicatures, or pragmatic presuppositions.
(iv) Less commonly recognized illocutionary forces, as in the incredulity construction (14) or the construction that announces an observed incongruity and requests an explanation for it (as in, e.g., *What are you doing smoking?*)
(v) Metalinguistic comments, as in metalinguistic negation (e.g., *It's not good, it's great!*) or the metalinguistic comparative (e.g., *He's more annoying than dangerous.*)

4 Model-theoretic and truth-conditional meaning

Normally, a construction specifies a syntactic configuration, usually (in some constructional approaches, always) a local tree, consisting of a mother node and one or more daughter nodes. Sign-Based Construction Grammar (Sag 2010) distinguishes between lexical constructions, which describe lexeme classes, and combinatoric constructions, which describe phrasal types. (For recent precursors to this approach, see the constructional HPSG of Ginzburg & Sag 2000, and the constructional approaches of Kay & Fillmore 1999; Kay 2002, 2005; Michaelis & Lambrecht 1996 and Michaelis 2004.) The construction also specifies how the semantics of the daughters are combined to produce the semantics of the mother, and what additional semantics, if any, is contributed by the construction itself. Current Sign-Based Construction Grammar (Sag 2010) uses a modified form of Minimal Recursion Semantics (Copestake et al. 2005), but constructional approaches in general are not constrained to any particular semantic theory, formal or informal. A fully developed formal analysis of the semantics and syntax of a very wide range of English interrogative clauses is given in Ginzburg & Sag 2000. That work represents perhaps the most extended formal fragment of any grammar that deals in full detail with both the syntactic and semantic phenomena of a large domain, as well as the exact specifics of their interrelations. As such it presents arguably the fullest available concrete demonstration of the principle of compositionality. Ginzburg & Sag implement the notion of construction in the formal device of typed feature structures (briefly 'types') organized as a multiple inheritance hierarchy. This enables them to build a hierarchy of types, with initially separate syntactic and semantic branches, which however are mixed and matched by virtue of multiple inheritance into hybrid syntactico-semantic types that pair structure and meaning. These hybrid types are intended as fully explicit implementations of the traditional notion of a construction as a conventional (specifically, grammatical) association of form and meaning. This expansive, tightly-written treatise contains too much material to be summarized here, but some idea of the coverage – if not the novel semantic theory of interrogatives – can be given by the leaves (maximal subtypes) of the hierarchy of interrogative clauses, which present fully explicit constructions specifying the syntax and semantic of the six major types of interrogative clauses given in (16), plus the thirteen subtypes suggested by multiple examples.

(16) a. polar interrogative clause: *Did Kim leave?*
 b. non-subject *wh* interrogative clause: *What did Kim see? [I wonder] what Kim saw*
 c. subject *wh* interrogative clause: *Who left? [I wonder] who left*
 d. reprise [i.e., echo] interrogative clause: *You saw WHO? Did I see WHO? Go WHERE? You're leaving?*
 e. direct in-situ interrogative clause: *You saw WHO? Kim saw Sandy?*
 f. sluiced interrogative clause: *Who? I wonder who.*

Ginzburg & Sag (2000) present separate constructions specifying the full syntax and semantics of each of these thirteen interrogative-clause types, as well as the complex interrelations of the various syntactic and semantic types they inherit. Sag (2010) generalizes the Ginzburg & Sag analysis by analyzing the interrogative patterns in (16 b–f) as subtypes of the head-filler filler-gap construction, along with other constructions that license long-distance dependencies, including topicalization, *wh*-exclamatives, relative clauses and the clauses of the biclausal correlative conditional discussed in section 2 above. Sag observes that while the clause type in (16b), e.g., exhibits an extraction dependency between a clause-initial filler phrase and a gap in the clausal head daughter, there are several parameters of variation that distinguish these types from one another, including: the type of the filler (i.e., whether it contains a *wh*-element and, if so, of what kind), the possible syntactic categories of the filler daughter, the semantics and/or syntactic category of the mother and the semantics and/or syntactic category of the head daughter. He shows that each of the five subtypes of the filler-gap construction imposes a distinct condition: the filler daughter of a topicalized clause must contain no distinguished element (*wh*-phrase or *the*-phrase), *wh*-interrogative, *wh*-relative, and *wh*-exclamative clauses each require the filler daughter to contain a distinct type of *wh*-element and the filler of a *the*-clause must contain the definite degree marker *the*. Paralleling these syntactic differences are semantic and discourse-pragmatic differences; for example, while interrogative clauses denote propositional functions, exclamatory clauses like *What a nice person Sandy is* denote 'facts' (presupposed propositions). Because the type descriptions that define constructions in this system can involve any combination of syntactic, semantic and use conditions, the model can incorporate types that have even more specific formal, interpretive and pragmatic constraints than those just discussed. These types include the interrogative construction illustrated in (17), which Kay & Fillmore (1999) refer to as the WXDY construction:

(17) a. What's this fly doing in my soup?
 b. What's this scratch doing on the table?
 c. Can you tell me what this scratch is doing on my favorite table?

What makes the construction undeniably idiomatic is that it is a *why* question that takes the form of a *what* question. At the same time, as Kay & Fillmore (1999) demonstrate, the pattern interacts with many semantic regularities. First, the predication expressed by Y is applied to x in the standard way that any (one-place) predicate is applied to its argument, resulting in the proposition $||Y(x)||$; it is this proposition, *e.g.*, 'There's a fly in my soup', that is subject to the special, explanation-seeking illocutionary force. Second, within the Y constituent, the semantics is assembled according to the familiar rules for assembling the semantics of prepositional phrases (17), adjective phrases (18a), gerundial clauses (18b), and predicational noun phrases (18c):

(18) a. What are you doing stark naked?
   b. What was he doing running for office?
   c. What's she doing only the runner up?

So sentences exemplifying the WXDY construction seamlessly interweave the semantic structures of the familiar constructions involved, *e.g.*, those that license the Y predicate, non-subject *wh* interrogatives (main clause with inverted head daughter or embedded and canonical), with a special illocutionary force to compose their meaning. Constructional approaches recognize the responsibility to account in a compositional way for the meanings of wholes in terms of the meanings of their parts and the rules of combination, that is, the constructions.

5 Argument structure

The principal contribution of constructional approaches to the semantics of argument structure has been the thesis that patterns of argument structure (argument-structure constructions) exist independently of lexical argument-taking predicates. Adele Goldberg has been the leading exponent of this view (see, e.g., Goldberg 1995, 2006; Kay 2005 and Michaelis 2004). Among the argument-structure constructions proposed by Goldberg are the Caused Motion Construction, the *Way* Construction and the Ditransitive Construction. The Caused Motion Construction is motivated by examples like (19)–(22):

(19) a. They laughed him off the stage.
   b. *They laughed him.

(20) a. Frank sneezed the tissue off the table.
   b. *Frank sneezed the tissue.

(21) a. She let the water *(out of the bathtub).
   b. *She let.

(22) a. Frank squeezed the ball through the crack.
   b. Frank squeezed the ball.

In (19)–(20) the verb can be used intransitively (not illustrated above) but cannot be used transitively without the path expression (as shown in the b versions). In (21) the verb also cannot be used transitively without the path expression and cannot be used intransitively either. In (22) the verb can be used transitively but does not have a motion-causing meaning when so employed. Clearly, the verb itself does not license the path PPs in (19)–(22), so something else must. Goldberg posits a Caused Motion Construction, an independent argument-structure construction, as the licenser. This construction adds the notion of caused motion to the semantics of the verb and the preposition. Gawron (1985, 1986) and others had argued that pragmatic inference is sufficient to complete the picture in the interpretation of, e.g., (20) by adding to the explicitly expressed propositions that (1) Frank sneezed and (2) the tissue found itself off the table and (3) the pragmatic inference that Frank's sneezing must have caused the tissue to find itself off the table.

Goldberg's counterarguments include the observation that many languages do not permit this kind of construction, owing to the prohibition against the manner and fact-of-motion event components in verb-framed languages (Goldberg 1995: 155, citing Talmy 1985) and the observation that some of the criticism is based on the confusion of merely decoding idioms with true encoding idioms – the latter requiring representation in the grammar because they are not deducible from anything else in the grammar. Kay (2005) acknowledges Goldberg's main point: that something has to be added to the grammar to license the path expressions, but suggests that both agentive transitivizing constructions and path adjunct constructions are independently required to derive (23b) and (23c), respectively, from (23a). He argues that if an independent Caused Motion Construction is posited, the analysis attributes to (23d) a spurious ambiguity.

(23) a. The top was spinning.
  b. Kim was spinning the top.
  c. The top was spinning off the table.
  d. Kim was spinning the top off the table.

Kay also argues that the proposed Caused Motion Construction overgenerates, presenting examples like those in (24):

(24) a. *He bragged her to sleep. (cf. *He bored her to sleep.*)
  b. *The storm raged the roof off the house. (cf. *The storm tore the roof off the house.*)

While this argument provides an alternative analysis for examples like (22), it does not provide an account for examples like (19)–(21), in which there is no independent active transitive version of the verb, or, if there is, it lacks the appropriate second argument. The argument against the Caused Motion Construction becomes somewhat fractionated at this point, different authors taking different views on the troublesome examples. Example (19) can be seen as semi-lexicalized; compare ??*They snored him off the stage*. According to this argument, (19) participates in a pattern of coinage that is not productive synchronically, like the pattern exemplified by the metaphorical comparatives *heavy as lead, light as a feather, old as the hills/Methuselah, happy as a lark* and *easy as pie*. But there are those who argue that such patterns of coinage, although not productive synchronically, should nevertheless be considered constructions of the language and included in the grammar. The argument against the Caused Motion Construction holds that tokens like (19)–(22) are analogical, nonce creations, not licensed by the grammar. Again, there does not seem to exist convincing evidence either for or against the nonce-creation view. Examples of this kind occur relatively rarely (an observation that supports the nonce-creation view) but with a relatively wide variety of verbs (an observation that undermines it); they sound strained or poetic to proponents of the nonce-creation view but (apparently) less so to advocates of the Caused Motion Construction. Whether or not it is decided that English contains a Caused Motion Construction, Goldberg's larger claim that caused-motion phenomena motivate the existence of argument-structure constructions that expand the semantic and syntactic valences of verbs appears sound.

The *Way* construction, exemplified in (25) provides a straightforward (although not necessarily simply analyzed) example of an argument-structure construction (Goldberg 1995: 202ff; Levin & Rapoport 1988; Jackendoff 1990):

(25) a. She was hacking her way through the brush, when . . .
 b. He whistled his way home.
 c. *He whistled her way home.

The construction requires an intransitive verb (or a transitive verb used intransitively, such as *eat* or *drink*) and adds to its valence a NP that occurs in what is normally object position – but which does not passivize to subject – and an additional phrase of any syntactic category denoting a path or destination. The pseudo-object NP is determined by a possessive pronoun that is co-construed with the subject. One is inclined to dub this NP a pseudo-object because it cannot co-occur with an object, as illustrated in (26):

(26) a. She entertained her way into café society.
 b. *She gave parties her way into café society.

In all cases the path or destination predicate is interpreted as predicated of the denotatum of the subject. Hence the denotatum of the subject is understood as moving either to a destination or along a path (or both). Thus in (25a) 'she' was traveling through the brush and in (25b) 'he' got home. In examples like (25a) the type of eventuality denoted by the verb is interpreted as providing a means that enables the movement (along the path or to the destination), overcoming some presupposed obstacle or other difficulty. The presumption of difficulty explains the sort of contrast exemplified in (27), according to which ordinary verbs of locomotion require a special context that provides an image of difficulty to sound acceptable in such sentences.

(27) a. ??She walked her way home.
b. ??She swam her way across the pool.
c. Exhausted by the struggle, she barely managed to swim her way to safety.

In examples like (25b), the type of eventuality denoted by the verb is interpreted as an accompaniment or a manner of the movement. Goldberg (1995: 210ff) sees the availability of both means and manner readings as evidence of constructional polysemy, pointing to precedents in the lexicon.

(28) a. Bob cut the bread with a knife. (means) [Goldberg 1995: 211, (37)]
b. Bob cut the bread with care. (manner) [Goldberg 1995: 211, (38)]

(29) a. Pat found a way to solve the problem. (means) [Goldberg 1995: 211, (40)]
b. He had a pleasant way about him. (manner) [Goldberg 1995: 211, (41)]

More formal, constraint based approaches, such as SBCG, would analyze the relations between examples like (25a) and (25b) as illustrating inheritance of identical syntax and largely overlapping semantics by two distinct constructions, leaving discussion of the extension of means to manner semantics as belonging to the history of the language rather than the synchronic grammar.

Most constructional approaches to argument structure have considered either additions to the argument structure of verbs or alternate syntactic valences with possible semantic consequences as in the dative alternation. Goldberg (1995: 141–151) and Kay (2005: 71–98) have provided analyses of the 'Dative Movement' alternation in somewhat differing constructional frameworks, Goldberg's relying on the notion of constructional polysemy, radial categories of argument-structure constructions, and various types of links among senses of a construction. This approach is close in spirit to much of the work in cognitive linguistics. Kay's approach is more similar to SBCG and the more formal constraint-based approaches to grammar. Both approaches agree that one or more argument-structure constructions are necessary to provide the special syntax of sentences like (30):

(30) Kim sent Sandy a letter.

and to account for the well known contrast of acceptability illustrated in (31).

(31) a. Kim forwarded the letter to Sandy.
     b. Kim forwarded Sandy the letter.
     c. Kim forwarded the letter to Oshkosh General Delivery.
     d. *Kim forwarded Oshkosh General Delivery the letter.

Whereas the destination of the transfer in (31a) and (31c) is not constrained to be a recipient, it is so constrained in (31b) and (31d). Before leaving the topic of argument structure constructions, we should note that argument-structure constructions do not always add arguments or shuffle them around arguments furnished by the lexical predicator. Argument-structure constructions may also delete arguments, as is the case of certain French reflexives, which inchoativize inherent transitives. Some French reflexives are presumably derived from transitive counterparts by removing an agentive subject valent both semantically and syntactically, rather than indicating that the subject's denotatum is performing a reflexive action. For example *démocratiser* is necessarily transitive and means 'to make [something] democratic'; similarly *ameliorer* is necessarily transitive and means to 'improve [something]', but the reflexive versions *se démocratiser* and *s'ameliorer* do not mean 'to democratize itself/oneself' or 'to improve itself/oneself', but merely 'to become democratic' and 'to improve' (J.-P. Koenig, p.c.).

6 Conventional implicature, or pragmatic presupposition

One of the areas in which constructional approaches have contributed to semantics is that of conventional implicature or pragmatic presupposition. It seems appropriate to allow the notion of compositionality to comprise these 'pragmatic' instructions embedded in the grammar that provide the addressee with a certain semantic structure and instruct him or her to find content in the context that satisfies that structure. Consider utterance of a sentence like (32):

(32) Kim won't (even) get question eight right let alone Sandy get question nine.

Sentence (32) asserts that Kim and Sandy won't get the correct answers to questions eight and nine, respectively. But there is rich content to (32) beyond these truth conditions (Fillmore, Kay & O'Connor 1988). The use of *let alone* to connect the two clauses signals that the first unilaterally entails the second, and thus suggests the paraphrase in (33).

(33) Kim won't get problem eight right; *a fortiori* Sandy won't get problem nine right.

And this entailment takes a particular form. In this example, we have to think that the problems can be arranged on a scale (presumably of difficulty) and students arranged on a scale (presumably of ability) where the scales are interrelated in such a way that a more able student will answer correctly any problem that a less able one will and a less able student will miss any problem that a more able one misses. A network of propositions connected by entailments of this kind has been called a scalar model (Kay 2004: 684). Scalar models have several interesting general properties. Two of these properties are that the form of a scalar model can be made mathematically precise (for the formal details, see Kay 1990), and that its content is left entirely open to retrieval from context, including background knowledge (Fillmore, Kay & O'Connor 1988; Kay 1997). The latter property is perhaps more readily appreciated with an example like (34).

(34) SANDY doesn't eat CHICKEN let alone KIM eat DUCK.

An utterance of (34) could be readily interpreted in a context in which duck is viewed as more expensive than chicken and Kim as more frugal than Sandy – or in a context in which duck is viewed as meatier than chicken and Kim is viewed as a stricter vegetarian than Sandy – or in a context in which duck is viewed as more exotic than chicken and Kim as more squeamish than Sandy. The *let alone* operator instructs the addressee to find in the context a scalar model that is induced by two unidimensional scales, here of eaters $<x_1, x_2, \ldots x_n>$ and foods $<y_1, y_2, \ldots, y_m>$, and a propositional function (here: x_i doesn't eat y_j), such that whatever Kim will eat Sandy will eat and whoever doesn't eat chicken necessarily doesn't eat duck. In the *let alone* construction the content of the scalar model is left for the addressee to extract from the context although the form of the model is strictly fixed. It is this property of directing the addressee to extract information of a prescribed form from the context that motivates the appellation 'contextual operator'.

An additional component of the meaning of the *let alone* is discussed further in section 9: the negation of the proposition denoted by the second clause is taken to be in the context. For example, a successful utterance of (34) requires a conversational context in which the proposition that Kim will eat duck is on the floor although not necessarily taken for granted: for instance, the context proposition might have been introduced in a question: *Does Kim eat duck?* The construction seems designed for use in a circumstance in which the demands of Gricean Quantity conflict with those of Relevance (Relation). For example, an utterance of (34) would be most appropriate in a context where the proposition that Sandy eats chicken has been asserted or questioned, and the speaker feels that rather than respond directly with a denial it would be more informative to reply that Kim does not eat duck, since the latter entails the correct answer to the former and provides additional, presumably relevant, information.

Contextual operators can be parasitic upon one another, by which we mean that when two occur in the same utterance the conceptual output of one can serve as input to the other. Consider *respective* and *vice versa*. First we establish that each of these expressions is a contextual operator. *Respective* (and *respectively* in a somewhat different fashion) presuppose a mapping (usually bijective) relating two sets, but in effect instruct the addressee to discover in the context the rule establishing the mapping (Kay 1989). Consider a sentence like (35):

(35) The teachers called their respective mothers.

An utterance of this sentence could of course be used in a context where the teachers' female parents were the intended receivers of calls but it could also be used in a context of a parent-teacher association function where each teacher has been assigned one (or more) mother to call. Figuring out from context the mapping relation that yields the codomain is the responsibility of the addressee.

Interpreting a sentence containing *vice versa* can likewise be shown to depend crucially on the addressee's finding needed information in the context. This can be seen by first considering a sentence that presents an ambiguity that can only be resolved by context. In (36) only context can decide the ambiguity between the anaphoric (*John*) and bound variable (*Every boy*) reading of the pronoun.

(36) John$_i$ thinks [every boy]$_j$ loves his$_{i,j}$ mother.

If we embed a sentence with this kind of ambiguity under the *vice versa* contextual operator, we see that the ambiguity is maintained.

(37) John thinks that every boy loves his mother and vice versa.

Sentence (37) will convey John's conviction of mutual love between himself and every boy's mother only if the referential interpretation is dictated by the context in which the sentence is heard. An ambiguity comparable to but distinct from that created by the referential versus bound variable reading of the pronouns in (36) can be created by *respective*.

(38) The secretaries called their respective senators.

In (38), the relation pairing secretaries and senators must be recovered from context. The senators may be the employers of the secretaries, pen pals, and so on. If we put both contextual operators into the same sentence, as in (39), the one with wider scope will take the conceptual output of the one with narrower scope as its input.

(39) The secretaries called their respective senators and vice versa.

Whatever relation is contextually recovered as pairing secretaries $<x_1, x_2, \ldots x_n>$ with senators $<y_1, y_2, \ldots, y_n>$ will establish the relation $\{<x,y>|$ x called y$\}$ as the meaning that is fed into the *vice versa* operator, which in turn will yield the meaning $\{<x,y>|$ x called y & y called x$\}$. (For further discussion of these and other examples of contextual operators, see Kay 1997; Michaelis 1994b on Vietnamese markers of expectation violation and Michaelis 1996 on the aspectual adverb *already*.)

A view closely related to that of contextual operator is that of Fillmorean frames, which provide an alternative explanation for many of the phenomena that go under the heading of presupposition in the formal semantic literature. Gawron (cf. article 3 [Semantics: Theories] (Gawron) *Frame Semantics*) discusses Fillmore's well-known example of *on the ground* versus *on land* (Fillmore 1985). An utterance employing the former expression is likely to presuppose a context including an air voyage while the latter is likely to presuppose a sea voyage. The striking aspect of the example is that these expressions appear to denote the same thing and differ only in the background frame they rely on and therefore evoke when uttered. Somewhat similarly, Fillmore has discussed at length the "commercial-event frame", which seems to provide background for and be evoked by a rather long list of words, including *buy, sell, cost, price, goods, etc.* Frame semantics provides a persuasive semantic theory at the lexical level; the mechanism that combines the meanings of words and elementary constructions into the meanings of sentences has received less attention in this tradition. (For further discussion see article 3 [Semantics: Theories] (Gawron) *Frame Semantics* and the Fillmore references cited therein.)

7 Less commonly recognized illocutionary forces

A number of constructions appearing in recent constructionist writings have involved special illocutionary forces, beyond the familiar ones of imperatives, questions, and a handful of others. Perhaps the most familiar such special illocutionary force is that associated with the "Mad Magazine" sentence type (Akmajian 1984; Lambrecht 1990); it is illustrated by (14), repeated below:

(14) Him get first prize?!

The force of this sort of sentence appears to be an expression of incredulity, but perhaps a particular nuance of that attitude expressible only in this or a small number of other forms.

Somewhat similarly perhaps, it is difficult to gloss the force of the construction illustrated in (7), repeated below:

(7) Watch me get wet.

The particular attitude conveyed by using this form has been described as "conjuring fate", but capturing the exact signification of this sentence form is not easy. Again, it is possible that this particular illocutionary meaning is expressible in English only in this form.

Another special illocutionary force displayed by a construction discussed above is that of examples (17a,b) repeated.

(17) a. What's this fly doing in my soup?
b. What's this scratch doing on the table?

The illocutionary force conveyed by this construction seems roughly to be that of pointing out an anomaly and expressing a desire for an explanation of it.

The special force or forces of the pseudo-conditional construction, exemplified in (1–2) above and in (40) below, seem especially hard to pin down. The examples in (40) present the first five relevant Google hits that matched the pattern "If you're x * you . . .". After viewing quite a few attested examples we confess to failure in isolating what the choice of the pseudo-conditional construction adds to or subtracts from a simple assertion of the proposition (or posing the question or imperative) formed from the pseudo-apodosis by substituting the person the (pseudo-) addressee is identified with in the pseudo-protasis substituted for "you". We leave figuring out the illocutionary function of this construction as an entertainment for the reader.

(40) a. We make a living by what we get, Churchill said, but we make a life by what we give. And to save a life? If you're Bill Gates, the richest man in the world, you give fantastic sums of money [. . .]. If you're a rock star like Bono, you give money. [. . .] If you're Bill Clinton and George H.W. Bush, you raise money – but you also give the symbols of power and the power of symbols[. . .].
b. Look, Davis is the boss and can sign and cut whoever he wants. It's just that communication is not one of his strengths. If you're the coach of the Raiders, you deal with it.
c. [I]f you're Britney Spears' publicist you might as well go ahead and kill yourself. Unless you have a time machine, there's no way to fix this.
d. The Firearms Waiting Period: No, that's not the waiting period to *buy* a gun. If you're Dick Cheney, that's the time you take until you get around to reporting you've shot somebody.
e. If You're Barack Obama, How Much Do You Trust Howard Dean?

8 Metalinguistic constructions

Metalinguistic constructions convey a comment on the form or meaning (or both) of the utterance in which they occur. The best-known example is Horn's (1985) analysis of metalinguistic negation (see also Horn 1989: Chapter 6), which relies on works by Grice (1967/1989, 1975), Wilson (1975) and Ducrot (1972, 1973), the last of whom was, to our knowledge, the first to use the term metalinguistic negation (*négation métalinguistique*). Horn showed that a sentence like (40) could not be analyzed by positing either a very general kind of propositional negation or two separate propositional negation operators in English (or languages with a similar phenomenon), primarily based on examples like those in (41).

(40) The King of France is not bald, because there is no King of France.

(41) a. Her name isn't [æn'drijə]; it's [andrej'ə].
b. It's not pretty; it's gorgeous.
c. It's not the unique criteria; its the unique criterion.
d. The cow isn't pissing, son, she's urinating.

None of the examples in (41) expresses negation of a proposition: (41a) involves correction of pronunciation; (41b) expresses cancellation of a Quantity implicature; (41c) concerns a grammatical correction; (41d) involves a correction of register. The point is that metalinguistic negation can object to any aspect of an utterance, not just the propositional content.

The metalinguistic negation phenomenon is of particular interest to constructional approaches because, along with the special semantic behavior just described, it possesses special morphosyntactic properties, so that it is appropriate to speak of the metalinguistic negation construction. First, metalinguistic negation does not act as a negative polarity trigger, not surprisingly since semantically it does not negate a proposition.

(42) a. John didn't manage to solve *any/some of the problems, he managed to solve all of them. (Horn 1985: 135)
 b. I wouldn't rather walk, but I'm willing to. (Kay 2004: 688)

In (42a) the negative polarity item *any* is rejected and in (42b) the positive polarity item *rather* is welcomed.

Secondly, metalinguistic negation does not allow morphologically or lexically incorporated negation.

(43) a. A bad outcome is *improbable/not probable; it's certain.
 b. I *doubt/don't believe he'll come; I'm sure of it.

Finally, a rectification clause, which is almost always present and always understood, cannot be introduced by *but*.

(44) a. He's not happy; (*but) he's delirious.
 b. Her name isn't [dʒæ'kwalIn]; (*but) it's [ʒaklin'].

The metalinguistic comparative construction was discussed briefly in section 3, as was metalinguistic negation. Again, we see evidence of a grammatical construction, as against an implicature or trope, in observing special constraints on the syntax.

(45) a. This cat is more stupid than malicious.
 b. *This cat is stupider than malicious.
 c. This cat is more stupid than he is malicious.
 d. This cat's stupidity exceeds his malice.

The metalinguistic comparative in version (45a) is read as proposing that *stupid* is a more apt description of the cat than *malicious*; it does not mean the same as (45d). The metalinguistic comparative also resists morphological incorporation, as shown in (45b). Example (45c), with a non-ellipted *than*-clause, does not yield a metalinguistic interpretation, but rather means roughly the same as (45d).

The class of metalinguistic operators includes the expressions dubbed *hedges* by Lakoff (1973). English hedges include the expressions *strictly speaking, loosely speaking, technically (speaking), kinda* (equivalently *kind of, sorta, sort of*). According to Kay (1984), a hedged sentence, when uttered, contains a comment on itself, its utterance or some part thereof. For example, in uttering the statement *Loosely speaking France is hexagonal*, a speaker has made a certain kind of comment on the locution *France is hexagonal*. "In this sort of metalinguistic comment, the words that are the subject of the comment occur both in their familiar role as part of the linguistic stream and in a theoretically unfamiliar role as part of the world the utterance is about" (Kay 1984: 129). That is, in saying *Loosely speaking France is hexagonal* a speaker at once claims that France is hexagonal and signals that there is something 'loose' about the claim being made, or the way it's being made.

The attested sentence (46) similarly makes a claim, and the same time makes a comment on the making of that claim:

(46) Chomsky has a very sorta classical theory of syntax.

The adverb *very* intensifies the adjective *classical*, but the metalinguistic hedge *sorta* signals that the speaker is unsure that *classical* is the *mot juste*. If *sorta* were simply an attenuator, like *slightly* for example, sentence (46) would mean something close to (47) but it clearly does not.

(47) Chomsky has a very slightly classical theory of syntax.

Rather, the intensification of *very* is heard as part of the interpretation of (46) and *sorta* is heard as a comment on the aptness of the word *classical* as a name for the property (of Chomsky's theory of syntax) the speaker has in mind.

Kinda and *sorta* also have a syntax that distinguishes them from ordinary deintensifiers, like *slightly*. Briefly, *kinda/sorta* can modify any projection of any major category. Kay (2004: 699) gives the following examples distinguishing the syntactic behavior of *kinda/sorta* from that of deintensifying adverbs.

(48) a. a very slightly but unevenly worn tire
      b. *a very sorta but surprisingly classical theory

(49) a. That tire is worn very slightly.
      b. *That tire is worn very sorta.

(50) a. That tire is worn, but only very slightly.
  b. *That tire is worn, but only very sorta.

(51) a. That [very slightly]$_i$ worn tire is proportionately$_i$ discounted.
  b. *That [very sorta]$_i$ classical theory is correspondingly$_i$ admired.

Metalinguistic constructions often mimic fairly closely the syntax of non-metalinguistic constructions, although usually with some variation.

9 Information flow

The central question addressed by theories of information structure is: why do grammars provide so many different ways of expressing the same proposition? The answer given is that the construction space of English and other languages is shaped by level-mapping constraints involving the three-termed relationship among syntactic roles, semantic roles and pragmatic roles, in particular topic and focus (Lambrecht 1995). The examples in (52) illustrate the range of syntactic and prosodic means available for expressing the proposition 'The dog ate the leftovers' in English (points of prosodic prominence are marked by small caps):

(52) a. The dog ate the LEFTOVERS.
  b. The DOG ate the LEFTOVERS.
  c. The LEFTOVERS, the DOG ate.
  d. It's the DOG that ate the leftovers.

Lambrecht (1994) and Lambrecht & Michaelis (1998) propose that the prosodic and syntactic permutations in (52) amount to differences in the presuppositional content of the constructions that license them. The relevance of presupposition to the pattern in (52d) is no doubt relatively obvious: as a cleft sentence, (52d) presupposes the propositional function 'The dog ate x', and the prosodic peak marks the focus, or 'new information': the identity of the variable (Jackendoff 1972: chapter 6). It is less obvious how presupposition comes into play in the other sentences: (52a), for example, can, but need not, presuppose the propositional function evoked by (52d); (52a) could answer the question (53a) as readily as it could (53b):

(53) a. What did the dog do NOW?
  b. What did the dog eat?

In the context of (53a), (52a) represents a predicate-focus sentence, and as such it is interpreted according to Lambrecht & Michaelis's (1998: 498ff) Principle of Accent Projection: an accented argument expression (in this case, *the leftovers*) can extend its semantic value to an unaccented predicate (in this case, *ate*), in which case the predicate and argument form a single information unit. In the case of (52a), this unit is a focal unit.

But what of (52b)? If the two peaks of (52b) were each presumed to represent foci, we could not easily explain why it, just like its single-peak analog (52a), can serve as an answer to the 'broad' question (53a). Lambrecht (1994: chapter 4) and Lambrecht & Michaelis (1998) propose that both the single- and double-peak prosodic patterns are the products of focus constructions, which affect the presuppositional properties of predicate-argument combinations. Lambrecht (1994: chapter 5) proposes three focus constructions, which are listed and exemplified in (54), along with the communicative function associated with each pattern:

(54) a. Argument focus, e.g., SOCIETY's *to blame*. Function: identifying a variable in a presupposed open proposition.
 b. Predicate focus, e.g., *She speaks several* LANGUAGES. Function: predicating a property of a given topic.
 c. Sentence focus, e.g., *Your* SHOE's *untied*. Function: introducing a new discourse referent or reporting an event or state involving such a referent.

Focus constructions behave much like argument-structure constructions, in that they impose interpretive and formal constraints on predicators and their valence members. In English, such constructions assign prosodic peaks to one or more arguments and potentially to the verb itself. According to Lambrecht & Michaelis (1998), the assignment of prosodic peaks is constrained by general principles governing the prosodic expression of the topic and focus roles in a predication. In contrast to theories of sentence prosody based on the Nuclear Stress Rule of Chomsky & Halle (1968) (see, e.g., Neeleman & Reinhart 1998), the accent-placement principles proposed by Lambrecht & Michaelis (1998) make no reference to either linear order of constituents or hierarchical structure. Such accent-placement principles are analogous to case-marking principles based on semantic role ordering (rather than syntactic position), and they are equally critical to the functioning of a declarative, nonprocedural model of grammar: no movement transformations are required to model focus marking in flexible word-order languages and only one set of principles is needed for both local and nonlocal argument instantiation, as in (55):

(55) a. It's called Republic PLAZA.
      b. Republic PLAZA it's called.

Both (55a) and (55b) illustrate the argument-focus pattern, whose accentual properties are described by a principle referred to by Lambrecht & Michaelis (1998: 498) as the Discourse Function of Sentence Accents, viz., "A sentence accent indicates an instruction from the speaker to the hearer to establish a pragmatic relation between a denotatum and a proposition". Sentence (55a) has a locally instantiated second argument while (55b) is an instance of focus fronting (Prince 1981), but the establishment of the focus relation relative to the open proposition 'It's called x' proceeds identically in the two cases. Similarly, predicates may fall under the pragmatic scope of their accented arguments whether they precede or follow them. The Principle of Accent Projection mentioned above accounts for the 'spreading' of an accented argument's focal value to its predicate – not only within the VP, as in (52a), but also in the sentence-focus pattern exemplified in (54c), in which the accented argument precedes the verb that licenses it. In both cases, predicate and argument are integrated into a single focal unit.

According to Accent Projection, while a focal predicate need not be accented, a focal argument is always accented. Is an accented argument necessarily a focus? The answer given by this model is no: an accented argument may also be a topic. Sentence (52b), repeated below as (56), illustrates this point:

(56) The DOG ate the LEFTOVERS.

The two prosodic peaks in (56) have distinct discourse-pragmatic significances. Removing the peak on *leftovers* changes (56) from a predicate-focus to an argument-focus sentence, but removing the peak on *dog* has no effect on the sentence's focus articulation: it remains a predicate-focus sentence. If the subject accent in (56) is not a focus accent, what is it? According to the principle referred to above as the Discourse Function of Sentence Accents, sentence accents establish a pragmatic relation, whether it is a focusrelation or a topic relation. This means that the referent of an accented argument expression can be either focal or topical. Lambrecht & Michaelis (1998: 499) use the term *topic accent* to refer to a sentence accent that marks a discourse-new or 'unratified' topic argument rather than a focus. In declarative sentences, a topic accent is necessarily accompanied by a focus accent elsewhere in the clause. (The one exception to this principle, discussed by Lambrecht & Michaelis (1998), is found in *wh*-questions, in which the focal constituent, the *wh*-word, is typically unaccented and accents in the gapped portion of the clause represent topic accents, as in, e.g., *Where did the POPE stay when he was in NEW YORK?*) While that focus accent falls within the

VP in subject-predicate sentences like (56), it may also fall within the gapped clause of a filler-gap construction like topicalization, as in (52c): *The LEFTOVERS the DOG ate*. While (52c) and (56) feature identical accented words, these accents reverse their roles in (52c): the topicalized NP *the leftovers* bears a (contrastively interpreted) topic accent, while the subject of the gapped clause (*the dog*) bears a focus accent (see Prince 1981, 1986 for discussion of the presuppositional properties of topicalization). The principle that governs the discourse function of sentence accents treats both patterns under a single umbrella, but the two patterns create a potential paradox for a movement-based account: how does the accented object NP change its pragmatic construal (from focus to topic) after its focus accent has been assigned *in situ*?

Let us now return to the question with which we began this section: what is presupposed by predicate-focus sentences like (56) and (52a)? Sentence (52a) is repeated below as (57):

(57) The dog ate the LEFTOVERS.

The answer given by Lambrecht & Michaelis (1998) relies on the distinction between *knowledge* presuppositions and *topicality* presuppositions. Knowledge presuppositions concern the assumed knowledge state of an addressee at the time of an utterance. Knowledge presuppositions correspond to those described in linguistic philosophy as the propositions evoked by factive verbs, definite descriptions, sentential subjects, aspectual verbs and argument-focus constructions of various kinds (Prince 1986). Topicality presuppositions concern the assumed statuses of referents as topics of current interest in a conversation. Sentence-focus sentences like *Your SHOE'S untied*, *My CAR broke down* and *Your PHONE'S ringing* illustrate the difference between the two types of presupposition: while all of the foregoing sentences, by virtue of their definite subjects, could be said to trigger the existential presupposition (a knowledge presupposition), all lack the topicality presupposition: their subject-referents are not presumed to be topics of current interest in the conversation. But the assumption that the subject referent is a topic (or predictable argument) in the predication is precisely what predicate-focus utterances convey. Put differently, the predicate-focus construction triggers the topicality presupposition. It does so, according to Lambrecht (1994), because of a communicative constraint originating from the Gricean lower bound on informativeness: the Principle of Separation of Reference and Role (PSRR). He describes this constraint by means of a maxim: "Do not introduce a referent and talk about it in the same clause" (Lambrecht 1994: 185). Michaelis & Francis (2007) observe the operation of this constraint in the distribution of lexical versus pronominal subject NPs in the Switchboard conversational corpus

(Marcus, Santorini & Marcinkiewicz 1993). Of approximately 31,000 subjects of declarative sentences, they find that only 9 percent are lexical NPs, while 91 percent are pronouns. (By contrast, about 66 percent of the approximately 7500 objects of transitive verbs are lexical.) The subject-coding trends indicate that conversants tend to adhere to the PSRR: they do not typically predicate properties of discourse-new entities. Conversely, and as suggested by the relative frequency of lexical object-expression in the corpus, speakers tend to introduce new referents in postverbal position and then resume them as pronominal subjects in subsequent predications. This strategy is exemplified in the following excerpt from the Fisher corpus of conversational speech:

(58) I have a friend of mine who used to be really involved in the beach volleyball circuit but uh he's not anymore but he still watches it. He coaches his daughter and all kinds of stuff.

At the same time, the presence of some 3,000 lexical-subject predications in the Switchboard corpus indicates that the PSRR is a violable constraint. The passage in (59), also from the Fisher corpus, exemplifies the use of a lexical subject (shown in boldface):

(59) [In a conversation about the Red Lobster restaurant] **My friend** used to work at Red Lobster actually, and she used to be so fed up with people coming in and being like oh it's mostly seafood.

Michaelis & Francis (2007) argue that the use of a lexical subject represents a short-circuited form of referent introduction that privileges speaker-based effort conservation at the expense of hearer-based explicitness. The lexical-subject strategy subserves effort conservation because it allows the speaker to accomplish something in a single clause that otherwise requires two clauses: introducing a referent and saying something about it. Michaelis & Francis argue that if one assumes the presuppositional analysis of predicate-focus sentences described above, the lexical-subject strategy can be seen as a brand of presupposition manipulation akin to those described by Lewis's (1979) rule for accommodation of presupposition: "If at time t something is said that requires presupposition p to be acceptable, and if P is not presupposed just before t, then – ceteris paribus and within certain limits – presupposition P comes into existence at t" (Lewis 1979: 172). Applied to the case at hand, this means that if a speaker uses a predicate-focus predication when the topicality presupposition is not satisfied, the hearer is capable of supplying it, insofar as the associated existential presupposition is banal (Kay 1992): the speaker has a friend, sister, etc. Accommodation of the topicality presupposition is also potentially facilitated by the linguistic mark carried by most new topics: the topic-establishing accent found in double-peak sentences like (56).

Presuppositional properties of focus constructions are relevant not only for the description of prosody and conversational referring behavior, but also for the establishment of inheritance relations among pragmatically specialized constructions, as shown by Birner, Kaplan & Ward (2007) in their study of the family of argument-structure constructions comprising *th*-clefts (e.g., *That's John who wrote the book*), equatives with epistemic *would* and a demonstrative subject (e.g., *That would be John*) and simple equatives with demonstrative subjects (e.g., *That's John*). The latter two constructions, they argue, should not be analyzed as truncated clefts (*pace* Hedberg 2003). Instead, as they demonstrate, all three constructions inherit formal, semantic and information-structure properties from an argument-focus construction used for equative assertions. The construction contains a copular verb, requires a demonstrative subject and presupposes an open proposition whose variable is referred to by the demonstrative subject. (The postcopular focal expression identifies this variable, as in other argument-focus constructions.) Thus, for example, in the sentence *That will be John*, the demonstrative subject refers to the variable in a presupposed open proposition (e.g., 'x is at the door'). They argue that the family of equative constructions exhibits functional compositionality, as cases which "the discourse-functional properties of a complex structure are determined by the functional and semantic properties of its component parts" (Birner, Kaplan & Ward 2007: 319, fn. 1). Birner, Kaplan & Ward's analysis is elegant and intuitively appealing, and further supports the claim that constructional and compositional modes of analysis are compatible.

10 Conclusion

In asking what constructions mean we must also ask how constructions mean. Constructions invoke formal properties ranging from syntactic categories to prosodic features to fixed lexical forms. All such patterns must interact in the licensing of utterances. The recursive nature of a language comes from the fact that we can use in one construction a sign that is an instance of another construction. While no current syntactic theory has failed to acknowledge that verbal idioms and their ilk can be embedded as the terminal nodes of regularly constructed phrases, non-constructionists have been less apt to acknowledge another fact about embedding: regular patterns can be embedded in idiomatic ones. Examples include the WXDY interrogative construction analyzed by Kay & Fillmore (1999), the subjectless tag sentences analyzed by Kay (2002) and the double-copula construction analyzed by Brenier & Michaelis (2005). We believe that the seamless integration of relatively idiomatic constructions with more productive ones in actual sentences provides an additional challenge to the notion of a privileged 'core' grammar.

11 References

Akmajian, Adrian 1984. Sentence types and the form-function fit. *Natural Language and Linguistic Theory* 2, 1–23.
Birner, Betty, Jeffrey Kaplan & Gregory Ward 2007. Functional compositionality and the interaction of discourse constraints. *Language* 83, 317–343.
Borsley, Robert 2004. An approach to English comparative correlatives. In: S. Müller (ed.). *Proceedings of the Fourth Conference on Head-Driven Phrase Structure Grammar*. Stanford, CA: CSLI Publications, 70–92.
Brenier, Jason M. & Laura Michaelis 2005. Optimization via syntactic amalgam: Syntax-prosody mismatch and copula doubling. *Corpus Linguistics and Linguistic Theory* 1, 45–88.
Chomsky, Noam 1995. *The Minimalist Program*. Cambridge, MA: The MIT Press.
Chomsky, Noam & Morris Halle 1968. *The Sound Pattern of English*. New York: Harper & Row.
Copestake, Ann, Dan Flickinger, Carl Pollard & Ivan A. Sag 2005. Minimal recursion semantics: An introduction. *Research on Language and Computation* 3, 281–332.
Cornulier, Benoît de 1986. *Effets de sens*. Paris: Editions de Minuit.
Culicover, Peter 1970. One more can of beer. *Linguistic Inquiry* 1, 366–369.
Culicover, Peter 1997. *Syntactic Nuts: Hard Cases in Syntax*. Oxford: Oxford University Press.
Culicover, Peter & Ray Jackendoff 1999. The view from the periphery: The English comparative correlative. *Linguistic Inquiry* 30, 543–571.
Ducrot, Oswald 1972. *Dire et ne pas Dire*. Paris: Hermann.
Ducrot, Oswald 1973. *La Preuve et le Dire*. Paris: Mame.
Fillmore, Charles J. 1985. Frames and the semantics of understanding. *Quaderni di Semantica* 6, 222–254.
Fillmore, Charles J. 1986. Varieties of conditional sentences. In: F. Marshall, A. Miller & Z.-S. Zhang (eds.). *Proceedings of the Eastern States Conference on Linguistics (= ESCOL) 3*. Columbus, OH: Ohio State University, 163–182.
Fillmore, Charles J., Paul Kay & Mary C. O'Connor 1988. Regularity and idiomaticity in grammatical constructions: The case of "let alone". *Language* 64, 501–538.
Gawron, Jean Mark 1985. A parsimonious semantics for prepositions and CAUSE. In: W. Eilford et al. (eds.). *Papers from the Regional Meeting of the Chicago Linguistic Society (= CLS) 21, Part II: Parasession on Causatives and Agentivity*. Chicago, IL: Chicago Linguistic Society, 32–47.
Gawron, Jean Mark 1986. Situations and prepositions. *Linguistics & Philosophy* 9, 427–476.
Ginzburg, Jonathan & Ivan A. Sag 2000. *Interrogative Investigations: The Form, Meaning and Use of English Interrogatives*. Stanford, CA: CSLI Publications.
Goldberg, Adele 1995. *Constructions: A Construction Grammar Approach to Argument Structure*. Chicago, IL: The University of Chicago Press.

Goldberg, Adele 2006. *Constructions at Work: The Nature of Generalizations in Language*. Oxford: Oxford University Press.

Grice, H. Paul 1967/1989. *Logic and Conversation: The 1967 William James Lectures*. Ms. Cambridge, MA, Harvard University. Reprinted as: H. P. Grice. *Studies in the Way of Words*. Cambridge, MA: Harvard University Press, 1989.

Grice, H. Paul 1975. Logic and conversation. In: P. Cole & J. L. Morgan (eds.), *Syntax and Semantics 3: Speech Acts*. New York: Academic Press, 41–58.

Hedberg, Nancy 2000. The referential status of clefts. *Language* 76, 891–920.

Horn, Laurence R. 1985. Metalinguistic negation and pragmatic ambiguity. *Language* 61, 121–174.

Horn, Laurence R. 1989. *A Natural History of Negation*. Chicago, IL: The University of Chicago Press.

Jackendoff, Ray 1972. *Semantic Interpretation in Generative Grammar*. Cambridge, MA: The MIT Press.

Jackendoff, Ray 1990. *Semantic Structures*. Cambridge, MA: The MIT Press.

Jackendoff, Ray 1997. *The Architecture of the Language Faculty*. Cambridge, MA: The MIT Press.

Kay, Paul 1984. The *kind of/sort of* construction. In: C. Brugman et al. (eds.), *Proceedings of the Annual Meeting of the Berkeley Linguistics Society (= BLS) 10*. Berkeley, CA: Berkeley Linguistics Society, 128–137.

Kay, Paul 1989. Contextual operators: Respective, respectively, and vice versa. In: K. Hall, M. Meacham & R. Shapiro (eds.), *Proceedings of the Annual Meeting of the Berkeley Linguistics Society (= BLS) 15*. Berkeley, CA: Berkeley Linguistics Society, 181–192.

Kay, Paul 1990. Even. *Linguistics & Philosophy* 13, 59–111.

Kay, Paul 1992. The inheritance of presuppositions. *Linguistics & Philosophy* 15, 333–381.

Kay, Paul (ed.) 1997. *Words and the Grammar of Context*. Stanford, CA: CSLI Publications.

Kay, Paul 2002. English subjectless tagged sentences. *Language* 78, 453–481.

Kay, Paul 2004. Pragmatic aspects of constructions. In: L. Horn & G. Ward (eds.), *The Handbook of Pragmatics*. Oxford: Blackwell, 675–700.

Kay, Paul 2005. Argument-structure constructions and the argument-adjunct distinction. In: M. Fried & H. Boas (eds.), *Grammatical Constructions: Back to the Roots*. Amsterdam: Benjamins, 71–98.

Kay, Paul & Charles J. Fillmore 1999. Grammatical constructions and linguistic generalizations: The 'what's X doing Y' construction. *Language* 75, 1–33.

Lakoff, George 1973. Hedges: A study in meaning criteria and the logic of fuzzy concepts. *The Journal of Philosophical Logic* 2, 458–508.

Lambrecht, Knud 1990. What, me, worry? Mad magazine sentences revisited. In: K. Hall et al. (eds.), *Proceedings of the Annual Meeting of the Berkeley Linguistics Society (= BLS) 16*. Berkeley, CA: Berkeley Linguistics Society, 215–228.

Lambrecht, Knud 1994. *Information Structure and Sentence Form*. Cambridge: Cambridge University Press.

Lambrecht, Knud 1995. The pragmatics of case: On the relationship between semantic, grammatical and pragmatic roles in English and French. In: M. Shibatani & S. Thompson (eds.), *Essays in Semantics in Honor of C.J. Fillmore*. Cambridge: Cambridge University Press, 145–190.

Lambrecht, Knud & Laura A. Michaelis 1998. Sentence accent in information questions: Default and projection. *Linguistics & Philosophy* 21, 477–544.

Levin, Beth & Tova Rapoport 1988. Lexical subordination. In: D. Brentari, G. Larson & L. MacLeod (eds.), *Papers from the Regional Meeting of the Chicago Linguistic Society (= CLS) 24*. Chicago, IL: Chicago Linguistic Society, 275–289.

Lewis, David 1979. Scorekeeping in a language game. *Journal of Philosophical Logic* 8, 339–359.
Makkai, Adam 1972. *Idiom Structure in English*. The Hague: Mouton.
Marcus, Mitchell, Beatrice Santorini & Mary Ann Marcinkiewicz 1993. Building a large annotated corpus of English: The Penn Treebank. *Computational Linguistics* 19, 313–330.
Michaelis, Laura A. 1994a. A case of constructional polysemy in Latin. *Studies in Language* 18, 45–70.
Michaelis, Laura A. 1994b. Expectation contravention and use ambiguity: The Vietnamese connective *cung*. *Journal of Pragmatics* 21, 1–36.
Michaelis, Laura A. 1996. On the use and meaning of *already*. *Linguistics & Philosophy* 19, 477–502.
Michaelis, Laura A. 2004. Type shifting in construction grammar: An integrated approach to aspectual coercion. *Cognitive Linguistics* 15, 1–67.
Michaelis, Laura A. & Knud Lambrecht 1996. Toward a construction-based model of language function: The case of nominal extraposition. *Language* 72, 215–247.
Michaelis, Laura A. & Hartwell Francis 2007. Lexical subjects and the conflation strategy. In: N. Hedberg & R. Zacharski (eds.). *Topics in the Grammar-Pragmatics Interface: Papers in Honor of Jeanette K. Gundel*. Amsterdam: Benjamins, 19–48.
Neeleman, Ad & Tanya Reinhart 1998. Scrambling and the PF-interface. In: M. Butt & W. Geuder (eds.). *The Projection of Arguments: Lexical and Compositional Factors*. Stanford, CA: CSLI Publications, 309–353.
Nunberg, Geoffrey, Ivan A. Sag & Thomas Wasow 1994. Idioms. *Language* 70, 491–538.
Prince, Ellen 1981. Topicalization, focus movement, and Yiddish movement: A pragmatic differentiation. In: D. Alford et al. (eds.). *Proceedings of the Annual Meeting of the Berkeley Linguistics Society (= BLS) 7*. Berkeley, CA: Berkeley Linguistics Society, 249–264.
Prince, Ellen 1986. On the syntactic marking of presupposed open propositions. In: A. Farley, P. Farley & K.-E. McCullogh (eds.). *Papers from the Regional Meeting of the Chicago Linguistic Society (= CLS) 22*. Chicago, IL: Chicago Linguistic Society, 208–222.
Sag, Ivan A. 2010. English Filler-gap Constructions. *Language* 86, 486–545.
Szabó, Zoltán 2007. Compositionality. *The Stanford Encyclopedia of Philosophy*, http://plato.stan ord.edu/archives/spr2007/entries/compositionality/, May 5, 2011.
Talmy, Leonard 1985. Lexicalization patterns: Semantic structure in lexical forms. In: T. Shopen (ed.). *Language Typology and Syntactic Description, vol. 3*. Cambridge: Cambridge University Press, 57–149.
Wilson, Deirdre 1975. *Presupposition and Non-Truth-Conditional Semantics*. New York: Academic Press.

Gennaro Chierchia, Danny Fox, and Benjamin Spector
10 Scalar implicature as a grammatical phenomenon

1 Introduction —— 325
2 Embedded implicatures: a first crack in the Gricean picture —— 333
3 A new argument for embedded implicatures in UE contexts: Hurford's constraint —— 340
4 Further cracks in the Gricean picture —— 350
5 Concluding remarks —— 363
6 References —— 364

Abstract: This article develops various arguments for the view that scalar implicatures should be derived within grammar and not by a theory of language use (pragmatics). We focus primarily on arguments that scalar implicatures can be computed in embedded positions, a conclusion incompatible with existing pragmatic accounts. We also briefly review additional observations that come from a variety of empirical domains, all incompatible with pragmatic accounts, yet predicted by the grammatical alternative.

1 Introduction

Since the late 1990's there has been a lively revival of interest in implicatures, particularly scalar implicatures (SIs for short). Building on the resulting literature, our main goal in the present article is to present several arguments for the claim that SIs can occur systematically and freely in arbitrarily embedded positions. We are not so much concerned with the question of whether drawing implicatures is a costly option (in terms of semantic processing, or of some other markedness measure). Nor are we specifically concerned with how implicatures come about (even though, to get going, we will have to make some specific assumptions on this matter). The focus of our discussion is testing the claim of the pervasive embeddability of SIs in just about any context, a claim that remains so far controversial.

Gennaro Chierchia and Danny Fox, Cambridge, MA, USA
Benjamin Spector, Paris, France

While our main goal is the establishment of an empirical generalization, if we succeed, a predominant view on the division of labor between semantics and pragmatics will have to be revised. A secondary goal of this article is to hint at evidence that a revision is needed on independent grounds. But let us first present, in a rather impressionistic way, the reasons why a revision would be required if our main generalization on embedded SIs turns out to be correct.

In the tradition stemming from Grice (1989), implicatures are considered a wholly pragmatic phenomenon (cf. article 15 [this article] (Simons) *Implicature*, article 5 [Semantics: Foundations, History and Methods] (Green) *Meaning in language use*, and also Davis 2005) and SIs are often used as paramount examples. Within such a tradition, semantics is taken to deal with the compositional construction of sentence meaning (a term which we are using for now in a loose, non technical way), while pragmatics deals with how sentence meaning is actually put to use (i.e. enriched and possibly modified through reasoning about speakers' intentions, contextually relevant information, etc.). Simply put, on this view pragmatics takes place at the level of complete utterances and pragmatic enrichments are a root phenomenon (something that happens globally to sentences) rather than a compositional one. So if SIs can be systematically generated in embedded contexts, something in this view has got to go. Minimally, one is forced to conclude that SIs are computed compositionally on a par with other aspects of sentence meaning. But more radical task reallocations are also conceivable. While we may not be able to reach firm conclusions on this score, we think it is important to arrive at a consensus on what are the factual generalizations at stake, how they can be established, and what range of consequences they may have.

Let us rephrase our point more precisely. The semantics/pragmatics divide can usefully be lined up with compositional vs. postcompositional interpretive processes. In the compositional part, basic meanings are assigned to lexical entries, which are then composed bottom up using a restricted range of semantic operations on the basis of how lexical entries are put together into phrases. These operations apply in an automatic fashion, blind to external considerations, e.g., speaker intentions and relevant contextual knowledge. Sentence meaning is, thus, constructed through the recursive application of semantic rules – typically, functional application. But what is sentence meaning? Such a notion is often identified with truth conditions. While semantics, as we understand it, falls within this tradition, we would like to keep our options open on the exact nature of sentence meaning. For the notions of sentence content that have emerged from much recent work are way more elaborate than plain truth conditions (cf. article 10 [Semantics: Sentence and Information Structure] (Hinterwimmer) *Information structure* and 17 [this volume] (Potts) *Conventional implicature and expressive content*). For example, sentence meaning has been argued to involve the computation of alternative meanings and hence to be a multidimensional phenomenon (cf. the semantics of questions, focus, etc); or sometimes sentence meaning has been assimilated to context change potentials (cf. dynamic approaches to presuppositions and anaphora). We remain neutral here on these various options, and we do so by simply taking sentence meaning as equivalent to the output of the compositional process of interpretation as determined by UG, whatever that turns out to be.

In understanding the compositional/postcompositional divide, one further preliminary *caveat* must be underscored. Sentence meaning is blind to context, but not independent of it. Virtually every word or phrase in Natural Language is dependent on the context in some way or other. In particular, the meaning of sentences will contain variables and indexicals whose actual denotation will require access to factual information accessible through the context. To illustrate, consider the following standard analysis of *only* and focus association, along the lines of Rooth (1985, 1992) and Krifka (1993) (an example that will turn out to be very useful for our approach to SIs). According to Rooth a sentence like (1a) is analyzed along lines explicated in (1b-d):

(1) a. Joe only upset [$_F$Paul and Sue]
 (where [$_F$] indicates the constituent bearing focal stress)
 b. **LF:** only [Joe upset [$_F$Paul and Sue]]
 c. **Interpretation:**
 [[Only$_{ALT(D)}$Joe upset [$_F$Paul and Sue]]]^{wo} =1 iff
 UPSET(JOHN, PAUL + SUE) (w_o) = 1 $\wedge$ $\forall p \in$ ALT(D) [λw.UPSET(JOHN, PAUL + SUE) (w) $\not\subseteq p \rightarrow p(w_o) = 0$]
 d. ALT(D) = {λw.UPSET(JOHN, u) (w) : $u \in D$} =
 {The proposition that Joe upset Lee, the proposition that Joe upset Sue, the proposition that Joe upset Kim, the proposition that Joe upset Lee and Sue, ... }

Something like (1a) has the Logical Form in (1b), where *only* is construed as a sentential operator, and is interpreted as in (1c). Such an interpretation, informally stated, says that Joe upset Paul and Sue and that every member of the contextually restricted set of alternatives ALT not entailed by the assertion must be false. Thus, in particular, *Joe upset Paul* is entailed by the assertion, and hence has to be true, but *Joe upset Kim* is not, and hence must be false. The set ALT is specified as in (1d). Such a set is generated by UG-driven principles through a separate recursive computation (and this is part of what makes sentence meaning multidimensional). In (1c), there is one variable whose value has to be picked up by pragmatic means: D, the quantificational domain. The determination of D's value is a pragmatic, 'postcompositional' process.

So, pragmatics, as understood here, is the process whereby speakers converge on reasonable candidates as to what the quantificational domain may be; it is also the process whereby a sentence like (1a) may wind up conveying that the meeting was a success (because, say, Joe managed to keep the number of upset people to a minimum), or the process whereby (1a) may result in an ironical comment on Joe's diplomatic skills, etc. Such processes are arguably postcompositional, in the sense that they presuppose a grasp of sentence meaning, plus an understanding of the speaker's intentions, etc. We have no doubt that such processes exist (and, thus, that aspects of the Gricean picture are sound and effective). The question is whether SIs are phenomena of the latter postcompositional sort or are UG-driven like, say, the principles of focus association sketched in (1).

1.1 Background

In his seminal work, Grice (1989) argues that the main source of pragmatic enrichment is a small set of maxims (Quality, Quantity, Relation, Manner) that govern, as overridable defaults, cooperative conversational exchanges (Oswald Ducrot developed related ideas independently, e.g. Ducrot 1973. Another approach, broadly inspired by Grice but which departs more radically from the original formulations, can be found within the tradition of Relevance Theory – see, e.g., Sperber & Wilson 1986, Carston 1988).

In discussing the various ways in which these maxims may be used to enrich basic meanings, Grice considers the case of how *or* might strengthen its classical Boolean inclusive value (according to which 'p or q' is true if at least one of the two disjuncts is true) to its exclusive construal ('p or q' is true if one and only one of the two disjuncts is). In what follows, we offer a reconstruction of the relevant steps of this enrichment process, as is commonly found in the literature (cf., e.g., Gamut 1991). The basic idea is that, upon hearing something like (3a), a hearer considers the alternative in (3b) and subconsciously goes through the reasoning steps in (3i–vi)

(3) a. Joe or Bill will show up
    b. Joe and Bill will show up
       i. The speaker said (3a) and not (3b), which, presumably, would have been also relevant [Relevance]
      ii. (3b) asymmetrically entails (3a), hence is more informative
      iii. If the speaker believed (3b), she would have said so [Quantity]
      iv. It is not the case that the speaker believes that (3b) holds

v. It is likely that the speaker has an opinion as to whether (3b) holds.
Therefore:
vi. It is likely that the speaker takes (3b) to be false.

This example illustrates how one might go from (3a) to (3vi) by using Grice's maxims and logic alone. The conclusion in (3vi) is close to the desired implicature but not quite. What we actually want to draw is that the speaker is positively trying to convey that Joe and Bill will not both come. Moreover, we need to be a bit more precise about the role of relevance throughout this reasoning, for that is a rather sticky point. We will do this in turn in the next three subsections.

1.2 SIs as exhaustifications

To understand in what sense the conclusion in (3vi) should and could be strengthened, it is convenient to note that the reasoning in (3) can be viewed as a form of *exhaustification* of the assertion, i.e., tantamount to inserting a silent *only*. Using B_s as a short form for 'the speaker believes that', the assertion in (3a) would convey to the reader the information in (4a), while the alternative assertion in (3b) would convey (4b).

(4) a. B_s (show up(j) $\vee$ show up(b))
    b. B_s (show up(j) $\wedge$ show up(b))

If you now imagine adding a silent *only* (henceforth, O) to (4a) (and evaluating it with respect to the alternative in (4b)), we get:

(5) $O_{ALT}(B_s$ (show up(j) $\vee$ show up(b)))
    = B_s (show up(j) $\vee$ show up(b)) $\wedge \neg B_s$ (show up(j) $\wedge$ show up(b))

The result in (5) is the same as (3iv) and entitles the hearer only to the weak conclusion in (3vi) (and for the time being, we might view this use of O as a compact way of expressing the reasoning in (3)). Now, the conclusion we would want instead is:

(6) B_s (O_{ALT}(show up(j) $\vee$ show up(b)))
    = B_s (show up(j) $\vee$ show up(b) $\wedge \neg$ (show up(j) $\wedge$ show up(b)))

The speaker, in other words, by uttering (3a), is taken to commit herself to the negation of (3b). The reading in (6) can be derived if we are allowed to go from something like *it is not the case that x believes that p* to *x believes that not p*. Sauerland (2004) calls this 'the epistemic step'. What is relevant in the present connection is that in the computation of SIs such a step does not follow from Gricean maxims and logic alone. It is something that needs to be stipulated. This seems to be a gap in the Gricean account of SIs (see for instance Soames 1982, Groenendijk & Stokhof 1984). And this problem interacts with another, even more serious one, having to do with seemingly innocent assumption that in uttering (3a), something like (3b) is likely to be relevant. Let us discuss it briefly.

1.3 Relevance

Let us grant that in uttering (3a), (3b) is also indeed relevant, whatever 'relevant' may mean. Now, a natural assumption is that the property of 'being relevant' is closed under negation, i.e., if a proposition ϕ is relevant, then $\neg \phi$ is relevant as well. To say that ϕ is relevant must be to say that it matters whether ϕ is true or false (this follows from several formal definitions of relevance proposed in the literature, e.g., Carnap 1950; Groenendijk & Stokhof 1984, 1990). If this is so, the negation of (3b) will also be relevant. But then the set of relevant alternatives changes. Assuming that relevance is also closed under conjunction (if A and B are both relevant, then so is *A and B*), it now includes:

(7) a. show up(j) ∨ show up(b)
    b. show up(j) ∧ show up(b)
    c. ¬(show up(j) ∧ show up(b)))
    d. (show up(j) ∨ show up(b)) ∧ ¬(show up(j) ∧ show up(b)))

Now, note that both (7d) and (7b) a-symmetrically entails (7a) (i.e., (3a)). So if we run the Gricean reasoning in (3) over this expanded set of alternatives or, equivalently, if we exhaustify the assertion along the lines discussed in (4), we must conclude that the speaker's only relevant belief is (7a), and, in particular, that he does not have the belief that (7b) is true, nor than (7d) is true. In other words, we conclude that a) the speaker believes that John or Bill will show up, b) that she does not have the belief that both will show up and c) that she does not have the belief that only one of the two will show up. Notice that in this case, the epistemic step would lead to a contradiction. In other words, we have to conclude that if the speaker utters *p or q*, he must not have an opinion as to whether *p and q* is the case, which blocks the possibility that he believes *p and q* to be false (a precursor of this argument, which was made explicit by von Fintel & Heim in their 1997 pragmatics class notes, can be found in Kroch 1972 – see also Davis 1998). This problem is a general one: the assumption that relevance is closed under negation (which is hard to avoid) has the effect of blocking any potential SI.

So we see that on the one hand, by logic alone, we are not able to derive SIs in their full strengths from the Gricean maxims. And, if we are minimally explicit about relevance, we are able to derive no implicature at all (except for 'ignorance' implicatures). Something seems to be going very wrong in our attempt to follow Grice's ideas. However, post-Gricean scholars, and in particular Horn (1972, 1989), have addressed some of these problems and it is important to grasp the reach of such proposals.

1.4 Scales

Horn's important point is that if we want to make headway in understanding how SIs come about, then the set of relevant alternatives needs to be constrained. In the most typical cases, they will be *lexically* constrained by items of the same category whose entailments line them up in a scale of increasing informativeness. Examples of Horn's scales are the following:

(8) a. The positive quantifiers: *some, many, most, all*
 b. The negative quantifiers: *not all, few, none*
 c. Numerals: *one, two, three*, ...
 d. Modals: *can, must*
 e. Sentential connectives: *or, and*
 f. Gradable adjectives: *warm, hot, boiling / chilly, cold, freezing*, etc.

These series are characterized by the fact that the items on the right are stronger than the items on their left. For example, if all of the students did well, then most of them did and surely some of them did. Similarly for the other scales. Horn's proposal is that if you use *some*, other members of the scale may be activated and provide the alternatives against which the assertion is evaluated. Not all have to be activated; perhaps none of them will. But if they are activated, they must look like in (8). What is crucial about these scales is that one cannot mix elements with different monotonicity/polarity properties (see Fauconnier 1975b and Matsumoto 1995). Thus for example, one cannot have positive and negative quantifiers as part of the same scale. This is the way the problem considered in section 1.3. is circumvented.

Horn's suggestions can be extended to other seemingly more volatile/ephemeral scales. Consider the following example, modeled after Hirschberg (1985):

(9) A: Did John mail his check?
    B: He wrote it.

This dialogue suggests that B's intention is to convey that John didn't mail the check. The 'scale' being considered here must be something like {write the check, mail the check}. What is crucial is that we do not consider mailing vs. not mailing, or mailing vs. stealing, for otherwise we would only derive ignorance implicatures (on the role played by questions for determining alternatives, see also van Kuppevelt 1996 and Spector 2006).

The main moral is that the notion of 'relevance' to be used in implicature calculation is, yes, context dependent but constrained in at least two ways: through the lexicon (certain classes of words form lexical scales) and through a monotonicity constraint: all scales, even scales that are not lexically specified, such as those needed for (9), cannot simultaneously include upward and downward entailing elements.

1.5 Monotonicity and scale reversal

There is a further important point to make. Let us consider an example like (10).

(10) A: Who will come to the party?
     B: I doubt that Joe or Sue will come.

Here no implicature comes about, even though the conjunctive statement *Joe and Sue will come to the party* must be relevant on the background of the question in A. The reason is the following. The active alternative to B is *I doubt that Joe and Sue will come to the party*. Since B's utterance *entails* this alternative, the latter cannot be excluded and no implicature comes about (operators which, like negation and the verb *doubt*, reverse the direction of entailment are called downward entailing, or monotone decreasing; operators which *preserve* entailment patterns are called upward entailing, or monotone increasing). In our terms, use of covert *only* in cases like these is simply vacuous. It is useful to compare (10) with:

(11) A: Who will come to the party?
     B: I doubt that all of the students will
     B-ALT: I doubt that (some of the) students will come to the party

If B's answer is as indicated, its alternative would presumably be something like B-ALT. (B-ALT might be somewhat less than felicitous because *some* is a positive polarity item – whence the parentheses.) So, exhaustifying B's utterance will bring about the negation of B-ALT, namely:

(12) It is not true that I doubt that (some of the) students will come to the party
= I believe that some of the students will come to the party.

This appears to be the right result: B's response to A does seem to implicate (12). This effect of scale reversal under negation and other downward-entailing operators, emphasized by several authors (cf., among others, Fauconnier 1975a, 1975b; Atlas & Levinson 1981, Horn 1989) is a welcome result.

2 Embedded Implicatures: a first crack in the Gricean picture

As mentioned, the goal of this article is to challenge the 'neo-Gricean' approach to SIs. We use the term "neo-Gricean" to characterize theories that attempt to derive SIs from Grice's maxims of conversation, generally supplemented with the notion of *scale*, and view SIs as resulting from a reasoning process about speakers' intentions (as in Horn 1972, 1989: Fauconnier 1975a, 1975b, and Levinson 1983, but also, more recently, Spector 2003, 2006, 2007b; Sauerland 2004; van Rooij & Schulz 2004, 2006). Chierchia (2004), in an article which began circulating in 2000, partly building on ideas by Landman (1998), challenged this neo-Gricean approach on the basis of embedded scalar implicatures, and concluded that SIs are derived by means of compositional rules which apply recursively to the constituents of a given sentence (see also Récanati 2003 for a version of this position). Chierchia (2004) thus argues for a *grammatical approach* to scalar implicatures. Several works reacted to this proposal by refining the neo-Gricean approach so as to enable it to account for some of Chierchia's empirical observations. (See for instance Spector 2003, 2006, 2007b; Sauerland 2004; van Rooij & Schulz 2004, 2006; Russell 2006. Horn 2006 is a recent assessment of several aspects of this dispute, from the neo-Gricean standpoint. See also Geurts 2009 for a nuanced defense of the globalist view.)

We are not going to review this literature in details; our goal here is to present what seem to us to be some of the most compelling arguments for a grammatical approach to scalar implicatures. The arguments (some of which are new) will be based on the existence of embedded SIs, and on a variety of additional considerations

We will begin in section 2 with an illustration of what a grammatical approach to SIs might look like, followed by a preliminary argument in favor of such an approach, based on a sub-case of the generalization mentioned in the introduction, namely that embedded implicatures are possible in downward entailing and non-monotonic contexts (non-monotonic operators are operators which are neither upward- nor downward-entailing). Section 3 will provide a detailed new argument for the existence of embedded implicatures in upward entailing contexts. Finally, section 4 will review other arguments that have been recently given for a grammatical approach to SIs.

2.1 Exhaustification as a grammatical device

Does Grice's approach, emended as proposed by Horn, provide us with a framework in which SIs may be properly understood? Horn's move helps us get around the problem raised by the appeal to relevance; but the epistemic step remains unaccounted for: reasoning via the maxims about the speaker's intentions gets us at best from something like (13a) to (13b):

(13) a. John or Bill will show up
     b. The speaker has no evidence that they both will show up

For the time being, let us simply stipulate that the epistemic step can take place and that an utterance of (13a) could be understood as conveying something such as (14a), which we represent as (14b):

(14) a. John or Bill and not both will show up
     b. O_{ALT}(John or Bill will show up)

For concreteness, we may assume that if the alternatives are active (and hence the set ALT is non empty), such alternatives are obligatorily factored into meaning via O. Otherwise, if the alternatives are not active, the plain unenriched meaning is used, and no SI comes about. (see also section 4.1.)

So far, we have regarded our silent *only* as way to express, in compact form, Gricean reasoning of the type exemplified in (3). However, a different interpretation of O is possible. One might imagine that a silent *only* can be present in the sentence's logical form, and that the scalar implicatures of a given sentence S are in fact *logical entailments* of S when construed as corresponding to an LF in which a silent *only* occurs and takes maximal scope. In this case, exhaustification would be more than just a way of expressing Gricean reasoning compactly. It would become a grammatical device. What lends preliminary plausibility to this interpretation is the observation, stemming from Horn's work, that grammar seems to constrain (via a specification of lexical scales) the set of alternatives.

Before further elaboration, we should state explicitly how our operator O is interpreted. Given a sentence S and a set of alternatives, $O_{ALT}(S)$ expresses the conjunction of S and of the negations of all the members of ALT that are not entailed by S. Equivalently, it states that the only members of ALT that are true are those entailed by S:

(15) $||O_{ALT}(S)||^w = 1$ iff $||S||^w = 1$ and $\forall \phi \in ALT\ (\phi(w) = 1 \rightarrow ||S|| \subseteq \phi)$

In section 3.4.2., we will need to modify this definition, but for the time being (15) is sufficient. Quite often in this article, we'll omit the subscript *ALT* (we make the simplifying assumption that ALT is fully determined by the scalar items that occur in the scope of O). A word of caution is in order: O, so defined, is not exactly equivalent to *only*, for *only* is usually assumed to trigger various presuppositions which *O*, according to the above entry, does not. Note also that the above definition does not encode any direct relationship between *O* and focus marking (see Fox & Katzir 2009).

We can now properly address the main issue of the present article. So far, we have been discussing implicatures that occur in unembedded contexts (like our original case in (3)). And even when we consider cases where implicature triggers (Horn Scale members, a.k.a. scalar items) occur in an embedded position, as in (11) and (12), the relevant implicatures appear to be computed at the root level. This is in keeping with Grice's insight that implicatures arise by reasoning on speakers intention given a particular speech act (i.e. a whole utterance).

The question we would like to investigate now is whether SIs are *always* computed at the root level. If Grice is right, it should indeed be so. In this respect, the view we are developing that implicatures arise via something like a covert use of *only*, suggests that a different answer to the question might be right. For there is no *a priori* reason for thinking that covert uses of *only* are restricted to the root. If such an operator exists, it is unclear what should prevent its deployment at embedded scope sites. However, whether we are right or wrong on how SIs come about, the issue of whether they can systematically arise in embedded positions clearly deserves close inspection.

Summing up, the Gricean view, emended *à la* Horn with grammatically based constraints on scales, and with the extra assumption of an epistemic step, is able to derive basic SIs. However, such an approach seems to clearly predict that SIs are a root, postcompositional phenomenon. This prediction seems to be confirmed in cases of 'scale reversal' such as those in (11)–(12). The question is whether it withstands further scrutiny.

The rest of this section argues that it does not, based on the existence of so-called 'intrusive' implicatures (see Levinson 2000), i.e., cases where a scalar item retains its 'strengthened' meaning under the scope of a downward entailing (DE) or non-monotonic (NM) operator. In section 3, we'll turn to SIs embedded in UE contexts. As we will see, they are expected to be harder to detect. Nonetheless, we will present various tools that will allow us to see very clear consequences of the presence of such implicatures.

2.2 Implicatures embedded in DE and NM contexts

Sometimes scalar items receive an enriched interpretation under the scope of negation. Examples that seem to force such an enrichment are the following.

(16) a. Joe didn't see Mary or Sue; he saw both.
 b. It is not that you *can* write a reply. You must.
 c. I don't expect that some students will do well, I expect that all students will.

The first example in (16a) receives a coherent interpretation only if the embedded *or* is interpreted exclusively. Similarly, the modal in (16b) has to be interpreted as *can though need not*, and the quantifier *some* in (16c) as *some though not all*. For all the sentences in (16), in other words, it looks as if the implicature gets embedded under the negative operator. In our notation, the LF of, e.g., (16a) could be represented as:

(17) not O_{ALT}(John saw Mary or Sue)

Examples of this sort have been widely discussed in the literature (especially in Horn 1985, 1989); they seem to require either focal stress on the implicature trigger and/or a strong contextual bias. Horn argues that cases of this sort constitute metalinguistic uses of negation, i.e., ways of expressing an objection not to a propositional content but to some other aspect of a previous speech act. The range of possible speaker's objection can be very broad and concern even the choice of words or the phonology.

(18) You don't want to go to [leisister] square, you want to go to [lester] square

In particular, with sentences like (16), the speaker objects to the choice of words of his interlocutor, presumably for the implicatures they might trigger.

While the phenomenon of metalinguistic negation might well be real (if poorly understood) there are other examples of DE contexts not involving negation that seem to require embedded implicatures, as noted by Horn himself (Horn 1989). In what follows, we will consider several such cases, modelled mostly after Levinson (2000). To begin with, consider the contrast in (19).

(19) a. If you take salad or dessert, you'll be really full.
b. If you take salad or dessert, you pay $ 20; but if you take both there is a surcharge.

The most natural reading of (19a) involves no implicature (*or* is construed inclusively); on the other hand, on the inclusive reading, (19b) would be contradictory. If an indicative conditional sentence is analyzed as a material or a strict conditional, a coherent interpretation, which is clearly possible in the case of (19b), requires an embedded implicature. Let us go through the reasons why this is so. Suppose that in the context where (19b) is uttered, the alternative with *and* is active. Then, there may be in principle two sites at which the implicature is computed. Using our notation, they can be represented as follows:

(20) a. O_{ALT}(if you take salad or dessert, you pay $ 20)
b. if O_{ALT}(you take salad or dessert), you pay $ 20

If the option in (20a) is taken, the relevant alternative set would be as in (21b):

(21) a. If you take salad or dessert, you pay $ 20
b. ALT = {If you take salad or dessert, you pay $ 20, If you take salad and dessert, you pay $ 20}
c. O_{ALT} (if you take salad or dessert, you pay $ 20) = 1 iff
If you take sale or dessert, you pay $ 20 $\wedge$ $\forall p \in$ ALT such that p is not entailed
by 'if you take salad or dessert, you pay $ 20', p is false.

Since the assertion (21a) entails all its alternatives, the truth conditions of (20a) wind up being the same as those of (21a) (i.e., no implicature comes about – cf. the computation in (21c)). And as already noted, this reading is too strong to be compatible with the continuation in (19b). So the LF in (20a) cannot account for the coherent interpretation of (19b). On the other hand, if the implicature is computed at the level of the antecedent, as in (20b), we get the equivalent of:

(22) If you take salad or dessert and not both, you pay $ 20

The truth conditions of (22) are weaker than those of (20a), and this makes them compatible with the continuation in (19b). Thus, the fact that sentences such as (19b) are acceptable seems to constitute prima facie evidence in favor of the possibility of embedding SIs.

One might wonder whether an alternative, non-monotonic analysis of conditionals, e.g., that of Stalnaker (1968) or Lewis (1973) could provide an account which would not rely on embedded implicatures. Although space limitations do not allow us to discuss this in any detail, we would like to point out that any such account would also have to explain the different behavior of conditional sentences in which the antecedent does not license a scalar implicature in isolation. (#*If you take salad or dessert or both, you pay exactly $ 20; but if you take both there is a surcharge.*).

This phenomenon seems to be quite general. Here are a few more examples involving the antecedents of conditionals, as well as further DE contexts like the left argument of the determiner *every*.

(23) a. If most of the students do well, I am happy; if all of them do well, I am even happier
b. If you can fire Joe, it is your call; but if you must, then there is no choice
c. Every professor who fails most of the students will receive no raise; every professor who fails all of the students will be fired. (M. Romero p.c.)

It should be noted that these examples can be embedded even further.

(24) John is firmly convinced that if most of his students do well, he is going to be happy and that if all of them will do well, he'll be even happier.

(25) Every candidate thought that presenting together his unpublished papers and his students evaluation was preferable to presenting the one or the other.

Without adding implicatures at a deeply embedded level, all of these examples would be contradictory. For instance, in (24) the implicature is embedded within the antecedent of a conditional, which is in turn embedded under an attitude verb. In (25), a coherent interpretation is possible only if *or* (in *the one or the other*) is interpreted as exclusive; note indeed that structures of the form *A is preferable to B* are perceived as contradictory when A entails B, as evidenced by the oddness of, e.g., *Having a cat is preferable to having a pet*. Thus if disjunction were inclusive in (25), it should sound odd as well.

A similar argument can be replicated for non-monotonic contexts. Consider for instance:

(26) Exactly two students wrote a paper or ran an experiment

It seems relatively easy to interpret *or* in (26) exclusively. As a first step towards seeing that this is the case, it is useful to note that the truth conditions associated with the exclusive and inclusive construals of *or* under the scope of a non-monotonic quantifier as in (26) are logically independent. For example, in a situation in which one student writes a paper and another writes a paper and also runs an experiment (and nobody else does either), the sentence is true on the inclusive construal of *or*, but false on the exclusive construal. On the other hand, in a situation in which one student only writes a paper, another only runs an experiment and other students do both, the inclusive interpretation of *or* in (26) is falsified; in such a scenario, (26) is only true on the (embedded) exclusive construal. Now the exclusive reading can be easily observed when we consider environments in which it forced:

(27) Exactly two students wrote a paper or ran an experiment. The others either did both or made a class presentation.

For (27) to be coherent, the implicature must be computed under the scope of *exactly two*. Cases of this sort are pretty general and can be reproduced for all scalar items: sentence (28) below must be interpreted as 'exactly three students did most though not all of the exercises'

(28) Exactly three students did most of the exercises; the rest did them all.

Taking stock, we have discussed a number of example sentences involving a variety of DE and NM contexts. Such sentences appear to have coherent interpretations that can only be derived if an implicature is computed at an embedded level (i.e., within the scope of a higher verb or operator). It should be noted that focal stress on the scalar item often helps the relevant interpretation. From our point of view, this is not surprising. The mechanism we have sketched for implicature calculation is, in essence, covert exhaustification, one of the phenomena triggered by focus. More generally, for the time being, we make no claim as to the frequency or marked status of embedded implicatures (but see our discussion in section 4.6 below). Our point is simply that they can and do naturally occur and that there are ways in which embedded implicatures can be systematically induced. This fact seems to be incompatible with the claim that SIs are a postcompositional semantic process, as the Gricean or Neo-Gricean view would have it. Of course, to establish our claim fully, we would like to be able to show that SIs can also be embedded in UE contexts, which, as we will see shortly, calls for more sophisticated methods.

3 A new argument for embedded implicatures in UE contexts: Hurford's constraint

If embedded implicatures exist, we expect many sentences to be multiply ambiguous, depending on whether an SI is computed in a given embedded position or not. Furthermore, in UE contexts, the various readings that are predicted are all stronger than the 'literal' reading, and in many cases, the presence of an embedded implicature yields a reading which is stronger than both the literal reading and the reading that results from applying the standard Gricean reasoning to the sentence as a whole (in our terms, the reading that results from applying O to the whole sentence). So, it may prove hard to establish the possibility of embedded implicatures by mere inspection of truth-conditions (since if a certain reading R1 entails another reading R2, there can be no situation where R1 is accepted as true and R2 is not; see, e.g., Meier & Sauerland 2008 for a related methodological discussion).

In order to circumvent this difficulty, it would be useful to have constructions in which only one of the potentially available readings is licensed. In this section, we are going to argue that such constructions exist: we'll show that some sentences will *have* to contain a local exhaustivity operator in a UE context for a certain constraint (Hurford's constraint) to be met. The general line of argumentation is presented in a more detailed way in Chierchia, Fox & Spector (2009).

3.1 Hurford's constraint

Hurford (1974) points to the following generalization:

(29) Hurford's constraint (HC): A sentence that contains a disjunctive phrase of the form S *or* S' is infelicitous if S entails S' or S' entails S.

This constraint is illustrated by the infelicity of the following sentences:

(30) a. # Mary saw an animal or a dog.
      b. # Every girl who saw an animal or a dog talked to Jack.

However (31) below, which is felicitous, seems to be a counterexample to HC:

(31) Mary solved the first or the second problem or both

If *or* is interpreted inclusively, then clearly (31) violates HC, since 'Mary solved both problems' entails 'Mary solved the first problem or the second problem'. On the basis of such examples, Hurford reasoned that *or* has to be ambiguous, and that one of its readings is the exclusive reading. On an exclusive construal of the first disjunction in (31), the sentence no longer violates HC. Gazdar (1979) noticed other cases where HC appears to be obviated, such as (32):

(32) Mary read some or all of the books

By analogy with Hurford's reasoning about disjunction, one might conclude that *some* is ambiguous as well, and means *some but not all* on one of its readings. But Gazdar argued that multiplying lexical ambiguities in order to maintain HC misses an obvious generalization. Gazdar, thus, proposed to weaken Hurford's generalization in the following way:

> Gazdar's generalization: A sentence containing a disjunctive phrase *S or S'* is infelicitous if *S* entails *S'* or if *S'* entails *S*, unless *S'* contradicts the conjunction of *S* and the implicatures of *S*. (Note that Gazdar's generalization is asymmetric, i.e., allows for cases where *S'* entails *S* but not for cases where *S* entails *S'*. We do not address this point here. See also Singh 2008)

In both (31) and (32), the SI associated with the first disjunct (*Mary did not solve both problems*, *Mary did not read all of the books*) contradicts the second disjunct, and so both sentences are predicted to be felicitous by Gazdar's generalization. Gazdar himself did not offer an account of his generalization. We will provide such an account, along the following lines:
– HC is correct as originally stated
– All apparent violations of HC involve the presence of an implicature-computing operator within the first disjunct, ensuring that HC is met – hence the presence of a 'local implicatures'

In a sense, we extend Hurford's original account based on ambiguity to all scalar items, even though we do not assume a *lexical* ambiguity, and instead derive the various readings with our implicature-computing operator. It should be clear that we derive something close to Gazdar's generalization: suppose S2 entails S1; then 'S1 or S2' violates HC; yet 'O_{ALT}(S1) or S2' may happen to satisfy HC; this will be so if S1 together with its implicatures is no longer entailed by S2, which will be the case, in particular, if S2 contradicts S1 together with its implicatures

However, as we will show in the next subsections, our proposal turns out to make very precise and new predictions in a number of cases – predictions that do not fall out from anything that Gazdar has said.

3.2 Forcing embedded implicatures

Gazdar's generalization, as such, does not make any particular prediction regarding the *reading* that obtains when there is an apparent violation of HC. But consider now the following sentence (in a context where it has been asked which of a given set of problems Peter solved):

(33) Peter either solved both the first and the second problem or all of the problems.

In the absence of an exhaustivity operator, (33) would violate HC, since solving all of the problems entails solving the first one and the second one. And (33) would then be equivalent to (34):

(34) Peter solved the first problem and the second problem.

Therefore, we predict that an exhaustivity operator has to be present, with the effect that (33)'s logical form is the following:

(35) O_{ALT}(Peter solved the first problem and the second problem) or he solved all of the problems

Recall that the meaning of our operator is supposed to be – as a first approximation – the same as that of *only*. If we are right, the meaning of (33) could be given by the following paraphrases (which are themselves equivalent):

(36) a. Peter only solved the first problem and the second problem, or he solved all of the problems
   b. Either Peter solved the first problem and the second problem and no other problem, or he solved all the problems

It turns out that this is indeed the only possible reading of (33). In other words, (33) is clearly judged *false* in a situation in which Peter solved, say, the first three problems and no other problem (out of a larger set). So (33) seems to be a clear case of an embedded implicature. What distinguishes (33) from cases like (31) and (32) is that exhaustifying the first disjunct has a semantic effect in this case.

In Chierchia, Fox & Spector (2009), we discuss more complex cases in which exactly the same logic is at play. But the general form of the argument should be clear: if HC is correct as originally formulated, then, in some cases, the only way to satisfy HC is to insert O locally at an embedded level, and this gives rise to readings which turn out to be the only possible ones. The next section develops a similar, though more complex, argument.

3.3 HC and recursive exhaustification

In this section, we are going to show that even in cases where the obligatory presence of embedded O does not have any direct effect on the literal truth-conditions of a sentence, it nevertheless has consequences that can be detected by investigating the *implicatures* of the sentence in question (or lack thereof). In our terms, the presence of the embedded implicature-computing operator turns out to have a truth-conditional effect when the sentence is itself embedded under another implicature-computing operator. First, we'll look at the interpretation of disjunctions of the form 'A or B or both' in the scope of necessity modals (3.3.1). Then we'll offer an account of the 'cancellation effect' triggered by *or both* in non-embedded contexts (3.3.2).

3.3.1 *Or both* in the scope of necessity modals

Consider the following two sentences:

(37) We are required to either read *Ulysses* or *Madame Bovary*

(38) We are required to either read *Ulysses* or *Madame Bovary* or both

Both these sentences implicate that we are not required to read both *Ulysses* and *Madame Bovary*. At first sight, they do not seem to trigger different implicatures. But upon further reflection, they, in fact, do. Suppose that we are actually required to read *Ulysses* or *Madame Bovary* and that we are *not* allowed to read both of them. Then (37) would be an appropriate statement, while (38) would not. Sentence (37), on its most natural reading, is silent as to whether or not we are allowed to read both novels. But (38) strongly suggests that we are allowed to read both novels. So (38) seems to trigger an implicature that (37) does not.

This is further confirmed by looking at the following dialogues:

(39) A: We are required to either read *Ulysses* or *Madame Bovary*
B: No! we have to read both

(40) A: We are required to either read *Ulysses* or *Madame Bovary*
B: ## No! We are not allowed to read both

(41) A: We are required to either read *Ulysses* or *Madame Bovary* or both
B: No! We are not allowed to read both

(39) serves to set the stage. It shows what we've already seen in section 2, namely that an implicature can be embedded below negation: Speaker B, in (39), is objecting, not to the literal meaning of A's utterance but to an implicatures of this utterance, namely, that we are not required to read both novels. In section 2 we've argued that phenomena of this sort argue for embedded implicatures, but this is not important in the current context. What is important here is that the relevant phenomena could be used to investigate the implicatures of various utterances, and as such they distinguish between (37) and (38). In (40), B's reply is clearly deviant. This shows that A's utterance in (40) (= (37)) does *not* implicate that we are allowed to read both novels; indeed, if A's sentence did trigger this implicature, then B's objection would be perfectly felicitous, since it would count as an objection to an implicature of A's utterance. But now notice the contrast with (41). B's objection in (41) is completely natural, and hence confirms our claim that in (41), A's sentence (= (38)) does implicate that we are allowed to read both novels.

How are these facts to be explained? Why does (38) have an implicature that (37) doesn't? Note that (modulo the effects of matrix *O*) (37) and (38) have the same truth-conditions. Yet they trigger different implicatures. We are going to show that this phenomenon is in fact entirely expected from our perspective. The implicatures associated with (37) and (38) are, in fact, instances of the following generalization:

(42) A sentence of the form $\Box(A \text{ or } B)$ triggers the following implicatures (where $\Box$ stand for any modal operator with universal force): $\neg\Box A$, $\neg\Box B$

To illustrate this generalization let us begin with (37), repeated here as (43), which implicates that we have a choice as to how to satisfy our obligations.

(43) We are required to either read *Ulysses* or *Madame Bovary*

The reading of (43), 'pragmatically strengthened' on the basis of the generalization in (42), is given in (44a), which is equivalent to (44b) (because 'being not required to do X' is equivalent to 'being allowed not to do X') and then to (44c).

(44) a. We are required to either read *Ulysses* or *Madame Bovary* and we are not required to read *Ulysses* and we are not required to read *Madame Bovary*.

b. We are required to either read *Ulysses* or *Madame Bovary*, we are allowed not to read *Ulysses* and we are allowed not to read *Madame Bovary*.
c. We are required to either read *Ulysses* or *Madame Bovary*, and we are allowed to read either one without reading the other

Now, let's see the consequences of this generalization for the case of (38) ("We are required to read *Ulysses* or *Madame Bovary* or both"), schematized as follows:

(45) □ [O_ALT(A or B) or (A and B)]

(45) is predicted to implicate the following:

(46) a. ¬□(O_ALT(A or B))
      b. ¬□(A and B)

The end-result is the following proposition, which indeed corresponds to the most natural reading of (38):

(47) We are required to read *Ulysses* or *Madame Bovary*, we are not required to read only one of the two novels, we are not required to read both novels.

From (47) it follows that we are allowed to read both novels, which was the desired result. So far we have shown that given the generalization in (42), the observed interpretation of (38) follows directly from the assumption that O is present in the first disjunct. Of course, it is also desirable to understand why generalization (42) should hold. It turns out that the exhaustivity operator as we have defined it so far (adding the negations of all non-weaker alternatives) can derive all the inferences that we observed, provided we now assume that the scalar alternatives of a disjunctive phrase *X or Y* include not only the phrase *X and Y* but also each disjunct *X* and *Y* independently. If so, then (43) has the following alternatives (using now the sign '□' to abbreviate 'we are required to', 'U' to abbreviate 'read *Ulysses*', and 'MB' to stand for 'read *Madame Bovary*'):

(48) ALT((43)) = {□(U or MB), □U, □MB, □(U and MB)}

To get the 'strengthened meaning' of (43), we simply assume that (43) gets exhaustified yielding the Logical Form in (49), which involves adding the negation of each of its alternatives that is not weaker than the assertion. The result is:

(49) $O_{ALT}((43)) = O_{ALT}\Box(U \text{ or } MB)) = \Box(U \text{ or } MB) \land \neg\Box U \land \neg\Box MB$

Let us now go back to our original example (38) to see how this assumption plays out:

(50) a. We are required to either read *Ulysses* or *Madame Bovary*, or both
 b. $O_{ALT}(\Box(O_{ALT}(U \text{ or } MB) \text{ or } (U \text{ and } MB)))$

The logical form of (50a) must be (50b), where the embedded exhaustivity operator is forced by HC and the matrix one exhaustifies the entire sentence. Given our new assumptions about the alternatives of a disjunctive phrase, (50)'s alternatives include, among others, '$\Box(O_{ALT}(U \text{ or } MB))$' (i.e., "we are required to read either *Ulysses* or *Madame Bovary* and we are forbidden to read both") and '$\Box(U \text{ and } MB)$'. Focussing (for simplicity) on just these two alternatives, (50b) tantamounts to

(51) a. $\Box(U \text{ or } MB)) \land \neg\Box(O_{ALT}(U \text{ or } MB)) \land \neg\Box(U \text{ and } MB)$
 b. We are required to either read *Ulysses* or *Madame Bovary*, and we are not required to read only one of them, and we are not required to read both
 c. We are required to read *Ulysses* or *Madame Bovary* and we are allowed to read both of them and we are allowed to read only one of them

This is exactly what we wanted to derive. Let us sum up what has been shown. The obligatory presence of an exhaustivity operator applying to the first disjunct in sentences like (38), together with the assumption that each member of a disjunctive phrase contributes to the alternatives of the disjunctive phrase, immediately predicts that (38), though equivalent to (37), has more alternatives. One of these alternatives, crucially, contains an exhaustivity operator. Due to this additional alternative, (38) triggers an inference that (37) does not (the inference that we are not required to read *only* one of the two novels), a prediction that appears to be correct.

3.3.2 Symmetric alternatives and Innocent Exclusion

In the next sub-section we will show that our perspective enables us to derive the fact that disjunctions of the form *A or B or both*, or *some or all*, do not trigger any SI if they are not embedded (a fact that is sometimes described as a 'cancellation' effect). But first we need to elaborate a bit on the idea that the disjuncts are alternatives of a disjunctive sentence. This idea, which seems to be needed for a variety of purposes in addition to the one mentioned above (see Sauerland 2004; Spector 2003, 2007b and Fox 2007), doesn't follow from the Horn set for disjunction given in (9d). One way of modifying the Horn set for binary connectives along the lines we have discussed is suggested by Sauerland (2004), namely expanding such a set to include the abstract elements L and R, where *p L q* is equivalent to *p* and *p R q* is equivalent to *q*:

(52) **Sauerland's alternatives for disjunction:** {*or, L, R, and*}

(For alternatives see Spector 2006, Katzir 2007, and Alonso-Ovalle 2005). The obvious problem with the proposal that the disjuncts are among the alternatives of a disjunctive statement is that our operator *O*, as we have defined it in section 2, now yields a contradiction when it applies to a simple disjunctive sentence: according to our definition, *O(p or q)* states that the disjunctive sentence is true and each of its alternatives (none of which it entails) is false. In particular, it would now follow that each of the disjuncts is false, but this of course contradicts *(p or q)*. The problem arises whenever the set of alternatives has a property that we might call 'symmetry', i.e., whenever it contains two or more alternatives that can be excluded separately but not together (e.g., *p or q* is consistent with the exclusion of *p* or with the exclusion of *q*, but the moment both are excluded the result is contradictory).

In order to correct for this problem, we have to revisit the question of which alternatives get to be excluded. Our previous definition stated that entailed alternatives don't get excluded. But, why? The reason seems rather obvious. Exclusion of weaker alternatives would lead to an automatic contradiction. But, as we've just seen, there are other exclusions that would lead to a contradiction, namely the simultaneous exclusion of two symmetric alternatives. We might therefore suggest that *O* be modified to avoid contradictions in situations of symmetry. In particular, given a sentence S and a set of alternatives C, we could define a set of innocently excludable alternatives, I-E(S,C), as the set of sentences that can all be false while S is true. We take this definition from Fox (2007), who took his inspiration from Sauerland's algorithm for the computation of SIs. (See also Spector 2003, 2007b and van Rooij & Schulz 2004, 2006 for related proposals.)

The definition of I-E(S,C) proceeds in two steps. First we look at the biggest subsets C' of C such that {¬S': S'∈C} ∪ {S} is a consistent set of propositions. Each such set corresponds to a way of excluding as many alternatives as possible in a consistent manner (i.e., consistent with the basic assertion). For instance, if S is of the form *p or q* and C is {*p or q, p, q, p and q*}, there are two sets which meet this condition, namely C' = {*p, p and q*} and C" = {*q, p and q*}. This is so because (a) {*p or q,* ¬*p,* ¬*(p and q)*} is consistent (every member of this set is true if q is true and p is false), and so is {*p or q*, ¬*q*, ¬(*p and q*)}, and (b) C' and C'' are, furthermore, maximal such sets, since the only bigger subset of C that does not include S is {*p, q, (p and q)*}, whose members cannot be consistently denied together if S itself (*p or q*) is asserted. The set of innocently excludable alternatives, I-E(S,C), is then constructed by collecting the alternatives which belong to *every* such maximal set. These are the alternatives which we know can be excluded safely (i.e., consistently), irrespective of which other alternatives have been already excluded. O is then defined in terms of innocent exclusion: when applied to a sentence S relative to a set of alternatives C, it returns the conjunction of S and the negations of all the innocently excludable members of C (i.e., of all the members of I-E(S, C)). This definition of O is summarized below:

(53) a. $O_C(S)$ is true iff S is true and for any S' in I-E(S,C): S' is false
 b. I-E(S,C) is the intersection of maximal excludable alternatives of C given S.
 c. $M \subseteq C$ is an excludable alternative of C given S, if the conjunction of S and the negation of all members of M is consistent.
 d. M is a maximal excludable alternative of C given S if M is an excludable alter-native of C given S and there is no superset of M included in C which is an excludable alternative of C given S.

The result of applying O, at times, could be rather difficult to compute, but the notion itself is rather simple. All stronger alternatives are excluded unless there is symmetry, in which case all alternatives that do not partake in symmetry are excluded. However, in most cases we do not need consider the definition in (53). Specifically, whenever using our initial definition of O does not result in a contradiction, we can continue to use it, and the reason is simple. If using our previous definition yields a non-contradictory result, then the set of innocently excludable alternatives is precisely the set of sentences in C not entailed by S. We will, thus, continue to use our initial definition of O whenever the result is consistent.

3.3.3 Cancellation

Consider the two following sentences:

(54) a. John bought some of the furniture.
 b. John bought some or all of the furniture.

Since the early days of theorizing on the nature of SIs, the fact that (54b) is not associated with the same SIs as the simple sentence in (54a) has been highly problematic. We will see that the problem is eliminated the moment the role of embedded exhaustification is understood.

The two sentences in (54) are equivalent. Under the Neo-Gricean Theory, as well as the grammatical alternative we are considering, the only way two equivalent sentences can be systematically associated with different SIs is if they have different scalar alternatives. The problem is that, without an embedded exhaustivity operator, (54a) and (54b) have equivalent scalar alternatives. Consider indeed the scalar items in (54b): *some*, *all*, and *or* with the following Horn Sets.

(55) a. Connectives: {*or, L, R, and*}
 b. Quantifiers: {*some, all*}

We thus get the following sentential alternatives:

(56) a. Alternatives for (54a):
 {John bought some of the furniture, John bought all of the furniture}
 b. Alternatives for (54b):
 {John bought some of the furniture, John bought some or all of the furniture, John bought some or some of the furniture, John bought some and some of the furniture,

 John bought all of the furniture, John bought all or all of the furniture, John bought some and all of the furniture, John bought all and all of the furniture}

Although there are more alternatives in (56b) than in (56a), they divide into two sets of equivalent alternatives (separated by a line). One set is equivalent to the *some* alternative in (56a) and the other to the *all* alternative. It follows that the same SI is predicted. The same holds if we use a more traditional Horn set, hence this recalcitrant problem in the Neo Gricean tradition is fairly independent of the particular perspective on alternatives we've been taking.

Interestingly the problem is obviated the moment O applies to the first disjunct. We now have another alternative, namely the first disjunct *O(John bought some of the furniture)*, which states that John bought some but not all of the furniture. This alternative is symmetric relative to the alternative based on *all*. One cannot exclude both, and, hence neither is innocently excludable. There are thus no innocently excludable alternatives, and matrix application of O is vacuous, precisely the result we want. We now see clearly why the addition of *or both* in sentences such as (54) has the effect of canceling the exclusive implicature typically associated with *or*.

3.4 Conclusion

In this section, we have offered a theory of the interaction of SIs and Hurford's Constraint. HC provides us with a way of probing the existence of embedded implicatures. Sometimes O has to be embedded for HC to be satisfied. Moreover, once we allow for embeddings of O, as we sometimes have to, we make a host of complex predictions that we have pain stakingly laid out and argued to be borne out. This further corroborates our main hypothesis, namely that scalar implicatures can be freely embedded.

4 Further cracks in the Gricean picture

As we mentioned at the very beginning, it is not clear how the availability of embedded scalar implicatures could be made consistent with a Gricean approach to SIs. More specifically, the facts suggest that SIs are not pragmatic in nature but arise, instead, as a consequence of semantic and syntactic mechanisms, which we have characterized in terms of the operator, O.

In this concluding section we would like to mention a few other observations that support this conclusion. Our discussion will be extremely sketchy given the limited space we have available. Nevertheless, we will try to introduce the pertinent issues and will refer the reader to relevant literature.

4.1 Obligatory SIs

A property that is commonly attributed to SIs is their optionality, sometimes referred to as "cancelability":

(57) a. John did some of the homework. In fact, he did all of it.
b. John did the reading or the homework. He might have done both.

The first sentences in (57a) and (57b) would normally lead to SIs (*not all* and *not both*, respectively). But these SI are not obligatory, else the continuation would lead to a contradiction.

The optionality observed in (57) is a necessary attribute of SIs from the (neo-) Gricean perspective. According to the latter, SIs are not automatic but rather follow from two assumptions that don't always hold, namely the assumption that the speaker is opinionated about stronger alternatives (which justifies the epistemic step alluded to in section 1.2.), and the assumption that the stronger alternatives are contextually relevant. The fact that these assumptions are not necessarily made in every context explains optionality.

This optionality is also captured by our grammatical mechanism. Given what we've said up to now, there is nothing that forces the presence of the operator O in a sentence containing a scalar item. Optionality is thus predicted, and one can capture the correlation with various contextual considerations, under the standard assumption (discussed in the very beginning of this article) that such considerations enter into the choice between competing representations (those that contain the operator and those that do not). An alternative way of capturing optionality is to assume that there is an optional process that activates the alternatives of a scalar item, but that once alternatives are active, SIs are obligatory (see Chierchia 2006 for an implementation). Under the latter view, what is optional is the activation of alternatives; if alternatives are activated, they must be factored into meaning via O.

This second option has a consequence. If under certain circumstances scalar alternatives have to be actived, *obligatory* SIs are expected to arise. The claim that this is so is, in fact, implicitly present in Krifka (1995) and Spector (2007a), and has been explicity defended in Chierchia (2004, 2006) and Magri (2009). We cannot go over all of the arguments and will narrow our attention to an argument made by Spector (2007a) in the domain of plural morphology.

Consider the contradictory status of the utterance in (58).

(58) #John read (some) books; maybe he read only one book.

This contradiction suggests that the first sentence *John read (some) books* (on both its variants) is equivalent to the statement that there is more than one book that John read. However, assuming this as the basic meaning doesn't account for its behavior in downward entailing environments. Consider the sentences in (59). Their interpretation (at least the one that immediately springs to mind) is stronger than what would be predicted under the putative meaning for the first sentence in (58).

(59) a. John didn't read books.
 b. I don't think that John read (some) books.

To see this, focus on (59a). The sentence (under its most natural interpretation) is false if John read exactly one book. The same point can be made for (59b), and both points are illustrated by comparison with sentences in which *John read (some) books* is substituted by a sentence that clearly has the putative meaning, namely *John read more than one book*:

(60) a. John didn't read more than one book.
b. I don't think that John read more than one book.

We seem to be facing something close to a paradox. In order to account for the meaning of (58), *John read (some) books* must have a strong meaning, namely that John read *more* than one book, and in order to account for the meaning of (59), it must have a weaker meaning, namely that John read *at least* one book.

Building on suggestions made by Sauerland (2003), Spector argues that the basic meaning is the *at least one* meaning, and that the stronger meaning (i.e., the *more than one* meaning) is a scalar implicature. Explaining how the strong meaning is derived is a rather complicated matter, which we will have to skip in this context. What is important, however, is that implicatures can easily disappear in downward entailing contexts, which accounts for the most natural readings of (59a) and (59b). As explained in section 2.1., the fact that scalar items need not retain their strengthened meaning in DE contexts is an automatic consequence of the neo-Gricean approach. It is also an automatic consequence of the grammatical perspective that we are advocating, since an exhaustivity operator (even if obligatorily present) need not be inserted below a DE operator. Let us see how things work in the case at hand.

If we assume that the plural morpheme *pl* makes it *obligatory* to insert the operator O in some syntactic position that c-commands *pl*, we expect the following: in a simple, non-embedded context, O can only be inserted just above the plural morpheme, which gives rise to an *at-least two* reading (as demonstrated in Spector's work); but if *pl* occurs in the scope of a DE-operator, more options are available; in particular, O may be inserted at the top-most level, i.e., above the DE-operator, in which case no implicature will arise (because inserting O at the top-most level always gives rise to the reading that is predicted by the pragmatic, neo-Gricean, approach). In the case of the plural morpheme, we therefore predict that the *at least two*-reading *can* disappear in DE-contexts, while it is obligatory in non-embedded UE contexts. This will generally be a property of *obligatory scalar implicatures*: the strengthened meaning of an item that *must* occur under the scope of O will be the only option in non-embedded UE contexts, but will appear to be optional in DE contexts. In the case of the plural morpheme, this seems to be just right. Notice that, as expected, the *at-least-two* reading actually *can* be maintained in DE-contexts, with the appropriate intonation pattern:

(61) Jack may have read *one* book; but I don't think he has read book*s*.

If all this is correct, it means that the implicature generated by plural morphology is obligatory (which is why (58) is contradictory in every context). As mentioned, this cannot be captured under neo-Gricean assumptions but can be made to follow from a grammatical theory that incorporates the operator *O*. Specifically, under the grammatical theory, one can maintain that for plural morphology, in contrast with standard scalar items, alternatives are automatically activated. Once alternatives are active, they must be associated with the operator *O*. This operator yields the *more than one* interpretation for (58). However, once (58) is embedded under a downward entailing operator (e.g., ((59)), the stronger alternatives are now weaker, and the relevant implicatures can be eliminated.

While our discussion has been extremely sketchy (as promised), we hope that the nature of the argument is clear. Gricean implicatures must be optional/cancelable. But if implicatures are derived by a grammatical mechanism, they are optional only when the mechanism is optional, and that, in turn, may depend on various grammatical factors. A similar argument has been made in other domains. Most famously, Krifka (1995) has argued that negative polarity items are obligatorily associated with alternatives, and that these alternatives yield obligatory implicatures which account for their distributional properties. This argument has been developed by Chierchia (2004) to account for intervention effects (discussed in section 4.3 below) and has been extended to other polarity items in Chierchia (2006).

4.2 Encapsulation

Consider the oddness of the following:

(62) John has an even number of children. More specifically, he has 3 (children).

The source of the oddness is intuitively clear: the second sentence seems to contradict the first sentence. However, it is not trivial to account for the contradiction. The second sentence *John has 3 children* (henceforth just *3*) has an interpretation which is consistent with the first sentence, e.g., an interpretation consistent with John having exactly 4 children, which is, of course, an even number. So, why should the two sentences feel contradictory? If in the context of (62), *3* was required to convey the information that John has exactly 3 children, the contradiction would be accounted for. But what could force this "exactly" interpretation on the sentence?

It is tempting to suggest that the theory of SIs should play a role in the account. If in (62) the implicature is obligatory, then the second sentence would contradict the first. And indeed, as we see in (63), and as we've already seen in the previous sub-section, there are some cases where implicatures are obligatory:

(63) Speaker A: Do you know how many children John has?
Speaker B: Yes, he has 4 children. #In fact, he has 5.

However, it turns out that the Gricean reasoning that has been proposed to account for SIs does not derive the attested contradiction. This is a point that was made in a different context by Heim (1991), and was discussed with reference to (62) and similar examples in Fox (2004) and most extensively in Magri (2009). To understand the argument, it is useful to try to derive the SI, along the lines outlined in section 1, and to see where things break down.

So, let's try. Upon hearing the utterance of 3, the addressee (h, for hearer) considers the alternative sentences in (64), and wonders why the speaker, s, did not use them to come up with alternative utterances.

(64) a. More specifically, he has 4 children.
b. More specifically, he has 5 children.
c. ...

Since all these (clearly relevant) alternatives are stronger than s's actual utterance, h concludes based on (the assumption that s obeys) the Maxim of Quantity that s does not believe any of these alternatives. i.e., s derives the conclusions in (65), which together with the basic utterance, 3, can be summarized as (66).

(65) a. $\neg B_s$(John has 4 children).
b. $\neg B_s$(John has 5 children).
c. ...

(66) O_{ALT} [B_s(John has 3 children)].

Now, based on the assumption that s is opinionated with respect to the alternatives in (64), h might take 'the epistemic step' (tantamount to 'neg-raising'), which leads to the conclusions in (67), summarized in (68).

(67) a. $B_s\neg$(John has 4 children).
b. $B_s\neg$(John has 5 children).
c. ...

(68) $B_s[O_{ALT}$ (John has 3 children)].

This conclusion clearly contradicts the first sentence in (62), thus, accounting for the observed phenomenon. We thus seem to have a purely neo-Gricean account of the deviance of (62). But this impression is mistaken, as the following illustrates.

The problem is that we were too quick to derive the conclusions in (65) based on the Maxim of Quantity. It is true that all of the utterances in (64) are *logically* stronger than 3, but are they all also *more informative*, given the special properties of the immediate context? To answer this question we have to understand what is taken to be true at the point at which 3 is uttered (i.e., after the first sentence in ((62)). If the first sentence in (62) is already taken to be true, i.e., if it is assumed that John has an even number of children, the proposition that John has at least 3 children (the relevant meaning of *3*), and the proposition that John has at least 4 children (the relevant meaning of (64a)) provide *exactly the same information*, namely that John has an even number of children greater or equal to three, i.e., that he has 4 or more children.

So, the Maxim of Quantity does not require s to prefer (64a) to 3. Therefore, the inference in (65a) does *not* follow from the assumption that s obeys the maxim. Moreover, since (65a) and the second sentence in (62), which uses the number 3, convey exactly the same information, they are predicted to yield exactly the same SI, which together with the basic contextual meanings amounts to the proposition that John has an even number of children greater or equal to 3, but does not have an even number of children greater or equal to 5, which is, of course, tantamount to saying that John has exactly 4 children. So the only implicature we get by employing this purely Gricean reasoning fails to make (62) incoherent.

In other words, on closer scrutiny, it turns out that we fail to account for the contradictory nature of (62). The Gricean reasoning predicts that (62) will be just as appropriate as the following:

(69) John has an even number of children. More specifically, he has 4 children.

This is in sharp contrast with what happens if SIs are derived within the grammar, using the operator O. Under such a view, the contradiction is derived straightforwardly. The sentence 3 activates alternatives which are operated on by O 'blindly', as it were, and when this happens we obtain the proposition that John has exactly 3 children, and this proposition directly contradicts the earlier sentence which asserts that John has an even number of children.

To couch it differently, what (62) seems to teach us is that the notion of informativity relevant to SI computation is logical entailment, rather than entailment given contextual knowledge. This means that the module that computes SIs has to be encapsulated from contextual knowledge, which makes sense if the module is (part of) grammar but not if it is (part of) a "central system" used for general reasoning about the world, as Grice envisioned. For further arguments to this effect, see Fox & Hackl (2006) and in particular Magri (2009).

As various examples in Magri (2009) illustrate, our argument does not specifically rely on the use of numerals, which we selected here to simplify the exposition. The general point can be made with other scalar items, even though one has to construct more complicated discourses, such as the following:

(70) Every student, including Jack, solved either none of the problems or all of the problems. #Jack solved some of the problems.

In this case, the second sentence, under its non-strengthened, logical meaning, is compatible with the first (and contextually entails that Jack solved all of the problems). Yet it is felt as contradictory. So even if numerals only had an 'exact' meaning, as suggested by Breheny (2008), our general point would remain.

4.3 Negative polarity items and intervention effects

Negative Polarity Items (NPIs) (e.g., *any*) are generally licensed in downward entailing contexts (Ladusaw 1979, Fauconnier 1975a). However, as pointed out by Linebarger (1987), certain logical operators appear to disrupt this licensing:

(71) a. John didn't introduce Mary$_1$ to anyone she$_1$ knows
b. *John didn't introduce [every woman]$_1$ to anyone she$_1$ knows.

This intervention effect has been studied extensively in the literature. Among the important observations that have come out of this study is a typology of the logical operators that yield an intervention effects, henceforth intervening operators (cf., among others, Linebarger 1987; Guerzoni 2004, 2006). Compare (71b) to (72), and (73a) to (73b).

(72) John didn't introduce [a single woman]$_1$ to anyone she$_1$ knows

(73) a. John didn't talk either to Mary or to any other girl.
b. *John didn't talk both to Mary and to any other girl.

This comparison leads to the conclusion that existential quantification and disjunction do not yield intervention affects, but universal quantification and conjunction do (Guerzoni 2004, 2006). Why should this be the case? Chierchia (2004) suggests that the answer follows from the theory of SIs. We cannot go over the details of the proposal but we can introduce the basic idea. Assume first that licensing of NPIs requires them to be in a DE context. Assume, furthermore, that

SIs are obligatorily factored into the meaning of (71)–(73) (i.e., that we are here in presence of obligatory SIs, just like in the examples considered in section 4.1). It can be shown that SIs in (71)a, (72) and (73)a do not affect the DE character of the context, wheareas they do in (71b) and (73b). Thus, in these latter cases, we no longer have DE contexts once SIs are factored in and hence the condition for the proper licensing of NPIs is not met.

To see how SIs could affect downward entailingness, consider the relationship between the sentences in (74).

(74) a. John didn't talk both to students and professors
b. John didn't talk both to students and physics professors

(74a) entails (74b) as long as their potential scalar implicatures are not taken into account. But otherwise, this is no longer the case. The reason for this is that (74a) triggers the SI that the stronger alternative with disjunction – (75a) below–is false, namely the implicature that the speaker talked either to students or to professors. If we factor SIs into basic meanings (deriving *strengthened meanings*), (74a) no longer entails (74b): in a situation where John talked to two biology professors and to no one else, (74a) is true on its strengthened meaning but (74b), while true on its weak meaning, is false on its strengthened meaning. In other words, there is no entailment between the sentences in (74), if they receive the syntactic parse in (74)'.

(74)' a. O_{ALT}[John didn't talk both to students and to professors].
b. O_{ALT}[John didn't talk both to students and to physics professors].

The situation in (75) is very different. (75a) has no SIs, because the alternative with conjunction – (74a) – is a weaker alternative and is therefore not excluded by any of the approaches to SIs.

(75) a. John didn't talk to students or to professors.
b. John didn't talk to students or to physics professors.

So, even if (75) received a parse with *O*, parallel to (74)', this will not interfere with downward-entailingness:

(75)' a. O_{ALT}[John didn't talk both to students or to professors].
b. O_{ALT}[John didn't talk both to students or to physics professors].

O is vacuous in (75)', and therefore does not affect the entailment between the (a) and the (b) sentence. In other words, if *O* is inserted above negation, the NPI in

(73b) is no longer in a downward entailing environment, while in (73b) downward entailment is not affected.

The same applies, arguably, to all interveners. For example, we can make sense of the fact that universal quantifiers are interveners but existential quantifiers are not. Existential quantifiers, in contrast to universal quantifiers, are the lowest members of their scale. Existential quantifiers and universal quantifiers form a Horn scale in which the universal is the logically strong member. Since, strength is reversed under downward entailing operators, universal quantifiers lead to matrix implicatures when embedded under such operators and existential quantifiers do not. The relevant implicatures, in turn, destroy downward entailingness, thus yielding the intervention effect.

But of course, none of this can work if SI are computed outside grammar. Under such an architecture, there is no reason why they should affect the licensing of NPIs. Moreover, Chierchia shows that his account can work only under very specific assumptions about the effects of SIs on syntactic intervention effects. If there is something to the account, SIs clearly must be computed within grammar.

4.4 Free choice

An utterance of the sentence in (76) is typically interpreted as a license to choose freely between two available options (the free choice inference, henceforth Free Choice).

(76) You are allowed to eat cake or ice cream.
There is at least one allowed world where you eat cake or ice cream.

More specifically, (76) licenses the two inference in (77).

(77) Free Choice (inference of ((76))
  a. You are allowed to eat cake.
     There is at least one allowed world where you eat cake.
  b. You are allowed to eat ice cream.
     There is at least one allowed world where you eat ice cream.

Free Choice, however, does not follow in any straightforward way from the basic meaning of the sentences. (76) – which contains two logical operators: the existential modal *allowed* and the disjunction *or* – should express the proposition that the disjunction holds in at least one of the allowed worlds [$\Diamond(C \lor IC)$]. And, the truth of this proposition does not guarantee that for each disjunct there is an allowed world in which the disjunct is true. [◊(C ∨IC) ≠> ◊(C) ∧ ◊(IC).]

Kamp (1973), who identified the puzzle, suggested that it be resolved by strengthening the basic semantics of the construction and a solution along such lines has been worked out also in Zimmermann (2000) and Geurts (2005) (see also Simons 2005). However, Kratzer & Shimoyama (2002) – henceforth K&S – and Alonso-Ovalle (2005) pointed out that such a revision would get the wrong result when the construction is embedded in a downward entailing environment:

(78) No one is allowed to eat cake or ice cream

If (76) – as part of its basic meaning – were to entail Free Choice, we would expect (78) to be true if one of the free choice inferences in (77) were false for every individual in the domain (e.g., if half the people were allowed to eat cake the other half were allowed to eat ice cream, but no one was free to choose between the two desserts). But (78) seems to express a much stronger proposition, namely that no one is allowed to eat cake and that no one is allowed to eat ice cream.

We've already seen this pattern in section 4.1, namely an inference that appears when a sentence is uttered in isolation, but is not incorporated into its meaning when the sentence is further embedded in a downward entailing environment. We've also seen that this otherwise puzzling pattern would follow straightforwardly if the inference could be derived as an SI. In the case of Free Choice, K&S suggest that the inference should follow from a reasoning process about the belief state of the speaker that one might call meta-implicature (see also, e.g., Schulz (2005), Klinedinst (2006), Chemla (2008), for related proposals).

Specifically, K&S suggest that the sentences in (76) has the alternatives given in (79) below, for which we've argued on independent grounds in section 3.

(79) Alternatives for (76) proposed by K&S/Alonso-Ovalle:
   a. You are allowed to eat the cake.
   b. You are allowed to eat the ice cream.

Furthermore, they suggest that when a hearer h interprets s's utterance of (76), h needs to understand why s preferred (76) to the two alternatives. K&S, furthermore, suggest that it is reasonable for h to conclude that s did not choose the alternative because she was not happy with their strong meaning (basic meaning + implicatures) – hence our term meta-implicature. Specifically, K&S suggest that h would attribute s's choice to the belief that the strong meanings of (79a) and (79b) (stated in (80)) are both false.

(80) Strong meaning of the alternatives for (76)
   a. You are allowed to eat the cake and you are not allowed to eat the ice cream.
   b. You are allowed to eat the ice cream and you are not allowed to eat the cake.

And, as the reader can verify, if (76) is true and the strengthened alternatives in (80) are both false, then the Free Choice inferences in (77) have to be true.

We believe this logic is basically correct, but we don't see a way to derive it from basic principles of communication (Maxims). In fact, if s believed that the Free Choice inferences hold, the Maxim of Quantity would have forced s to prefer the sentences in (79) and to avoid an utterance of (76) altogether. The fact that s did not avoid (76) should, therefore, lead h to the conclusion that s does not believe that the sentences in (79) are true (see our discussion in section 1.1.).

This has led Chierchia (2006) and Fox (2007) to provide a formal/grammatical alternative to K&S. We cannot go over the details of the proposals, but would like to point out Fox's observation, namely that K&S's results follow from a representation in which two instances of the operator, O, are appended to (76):

(81) Alternatives for a logical form for (76) that derives Free Choice:
O[O(You are allowed to eat cake or ice cream)].
There is at least one allowed world where you eat cake or ice cream.
And (80)a,b, are both false.

So while there are reasons to believe that free choice effects can be explained in a principled way as meta- (or higher order) implicatures (Spector 2007a, which we briefly discussed in subsection 4.1, also makes use of higher-order implicatures) and while the basic idea might seem at first compatible with a Gricean system, working it out turns out to be in conflict with the basic maxims. Furthermore, Chierchia (2006) further develops this logic arguing that constraints on the relevant grammatical representations yields an account of the cross-linguistic distribution of Free Choice items. If these proposals are anywhere close to the mark, then clearly implicatures must be part of grammar

4.5 Non-monotonic contexts: negating alternatives that are neither stronger nor weaker

Consider the following sentence:

(82) Exactly one student solved some of the problems

Let's assume that (82)'s only scalar alternative is (83).

(83) Exactly one student solved all of the problems

(83) is neither stronger nor weaker than (82): both sentences can be true in a situation where the other is false. Since (83) is not more informative than (82), Grice's maxim of quantity, under its most natural understanding, does not require that one utter (83) rather than (82) even when both are believed to be true and relevant. So the Gricean approach, unless supplemented with quite specific assumptions, predicts no SI in the case of (82). In contrast to this, a theory that incorporates the exhaustivity operator, which is modeled on the semantics of *only*, does predict an implicature for (82) when the exhaustivitiy operator takes matrix scope (it also predicts the possibility of an embedded implicature under the scope of *exactly one*, as discussed in section 2.2).

Indeed, applying the exhaustivity operator to a given sentence S with alternatives ALT(S) generally returns the conjunction of S and of the negations of all the alternatives of S that are not entailed by S (modulo the modification we have introduced above in order to reach a correct treatment of disjunctive sentences), which include both alternatives that are stronger than S and possibly alternatives that are neither stronger nor weaker than S. So the meaning of (82) (under the parse O(*Exactly one student solved some of the problems*)) is predicted to be the proposition expressed in (84a) which is equivalent to (84b) (Note that the fact that exactly one student solved at least one problem entails that no student except one solved any problem at all):

(84) a. Exactly one student solved at least one of the problems and it is false that exactly one student solved all of the problems
b. There is a student *x* who solved at least one of the problems, no student except *x* solved any problem, and *x* did not solve all of the problems.

It seems to us that this prediction is borne out: (84a), which is equivalent to (84b), is indeed a very natural interpretation for (82). The fact that implicature computation seems to involve the negation of non-stronger alternatives is quite unexpected from the Gricean perspective, unless further assumptions are made (for instance the assumption that the set of alternatives of any sentence is closed under conjunction, cf. Van Rooij & Schulz 2004, 2006 and Spector 2003, 2006, 2007b; see Fox 2007 for an argument against this assumption).

4.6 Constraints on the placement of the exhaustivity operator

We have observed that a hallmark of SIs is that they tend to disappear in downward-entailing environments – i.e., the strengthened reading of scalar items is dispreferred under, say, negation or in the restrictor of a universal quantifier. At first sight, this phenomenon makes the pragmatic, neo-Gricean, account of SIs particularly appealing: indeed, as we have seen, the absence of the strengthened reading in DE contexts is directly predicted by the neo-Gricean perspective.

However, as we pointed out in section 2, the strengthened meaning of a scalar item is actually not entirely ruled out in DE contexts; it is only dispreferred. From a purely Gricean perspective, it is a challenge to explain why a scalar item could ever be interpreted under its strengthened meaning in a DE context (so called 'intrusive implicatures'). To account for such cases, advocates of the purely pragmatic perspective are forced to introduce new mechanisms, such as a mechanism of metalinguistic negation, which then has to be generalized (cf. Horn 1989) to other operators (but if our previous arguments are conclusive, these 'repairs' are anyway unable to account for the full range of phenomena). The grammatical view does not face a similar challenge; but it clearly needs to be supplemented with some principles that determine which particular readings are preferred and which ones are dispreferred (and hence marked).

One possibility that suggests itself is that, when a sentence is potentially ambiguous, there is a preference for the strongest possible interpretation. Such a general principle has been suggested independently by various researchers beginning with Dalrymple et al. (1998) – the 'strongest meaning hypothesis'. If a principle of this sort is adopted, then inserting O in a DE context would be dispreferred: indeed, for any sentence S, O(S) is stronger than S; hence, inserting O(S) in the (immediate) scope of a DE operator X, i.e., an operator that reverses logical strength, gives rise to a sentence X(O(S)) that is now *weaker* than what would have resulted if O were absent, i.e., weaker than X(S).

How exactly such a principle should be stated is far from trivial. Given our general perspective, it should state that a Logical Form S in which O occur is dispreferred in case S is a-symmetrically entailed by some well-defined competitor S'. That is, we have to define, for any such S, its *comparison class*. One possibility we will briefly consider is the following: an occurrence of the exhaustivity operator is dispreferred if and only if it gives rise to a reading that is weaker than what would have resulted in its absence.

(85) Strongest Meaning Hypothesis

Let S be a sentence of the form $[_S \ldots O(X) \ldots]$. Let S' be the sentence of the form $[_{S'} \ldots X \ldots]$, i.e., the one that is derived from S by replacing O(X) with X, i.e. by eliminating this particular occurrence of O. Then, everything else being equal, S' is preferred to S if S' is logically stronger than S.

(85) predicts that O should be dispreferred under DE-operators. However, it does not predict any preference between matrix exhaustification and embedded exhaustification in UE-contexts. This can be illustrated by the following example:

(86) For this class, we must read most of the books on the reading list

An exhaustivity operator could be inserted either above or below the modal *must*, giving rise to the following readings:

(87) a. O(we must read most of the books on the reading list)
 = we must read most of the books on the reading list and we don't have to read all of then
 b. We must O(read most of the books on the reading list)
 = we must read most of the books on the reading list and we have the obligation no to read them all

(87b) a-symmetrically entails (87a). Yet the principle in (85) does not predict that (87b) should be preferred to (87a) (or the other way around). This is so because according to (85), (87a) and (87b) do not belong to each other's comparison classes. Rather, each of them is to be compared to the proposition that one gets be deleting the operator, namely to the non-strengthened reading of 'We must read *Ulysses* or *Madame Bovary*". Plainly, the condition stated in (85) is met in both cases, since in both cases the presence of O has a strengthening effect, and so no preference is predicted. More generally, in UE contexts, (85) does not favor one particular insertion site for the exhaustivity operator. Of course, more general considerations (such as, for instance, the plausibility of a given reading) might create a preference for certain readings.

5 Concluding remarks

In this article we tried to show that SIs can occur in all sorts of embedded context. If this attempt has been successful, we think it calls for a reassessment of the semantics/pragmatics interface. In order to establish our point, we have adopted the view that implicatures arise through a silent exhaustification operator, akin to *only*, which acts on scalar alternatives. We think that the idea – while leaving many open issues – has significant benefits: in many cases (involving Hurford's Constraint, iterated applications of O, etc.) it makes just the right predictions.

The grammatical view of SIs retains the most beautiful feature of the Gricean insight: the sensitivity of SIs to embeddings within polarity affecting contexts. And, through the link to alternative sensitive operators, this view also creates a powerful bridge to a host of like phenomena occurring in very diverse corners of grammars (from the analysis of plurals, through free choice, to intervention and the like). Within the limits of the present article, these remain largely promissory notes. But we hope that we were able to lay out the strategy that needs to be pursued in a fairly clear manner. Finally, we hope that it will be possible begin to reap additional benefits from the entrance of SIs (and of, possibly, implicatures of other sorts) into the computational system of grammar.

We would like to thank participants in various classes, colloquia and seminars in which this work was presented (by at least one of us), in particular Columbia University (2008), Institut Jean-Nicod (2008), the LSA summer institute (2005), University of Georgetown (2006), LOGOS (Barcelona 2008), Harvard-MIT seminar in semantics (2006), MIT-Paris workshop in linguistics (2007), and the University of Vienna (2009). Special thanks to Emmanuel Chemla, Irene Heim, Maribel Romero, Daniel Rothschild and Philippe Schlenker.

6 References

Alonso-Ovalle, Luis 2005. Distributing the disjuncts over the modal space. In: L. Baterman & C. Ussery (eds.). *Proceedings of the North Eastern Linguistic Society (= NELS) 35.* Amherst, MA: GLSA, 75–86.

Atlas, Jay D. & Stephen Levinson 1981. *It*-clefts, informativeness, and logical form: Radical pragmatics (revised standard version). In: P. Cole (ed.). *Radical Pragmatics.* New York: Academic Press, 1–61.

Breheny, Richard 2008. A new look at the semantics and pragmatics of numerically quantified noun phrases. *Journal of Semantics* 25, 93–140.

Carnap, Rudolf 1950. *Logical Foundations of Probability.* Chicago, IL: The University of Chicago Press.

Carston, Robyn 1988. Implicature, explicature, and truth-theoretic semantics. In: R. Kempson (ed.). *Mental Representations: The Interface Between Language and Reality.* Cambridge: Cambridge University Press, 155–181.

Chemla, Emmanuel 2008. *Présuppositions et implicatures scalaires. Etudes formelles et expérimentales.* Ph.D. dissertation. Ecole des Hautes Etudes en Sciences Sociales, Paris.

Chierchia, Gennaro 2004. Scalar implicatures, polarity phenomena, and the syntax/pragmatics interface. In: A. Belletti (ed.). *Structures and Beyond 3.* Oxford: Oxford University Press, 39–103.

Chierchia, Gennaro 2006. Broaden your views. Implicatures of domain widening and the "logicality" of language. *Linguistic Inquiry* 37, 535–590.

Chierchia, Gennaro, Danny Fox & Benjamin Spector 2009. Hurford's constraint and the theory of scalar implicatures. In: P. Egré & G. Magri (eds.). *Presuppositions and Implicatures. Proceedings of the MIT-Paris Workshop* (MIT Working Papers in Linguistics 60). Cambridge, MA: MIT, 47–62.

Dalrymple, Mary, Makoto Kanazawa, Yookyung Kim, Sam Mchombo & Paul S. Peters 1998. Reciprocal expressions and the concept of reciprocity. *Linguistics & Philosophy* 21, 159–210.

Davis, Wayne 1998. *Implicature: Intention, Convention, and Principle in the Failure of Gricean Theory*. Cambridge: Cambridge University Press.
Davis, Wayne 2005. Implicature. In: E.N. Zalta (ed.). *The Stanford Encyclopedia of Philosophy (Summer 2005 Edition)*. http://plato.stanford.edu/entries/implicature/, February 26, 2012.
Ducrot, Oswald 1973. *La preuve et le dire*. Paris: Mame.
Fauconnier, Gilles 1975a. Polarity and the scale principle. In: R. Grossman, L. San & T. Vance (eds.). *Papers form the Eleventh Regional Meeting of the Chicago Linguistic Society (= CLS)*. Chicago, IL: Chicago Linguistic Society, 188–199.
Fauconnier, Gilles 1975b. Pragmatic scales and logical structure. *Linguistic Inquiry* 6, 353–376.
Fox, Danny 2004. *Implicatures and Exhaustivity*. Lecture notes (Class 4: Back to the Theory of Implicatures, University of Southern California, November 2004). http://web.mit.edu/linguistics/people/faculty/fox/class_4.pdf, February 26, 2012.
Fox, Danny 2007. Free choice disjunction and the theory of scalar implicatures. In: U. Sauerland & P. Stateva (eds.). *Presupposition and Implicature in Compositional Semantics*. New York: Palgrave Macmillan, 71–120.
Fox, Danny & Martin Hackl 2006. The universal density of measurement. *Linguistics & Philosophy* 29, 537–586.
Fox, Danny & Roni Katzir 2009. On the characterization of alternatives for implicature and for focus. In: P. Egré & G. Magri (eds.). *Presuppositions and Implicatures. Proceedings of the MIT-Paris Workshop* (= MIT Working Papers in Linguistics 60). Cambridge, MA: MIT, 101–110.
Gamut, L. T. F. 1991. *Logic, Language, and Meaning*. Chicago, IL: The University of Chicago Press.
Gazdar, Gerald 1979. *Pragmatics: Implicature, Presupposition and Logical Form*. New York: Academic Press.
Geurts, Bart 2005. Entertaining alternatives: Disjunctions as modals. *Natural Language Semantics* 13, 383–410.
Geurts, Bart 2009. Scalar implicature and local pragmatics. *Mind & Language* 24, 51–79.
Grice, Paul 1989. *Studies in the Way of Words*. Cambridge, MA: Harvard University Press.
Groenendijk, Jeroen & Martin Stokhof 1984. *Studies on the Semantics of Questions and the Pragmatics of Answers*. Ph.D. dissertation. University of Amsterdam.
Groenendijk, Jeroen & Martin Stokhof 1990. *Partitioning Logical Space*. Annotated handout for the *European Summer School in Language, Logic and Computation (= ESSLI)*, Leuven, August 1990. http://staff.science.uva.nl/~stokhof/pls.pdf, February 26, 2012.
Guerzoni, Elena 2000. Towards a movement-based account of the locality constraints on negative polarity items. In: C. Czinglar et al. (eds.). *Proceedings of the Conference of the Student Organisation of Linguistics in Europe (= CONSOLE) 8*, Leiden: SOLE, Leiden University, 125–138.
Guerzoni, Elena 2004. Even-{NPI}s in yes/no questions. *Natural Language Semantics* 12, 319–343.
Guerzoni, Elena 2006. Intervention effects on NPIs and feature movement: Towards a unified account of intervention. *Natural Language Semantics* 14, 359–398.
Heim, Irene 1991. Artikel und Definitheit. In: A. v. Stechow & D. Wunderlich (eds.). *Semantik – Semantics. Ein internationales Handbuch der zeitgenössischen Forschung – An International Handbook of Contemporary Research* (HSK 6). Berlin: de Gruyter, 487–535.
Hirschberg, Julia 1985. *A Theory of Scalar Implicature*. Ph.D. dissertation. University of Pennsylvania, Philadelphia, PA.

Horn, Larry 1972. *On the Semantic Properties of Logical Operators in English*. Ph.D. dissertation. University of California, Los Angeles, CA.
Horn, Larry 1985. Metalinguistic negation and pragmatic ambiguity. *Language* 61, 121–174.
Horn, Larry 1989. *A Natural History of Negation*. Chicago, IL: The University of Chicago Press.
Horn, Larry 2006. The border wars: A neo-Gricean perspective. In: T. Turner & K. von Heusinger (eds.). *Where Semantics meets Pragmatics*. Amsterdam: Elsevier, 21–48.
Hurford, James 1974. Exclusive or inclusive disjunction. *Foundation of Language* 11, 409–411.
Kamp, Hans 1973. Free choice permission. *Proceedings of the Aristotelian Society* 74, 57–74.
Katzir, Roni 2007. Structurally-defined alternatives. *Linguistics & Philosophy* 30, 669–690.
Klinedinst, Nathan 2006. *Plurality and Possibility*. Ph.D. dissertation. University of California, Los Angeles, CA.
Kratzer, Angelika & Junko Shimoyama 2002. Indeterminate pronouns: The view from Japanese. In: Y. Otsu (ed.). *Proceedings of the Tokyo Conference on Psycholinguistics 3*. Tokyo: Hituzi Syobo, 1–25.
Krifka, Manfred 1993. Focus and presupposition in dynamic interpretation. *Journal of Semantics* 10, 269–300.
Krifka, Manfred 1995. The semantics and pragmatics of polarity items. *Linguistic Analysis* 25, 209–257.
Kroch, Anthony 1972. Lexical and inferred meanings for some time adverbs. *Quarterly Progress Reports of the Research Laboratory of Electronics* 104, 260–267.
van Kuppevelt, Jan 1996. Inferring from topics: Scalar implicatures as topic dependent inferences. *Linguistics & Philosophy* 19, 393–443.
Ladusaw, Bill 1979. *Polarity Sensitivity as Inherent Scope Relations*. Ph.D. dissertation. University of Texas, Austin, TX.
Landman, Fred 1998. Plurals and maximalization. In: S. Rothstein (ed.). *Events and Grammar*. Dordrecht: Kluwer, 237–272.
Levinson, Stephen C. 1983. *Pragmatics*. Cambridge: Cambridge University Press.
Levinson, Stephen C. 2000. *Presumptive Meaning*. Cambridge, MA: The MIT Press.
Lewis, David 1973. *Counterfactuals*. Oxford: Blackwell.
Linebarger, Marcia 1987. Negative polarity and grammatical representation. *Linguistics & Philosophy* 10, 325–387.
Magri, Giorgio 2009. A theory of individual level predicates based on blind scalar implicatures. *Natural Language Semantics* 17, 245–297.
Matsumoto, Yo 1995. The conversational condition on Horn scales. *Linguistics & Philosophy* 18, 21–60.
Meier, Marie-Christine & Uli Sauerland 2008. A pragmatic constraint on ambiguity detection. *Natural Language and Linguistic Theory* 27, 139–150.
Récanati, François 2003. Embedded implicatures. *Philosophical Perspectives* 17, 1299–1332.
van Rooij, Robert & Kathrin Schulz 2004. Exhaustive interpretation of complex sentences. *Journal of Logic, Language and Information* 13, 491–519.
van Rooij, Robert & Kathrin Schulz 2006. Pragmatic meaning and non-monotonic reasoning: The case of exhaustive interpretation. *Linguistics & Philosophy* 29, 205–250.
Rooth, Mats 1985. *Association with Focus*. Ph.D. dissertation. University of Massachusetts, Amherst, MA.
Rooth, Mats 1992. A theory of focus interpretation. *Natural Language Semantics* 1, 117–121.
Russell, Benjamin 2006. Against grammatical computation of scalar implicatures. *Journal of Semantics* 23, 361–382.

Sauerland, Uli 2003. A new semantics for number. In: R. Young & Y. Zhou (eds.). *Proceedings of Semantics and Linguistic Theory (= SALT) XIII*, Ithaca, NY: Cornell University, 258–275.

Sauerland, Uli 2004. Scalar implicatures in complex sentences. *Linguistics & Philosophy* 27, 367–391.

Schulz, Kathrin 2005. A pragmatic solution for the paradox of free choice permission. *Synthese* 147, 343–377.

Simons, Mandy 2005. Dividing things up: The semantics of *or* and the modal/*or* interaction. *Natural Language Semantics* 13, 271–316.

Singh, Raj 2008. On the interpretation of disjunction: Asymmetric, incremental, and eager for inconsistency. *Linguistics & Philosophy* 31, 245–260.

Soames, Scott 1982. How presuppositions are inherited: A solution to the projection problem. *Linguistic Inquiry* 13, 483–545.

Spector, Benjamin 2003. Scalar implicatures: Exhaustivity and Gricean reasoning. In: B. ten Cate (ed.). *Proceedings of the European Summer School in Logic, Language and Information Student Session (= ESSLLI Student Session) 8*. Vienna, Austria, 277–288. http://users.soe.ucsc.edu/~btencate/esslli03/stus2003proc.pdf, May 8, 2011.

Spector, Benjamin 2006. *Aspects de la pragmatique des opérateurs logiques*. Ph.D. dissertation. Université Paris 7.

Spector, Benjamin 2007a. Aspects of the pragmatics of plural morphology. In: U. Sauerland & P. Stateva (eds.). *Presupposition and Implicature in Compositional Semantics*. New York: Palgrave Macmillan, 243–281.

Spector, Benjamin 2007b. Scalar implicatures: Exhaustivity and Gricean reasoning. In: M. Aloni, A. Butler & P. Dekker (eds.). *Questions in Dynamic Semantics*. Amsterdam: Elsevier, 225–249.

Sperber, Dan & Deirdre Wilson 1986. *Relevance: Communication and Cognition*. Oxford: Blackwell.

Stalnaker, Robert 1968. A theory of conditionals. In: N. Rescher (ed.). *Studies in Logical Theory*. Oxford: Blackwell, 98–112.

Zimmermann, Thomas E. 2000. Free choice disjunction and epistemic possibility. *Natural Language Semantics* 8, 255–290.

Katarzyna M. Jaszczolt
11 Semantics/pragmatics boundary disputes

1   Sentences, utterances, and truth conditions —— 368
2   The pragmatic wastebasket: Grice on *what is said* and *what is implicated* —— 370
3   Redrawing the boundary —— 376
4   Delimiting implicatures —— 383
5   Minimalism, contextualism, and beyond —— 394
6   Summary: The significance of the boundary disputes —— 397
7   References —— 398

Abstract: The boundary between semantics and pragmatics has been the subject of heated debates, most notably in post-Gricean theories of meaning and communication. I present a survey of the standpoints on the boundary issue beginning with Grice's distinction between what is said and what is implicated, through various attempts at redrawing the boundary towards a version of the contextualist stance in which the truth-conditional content of the utterance is enriched in a way that reflects the speaker's intentions and the addressee's intuitions about what is said. I acknowledge the role of radical pragmatics in the 1970s in putting forward the idea of semantic underdetermination and move on to discussing the most influential concepts and approaches in post-Gricean accounts. I present some differences between contextualist accounts, mainly with respect to the acceptance or rejection of unarticulated constituents, and place contextualism in the wider perspective of the debate concerning the scope of semantic content, ranging from the minimalist accounts (Borg, Cappelen & Lepore, Bach) to the late Wittgensteinian view of so-called meaning eliminativism. I conclude with a brief discussion on the significance of the boundary disputes.

1 Sentences, utterances, and truth conditions

Truth-conditional semantics is at present the best developed approach to sentence meaning, benefiting from high predictive power, formal rigour, and intuitive plausibility in that it associates sentence meaning with the truth and falsity understood as correspondence with eventualities in a model. But there are some aspects of meaning that go beyond the meaning of sentences so understood. For example, while the sentential connective *and* in English acquires a truth-conditional analysis that is founded on the properties of its formal equivalent of conjunction in propositional logic, it is evident that English *and* conveys more than its formal equivalent does. Sentence (1) should be true when both conjuncts are true and its truth value should be resistant to the change in the order of the conjuncts as in (1a).

(1)   The janitor left the door open and the prisoner escaped.
(1a) The prisoner escaped and the janitor left the door open.

It is clear, however, that (1a) is not as felicitous as (1). In fact, according to the judgment of many native speakers of English, it is plainly false as a description of the situation depicted in (1). This shows that there is more to the meaning of *and* than the straightforward conjunction of two phrases. In (1) and (1a), *and* also conveys the consequential meaning *as a result*, as in (1b).

(1b) The janitor left the door open *and as a result* the prisoner escaped.

Alternatively, we can surmise that it is not the connective *and* that is responsible for the meaning of consequence but rather the very juxtaposition of the description of two events: leaving the door open and the prisoner's escaping. Be that as it may, there is more to the meaning of (1) than the truth-conditional analysis of the sentence reveals. The translation into the metalanguage of first-order logic leaves the consequence relation between the clauses unaccounted for.

It seems that in addition to the analysis of the structure of the sentence and the encoded lexical content attended to in standard truth-conditional analysis, we have to look for information about meaning that comes from other sources. The most important of these sources is the context of utterance, understood broadly as the background knowledge of the interlocutors, information conveyed in other parts of the conversation or written text (co-text), as well as the baggage of world experience brought to the situation of discourse by the interlocutors. But we can only bring this information in when we agree to alter the object of study of the theory of meaning to something more intuitively appealing and useful than an abstract unit of a sentence. The speaker and the addressee attend to the meaning of the *utterance*: the real, concrete unit of meaning that carries some information content through the words used, the structure, the exact placement in the structure of the conversation, the additional senses it brings to mind in the particular context, the immersion in the overall system of gestures and other ways of conveying meaning, and so forth.

Examples that testify to the importance of the extra-sentential means of conveying information are ample. Deictic expressions such as pronouns and demonstrative noun phrases rely on the context of utterance to convey meaning. In fact, they even rely on the context in order to make a contribution to the sentence that would make this sentence truth-evaluable. Definite descriptions such as 'the best Austrian novelist' are also dependent on the context in their interpretation: they can refer to a particular individual (say, for me, it is Robert Musil and I can make it clear in the conversation that when I use this description I indeed mean Robert Musil) or they can be used attributively, to mean whoever happens to be the best Austrian novelist. Once a truth-conditional semanticist has recognised the importance of these extra-sentential factors and contemplated the alteration of the object of study from the sentence to the utterance, and from sentence meaning to the speaker's meaning, he/she has two options to choose from: either to (i) reject truth-conditional semantics and look for an alternative theory, or (ii) try to preserve truth-conditional semantics and adapt it to the new object of study. Let us assume that our semanticist is a devoted supporter of the methods of truth-conditional semantics and opts for the latter solution. At this juncture he/she is faced with two options again: either (ii.a) to advocate that there is more to meaning than truth conditions alone and allow for a pragmatic overlay to the thereby saved semantic theory, or (ii.b) to propose that pragmatic factors contribute to the truth-conditional content and 'shift' the truth-conditional analysis from sentences to utterances. The latter avenue opens up the option of adding information about meaning that comes from sources other than the lexicon and the structure.

Let us now see what actually happened in the history of the semantics/pragmatics interface, beginning with the philosopher who is generally recognised as the founder of modern pragmatic theory: Paul Grice. Grice pursued the path of preserving the truth-conditional analysis but was rather ambivalent as to the options (ii.a) and (ii.b) above: he allowed some pragmatic input in the truth-conditional content, while keeping most of it outside of this content. Needless to say, this kind of proposal had to generate a heated debate, a debate that is still at the forefront of theorising in semantics and pragmatics and that is still producing cutting edge analyses.

2 The pragmatic wastebasket: Grice on *what is said* and *what is implicated*

It is a common fact of conversation that speakers often mean more than they physically utter. They also often mean something different from what they actually utter. In the exchange in (2), speaker B communicates that Smith may in fact have a girlfriend, contrary to what A assumes:

(2) A: Smith doesn't seem to have a girlfriend these days.
    B: He has been paying a lot of visits to New York lately.

(from Grice 1975: 32). In order to retrieve the relevance of B's statement, one has to perform some basic inference. B's response is relevant and informative but not in virtue of the truth-conditional content of the sentence alone, but rather in virtue of what it implies (or, to use Grice's term, *implicates*) in this conversation. This implicated meaning, called a conversational implicature, is pragmatic through and through. The implicature 'Smith may have a girlfriend in New York' bears no structural resemblance to the sentence uttered by B, it is constructed by the addressee entirely on the basis of pragmatic inference.

Now, it seems that in the interest of shifting the object of study from sentence meaning to speaker's meaning we may have obliterated the differences in the understanding of the term 'meaning'. In order to clarify the term, we have to go to Grice's (1957) seminal paper 'Meaning' and look for the principles on which his notion of meaning is founded. Grice stresses that he is not interested in the instances of the so-called *natural meaning*, where meaning that p entails that it is the fact that p. 'These spots mean meningitis' is an example of the natural meaning: there is a natural connection between the symptom and the disease. Instead, he is interested in speaker's meaning which he calls *non-natural meaning* (meaning$_{NN}$). This meaning is conventional but not natural; it does not carry the strong requirement of entailment. Meaning$_{NN}$ will henceforth be the object of study in post-Gricean pragmatics, and also the object of the following discussion of the semantics/pragmatics interface in the remainder of this article. Grice defines this meaning by resorting to speaker's intentions and the recognition of these intentions by the addressee: "'A meant$_{NN}$ something by x' is roughly equivalent to 'A uttered x with the intention of inducing a belief by means of the recognition of this intention'." (Grice 1957: 219).

The role of intention, also stressed in the speech-act literature of that period (e.g. Austin 1962; Searle 1969), is further spelled out in Grice's 'Utterer's Meaning and Intentions' (1969):

"'U meant something by uttering x' is true iff [if and only if], for some audience A, U uttered x intending:
[1] A to produce a particular response r
[2] A to think (recognize) that U intends [1]
[3] A to fulfill [1] on the basis of his fulfillment of [2]" (Grice 1969: 92).

In some cases, the recognition of the speaker's intentions is short-circuited, so to speak, in that the response is secured because the meaning is so conventionalized in a language that conventions create a 'shortcut' through the recognition of the intentions. By a response Grice means here any physical or a cognitive reaction to the speaker's utterance, including an understanding of what was intended to be communicated. It also has to be stressed that by an 'utterance' he means any act of communication, not only a linguistic one. So, drawing a picture for the addressee or making clearly recognisable facial expressions such as a smile of approval or contempt are also subsumed under the category of an utterance. Bearing in mind this possibility of a conventional uptake, we can sum up that on this account communication is explained in terms of intentions and inferences. An intention to inform the addressee is fulfilled simply by the recognition of this intention by the addressee.

This intention-based theory of meaning lays the foundations for the theory of implicature in which Grice spells out the principles of a cooperative conversational behaviour. Most implicatures are considered to be meanings intended by the speaker but in the case of literary texts, for example poetry, the speaker or writer may intend to leave the range of plausible implicatures deliberately open (see also Davis 1998 on speaker's implicature vs. sentence implicature). *Nota bene*, originally, the term 'implicature' referred to the process of implicating some meaning, while the product was dubbed an 'implicatum' (plural: 'implicata'). In the post-Gricean literature, however, the Latin nominal has gone out of use and the term 'implicature' now serves to name the product of implicating. An utterance can give rise to a number of additional thoughts called implicatures.

In his theory of conversational behaviour, Grice (1975) makes the important assumptions that participants in a discourse are rational agents and that they are governed by principles of rational communicative behaviour. Their behaviour is predictable in the sense that meaning is implicated according to some principles of rationality. The umbrella term for this rationality is the Cooperative Principle:

> "Make your conversational contribution such as is required, at the stage at which it occurs, by the accepted purpose or direction of the talk exchange in which you are engaged."
> (Grice 1975: 26. See also Mill 1872: 517; Ducrot 1972: 134.)

Subsumed under this principle are particular so-called maxims of conversation, stating that the speaker's contribution is to be sufficiently but not overly informative (the maxims of quantity); that the contribution is to be true in the sense that the speaker has to say what he/she believes to be true and supported by sufficient evidence (the maxims of quality); that the contribution is to be relevant (the maxim of relation); and that the form of the contribution is to be clear (perspicuous): not obscure, ambiguous, excessively long, or reporting events in the wrong order (the maxims of manner). The exact content of the maxims will not concern us here, especially in view of the later developments of the theory in which it was demonstrated that there was a considerable overlap and redundancy among the maxims and that we could make do with fewer, perhaps two (Horn 1984, 1988, 2004), three (Levinson 1987, 1995, 2000 and section 4.5 below), or even one (Sperber & Wilson 1986 and section 4.2 below) principle instead (See Jaszczolt 2002: chapter 10 and Jaszczolt 2010a for an overview).

It has to be remembered that although Grice's maxims are formulated as if they were prescriptive laws, their raison d'être is to spell out the principles that the human mind naturally follows. Although it is possible to consciously disobey the maxims or even overtly opt out of them, the standard presumption in every conversation is that they do apply. In (3), which we can imagine to be an extract from a review of a piano recital, the implicature that the pianist was a bad one comes from the unnecessary prolixity with which information was conveyed.

(3) The pianist sat down at the instrument and hit the keys in a way resembling Chopin's nocturne in C minor.

Since the description of the performance is clearly more demanding on the reader's time and effort than just reading that the pianist played Chopin's nocturne in C minor, the reader rationally infers that there must be some implicated meaning to it such as that the performance was a particularly bad one. To sum up, implicatures can arise through observing or violating the maxims of conversation.

Implicatures are clearly pragmatic constructs: they are thoughts and do not have direct counterparts in sentences or in physical utterances. So, by the very nature of being inferred meanings, they have to be weaker than meanings of sentences or utterances. They are also weaker than deductive inferences of the type of *modus ponens* (if p then q; p; therefore: q). Implicatures are cancellable. We can always cancel the implicatures in (2) or (3) by adding (2a) and (3a) respectively.

(2a) But I don't mean to suggest that he has a girlfriend in New York. His company is based there and he is very busy commuting.

(3a) After a few bars, I realised it *was* Chopin's nocturne in C minor, played with unprecedented skill, insight and feeling.

We are now in a position to discuss and assess Grice's view on the boundary between semantics and pragmatics. The motivation behind the proposal of the cooperative principle and the maxims was to explain how expressions of a natural language differ in their properties from their translations in the metalanguage of first-order logic. The assumption was that the truth-conditional semantic analysis is to be preserved and the discrepancies are to be explained as a pragmatic overlay. But the boundary is not as clear-cut as it may seem. Firstly, words and structures can be ambiguous. In order to assign truth conditions to such constructions, they have to be disambiguated and this disambiguation is a pragmatic process. Next, there are context-dependent expressions such as personal and demonstrative pronouns and demonstrative noun phrases that do not pick out a referent on their own: the referent has to be assigned in a context, in a pragmatic process. Hence, Grice (1978) had to admit the output of such pragmatic processes into the truth-conditional part of meaning$_{NN}$. The remainder, what is implicated, is a graded category: some types of implicatures are closer in their characteristics to the semantic content than others. The implicatures in (2) and (3) are far removed from what is said in that they rely on the particular context: they are what Grice called particularized conversational implicatures (PCIs). But there are also implicatures that occur in virtue of the sentence alone: they are standard, normal predictions, or salient meanings, that arise independently of the context—unless, of course, the context makes it clear that they have to be cancelled or should not be computed. The implicature of (4) in (4a) is an example of such a generalized prediction, called by Grice a generalized conversational implicature (GCI).

(4) Some of the guests like oysters.
(4a) Not all of the guests like oysters.

The inference from *some* to *not all* is a standard prediction that goes through in virtue of the words used rather than in virtue of the context. Such examples subsequently gave rise to a theory of scalar implicature: lexical items <all, some> form a semantic scale and when the weaker term (the term to the right) is used, it is implicated that the stronger terms (here: *all*) do not apply to the situation talked about. It is possible to expand the scale to <all, most, many, some, few, ... >, possibly adding some more terms. Scalar predicates are then semantically lower-bounded: *some* means *at least some*, and pragmatically upper-bounded: *some* means *at most some (not all)*. This upper bound is provided by the maxim of quantity (see Horn, e.g. 1988, 2004). While it has been demonstrated that scales themselves can sometimes be context-dependent, the fact remains that it is easy to pinpoint a class of implicatures that do not rely on the context of the utterance but instead arise as assumed meanings. And context-free scalar implicatures make a substantial part of such generalized predictions.

When Grice presented his maxims of conversation as a natural complement to the truth-conditional semantics, he thus offered a tool for explaining the behaviour of sentential connectives such as *and* and *or*. Disjunction (*or*) in propositional logic is inclusive: *p or q* means *p, q, or both*. In English, we normally use *or* with an exclusive meaning: *either p, or q, but not both*. This discrepancy can be explained by means of adding an implicature of exclusiveness that comes from a semantic scale: <and, or> form such a scale and when the speaker utters 'or', he/she implicates that 'and' does not hold for the described situation. This implicature can, of course, be cancelled as in (5).

(5) In August I will go to the seaside or to the mountains, or both.

GCIs are thus closer to the truth-conditional content than PCIs: they arise in virtue of the words and constructions used, and hence have a strong semantic flavour.

Grice also distinguished another category that blurs the distinction between semantics and pragmatics even further: this is the category of a conventional implicature. This implicature does not share the properties with conversational implicatures: it is not cancellable, not calculable, and detachable when a synonymous sentence is substituted. So, it is in fact a species of lexical content. Words such as 'but', 'manage', or 'therefore' are said to convey conventional implicatures of contrast, overcome difficulty, and consequence respectively. One may wonder why complicate the theory by distinguishing such meanings from lexical, coded content *simpliciter*. The reason was that there are no obvious translations of such expressions into the metalanguage of first-order logic, and Grice assumed that the translation is an indispensable component of truth-conditional semantics, where the latter was itself regarded as indispensable, just in need of some patching up. So, 'but' became translated as logical conjunction, on a par with 'and', and the contrast sense was dubbed a conventional implicature. To sum up, for Grice, truth-conditional semantics is the core of the analysis of meaning, and pragmatic inference is added as and when it fits—within the truth-conditional content (disambiguation and reference assignment), or outside it, but with varying degrees of 'semanticity': from conventional implicatures that are a species of coded content, through generalized implicatures that arise in virtue of such coded meanings, and finally context-dependent particularized implicatures that are most 'pragmatic' of them all.

Retrospectively, we are in a position to say that the fact that Grice (i) admitted the output of some pragmatic processes in the truth-conditional aspect of meaning and (ii) arranged implicatures on a scale of progressive detachment from the semantic content opened a door for the current boundary disputes in that once some pragmatic inference finds its way into the propositional representation, it becomes a matter of debate (and empirical evidence) how much exactly should be allowed in.

Moreover, Grice employed the theory of implicature to argue against the methodological superiority of postulating ambiguities where a unitary semantic account can be given. For disjunction in English, for example, it suffices to admit the meaning of its propositional-logic equivalent as its semantic content and account for the exclusive reading by means of an implicature: there is no need to postulate semantic ambiguity on a par with the lexical ambiguity of 'bank' or 'port'. This economy of senses was spelled out as a Modified Occam's Razor (Grice 1978: 47):

Senses are not to be multiplied beyond necessity.

Again, retrospectively, we can judge that this was a landmark in pragmatic theory and in the semantics/pragmatics boundary disputes. Once unnecessary ambiguities are exorcised on methodological grounds, we are left with semantic meanings that cannot always be precisely delineated. And this was the foundation stone for the radical pragmatics in the 1970s and for the idea of semantic underdetermination to which we now turn.

3 Redrawing the boundary

Grice's proposal to assign a different status to disambiguation and reference assignment than to the other kinds of pragmatic elaborations of what is contained in the sentence generated many theoretical discussions: if the result of the process of reference assignment and disambiguation belonged to the semantic, truth-conditional content, then why not also include the results of other pragmatic processes that shed light on what is said by the speaker? The slogan 'pragmatics equals meaning minus truth conditions' started to lose its appeal when it was recognised that the truth-conditional content does not correspond to a clear-cut semantic object. Let us take sentential negation for example. Sentence (6) seems to allow for two interpretations, depending on whether the presupposition of the existence of the king of France is fulfilled at the time of the utterance.

(6) The king of France is not bald.

On the reading (6a), there is a king of France and he doesn't have a property of being bald.

(6a) There is somebody who fulfils the property of being the king of France, there is only one such person, and whoever fulfils this property is not bald.

Or, formally:

(6a') $\exists x\, (KoF(x) \land \forall y\, (KoF(y) \rightarrow y = x) \land \neg Bald\,(x))$

The other reading is (6b).

(6b) It is not true that the king of France is not bald.

—for example, because there is no such person. Let us try to represent this reading formally just by varying the position of the negation operator as in (6b') which contains a wide-scope, sentential negation and states that it is not the case (for whatever reason) that there is a king of France who is bald. This reason can be that France is not a monarchy or that the king is not hairless.

(6b') $\neg \exists x\, (KoF(x) \land \forall y\, (KoF(y) \rightarrow y = x) \land Bald\,(x))$

It says that it is not the case that there is somebody who fulfils the following two conditions: being the (unique) king of France and being bald. It would be easy and natural to assume on the basis of this analysis that negation is ambiguous in that it can take wide or narrow scope as represented formally by the above logical forms advocated by Bertrand Russell. However, the two logical forms in (6a') and (6b') are not disjoint: the former entails the latter. So, representing the difference between the two readings of (6) by invoking these logical forms and ambiguity of negation is not very satisfactory. Moreover, there is no strong intuition among native speakers that negation in English is indeed ambiguous, Instead, why not assume that the semantics of sentential negation in English underdetermines the meaning? According to such a view, the processing of the lexicon and the structure of (6) results in an underspecified semantic representation and the exact reading, (6a) or (6b), is given by pragmatic enrichment performed in the particular context of discourse. This position of *semantic underdetermination*, also called *sense-generality*, was an important landmark in semantic theory. We owe it to a group of Gricean pragmaticists working in the 1970s, and among others to Jay Atlas's and Ruth Kempson's remarks on the underdetermination of negation—the so-called Atlas-Kempson thesis (see Atlas 1977, 1979, 1989, 2005a, 2006a; Kempson 1975, 1979, 1986; see also Wilson 1975). The movement resulted in the increasing acceptance of the standpoint that there is no semantic ambiguity and the cases such as that of the scope of negation can be handled by the pragmatic additions to the semantically underspecified representation. Semantic analysis takes us part-way, and pragmatic enrichment completes the recovery of utterance meaning. The movement also came to be known as *radical pragmatics* (Cole 1981). To sum up, while lexical and syntactic ambiguity can be represented as two independent logical forms pertaining to the ambiguous sentence, semantic underdetermination is the case where one underspecified logical form ensues in processing and further determinations of meaning take place through pragmatic inference or through some other pragmatic process such as an application of presumed, salient, default interpretations. Underdetermination and inference are two interconnected aspects of utterance interpretation, as is well captured in Atlas's apt pastiche of Kant: "Pragmatic inference without sense-generality is blind, but sense-generality without pragmatic inference is empty." (Atlas 1989: 124). There have been various terms used in the literature for the underdetermination of meaning: underdetermination, underspecification, indeterminacy, sense-generality, vagueness, neutrality, and others (see Zwicky & Sadock 1975: 2; Green 1996: 1). I use 'underdetermination' of meaning as a general concept for the phenomenon and 'underspecified representation' for the property of the logical form as the output of syntactic processing (see van Deemter & Peters 1996; Jaszczolt 1999, 2005). Zwicky & Sadock (1975) presented a battery of tests that can be used to tell ambiguity and underdetermination apart. Perhaps the most important of them is the identity test: conjoining reduced constituents should be possible only when the conjuncts have matching readings. For example, let us take (7) and (8).

(7) They saw her duck.

(8) They saw her swallow.

The conjunction reduction to (9) allows only to juxtapose matching senses: the action of ducking with the action of swallowing, and a duck with a swallow.

(9) They saw her duck and her swallow.

Crossed readings are not semantically well-formed, unless they are used for punning effect (see Lascarides, Copestake & Briscoe 1996). This test is modelled on Lakoff's (1970: 357) 'and the same goes for . . .' reduction. Mixed readings are supposed to be freely available for semantic underdeterminacy. However, as in other aspects of the boundary dispute, even here we cannot point to clear-cut distinctions: some examples of underdetermination fare better than others with the tests and hence the tests are not conclusive. The condition of entailment of the logical form is a much safer criterion to follow.

Semantic underdetermination, a revolutionary idea for the theory of linguistic meaning, was a reaction to a widespread attempt in the 1960s and early 1970s to give syntactic explanations to pragmatic phenomena. This tendency was called Generative Semantics. The influence of the Oxford ordinary language philosophy, and most notably John L. Austin, H. Paul Grice, Peter F. Strawson, late views of Ludwig Wittgenstein in Cambridge, as well as subsequent arguments put forward by Bruce Fraser, Gerald Gazdar, Jerry Morgan, Jay Atlas, Ruth Kempson, Deirdre Wilson, and others contributed to the fall of generative semantics and opened up a way to *pragmatic* explanation of clearly *pragmatic* phenomena such as various uses of negation and other sentential connectives. In his 'A Personal History of Linguistic Pragmatics 1969–2000', Jay D. Atlas recollects as follows:

> "I read the first, introductory paragraph to Sadock and Zwicky's paper, and I thought to myself, 'That's it. If 'not' is not ambiguous, it's semantically non-specific. Let's try the tests.' Ten minutes later I had satisfied myself that 'not' in definite description sentences failed Sadock's ambiguity tests. And then the power of Grice's notion of generalized conversational implicatural inference hit me full on. The solution had to be in the utterance-meanings, in one of two ways. Either the utterance-meanings were produced by a Griceanish inference, not from classical logical forms as Grice thought, e.g. sentential exclusion negation, but from a non-specific, semantical representation of a sentence-type whose meaning was not that of either a choice or an exclusion negation proposition, or the utterance-meanings were produced by a classical Gricean inference from the sentential exclusion negation logical form, which on classical Gricean grounds one would have to 'posit' as the semantic content of 'what is said' in the asserted sentence—Grice's version of the 'minimal proposition'."
>
> Atlas (2006a: 4).

In short, either there is some underspecified semantic representation given by the processing of the structure, or we adopt (6b') as such an underspecified representation.

The most interesting aspect of radical pragmatics is that such pragmatic resolution of the exact meaning of semantically underdetermined expressions is admitted into truth-conditional semantics. The unit of which we now predicate truth conditions is the *utterance* rather than the *sentence*: it is (6') or (6") that has truth conditions in any interesting sense, not the sentence in (6). So, the boundary between semantics and pragmatics is shifted even more in the direction of pragmatics. A variety of pragmatic processes of different kinds was allowed to contribute to the truth-conditional representation. For example, in (1) repeated below, the consequence sense of *and* is a pragmatic addition to the semantic content.

(1) The janitor left the door open and the prisoner escaped.

This blurring of the boundary called for further terminological tidying. Carston (1988) proposed to call the output of syntactic processing of the sentence *linguistic semantics*, reserving the term *truth-conditional semantics* for the amalgam of the output of linguistic semantics and pragmatic inference. In (1), $p \wedge q$ is a representation in linguistic semantics, while *p and therefore q* is a representation in truth-conditional semantics. At this point we should add a terminological distinction: the representations in linguistic semantics are called logical forms in that they are the same logical forms as those recognised as the semantic structure of sentences in truth-conditional Montagovian semantics (see Dowty, Wall & Peters 1981; Lycan 1984). The enriched representations of truth-conditional semantics in the above (contextualist) sense will be called semantic representations.

The exact scope of application of semantic underdetermination is still a matter of debate. For example, it has often been argued that number terms such as 'three' are semantically underdetermined. According to Horn's early analysis (1976: 33), a sentence containing a cardinal number term n asserts lower boundedness 'at least n', while the upper boundary 'at most n' is just an optional addition executed through pragmatic inference. The final product, the 'exactly n' meaning, is the output of the two. However, there are also sentences in which the 'at most n' meaning is dominant, as in (10).

(10) She can miss the target three times without dropping out of the competition.

According to some subsequent analyses, number terms are just semantically underdetermined: semantically, they are neither *at least n*, nor *at most n*, nor *exactly n* (see Carston 1998). But more recently, this analysis of number terms has been questioned. Examples such as (11) and (12) strongly suggest that the *exactly n* reading is not arrived at pragmatically but instead is the straightforward coded meaning.

(11) I have at least three pounds in my pocket.
(12) Three men carried the piano up the stairs.

Qualifying the number term by 'at least' or 'at most' strongly suggests that the basic meaning is just 'three'. Similarly, (12), where the reading is clearly collective (*three men together*), does not allow for entailments: three men carrying the piano together does not entail that two did. Neither does it mean that perhaps more than three did. So, perhaps the exactly (punctual) semantics of number terms is correct after all (see e. g. Koenig 1993; Geurts 1998; Bultinck 2005; Jaszczolt 2005; Horn 1992, 2006). While experimental evidence is still inconclusive, it suggests that number terms behave very differently from scalar terms. It also shows that the 'exactly n' interpretation is much more psychologically salient (see e.g. Musolino 2004). The example of number terms shows that semantic underdetermination has to be approached with caution: the correct analysis of the particular expression type need not exhibit it just because from the theoretical point of view it seems to apply.

Once a wide variety of pragmatic additions was allowed in semantic representation, it had to be decided what really matters for the boundary: (i) the distinction between the (by now eclectic, semantico-pragmatic) semantic representation and the separate senses that this meaning gives rise to, or (ii) the distinction between the logical form as the 'pure' output of syntax and the 'pure' what is physically uttered on the one hand, and the whole array of implicatures on the other, irrespective of whether they contribute to the semantic representation or to some additional senses this primary meaning of the utterance gives rise to. In the following sections I present and assess various views on this matter.

There have also been other attempts to redraw the semantics/pragmatic boundary that can be subsumed under broadly understood contextualism in that they propose various solutions on how to incorporate contextual information into the semantic representation. The most influential ones are perhaps the unarticulated constituents view and Kaplan's two-dimensional theory. The unarticulated constituents view is an attempt to explain various pragmatic additions to the semantic structure as elements of the unarticulated syntactic structure. On this account, pragmatic enrichment has a syntactic provenance and amounts to filling in slots in the logical form: "[m]uch syntactic structure is unpronounced, but no less real for being unpronounced" (Stanley 2002: 152; see also Stanley & Szabó 2000; King & Stanley 2005). For example, according to Stanley & Szabó, sentence (13) obtains an analysis as in (14), where the node N contains information about the contextual restriction of the domain of the universal quantifier 'every': f(i), where f stands for a function mapping objects onto quantifier domains and i for an object provided by the context. As a result, the enriched meaning in (15) is accounted for by means of the syntactic analysis because 'everybody' is taken to refer to a restricted domain of, say, invited guests (see Stanley & Szabó 2000 for other possible syntactic analyses using unarticulated constituents and their limitations as compared with that in (14)).

(13) Everybody came to the party.

(14)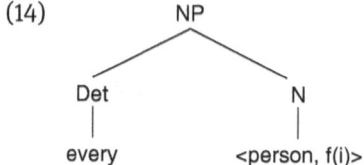

(15) Every invited guest came to the party.

In a similar vein, Chierchia (e.g. 2004) attempts to derive scalar implicatures such as for example from *some* to 'not all' from the logical form of a sentence. He says that grammar (on his understanding: syntax and semantics) allows for two interpretive procedures which give two kinds of values to expressions: a plain value, say, 'some', and a strengthened, 'scalar' value, say, 'some but not all'. The latter value is normally selected by the system but is defeasible by context. As he says, "some of the Grice-inspired pragmatics is probably part of the computational system of grammar" (Chierchia 2004: 59). Reversing the monotonicity removes the implicatures. So, downward entailing contexts (such as embedding a sentence *p* under 'I doubt that...') remove any scalar implicatures of *p* and add new, indirect ones through a process which is governed by a general rule that implicatures must lead to strengthening.

Another view which is represented in current research is a rather less radical Montagovian formal pragmatics as elaborated by Kaplan (1978, 1989) in his two-dimensional semantics. Context is represented there by an index with respect to which sentences are interpreted. The interpretation provides contents or, as we could say, propositions (functions from possible worlds to truth values). The scope of pragmatic information contained in the index is, however, rather limited as compared with the free pragmatic modulation of radical contextualism (see e.g. Stalnaker 1999, but also Predelli 2005a, b, 2006 for a defence). Kaplan's semantics is two-dimensional in that he distinguishes content from character, where the latter is a way of getting from the context to the content. To repeat, content in turn yields a truth value relative to a possible world ('circumstances of evaluation'). Or, as Chalmers (2006: 59) puts it,

"The core idea of two-dimensional semantics is that there are two different ways in which the extension of an expression depends on possible states of the world. First, the actual extension of an expression depends on the character of the actual world in which an expression is uttered. Second, the counterfactual extension of an expression depends on the character of the counterfactual world in which the expression is evaluated. Corresponding to these two sorts of dependence, expressions correspondingly have two sorts of intensions, associating possible states of the world with extensions in different ways. On the two-dimensional framework, these two intensions can be seen as capturing two dimensions of meaning."

There are different varieties of two-dimensional semantics. Kaplan's (1978, 1989) character and content have their equivalents, albeit exhibiting important conceptual differences, in Stalnaker's (1978) diagonal proposition and proposition expressed, Chalmers' (1996) primary and secondary intension, and several other pairs of constructs (see Chalmers 2006: 62). It is still a matter of debate as to whether this approach can handle a wide range of contextual enrichment. While its utility for indexical terms is unquestionable, the scope of application is still a matter of vivid debates (see also e. g. Stalnaker 1999; Chalmers 2006; Predelli 2005a, b, 2006; Balaguer 2005).

In what follows I focus on approaches to the semantics/pragmatics interface which developed more elaborate, albeit less formal and arguably less formalizable, accounts of the role of various types of pragmatic enrichment for semantic analysis.

4 Delimiting implicatures

4.1 Intentions and intuitive truth conditions

Post-Griceans held different views on how to classify the output of syntactic processing, the pragmatic additions to the semantic representations, and the implicatures proper, understood as separate thoughts implied by the utterance. While for some the main boundary lies between the pragmatically enriched semantic representation and implicatures proper, for others the component of the pragmatic enrichments to the semantic representation is sufficiently distinct in its provenance as compared with the logical form to call for a separate, middle level of meaning. Yet for others all pragmatic aspects of meaning, be it developments of what is said or separate thoughts, should be grouped together as the traditional Gricean category of the implicature. Different views that are in the forefront of the current discussions are presented in the following sub-sections. But before we attend to the differences, it has to be emphasised that there is a lot that unites these views. They are all Gricean in spirit in that they all recognise the important role of intentions in the analysis of meaning. The unit of meaning is an utterance (meaning$_{NN}$) rather than a sentence, and the route to the recovery of the speaker's meaning is the recognition of the speaker's intentions. Intentions have received a lot of attention in pragmatic literature. For Bach & Harnish (1979), an intention to communicate certain content is fulfilled when it is recognised by the addressee (see also Bach 1987a, b, 1999; Jaszczolt 1999, Haugh & Jaszczolt 2012). They call it an *illocutionary informative intention* and say that it comes with a so-called *communicative presumption*: when the speaker produces an utterance, the hearer assumes that the speaker produced it with some intention. The next common characteristic is the foregrounding of the intuitive truth conditions. With the growth of Gricean pragmatics, and undoubtedly, in virtue of the general tendency in philosophy of language since the late 1950s to talk about speaker's meaning rather than sentence meaning, the balance shifted from the truth conditions of sentences to those of utterances. Although (16) and (16a) 'mean the same' in virtue of the equivalence of $p \wedge q$ and $q \wedge p$, their utterances normally do not.

(16) They earned a lot of money and went to live in London.
(16a) They went to live in London and earned a lot of money.

What became foregrounded instead was the fact that the addressee would be likely to deny (16a) arguing as in (17).

(17) It's not true that they earned a lot of money and went to live in London; they moved to London first and got good jobs there.

The truth conditions of the pragmatically enriched proposition (p *and then* q), that is the proposition intuitively understood as the one meant by the speaker, became the object of analysis in post-Gricean contextualism.

4.2 The explicit/implicit boundary

The pressing problem became to delimit the primary, explicit content of the utterance. To repeat, for some contextualists, what is said includes all sorts of developments of the semantic content of the uttered proposition. Sperber & Wilson (1986) and Carston (1988, 1998) dubbed such a development of the utterance's logical form an *explicature*. This unit of 'explicit' content is particularly useful when a sentence seems to convey an obvious truth, as in (18), or a blatant falsehood, as in (19). The enriched proposition, the explicature, is then the intended meaning of he speaker's—as in (18a) and (19a).

(18)   I have eaten.
(19)   Everybody was there.

(18a) The speaker has already eaten lunch on that day.
(19a) Everybody who was invited was there.

Explicatures are also helpful when a sentence uttered does not convey a complete proposition, as in (20). Pragmatic processing can then result in a proposition that is assumed by the addressee to have been intended by the speaker.

(20)   Tom is not experienced enough.
(20a) Tom is not experienced enough to lead a Himalayan expedition.

It has to be remembered, however, that while Grice's programme was to account for *speaker's* meaning, relevance theorists give an account of utterance *interpretation* (see Saul 2002 and Horn 2004: 22). Explicatures were said to be created by means of pragmatic processes that do not differ from those producing separate, implicit meanings. In other words, both the pragmatic developments of the logical form of the sentence and the truly implicated meanings are arrived at through the same kind of pragmatic inference (but see Recanati 2004, 2007, 2010; Carston 2007).

The problem is that, in principle, such developments of the logical form of the sentence could proceed *ad infinitum*: we need a demarcation line somewhere in order to understand how and when they stop. Carston (1988: 169) suggests that the enrichments stop as soon as optimal relevance is achieved, where by relevance she means the cognitive and communicative principle proposed by Sperber & Wilson (1986, 1995), according to which the effort invested by the addressee in the processing of the speaker's utterance is offset by the so-called 'cognitive effect': gained information or any other improvement to the addressee's information state. The cognitive principle of relevance says that 'Human cognition tends to be geared to the maximization of relevance' (Sperber & Wilson 1995: 260), while the communicative counterpart says that 'Every act of ostensive communication communicates a presumption of its own optimal relevance' (Sperber & Wilson 1986: 158). To bring the idea down to common-sense intuitions, it says that we stop interpreting what the speaker said once we have reached the satisfactory interpretation. But it does not say more than this intuitive claim: it offers no way of measuring or predicting the explicature in particular cases.

What we also need is a criterion that would tell us which kind of output of pragmatic inference qualifies as part of the explicature and which has to be relegated to implicatures proper. Carston proposes such a criterion. She says that implicatures are *functionally independent* from the explicature. This means that implicatures, if we wanted to spell them out, would have to have their own logical forms which are independent from the logical form of the sentence. They function as independent premises in reasoning. For example, in (18) repeated below, (18a) is the explicature, while (18b) is a possible implicature.

(18) I have eaten.
(18a) The speaker has already eaten lunch on that day.
(18b) The speaker is not hungry.

By the criterion of functional independence, sentence (1b) repeated below is the explicature of (1).

(1b) The janitor left the door open *and as a result* the prisoner escaped.
(1) The janitor left the door open and the prisoner escaped.

However, functional independence is not a sufficiently precise criterion. When we try to formulate it in terms of entailment, problems arise. The criterion that the implicature must not entail the explicature works for most examples: (1b) entails (1) and hence it would not be plausible to assume that the interlocutors store both propositions in the mind; the propositions are not functionally independent. But entailment does not work when construed in the other direction: it is perfectly normal for an explicature to entail an implicature, as in (21). B's answer entails and implicates that B bought some flowers.

(21) A: Did you buy flowers for Mary's birthday?
B: I bought some roses.

On some scenarios, it is also problematic to take functional independence to mean the relation of entailment even when it proceeds from implicature to explicature (see Recanati 1989 and Carston 1998 for response; see also Carston 2001).

Now, as can be seen from examples (18) and (19), the sentence uttered by the speaker can be perfectly complete, have a complete logical form, and yet pragmatic inference can take place. According to some pragmaticists then, pragmatic enrichment can be free, not syntactically controlled (see e. g. Bach 2000; Carston 1988, 2002; Recanati 1989, 1993, 1994, 2001, 2002a, 2004, 2010; Levinson 2000, Jaszczolt 2005, 2010b). This argument is often used against the unarticulated constituents view discussed in section 3. As Recanati (2002a) says, there are unarticulated constituents that do not pertain to any slots in the logical form: they are aspects of the explicit content that are entirely pragmatic in their provenance.

Whether this stance necessitates a contextualist orientation will be discussed in sections 4.4 and 5.

4.3 The pragmatic aspects of *what is said*

The criteria for distinguishing the explicit content from implicatures became an important preoccupation of some post-Griceans in the late 1980s. Recanati (1989: 98) agreed with relevance theorists on the scope of the explicit content, called by him *what is said*—not to be confused with Grice's rather minimal 'what is said'. He distinguishes pragmatic processes of filling in slots in the logical form as in the case of the assignment of reference to personal pronouns (*saturation*) such as 'I' in (18), and a free, not grammatically controlled process of *strengthening* (or sense modulation, Recanati 2004, 2005, 2010), exemplified in (1), (18)–(20) above. Strengthening, or modulation, is a 'top-down' process: it is independent of the constitution of the logical form, where the latter is the output of the processing of grammar. He admits that postulating slots in the logical form is theoretically possible but encounters a quandary: in order to postulate the necessary slots to be filled we already have to know what is said. So, we have circularity in the explanation.

Having objected to compulsory syntactic slots as well as to some aspects of the functional independence principle, Recanati (1989) proposes his own criteria for delimiting what is said. What is said is to be specified intuitively and corresponds to 'pre-theoretic intuitions', as his Availability Principle states:

> "In deciding whether a pragmatically determined aspect of utterance meaning is part of what is said, that is, in making a decision concerning what is said, we should always try to preserve our pre-theoretic intuitions on the matter."
>
> Recanati (1989: 106).

This principle, being rather general, is adopted in conjunction with the Scope Principle, adapted from Cohen (1971) who, *nota bene*, used it to the opposite effect; to argue for the rich *lexical* meaning of sentential connectives:

> "A pragmatically determined aspect of meaning is part of what is said (and, therefore, not a conversational implicature) if—and, perhaps, only if—it falls within the scope of logical operators such as negation and conditionals."
>
> Recanati (1989: 114).

So, to invoke Cohen's own example, in (22) below, the temporal 'and then' meaning of conjunction *and* in English is part of what is said because in the scope of implication (*if... then*) it is necessary in order to make sense of the assertion.

(22) If the old king died of a heart attack and a republic was declared Sam will be happy, but if a republic was declared and the old king died of a heart attack Sam will be unhappy.

Formally, the first of the contrasted conjuncts can be represented as in (22a) and the second as in (22b). Since in our metalanguage of propositional logic $(p \wedge q) \leftrightarrow (q \wedge p)$, the contrast in r and $\neg r$ only makes sense when we enrich $\wedge$ to mean 'and then'.

(22a) $(p \wedge q) \to r$
(22b) $(q \wedge p) \to \neg r$

Another interesting aspect of Recanati's solution is his claim that what is said is the smallest constituent available consciously. In other words, what is said is arrived at through a pragmatic process which is not consciously available. It is sub-personal, automatic, and it cannot be properly called 'inferential': "communication is as direct as perception" (Recanati 2002b: 109). He dubs this process a primary pragmatic process, to distinguish it from a secondary type of inference proper that produces implicatures (see e.g. Recanati 2004: 38–44, 2007). All in all, the truth conditions of the utterance depend on the interplay of a variety of sources of information. As a result, we obtain what is sometimes dubbed Truth-Conditional Pragmatics (Recanati 2002a).

Recanati advocates a rather strong view of pragmatic enrichment (modulation). He claims that such contextual modulation is *always* present: "there is no level of meaning which is both (i) propositional (truth-evaluable) and (ii) minimalist, that is, unaffected by top-down factors" (2004: 90). This view is thus a strong variety of contextualism and it is currently the subject of heated debates with those who would rather keep semantics simple, 'minimal', close to what is physically uttered.

4.4 The middle level: An impl/citure

Kent Bach (1994, 2001) recognises the difficulty with subsuming the output of pragmatic inference under the label 'explicit' content and offers a more intuitively acceptable solution: there is what is said and what is implicated, but there are also parts of the content that are *implicit in what is said* and yet are not implicatures proper. He acknowledges that people often speak loosely, non-literally, and that fact is not a deficiency of human communication but rather a positive trait: it is more efficient to do so and to rely on the addressee to recover the missing aspects. For example, when a mother reacts to a child's crying about a cut finger in saying (23), she uses the sentence non-literally:

(23)   You are not going to die, Peter.

(from Bach 1994: 267). While the content of the sentence (called the *minimal proposition*) is that Peter is going to live forever, the implicit constituents inferred by him from his mother's utterance ensure that the message is something to the effect of (23a).

(23a) You are not going to die from this cut, Peter.

So, what is meant by the speaker is the expansions of such a minimal proposition.
Similarly, sentences that are semantically incomplete in that they do not have clear truth conditions such as (20) repeated below, require implicit constituents of what is said.

(20)   Tom is not experienced enough.

Sentence (20), Bach argues, does not express a proposition; it only expresses a *propositional radical* which is in need of pragmatic completion in order to produce the intended meaning, such as, for example, (20a).

(20a) Tom is not experienced enough to lead a Himalayan expedition.

In short, we have two similar phenomena here: sentence non-literality, where the minimal proposition requires expansion, or, as Bach calls it 'fleshing out', and semantic underdetermination, where the propositional radical requires completion, or 'filling in' (see Bach 1994: 269). Such expansions and completions constitute a 'middle ground' between what is said and what is implicated: they do not belong to what is said and they are not implicatures either. There is no clear boundary to discern. A proposition enriched through expansion and completion he calls an impliciture. For Bach (2004, 2006, 2007), although there is a middle ground between what is said and what is implicated, this does not mean that the boundary between semantics and pragmatics is blurred: semantic properties belong to sentences, and pragmatic to acts of uttering them. "Sentences have the properties they have independently of anybody's act of uttering them. Speakers' intentions do not endow them with new semantic properties..." (Bach 2004: 27). Here Bach takes issue with the contextualist idea that semantics must produce truth conditions and when it does not produce them as in (20) or produces 'wrong ones' as in (18), context 'intrudes' into the domain of semantics in the form of pragmatic inference and supplies missing information. So, he takes issue with relevance-theoretic and Recanati's positions. For Bach, the semantic content of sentences and the intended content of utterances have to be kept apart. Sentences uttered normally underdetermine what the speaker means but there is nothing extraordinary about this fact: semantics ends with the sentence meaning, even if it is counterintuitive or incomplete, and pragmatics begins with utterance meaning. In this perspective, the middle level of implicitures is not the middle level between semantics and pragmatics: it is fully pragmatic, it is just not the level of implicatures proper.

This dissociation of semantics from truth conditions has important consequences for the current minimalism-contextualism debate to which I turn in section 5. At this point however it is important to add that the impliciture view is gaining popularity in the latest discussions on the boundary dispute. Horn (2004: 22) stresses its compatibility with other neo-Gricean approaches, and most notably with the observation that Grice's account concerned speaker's meaning, not utterance interpretation (Saul 2002). In Horn (2006: 24), he adopts Bach's traditional semantics/pragmatics distinction, as well as his notion of impliciture. Similarly, Atlas (2005b, 2006b) argues for keeping semantics and truth conditions apart. The conclusion that must be drawn from these recent developments is this. After three decades of the emotions stirred up by semantic underdetermination, it is now being emphasized that there is nothing so very interesting in the fact that semantic content underdetermines the speaker's intended meaning. The fault lies in the repeated attempts to use truth conditions as theoretical framework and argue from this that, since the analysis is truth-conditional, it has to be semantic and semantics has to be construed as allowing for the intrusion of context and the result of pragmatic inference. For Bach and his sympathisers, this is an obvious *non sequitur*.

4.5 Presumptive meanings: Between semantics and pragmatics

Bach's tri-partite distinction is not the only way to cut the pie. Levinson (1995, 2000) proposes a level of meaning that lies between semantics and pragmatics while retaining the contextualist assumptions. Unlike Bach, he allows for the contribution of pragmatic inference to the propositional representation, and unlike Bach, he retains the dominant role of truth-conditional analysis of meaning in semantics. But unlike relevance theorists, he does not emphasise the importance of such an expanded and embellished representation of meaning. For him, there is a sub-category of such embellishments that is neither semantic nor pragmatic. These are presumed, default interpretations, arrived at by virtue of the repeated scenarios from the past, knowledge of language and the world, and other salient information, processed with the aid of some general principles of human reasoning. These general principles correspond loosely to Grice's generalized conversational implicatures and hence Levinson's theory of presumed ('presumptive') meanings is also called a theory of generalized conversational implicature (Levinson 2000; for other default-based approaches see Asher & Lascarides 2003 and article 13 [Semantics: Theories] (Zeevat) *Rhetorical relations*; Blutner & Zeevat 2004; and an overview in Jaszczolt 2006).

According to Levinson, there are three levels of meaning: sentence meaning, utterance-type meaning, and utterance-token meaning. Default interpretations, and among them most notably GCIs, belong to the middle level of utterance-type meaning. Such middle-level meanings are neither properly semantic nor properly pragmatic. Presumptive meanings are dubbed GCIs but they have one important feature that distinguishes them from Grice's GCIs. For Grice, pragmatic inference operated post-propositionally. The output of syntactic processing had to be completed and had to deliver a logical form of the sentence before the speaker's utterances were inferred on the basis of the maxims of conversation. Levinson's GCIs are 'local': they arise at the point at which they are triggered. For example, the word 'some', even when it is the first word of an utterance, gives rise to the default presumption 'not all', unless there are contextual clues that prevent it from arising. Naturally, the presumptive meaning can be cancelled at any later stage as the utterance continues.

Presumed meanings are very useful for human communication. Levinson observes that human speech is transmitted quite slowly: phonetic representations are encoded as acoustic signals with a rate of approximately 7 syllables per second. This is very significantly slower than the rate at which standard personal computers work. On the other hand, humans' mental capacity for speech production and speech comprehension is much higher. He calls this situation a 'bottleneck in the speed of human communication' (Levinson 2000: 28) and presents it as a motivation for communicating through implicatures: while producing speech slows communication down as compared to what it could have been given the mental architecture, inference can help speed it up. As he says, "inference is cheap, articulation expensive, and thus the design requirements are for a system that maximizes inference" (Levinson 2000: 29).

Pragmatic inference proceeds according to three general heuristics which constitute one of three main attempts at a revision of the Gricean maxims of conversations, along with Horn's Q and R principles and Sperber & Wilson's principle of relevance. On the most general formulation, they say the following (from Levinson 2000: 35–39):

Q-heuristic: 'What isn't said isn't.'

This heuristic is responsible for scalar implicatures: if the speaker utters (24), a Q-implicature as in (24a) is normally produced.

(24)   Some people have a sense of humour.
(24a)   Not all people have a sense of humour.

I-heuristic: 'What is expressed simply is stereotypically exemplified.'
   For example, the phrase 'three men' in (25) is presumed to give rise to the collective interpretation ('together') by force of the I-heuristic.

(25)   Three men pushed a lorry out of a snowdrift.

M-heuristic: 'What's said in an abnormal way isn't normal.'

   This heuristic works as a complement to the I-heuristic in that while the I-heuristic takes the addressee to the standard, stereotypical interpretation, the M-heuristic captures the fact that when the speaker used a marked rather than an ordinary expression, the intended interpretation is also marked. For example, in (26), the use of 'it is not impossible that...' construction rather than the standard 'it is possible' signals that the probability is low: lower than in the case of the alternative expression.

(26)   It is not impossible that she will win the piano competition.

To sum up, presumptive meanings are default interpretations in the sense of being context-free. As such, they are also 'cheap' in that they require less effort to process than consulting the particular context would. But it seems that they also demand some effort in that, if they are produced on-line, locally, as soon as the triggering word or construction arises, they are likely often to be cancelled.

4.6 Radical contextualism of Default Semantics

Default Semantics (Jaszczolt 2005, 2009, 2010b) goes further than the contextualist accounts discussed earlier in that the explicit (called: *primary*) meaning of an utterance does not have to bear any structural resemblance to the logical form of the sentence. It need not constitute a development of the logical form of the sentence or, in other words, need not obey the *syntactic constraint*. All sources of information about meaning identified there are treated on a par: the output of any of them can override the output of any other. For example, the most salient meaning of B's response in (2) repeated below is something like (2Ba).

(2)   A: Smith doesn't seem to have a girlfriend these days.
      B: He has been paying a lot of visits to New York lately.

(2Ba) Smith may have a girlfriend.

On the Default-Semantics construal, (2Ba) is the primary content of B's utterance and it is this content that enters into the compositional semantic representation (called *merger representation*) of (2B). So, semantics is understood here as the theory that provides the intuitive truth conditions of utterances, but these truth conditions are even 'more intuitive', so to speak, than those of truth-conditional pragmatics discussed above. We drop the restriction that one of the sources of speaker's meaning, namely the logical form of the sentence, has priority over the others and that the contribution of inference and presumed, salient enrichments is to be limited to embellishments of this logical form. This view does not come free though. It requires a substantial rethinking of the principle of compositionality of meaning. Recanati (2004) already observed that, with intuitive truth conditions of truth-conditional pragmatics, we need a more 'pragmatic' approach to compositionality: composition of meaning will have to proceed not on the level of the logical form of the sentence but rather on the level of the semantic representation of the intended proposition. In the above spirit, merger representation is conceived of as the result of an interaction of various sources of meaning identified in the theory. What a semantic theory needs is an algorithm to show how all the sources of information about meaning interact. Another (related) consequence of extending what is said in this way is that we need a new criterion for distinguishing what is said (and a merger representation) from implicatures proper. In Default Semantics, implicatures are produced by two out of the four sources that also build merger representations: conscious pragmatic inference and socio-cultural defaults. The source of information and the process through which the implicature arises cannot differentiate it from the explicit content. In this Default Semantics is closer in spirit to relevance theory than to Recanati's truth-conditional pragmatics. To repeat, in relevance theory, the same processes are responsible for the explicatures and the implicatures, while in truth-conditional pragmatics, all modulation is automatic, unconscious (i.e. *subdoxastic*), while the processing of implicatures is conscious and more effortful.

In the following section I attend to some differences in the contextualist views and to the opposing view according to which no contextual information is allowed in the semantics (semantic minimalism). This overview will allow us to better assess and compare different stances discussed here.

5 Minimalism, contextualism, and beyond

In the preceding sections I discussed the view that every instance of utterance interpretation involves 'top-down' processing, called contextualism. I also mentioned briefly one non-contextualist view while introducing Bach's notion of impliciture. In more general terms, contextualism is a position in the philosophy of language that a sentence expresses fully determined content only in the context of a speech act. This view did not arise in a void. It is a development of the position held in the 1950s by ordinary language philosophers such as later Wittgenstein, J. L. Austin, and subsequently J. Searle. Contextualism has now become one of the leading orientations in the study of meaning. To repeat, on the assumption that we want to retain truth conditions in semantic theory, we have to admit context into that theory. And once it is admitted, there is one step from there to saying that talk about meaning only makes sense when the sentence is immersed in the context in which it was uttered. This view holds equally of the Gricean developments and Montagovian approaches such as two-dimensional semantics introduced in section 3 which, to repeat, are also contextualist in a broad sense.

Contextualism is best seen as a reaction to the traditional view that sentences themselves can be ascribed truth conditions. The latter view we shall call, after Recanati (2004, 2005), *literalism*. Examples of semantic underdetermination and sentence non-literality discussed in section 4.4 testify to the deficiencies of this view, and so does the requirement of psychological reality of the object of study (see e. g. Clapp's (2007) argument against minimal semantics). Now, according to Recanati's (2005) historical overview, literalism has gone through a 'gradual weakening': it has become less and less radical, until it gave rise to stronger and stronger forms of contextualism.

In the current debates on the semantics/pragmatics boundary, only the weakest form of literalism, called *minimalism*, is a real contender. Minimalism itself has two versions. One says that truth-conditional content is indeed permeated with the result of pragmatic inference but this inference is constrained by the grammar: there are slots in the syntactic representation that are to be filled in. This is how utterance meaning is kept very close to the meaning of the sentence type. The main representative of this view is Peter Stanley whose views were briefly introduced in section 3. The other version, dubbed by Recanati 'the syncretic view', holds that there is a minimal semantic content, but on the other hand there is also intuitive utterance content. Since the latter can be freely modulated to reflect the speaker's intended meaning as assessed by the addressee, the first can be kept even 'more minimal': slots provided by deictic and other context-dependent expressions have to be filled but there is no temptation to postulate any other contentious slots just in order to capture the intuitive meaning of the utterance: sentence-type meaning and speaker's meaning can be safely kept apart. A syncretist, Emma Borg (2004), claims in her theory of *Minimal Semantics* that semantic theory is unaffected by any intrusion of aspects of meaning that are not present in the sentence itself. Semantic theory is a theory of 'literal linguistic meaning' and its task is only to provide 'pure' sentence meaning. She assumes that the understanding of sentence meaning is modular and should be kept apart from the understanding of speaker's intentions and from any non-deductive inference. Sentences have truth conditions even if it would not be possible to tell what situation would make the sentence true. There is no need for the intrusion of the contextual enrichment. Truth conditions are not conditions of verification as contextualists have it. A similar orientation is presented in Cappelen & Lepore's (2005) *Insensitive Semantics*: a truth condition can be produced for a sentence even if we are not in a position to discern possible situations that would verify the sentence. So, on this account, Tarski's T-sentence (27) produces a truth condition just in virtue of having a form of a T-sentence (see Bach 2006 for criticism).

(27) 'Tom is not strong enough' is true if and only if Tom in not strong enough.

Cappelen & Lepore claim that it is a mistake to assume that a semantic theory should account for speakers' intuitions about the content of the utterance, i.e. about the speaker's meaning. They argue that there is no strong connection between the content of speech acts and the content of sentences and that they should be kept apart. By the same reasoning, semantics and pragmatics should be kept apart.

The boundary dispute would be simple indeed to solve if semantics and pragmatics could be delimited in the way Cappelen & Lepore suggest. However, they seem to cut off parts of each discipline in order to keep the boundary clear: composing sentence meaning is not a simple enterprise of combining clear-cut word meanings in the way provided by the grammar. Neither is pragmatics merely a description of what people say. Post-Gricean pragmaticists aim at generalizations about the speaker's meaning that stem out of the principles of rational conversational behaviour. Most of them are also interested in the psychology of utterance interpretation and in the application of such principles during this process. So, even leaving aside the debate concerning the unit of which truth conditions should be predicated, it is evident that one must resort to unwarranted simplifications in order to force semantics and pragmatics into separate moulds.

Semantic minimalism gave rise to ample criticism from the contextualists. As we know from the earlier discussion of Recanati's version of contextualism, the main objection to the first version of minimalism is that there is no evidence for the kinds of syntactic slots that have to be postulated in order to maintain the view that syntactic form alone accounts for the intuitive truth conditions. The main objection to the second version of minimalism, the syncretic view, is the lack of practical utility of a minimal proposition. The syncretists who opt for verification-free truth conditions are also attacked on the count of redefining truth conditions:

> "This move strikes me as an unacceptable weakening of the notion of truth-condition. The central idea of truth-conditional semantics (...) is the idea that, via truth, we connect words and the world. If we know the truth-conditions of a sentence, we know *which state of affairs must hold for the sentence to be true*."
>
> Recanati (2005: 185).

The truth conditions of syncretists do not have to fulfil this requirement of 'connecting words with the world': they only provide a formal procedure for a theory of meaning. The debate is at present in the focus of attention of most post-Griceans and is likely to occupy us for some time. Suffice it to say that objections to weakening truth conditions should not be taken lightly.

There is another view that we should consider in that it shares some assumptions with the above versions of minimalism, while rejecting others. We have seen in section 4.4 that Kent Bach advocates a clear-cut boundary between the tasks of semantics and those of pragmatics. He does so by claiming that the semantic analysis of a sentence need not result in a truth-conditional content: not every declarative sentence expresses a proposition, even if it is free from indexical expressions. Instead, sentences can just express propositional radicals. Bach (2006) calls this view Radical Semantic Minimalism. This view seems to have been increasing in popularity recently (see e. g. Horn 2006; Atlas 2005b). But, as we have seen, other minimalists do not share this view of the dissociation of semantics from truth conditions, so it has to be distinguished as a separate variety, only tentatively subsumed under the umbrella label of 'minimalism'.

Returning to contextualism, we can go even further in the direction of context-dependence. We can assume that words don't have determined, coded sense. Instead, they act like pointers to particular senses in particular contexts. Truth conditions are then assigned to utterances that owe nothing to sentence-type meaning, but neither do they owe anything to lexical meanings. Neither of the two exists. Words have only a so-called *semantic potential*. All they have is particular uses. This view is thus clearly reminiscent of later Wittgenstein's view that meaning *is* language use and thus of the theoretical orientation of ordinary language philosophy. Although this view is not currently in the forefront of theorizing, it is the next logical step from the contextualist stance represented in truth-conditional pragmatics and other approaches that allow top-down pragmatic enrichment which is not dictated by grammar.

6 Summary: The significance of the boundary disputes

The current state of the debate concerning the interface between semantics and pragmatics is to a large extent the upshot of the revolutionary period in the study of meaning known as radical pragmatics, aided by the views of ordinary language philosophers. Two relatively separate disciplines, the formal study of sentence meaning and the relatively informal study of the properties of speech acts became more and more intertwined as a result of the adoption of semantic underdetermination and the admittance of pragmatic inference about the speaker's intentions, as well as some other context-bound information, into the semantic content. This facilitated the shift of the centre of attention from the sentence to the utterance. However, the direction of change has not been steady throughout the past three decades. There are attempts to keep semantics and pragmatics apart either through denying that semantics has to provide propositions and hence truth-conditional content, or through keeping the objectives of semantics and pragmatics apart and stressing the theoretical utility of the sentence's truth conditions, like minimalists of the syncretic flavour do. At present the dominant orientations seem to be various forms of contextualism. This state of affairs is undoubtedly aided by the overall desideratum to stay faithful to speakers' intuitions about meaning and to the view that semantic theory should not ignore these intuitions. The desideratum to account for *all* kinds of enrichment by postulating one type of mechanism is also an important consideration. Whether contextualism will retain its power, succumb to minimalism, or evolve into a radical form of occasion-meaning of meaning eliminativism remains to be seen.

7 References

Asher, Nicholas & Alex Lascarides 2003. *Logics of Conversation*. Cambridge: Cambridge University Press.

Atlas, Jay D. 1977. Negation, ambiguity, and presupposition. *Linguistics & Philosophy* 1, 321–336.

Atlas, Jay D. 1979. How linguistics matters to philosophy: Presupposition, truth, and meaning. In: C. K. Oh & D. Dinneen (eds.). *Syntax and Semantics 11: Presupposition*. New York: Academic Press, 265–281.

Atlas, Jay D. 1989. *Philosophy without Ambiguity: A Logico-Linguistic Essay*. Oxford: Clarendon Press.

Atlas, Jay D. 2005a. *Logic, Meaning, and Conversation: Semantical Underdeterminacy, Implicature, and Their Interface*. Oxford: Oxford University Press.

Atlas, Jay D. 2005b. Whatever happened to meaning? A morality tale of Cappelen's and LePore's insensitivity to lexical semantics and a defense of Kent Bach, sort of. Paper presented at the *International Pragmatics Association Conference*, Riva del Garda.

Atlas, Jay D. 2006a. A personal history of linguistic pragmatics 1969–2000. Paper presented at the *Jay Atlas – Distinguished Scholar Workshop*, University of Cambridge.

Atlas, Jay D. 2006b. Remarks on Emma Borg's *Minimal Semantics*. Ms. Claremont, CA, Pomona College.

Austin, John L. 1962. *How to Do Things with Words*. Oxford: Oxford University Press. 2nd ed. 1975.

Bach, Kent 1987a. *Thought and Reference*. Oxford: Clarendon Press.

Bach, Kent 1987b. On communicative intentions: A reply to Recanati. *Mind & Language* 2, 141–154.

Bach, Kent 1994. Semantic slack: What is said and more. In: S. L. Tsohatzidis (ed.). *Foundations of Speech Act Theory: Philosophical and Linguistic Perspectives*. London: Routledge, 267–291.

Bach, Kent 1999. The semantics-pragmatics distinction: What it is and why it matters. In: K. Turner (ed.). *The Semantics/Pragmatics Interface from Different Points of View*. Amsterdam: Elsevier, 65–84.

Bach, Kent 2000. Quantification, qualification and context: A reply to Stanley and Szabó. *Mind & Language* 15, 262–283.

Bach, Kent 2001. You don't say? *Synthese* 128, 15–44.

Bach, Kent 2004. Minding the gap. In: C. Bianchi (ed.). *The Semantics/Pragmatics Distinction*. Stanford, CA: CSLI Publications, 27–43.

Bach, Kent 2006. The excluded middle: Semantic minimalism without minimal propositions. *Philosophy and Phenomenological Research* 73, 435–442.

Bach, Kent 2007. Regressions in pragmatics (and semantics). In: N. Burton-Roberts (ed.). *Pragmatics*. Basingstoke: Palgrave Macmillan, 24–44.

Bach, Kent & Robert M. Harnish 1979. *Linguistic Communication and Speech Acts*. Cambridge, MA: The MIT Press.

Balaguer, Mark 2005. Indexical propositions and *de re* belief ascriptions. *Synthese* 146, 325–355.

Blutner, Reinhard & Henk Zeevat (eds.) 2004. *Optimality Theory and Pragmatics*. Basingstoke: Palgrave Macmillan.

Borg, Emma 2004. *Minimal Semantics*. Oxford: Oxford University Press.

Bultinck, Bert 2005. *Numerous Meanings: The Meaning of English Cardinals and the Legacy of Paul Grice*. Amsterdam: Elsevier.
Cappelen, Herman & Ernie Lepore 2005. *Insensitive Semantics: A Defense of Semantic Minimalism and Speech Act Pluralism*. Oxford: Blackwell.
Carston, Robyn 1988. Implicature, explicature, and truth-theoretic semantics. In: R. M. Kempson (ed.). *Mental Representations: The Interface Between Language and Reality*. Cambridge: Cambridge University Press, 155–181.
Carston, Robyn 1998. Postscript (1995) to Carston 1988. In: A. Kasher (ed.). *Pragmatics: Critical Concepts, vol. 4*. London: Routledge, 464–479.
Carston, Robyn 2001. Relevance theory and the saying/implicating distinction. In: C. Iten & A. Neleman (eds.). *UCL Working Papers in Linguistics 13*. London: University College London, 1–34.
Carston, Robyn 2002. *Thoughts and Utterances: The Pragmatics of Explicit Communication*. Oxford: Blackwell.
Carston, Robyn 2007. How many pragmatic systems are there? In: M. J. Frápolli (ed.). *Saying, Meaning and Referring: Essays on François Recanati's Philosophy of Language*. Basingstoke: Palgrave Macmillan, 18–48.
Chalmers, David J. 1996. *The Conscious Mind: In Search of a Fundamental Theory*. Oxford: Oxford University Press.
Chalmers, David J. 2006. The foundations of two-dimensional semantics. In: M. García-Carpintero & J. Macià (eds.). *Two-Dimensional Semantics*. Oxford: Clarendon Press, 55–140.
Chierchia, Gennaro 2004. Scalar implicatures, polarity phenomena, and the syntax/pragmatics interface. In: A. Belletti (ed.). *Structures and Beyond: The Cartography of Syntactic Structures, vol. 3*. Oxford: Oxford University Press, 39–103.
Clapp, Lenny 2007. Minimal (disagreement about) semantics. In: G. Preyer & G. Peter (eds.). *Context-Sensitivity and Semantic Minimalism*. Oxford: Oxford University Press, 251–277.
Cohen, L. Jonathan 1971. Some remarks on Grice's views about the logical particles of natural language. In: Y. Bar-Hillel (ed.). *Pragmatics of Natural Languages*. Dordrecht: Reidel, 50–68.
Cole, Peter (ed.) 1981. *Radical Pragmatics*. New York: Academic Press.
Davis, Wayne A. 1998. *Implicature: Intention, Convention, and Principle in the Failure of Gricean Theory*. Cambridge: Cambridge University Press.
van Deemter, Kees & Stanley Peters (eds.) 1996. *Ambiguity and Underspecification*. Stanford, CA: CSLI Publications.
Dowty, David R., Robert E. Wall & Stanley Peters 1981. *Introduction to Montague Semantics*. Dordrecht: Reidel.
Ducrot, Oswald 1972. *Dire et ne pas dire*. Paris: Hermann.
Geurts, Bart 1998. Scalars. In: P. Ludewig & B. Geurts (eds.). *Lexikalische Semantik aus kognitiver Sicht*. Tübingen: Narr, 95–117.
Green, Georgia M. 1996. Ambiguity resolution and discourse interpretation. In: K. van Deemter & S. Peters (eds.). *Ambiguity and Underspecification*. Stanford, CA: CSLI Publications, 1–26.
Grice, H. Paul 1957. Meaning. *Philosophical Review* 66, 377–388. Reprinted in: H. P. Grice. *Studies in the Way of Words*. Cambridge, MA: Harvard University Press, 1989, 213–223.
Grice, H. Paul 1969. Utterer's meaning and intentions. *Philosophical Review* 78, 147–177. Reprinted in: H. P. Grice. *Studies in the Way of Words*. Cambridge, MA: Harvard University Press, 1989, 86–116.

Grice, H. Paul 1975. Logic and conversation. In: P. Cole & J. L. Morgan (eds.). *Syntax and Semantics 3: Speech Acts*. New York: Academic Press. Reprinted in: H. P. Grice. *Studies in the Way of Words*. Cambridge, MA: Harvard University Press, 1989, 22–40.
Grice, H. Paul 1978. Further notes on logic and conversation. In: P. Cole (ed.). *Syntax and Semantics 9: Pragmatics*. New York: Academic Press. Reprinted in: H. P. Grice. *Studies in the Way of Words*. Cambridge, MA: Harvard University Press, 1989, 41–57.
Haugh, Michael & Kasia M. Jaszczolt 2012. Intentions and intentionality. In: K. Allan & K.M. Jaszczolt (eds.). *The Cambridge Handbook of Pragmatics*. Cambridge: Cambridge University Press, 87–112.
Horn, Laurence R. 1976. *On the Semantic Properties of Logical Operators in English*. Bloomington, IN: Indiana University Linguistics Club.
Horn, Laurence R. 1984. Toward a new taxonomy for pragmatic inference: Q-based and R-based implicature. In: D. Schiffrin (ed.). *Georgetown University Round Table on Languages and Linguistics 1984*. Washington, DC: Georgetown University Press, 11–42.
Horn, Laurence R. 1988. Pragmatic theory. In: F. J. Newmeyer (ed.). *Linguistics: The Cambridge Survey, vol. 1*. Cambridge: Cambridge University Press, 113–145.
Horn, Laurence R. 1992. The said and the unsaid. In: C. Barker & D. Dowty (eds.). *Proceedings of Semantics and Linguistic Theory (= SALT) II*. Columbus, OH: The Ohio State University, 163–192.
Horn, Laurence R. 2004. Implicature. In: L. R. Horn & G. Ward (eds.). *The Handbook of Pragmatics*. Oxford: Blackwell, 3–28.
Horn, Laurence R. 2006. The border wars: A neo-Gricean perspective. In: K. von Heusinger & K. Turner (eds.). *Where Semantics Meets Pragmatics: The Michigan Papers*. Amsterdam: Elsevier, 21–48.
Jaszczolt, Katarzyna M. 1999. *Discourse, Beliefs, and Intentions: Semantic Defaults and Propositional Attitude Ascription*. Amsterdam: Elsevier.
Jaszczolt, Katarzyna M. 2002. *Semantics and Pragmatics: Meaning in Language and Discourse*. London: Longman.
Jaszczolt, Katarzyna M. 2005. *Default Semantics: Foundations of a Compositional Theory of Acts of Communication*. Oxford: Oxford University Press.
Jaszczolt, Katarzyna M. 2006. Defaults in semantics and pragmatics. In: E. N. Zalta (ed.). *Stanford Encyclopedia of Philosophy (Winter 2006 Edition)*. http://plato.stanford.edu/archives/win2006/entries/defaults-semantics-pragmatics/ November 7, 2011.
Jaszczolt, Katarzyna M. 2009. *Representing Time: An Essay on Temporality as Modality*. Oxford: Oxford University Press.
Jaszczolt, Katarzyna M. 2010a. Semantics-pragmatics interface. In: L. Cummings (ed.). *The Pragmatics Encyclopedia*. London: Routledge, 428–432.
Jaszczolt, Katarzyna M. 2010b. Default Semantics. In: B. Heine & H. Narrog (eds.). *The Oxford Handbook of Linguistic Analysis*. Oxford: Oxford University Press, 193–221.
Kaplan, David 1978. Dthat. In: P. Cole (ed.). *Syntax and Semantics 9: Pragmatics*. New York: Academic Press, 221–243.
Kaplan, David 1989. Demonstratives. In: J. Almog, J. Perry & H. Wettstein (eds.). *Themes from Kaplan*. Oxford: Oxford University Press, 481–563.
Kempson, Ruth M. 1975. *Presupposition and the Delimitation of Semantics*. Cambridge: Cambridge University Press.
Kempson, Ruth M. 1979. Presupposition, opacity, and ambiguity. In: C.-K. Oh & D. A. Dinneen (eds.). *Syntax and Semantics 11: Presupposition*. New York: Academic Press, 283–297.

Kempson, Ruth M. 1986. Ambiguity and the semantics-pragmatics distinction. In: C. Travis (ed.). *Meaning and Interpretation*. Oxford: Blackwell, 77–103.

King, Jeffrey C. & Jason Stanley 2005. Semantics, pragmatics, and the role of semantic content. In: Z. G. Szabó (ed.). *Semantics vs. Pragmatics*. Oxford: Oxford University Press, 111–164.

Koenig, Jean-Pierre 1993. Scalar predicates and negation: Punctual semantics and interval interpretations. *Papers from the 27th Regional Meeting of the Chicago Linguistic Society (= CLS). Part 2: The Parasession on Negation*. Chicago, IL: Chicago Linguistic Society, 140–155.

Lakoff, George 1970. A note on vagueness and ambiguity. *Linguistic Inquiry* 1, 357–359.

Lascarides, Alex, Ann Copestake & Ted Briscoe 1996. Ambiguity and coherence. *Journal of Semantics* 13, 41–65.

Levinson, Stephen C. 1987. Minimization and conversational inference. In: J. Verschueren & M. Bertuccelli-Papi (eds.). *The Pragmatic Perspective. Selected Papers from the 1985 International Pragmatics Conference*. Amsterdam: Benjamins, 61–129.

Levinson, Stephen C. 1995. Three levels of meaning. In: F. R. Palmer (ed.). *Grammar and Meaning. Essays in Honour of Sir John Lyons*. Cambridge: Cambridge University Press, 90–115.

Levinson, Stephen C. 2000. *Presumptive Meanings: The Theory of Generalized Conversational Implicature*. Cambridge, MA: The MIT Press.

Lycan, William G. 1984. *Logical Form in Natural Language*. Cambridge, MA: The MIT Press.

Mill, John Stuart 1872. *An Examination of Sir William Hamilton's Philosophy*. 4th edn. London: Longmans, Green, Reader & Dyer.

Musolino, Julien 2004. The semantics and acquisition of number words: Integrating linguistic and developmental perspectives. *Cognition* 93, 1–41.

Predelli, Stefano 2005a. *Contexts: Meaning, Truth, and the Use of Language*. Oxford: Clarendon Press.

Predelli, Stefano 2005b. Painted leaves, context, and semantic analysis. *Linguistics & Philosophy* 28, 351–374.

Predelli, Stefano 2006. The problem with token-reflexivity. *Synthese* 148, 5–29.

Recanati, François 1989. The pragmatics of what is said. *Mind & Language* 4, 295–329. Reprinted in: S. Davis (ed.). *Pragmatics: A Reader*. Oxford: Oxford University Press, 1991, 97–120.

Recanati, François 1993. *Direct Reference: From Language to Thought*. Oxford: Blackwell.

Recanati, François 1994. Contextualism and anti-contextualism in the philosophy of language. In: S. L. Tsohatzidis (ed.). *Foundations of Speech Act Theory: Philosophical and Linguistic Perspectives*. London: Routledge, 156–166.

Recanati, François 2001. What is said. *Synthese* 128, 75–91.

Recanati, François 2002a. Unarticulated constituents. *Linguistics & Philosophy* 25, 299–345.

Recanati, François 2002b. Does linguistic communication rest on inference? *Mind & Language* 17, 105–126.

Recanati, François 2004. *Literal Meaning*. Cambridge: Cambridge University Press.

Recanati, François 2005. Literalism and contextualism: Some varieties. In: G. Preyer & G. Peter (eds.). *Contextualism in Philosophy: Knowledge, Meaning, and Truth*. Oxford: Clarendon Press, 171–196.

Recanati, François 2007. Reply to Carston 2007. In: M. J. Frápolli (ed.). *Saying, Meaning and Referring: Essays on François Recanati's Philosophy of Language*. Basingstoke: Palgrave Macmillan, 49–54.

Recanati, François. 2010. *Truth-Conditional Pragmatics*. Oxford: Clarendon Press.
Saul, Jennifer M. 2002. What is said and psychological reality; Grice's project and Relevance Theorists' criticisms. *Linguistics & Philosophy* 25, 347–372.
Searle, John R. 1969. *Speech Acts: An Essay in the Philosophy of Language*. Cambridge: Cambridge University Press.
Sperber, Dan & Deirdre Wilson 1986. *Relevance: Communication and Cognition*. Oxford: Blackwell.
Sperber, Dan & Deirdre Wilson 1995. *Relevance: Communication and Cognition*. 2nd edn. Oxford: Blackwell.
Stalnaker, Robert 1978. Assertion. In: P. Cole (ed.). *Syntax and Semantic 9: Pragmatics*. New York: Academic Press, 315–332.
Stalnaker, Robert 1999. Introduction. In: R. Stalnaker. *Context and Content: Essays on Intentionality in Speech and Thought*. Oxford: Oxford University Press, 1–28.
Stanley, Jason 2002. Making it articulated. *Mind & Language* 17, 149–168.
Stanley, Jason & Zoltán G. Szabó 2000. On quantifier domain restriction. *Mind & Language* 15, 219–261.
Wilson, Deirdre 1975. *Presuppositions and Non-Truth-Conditional Semantics*. New York: Academic Press.
Zwicky, Arnold & Jerrold Sadock 1975. Ambiguity tests and how to fail them. In: J. P. Kimball (ed.). *Syntax and Semantics 4*. New York: Academic Press, 1–36.

Thomas Ede Zimmermann
12 Context dependence

1 Contexts —— 403
2 Trivialities —— 408
3 Characters —— 413
4 Diagonals —— 421
5 Extensionality —— 430
6 Attitude reports —— 432
7 Monsters —— 443
8 Parameterization —— 452
9 References —— 459

Abstract: Linguistic expressions frequently make reference to the situation in which they are uttered. In fact, there are expressions whose whole point of use is to relate to their context of utterance. It is such expressions that this article is primarily about. However, rather than presenting the richness of pertinent phenomena (cf. Anderson & Keenan 1985), it concentrates on the theoretical tools provided by the (standard) two-dimensional analysis of context dependence, essentially originating with Kaplan (1989a) – with a little help from Stalnaker (1978) and Lewis (1979a, 1980), and various predecessors including Kamp (1971) and Vlach (1973). The current article overlaps in content with the account in Zimmermann (1991), which is however much broader (and at times deeper).

1 Contexts

Whether spoken, signed, written, telegraphed – whenever language is used, an utterance is produced, under circumstances to which we will henceforth refer as [*utterance*] *contexts*. It is a characteristic feature of certain expressions – words, phrases, constructions, features, etc. – that they directly relate to the very context in which they are uttered. Personal pronouns are cases in point. Given an utterance context c, the first-person pronoun *I* refers to whoever produced the utterance – SPEAKER(c) for short. We thus have:

(1) $/I/^c$ = SPEAKER(c),

Thomas Ede Zimmermann, Frankfurt/Main, Germany

https://doi.org/10.1515/9783110589849-012

where $/A/^c$ is the referent of a given (referential) expression A in a given utterance context c. It should be noted that the equation (1) is *schematic* in that it applies to any context c. Hence SPEAKER is a function assigning persons to utterance contexts. In fact, this particular function may be thought of as a *communicative rôle*, and (1) as saying that the pronoun *I* expresses that rôle in that it always, i.e. in any utterance context, refers to the person playing it. Utterance contexts may in turn be characterized as those situations in which someone plays the rôle expressed by *I*, i.e. those situations for which SPEAKER is defined.

In a similar vein, the (singular) pronoun *you* can be seen to express a communicative rôle in that it is used to refer to the person addressed in a given context c:

(2) $/you_{sg}/^c = \text{ADDRESSEE}(c)$

Traditionally, expressions of communicative rôles are categorized as *person deixis*. Languages not only differ as to the expressive means of person deixis, there is also ample variation as to the rôles expressed. Some languages (like French) distinguish more than one second person, depending on the social relationship between speaker and hearer, a phenomenon known as *social deixis*; another common distinction (to be found, e.g., in Tagalog) is between an inclusive and an exclusive first person plural, depending on whether the addressee does or does not belong to the group designated (and thus avoiding embarrassing misunderstandings caused by the indeterminacy of sentences like *We have been invited to the President's dinner*).

Communicative rôles are one example of *contextual parameters* that are commonly used to determine reference. Others include the *time* and *place* of utterance that help determining the referents of *today* (= the day on which the utterance is made); *tomorrow* (= the day after the utterance); *ago* (= before the utterance); and *here* (= the place of the utterance). Traditionally, such expressions are categorized as *temporal* and *local* deixis, respectively. Extending the above notation, one may capture them by means of functions assigning times and places to utterance contexts. Then the most basic deictic expressions directly denote the values of these functions:

(3) a. $/now/^c = \text{TIME}(c)$
    b. $/here/^c = \text{PLACE}(c)$

In (3), TIME and PLACE are functions assigning to any (utterance) context its temporal and spatial location, respectively. These locations may be thought of as points, intervals or more complex constructions, depending on the semantic operations performed on them. And the denotations of other deictic expressions may be expressed in terms of these functions, or derived from them with the help of standard temporal and spatial measures:

(4) a. $/today/^c$ = DAY(TIME(c))
 b. $/yesterday/^c$ = DAY(TIME(c) – 24HRS)
 c. $/ago/^c$ (X) = TIME(c)–X

While the expressions mentioned so far make reference to various *objective* features of utterances, a number of locutions and constructions seem to bring more *subjective* contextual factors into play (cf. Borg 2004: 29ff.):

(5) a. This belongs to me.
 b. He is an enemy.
 c. John's book is expensive.
 d. Everybody had a great time.

Demonstratives like the subject of (5a) are frequently accompanied by a pointing gesture that helps the hearer to identify their referents. Arguably, it is this *demonstration* that determines the referent. Of course, as a bodily movement, the gesture itself is as objective a part of the context as the speaker or the addressee. However, the referent of the demonstrative is not the gesture but its target, which may not be so easily identified (*pace* von Kutschera 1975: 127); arguably and within certain limits, what this target is, is up to the person performing the gesture, i.e. the speaker. Hence, inasmuch as the demonstration determines the referent of the demonstrative, the speaker's intentions are decisive, and they make this kind of expression context-dependent in a more subjective way; see Kaplan (1978, 1989b: 582ff.), Wettstein (1984), Bach (1987: 182ff., 1992), and Reimer (1991, 1992a, 1992b) for more (and different views) on the subject. Despite this subjectivity, there is little doubt that the referent of *this* depends on the utterance context and could therefore be provided by a (speaker-dependent) parameter:

(6) $/this/^c$ = DEMONSTRATUM(c) (SPEAKER(c))

Third person pronouns and *implicit arguments* seem to work in a similar way, except that they are not normally accompanied by demonstrations; but their referents are usually taken to be supplied by the background. This is illustrated by (5b), which may be used to subsume a male person as among the foes of a community to which the speaker belongs – which person and which community depending on the circumstances in which the sentence is uttered. Again, it would seem that, within certain limits, the speaker has the last word about who precisely is referred to by these, presumably context-dependent, devices.

Possessives come in a variety of guises and with a variety of functions (cf. article 6 [Semantics: Noun Phrases and Verb Phrases] (Barker) *Possessives and relational nouns*). A common core is that they express a relation between the referents of two nominal expressions. In many cases the relation is supplied by a (relational) possessor noun like *surface* or *father*; in others it is some default like ownership or a part-whole relation. In typical utterances of (5c) the relevant relation would be reading, writing, or, per default, owning; but it is not hard to imagine situations in which it is the relation holding between x and y if x writes a term paper about y, etc. (Williams 1982: 283). It thus seems that the relation a possessive construction expresses is a matter of the circumstances in which it is used; hence possessives are candidates for context-dependent expressions. More precisely, it is the grammatical construction itself, or the constellation in which possessor and possessee stand, that makes reference to context, possibly by introducing an un-pronouced functional morpheme that expresses a relation whose precise identity may depend on the utterance context (cf. Cresswell 1996: 50ff.). However, unlike the other contextual parameters mentioned above, the possessive relation cannot always be read off from the utterance context all that easily.

Quantifiers have domains that are understood as given by their linguistic and extra-linguistic environment. (5d), taken from von Fintel (1996: 28), is a case in point: if the sentence is used as an answer to *How was the party?*, its subject is likely to be construed as quantifying over the participants in the event mentioned in the question – as it would be if the sentence is uttered after said occasion, with happy people leaving the premises in the speaker's view. The phenomenon has aroused much interest among philosophers of language (e.g., Stanley & Williamson 1995; Reimer 1992c, 1998), not least because it is paralleled by definite descriptions whose quantificational status has been under dispute ever since Russell (1905). Again, it is hard to pin down objective features of contexts that would correspond to domains of quantifiers, which in general do not seem to be identifiable without knowing what the speaker has in mind. (But see Gauker 1997 for a skeptical view.)

What the phenomena illustrated in (5) have in common, and what distinguishes them from the classical cases of deixis, is their lack of objectivity: misunderstandings as to what was pointed to, who was left implicit, which possessive relation was alluded to, or who is quantified over arise rather easily – more easily than when it comes to determining who the speaker is, or where and when the utterance is made. If worse comes to worst, the speaker using a possessive would have to make herself clear. Of couse, this does not make speakers Humpty-Dumpties, who arbitrarily decide what their words mean: what is intended and left implicit must be salient and accessible to the audience (Lewis 1979b: 348ff.); otherwise the speaker may be perceived as uncooperative, obscure, or even deranged. But within a certain range, it seems to be at the speaker's discretion to decide what the sentences in (5) are about. So there is something ultimately subjective in the way quantifier domains, possessive relations, implict arguments, and the referents of 3rd person pronouns and demonstratives may depend on the context, which distinguishes them from the classical deictics in (1)–(4).

It is important to distinguish the subjective nature typical of the locutions in (5) from other sources of referential indeterminacy like vagueness and ambiguity. If a speaker uses the (complex) demonstrative *this mountain* to refer to the Eiger, this reference may be quite vague because the Eiger does not have clearly determined boundaries, and presumably the speaker does not (want to) impose or presuppose such boundaries by his utterance either. However, this vagueness has nothing to do with the subjective nature of the demonstrative; in fact, it also occurs with ordinary deictic expressions like *here* (cf. Klein 1978). The subjective nature of the demonstrative shows in the fact that the speaker may refer to the Eiger even though his gesture alone could be interpreted as relating to the Jungfrau, or even a heap of rocks. And these alternatives do not constitute different readings of the sentence; otherwise English syntax would have to supply indefinitely many underlying forms suiting the referential possibilities of arbitrary speakers in arbitray environments – which is highly implausible, to say the least (cf. Stanley & Szabó 2000: 223, fn. 16). In sum, it is not vagueness or ambiguity that distinguishes the cases in (5) from the context-dependencies in (1)–(4) but the fact that matters of referenc are – at least in part – determined by the speaker's intentions.

The subjectivity of certain context-dependent expressions and constructions must also be distinguished from uncertainties in the identification of the utterance situation. Thus, e.g., the hearer does not always know who is speaking or writing, anonymous phone calls and letters being cases in point; still, the hearer does know that the speker is referring to him- or herself when using a first-person pronoun. Similarly, if a speaker uses local or temporal deixis, the hearer may be uncertain as to which places she is referring to because he might not know where or when the utterance was made; still he does know that the speaker was referring to the time and place of utterance. This kind of ignorance may even occur with speakers who are confused as to where they are, what time it is, and maybe even who they are. (The latter possibility appears hard to imagine, but see Perry (1977: 492f.) and Lewis (1979a: 520f.) for pertinent *gedankenexperiments*.) In all these cases though, the deictic expressions work as usual; it is only the communicants that lack knowledge of the utterance situation and are thus not in a position to fully exploit their meaning. The epistemic uncertainty about the utterance context may also concern the question which situation should count as the context in the first place. For sometimes an utterance is properly understood only under the pretense that it had been uttered under different cirumstances. This is the case with certain recorded utterancs in which the speaker pretends to be speaking at a later time (as in some TV shows), but also in more remote 'utterances' like first-person inscriptions on tombstones (Kratzer 1978: 17ff.), where the intended utterance context may well be an impossible scene! Note that in all such cases despite the pretense concerning the exact circumstances, the utterance as such is not taken to be fictional as it would be the case in a theatre performance. In sum, even with classical deictics like those in (1)–(4) matters of reference are not always as clear as we have been assuming; but the unclarity lies in the utterance situations at large, not in the meanings of these expressions.

What follows is a survey of one type of semantic analysis of context dependence. In it we will not bother to distinguish between various forms of context dependence. In fact, most of the time we will concentrate on the 1st person pronoun as given in (1), with occasional glimpses of other deictic expressions like those in (2)–(4). Still whatever will be said below is meant to apply, *mutatis mutandis*, to all context-dependent expressions alike, whether relating to objective features of the utterance situation or to more subjective, intentional aspects like those in (5), which may be thought to be interpreted by subjective, speaker-dependent contextual parameters as indicated in (6).

2 Trivialities

In the above examples (aspects of) the utterance situation played a crucial role in determining the reference of the expressions under scrutiny. However, this alone is not what makes these expressions deictic or context-dependent. In fact, to the extent that an expression can be said to refer to anything at all, what it refers to usually depends on the utterance situation. For instance, when used around the time of writing this contribution, the definite description *the German chancellor* refers to Angela Merkel, whereas some ten years ago its referent would have been Gerhard Schröder. Hence what the expression refers to may change with, and depends on, when it is or was uttered, and thus on the utterance situation. In this respect the definite *the German chancellor* is like the first-person pronoun *I*. To highlight the context-dependence of the referent of the description and bring out the analogy with the personal pronoun, we may use the same kind of notation:

(1) $/I/^c = \text{SPEAKER}(c)$
(7) $/\text{the German chancellor}/^c = \text{GC}(c)$,

where GC is a function assigning to any utterance context c that person (if any) that happens to be the German chancellor at the utterance time, TIME(c). To be sure, there is an obvious difference between (1) and (7): while the SPEAKER rôle is likely to be associated with the pronoun *I* for lexical reasons, the equation in (7) would have to be derived by general compositional mechanisms from the meanings of the lexical items that somehow conspire to express GC. This difference also accounts for the relatively idiosyncratic nature of the function GC as opposed to the arguably more natural and straightforward SPEAKER aspect of utterance contexts. These differences notwithstanding, it would still seem that both the reference of the first person pronoun *I* and that of the definite description *the German chancellor* depend on the utterance context, and this common feature shows clearly in (1) and (7).

Given the rough analogy between (1) and (7), it is tempting to regard context dependence as a special case of the more general phenomenon of the situation dependence of reference. Yet although (1) and (7) will fall out of the standard approach to context dependence, these equations are deceptively simple: as it turns out, the two cases at hand differ fundamentally in the precise way reference depends on the utterance context. This can be seen by looking at *uninformative* statements like the following:

(8) No bachelor is married.
(9) The German chancellor is a politician.
(10) I am here.

(8) is clearly trivial: being a bachelor means, among other things (like being a male person), never having married. Consequently, an utterance of (8) is likely to be construed in some non-literal sense, or to be used in some purely rhetorical function. We may take it for granted that, whatever the communicative effects of utterances of (8) may be, and however they may come about, they do not constitute the literal, conventional meaning of the sentence. If it were only for its literal meaning, (8) would be totally pointless. And it is easy to see why this is so: to use a Kantian phrase, the predicate concept of being married is contained in the subject concept of not applying to bachelors. Extending our notation to nouns and (predicative) adjectives, we may write the two extensions as /*bachelor*/^{c} and /*married*/^{c}, the upper index indicating that the extension depends on the utterance context c. Since the function of the determiner *no* is to express disjointness of the two extensions, the *truth condition* (8) imposes on c can now be formulated as follows:

(11) /*bachelor*/^{c} ∩ /*married*/^{c} = ∅

Indeed, it is hard to see how any context *c* could fail to meet (11), which is why (8) is trivial.

(9) too has an air of triviality: being the chancellor of Germany means holding a particular political office, and holding a political office makes a politician. Maybe (9) is not *entirely* trivial in that there are (or rather: were) contexts in which Germany did not have a chancellor. However, as long as we fix the general political situation, (9) is not really helpful. Consequently, an utterance of (9) is likely to be construed in some non-literal sense, perhaps as an allusion to certain stereotypes. Again we take it that whatever the communicative effects of (9) may be, and however they may come about, they do not constitute the literal, conventional meaning of the sentence. Rather, given a context *c*, (9) is literally true just in case (12) obtains:

(12) $GC(c) \in /politician/^c$

This truth condition is trivially satisfied by any context *c* in which the subject of (9) has a referent; and for simplicity we will not bother about other contexts, in which the use of (9) would be inappropriate anyway.

(10) parallels (8) and (9) in its triviality: given an utterance context, the speaker in that context is certainly located at the place where the utterance is made. This truth condition can be brought out in terms of a binary 'locality' relation between objects and their locations, which we take to be the extension of the preposition *at* (in its locative sense) and which depends on the context *c*, because in different contexts, things may be in different places:

(13) $(SPEAKER(c), PLACE(c)) \in AT(c)$ [= $/at/^c$]

Again it would seem that no context could fail to satisfy (13), which is why (10) cannot be uttered falsely and thus appears trivial.

While there is doubtlessly something trivial about (10), the sentence is not quite as uninformative as (8), and not in the same way. In fact, an utterance of (10) may tell the hearer something she did not know before – which is hardly possible with (8). One may imagine John coming home unexpectedly early to hear his wife speak to someone over the phone, saying that she is not expecting her husband before the end of the week – whereupon he enters the room uttering (10), and surprising Mary. Though the surprise effect may be attributed to the very fact that John is standing there visibly and audibly, it also appears that the very *content* of John's utterance, i.e. what is (literally) said by it, expresses precisely what Mary is surprised about. For even though the surprise could not have been smaller had John uttered (8), say, the content of that utterance would not have been the object of her surprise, only the fact that an utterance with such content is made.

The contrast between (8) and (10), then, turns on a difference in their *content*, i.e. what is (or can be) said, or expressed, by uttering these sentences. To the extent that content is a semantically relevant notion, so is the difference in the kind of triviality these two sentences exemplify. Indeed, it would seem that the content of a sentence depends on its meaning. However, it is not determined by its meaning alone. Had Mary's son Peter uttered (10) on the same occasion, he would have expressed something much less surprising – as John might have, had he made his utterance somewhere else. In other words, what John expressed with (10) in the circumstances was that he, John, was at the place of his utterance, viz. John and Mary's home; whereas Peter would have expressed that he, Peter, was at that same place; etc. And clearly, none of these contents would have been as trivial as what anybody would (literally) express by uttering (8). Hence which content is expressed by a given sentence may depend on the context in which the utterance is made. So while (8) and (10) are both trivially true whenever uttered, the content of the latter need not be trivial, whereas that of the former always is. That the content of (10) as uttered on the occasion described above is non-trivial can be seen from the fact that there are many circumstances that it rules out. In this respect, it differs from what is expressed by (8), in whichever context it may be uttered: even if things get as crazy as one may imagine, there will be no married bachelors. However, things do not have to be particularly wild for John to not be at home; in fact, this is what Mary thought would be the case, and she is pretty down to earth.

In order to model these differences in informativity, we will identify the content of a sentence with the circumstances to which it truthfully applies, i.e. those situations that it does not rule out. (Cf. article 7 [Semantics: Theories] (Zimmermann) *Model-theoretic semantics*, sec. 2, for more on the general setting.) More specifically, we will take the content $[\![S]\!]^c$ of a sentence S to be a subset of the stock of all possible situations, a set called *Logical Space*: $[\![S]\!]^c \subseteq LS$. Thus, if c^* is the above context in which John utters (10), we find that $[\![10]\!]^{c^*} \neq LS$, because $[\![10]\!]^{c^*}$ only contains the situations in which John is at home, leaving out innumerable situations in which he is not. More generally, if a speaker x utters (10) at a place y, x thereby expresses a content that rules out the situations in which x is not located at y. We thus have:

(14) a. $[\![(10)]\!]^{c^*} = \{s \mid (\text{John}, \text{Home}) \in \text{AT}(s)\}$
 b. $[\![(10)]\!]^c = \{s \mid (\text{SPEAKER}(c), \text{PLACE}(c)) \in \text{AT}(s)\}$

According to (14a), whether a situation s ends up in the content expressed by (10) in c^*, then, depends on John's location in that situation: if s is such that John is at his (actual) home, then $s \in [\![10]\!]^{c^*}$; otherwise $s \notin [\![10]\!]^{c^*}$. Hence $[\![10]\!]^{c^*} \neq LS$ because there are various possible (and actual) scenarios in which John is not at home; so the content of (10) as uttered in c^* is not trivial in that it excludes a host of possible situations. On the other hand, in c^*, John is at home, and thus $c^* \in [\![10]\!]^{c^*}$. According to (14b), whether a situation s ends up in the content expressed by (10) in an arbitrary context c, depends on where the speaker in c is in that situation: if s is such that the speaker (in c) is at the place where c is located, then $s \in [\![10]\!]^c$; otherwise $s \notin [\![10]\!]^c$. Hence $[\![10]\!]^c \neq LS$ because the location of individuals is a contingent matter; so the content of (10) is never trivial. On the other hand, quite generally the speaker is where the utterance is made, and thus $c \in [\![10]\!]^c$. This is what makes (10) trivial, although its content ist not.

Readers are advised to briefly stop to ponder over the difference between the truth condition (13) of (10) and the general characterization (14b) of its content (in a context c). On the one hand, a context c satisfies condition (13) just in case it is a member of the set in (14b); in other words, (10) is true in c just in case it is among the situations the content of (10) *as expressed in c*, applies to:

(15) $c \in \{s \mid (\text{SPEAKER}(c), \text{PLACE}(c)) \in \text{AT}(s)\}$
        iff $(\text{SPEAKER}(c), \text{PLACE}(c)) \in \text{AT}(c)$

On the other hand, the set characterized in (14b) is not the set of contexts in which (10) is true. To begin with, as we have just seen, the content of (10) in a given context c does not only contain utterance contexts, but all sorts of possible situations including ones in which no utterance is made. More importantly, not every context in which (10) is true, ends up in $[\![10]\!]^c$: what (10) expresses *in a context c* – viz. that the speaker *in c* is at the place *of c* – need not be true in a context d. Take c^* again where John is speaking at home. Since John's home is far away from Rome, $(\text{SPEAKER}(d^*), \text{PLACE}(d^*)) = (\text{John, Rome}) \in \text{AT}(d^*)$, $(\text{SPEAKER}(c^*), \text{PLACE}(c^*)) = (\text{John, Home}) \notin \text{AT}(d^*)$. Consequently, $d^* \notin [\![10]\!]^{c^*}$, though (10) is true in d^* as in any other context; indeed, $d^* \in [\![10]\!]^{d^*}$.

What makes (10) trivial, then, is the fact that its content is true in that context – despite the fact that its content does not apply to every context; in particular, its content varies from context to context. In this respect, (10) differs from (8); for no matter what the context is, the content of (8) is always the same triviality, applying to all possible situations alike, whether utterance contexts or not. Plainly, for any context c we have:

(16) $[\![(8)]\!]^c = LS$

Now for (9), which we placed in the middle, because it seems to share features of both (8) and (10). We have already said that it is next to tautological. However, its triviality notwithstanding, there is a sense in which it conveys, or may convey, genuine information. For instance, if it is used as (part of) an explanation of, or a comment on, what Angela Merkel did in a certain situation, it may be understood as expressing the content that she, Angela Merkel is a politician. This content is by no means trivial, and the way it relates to the trivial, tautological construal of (9) may be reminiscent of the triviality of (10) and its content in a given utterance context: the non-trivial content (17a) associated with (9) results from understanding the subject as getting its referent 'directly' from the utterance context – just like the 1st person pronoun and the locative adverb in (10); cf. (15). On the other hand, on its near-tautological construal, subject and predicate are 'evaluated' relative to the same situation:

(17) a. $\{ s \mid GC(c) \in /politician/^s \}$ $[\neq LS]$
      b. $\{ s \mid GC(s) \in /politician/^s \}$ $[\approx LS]$

The squiggly equality in (17b) is meant to capture the fact that GC is not defined throughout *LS*, because there are situations *s* without German chancellors; however, whenever it is defined, its value is a member of $/politician/^s$, or so we have been assuming. It seems that both sets in (17) are plausible candidates for the content expressed by (9). We will return to the shifty 'character' of (9) in due course.

(8)–(10) show that there are at least two different ways in which a (declarative) sentence may be trivial: it may be that, in any context in which it could be uttered, it carries a content that does not exclude any possibilties whatsoever; and it may so happen that, in any context in which it could be uttered, it carries a content that does not exclude the context itself. To be sure, both kinds of triviality result in total pointlessness; for in both cases the sentence is guaranteed to be true no matter where and when it is uttered, or by whom. But the cases differ in that the pointlessness of the utterance is not due to its content; that this is possible is due to the fact that this content varies from context to context.

3 Characters

Summing up these observations, we arrive at the following general picture, not just of informational voidness but also of (sentential) meaning at large. The content of a sentence is a set of possible situations, and what the content of a particular sentence is, depends on the context of utterance. A sentence has trivial content in a given context if its content in that context coincides with the set *LS* of all possible situations; it is trivially true when uttered if every context of utterance is itself a member of its content at that context. The following definitions reformulate these findings in standard terminology, mostly due to Kaplan (1989a):

Definition

Let S be a (declarative) sentence, and let $C \subseteq LS$ be the set of all utterance contexts.
a) The *character of S* is a function $[\![S]\!]: C \to \wp(LS)$ that assigns to any utterance context $c \in C$ a set $[\![S]\!]^c \subseteq LS$ of (possible) situations, the *content* of S in c.
b) S is *true of a situation* $s \in LS$ in a context $c \in C$ iff $s \in [\![S]\!]^c$; and S is *false of* s in c iff $s \notin [\![S]\!]^c$.
c) S is *necessarily true [false]* in a context $c \in C$ iff S is true of every possible situation, i.e. iff $[\![S]\!]^c = LS\ [\ldots = \emptyset]$.
d) S is *true [false] in* a context $c \in LS$ iff S is true [false] of c in c, i.e. iff $c \in [\![S]\!]^c$ $[c \notin [\![S]\!]^c]$.
e) S is *a priori true [false]* iff S is true [false] in every context $c \in C$.

Some remarks on these definitions are in order. Taken together, they form the core of the *two-dimensional* theory of context-dependence; note that they presuppose the general notions of a possible situation, an utterance situation, and Logical Space. *a)* should be read as programmatic rather than abbreviatory: a full account of linguistic meaning must be inclusive enough so that the character function can be determined from it. This need not mean that meaning, or even literal meaning, *coincides* with character. Neither does the notion of character have to be confined to sentences; in fact we will soon see how to construct characters of arbitrary expressions. – *b)* brings out that, once characters come into play, truth and falsity is a matter of two parameters, viz. the context in which the sentence is uttered and the situations to which its content may be applied. Intuitively, this difference may be described as that between the situation in which an utterance is made and the situations that the utterance is about. However, this characterization should be taken with a grain of salt. After all, characters are defined for all contexts of utterance whether or not the sentence (or expression) analyzed is uttered in it; and it is not obvious which situations intensions are about, given that they are defined for all of LS (for the time being, anyway). – *c)* defines the kind of triviality exemplified by (8). However, note that (8) is special in that its content is the same across arbitrary contexts (or so we have assumed); this is not a requirement of necessity as defined in *c)*. We will later see examples of necessary truths and falsehoods with 'unstable' characters. – *d)* shows how the ordinary notion of truth (and falsity) relative to an utterance context is grounded in the binary notion defined in *b*), viz. by having the context play two rôles: determining content, and applying the latter to it. This rôle identification is a key tool of the theory presented here, known as *diagonalisation*. We will meet it in various guises as we go along. – To prove the point, it already makes an appearance in *e*), where the kind of triviality exemplified by (10) is defined.

In order to generalize characters from sentences to (almost) arbitrary expressions, we return to the dependence of reference and extension on situations but now take the two parameters into account. We illustrate the general strategy with a few simple examples:

(18) ⟦*I am married*⟧^{c} = {s | SPEAKER(c) ∈ /*married*/^{s}}

In (18), *c* is an arbitrary context, and the extension of *married* consists of all persons that are married in the situation at hand. Then, like (14b), (18) reflects the fact that the content of the sentence depends on the utterance context: if John utters it, he expresses that he is married, and the content consists of the (possible) situations in which John is married; if Jane utters it, she expresses that she is married, etc. Of course, this time there are contexts to which the resulting content does not truthfully apply: *I am married* is not *a priori* true. Still what (18) and (14b) have in common is the fact that the referent of the subject solely depends on the context *c* whereas the extension of the predicate solely depends on the situation *s* the content is applied to. This asymmetry of subject and predicate is somewhat coincidental, as the following example shows:

(19) ⟦*No politician is married*⟧^{c} = {s | /*politician*/^{s} ∩ /*married*/^{s} = ∅}

If uttered in a context $c \in C$, the sentence whose character is described in (19), expresses that there are no married people among the politicians, thereby ruling out those possible (in fact, likely) situations in which the extensions of *politician* and *married* overlap. Hence neither the extension of the subject nor that of the predicate depend on the utterance context. (Remember that we ignore temporal reference altogether.) So it is not in the nature of subjects to bring context into play, as (18) may have suggested; rather it is the very context-dependence of the personal pronoun that does. The following example confirms this, at least at first blush:

(20) ⟦*The German chancellor is married*⟧^{c} = {s | GC(s) ∈ /*married*/^{s}}

The sentence interpreted in (20) may be used to rule out the possibility that the German chancellor is unmarried, i.e. those situations in which there is a spouseless German chancellor – *whoever he or she may be*. Given this, the referent of the subject should not depend on the utterance context; otherwise the content of the sentence would come out as ruling out that Angela Merkel – *chancellor or not* – is unmarried (given a realistic context at the time of writing this). So, as in (19) there is no context-dependence in the subject (nor elsewhere in the sentence). On the other hand, it would seem that the sentence may be used to convey precisely a piece of information about a certain person. If so, its content would have to look different. To avoid ambiguity, we may use a notational device distinguishing this, somewhat more unusual construal:

(21) $[\![\textit{The}_d \textit{ German chancellor is married}]\!]^c = \{s \mid GC(c) \in /married/^s\}$

The above examples may suggest that the reference (or extension) of subjects is always exclusively a matter of context or else not a matter of context at all. However, there are also mixed cases, i.e. subjects whose referents depend on both the context of utterance and the situation to which the content is applied:

(22) $[\![\textit{No friend of mine is married}]\!]^c = \{s \mid /friend/^s(\text{SPEAKER}(c)) \cap /married/^s = \emptyset\}$

In (22) we have assumed that the extension of the relational noun *friend* is the function assigning to each individual the set of his or her friends. If uttered by John, say, the sentence rules out the possible situations in which John has any married friends. Hence, obviously, the 1st person possessive relates to the speaker at the context of utterance. Had the set of friends been determined by context too (i.e. had we written '$/friend/^c$' instead of '$/friend/^s$'), the content would have ruled out that any of a particular group of people, viz. those who happen to be John's friends at the context of utterance, is married. Now, even though – somewhat analogously to (20) – the sentence might be interpreted that way (which we will leave open here), this is certainly not its most straightforward reading, let alone the only one. It appears that a more obvious way of understanding what it says is given in (22), according to which the extension of the subject partly depends on the utterance context, but not entirely so.

In general, nominal constituents (noun phrases, determiner phrases, quantifiers, etc.), like sentences, have extensions that depend on both the context of utterance and the situation to which the (sentential) content is ultimately applied. As it turns out, the same goes for verbal constituents, and almost any other kind of expression (logical words being famous exceptions). In order to combine these extensions in a consistent and compositional way, it is thus natural to assume that the extensions of *all* expressions depend on the utterance context and a situation to which the content is applied. Hence, we may generalize (and slightly adjust) the above definition *a*):

Definition

Let α be an expression (of any category), and let $C \subseteq LS$ be the set of all utterance contexts.

a*) The *character of* α is a function $[\![α]\!]$ that assigns to any utterance context $c \in C$ a function $[\![α]\!]^c: LS \to D_α$, the *intension of* α *in* c, where $D_α$ is the set of possible extensions of α.

a*) presupposes the notion of a possible extension of a given expression, which needs to be settled independently. For the purpose of this survey we continue to assume that certain category-dependent restrictions apply; in particular, we take it that the extensions of (declarative) sentences are truth values, that those of nouns and predicates are sets of individuals, and that the extensions of referential expressions like proper names, personal pronouns, and definite descriptions coincide with their referents.

To see that a*) does generalize a), one needs to identify sets $M \subseteq LS$ of possible situations with their *characteristic functions* f_M, which distinguish members of M from other situations by assigning corresponding truth values: $f_M(s) = 1$ if $s \in M$; and $f_M(s) = 0$ if $s \in LS \setminus M$. Due to this correspondence, the contents assigned to sentences by characters conforming to a) may be represented by their characteristic functions, which assign truth values to situations. Since truth values may be regarded as the extensions of sentences, sentential characters according to a) turn out to be special cases of a*); and the intensions of sentences come out as functional representatives of their contents as conceived above. But, of course, a*) is much more general. In particular, the characters of referential expressions α are said to assign *individual concepts* to contexts, i.e. functions from possible situations to indviduals; and the extensions of predicates will be *properties*, i.e. sets of individuals depending on contexts and situations.

Following a*), the extensions of the context-dependent expressions considered above can now be assigned by their characters:

(23) a. $[\![I]\!]^c(s) = \text{SPEAKER}(c)$
b. $[\![you]\!]^c(s) = \text{ADDRESSEE}(c)$
c. $[\![now]\!]^c(s) = \text{TIME}(c)$
d. $[\![here]\!]^c(s) = \text{PLACE}(c)$

The equations in (23), which must be read as generalizing over abirtrary utterance contexts $c \in C$ and situations $s \in LS$, all conform to a*). In each case, the character of an expression α assigns to a given context an individual concept (assuming that times and places are individuals). However, in each of these cases, the individual concept is constant across all of Logical Space: $[\![\alpha]\!]^c(s) = [\![\alpha]\!]^c(s')$ whenever s, s' $\in LS$. This is so because the referent of a deictic expression only depends on the context in which it is uttered, not on the situation to which the content of the sentence in which it occurs is applied; this much can be gleaned from the above description of a typical sentence like (18):

(18) $[\![I\ am\ married]\!]^c = \{s \mid \text{SPEAKER}(c) \in /married/^s\}$

So the situations s in (23) are there but for uniformity: characters in general need them, even though these particular ones could do without them. This hybrid treatment pays once we turn to the predicates considered above, which come out as the mirror images of deictic expressions in that their extensions are determined exclusively relatively to the situations that make up sentence content, without the utterance context coming in. Again, this can be seen from a typical case like (18) above, where *be married* is the predicate under scrutiny and its extensions are all of the form $/married/^s$ where s is a situation in Logical Space. According to a^*), these extensions should be thought as given by the character of the predicate, which for reasons of uniformity again, comes out as somewhat redundant in that it assigns the same property to every context:

(24) a. $[\![be\ married]\!]^c(s) = /married/^s = \{x \mid x \text{ is married in } s\}$
 b. $[\![be\ a\ politician]\!]^c(s) = /politician/^s = \{x \mid x \text{ is a politicianins}\}$

The difference in character between the deictic expressions in (23) and the predicates in (24) gives rise to a natural distinction (cf. Zimmermann 1991: 162):

Definition

f) An expression α is *direct* iff $[\![\alpha]\!]^c(s) = [\![\alpha]\!]^c(s')$, for any context c and situations s and s'.
g) An expression α is *absolute* iff $[\![\alpha]\!]^c(s) = [\![\alpha]\!]^{c'}(s)$, for any contexts c and c' and situations s.

Hence the deictic expressions under (23) are direct, whereas the predicates in (24) are absolute. Note that directness does not *per se* imply context dependence in that a character may be *both* direct *and* absolute, and thus the extension would not depend on the utterance context after all. Logical words like *and* and *every* are cases in point; so may be proper names (according to Kaplan 1989a: 558ff., anyway). The term (which generalizes the more common *directly referential*) is meant to suggest that no content layer gets in the way between context and extension: the intension is a degenerate, constant function; such intensions are also called *rigid*, in the tradition of Kripke (1972) where, famously, proper names are argued to be 'rigid designators'. The term defined in g) is meant to suggest independence from context.

One should note that characters may be *mixed*, i.e. neither direct nor absolute. As a case in point, the truth of the sentence *I am married* as analyzed in (18), depends on both the context of utterance and a situation to which its content is applied. In other words, it is neither direct, because its content (in a given context) may assign different truth values to different situations, nor absolute, because its character may assign different contents to different contexts. (We note in passing that none of our sample lexical items has a mixed character, which gives rise to the conjecture that this is always so; cf. Zimmermann 1995 and Bierwisch 2004 for more on this so-called *Hypothesis (L)*, originating with Zimmermann 1991: 164.) It is obvious how the predicates analyzed in (24) combine with deictic subjects to produce doubly-dependent sentence characters, viz. by way of the following *character composition* rule:

(25) $[\![SUBJ\ PRED]\!]^c(s) = \begin{cases} 1, \text{if } [\![SUBJ]\!]^c(s) \in [\![PRED]\!]^c(s) \\ 0, \text{otherwise} \end{cases}$

(25) is a *pointwise* characterization of the characters of sentences with referential subjects: for each context $c \in C$ it says which truth value the content of the sentence in c assigns to any situation $s \in LS$; under the assumption that a function is completely characterized by its course of values (i.e. the set of its argument-value pairs), this fixes the content at each c, which in turn fixes the character. Alternatively, the combination defined in (25) may be formulated in terms of characteristic functions, rather than sets, as predicate extensions:

(25') $[\![SUBJ\ PRED]\!]^c(s) = [\![PRED]\!]^c(s)([\![SUBJ]\!]^c(s))$

As long as it is unlikely to lead to confusion, we will not bother to distinguish between (25) and (25').

It is readily seen that (25) yields (18) when applied to the characters given in (23a) and (24a). And we also obtain the intended (and expected) result when applying the combination to sentences with non-deictic subjects, like (9) above:

(26) $[\![\text{the German chancellor is married}]\!]^c(s) = 1$
 iff $[\![\text{the German chancellor}]\!]^c(s) \in [\![\text{is married}]\!]^c(s)$
 iff $/\text{the German chancellor}/^s \in \{x \mid x \text{ is married in } s\}$

Sentences with quantificational subjects may be treated in a similar way, the difference lying in the direction of application: whereas the truth value in a predication like (26) ensues from applying the extension of the predicate to that of the subject, quantificational subjects work the other way round. The tautology (8) discussed earlier is a case in point:

(27) $[\![no\ bachelor\ is\ married]\!]^c(s) = 1$
  iff $[\![is\ married]\!]^c(s) \in [\![no\ bachelor]\!]^c(s)$
  iff ...
  iff $\{x \mid x\ is\ a\ bachelor\ in\ s\} \cap \{x \mid x\ is\ married\ in\ s\} = \emptyset$

The intermediate steps, which only involve standard combinations and denotations of quantifier extensions, have been skipped. Since the condition in the final line of (27) does not mention the context, (8) turns out to be absolute in the sense of g), i.e. it has the same content in every utterance situation; and since the condition is met by any situation $s \in LS$, this content coincides with LS. As a consequence, (8) also comes out as an *a priori* truth: its (rigid) content contains all situations whatsoever – and thus *afortiori* the (changing) utterance context.

The character (14b) of (10) is different:

(14) b. $[\![(10)]\!]^c = \{s \mid (SPEAKER(c), PLACE(c)) \in AT(s)\}$

In order to derive it compositionally, we first have to dissect its predicate into the locative adverbial and a corresponding reading of the copula. Since the latter relates the referent of the subject and a location in the situation the content is applied to, it is absolute:

(28) $[\![be_{LOC}]\!]^c(s) = AT(s) = \{(x,y) \mid in\ s,\ x\ is\ located\ at\ y\}$

The general definition of the character composition corresponding to locative predicate formation is left to the reader. Its effect on the case at hand is straightforward:

(29) $[\![be_{LOC}\ here]\!]^c(s)$
  $= \{x \mid (x, [\![here]\!]^c(s)) \in [\![be_{LOC}]\!]^c(s)\}$
  $= \{x \mid (x, PLACE(c)) \in AT(s)\}$

Note that according to (29), the predicate of (10) is no longer absolute, due to the directness of *here*. Neither is the whole sentence whose character can now be determined with the help of (25):

(30) ⟦I am$_{LOC}$ here⟧^{c}(s)= 1
  iff ⟦I⟧^{c}(s) ∈ ⟦am here⟧^{c}(s)
  iff (SPEAKER(c),PLACE(c)) ∈ AT(s)

Thus unlike (8), (10) never expresses a necessary truth, for reasons we have already seen: the location of any individual, including the speaker at a given context, is instable across Logical Space, and so the content will never cover all of the latter. However, it will always contain the utterance situation, which means that the sentence comes out true in every context and is thus *a priori* true, in the sense of Definition e).

4 Diagonals

The two kinds of triviality thus come out as reflected by a difference in character. Sentences like (8) are necessarily true and express trivial content, coinciding with Logical Space. Sentences like (10) are *a priori* true and thus true in every context. The difference did not show in their respective truth conditions (11) and (13), which are equivalent because (8), apart from always being necessarily true, is an *a priori* truth too:

(11) /bachelor/^{c} ∩ /married/^{c} = ∅
(13) (SPEAKER(c), PLACE(c)) ∈ AT(c)

From the character point of view, these truth conditions pertain to the unary notion of truth in a context, as introduced in Definition d), and thus water down the binary one of Definition b) by selecting those contexts to which the content expressed by the sentence applies. Technically this step comes down to an identification of the two parameters, which is quite a general procedure:

Definition

h) The *extension* /α/^{c} of an expression α in a context c∈C is the value α's intension at c assigns to c itself: /α/^{c} = ⟦α⟧^{c}(c).
i) The *diagonal* of a character /α/ (of an expression α) is the function /α/: C → D$_α$ that assigns to each context c the extension of α at c: /α/(c) = /α/^{c}.

Using the above terminology (and our identification of sets with their characteristic functions), we thus see that the diagonal of a sentence is the set of contexts in which it is true. In particular, *apriority* turns out to be a matter of the diagonal: according to Definitions d) and e) a sentence S is *a priori* true iff for any $c \in C$, $c \in [\![S]\!]^c$, which means that $/S/ = C$, by Definition i); and similarly for *a priori* falsehoods, whose diagonal is empty. Given that contexts are situations, i.e. $C \subseteq LS$, diagonals may be conceived of as (possible) sentence contents. Hence *apriority* is to the diagonal what necessity is to content. It is in view of this distinction between the content of a sentence (or more generally: the intension of an expression) on the one hand and the diagonal of its character on the other, that the current approach has been dubbed 'two-dimensional'. Hence the dimensions are not the two parameters extensions depend on but the two kinds of content deriving from this dependence: ordinary content as expressed in a given context distinguishing between genuine possibilities and situations that may be ruled out; and diagonal content as determined by the character at large and distinguishing between contexts in which the sentence is (or would be) true or false when uttered. The current section takes a closer look at the relation between these two dimensions.

The term 'diagonal' derives from a representation of characters in terms of look-up tables with lines (conventionally) corresponding to contexts of utterance, columns to arbitrary possible situations, and cells containing the extensions. This is what the character of the first-person pronoun I looks like:

Tab. 12.1: The character of I

	c_0	c_1	c_2	c_3	...	s^0	s^1	...
c_0	Σ_0	Σ_0	Σ_0	Σ_0	...	Σ_0	Σ_0	...
c_1	Σ_1	Σ_1	Σ_1	Σ_1	...	Σ_1	Σ_1	...
c_2	Σ_2	Σ_2	Σ_2	Σ_2	...	Σ_2	Σ_2	...
c_3	Σ_3	Σ_3	Σ_3	Σ_3	...	Σ_3	Σ_3	...
...	...	...	...	...	...	...	...	...

Each row represents the intension of I in a given context c, by running through LS (as represented by the columns) and assigning the referent of I in c to each of the situations. Since the referent coincides with the speaker in c, it will be the same one in each situation; consequently the columns all look the same. For convenience we abbreviated 'SPEAKER(c_n)' by 'Σ_n'; this is not meant to exclude that in some cases $\Sigma_n = \Sigma_m$, even though $n \neq m$ and consequently $c_n \neq c_m$. Note that we are using subscripts to distinguish different contexts and superscripts to distinguish possible situations that do not happen to be utterance contexts. Also note that the columns have been arranged so that the contexts $c \in C \subseteq LS$ come first, and in the same order as in the rows. This helps keeping track of the diagonal, which we have moreover shaded. Finally note that the diagonal only cuts through part of the character, because there are no rows for non-contexts.

Using similar notational devices, our representation of the character of *here*, or in fact any direct expression, would look almost the same, with each row repeating the place of utterance ('Π_n') all over the place (= LS); we do not bother to write this down. Absolute expressions are, of course, a different matter. Thus, e.g., the character of locative *be* has the following form:

Tab. 12.2: The character of be_{LOC}

	c_0	c_1	c_2	c_3	...	s^0	s^1	...
c_0	AT_0	AT_1	AT_2	AT_3	...	AT^0	AT^1	...
c_1	AT_0	AT_1	AT_2	AT_3	...	AT^0	AT^1	...
c_2	AT_0	AT_1	AT_2	AT_3	...	AT^0	AT^1	...
c_3	AT_0	AT_1	AT_2	AT_3	...	AT^0	AT^1	...
...	...	...	...	...	...	...	...	...

Of course, $AT_n = AT(c_n)$, and $AT^n = AT(s^n)$. In this case the rows all look the same; this is of course, due to the fact that the extension of locative *be*, like that of any absolute expression, does not depend on the context of utterance. One restriction, not visible in the table but important in what follows is that for any subscript n, it holds that $(\Sigma_n, \Pi_n) \in AT_n$ (cf. Kaplan 1979: 89, clause 10). Given this restriction and the fact that according to our above analysis (30), (10) is true of a situation s in a context c_n if $(\Sigma_n, \Pi_n) \in AT(s)$, we may conclude that the diagonal of its character is entirely made up of 1s; the other truth values depend on the specifics of the situations s and contexts c_n and have been filled in arbitrarily:

Tab. 12.3: The character of (10)

	c_0	c_1	c_2	c_3	...	s^0	s^1	...
c_0	1	1	0	0	...	0	1	...
c_1	1	1	0	0	...	1	1	...
c_2	0	0	1	1	...	0	0	...
c_3	1	1	1	1	...	1	1	...
...	...	...	...	...	...	...	...	...

To get a grip on Tab. 12.3, suppose that Σ_0 = Mary and Π_0 = Frankfurt. Then the first row has a 1 in a given column representing a situation s if s is a situation in which Mary is in Frankfurt (which we take to be immovable). Arguably, this row represents the content of:

(31) *Mary is in Frankfurt.*

To actually derive the equivalence in content between (31) and (10) as used in c_0, we must make the (debatable) assumption that the reference of proper names is neither context-dependent nor a matter of intension. Consequently, their characters are completely degenerate, with all cells filled in by the same individual (per name):

Tab. 12.4: The character of *Mary*

	c_0	c_1	c_2	c_3	...	s^0	s^1	...
c_0	m	m	m	m	...	m	m	...
c_1	m	m	m	m	...	m	m	...
c_2	m	m	m	m	...	m	m	...
c_3	m	m	m	m	...	m	m	...
...	...	...	...	...	...	...	...	...

Tab. 12.4 gives the simplistic character of *Mary*; a similar table, full of 'f's would represent that of *Frankfurt*. Hence, given the above treatment of locative predications, (31) comes out as having an absolute character:

(32) $[\![(31)]\!]^c(s) = 1$
         iff $(m,f) \in AT(s)$
         iff $(\Sigma_0, \Pi_0) \in AT(s)$
         iff $[\![(10)]\!]^c(s) = 1$

Note that (32) holds for any context $c \in C$; indeed, (31) is absolute, with the first line of Tab. 12.3 repeating itself all the way down (C):

Tab. 12.5: The character of (31)

	c_0	c_1	c_2	c_3	...	s^0	s^1	...
c_0	1	1	0	0	...	0	1	...
c_1	1	1	0	0	...	0	1	...
c_2	1	1	0	0	...	0	1	...
c_3	1	1	0	0	...	0	1	...
...	...	...	...	...	...	...	...	...

The treatment of *Mary* as in Tab. 12.4 also gives rise to the construction of a kind of sentence character that we have not met so far, exemplified by:

(33) *I am Mary.*

Under the (uncontroversial) assumption that *identity statements* are true just in case the extensions of the equated expressions coincide, the character of (33) is split into two parts: in any context c in which Mary is speaking, it is necessarily true, because all situations are such that Mary (= SPEAKER(c)) is identical with Mary (= the extension of *Mary* according to Tab. 12.4); but in a context c in which Mary is not the speaker, (33) is necessarily false, because all situations are such that SPEAKER(c) ≠ Mary. We thus arrive at the following character, where Mary is speaking in c_0 and c_1, but not in c_2 and c_3:

Tab. 12.6: The character of (33)

	c_0	c_1	c_2	c_3	...	s^0	s^1	...
c_0	1	1	1	1	...	1	1	...
c_1	1	1	1	1	...	1	1	...
c_2	0	0	0	0	...	0	0	...
c_3	0	0	0	0	...	0	0	...
...	...	...	...	...	...	...	...	...

As one can immediately tell from the diagonal of its character depicted in Tab. 12.6, sentence (33) is not *a priori* true; in particular it is not tautological in the way (8) is. Still, like (8), it is necessarily true in some contexts, viz. those in which Mary is speaking. Hence (33) comes out as trivial in the restricted sense that its content may be uninformative, depending on the context. The fact that it is not trivially true in every context may be seen as the beginning of an explanation why it is not uninformative *tout court* even though its content is. A hearer who is not fully informed about the context – and particularly about who is speaking – may rule out (being part of) any context in which the speaker is not Mary, as long as (s)he is prepared to trust the speaker. Such a hearer could take the diagonal of the character as a substitute for the content expressed by the sentence, thereby eliminating all contexts in which Mary is not speaking and thus learning that Mary is the speaker. This *pragmatic* analysis, which makes heavy use of the diagonal, may even be applied to utterance situations in which the speaker does not know which person is being referred to by the name *Mary*, thus extending well beyond the semantics-pragmatics divide. However, it also has to rely on a wider conception of contexts and characters and thus goes far beyond this short survey. A fuller story along these lines can be found in Stalnaker (1978) and Haas-Spohn (1991); see also Haas-Spohn (1995) for a different (though related) approach.

The diagonal may also be seen to play a rôle in the shifty interpretation of the (surface) sentence (9), to which we attributed two different characters, repeated here:

(20) 〚*The German chancellor is married*〛^{c} = {s | GC(s)∈/married/^{s}}
(21) 〚*The$_d$ German chancellor is married*〛^{c} = {s | GC(c)∈/married/^{s}}

The difference between the two analyses lies in the interpretation of the subject, which is absolute according to (20) and direct according to (21):

(34) 〚*the German chancellor*〛^{c}(s) = GC(s)
(35) 〚*the$_d$ German chancellor*〛^{c}(s) = GC(c)

Comparing the corresponding character tables reveals how one can be derived from the other:

Tab. 12.7: The character of *the German chancellor*

	c_0	c_1	c_2	c_3	...	s^0	s^1	...
c_0	CG_0	GC_1	GC_2	GC_3	...	GC^0	GC^1	...
c_1	GC_0	GC_1	GC_2	GC_3	...	GC^0	GC^1	...
c_2	GC_0	GC_1	GC_2	GC_3	...	GC^0	GC^1	...
c_3	GC_0	GC_1	GC_2	GC_3	...	GC^0	GC^1	...
...	...	...	...	...	...	...	...	...

Tab. 12.8: The character of *the$_d$ German chancellor*

	c_0	c_1	c_2	c_3	...	s^0	s^1	...
c_0	GC_0	GC_0	GC_0	GC_0	...	GC_0	GC_0	...
c_1	GC_1	GC_1	GC_1	GC_1	...	GC_1	GC_1	...
c_2	GC_2	GC_2	GC_2	GC_2	...	GC_2	GC_2	...
c_3	GC_3	GC_3	GC_3	GC_3	...	GC_3	GC_3	...
...	...	...	...	...	...	...	...	...

A quick inspection shows that both tables contain the same function f from contexts c to the German chancellor GC_c in c, only arranged in different ways: whereas Tab. 12.8 repeats f in every column, Tab. 12.7 has f on the left side of every row. Hence the character in Tab. 12.8 can be obtained from that in Tab. 12.7 by inserting its diagonal into each column; in fact, this operation is perfectly general and does not even require absoluteness:

Definition

j) The *direct interpretation* $\nabla\alpha$ of an expression α is that character that assigns to every context $c \in C$ the intension that assigns to every situation $s \in LS$ the extension of α in c: $\nabla\alpha(c)(s) = /\alpha/^c = [\![\alpha]\!]^c(c)$.

Obviously, the direct interpretation of an expression is always direct in the sense of Definition f) – thence the term; moreover, it is easy to verify that the direct interpretation of a direct expression coincides with its ordinary character: $\nabla\alpha = [\![\alpha]\!]$. If direct interpretation could be shown to be the result of a general interpretative strategy of applying the intension directly to the context of utterance, then the uncertainty as what kind of content is expressed by sentences like (9) might be approached in pragmatic terms (cf. Kripke 1977); in fact, it is even conceivable that separate pragmatic processes make use of the (ordinary) character and the direct interpretation of one expression at the same time. Alternatively, one may try and seek an explanation in terms of ambiguity, in which case ∇ would have to be an operator in the object language embedding (suitable) expressions α (cf. Kaplan 1978, relating to Donnellan 1966):

(36) $[\![\nabla\alpha]\!]^c(s) = [\![\alpha]\!]^c(c)$

When restricted to referential expressions α, the operator in (36) is also known as *dthat*, which is short for 'demonstrative *that*' and pronounced [dðæt]; applied to sentences α, it boils down to a combination of the operations expressed by certain readings of *actually* and *now* (cf. Kaplan 1979).

It is tempting and natural to consider a reversal Δ of direct interpretation that turns any character into an absolute one. Whereas ∇ pastes the diagonal into each column, Δ would have to insert it in the rows of the resulting table. In analogy with (36), Δ would thus have to satisfy the equations:

(37) $\Delta\alpha(c)(s) = [\![\alpha]\!]^s(s)$

However, there is an obvious problem with this construction, due to the asymmetry of characters: they are only defined for utterance contexts, and not for the remaining situations in Logical Space. In the case of absolute expressions α the intension assigned by their character is the same across C and may thus be generalized to all of LS. However, with direct or even mixed expressions, this "extrapolation" obviously does not work. Hence the right side of (37) is not always defined; as a consequence, the intensions assigned by characters Δα would have to be partial, only defined for situations $s \in C$.

Definition

k) The *diagonal character* Δα of an expression α is that function that assigns to every context $c \in C$ the partial intension that assigns to every utterance situation $s \in C$ the extension of α in s: $Δα(c)(s) = /α/^c = [\![α]\!]^s(s)$.

Note that we continue to use 's' as a variable for situations to which intensions apply, even if they are restricted to members of C, as in k); this should remind of their rôle as determining extensions. Obviously, the diagonal character of an expression is always absolute in the sense of Definition g); moreover, it is easy to verify that the diagonal character of an absolute expression coincides with its ordinary character if the values are restricted to utterance contexts (or "extrapolated" in the sense indicated above): $Δα ≈ [\![α]\!]$.

The partiality of the intensions assigned by diagonal characters may be construed as presuppositional. Take the character of the first-person pronoun, *I*, given in Tab. 12.1. The result of applying the operation defined in (37) to it may be represented as in Tab. 12.9, where '#' stands for undefinedness:

Tab. 12.9: The partial character Δ*I*

	c_0	c_1	c_2	c_3	...	s^0	s^1	...
c_0	$Σ_0$	$Σ_1$	$Σ_2$	$Σ_3$	...	#	#	...
c_1	$Σ_0$	$Σ_1$	$Σ_2$	$Σ_3$	...	#	#	...
c_2	$Σ_0$	$Σ_1$	$Σ_2$	$Σ_3$	...	#	#	...
c_3	$Σ_0$	$Σ_1$	$Σ_2$	$Σ_3$	...	#	#	...
...	...	...	...	...	...	...	...	...

The character depicted in Tab. 12.9 is gappy for a systematic reason: there are no extensions $Σ^n$ = SPEAKER(s^n) because only utterance situations have (uniquely defined) speakers. Hence the partial character presupposes that the content is applied to utterance situations only, i.e. to situations with speakers. This partial character may be described somewhat more perspicuously (and revealingly) by the following equation:

(38) $\Delta I(c)(s) = \begin{cases} \text{SPEAKER}(s), \text{ if } s \in C \\ \#, \text{ otherwise} \end{cases}$

According to (38), the intension ΔI assigns to a context is always the SPEAKER function. Hence ΔI coincides with the (ordinary) character of *the speaker*, which refers to the speaker in a given utterance situation. In a similar vein, Δ may be combined with other deictics like *here* and *now*, always resulting in absolute expressions that turn their context-dependence into a partial intension: $\Delta here$ comes out as expressing the character of *the place of utterance*; Δnow corresponds to *the time of utterance*; etc. In order to better understand operation Δ, one may study its effect on various kinds of sentences:

(39) a. ΔI *am married*$(c) = \{s \in C \mid \text{SPEAKER}(s) \in /married/^s\}$
b. ΔI *am here*$(c) = \{s \in C \mid \text{SPEAKER}(s), \text{PLACE}(s)) \in \text{AT}(s)\}$
c. ΔI *am Mary*$(c) = \{s \in C \mid \text{SPEAKER}(s) = \text{Mary}\}$

For simplicity, (39) ignores the differentiation between utterance contexts of which the content (intension) is false and non-utterance situations of which it is undefined. In any case, due to the presupposition introduced by Δ, the situations to which it assigns the truth value 1 are confined to utterance situations; and these are the ones mentioned in (39). As expected, these diagonal characters (which may be derived by combining interpretive mechanisms introduced above) correspond to certain absolute expressions:

(40) a. $[\![$*The speaker is [identical with] Mary*$]\!]^c(s) = \{s \in LS \mid \text{SPEAKER}(s) = \text{Mary}\}$
b. $[\![$*The speaker is married*$]\!]^c(s) = \{s \in LS \mid \text{SPEAKER}(s) \in /married/^s\}$
c. $[\![$*The speaker is at the place of the utterance*$]\!]^c(s)$
$= \{s \in LS \mid (\text{SPEAKER}(s), \text{PLACE}(s)) \in \text{AT}(s)\}$

The sentences analyzed in (40) all have straightforward presuppositional readings, which on closer inspection coincide with the corresponding diagonalized characters given in (39), due to the fact that the SPEAKER function is defined for utterance situations and only them and provided that *the place of the utterance* expresses a partial intension defined on utterance situations and assigning their respective location to them. So the characters in (40) may be seen as equivalent to the diagonal characters in (39), thereby offering a glimpse of what diagonalization in general amounts to: instead of taking their referents directly from the utterance situations, the diagonal character takes them from the situation described by the content of the sentence. In the case of (40a), which has been disambiguated to avoid unwelcome (e.g., information-structural) side-effects, we have already seen that this is the non-trivial content that a hearer who is initially unaware of the speaker's identity, may associate with an utterance of *I am Mary*; such a hearer may thus be said to *diagonalize* the utterance, thereby learning who is speaking. And a hearer who does not know who is uttering *I am married*, may still learn that the speaker – *whoever she is* – is married; again he may do so by diagonalization (Stalnaker 1978). But nothing can be gained by diagonalizing *I am here*: the result is just as uninformative as the content it expresses according to its ordinary character.

The uses of diagonalization indicated here are all pragmatic. As we already mentioned, we will not go into the full story here, because it ultimately necessitates a much more refined setting. Apart from these pragmatic applications, there is reason to believe that diagonalization is of no avail to semantic analysis. In particular, we will soon (in Section 7) see reasons why it should not be rendered by an operator in the object language, modelled after (and mirroring) ∇ as analyzed in (36):

(41) $[\![\Delta\alpha]\!]^c(s) = [\![\alpha]\!]^s(s)$

5 Extensionality

The examples discussed so far suggest that the characters of complex expressions can be derived by combining those of their immediate parts. In fact, in all the above cases, this could be achieved by pointwise combinations, proving them to be extensional:

Definition

1) A syntactic construction Σ is *extensional* if, for every context $c \in C$ and situation $s \in LR$, there is a corresponding operation $\Gamma^{c,s}$ on (possible) extensions such that for any expression α built up by Σ from expressions $\beta_1, \ldots, \beta_n$, the following equation holds:
$[\![\alpha]\!]^c(s) = \Gamma^{c,s}([\![\beta_1]\!]^c(s), \ldots, [\![\beta_n]\!]^c(s))$.

As is common in the algebraic approach to compositionality (cf. Janssen 1997), we take syntactic constructions (or environments, constellations, ...) Σ to be n-place structure-building operations. Note that the combination of extensions corresponding to an extensional construction may depend on the context and situation relative to which the extension of the whole expression is determined. If it does not, i.e. if $\Gamma^{c,s}$ is the same for all $c \in C$ and $s \in LR$, the construction Γ is called *canonically extensional*:

m) An extensional syntactic construction Σ is *canonically extensional* if there is a corresponding operation Γ on (possible) extensions such that for every context $c \in C$, situation $s \in LR$, and any expression α built up by Σ from expressions $\beta_1, \ldots, \beta_n$, the following equation holds:
$[\![\alpha]\!]^c = \Gamma([\![\beta_1]\!]^c(s), \ldots, [\![\beta_n]\!]^c(s))$.

Also note that for the equations in Definitions *l*) and *m*) to hold, it is not enough (though, of course, necessary) that the extensions of α *in all contexts c* behave compositionallly:

(42)　$/\alpha/^c = \Gamma^{c,c}(/\beta_1/^c, \ldots, /\beta_n/^c)$

Rather, in order for the construction building up α to be extensional, *all* extensions determined by α's intension (in arbitrary contexts *c*) must behave compositionally. As a consequence, the equations in Definition *l*) and *m*) fully determine the character of α. In Section 3, we have already seen an example of such a pointwise definition of the character combination corresponding to an extensional construction, viz. *subject predication*:

(25′)　$[\![SUBJ\ PRED]\!]^c(s) = [\![PRED]\!]^c(s)([\![SUBJ]\!]^c(s))$

In (25′), the syntactic construction is the formation of simple sentences by putting together referential subjects with their predicates; and the corresponding operation on extensions is *functional application* – 'APP', for short – combining a (characteristic) function f with its argument x to yield the value $f(x)$: APP$(f, x) = f(x)$. (To shun set-theoretic paradoxes, one must restrict APP and, e.g., prevent it from applying to itself; we are ignoring such complications here.) Using this notation, (25′) can be reformulated as:

(25″)　$[\![SUBJ\ PRED]\!]^c(s) = $ APP$([\![PRED]\!]^c(s), [\![SUBJ]\!]^c(s))$

Note that, since APP in (25″) does not depend on *c* or *s*, subject predication turns out to be canonically extensional; in fact, it may well be that all extensional constructions are canonical (Zimmermann 1991: 167).

Given the generality of (25″), the equation fully determines a function that combines the characters of (referential) subjects and predicates into the characters of the corresponding sentences. More specifically, the relevant character composition is *(pointwise) functional application* – APP*, for short – combining two characters χ_1 and χ_2 into one that assigns to each context $c \in C$ an intension $F(c)$ that in turn assigns APP($\chi_1(c)(s),\chi_2(c)(s)$) to each situation $s \in LR$. Using this notation, (25″) can be reformulated as:

(25*) ⟦*SUBJ PRED*⟧ = APP*(⟦*PRED*⟧,⟦*SUBJ*⟧)

Generalizing from this example, it is readily seen that for any (not necessarily canonically) extensional construction Σ satisfying the equation in Definition *1*) there is a (unique) corresponding pointwise operation Γ^* on characters satisfying the general compositionality equation (43); the pointwise definition of Γ^* is given in (43*), where the $\Gamma^{c,s}$ are as in Definition *1*) and $\chi_1, \ldots, \chi_n$ are (suitable) characters:

(43) ⟦α⟧ = Γ^*(⟦β_1⟧,…,⟦β_n⟧)
(43*) $\Gamma^*(\chi_1,\ldots,\chi_n)(c)(s) = \Gamma^{c,s}(\chi_1(c)(s),\ldots,\chi_n(c)(s))$

A function like Γ^* that combines the characters of the (immediate) parts of an expression α into the character of α itself, will be called the *character composition* associated with the pertinent syntactic construction. Hence APP* is the character composition associated with subject predication, which is (canonically) extensional, given (25″); derivatively, APP* will also count as (canonically) extensional. As pointed out above, many more syntactic constructions and their associate character compositions are extensional, prime examples being the combination of determiners with noun phrases, and of (ordinary, 'extensional') verbs with their quantificational subjects or any kind of (nominal) objects.

6 Attitude reports

It has been well known since the beginnings of modern semantics that not all syntactic constructions are extensional (let alone canonical). In particular, classical substitution arguments show that *clausal embedding* cannot be so interpreted (Frege 1892). Sentences of the following form are cases in point (where *S* is any declarative sentence):

(44) *John thinks that S*

Whatever the exact parts of such *attitude reports* are – *John*; *think*; *thinks that S*; ...–, as long as *S* itself is one of them, the whole sentence is a (possibly quite complex) syntactic combination Σ of them. Now, if all syntactic constructions were extensional, then so would be all combinations of them. In particular, Σ would have to be associated with an extensional character composition Γ^*. By (42), then, the following equation would hold for any sentences *S* and contexts *c*:

(45) /*John thinks that S*/^{c} = $\Gamma^{c,c}$(/*John*/^{c},...,/*S*/^{c})

Obviously, this cannot be right. Otherwise any two sentences of the form (44) would have to have the same truth value as long as the embedded clauses do; in other words, substituing the embedded clause in (44) by an extensionally (or 'materially') equivalent one would not affect the truth value of the attitude report:

(46) If /S_1/^{c} = /S_2/^{c}, then /*John thinks that S_1*/^{c} = /*John thinks that S_2*/^{c}.

Readers are invited to instantiate the well-known absurdity (46) by their favourite counter-example.

While such *substitution arguments* show that not all syntactic constructions are extensional, they do not affect the compositionality of characters, i.e. the assumption that any (*n*-place) syntactic construction Σ may be associated with a character composition Γ that determines the characters of expressions constructed by Γ from the characters of its immediate parts (Montague 1970):

(47) $[\![\Gamma(\beta_1,\ldots,\beta_n)]\!] = \Gamma([\![\beta_1]\!],\ldots,[\![\beta_n]\!])$

In particular, (47) could still be applicable to the constructions involved in building up sentences of the form (44). Instead of (45) we would just have.

(48) $[\![\textit{John thinks that S}]\!] = \Gamma([\![\textit{John}]\!],\ldots,[\![S]\!])$

And the consequences from the corresponding substitution argument would be far less absurd than (46):

(49) If $[\![S_1]\!] = [\![S_2]\!]$, then $[\![\textit{John thinks that }S_1]\!] = [\![\textit{John thinks that }S_2]\!]$

All (49) says is that substituting the complement of *think* by a clause with the same character, preserves the character of the original sentence of the form (44). And, indeed, purported counter-examples to the validity of (49) appear far less obvious than the ones against (47). For the purpose of this survey, we will simply ignore them and assume that characters do behave compositionally. (Cf. Cresswell (1985) and Stalnaker (1991, 1999) for some discussion of compositionality challenges in attitude reports.)

A closer look at pertinent examples suggests that the general mechanisms involved in deriving attitude reports are more restricted than (48) would suggest. Thus, in a context c_{50} in which Mary is talking to Jane on a Thursday and they are both in Rome, the following two reports amount to the same:

(50) a. *John thinks that I met you here yesterday.*
b. *John thinks that Mary met Jane in Rome on Wednesday.*

Of course, in normal circumstances, Mary would not be inclined to express herself by (50b); in particular, she would not refer to herself as *Mary* and to her addressee as *Jane*. These preferences, which are not restricted to attitude reports, ought to be explicable in pragmatic terms, most likely by a principle of *presupposition maximization* (cf. Heim 1991, 2008; Sauerland 2008). Yet apart from its awkwardness, it is hard to see how, in the context given, (50b) could differ from (50a) in truth value; in fact, in the context at hand the two sentences seem to say the same thing. This might not come as a surprise. After all, the two sentences differ only as to their embedded clauses, and the latter coincide in their content in the context assumed here:

(51) $[\![\textit{I met you here yesterday}]\!]^{c_{50}} = [\![\textit{Mary met Jane in Rome on Wednesday}]\!]^{c_{50}}$

Indeed it would seem that the substitution of co-intensional clauses goes through precisely because attitude reports report a relation holding between the referent of the subject and the truth-conditional content of the embedded clause, i.e. its intension. This impression is confirmed by an influential analysis of attitude reports (Hintikka 1969; cf. article 16 [Semantics: Noun Phrases and Verb Phrases] (Swanson) *Propositional attitudes* for alternatives). According to it, an attitude verb expresses a (situation-dependent) relation between persons – the attitude *subjects* – and situations, which make up the person's pertinent *perspective* in a given situation s; in the case of *think* (as appearing in (44)), this would be the so-called *doxastic* perspective, which consists of the set of situations that, for all the subject believes (in s), he cannot exclude to be a situation he is in. And a report of the form (44) is true of a situation s just in case the content of the complement clause is a superset of John's doxastic perspective in s, i.e. if that content applies to all situations that John does not exclude – and thus excludes all situations in which it does not; hence (44) comes out as reporting that John's doxastic perspective is a subset of the content expressed by S:

(52) $[\![(44)]\!]^c = \{s \in LS \mid DOX_{John,s} \subseteq [\![S]\!]^c\}$

... where $c \in C$ is an arbitrary context and $DOX_{x,s}$ is a person x's doxastic perspective in a situation $s \in LS$. There are various options of deriving (52) compositionally. E.g., one may determine the character of *think* as in (53) and then employ the general rule (54) for determining the extension of a predicate from the extension of the attitude and the intension of its complement clause:

(53) $[\![think]\!]^c(s) = \{(x,p) \mid DOX_{x,s} \subseteq p\}$
(54) $[\![AttVerb\ [that]\ S]\!]^c(s) = \{x \mid (x, [\![S]\!]^c) \in [\![AttVerb]\!]^c(s)\}$

More generally, a simple (non-quantified) attitude report that derives from (44) by replacing *John* and *thinks* by a (suitable) referential subject and an attitude verb, respectively, comes out as true of s just in case the content of the complement clause is a superset of the subject's pertinent perspective in s (supplied by the lexical meaning of the verb). In the case at hand, this means that Mary's report (50a), as uttered in c_{50}, is true of a situation s just in case John's doxastic perspective in s only contains situations s' in which SPEAKER(c_{50}) met ADDRESSEE(c_{50}) in PLACE(c_{50}) at DAY(TIME(c_{50})) – 24HRS). Given our characterization of c_{50}, (50a) comes out as reporting a situation (s) in which whatever John believes excludes the possibility (s') that Mary did not meet Jane in Rome on Wednesday. At first blush, this looks like an adequate truth condition for (the utterance of) (50a). And it obviously does make (50b) come out equivalent in c_{50}, precisely because, in that context, they express the same content.

So the Hintikka-style analysis of attitude reports supports the initial impression that the substitution of intensionally equivalent complement clauses of attitude reports of the form (44) preserves the content of the report. However, this approach has its limits. In particular, it faces two challenges that go by the name of beliefs (or, more generally: attitudes) *de re* and *de se*:

- A belief *de re* by John is a belief John has *about an object* (= lat. *de re*), i.e. something that he believes *of* something (or someone).
- A belief *de se* (by John) is one that John has *about himself* (= lat. *de se*) *as himself* (as opposed to having it about himself without being aware of this fact); hence every belief *de se* is also a belief *de re* though not *vice versa*.

It is easy to see that (some) sentences of the form (44) can be used to truthfully ascribe beliefs *de re* to John – and thereby present a challenge to semantic analysis, especially (but not exclusively) as based on a Hintikka-style model of attitudes. This is mainly due to two characteristic features of beliefs *de re*:

(i) In order for John to form a belief *de re* about an *object* (lat. *res*) with a certain property, it is necessary for such an object to exist but not for John to know that it has that property (Quine (1956)). Thus, e.g., if John believes of Mary that she is Swiss and Mary happens to be the shortest Vatican spy, then there is such a spy and John has a belief (*de re*) about her, even though he may not make the connection between her and the Pope (because he only knows her as his polite neighbour, say).

(ii) Still, in order for John to form a belief *de re*, it is necessary for him to somehow be acquainted with the *res* (Kaplan 1968). Thus, e.g., if John believes that there are Vatican spies without having any specific suspicions, he may deduce, and thus believe, that among them, one is the shortest; yet it seems that even if there is a shortest Vatican spy, John cannot be said to believe of her that she is the shortest spy if there is no connection between him and her.

One problem arising from (i) is that in reports of the form (44), referential expressions occurring within the complement clause *S* may refer to objects of belief. Hence their content should not contribute to the content of the sentence characterizing the subject's attitude. For example, the scenario in (i) may be reported by the following instance of (44), even though under the circumstances John may be quite neutral as to the existence of Vatican spies, or may even exclude the possibility that there are any:

(55) *John thinks that the shortest Vatican spy is Swiss.*

This observation suggests that the referent of the underlined expression in (55) needs to be determined relative to the situations in which John is reported as holding his belief (*de re*), rather than relative to his doxastic perspective; the latter would then have to only contain situations in which Mary – Vatican spy or (more likely) not – is Swiss. However, closer inspection of that alleged perspective reveals that it would require John to have some error-proof way of identifying the *res* (Mary) – which is beyond his cognitive capacities: ordinary identification procedures mostly rely on perception and memory and are principally prone to mistakes, however improbable. The (vast) literature on attitudes *de re* is full of pertinent (and sometimes rather exotic) examples to prove this point; *vide*, e.g., Lewis (1981) or Aloni (2001). In fact, it seems that the subject's acquaintance with the *res* observed in (ii) comes in here: in the case at hand, the situations that make up John's doxastic perspective would all have to contain someone who fits his way of identifying Mary and at the same time is Swiss; but this individual does not have to be the same across John's perspective, and *afortiori* it does not always have to be Mary. If this reasoning – basically due to Kaplan (1968) – is on the right track, then the relation between the contents of the complement clauses in *de re* attitude reports of the form (44) and the subjects' pertinent (doxastic, epistemic, . . .) perspectives is much more involved one than subsethood, which is all the Hintikka-style analysis has to offer. One strategy, inspired by Quine (1956), is to assimilate reports of the form (44) to sentences in which the *res* can be treated as an argument of the verb, as in certain infinitival constructions (*wants <u>the shortest spy</u> to leave*). To achieve this one neeeds to 'dissect' the complement clause in (44) into the expressions that correspond to the *res* (which may be plural!) and a remainder 'predicate' – in (55) this would be the underlined subject and the predicate –, and then describe the content of the report in terms of all these parts. (55) would then come out as akin to (55*), where the embedded clause must denote a property rather than a sentence content; and the verb could then express a ternary relation between a subject, a *res*, and a property:

(55*)   *John thinks of the shortest Vatican spy that <u>she</u> is Swiss.*

While compositional treatments of (55*) are conceivable according to which the underlined pronoun is interpreted as property-forming rather than deictic (cf. Chierchia 1989), it is not obvious how to adapt this strategy to (55) and reports of the form (44) in general, given that the number of *res* in them is unlimited; see, however, Cresswell & von Stechow (1982) for a systematic approach within a more fine-grained ('hyperintensional') framework. We will not delve into the details of this discussion but only note that part of the above conclusion that attitude reports only involve the contents of their complement clauses needs to be modified in the light of *de re* reports and depends on a solution of the problems surrounding them.

It should be noted in passing that although sentences like (55) can be used to report beliefs *de re*, they need not. In the scenario described in (ii), e.g., (55) may well be true despite there being no direct connection between John and the Vatican's employees: John may be convinced that only members of the Swiss Guard are eligible for the Vatican Secret Service. In this case, for the report (52) to come out true, the referent of the underlined description needs to be determined relatively to John's doxastic perspective: many possible situations are compatible with John's beliefs, and though they all contain Vatican spies, they do not all agree as to who is the shortes of them. The description is then said to be construed *de dicto* [= about the expression, or rather its content]. Of course, this is precisely as the Hintikka approach would have it. Given that the difference between reports about beliefs *de re* vs. *de dicto* appears to be an ambiguity (which we will not justify here), the Hintikka analysis turns out to cover part of the reports of the form (44) (which may be better than covering all of them insufficiently). But the *de re* cases remain a challenge to it (and, to be fair, any systematic approach to the semantics of attitude reports).

It should also be noted in passing that although sentences like (55) can be used to report beliefs *de dicto*, those under (50) most likely cannot (*pace* Kripke 1979), due to the fact that the only referential terms they contain are rigid and their truth under a *de dicto* construal would thus require the subject to have 'superhuman' identification procedures at his disposal (cf. Lewis 1981).

Beliefs *de se* pose a different kind of challenge to the two-dimensional approach. To see what is at stake here, let us first look at a famous example, due to David Kaplan (1989a: 533):

> If I see, reflected in a window, the image of a man whose pants appear to be on fire, my behavior is sensitive to whether I think, '**His** pants are on fire' or '**My** pants are on fire' [. . .]

Kaplan characterizes beliefs in terms of the characters of sentences the subject (Kaplan, in this case) would use to describe them. In the scenario at hand he initially has a certain belief *de re* about himself, and subsequently comes to hold the corresponding belief *de se*, which (by definition) is also a belief *de re*, with the same *res*; in fact, he continues to hold his original belief, but this is of no importance here, only the difference is. And there *is* a difference in his beliefs, a dramatic change indeed: his initial belief might lead Kaplan to start looking for the unfortunate person to warn him; given his updated belief, he is more likely to feel an urge to look for a hose or a bucket, cry for help, etc. The difference is reflected in the way the subject would describe himself, viz. by a certain 3rd person description (*the man whose reflection is visible in the window*) vs. the 1st person pronoun (*I*). Unlike the former belief *de re*, the latter is also a belief *de se*, a belief the subject holds not only about himself but also about himself *as himself*. As Frege (1919: 66) [(1956: 298)] put it, 'everyone is presented to himself in a particular and primitive way, in which he is presented to no-one else' (cf. Perry (1977), Kaplan (1989a: 529ff.), and Künne (1997) for reconstructions of Frege's views); and it is this peculiar mode of presentation, this subjective perspective the subject has on himself, that makes a belief *de re* a belief *de se*. The difference in perspective seems to be as obvious as it is hard to pin down. In particular, it does not show in the *contents* of the sentences that a subject is inclined to accept – as Kaplan's example makes clear: initially the subject would express his belief by (56) but not (57), though in the situation at hand the two sentences (as uttered by Kaplan) would express the same content, eliminating any possibility that Kaplan's pants are not on fire:

(56) *His pants are on fire.*
(57) *My pants are on fire.*

This substitution resistance is reminiscent of an observation made above, in connection with beliefs *de re*: (human) subjects' identification procedures are never quite immune against error, and thus Kaplan's doxastic perspective could not cover exactly the situations to which (56) and (57) apply. Rather, each situation compatible with his belief would have to contain a person – not necessarily Kaplan himself – whose reflection he sees and whose pants are on fire, whereas his own pants are not. Now, by the same reasoning, the underlined pronouns in this characterization of Kaplan's doxastic perspective would also have to correspond to some way in which Kaplan would describe himself. It is not obvious which description this could be if not the 1st person pronoun (or some synonym like *the person with whom I am identical*). Maybe it should contain everything Kaplan knows about himself (as himself, to be sure)? However, various, at times rather exotic scenarios constructed in the literature on beliefs *de se* make it appear unlikely that the descriptions a subject has of himself eventually add up to his subjective perspective; *vide*, e.g., Geach (1957); Castañeda (1967); Perry (1979); Lewis (1979a). Loosely (but intuitively) speaking, the descriptions a person can give of himself without referring to himself as himself all lack the immediacy of what Frege (*ibid.*) called the 'subjective and primitive way' of the self-presentation characteristic of beliefs *de se*. In fact, it seems that any description a subject may have of any object or situation is based on, or relative to, his subjective perspective – as is illustrated by the underlined pronouns in the above account of Kaplan's beliefs. Moreover, unlike other (human) identification procedures, the subject's identification of himself as himself does seem to be immune to error: though, from his own perspective, it could have turned out that the man Kaplan sees is not he himself after all (or even that there was no man in the first place, only what looked like a reflection of one), it is next to impossible to imagine that he misidentified himself as the observer of that scene. These observations turn out to be important for the reconstruction of subjective perspective, as we will soon see.

Despite their coincidence in content (in the situation at hand), (56) and (57) do display a semantic difference, to wit in character. As it turns out, the subjective perspective corresponds to first person reference in the sentences by which the subject would be inclined to (honestly) describe his beliefs: although he believes certain things about himself *de re*, it is only when he realizes that he himself is the *res*, that he refers to himself in the first person. It would thus seem that the subjectivity characteristic of beliefs *de se* is a matter of character. In fact, closer inspection shows that it is not the whole character but only the diagonal that matters when it comes to characterizing belief in terms of sentence meaning (Stalnaker 1981): in describing his beliefs by sentences, the subject takes them to be true in a context; and if he only accepts the first person in a sentence if he has the corresponding belief *de se*, the context is one in which he himself is the speaker. In sum, if the subject uses a sentence to describe something he believes, he takes himself to be the speaker in a context in which the sentence is true. It would thus appear that the doxastic perspective ought to be characterizable in terms of the diagonal of the sentences accepted by a subject; more generally, it would have to consist of the possible contexts the subject might be in, for all he believes. Unfortunately, this cannot be *quite* correct for the simple reason that subjects do not always take themselves to be in utterance situations. A more accurate characterization of the doxastic perspective (in a situation s) thus necessitates a substitution of the SPEAKER parameter by a subject parameter: whereas the word *I* refers to SPEAKER(c) in any given context c, a subject takes himself to be SUBJECT(s), i.e. the subject, in any situation he finds himself in. As a case in point, Kaplan's perspective shifts from a set of situations in which someone other than the subject is reflected in the window, to the corresponding situations in which the (respective) subject's pants are burning. More generally, the *epistemological reinterpretation* [*erkenntnistheoretische Umdeutung*] of the two-dimensional approach to context dependence (Zimmermann 1991: 178ff.) has all pertinent aspects of the context replaced ('subjectivized') by corresponding subjective categories: subject, subjective time, subjective spatial perspective, etc. and assigns to sentences S corresponding epistemological characters whose diagonals then turn out to be supersets of the epistemic perspectives of the subjects that would use them to characterize their beliefs. Technically, this shift involves a revision of Logical Space the details of which need not concern us here; it is usually carried out in terms of the parameterization to be discussed in Section 8 and will briefly be addressed there. Varieties of epistemological reinterpretation have some success in current metaphysics and philosophy of mind (e.g., Chalmers 1996, Spohn 2009: Part V), in particular when it comes to tease apart *metaphysical* ('objective', 'perspectiveless') and *epistemic* ('subjective', 'perspectival') informational content. In the semantics of attitude reports, it may therefore be employed to correct the simplified Hintikka-style approach to psychological attitudes. As a case in point, we may look at a report about Kaplan's unfortunate (though, presumably, imaginary) experience where we take it that the possessive pronoun *his* is anaphoric to the matrix subject and may therefore be interpreted as (directly) referring to David Kaplan:

(58) *Kaplan thinks his pants are on fire.*

Since (58) does not contain any context-dependent material (or so we assume), it is absolute and has the same content across all utterance contexts. And it appears that this content applies to both the initial and the subsequent stage of Kaplan's learning process, to which we will refer as 's_0' and 's_1', respectively. This has to do with the fact that the complement clause shares its content with the contents of the sentences under (56) and (57) as uttered by Kaplan. Yet the connection is not as direct as it might seem: as was already remarked, Kaplan's doxastic perspectives in the situations s_0 and s_1 do not cover this content. On the other hand, in s_1 Kaplan sees himself in a position to assent to (57), and the content he expresses (or would express) by (57) in s_1 is precisely the content of the complement in (58). And although he does not assent to (57) in s_0, he does see himself in the mirror and thus could have described his belief by uttering (56), which again coincides in content with the complement of (58). Now, from this observation we might jump to the general conclusion that, for an attitude report to apply to a situation s, it is necessary and sufficient that (*) the content of the embedded clause must coincide with the content of some sentence that the subject would be inclined to agree to in s. Alas, things are not so simple, basically due to a radical generalization of Kaplan's (1968) infamous shortest spy problem (ii): given certain harmless side-conditions, (*) is met as soon as the complement of the embedded clause happens to be true of s; rather than pursuing this line of reasoning, we refer the reader to the concise presentation in article 17 [Semantics: Noun Phrases and Verb Phrases] (Schlenker) *Indexicality and de se* (p. 1572), based on Crimmins (1998) and von Stechow & Zimmermann (2005). In any case, a more sophisticated account is called for. And though, e.g., the 'hyperintensional' approach (Cresswell & von Stechow 1982) smoothly generalizes from *de re* to *de se* reports (von Stechow 1984), a treatment that conforms to more orthodox compositionality standards is yet to be found.

Sentences of the form (44), then, may be used to report *de se* beliefs. However, as with *de re* beliefs in general, this does not mean that the complement of the attitude verb is something the subject could truthfully utter in the situation described. Otherwise (58*) would be an adequate report about s_1 – no matter who utters the sentence:

(58*) *Kaplan thinks my pants are on fire.*

However, unless (somewhat unidiomatically) Kaplan himself uses (58*), the sentence would be a false report of s_1 – for the simple reason that the content the embedded clause expresses in the reporting context does not match the content of any sentence Kaplan would assent to in s_0; in particular, Kaplan does not believe that the person who happens to describe s_1 by uttering (58*), has burning pants. So although the 1st person as used by the attitude subject expresses his own subjective perspective, in the report it refers to the speaker – despite the fact that it occurs in the clause he uses to describe the subject's attitude. We will return to this elementary observation in the next section.

The fact that sentences of the form (44) (and similar) can be used to report about attitudes *de re* and *de se* does not mean that they are ambiguous in this respect: by definition, attitudes *de se* are attitudes *de re*, and these reports appear to cover them all. That no ambiguity is likely to be involved is suggested by the observation (frequently misattributed to Zimmermann 1991, methinks) that *quantified attitude reports* may generalize over a mixed bag of attitudes *de re* and *de se*:

(59) a. *Each of these men thinks that his pants are on fire.*
     b. *Only one of these men thinks that his pants aren't on fire.*

The reader is invited to fill in the details and then check her intuition: (59a) may be true (though a misleading thing to say) if all but one of the men wrongly think their own pants are on fire (*de se*) and one of them believes that he is watching (precisely) one man with burning pants without realizing he is watching himself (purely *de re*). At the same time, (59b) may be judged true in the same scenario, which does indicate that reports of the form (44) have separate *de se* reading after all. However, it is not obvious how to tell apart semantic and pragmatic effects in these cases. In particular, the source of the ease with which attitudes *de se* can be attributed is not obvious; cf. Percus & Sauerland (2003), Maier (2006), and Anand (2006) for different approaches. Unequivocal *de se* readings may still be found beyond the realm of clausal reports like (44), viz. in certain infinitival constructions involving control-verbs (Chierchia 1989).

(60) a. *John wants to be president.*
     b. *John wants himself to be president.*

Whereas (60b) can be applied to a situation in which John, who has given up on his political career, sees someone on TV who he judges to be a good candidate without realizing that it was himself, no such interpretation is available to (60a). But for the attitude, the example is quite parallel to Kaplan's scenario. This suggests that, unlike the reflexive in (60b), which is *de re*, the implicit subject (PRO) of the infinitive in (60b) needs to be restricted to a *de se* interpretation, i.e. as standing for the first person were the subject to describe his wishes. Unlike the *de re* construals of reports of the form (44), neither form in (60) presents a compositionality challenge, because in both cases the position of the *res* is structurally identifiable. In particular, the main verb in (60b) can be interpreted as expressing a ternary relation holding between the attitude subject (John), a *res* (John), and the intension of the infinitive, i.e. a function assigning sets of individuals (the presidents) to possible situations; roughly, the relation holds in a given situation *s* just in case the subject's pertinent (in this case: *bouletic*) perspective 'implies' that there is someone he is acquainted with in some way he is actually acquainted with the *res* (as the guy on TV, say) and who is the president. The details of this treatment depend on the precise reconstruction of subjective perspectives within an epistemological reinterpretation. The same goes for the *de se* attitude expressed by (60a), to which we will return in the next section.

In sum, sentences of the form (44) are most easily interpreted as reports about attitudes *de dicto*. As reports about attitudes *de re* they present a serious challenge to compositional interpretation, Hintikka-based or otherwise. The special case of *de se* attitudes adds the complication that the subject's perspective must be taken into account when it comes to characterizing his attitude and his relation to the *res*; moreover it is not clear in which cases they constitute separate readings.

7 Monsters

Let us take a step back. In Section 2 we saw that the 'one-dimensional' approach to extensions as solely depending on contexts cannot explain the difference between two kinds of trivialities: those that come out true whenever uttered, and those that express trivial content. The two-dimensional account of extensions in terms of characters introduced in Section 3 was designed to capture this distinction by sneaking in intensions mediating between contexts of utterance and extensions. In Section 4 we saw that, apart from the ordinary content that excludes possibilities in Logical Space, characters also encode diagonal content, which may serve various pragmatic purposes. However, even though we insisted right from the beginning that the observations and subtleties captured by the two-dimensional approach somehow depend on literal meaning, it is not all that obvious that they are themselves semantically relevant. In particular, one may wonder whether the notion of (ordinary) content that was crucial to the distinction between necessity and *apriority* has a rôle to play in semantics, or whether it is just derived from literal meaning by some pragmatic processes. As it turns out though, there is hope to give a purely semantic motivation of the notion of content (and intension in general). To this we will now turn.

The starting point of the preceding section was a classical substitution argument to the effect that clausal embedding under attitude verbs is not extensional. On the other hand, we also observed that once the utterance context is fixed, substitution of intensionally equivalent material does not bear on the truth value of the report (though it may affect its pragmatic acceptability); hence in a suitablae context (like c_{50}) the following two sentences come out as extensionally equivalent because the embedded clauses coincide in their content:

(50) a. *John thinks that I met you here yesterday.*
b. *John thinks that Mary met Jane in Rome on Wednesday.*

Now, it is worth noting that these substitution facts are independent of the *de re/de dicto* ambiguities:

(61) a. *John thinks that <u>Mary's husband</u> is Greek.*
b. *John thinks that <u>the man who is married to Mary</u> is Greek.*

Given that the underlined descriptions in (61) are intensionally equivalent, both sentences report John to either hold a certain belief *de re* about Mary's husband (whom John need not associate with Mary then), or else to think that whoever is married to Mary is Greek (in which case Mary could well be husbandless).

Abstracting from the details of the case, we may thus venture the hypothesis that replacing a complement clause in an attitude report of the form (44) by one with the same content does not affect the truth value of the report at large. Instead of the absurd extensional substitution principle (46), the general compositionality principle (49) can be strengthened to (62):

(46) If $/S_1/^c = /S_2/^c$, then $/$John thinks that $S_1/^c = /$John thinks that $S_2/^c$.
(49) If $[\![S_1]\!] = [\![S_2]\!]$, then $[\![$John thinks that $S_1]\!] = [\![$John thinks that $S_2]\!]$.
(62) If $[\![S_1]\!]^c = [\![S_2]\!]^c$, then $[\![$John thinks that $S_1]\!]^c = [\![$John thinks that $S_2]\!]^c$.

Similar observations can be made with other non-extensional constructions. Thus, e.g., in the above context c_{50}, the following sentences appear to pairwise express the same content:

(63) a. *It is possible that <u>I met you here yesterday</u>.*
b. *It is possible that <u>Mary met Jane in Rome on Wednesday</u>.*

(64) a. *I want to <u>meet you tomorrow</u>.*
b. *Mary wants to <u>meet Jane on Friday</u>.*

(65) a. *John is looking for <u>a book about Jane</u>.*
b. *John is looking for <u>a book about you</u>.*

In each of these cases the underlined constituent can be shown to resist substitution by co-extensional expressions *salva veritate* (= thereby preserving truth [values]). Hence, just like in attitude reports of the form (44), the pertinent syntactic construction cannot be extensional. However, the substitutions in (63)–(65) do go through because the underlined constituents happen to have the same (pairwise) intensions in the context at hand. Hence, though not extensional, the constructions in question do seem to have a special property that would explain the subsitutivity facts:

Definition

n) A syntactic construction Σ is *intensional* if, for every context $c \in C$, there is a corresponding operation Γ^c on (possible) intensions such that for any expression α built up by Σ from expressions $\beta_1, \ldots, \beta_n$, the following equation holds:
 - $[\![\alpha]\!]^c = \Gamma^c([\![\beta_1]\!]^c, \ldots, [\![\beta_n]\!]^c)$

A comparison of Definitions l) and n) reveals that every extensional construction is intensional: Γ^c in n) can always be constructed from the $\Gamma^{c,s}$ as given in l) by putting: $\Gamma^c(\iota_1, \ldots, \iota_n)(s) = \Gamma^{c,s}(\iota_1(s), \ldots, \iota_n(s))$, for any situation $s \in LS$ and (suitable) intensions $\iota_1, \ldots, \iota_n$. (The verification of the details are left to the reader.) Hence 'intensional' means 'at most intensional'; if a construction is intensional without being extensional, we may say that it is *properly intensional*.

In general, properly intensional constructions are characterized by a failure of extensional substitution, i.e. the fact that the extension of the whole (partly) depends on the intension of (at least) one of its (immediate) parts; since this intension itself consists of the extensions of that part at all possible situations, one may think of intensional constructions as having the extension of the whole at a given situation depend on the extensions of one of the parts at other situations than that situation alone (otherwise the construction would be extensional and not properly intensional). So an intensional construction can be loosely characterized as involving a *shift* from the situation at hand to other situations relevant to determine the extension of the substitution-resistant part, and thus the extension of the whole. As a case in point, if analysed à la Hintikka (1969), belief reports (and attitude reports in general) involve a shift from the situation reported to the subject's doxastic (or otherwise pertinent) perspective. Though this characterization is not without intuitive appeal (which explains its popularity among semanticists, logicians, and philosophers of language alike), one should be aware that it is quite loose in that the purported 'shift' normally does not replace one situation by another *one*, but brings in a whole bagful of relevant alternative situations; it may even bring in all of Logical Space, as in the case of (a certain reading of) the adverb *necessarily* that characterizes a sentence as true if its intension holds of every possible situation. In fact, mere shifts that would replace the situation described by another *one* seem to be unattested; but we will meet something close to them in a minute. Given this, it would be more accurate to speak of *abstraction* from the situation at hand, or *generalizing* over possible situations. Despite these qualms, we will follow tradition and say that the hallmark of intensionality is the *shiftiness* of the situation described.

The case of clausal embedding and the examples in (63) indicate that not every intensional construction is extensional. Neither is every (conceivable) character composition intensional. In fact, we have already seen an example of a non-intensional 'construction', viz. diagonalization:

(41) $[\![\Delta\alpha]\!]^c(s) = [\![\alpha]\!]^s(s)$

Whatever the syntactic details of (presumed) expressions of the form '$\Delta\alpha$', they must involve some non-intensional construction if (41) is to hold. To see this, let us look at c_{50} again, where Mary is speaking in Rome and we thus have:

(66) $[\![I\ am\ here]\!]^{c_{50}} = [\![Mary\ is\ in\ Rome]\!]^{c_{50}}$

However, by the observations made in connection with (39) in Section 4, we may conclude:

(67) $[\![\Delta\ I\ am\ here]\!]^{c_{50}}$
     $= \{s\in LS|\ [\![I\ am\ here]\!]^s (s) = 1\}$
     $= \{s\in LS|\ [\![SPEAKER(s), PLACE(s))]\!] \in AT(s)\}$
     $= C$

The last line in (67) is due to the apriority of *I am here* (which takes care of the '$\supseteq$'-direction) and the fact that the SPEAKER function is defined for utterance contexts only ('$\subseteq$'). On the other hand, diagonalizing *Mary is in Rome* is useless because the sentence is absolute:

(68) $[\![\Delta\ Mary\ is\ in\ Rome]\!]^{c_{50}}$
     $= \{s\in C|\ [\![Mary\ is\ in\ Rome]\!]^s(s) = 1\}$
     $= \{s\in C|\ (Mary, Rome) \in AT(s)\}\ (= [\![Mary\ is\ in\ Rome]\!]^{c_{50}})$

Clearly, the set in (68) does not coincide with C: it misses out contexts in which Mary (speaker or not) is away from Rome (and, if "extrapolated", it also contains situations in which no word is spoken). Hence although *I am here* and *Mary is in Rome* have the same content (in the context at hand), their diagonalizations do not; as a consequence, diagonalization is not intensional (and cannot be achieved by combining intensional constructions either). Interestingly, its mirror image, direct interpretation operator ∇ (a.k.a. *dthat*), is:

(36) $[\![\nabla\alpha]\!]^c(s) = [\![\alpha]\!]^c(c)$

The intensionality of the construction in (36) is brought out by the following equation, where (for any $c \in C$) Γ^c is the operation assigning to any intension ι the extension $\iota(c)$:

(69) $[\![\nabla\alpha]\!]^c = \Gamma^c([\![\alpha]\!]^c)$

Since Γ^c obviously depends on c, direct interpretation is not a canonically intensional construction though; the verification of (69) and the definition of canonical intensionality are left to the reader.

In Section 4 it was mentioned that diagonalization, understood as replacing the content of an utterance by its diagonal, is a pragmatic repair strategy applied to natural language characters, particularly by hearers that lack sufficient knowledge of the context to determine the content of the utterance. If this is the only kind of use made by diagonalization, then there is no need for a diagonal operator in the (natural) object language, as in (41). Given that this was our only example of a (potential) non-intensional construction so far, one may now wonder whether there are any other ones. As it turns out, this is not obvious. In fact, one of the central tenets of the two-dimensional approach to context-dependence has it that there are none:

Ban on Monsters
All syntactic constructions are (at most) intensional.

The Ban goes back to David Kaplan's (1989a) *Demonstratives* (originally distributed in 1977, and actually dating from the early 1970s), the *locus classicus* of two-dimensionality. Its name alludes to a section heading ('VIII. Monsters Begat by Elegance', p. 510), under which diagonalization (as a language-internal operator) is discussed as a potential counter-example; another formulation is that there are no monsters, which are then defined as non-intensional constructions. The rationale of the Ban on Monsters is that two-dimensional interpretation comes in two steps: first the context fixes the referents of deictic (and similar) expressions, then compositionality takes over, combining extensions and intensions as in the pre-Kaplanian times of so-called Frege-Carnap semantics (Frege 1892, Carnap 1947). Hence the Ban finally gives an answer to the question of whether content has a rôle to play in semantics, or whether it is merely a derivative of sentence meaning that is primarily of pragmatic interest: like intensions in general, the contents of sentences are what counts for compositionality.

Ever since Kaplan placed the Ban on Monsters, ample confirmation has been found in terms of constructions that conform to it. However, Kaplan's Ban has also been subject to numerous attempts at refutation, especially since Schlenker (2003), a paper aptly titled *A Plea for Monsters*. To get the flavour of the most prominent kind of counter-example, it is instructive to once more return to the topic of the preceding section, where we noticed that (44) cannot be made true by plugging in a sentence *S* that John is inclined to agree to (in the circumstances described). Rather, the subject's 1st person reference would have to be replaced by a corresponding 3rd person referring to him as a *res* (given to him as his self). This is a brute fact about the system of personal pronouns in English and many other languages – but not all. For there happen to be languages in which (what looks like) a 1st person pronoun occurring in an attitude report may indicate the subject's perspective on himself, instead of referring to the producer of the report. The following example from the (Indoeuropean) language Zazaki (spoken in Turkey) and collected by Anand & Nevins (2004: 22) is a case in point:

(70) *Rojda ne va kɛ <u>mɨ</u> kes paci kɛrd.*

Word by word, the sentence reads 'Rojda not said that <u>I</u> anyone kiss did', but it means that Rojda did not say that <u>she</u> kissed anyone. The presence of the negative polarity item *kes* ['anyone'] shows that the embedded clause is not a quotation; hence according to the Ban on Monsters, the underlined pronoun ought to refer to the speaker of the report. Note that (70) is indirect speech rather than an attitude report. As a consequence, it is readily interpreted by *diagonalizing* the underlined pronoun, which then comes out as meaning *the speaker*. Moreover, the phenomenon of an unexpected contextual shift is not restricted to the speaker but also affects other contextual parameters such as the addressee, which can be treated in a parallel way. However, such 'local' diagonal operators are obviously monstrous. One way of avoiding them in the case at hand is to treat the personal pronouns as absolute expressions, lexically interpreted by the diagonal content of ordinary personal pronouns; however, this interpretive strategy would not explain the particular distribution of their readings, for which we have to refer the reader to Anand & Nevins (2004) and Anand (2006). More counter-examples to Kaplan's Ban along the lines of (70) have been observerd in a variety of languages. Their precise nature and pattern appears to be in need of further exploration but it is clear that the Ban will not emerge from this scrutiny unscathed; see article 17 [Semantics: Noun Phrases and Verb Phrases] (Schlenker) *Indexicality and de se* for the current state of research (and much more on the topic).

Apart from such diagonal readings of personal pronouns in reports there are some other phenomena that appear to be difficult (though not impossible) to reconcile with the Ban on Monsters. In particular, sometimes a deictic expression that would normally have its extension determined by the context of utterance, seems to be used in a more general way. Here are four quite different cases:

(71) a. *Never put off until <u>tomorrow</u> what you can do <u>today</u>.*
b. *Only I did <u>my</u> homework.*
c. *Every man faced an <u>enemy</u>.*
d. *Only one class was so bad that <u>no student</u> passed the exam*

(71a) is mentioned in Kaplan (1989a: 510, fn. 4) and attributed to Richmond Thomason. The natural way to understand this proverb is as a general advice to be followed on a day-to-day basis. In particular, the temporal adverbs *today* and *tomorrow* are not understood as referring to the day of utterance and its successor. Yet if they have their ordinary, deictic readings in (71a), this reference could only be overridden by a monster. However, even though a lexical ambiguity is unlikely here, a pragmatic analysis seems to be within reach; cf. Zimmermann (1991: 219) for some speculation and Predelli (1996) for a more specific proposal.

The crucial observation about (71b), due to Irene Heim (c. 1991), is that in it the 1st person possessive *my* does not seem to make reference to the speaker. Rather, the whole sentence quantifies over a domain (of students, most probably) and the object *my homework* is understood as 'co-varying' with the objects in that domain, i.e. the persons quantified over by the subject *only I*. Hence this particular use of the 1st person is not deictic but quantificational, and again no ambiguity seems to be involved. It may thus appear that (71b) presents another case of generalization over contexts, though one that cannot be explained in pragmatic terms. However a natural explanation may be found on the other side of the semantic interfaces: it is well known that morphological features (like number, gender, . . .) may generally carry meaning without always being semantically active (or *interpretable*). Thus, e.g., the underlined pronoun in (72), though morphologically plural, expresses singular meaning, co-varying with the persons quantified over by the subject:

(72) *Most students did <u>their</u> homework.*

In this case it is rather obvious that the pronoun *their* is both semantically and morphologically dependent on the quantifier *most students*, the former relation being one of binding, the latter consisting in number and person agreement. Arguably, something similar might be going on in (71b): although the form *my* carries first-person morphology due to its syntactic relation to the subject *only I*, and although this relation itself is semantically interpreted (as quantificational 'binding'), in this specific constellation, the morphological feature is not. In general, then, words like *I*, *you*, or *my* would have to be treated as complex expressions, with person features as their parts; and these person features are deictic expressions, which however need not be semantically active (or occur properly, i.e. semantically visibly). *Vide*, e.g., von Stechow (2003) for a detailed proposal along these lines, and Sternefeld (2008) for some principled criticism and a different approach.

In Section 1, we have seen that the context may supply the referents of implicit arguments of relational nouns like *enemy*:

(5) b. *He is an enemy.*

This construal is also available for (71c), borrowed from Partee (1984: 301): if, e.g., a Norwegian general utters the sentence, he may speak about a battle fought by the Norwegian army and thus express that each of his soldiers faced a member of the same guerilla army. Hence the general would use the subject as quantifying over Norwegian soldiers (in line with the context-dependence of quantifier domains observed in Section 1); and depending on the exact circumstances (including the general's intentions), the implicit argument might be the Norwegians or the Norwegian army. However, (71c) could also be used by someone who describes the same battle scene from a more neutral point of view, quantifying over Norwegian and guerilla soldiers alike. In that case, the implicit argument could not be supplied by the context; for it would have to depend on the respective soldiers quantified over. Again this means that we cannot treat the implicit argument as in (5b), where we took it to be the value of some contextual parameter. At first blush this looks like a monster is lurking somewhere behind the quantificational construction; but then it is not obvious how to arrive at the correct truth conditions of (the relevant reading of) (71c) by quantifying over contexts; presumably, the contexts quantified over would have to have soldiers as their speakers, but then the quantification should not affect the other contextual parameters. It seems more promising to treat implicit arguments like variables in logic and allow them to be bound by quantifiers in higher positions while the values of free variables depend on the context of utterance. This would also conform to Partee's (1984: 301) observation that there do not seem to be 'any cases of implicit arguments which can be interpreted *only* as bound variables or *only* as indexicals' [= deictic expressions]. We will soon return to this strategy.

(71d), which is von Fintel's (1996: 31) translation of a German example due to Heim (1991: 508), poses similar problems. Although the domain of the underlined quantifier ought to depend on the context, it does not but rather co-varies with the classes quantified over by the matrix subject. Again, a monster seems to be in sight, and again the remedy could be bindable variables on whose values quantificational domains (may) depend; cf. von Fintel (1996: 28ff.) and Stanley & Szabó (2000: 251ff.) for specific proposals along these lines. Hence sometimes what looks like a deictic expressions captured by a monster may turn out to be a variable bound by a quantifier.

The treatment of seemingly deictic expressions as variables can also be applied to 3rd person pronouns, which (as we have seen in Section 1) bear some similarity to demonstratives in that their referents are (sometimes) supplied by the context, to wit by whatever the speaker intends to refer to. However, it is well known that they too can be bound by nominal quantifiers; the following contrast may be used to illustrate this point:

(73) a. *Mary likes his teacher.*
 b. *Everyone likes his teacher.*

Ignoring irrelevant details and alternative readings, we may bring out the difference in the interpretation of the underlined (possessive) pronouns by a bit of (predicate) logical notation:

(74) a. LIKE(MARY,TEACHER($\underline{x}$))
 b. ($\forall x$) LIKE(x,TEACHER($\underline{x}$))

The formulae in (74) may be seen as approximations to the truth conditions of the corresponding sentences in (73), with underlined occurrences of the variable x corresponding to occurrences of the 3rd person pronouns. The occurrences in (74) differ in their status: the underlined 'x' in (74a) is free, the one in (74b) is bound (by the universal quantifier). As a consequence, unlike the closed formula (74b), (74a) only denotes a truth value relative to a variable assignment. This may be seen as parallel to the contrast in (73): in (73a) the referent of the pronoun is supplied by the context, in (74b) it is not. In fact, the denotations of both the pronoun in (73b) and the variable in (74b) seem to co-vary with the individuals in the domain of the respective quantifiers, *everyone* and $\forall$. Hence we would make the parallel perfect by assuming that the context is to the occurrence of *his* in (73a) what the variable assignment is to 'x' in (74a). In other words, it looks like we ought to identify 3rd person pronouns with variables and contexts with variable assignments (cf. Montague 1970). As a consequence, though, the very process of binding would come out as a monster: just like the logical formula in (74b) can only be evaluated by going through its truth values under more than one assignment, so would the sentence in (73b) have to be interpreted by comparing its extensions across different contexts. Hence either the parallel between (73) and (74) or the Ban on Monsters has to go (Zimmermann 1991: 201ff.; Rabern 2012a, 2012b).

As it turns out the question whether the Ban should be upheld is quite tricky, which is partly due to its shifty theoretical status. For it may come either in the guise of an empirical hypothesis (as suggested by the discussion so far) or as an analytic theorem. To the second option we now turn.

8 Parameterization

The examples discussed so far suggest that the rôle of the utterance situation in determining extensions is restricted to contributing certain aspects or parameters like SPEAKER, ADDRESSEE, TIME, PLACE, etc. We have treated such parameters as functions assigning extensions to specific (possible) situations. Of course, there are innumerable such functions only very few of which are relevant to determining the extensions of context-dependent expressions (via their characters) – as *contextual* parameters. We have left their precise nature and number open and will continue to do so. However, we will assume that there are enough of them to distinguish any two contexts; in other words, we take the correspondence between contexts and their parametric values to be one-one:

Definition

0) A *C-parameterization* is a finite list $\pi = (\pi_1; \ldots; \pi_n)$ of functions π_i with domain C (and arbitrary ranges) such that,
    (*) for any distinct contexts c and c':
    $\pi_i(c) \neq \pi_i(c')$, for some $i \leq n$.
    For any $c \in C$, $c^* := (\pi_1(c); \ldots; \pi_n(c))$; hence $c^* \neq c'^*$ whenever $c \neq c'$.

For definiteness, let us zoom in on a particular C-parameterization that includes the four contextual parameters mentioned a few lines earlier as well as the spatio-temporally maximal situation of which the utterance situation is part – its (possible) WORLD:

(75) $c^* = $ (SPEAKER(c); ADDRESSEE(c); WORLD(c); TIME(c); PLACE(c); …)

We will say that c^* *represents* the context $c \in C$ (relative to the parameterization given) just in case (75) holds. Since, by assumption, the contextual parameters suffice to determine all extensions, the utterance situations in all their specificity and abundance, may as well be replaced by their representations. More precisely, we may encode characters χ by functions χ* assigning intensions to representations of parametric values:

(75*) $\chi^*(c^*) = \chi(c)$

C-parameterizations are little more than standardizations of characters, and may even be perceived as notational overkill. Moreover, there may be Ockhamian reasons for mistrusting them, due to the danger of proliferation of contextual parameters *praeter necessitatem*, as caricatured by Cresswell (1972: 8, 1973: 111) with his infamous *previous drinks* coordinate, supposedly to account for *Just fetch your Jim another quart*. On the other hand, there seems to be something natural about parameterizing contexts; the technique has been popular ever since Scott (1970). In any case, it turns out to be useful when we step down from characters to intensions and replace the situations in their domains by corresponding lists.

Before doing so, we need to get clear about what should make the difference between a contextual parameter and one that may be employed in the description of (properly) intensional constructions. As was mentioned near the beginning of the previous section, there is quite some variation among such constructions. In particular, constructions differ as to which aspects of the situation they abstract from: modals tend to bring in other possible worlds (cf. article 14 [Semantics: Noun Phrases and Verb Phrases] (Hacquard) *Modality*); some 'frame-setting' temporal adverbs and prepositions go back and forth in time (see article 13 [Semantics: Noun Phrases and Verb Phrases] (Ogihara) *Tense* and the literature cited there for a fuller picture); and, *pace* Maienborn (2001), presumably the same holds for literal uses of locative frame adverbials (Thomason & Stalnaker 1973). Under the assumption (76) that modification by sentence adverbs is interpreted by combining the extension of the adverb with the intension of the modified sentence, we can illustrate each case by (extremely simplified) character descriptions as in (77):

(76) $[\![ADV_{\{mod, temp, loc,...\}}\, S]\!]^c(s) = 1$ iff $[\![S]\!]^c \in [\![ADV_{\{mod, temp, loc,...\}}]\!]^c(s)$

(77)   a. $[\![possibly]\!]^c(s) = \{X \subseteq LS \mid s' \in X,\ \text{for some}\ s' \in LS\ \text{such that}\ s \stackrel{W}{=} s'\}$
       b. $[\![now]\!]^c(s) = \{Y \subseteq LS \mid s' \in Y,\ \text{for some}\ s' \in LS\ \text{such that}\ s \stackrel{T}{=} s'\ \&\ \text{TIME}(s') = \text{TIME}(c)\}$
       c. $[\![in\ Rome]\!]^c(s) = \{Z \subseteq LS \mid s' \in Z,\ \text{for some}\ s' \in LS\ \text{such that}\ s \stackrel{P}{=} s'\ \&\ \text{PLACE}(s') = \text{Rome}\}$

In (77) the relation $\stackrel{W}{=}$ should be understood as holding between two situations that may be part of different *Worlds* but are otherwise (e.g., with respect to their time and place) as similar to each other as possible; and likewise for $\stackrel{T}{=}$ and $\stackrel{P}{=}$, and the *Times* and *Places* of the situations related rather than their *Worlds*. These maneuvers are necessary in order to account for nested occurrences of these adverbials, as the reader is invited to verify. Given this background, it is easy to pin down in which sense modal, temporal, and locative adverbials respectively *shift* the modal, temporal, and spatial parameter of the situation described:

(78) $\left[\!\!\left[\left\{\begin{array}{c} ADV_{mod} \\ ADV_{temp} \\ ADV_{loc} \end{array}\right\} S_1 \right]\!\!\right]^c (s) \neq \left[\!\!\left[\left\{\begin{array}{c} ADV_{mod} \\ ADV_{temp} \\ ADV_{loc} \end{array}\right\} S_2 \right]\!\!\right]^c (s),$

then for some $s' \in LS$ such that $\left\{\begin{array}{c} s \stackrel{W}{=} s' \\ s \stackrel{T}{=} s' \\ s \stackrel{P}{=} s' \end{array}\right\} : [\![S_1]\!]^c(s') \neq [\![S_1]\!]^c(s')$

We leave it to the reader to verify that each of the characters defined in (77a–c) satisfies one of the conditions in (78), though none satisfies any of the other two. Generalizing from (78), we will say that an *n*-place construction Γ *shifts* a function π defined on *LS* just in case there is a place $i \leq n$ such that the following equation holds for any $c \in C$, $s \in LS$, and characters $\chi_1, \ldots, \chi_n$ in the domain of the character composition Γ* associated with Γ:

(79) If $\Gamma^*(\chi_1, \ldots, \chi_i, \chi_n)(c)(s) \neq \Gamma^* (\chi_1, \ldots, \chi'_i, \ldots, \chi_n)(c)(s),$
then for some $s' \in LS$ such that $s \stackrel{\pi}{=} s'$: $\chi_i(c)(s) \neq \chi'_i(c)(s')$

The relations $\stackrel{\pi}{=}$ (and even the notation) are reminiscent of so-called *modified assignments* used in the compositional approach to variable binding in logic. However, situations not being assignments, their exact meaning is less clear. Thus, e.g., some $s \in LS$ could stand in any of these relations to more than one situation, or none at all; which of these cases applies, depends on the specific features of *s* as well as the structure of Logical Space at large. It seems that an approach to intensions in terms of parameters is far simpler in this respect. In fact, the examples in (77) suggest that three of the contextual parameters listed in (75) may also be used in the characterization of intensional constructions. Though not strictly necessary, one should then split up the interpretation of (sentence-) adverbial modification (76) into different cases (76⁺a–c) according to the parameters targeted by the modifying adverb; this seeming complication, which is independently supported by syntactic considerations, pays when it comes to adapting the extensions of adverbs, as is done in (77⁺):

(76⁺) a. $\llbracket ADV_{mod}\, S\rrbracket^c(w; t; p; \ldots) = 1$ iff $\{w' \mid \llbracket S\rrbracket^c(w'; t; p; \ldots) = 1\} \in \llbracket ADV_{mod}\rrbracket^c(t; p; w; \ldots)$
b. $\llbracket ADV_{temp}\, S\rrbracket^c(w, t; p; \ldots) = 1$ iff $\{t' \mid \llbracket S\rrbracket^c(w; t'; p; \ldots) = 1\} \in \llbracket ADV_{temp}\rrbracket^c(t; p; w; \ldots)$
c. $\llbracket ADV_{loc}\, S\rrbracket^c(w; t; p; \ldots) = 1$ iff $\{p' \mid \llbracket S\rrbracket^c(w; t; p'; \ldots) = 1\} \in \llbracket ADV_{loc}\rrbracket^c(t; p; w; \ldots)$

(77⁺) a. $\llbracket possibly\rrbracket^c(w; t; p; \ldots) = \{X \subseteq W \mid X \neq \emptyset\}$
b. $\llbracket now\rrbracket^c(w; t; p; \ldots) = \{Y \subseteq T \mid \mathrm{TIME}(c) \in Y\}$
c. $\llbracket in\ Rome\rrbracket^c(w; t; p; \ldots) = \{Z \subseteq P \mid \mathrm{Rome} \in Z\}$

Obviously, these equations can easily be adapted so that the character depends on the representation of the (arbitrary) context c. In any case, in (76⁺) and (77⁺) intensions are now taken to be functions defined on lists $(w; t; p; \ldots)$ of Worlds, Times, Places, and others.

(76⁺) shows more directly than (76) how an intensional construction may select particular parameters of a situation while leaving the others untouched; and according to (77⁺), these parameters are all the extensions of the sentence adverbs care about. Using the above terminology, we may say that modal, temporal, and locative adverbials respectively *shift* the WORLD, TIME, and PLACE parameter of the situation described. So the rationale behind the parameterization should be that it brings out in the open what was implicit in the earlier approach using situations at large: the *shifting* of particular parameters. We thus obtain the following natural construction, where functions that are shifted by some intensional construction are called *shifty*:

Definition

p) An *I-parameterization* is a finite list $\rho = (\rho_1; \ldots; \rho_m)$ of shifty functions π_i with domain LS (and arbitrary ranges) such that,
(⁺) for any distinct situations s and s':
$\rho_i(s) \neq \rho_i(s')$, for some $i \leq m$.
For any $s \in LS$, $s^+ := (\rho_1(s); \ldots; \rho_m(s))$; hence $s^+ \neq s'^+$ whenever $s \neq s'$.

Condition (⁺) is adopted mainly for parallelism; but it will turn out to be useful. As a matter of fact, it could be dropped if Definition q) is slightly strengthened; see below.

Not only elegance and transparency speak in favour of *I*-parameterization The construction of intensions in terms of lists rather than situations opens the possibility of *free variation* within these lists: instead of defining intensions as operating on lists of the form s^+, we may extend them to arbitrary combinations of parameters, including those that do not correspond to any situation. Such lists or *indices* are easily constructed if the *I*-parameterization is rich enough. For instance, in order to guarantee condition (⁺), one may include the identity mapping over *LS*; as a result, any minimal modification of a list s^+ would lead to an index that does not represent any situation. Still, free variation would not lead to any change in the formulation of general character descriptions like (76⁺) and (77⁺). In fact, it may even come in handy if parameters get shifted beyond Logical Space but without contradiction. One possible case is discussed in Zimmermann (1991: 170): if, as current-day physics has it, the universe came into existence 14.6 billion years ago, no sentence modified by *16 billion years ago* could be true in an actual situation, which seems to contradict intuition because there would be no way of negating the fact that something or other happened at that time. Again we have to leave the details of this argument for the reader to fill in.

In principle, free variation is also available for contextual parameters, which can be turned against *C*-parameterization (Lewis 1980): since the rôle of contextual parameters is to determine intensions relative to utterance contexts, there seems to be no use of combinations beyond the representations of the latter. However, *C*-parameterizations may still be helpful in reconstructing the ingredients of two-dimensional semantics in terms of *I*-parameterization. In particular, the internal structure of lists of contextual parameters may be exploited in the construction of *diagonals* – provided that the *C*- and *I*-parameters are in tune, in the following sense:

Definition

q) A *C*-parameterization $\pi = (\pi_1; \ldots; \pi_n)$ *fits* an *I*-parameterization $\rho = (\rho_1; \ldots; \rho_m)$ iff the following conditions hold:
 – $n \geq m$;
 – π_i is not shifty if $i < n-m$;
 – $\pi_i = \rho_i$, for any $i \geq n-m$.

In the absence of condition (⁺) in Definition *p*), a further constraint on fitting *I*-parameterizations would have to be imposed, viz. that $(\pi_{n-m}(c); \ldots ; \pi_n(c))$ uniquely determines *c*.

Hence fitting C-parameterizations only add parameters that are not shifty and thus only needed for determining context-dependent intensions (otherwise they shoud occur in the I-parameterization). Thus, e.g., the C-parameterization

(SPEAKER; ADDRESSEE; WORLD; TIME; PLACE; . . .)

is in tune with the I-parameterization

(WORLD; TIME; PLACE; . . .)

where $n = m + 2$ and the '. . .' stand for the same list of (shifty) parameters. Given Definition q), it is possible to construct diagonals in quite the same fashion as in Section 4 above. This may come as a surprise, given that lists of contextual parameters are longer than I-parameters and thus there appear to be more of them than there are indices – whereas the contexts of utterance form a proper subset of Logical Space. However, as long as we rule out free variation on C-parameters, things do not change dramatically, due to the restrictions (*) and (⁺) in Definitions o) and p): given fitting C- and I-parameterizations, any $c \in C$ will be represented by a unique list c^*, and any $s \in LS$ will be represented by a unique list s^+. Consequently, any c will be represented by a unique pair (c^*, c^+) – and this pair represents the diagonal point (c,c)! To be sure, characters still look slightly different after (fitting) parameterization, but only because of the free variation among I-parameters, which extends their right side but leaves the 'diagonalizable' left part untouched.

Parameterization, thus conceived, has deep repercussions on the two-dimensional approach to context-dependence. This is because it makes shiftability the criterion for distinguishing between context and index, and thus between intension and character. More specifically, the Ban on Monsters comes out as an analytic truth (i.e., true by definition) rather than an empirical hypothesis. The rationale behind this is that shifty parameters are more clearly identifiable than the contents of utterances (Lewis 1980; see also Rabern 2012b). In Section 2, following the tradition of Kaplan (1989a), we identified the latter with *what is said*. However, this locution is by no means unequivocal, as becomes clear from dialogues like:

(80) John: *Smith said to me: 'You are my best friend.'*
      Mary: <u>*What Smith said*</u> *is what he has been telling me all the time.*

Mary's reply may be (and may be meant to be) either reassuring or critical, depending on whether the underlined free relative refers to (a) the situations in which

John is Smith's best friend, or (b) the situations in which *Smith's addressee* is his best friend. Both readings seem plausible and, arguably, neither is the better choice for the literal referent of the underlined clause. But whereas (a) is the content of Smith's reported (alleged) utterance, (b) involves (local) diagonalization of the 2nd person pronoun. So not all is well with the pragmatic definition of content, and thus intension in general, in terms of what is said by (assertoric) utterances. On the other hand, shiftability does not presuppose the notion of content because it directly shows in, and affects, the truth conditions of utterances. This speaks in favour of an identification of intensions in terms of compositional semantics rather than pragmatics.

However, unlike the distinction between utterance situations and non-utterance situations, that between context and index is language-dependent, because it depends on the semantic properties of grammatical constructions. Therefore, any purported counter-examples to the Ban on Monsters can and must be dealt with by turning purported *C*-parameters into *I*-parameters. Thus, e.g., since the implicit argument in (5b) may be quantified, as (71c) shows, it would have to be provided by an *I*-parameter:

(5) b. *He is an enemy.*
(71) c. *Every man faced an <u>enemy</u>.*

The fact that the context still provides the value of the parameter thus comes out as merely a reflex of the general dependence of extensions on the utterance situation already observed in connection with Definition *h*) in Section 4: given an utterance context, the extension of an expression is determined by applying its intension to the context itself. As a result, in the absence of any intensional construction shifting the pertinent parameter, the context of utterance provides the values of the *I*-parameters. However, if taken to its limits, the strategy of pushing *C*-parameters into the index runs the risk of eventually emptying the list. Now, this would not make the distinction between context and index totally idle; after all, deictic expressions might coexist with 'bindable' ones and share the same parameter. Only in the absence of any deictic expressions would characters be superfluous because the intensions alone would suffice to determine all extensions relative to any (utterance) situation; and as a consequence, the Ban of Monsters too would be pointless in a language devoid of deixis. This should not come as a surprise, though; for it is deictic expressions that motivated the distinction between intension and character in the first place.

I am indebted to Jan Köpping for a number of critical comments and suggestions.

9 References

Aloni, Maria 2001. *Quantification under Conceptual Covers*. Ph.D. dissertation. University of Amsterdam.
Anand, Pranav 2006. *De De Se*. Ph.D. dissertation. MIT, Cambridge, MA.
Anand, Pranav & Andrew Nevins 2004. Shifty operators in changing contexts. In: R. B. Young (ed.). *Proceedings of Semantics and Linguistic Theory (= SALT) XIV*. Ithaca, NY: Cornell University, 20–37. http://elanguage.net/journals/salt/issue/view/284, June 13, 2012.
Anderson, Stephen R. & Edward L. Keenan 1985. Deixis. In: T. Shopen (ed.). *Language Typology and Syntactic Description, vol. 3: Grammatical Categories and the Lexicon*. Cambridge: Cambridge University Press, 259–308.
Bach, Kent 1987. *Thought and Reference*. Oxford: Oxford University Press.
Bach, Kent 1992. Intentions and demonstrations. *Analysis* 52, 140–146.
Bierwisch, Manfred 2004. Tertium evitari non potest: On Ede Zimmermann's bipartition of the lexicon. In: H. Kamp & B. H. Partee (eds.). *Context-Dependence in the Analysis of Linguistic Meaning*. Amsterdam: Elsevier, 375–382.
Borg, Emma 2004. *Minimal Semantics*. Oxford: Oxford University Press.
Carnap, Rudolf 1947. *Meaning and Necessity*. Chicago, IL: The University of Chicago Press.
Castañeda, Hector-Neri 1967. Indicators and quasi-indicators. *American Philosophical Quarterly* 4, 85–100.
Chalmers, David 1996. *The Conscious Mind*. Oxford: Oxford University Press.
Chierchia, Gennaro 1989. Anaphora and attitudes *de se*. In: R. Bartsch, J. van Benthem & P. van Emde Boas (eds.). *Semantics and Contextual Expression*. Dordrecht: Foris, 1–31.
Cresswell, Maxwell J. 1972. The world is everything that is the case. *Australasian Journal of Philosophy* 50, 1–13.
Cresswell, Maxwell J. 1973. *Logics and Languages*. London: Methuen.
Cresswell, Maxwell J. 1985. *Structured Meanings*. Cambridge, MA: The MIT Press.
Cresswell, Maxwell J. 1996. *Semantic Indexicality*. Dordrecht: Kluwer.
Cresswell, Maxwell J. & Arnim von Stechow 1982. *De re* belief generalized. *Linguistics & Philosophy* 5, 503–535.
Crimmins, Mark 1998. Hesperus and Phosphorus: Sense, pretense, and reference. *Philosophical Review* 107, 1–47.
Donnellan, Keith S. 1966. Reference and definite descriptions. *Philosophical Review* 75, 281–304.
von Fintel, Kai 1996. *Restrictions on Quantifier Domains*. Ph.D. dissertation. University of Massachusetts, Amherst, MA.
Frege, Gottlob 1892. Über Sinn und Bedeutung. *Zeitschrift für Philosophie und philosophische Kritik* 100, 25–50. English translation in: P. Geach & M. Black (eds.). *Translations from the Philosophical Writings of Gottlob Frege*. Oxford: Blackwell, 1980, 56–78.
Frege, Gottlob 1919. Der Gedanke. Eine logische Untersuchung. *Beiträge zur Philosophie des deutschen Idealismus* 2, 58–77. English translation by P. Geach: The thought: A logical inquiry. *Mind* 65, 1956, 289–311.
Gauker, Christopher 1997. Domain of discourse. *Mind* 106, 1–32.
Geach, Peter T. 1957. On beliefs about oneself. *Analysis* 18, 23–24.
Haas-Spohn, Ulrike 1991. Kontextveränderung. In: A. v. Stechow & D. Wunderlich (eds.). *Semantik – Semantics. Ein internationales Handbuch der zeitgenössischen Forschung – An International Handbook of Contemporary Research* (HSK 6). Berlin: de Gruyter, 229–250.

Haas-Spohn, Ulrike 1995. *Versteckte Indexikalität und subjektive Bedeutung*. Berlin: Akademie Verlag.
Heim, Irene 1991. Artikel und Definitheit. In: A. v. Stechow & D. Wunderlich (eds.). *Semantik – Semantics. Ein internationales Handbuch der zeitgenössischen Forschung – An International Handbook of Contemporary Research* (HSK 6). Berlin: de Gruyter, 487–535.
Heim, Irene 2008. Features on bound pronouns. In: D. Harbour, D. Adger & S. Béjar (eds.). *Phi Theory: Phi Features across Interfaces and Modules*. Oxford: Oxford University Press, 35–56.
Hintikka, Jaakko 1969. Semantics for propositional attitudes. In: J. W. Davis, D. J. Hockney & W. K. Wilson (eds.). *Philosophical Logic*. Dordrecht: Reidel, 21–45.
Janssen, Theo M.V. 1997. Compositionality (with an appendix by Barbara H. Partee). In: J. v. Benthem & A. G. B. ter Meulen (eds.). *Handbook of Logic and Language*. Amsterdam: Elsevier, 417–473.
Kamp, Hans 1971. Formal properties of 'now'. *Theoria* 37, 227–273.
Kaplan, David 1968. Quantifying in. *Synthese* 19, 178–214.
Kaplan, David 1978. Dthat. In: P. Cole (ed.). *Syntax and Semantics 9: Pragmatics*. New York: Academic Press, 221–243.
Kaplan, David 1979. On the logic of demonstratives. *Journal of Philosophical Logic* 8, 81–98.
Kaplan, David 1989a. Demonstratives. An essay on the semantics, logic, metaphysics and epistemology of demonstratives and other indexicals. In: J. Almog, J. Perry & H. Wettstein (eds.). *Themes from Kaplan*. Oxford: Oxford University Press, 481–563.
Kaplan, David 1989b. Afterthoughts. In: J. Almog, J. Perry & H. Wettstein (eds.). *Themes from Kaplan*. Oxford: Oxford University Press, 565–614.
Klein, Wolfgang 1978. Wo ist hier? Präliminarien zu einer Untersuchung der lokalen Deixis. *Linguistische Berichte* 58, 18–40.
Kratzer, Angelika 1978. *Semantik der Rede. Kontexttheorie – Modalwörter – Konditionalsätze*. Königstein/Ts.: Scriptor.
Kripke, Saul A. 1972. Naming and necessity. In: D. Davidson & G. Harman (eds.). *Semantics of Natural Language*. Dordrecht: Reidel, 253–355.
Kripke, Saul A. 1977. Speaker's reference and semantic reference. In: P. French et al. (eds.). *Midwest Studies in Philosophy, vol. 2: Studies in the Philosophy of Language*. Morris, MN: University of Minnesota, 255–276.
Kripke, Saul A. 1979. A puzzle about belief. In: A. Margalit (ed.). *Meaning and Use*. Dordrecht: Reidel, 239–283.
Künne, Wolfgang 1997. First person propositions: A Fregean account. In: W. Künne, A. Neven & M. Anduschus (eds.). *Direct Reference, Indexicality, and Propositional Attitudes*. Stanford, CA: CSLI Publications, 49–68.
von Kutschera, Franz 1975. *Sprachphilosophie*. 2nd edn. München: Fink.
Lewis, David K. 1979a. Attitudes de dicto and de se. *Philosophical Review* 88, 513–543.
Lewis, David K. 1979b. Scorekeeping in a language game. *Journal of Philosphical Logic* 8, 339–359.
Lewis, David K. 1980. Index, context, and content. In: S. Kanger & S. Öhman (eds.). *Philosophy and Grammar*. Dordrecht: Reidel, 79–100.
Lewis, David K. 1981. What Puzzling Pierre does not believe. *Australasian Journal of Philosophy* 59, 283–289.
Maienborn, Claudia 2001. On the position and interpretation of locative modifiers. *Natural Language Semantics* 9, 191–240.

Maier, Emar 2006. *Belief in Context*. Ph.D. dissertation. Radboud University Nijmegen.
Montague, Richard 1970. Universal grammar. *Theoria* 36, 373–398.
Partee, Barbara 1984. Compositionality. In: F. Landman & F. Veltman (eds.). *Varieties of Formal Semantics*. Dordrecht: Foris, 281–312.
Percus, Orin & Uli Sauerland 2003. On the LFs of attitude reports. In: M. Weisgerber (ed.). *Proceedings of Sinn und Bedeutung (= SuB) 7* (Arbeitspapiere des Fachbereichs Sprachwissenschaft 114). Konstanz: University of Konstanz, 228–242. http://ling.uni-konstanz.de/pages/conferences/sub7/, June 13, 2012.
Perry, John 1977. Frege on demonstratives. *Philosophical Review* 86, 474–497.
Perry, John 1979. The problem of the essential indexical. *Noûs* 13, 3–21.
Predelli, Stefano 1996. Never put off until tomorrow what you can do today. *Analysis* 56, 85–91.
Quine, Willard van Orman 1956. Quantifiers and propositional attitudes. *Journal of Philosophy* 53, 177–187.
Rabern, Brian 2012a. Monsters in Kaplan's logic of demonstratives. *Philosophical Studies* 158. DOI: 10.1007/s11098-012-9855-1.
Rabern, Brian 2012b. Against the identification of assertoric content with compositional value. *Synthese* 186. DOI: 10.1007/s11229-012-0096-9.
Reimer, Marga 1991. Do demonstrations have semantic significance? *Analysis* 51, 177–183.
Reimer, Marga 1992a. Demonstrating with descriptions. *Philosophy and Phenomenological Research* 52, 877–893.
Reimer, Marga 1992b. Three views of demonstrative reference. *Synthese* 93, 373–402.
Reimer, Marga 1992c. Incomplete descriptions. *Erkenntnis* 37, 347–363.
Reimer, Marga 1998. Quantification and context. *Linguistics & Philosophy* 21, 95–115.
Russell, Bertrand 1905. On denoting. *Mind* 14, 479–493.
Sauerland, Uli 2008. On the semantic markedness of phi-features. In: D. Harbour, D. Adger & S. Béjar (eds.). *Phi Theory: Phi Features across Interfaces and Modules*. Oxford: Oxford University Press, 57–82.
Schlenker, Philippe 2003. A plea for monsters. *Linguistics & Philosophy* 26, 29–120.
Scott, Dana 1970. Advice on modal logic. In: K. Lambert (ed.). *Philosophical Problems in Logic*. Dordrecht: Reidel, 143–173.
Spohn, Wolfgang 2009. *Causation, Coherence, and Concepts*. Berlin: Springer.
Stalnaker, Robert 1978. Assertion. In: P. Cole (ed.). *Syntax and Semantics 9: Pragmatics*. New York: Academic Press, 315–332.
Stalnaker, Robert 1981. Indexical belief. *Synthese* 49, 129–151.
Stalnaker, Robert 1991. The problem of logical omniscience, I. *Synthese* 89, 425–440. Reprinted in: R. Stalnaker. *Context and Content*. Oxford: Oxford University Press, 1999, 241–254.
Stalnaker, Robert 1999. The problem of logical omniscience, II. In: R. Stalnaker. *Context and Content*. Oxford: Oxford University Press, 255–273.
Stanley, Jason & Zoltán Gendler Szabó 2000. On quantifier domain restriction. *Mind & Language* 15, 219–261.
Stanley, Jason & Timothy Williamson 1995. Quantifiers and context-dependence. *Analysis* 55, 291–295.
von Stechow, Arnim 1984. Structured propositions and essential indexicals. In: F. Landman & F. Veltman (eds.). *Varieties of Formal Semantics*. Dordrecht: Foris, 385–403.
von Stechow, Arnim 2003. Feature deletion under semantic binding: Tense, person, and mood under verbal quantifiers. In M. Kadowaki & S. Kawahara (eds.). *Proceedings of the North Eastern Linguistic Society (= NELS) 33*. Amherst, MA: GLSA, 379–403.

von Stechow, Arnim & Thomas E. Zimmermann 2005. A problem for a compositional treatment of *de re* attitudes. In: G. N. Carlson & F. J. Pelletier (eds.). *Reference and Quantification. The Partee Effect*. Stanford, CA: CSLI Publications, 207–228.

Sternefeld, Wolfgang 2008. Pronominal features: How "interpretable" are they? *Korean Journal of Linguistics* 33, 305–340.

Thomason, Richmond & Robert Stalnaker 1973. A semantic theory of adverbs. *Linguistic Inquiry* 4, 195–220.

Vlach, Frank 1973. *'Now' and 'Then': A Formal Study in the Logic of Tense and Anaphora*. Ph.D. dissertation. University of California, Los Angeles, CA.

Wettstein, Howard 1984. How to bridge the gap between meaning and reference. *Synthese* 58, 63–84.

Williams, Edwin S. 1982. The NP cycle. *Linguistic Inquiry* 13, 277–295.

Zimmermann, Thomas E. 1991. Kontextabhängigkeit. In: A. v. Stechow & D. Wunderlich (eds.). *Semantik – Semantics. Ein internationales Handbuch der zeitgenössischen Forschung – An International Handbook of Contemporary Research* (HSK 6). Berlin: de Gruyter, 156–229.

Zimmermann, Thomas E. 1995. Tertiumne datur? Possessivpronomina und die Zweiteilung des Lexikons. *Zeitschrift für Sprachwissenschaft* 14, 54–71. English translation: Tertiumne datur? Possessive pronouns and the bipartition of the lexicon. In: H. Kamp & B. Partee (eds.). *Context-Dependence in the Analysis of Linguistic Meaning*. Amsterdam: Elsevier, 2004, 319–332.

Holger Diessel
13 Deixis and demonstratives

1 Introduction —— 463
2 Foundations of deixis —— 464
3 Participant deixis —— 472
4 Object deixis —— 475
5 Conclusion —— 489
6 References —— 489

Abstract: This paper provides an overview of the form, meaning, and use of deictic expressions from a cross-linguistic perspective. The first part of the paper is concerned with the psychological foundations for a linguistic theory of deixis. It is argued that the use of deictic expressions presupposes a theory-of-mind that enables the communicative partners to adopt the perspective of another person. The second part of the paper provides an overview of deictic expressions in the world's languages. Two basic types of deixis are distinguished: participant deixis, which concerns the speech participants, and object deixis, which concerns elements of the situational and discourse context. The paper argues that person deictics are used as anaphors and that participant deictics, notably demonstratives, are used to establish joint attention, which is one of the most fundamental functions of human communication, providing a prerequisite for social interaction, cognition, and discourse.

1 Introduction

The term deixis refers to a class of linguistic expressions that are used to indicate elements of the situational and/or discourse context, including the speech participants and the time and location of the current speech event (cf. Bühler 1934; Frei 1944; Lyons 1977, 1979; Fillmore 1982, 1997; Levinson 1983, 2004). English has a wide variety of expressions that are commonly analyzed as deictics: personal pronouns such as *I* and *you*, spatial adverbs such as *here* and *there*, demonstratives such as *this* and *that*, temporal adverbs such as *now*, *then*, *today*, *ago*, and *recently*, motion verbs such as *come* and *go*, and tense morphemes such as the

Holger Diessel, Jena, Germany

https://doi.org/10.1515/9783110589849-013

future auxiliary *will* and the past tense suffix *-ed* (cf. Lyons 1977; Fillmore 1997). In addition, grammatical constructions such as the imperative and the vocative are often characterized as deictics (cf. Levinson 1983).

Deictic expressions raise important issues for semantic theory (cf. article 4 [Semantics: Foundations, History and Methods] (Abbott) *Reference*). In (formal) semantics, deictic expressions (also called *indexicals*; cf. Peirce 1955) are defined as linguistic signs with "direct reference" (Kaplan 1989: 483). In contrast to content words, deictic expressions do not evoke a concept of some entity (Frege's *sense*) but establish a direct referential link between world and language (cf. article 17 [Semantics: Noun Phrases and Verb Phrases] (Schlenker) *Indexicality and de se*). Since the interpretation of deixis is immediately determined by aspects of the speech situation, deictic expressions require a particular treatment in semantic theory (cf. Kaplan 1989; see also papers in Davis 1991, vol. III and Kasher 1998, vol. III).

In the literature, deictic expressions are commonly distinguished from deictic uses (cf. Nunberg 1998; Levinson 2004). Deictic expressions are linguistic elements "with built-in contextual parameters" that must be specified by aspects of the situational or discourse context (Levinson 2004: 14). Other linguistic elements can be used deictically if they are combined with a genuine deictic or referential expression. For example, a noun such as *tree* may refer to a concrete entity in the situational context if it is accompanied by a demonstrative that relates the concept of tree to a concrete entity in the surrounding situation (cf. *that tree*). Alternatively, content words can be grounded in the speech situation by non-linguistic means such as gesture, eye-gaze, or the presentation of an object. In general, as Levinson (2004) has pointed out, just about any nominal expression can be used deictically if it is accompanied by a communicative device that indicates a direct referential link between language and context.

This paper surveys the form, meaning, and use of deictic expressions from a psycholinguistic and cross-linguistic perspective. Two basic categories of deixis are distinguished: participant deixis and object deixis. Participant deixis concerns the role of the speech participants and their social relationship to each other, whereas object deixis concerns linguistic expressions referring to aspects of the situational or discourse context. The two types of deixis serve radically different functions and are expressed by different types of words; but they also have important properties in common, which underlie their uniform classification as deictics.

2 Foundations of deixis

There is a long tradition in western philosophy of defining human cognition by formal operations over abstract symbols (cf. Montague 1974; see also article

10 [Semantics: Foundations, History and Methods] (Newen & Schröder) *Logic and semantics* and article 11 [Semantics: Foundations, History and Methods] (Kempson) *Formal semantics and representationalism*). However, recent work in cognitive psychology, philosophy, and linguistics has argued that this approach is not appropriate to characterize human cognition. Specifically, it has been claimed that cognitive processes are "embodied", i.e., grounded in our bodily experience with the environment (see Wilson 2002 for a review; see also Steels 1999; Clark 1997; Barsalou 1999). In this view, the sensory and motor activities of the body are important determinants of human cognition, which in turn influence the structure and use of language (Lakoff & Johnson 1980, 1999).

There is perhaps no other linguistic phenomenon that is so fundamentally rooted in our bodily experience than deixis. In fact, one of the reasons why indexicals have been discussed extensively in both linguistics and philosophy is that they pose a serious challenge to semantic theories in which linguistic meaning is decontextualized and disembodied. Philosophers such as Russell and Reichenbach tried to reduce all indexical expressions to a single deictic term that can be translated into some context-free expression in an artificial language; but this account does not provide an adequate description of the use and meaning of deictic expressions. In natural language, deixis is fundamentally grounded in our bodily experience and situated interactions between the interlocutors. Thus, any account of natural deixis has to start from a pragmatic theory of language use and human cognition (cf. article 5 [Semantics: Foundations, History and Methods] (Green) *Meaning in language use*).

2.1 Theory-of-mind

Language use is a triadic behaviour involving the speaker, the hearer, and the entities talked about (cf. Bühler 1934). The triadic nature of language presupposes that the interlocutors understand each other as "mental or intentional agents" (cf. Tomasello 1999). In order to communicate, speaker and hearer must realize that the communicative partner has mental representations and that she views the situation from a different perspective. In other words, language use presupposes a *theory-of-mind* that enables the language users to adopt the perspective of another person (cf. Tomasello 1999; Clark 1996). Interestingly, while other species may communicate in one way or another, it seems that human communication is the only form of communication that involves an understanding of the mind (cf. Butterworth 1998; Povinelli & Vonk 2003; Franco 2005; Tomasello 2006). As Tomasello (1999) and others have pointed out, the ability to adopt another person's perspective is a unique trait of human cognition that is reflected in the structure and use of language.

2.2 The deictic centre

A linguistic phenomenon that crucially relies on this ability is deixis. As Bühler (1934) and other theorists have pointed out, the use of deixis involves a particular viewpoint called the *deictic centre* or *origo* (cf. Bühler 1934; Lyons 1977). The deictic centre is the centre of a coordinate system that underlies the conceptualization of the speech situation. In the unmarked case, the deictic centre is defined by the speaker's location at the time of the utterance. Deictic expressions are used to indicate a location or point in time relative to the deictic centre. For instance, the spatial adverbs *here* and *there* can be used to express a contrast between two different locations based on their relationship to the origo: *here* marks the area that is conceptualized as the deictic centre, and *there* indicates a location that is not included in this area. In the literature, *here* and *there* are commonly characterized as proximal and distal deictics, but the attributes 'proximal' and 'distal' must not be taken in the absolute sense of these terms because the deictic centre and the speech situation are conceptual units that cannot be equated with the physical location in which the speech event occurs. Consider for instance the use of the spatial deictic *here* in examples (1a-e).

(1) a. *Here* where I am
    b. *Here* in this room
    c. *Here* in Jena
    d. *Here* in Germany
    e. *Here* on this planet

What these examples illustrate is that the area included in the deictic centre (denoted by *here*) varies with the construal of the speech situation. In (1a), *here* refers to a location that is further specified by the pronoun *I*, indicating that the deictic centre is basically identical with the speaker's body; but in all other examples the deictic centre includes a much larger area organized around the speaker's location at the time of the utterance: In (1b) the deictic centre is the room in which the speech event is taking place, in (1c) it is the city of Jena, in (1d) it is a country, and in (1e) the deictic centre consists of the whole planet. In other words, the referent of *here* varies with the conceptualization of the speech situation. The distal term *there* is used in contrast to *here*; it can refer to any location in the speech situation as long as it is not included in the area conceptualized as the deictic centre. In general, *here* and *there*, and other proximal and distal deictics, do not express absolute measures of distance, but differentiate between two different locations relative to the deictic centre within the current construal of the speech situation.

In conversation, the deictic centre is constantly changing between the communicative partners. Every time a new speaker adopts the turn, the speech event is conceptualized from a different point of view, which means that expressions such as *here* and *there* and *I* and *you* refer to different entities when used by different speakers. Adult speakers are so used to this procedure that they do not realize the constantly changing perspective that is involved in the use of deictic expressions; but children have great difficulties with the alternating point of view. Although English-speaking children begin to use deictic expressions very early, they often misinterpret their meaning and use (cf. Clark 1978; Tanz 1980; Wales 1986). For instance, it is well-known that some children begin to use the personal pronouns *I* and *you* as fixed expressions for the child and an adult speaker. Consider for instance the dialog in (2) between a two-year-old English-speaking boy and his mother (cf. Clark 1978: 101).

(2) Mother: What do you want?
    Child: Daddy toothbrush.
    Mother: Oh you want Daddy's toothbrush, do you?
    Child: Yes . . . *you* want to put the frog in the mug. [you = I]
    Mother: I think the frog is too big for the mug.
    Child: Yes *you* can put the duck in the mug [you = I]
           make bubble . . . make bubble.
    Mother: Tomorrow. Nearly all the water's run out.
    Child: *You* want Mummy red toothbrush . . . yes [you = I]
           you can have Mummy old red toothbrush.

In this example, both the boy and his mother use the pronoun *you* with reference to the child, suggesting that the boy misinterprets the term as some sort of proper name. The same absolute use of personal pronouns has been observed in many other studies. Consider for instance the following example from a diary study adopted from Clark (1978: 101).

(3) a. *I* carry.   [= you carry; a request to be picked up]
    b. Yacky tease *you*. [= Yacky is teasing me]
    c. Papa help *you*.   [= Papa help me]
    d. *You* want cake.   [= I want cake]

In these examples, the deictic pronouns *I* and *you* are used as fixed expressions for the child and one of his parents: the first person pronoun *I* refers to the parent, notably the father, and the second person pronoun *you* is used in self reference to the child.

2.3 The frame of reference

The deictic centre constitutes the centre of a relative frame of reference, which must be distinguished from two other reference frames for spatial orientation: the intrinsic frame of reference and the absolute frame of reference (Levinson 1996, 2003; Miller & Johnson-Laird 1976; Pederson et al. 1998). Each frame evokes a coordinate system, but is differently anchored in the speech situation. The relative frame of reference presupposes a viewpoint provided by the speaker or some other person; the intrinsic frame of reference involves an object-centred coordinate system determined by the inherent orientation of an object or person; and the absolute frame of reference is anchored by landmarks in the environment such as a mountain, a river, or the sun (see below).

While the conceptualizations of the three reference frames are in principle independent of language, they can be triggered by particular types of expressions. The relative frame of reference is commonly evoked by deictics such as *I* and *you* and *here* and *there* (cf. 4a-b); the intrinsic frame of reference is triggered by relational terms such as *in front of* and *behind* (cf. 5a-b); and the absolute frame of reference is established by expressions such as *uphill* and *downhill* or *east* and *west* that indicate a geographical location (cf. 6a-b).

(4) a. Peter is over *there*.
b. Can *you* show *me that*?

(5) a. The ball is *in front of* the car.
b. Peter stood on his uncle's *left* side.

(6) a. The cottage is *uphill*.
b. They were driving *west*.

Note that although the relative frame of reference provides the conceptual background for the interpretation of spatial deictics, it is in principle independent of the deictic center (cf. Levinson 1996). As can be seen in (7), the relative frame of reference can also be construed from the perspective of a third person (expressed in the *for*-phrase).

(7) For John, the ball is *in front of* the tree.

Interestingly, if we leave out *for John* the spatial arrangement is interpreted from the speaker's point of view, although the sentence does not include a deictic expression. Thus, while the relative frame of reference does not presuppose the use of deictics, it is construed from the speaker's point of view, i.e., the deictic centre, if there is no other point of reference, suggesting that the deictic centre provides the default viewpoint (or anchor) for this type of frame.

Like the relative frame of reference, the intrinsic frame of reference is derived from our bodily experience. It is based on the vertical and horizontal orientation of the human body, which is commonly expressed by relational terms such as *in front of* and *behind*, *left* and *right*, *up* and *down*, and *above* and *below*. Like deictic expressions, these expressions may involve the speaker's location at the time of the utterance (cf. 8a-c).

(8) a. The ball *in front of* me
    b. The ball to my *left*
    c. I put the ball *down*.

In examples (8a-c), relational expressions are used to indicate the location of an object based on the speaker's orientation in the speech situation. Note that these examples include a deictic expression referring to the speaker; but even if the utterance does not include a deictic term, relational expressions are commonly interpreted deictically, as in the following example in which *in front of* characterizes a location from the speaker's point of view, although the speaker is not mentioned in the sentence (Levinson 1996).

(9) The ball is *in front of* the tree.

However, in contrast to deictics relational expressions are in principle independent of the speaker's point of view and the human body. As can be seen in (10a-c), *in front of*, *left*, and *down* may indicate the location of an entity based on the inherent orientation of an object such as *house*, *car*, or *table*.

(10) a. A horse stood *in front of* the house.
     b. Peter's seat is in the back, on the *left* side of the car.
     c. The bottle fell *down* from the table.

What these examples show is that while relational expressions may involve the speaker's bodily orientation in the speech situation, their interpretation is not inherently tied to the speaker's body or location. That is, while relational expressions can be used deictically, they are distinct from genuine deictics in that they do not presuppose the deictic centre or the speaker's perspective (cf. Levinson 1996).

2.4 Deictic projection

Since the deictic centre is commonly defined by the speaker's location at the time of the utterance, deictic expressions are usually egocentric. However, the deictic centre can be transferred from the speaker to a person in an imaginary situation. This phenomenon, which Lyons (1977: 579) called "deictic projection" (cf. Jakobson 1957; Fillmore 1997), is characteristic of narratives and descriptions. In narratives the speaker creates a story world in which the protagonists provide the anchor for deictic expressions. This is particularly striking in the case of reported speech, in which deictic expressions are grounded by the person whose speech is reported; but the protagonists can also provide the anchor for deictic expressions in other contexts. For instance, if the story includes an I-narrator deictic expressions are commonly used within the narrator's coordinate system. Example (11), for instance, includes deictic expressions (i.e. *I, my, me, there*) that do not refer to the author and entities in his surrounding situation, but to the I-narrator and elements in the universe of discourse.

(11) The old man was dead. *I* removed the bed and examined the corpse. Yes, he was stone, stone dead. *I* placed *my* hand upon the heart and held it *there* many minutes. *There* was no pulsation. He was stone dead. His eye would trouble *me* no more.

[Edgar Allen Poe: The tell tale heart]

Interestingly, although deictic expressions presuppose a particular perspective, their occurrence does not entail the existence of a concrete person. As can be seen in the German example in (12) (adopted from Ullmer-Ehrich 1982: 233), spatial descriptions are often construed from the perspective of a fictive observer.

(12) Ja eh wenn man zur Tür reinkommt, gleich rechts davon ist der Schreibtisch an der Wand, im Anschluss daran ist das Bett, und *dann* kommt schon die Ecke zum Fenster, und *da* ist zwischen Fenster und Wand *dieses* Bücherregal, und an der anderen Seite, ja *da* is nich mehr viel Platz, *da* schließt sich *da* die andere Längswand an, *da* hab ich die Schlafcouch stehen, zwischen Schlafcouch und Bücherregal den Esstisch, an die Schlafcouch ran *kommt* der Kleiderschrank, neben m Kleiderschrank steht der Kühlschrank, und *dann* inner Ecke kommt das Waschbecken.

Well, er as you enter the door, immediately to the right of it is the desk against the wall, connected to it is the bed and *then* comes the corner going up to the window, and *there* between the window and the wall is *this* bookshelf, and on the other side, um, *there* isn't much space left, *there* I have the couch bed, between couch bed and bookshelf the dining table, by the sleeping couch *comes* the wardrobe, beside the wardrobe is the refrigerator, and *then* in the corner is the wash basin.

In this example, the speaker takes the hearer on an "imaginary gaze tour" through his student bedroom (Ullmer-Ehrich 1982: 241). In order to orient the hearer on this tour, the speaker uses various deictic expressions that are grounded by a fictive observer who describes the room as if individual pieces of furniture come in turn into view (cf. Linde & Labov 1975; Levelt 1989; Taylor & Tversky 1996).

2.5 Deictic categories

Deictic expressions are commonly divided into semantic categories; three categories are traditionally distinguished: person, place, and time (cf. Bühler 1934). In English, each category is associated with particular deictic expressions: *I* and *you* are person deictics, *here* and *there* and *this* and *that* are place deictic expressions, and *now* and *then*, and *today*, *yesterday* and *tomorrow* are temporal deictics. In addition to person, place and time, some studies assume two further deictic categories: discourse deixis and social deixis (cf. Lyons 1977; Levinson 1983, 2004; Fillmore 1997). Discourse deixis is concerned with expressions making reference to linguistic entities in the ongoing discourse, and social deixis is concerned with the social relationship between the interlocutors. Like person, place and time deixis, discourse deixis and social deixis may be expressed by particular terms. For instance, the English expressions *the latter* and *the aforementioned* are discourse deictics, and the French pronouns *tu* 'you.familiar' and *vous* 'you.unfamiliar' are instances of social deixis. Tab. 13.1 provides an overview of the deictic categories that are commonly distinguished in descriptive approaches to deixis (e.g., Levinson 1983, 2004; Fillmore 1997).

Tab. 13.1: Deictic categories

Category	Example
Person deixis	*I, you*
Place deixis	*here, there, this, that*
Time deixis	*now, then, today, yesterday, tomorrow*
Discourse deixis	*the latter, the aforementioned*
Social deixis	*tu, vous* [French]

While the traditional classification of deictic categories highlights important semantic distinctions, it ignores differences in their pragmatic use. If we consider the various deictic expressions from the perspective of their communicative function, they can be divided into two basic types: Participant deixis and object deixis. Participant deixis concerns deictic phenomena related to the speech participants, whereas object deixis concerns deictic phenomena that involve a referential link to elements of the situational or discourse context. The two types of deixis serve different communicative functions and are encoded by different types of expressions.

3 Participant deixis

Participant deixis subsumes the traditional categories of person and social deixis. In the literature, it is commonly assumed that person deictics function to identify the speech participants, but this assumption is not consistent with their use. Since speaker and hearer are usually aware of their communicative roles, person deictics are only rarely used to "identify" the speech participants in the surrounding situation (e.g., *I want to talk to you* [pointing to a person]); instead, they usually function to indicate the semantic roles of speaker and hearer in the event that is expressed by an utterance (e.g., *Peter noticed that I gave you the book*). Since the speech participants are aware of each other, the use of person deictics is similar to the use of anaphors: Both types of expressions function to denote a 'familiar' or 'activated' referent, i.e., a referent that is in the interlocutors' current focus of attention. The communicative function of participant deictics is reflected in the semantic features they encode. Four features are important:
1. Communicative role
2. Number
3. Gender
4. Social rank/relationship

All languages have particular expressions referring to speaker and addressee, but these expressions are not always deictic. In some South-east Asian languages, the speech participants are commonly expressed by common nouns (Cooke 1968). In Thai (Tibeto-Burman, Thailand), for instance, speaker and hearer are referred to by various nominal expressions such as *phom'* 'I' (lit. hair) and *tua* 'you' (lit. body/self), which are also used with their literal meaning (cf. Siewierska 2004: 228). However, the vast majority of the world's languages have deictic pronouns such as English *I* and *you* to indicate the communicative roles of the speech participants. In many languages, the speech participants are expressed by bound morphemes on the verb (cf. Siewierska 2004: Ch. 2), leaving the use of independent pronouns to situations in which the referent is especially emphasized (cf. example 13).

(13) wa-yį-ku:-wa
 1SG-2SG-give-REALIS
 'I give (it) to you'

In addition to the communicative role, number is a frequent feature of participant deixis. In a world wide sample of 260 languages, Dunn (2005) found only two languages, Acoma (Keresan, New Mexico) and Wari' (Chapacura-Wanhan, Brasil), in which first and second person pronouns do not have separate singular and plural forms; that is, the vast majority of the world's languages distinguish between *I* and *we* and *you*.SG and *you*.PL (English is unusual in this regard) (cf. Cysouw 2003; Siewierska 2004).

Note, however, that the plural of first person is conceptually distinct from the plural of other (pro)nominal expressions in that *we* does not denote multiple instances of *I* (cf. Cysouw 2003: Ch. 3). Rather, the plural of a first person pronoun refers to a group of people including the current speaker. Two basic types of first person plural pronouns can be distinguished: Inclusive pronouns, referring to a group of people including both speaker and hearer, and exclusive pronouns, referring to a group of people including only the speaker, i.e., excluding the addressee. For instance, as can be seen in Tab. 13.2, Chamorro (Austronesian, Guam) has three first person pronouns: *hu* meaning 'I', *ta* meaning 'I and you and possibly some others', and *in* meaning 'I and somebody else but not you'. While the inclusive-exclusive distinction is rare in Europe, it is a very frequent feature of participant deixis in other parts of the world (cf. Cysouw 2003).

Tab. 13.2: First person pronouns in Chamorro (Topping 1973: 106–108)

Meaning	Form
'I'	hu
'we' inclusive	ta
'we' exclusive	in

Another semantic feature that may be expressed by person deictics is gender. However, compared to number, gender is an infrequent feature of person deixis. In a world wide sample of 378 languages, Siewierska (2004) found only 21 languages in which first and/or second person pronouns carry a gender feature.

Moreover, in most of these languages gender marking is limited to the singular; in the plural, first and second person pronouns are almost always unmarked. Tab. 14.3 shows the personal pronouns in Ngala (Sepik, New Guinea), which is one of the few languages in Siewierska's sample in which both first and second person pronouns carry a gender feature, but only in the singular, i.e., in the dual and plural first and second person pronouns are unmarked.

Tab. 13.3: Personal pronouns in Ngala (Laycock 1965: 133)

	Singular		Dual	Plural
	Masculine	Feminine		
1. person	wn	ñən	öyn	nan
2. person	mən	yn	bən	gwn

In contrast to first and second person pronouns, third person pronouns are often gender-marked. In Siewierska's sample, gender marking in third person pronouns is about five times as frequent as gender marking in first and second person pronouns, suggesting that gender carries a greater functional load in third person anaphors than in participant deictics. While gender marking can help to differentiate between multiple antecedents of third person pronouns, it is irrelevant for the identification of the speech participants because speaker and hearer are sufficiently determined by the communicative interaction (cf. Siewierska 2004: 105).

Unlike gender marking, the marking of social relationships is very common in participant deictics, notably in expressions for the addressee. Many European languages employ two types of second person pronouns to indicate the social relationship between the speech participants. In German, for instance, *du* is used to address family members, friends, and young children, whereas *Sie* refers to strangers and people in professional relationships. A parallel contrast between familiar and respectful forms occurs in other European languages including French and Russian (cf. Tab. 13.4).

Tab. 13.4: Familiar and polite second person pronouns in three European languages

Language	Familiar form	Polite / respectful form
German	du	Sie
French	tu	vous
Russian	ty	vy

In German, French, and Russian, the polite forms are based on plural pronouns, but social deixis can also be expressed by special honorifics derived from common nouns such as 'master', 'servant', and 'king' (Siewierska 2004: Ch. 6). The use of (nominal) honorifics is characteristic of South-east Asian languages such as Thai and Vietnamese, which seem to lack genuine participant deictics (Cysouw 2003: 12–13; Siewierska 2004: 8–15).

4 Object deixis

Object deixis subsumes the deictic categories of place, time, and discourse. Place deictic expressions refer to concrete objects and locations in the situation surrounding the speech participants, but time and discourse deixis are more elusive. Time deictic expressions indicate a point in time relative to the moment of the speech event, and discourse deictic expressions locate linguistic elements in the ongoing discourse. Since time and discourse are abstract entities they are not immediately available for a concrete act of reference such as pointing. However, in language time and discourse are commonly conceptualized in spatial terms making them more objective (see below). This explains why time and discourse deixis are frequently expressed by spatial terms, suggesting that place deixis provides the conceptual and linguistic foundation for more abstract varieties of object deixis (cf. Lyons 1977: 718).

4.1 Place deixis

The core of place deixis constitutes a small class of expressions that are of fundamental significance to the organization of the deictic system: demonstratives such as English *this* and *that* and *here* and *there* (cf. Himmelmann 1997; Diessel 1999; Dixon 2003; see also article 1 [Semantics: Noun Phrases and Verb Phrases] (Büring) *Pronouns*). In the literature, demonstratives are commonly described as one type of place deixis, serving grammatical functions as pronouns, determiners, and adverbs; but this analysis does not adequately characterize their function and status in language (cf. Diessel 2006a).

4.1.1 The communicative function of demonstratives

In their basic use, demonstratives focus the interlocutors' attention on concrete entities in the surrounding situation; that is, demonstratives serve to establish joint attention, which is one of the most fundamental functions of human communication, providing a foundation for the organization of verbal interactions, the structuring of discourse, and the diachronic evolution of grammar (cf. Diessel 2006a).

Joint attention has been studied in interdisciplinary research on pointing, eye gaze, and theory-of-mind (for a review see Dunham & Moore 1995; Krause 1997; Eilan 2005); it involves three basic components: the speaker, the hearer, and the entities talked about (see above). Communication is thus a triadic behaviour in which the communicative partners are jointly focused on the same referent. In face-to-face conversations, the speaker can use eye gaze and pointing in addition to language to establish a joint focus of attention (cf. Bruner 1983; Carpenter et al. 1998; Tomasello 1999; Eilan 2005). While there are many linguistic means to create joint attention, demonstratives provide the primary linguistic device to manipulate the interlocutors' attention in the speech situation (cf. Clark 1996). The particular communicative function of demonstratives is reflected in a number of properties that characterize them as a particular word class (cf. Diessel 2006a).

To begin with, one of the most striking features of demonstratives is that they are commonly accompanied by a pointing gesture (cf. Bühler 1934; Enfield 2003; Levinson 2004; Diessel 2006a). Deictic pointing is a communicative device that is used in all cultures to establish joint attention (cf. Kita 2003); it usually involves the index finger, but there are also cultures in which lip pointing is used to direct the other person's attention (cf. Enfield 2002; Wilkins 2003). The frequent cooccurrence of demonstratives and deictic pointing supports the hypothesis that demonstratives function to establish joint attention, which is crucially distinct from the communicative function of person deixis. First and second person pronouns refer to the speech participants, which are automatically activated as part of the speech event, whereas demonstratives create a new focus of attention or else indicate a contrast between two previously established referents (cf. Levinson 2004; Diessel 2006a).

The frequent combination of demonstratives and deictic pointing is especially striking in early child language (cf. Clark 1978). When children begin to produce their first words, at around the age of 15 months, they typically use content words referring to persons, objects, and other entities in their environment (cf. Gentner 1982); but in addition to these words demonstratives are always among the first and most frequent expressions in early child language (cf. Clark 1978; Diessel 2006a). The early appearance of demonstratives is motivated by their communicative function to establish joint attention and their relationship to deictic pointing. The earliest pointing gestures children produce appear a few months prior to the onset of language and can be seen as a sign of the child's emerging ability to engage in triadic interactions, providing a prerequisite for the development of communication and language (cf. Tomasello 1999, 2003, 2006; Franco 2005).

The communicative importance of demonstratives is also reflected in their crosslinguistic distribution. Early work in linguistic typology was based on the assumption that grammatical categories are universal; but more recent work suggests that most linguistic categories have language-specific properties and are often restricted to a subset of the world's languages (cf. Croft 2001). For instance, while definite articles and auxiliaries are commonly found in Indo-European languages, they are often absent from languages in other genetic groups. However, in contrast to definite articles, auxiliaries, and other function morphemes, demonstratives are truly universal (cf. Himmelmann 1997; Diessel 1999, 2003, 2006a, 2006b; Dixon 2003).

What is more, demonstratives appear to be older than other closed-class items. In the literature, linguistic expressions are commonly divided into two basic types: content words and grammatical markers. Recent work in grammaticalization has shown that grammatical markers are frequently derived from content words. For instance, locational prepositions such as English *in front of* develop from relational nouns (or body part terms), and future tense auxiliaries such as English *going to* are often derived from motion verbs (cf. Hopper & Traugott 2003). The development of grammatical markers from content words is crosslinguistically so frequent that it has become a standard assumption of grammaticalization theory that all grammatical expressions are eventually derived from content words (cf. Hopper & Traugott 2003: 104). According to this view, demonstratives are function words, i.e., grammatical markers, that must have originated from a lexical source, i.e., from nouns or verbs. However, in sharp contrast to other closed-class expressions, there is no evidence that demonstratives are historically derived from lexical terms, suggesting that they are older than other closed-class items. If we consider the particular function of demonstratives to establish joint attention, it seems reasonable to assume that demonstratives may have emerged very early in the evolution of human language and independently of other linguistic terms (cf. Diessel 2006a).

4.1.2 The form and meaning of demonstratives

While demonstratives are universal, they can differ widely in terms of their form, meaning, and use (cf. Diessel 1999; Dixon 2003). The semantic features of demonstratives are divided into two basic types: (1) deictic features, which indicate the location of the referent relative to the deictic centre, and (2) non-deictic features, which characterize the type of referent (cf. Diessel 1999: Ch. 3; see also Fillmore 1982; Rauh 1983; Hanks 1990).

The deictic features of demonstratives are commonly characterized in spatial terms based on their relationship to the deictic centre. As can be seen in (14), if *this* and *that* are used contrastively, *this* denotes a referent that is closer to the deictic centre than the referent of *that*; that is, *this* is proximal and *that* is distal.

(14) *This* one (here) is bigger than *that* one (over there).

However, in non-contrastive situations *this* and *that* are often interchangeable (cf. 15), suggesting that they do not carry an inherent distance feature.

(15) I like *this/that* one better.

Considering the various uses of demonstratives in English, Levinson (2004) argues that while *this* always expresses some sense of proximity, *that* is only interpreted as a distal term if it is used in explicit contrast to *this*; that is, *that* is semantically unmarked for distance, but is interpreted as a distal term by pragmatic contrast via Grice's maxim of quantity ('Be as informative as circumstances permit'). Thus, Levinson concludes that the traditional analysis of demonstratives in terms of spatial features (i.e., proximal vs. distal) is not always adequate to characterize their meaning and use (cf. Enfield 2002).

However, while demonstratives do not generally indicate a contrast between proximal and distal referents, they are usually organized in paradigms of contrastive forms. English has a two-way deictic system, contrasting proximal and distal referents (in some uses); but many languages employ more than two deictic terms (cf. Diessel 2005a; see also Anderson & Keenan 1985 and Diessel 1999). For instance, as can be seen in Tab. 13.5, Irish (Celtic, Europe) has three demonstratives indicating three different locations on a distance scale: proximal, medial, and distal.

Tab. 13.5: Demonstratives in Irish (Bammesberger 1983: 60–61)

Proximal	*seo*
Medial	*sin*
Distal	*siúd*

In some languages the medial term is reserved for entities near the hearer. In Japanese, for instance, demonstratives differentiate between entities near the speaker, entities near the hearer, and entities away from both speaker and hearer (cf. Tab. 13.6).

Tab. 13.6: Demonstratives in Japanese (Kuno 1973)

	Pronouns	Determiners	Adverbs
Near speaker	kore	kono	koko
Near hearer	sore	sono	soko
Away from speaker and hearer	are	ano	asoko

Note that Japanese employs three different sets of demonstratives functioning as pronouns, determiners, and adverbs, which many languages do not formally distinguish; in particular the contrast between demonstrative pronouns and determiners is often formally unmarked (Diessel 2005b). But even if the demonstratives are divided into separate syntactic classes, as in Japanese, they tend to carry the same deictic features because they usually include the same deictic roots (cf. Diessel 1999: Ch. 2).

While two- and three-term systems are cross-linguistically very common, there are also languages with more than three deictic terms. In a world-wide sample of 234 languages, Diessel (2005a) found 127 languages with two deictic terms, 88 languages with three deictic terms, and 12 languages with more than three deictic terms (in addition, there were 7 languages in which some demonstratives are deictically not contrastive; cf. Diessel 1999: 37–39). If we look at the languages with more than three deictic terms, we find that they typically include a particular expression for objects and locations near the hearer (cf. the demonstratives in Tab. 13.7 from Hausa (Chadic, Africa)).

Tab. 13.7: Demonstratives in Hausa (Wolff 1993: 119–120)

Near speaker	nân
Near hearer	nan
Away from speaker and hearer	cân
Far away from speaker and hearer	can

Interestingly, in languages of this type there are two different ways of conceptualizing the deictic centre (see Fig. 13.1 below). Demonstratives such as Hausa *nân* 'near speaker' and *nan* 'near hearer' are interpreted relative to the area determined by the speaker's location alone, i.e., these two expressions exclude the hearer from the deictic centre (cf. deictic centre 1); whereas the two distal terms, *cân and can*, are interpreted relative to the common domain of the speech participants, i.e., in this case both speaker and hearer are included in the deictic centre (cf. deictic centre 2).

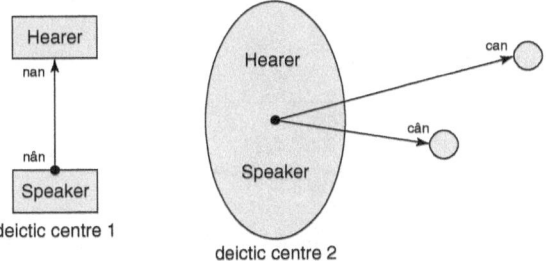

Fig. 13.1: The conceptualization of the deictic centre

Since the deictic centre of the distal terms is conceptualized as the common domain of the speech participants, the interpretation of these terms involves maximally three different entities: the deictic centre, consisting of the common domain of the speech participants, and two other entities that are 'away' and 'far away' from the deictic centre. Thus, although languages with a hearer-based demonstrative may employ four (or more) deictic terms, conceptually they are usually limited to spatial scenarios with maximally three distinct reference points (cf. Diessel 2005a).

In addition to distance, demonstratives may indicate whether the referent is visible or out-of-sight, at a higher or lower elevation, uphill or downhill, upriver or downriver, or in a particular direction along the coast line (see Diessel 1999: 41–47). While these features are not inherently deictic (cf. Fillmore 1982: 51), they are often expressed by particular demonstratives that are part of the deictic system. Many Native American languages, for instance, have a particular demonstrative for an invisible referent, i.e., a referent out of sight. As can be seen in Tab. 13.8, Tümpisa Shoshone (Uto-Aztecan, North America) has four demonstrative roots that differentiate between three (visible) entities in the surrounding situation and a fourth entity that is invisible from the speaker's point of view.

Tab. 13.8: Demonstrative roots in Tümpisa Shoshone (Dayley 1989)

Right here	i-
Here nearby	e-
There (visible)	a-
There (not visible)	u-

Similarly, semantic features such as 'uphill' and 'downhill' are commonly expressed by particular demonstrative forms. For instance, as can be seen in Tab. 13.9, Usan (Sepik, New Guinea) has four demonstratives locating a referent in the surrounding situation; two of them express the usual contrast between proximal and distal referents whereas the two other terms indicate whether the referent is above or below the deictic centre (see Diessel 1999: 41–47 for a survey of these features).

Tab. 13.9: Demonstrative roots in Usan

Here	e
There (vertical)	iré
Up there (horizontal)	ité
Down there (horizontal)	úmo
(Reesink 1987: 69)	

Turning to the non-deictic features of demonstratives, we may distinguish four different categories (cf. Diessel 1999: 47–52):
1. Ontology
2. Number
3. Gender
4. Boundedness

The most frequent non-deictic feature is ontology indicating the type of referent. This feature is well-known from Indo-European languages, where demonstratives such as English *here* and *there* are used with reference to locations, whereas *this* and *that* refer to other types of entities. The semantic contrast between *here/there* and *this/that* corresponds with their syntactic functions: While *here* and *there* are commonly used as adverbs, *this* and *that* function as pronouns and determiners. Note however that demonstrative adverbs are also commonly used as noun modifiers, as for instance in English *this book here* (cf. French: *ce livre-ci*; German: *das Buch hier*; Swedish: *det här huset*), suggesting that the semantic contrast between locations and other entities is in principle independent of the syntactic contrast between adverbs and pronouns (or determiners) (cf. Diessel 2006a).

Apart from 'ontology', 'number' is a frequent feature of demonstratives. In a world-wide sample of 85 languages, Diessel (1999) found 64 languages in which demonstratives mark the contrast between singular and plural referents. However, the occurrence of number in demonstratives varies with their syntactic function: Demonstrative pronouns are more often marked for number than demonstrative determiners, which in turn are more often number-marked than demonstrative adverbs.

The two other features, gender and boundedness, occur only in a minority of the world's languages (cf. Diessel 1999: 48–49). Gender, and the related features of animacy and humanness, are commonly found in languages that lack a particular class of third person pronouns so that unstressed demonstrative pronouns are commonly used as anaphors (cf. Siewierska 2004). Boundedness is a central feature of the deictic system in Inuktitut (Eskimo, North America), in which demonstratives indicate whether the referent is conceptualized as a "restricted" or "extended" entity (cf. Denny 1982).

4.1.3 Place deixis and motion

The demonstratives considered thus far give rise to a stationary construal of the speech situation; but demonstratives can also evoke a dynamic scenario involving direction and movement. For instance, Nunggubuyu (Gunwingguan, Australia) has three kinetic suffixes that are combined with demonstrative roots to indicate whether the referent is moving (1) toward the deictic centre, (2) away from the deictic centre, or (3) across the speaker's line of vision (cf. Tab. 13.10).

Tab. 13.10: Kinetic demonstratives in Nunggubuyu (Heath 1980: 152)

Form	Gloss	Translation
yuwa: - gi: - 'la	*that* - NounClass - toward speaker	'There he/she comes'
yuwa: - gi: - 'li	*that* - NounClass - away from speaker *that* -	'There he/she goes away'
yuwa: -gi: - yaj	NounClass - across field of vision	'There he/she goes across'

The Nunggubuyu demonstratives resemble the English demonstratives *hither* and *thither* in that they indicate direction away and towards a particular place. Very often, demonstratives of this type are combined with motion verbs, as in the following examples from German.

(16) a. hin-/her-kommen   'to come hither/thither'
     b. hin-/her-fahren   'to go by vehicle hither/thither'
     c. hin-/her-laufen   'to run hither/thither'
     d. hin-/her-kriechen 'to crawl hither/thither'
     e. hin-/her-schwimmen 'to swim hither/thither'

The verbs in (16a-e) are prefixed by two deictic preverbs, *hin* 'hither' and *her* 'thither', which occur with a large number of verbs expressing physical motion or metaphorically related activities (e.g., *hin/her-hören* 'to listen hither/thither'). The deictic preverbs are historically derived from the demonstrative root *hi*, which is also preserved in *hier* 'here' and *heute* 'today' (cf. Lockwood 1968: 36, 72). Interestingly, although motion verbs are often combined with directional demonstratives, some motion verbs do not need demonstratives to indicate direction towards the speaker because their interpretation involves the deictic centre by default. For instance, although the sentences in (17a-b) do not include a deictic expression, the verb *come* is interpreted deictically. With no further information given, *come* denotes a motion event directed towards the speaker's location, i.e., the deictic centre (cf. Fillmore 1997).

(17) a. Peter is coming.
     b. Come in!

Apart from *come*, there are several other verbs that have been analyzed as deictic motion verbs in English: *go, bring, take, leave, depart,* and a few others (cf. Talmy

2000). Note, however, that all of these verbs can also be used non-deictically. For instance, in examples (18a-b) *come* and *go* describe motion events between two lexically specified locations.

(18) a. Peter came from Berlin to John's party.
 b. Peter went from Jena to Weimar.

Since the interpretation of these sentences does not involve the speaker's location at the time of the utterance, *come* and *go* are non-deictic in these examples. In general, although motion verbs may have a deictic interpretation, they are different from demonstratives and other deictics in that they do not presuppose the deictic centre as a particular point of reference. Moreover, the deictic interpretation of demonstratives and motion verbs is based on different psychological mechanisms. Demonstratives are interpreted as deictics because they function to establish joint attention, which presupposes the speaker's body or location. In order to establish joint attention, the speaker indicates the direction of the referent from his point of view, i.e., the deictic centre. However, deictic motion verbs do not establish joint attention; rather, they denote a directed motion event between two locations. Since the speaker's location is a prominent reference point in the communicative interaction, it is often interpreted as the default endpoint or beginning of a motion event. But motion verbs do not generally involve the deictic centre as a designated endpoint or beginning, suggesting that verbs such as *come* and *go* are not genuine deictics. In other words, the interpretation of motion verbs is distinct from the interpretation of genuine deictics such as demonstratives, which always involve the deictic centre, while motion verbs are only deictic by default, i.e., if no other reference point is specified.

4.2 Time deixis

The deictic treatment of time is based on the time-as-space metaphor (Lakoff & Johnson 1980; Radden 2004; see also article 1 [Semantics: Theories] (Talmy) *Cognitive Semantics*). Since time is not directly amenable to experience, it is a more elusive concept than space. However, in language time is commonly objectified by the metaphorical structuring of time in terms of spatial concepts (cf. Lakoff & Johnson 1980; Lakoff 1993; Evans 2004). The conceptual relationship between space and time is reflected in the frequent development of temporal expressions from spatial terms. For instance, temporal adpositions such as *in* and *before* are commonly derived from body part terms (cf. Heine, Claudi & Hünnemeyer 1993), and temporal adverbs such as *then* are often based on spatial deictics (see below).

Spatial orientation involves three-dimensions: the front-back axis, the up-down axis, and the left-right axis; but the spatial interpretation of time is unidimensional. More precisely, time is commonly conceptualized as a straight line providing the conceptual ground for a fictive observer. There are two variants of the time-as-space metaphor, the ego-moving metaphor and the time-moving metaphor (cf. Lakoff 1993; Boroditsky 2002). In the ego-moving metaphor, the observer is moving along the time line into the future (e.g., *We are approaching Eastern*), whereas in the time-moving metaphor moving events on the time line are passing a stationary observer (e.g., *His birthday is coming up soon*). Since motion is commonly directed to the front, the conceptualization of the time line is usually based on the front-back axis of spatial orientation, but it may also involve the vertical dimension (cf. Radden 2004). For instance, in Chinese temporal expressions are commonly characterized based on the up-down axis: earlier times are up (e.g., *shang.ban.tian* [lit. upper.half.day] 'morning') and later times are down (e.g., *xia.ban.tian* [lit. lower.half.day] 'afternoon') (Yu 1998: 110) (for a recent study of the time-as-space metaphor in sentence processing see Ulrich & Maienborn 2010).

The time line is divided into three domains: present, past, and future. The present is conceptualized as the deictic centre, which in English is commonly referred to by *now*. Like the deictic centre of place, the deictic centre of time varies with the conceptualization of the speech situation: *Now* may refer to the very moment of the speech event, but may also refer to a larger time period that includes the time of the current speech event (e.g., *Peter is now thirty years old*). The deictic centre is distinguished from the time conceptualized as past and future, for which English has a variety of deictic expressions: *Then* can be used with reference to both past and future time (cf. 19a-b), but other time deictic expressions such as *soon* and *ago* refer only into one direction along the time line; that is, they are exclusively used with reference to the past or future (cf. 19c-d).

(19)   a. I was still in school *then*.   [past]
       b. I'll be ready *then*.   [future]
       c. I'll be there *soon*.   [future]
       d. Ten years *ago* I was a graduate student.   [past]

Time deixis often interacts with measures for time periods such as day, week, months, or year (cf. Levinson 1983: 73–76). In English, the two concepts, i.e., deixis and time measurement, are jointly expressed in complex NPs consisting of a demonstrative (or a sequential adjective) and a noun (e.g., *this week; next week*); but the combination of time deixis and time measurement can also be lexicalized, as in the temporal adverbs *today, yesterday*, and *tomorrow*, which indicate both a point in time, relative to the deictic centre, and a time unit, i.e., a day.

English has a variety of genuine time deictic expressions, but time deixis can also be expressed by demonstratives that are imported into the temporal domain. Anderson & Keenan (1985: 297–298) discuss examples from several languages in which time deictic expressions such as *now* and *then* are realized by demonstratives as in the following examples from German (Indo-European, Europe) and Urubu-Kaapor (Tupi-Guarani, South America), in which the spatial deictics *da* 'there' and *pe* 'there' occur with temporal reference.

(20) German
Da   war   ich   ganz   unglücklich.
There/then was   I   totally   unhappy
'Then (at that time) I was totally unhappy.'

(21) Urubu-Kaapor (Kakumasu 1986: 384)
Pe   ih?   koty   jangwate   keruh   u-jan   u-wyr
DEM   me   towards   jaguar   very.big   3.run   3.come
'Then the great jaguar came running towards me.'

What is more, temporal deictics are often diachronically derived from demonstratives, as for instance English *then,* which evolved from a deictic root with spatial meaning. Similar developments have been found in many other languages across the world. For instance, in Ainu (Isolate, Japan) temporal deictics such as *tap/tane* 'now' and *tanpa* 'this year' include the deictic root *ta* 'this/here' (Refsing 1986), which also functions as a demonstrative; and in Nama (Khoisan, South Africa) the formation of temporal deictics such as *nee-tse* 'today' and *//nāá-tse* 'on that day' is based on the demonstratives *nee* 'this' and *//nāá* 'that' (Hagman 1977). Tab. 13.11 shows another example from Mokilese (Austronesian, Pacific), in which nouns for time measurement are combined with the demonstrative suffixes *-e* 'this (near speaker)', *-oawe* 'that (near addressee)', and *-o* 'that (away from speaker and hearer)' if they are used deictically.

In general, since time is commonly conceptualized as motion in space, spatial deictics can function to 'locate' an event on the time line relative to the moment of

Tab. 13.11: Time deictic expressions in Mokilese (Harrison 1976)

Word	Gloss	Translation
wihkk-*e* lakapw	week-FUTURE tomorrow	Next week
wihkk-*oawe*	week-PRESENT	This week
wihkk-*o* aio	week-PAST yesterday	Last week

the speech event, i.e., the deictic centre. This explains why time deictic expressions are often realized by spatial terms, notably by demonstratives, which historically may develop into time deictics. However, although time deixis is commonly conceptualized in spatial terms, it remains an abstract concept, which is reflected in the fact that demonstratives usually loose some of their deictic force when they are imported into the temporal domain.

4.3 Discourse deixis

Like time deixis, discourse deixis is based on the metaphorical structuring of time as space. Discourse consists of words and utterances that are processed in sequential order, that is, one element at a time. The sequential ordering of discourse elements is commonly conceptualized as a string of linguistic entities, to which speakers may refer in the same way as they refer to temporal entities on the time line. Both time deixis and discourse deixis involve a band of successive elements that is divided into separate areas by the deictic centre. However, while the deictic centre of time deixis is defined as the time including the moment of utterance, the deictic centre of discourse deixis is defined by the location of a deictic word in the ongoing discourse, from where the interlocutors' attention is directed to linguistic elements along the string of words and utterances. Bühler (1934) described this as follows:

> If discourse deictic expressions could speak, "they would speak as follows: look ahead or back along the band of the present utterance. There something will be found that actually belongs here, where I am, so that it can be connected with what now follows. Or the other way round: what comes after me belongs there, it was only displaced from that position for relief." [Bühler 1934: 390]

Discourse deixis can be realized by a variety of expressions. English has a few linguistic terms that may be analyzed as genuine discourse deictics (e.g., *the aforementioned, the latter*); but more frequently discourse deixis involves deictic expressions from other conceptual domains. For instance, sequential adjectives such as *last* and *next*, which are commonly used as time deictic expressions, may be used with reference to linguistic elements in the ongoing discourse (cf. 22a-b).

(22) a. the last paragraph
b. the next chapter

The most frequent discourse deictic expressions are borrowed from the spatial domain. Across languages, demonstratives are used as discourse deictics, as in the following example from English.

(23) I was really interested particularly because he was saying that a lot of the leaning was going to be towards choreography and *that* was my particular interest. I really didn't like technique. I mean I'm too lazy really for *that*, I think, and that was my interest in it. *That*'s how I sort of got started in it. (International Corpus of English)

Example (23) includes four tokens of the distal demonstrative *that* referring to a previous chunk of discourse. Like *that*, the proximal demonstrative *this* can be used with reference to linguistic elements; but interestingly while *that* may only refer to previous discourse units *this* can also function as a cataphor announcing a following piece of discourse, as in example (24).

(24) I forgot to tell you *this* (*that). Uhm Matt Street phoned while I was out. (International Corpus of English)

Note that the demonstratives in (23) and (24) refer to propositions (or speech acts); whereas the demonstrative in (25) indicates a link between two discourse participant. In this example, the demonstrative *this* accompanies a noun (plus adjective), which together resume the referent of a prior NP.

(25) I had sardines once with a fly on it. I was just about to tuck into it and I noticed *this* great fly soaked in tomato sauce. (International Corpus of English)

If demonstratives refer to propositions, as in (23) and (24), they indicate a link between two states of affairs; but if they refer to an NP, as in (25), they continue a prior discourse participant (cf. Himmelmann 1996; Diessel 1999: Ch. 4). In the latter use, demonstratives are similar to third person pronouns in that both types of expressions track a previous discourse participant; they occur, however, in different contexts. Consider for instance the following example from German, contrasting the third person pronoun *er* 'he' with the anaphoric use of the demonstrative *der* 'this/that' (cf. Diessel 1999: 96)

(26) Peter   bemerkte   einen   Polizisten.   Als   er/der   ...
     Peter   noticed   a   police officer   when   he/that one
     'Peter noticed a police officer. When he ...'

Although both types of anaphors are coreferential with a previous NP, they have different antecedents. The third person pronoun *er* is coreferential with the subject of the previous sentence, i.e., *Peter*, whereas the demonstrative *der* can only be interpreted as being coreferential with the object, i.e., *einen Polizisten* 'a police man'. The two types of anaphors have different antecedents because they serve different discourse-pragmatic functions. Third person pronouns are used to continue a previously established discourse referent that is already in the interlocutors' focus of attention, whereas anaphoric demonstratives are used to indicate a topic shift, i.e., they direct the addressee's attention to a new discourse participant (cf. Diessel 1999). The same complementary use of third person pronouns and anaphoric demonstratives has been observed in Dutch and Russian (Comrie 1998), To'aba'ita (Lichtenberk 1996), Tagalog (Himmelmann 1997), and Montagnais (Cyr 1993, 1996). In all of these languages anaphoric demonstratives function to shift the interlocutors' attention on a new discourse participant that serves as the main topic in the subsequent discourse (cf. Diessel 1999: 96–98).

In English and German, discourse-related demonstratives are morphologically indistinguishable from demonstratives that are used with reference to concrete entities; but there are languages in which these uses are formally distinguished. In Latin, for instance, the demonstrative *is* 'this/that' can only function as an anaphor, whereas *hic* 'this (near speaker)', *iste* 'that (near hearer)', and *ille* 'that (away from speaker and hearer)' are primarily used for language-external reference. Likewise, in Usan (Sepik, New Guinea) the demonstratives *ende* and *ete* are exclusively used with reference to the previous (*ende*) or subsequent (*ete*) discourse (Reesink 1987; Himmelmann 1997; Diessel 1999: 103–104).

Since discourse referents are not visible, discourse-related demonstratives are not accompanied by a pointing gesture; however, they involve the same psychological mechanism as demonstratives that speakers use with language-external reference. In both uses, demonstratives focus the interlocutors' attention on a particular referent. In the language-external use (also called the exophoric use) they focus the interlocutors' attention on concrete entities in the physical world, and in the discourse use (also called the endophoric use) they focus their attention on linguistic elements in the surrounding context. In other words, in both uses demonstratives function to create a joint focus of attention. Joint attention is thus not only important to coordinate the interlocutors' attentional focus in the speech situation, it also plays a crucial role in the internal organization of discourse.

What is more, when anaphoric and discourse deictic demonstratives are routinely used in particular constructions, they often develop into grammatical markers. For instance, in English the definite article *the* and the third person pronouns *he* and *it* are historically derived from anaphoric demonstrative pronouns. The same developments occurred in many other languages across the world (cf. Himmelmann 1997; Diessel 1999). In general, demonstratives that are routinely used with reference to linguistic elements in discourse provide a common historical source for some of the most frequent grammatical markers including not only definite articles and third person pronouns but also relative pronouns, complementizers, conjunctions, copulas, directional preverbs, focus markers, and a wide variety of other grammatical morphemes (see Diessel 1999: Ch. 6 for an overview). The grammaticalization of demonstratives is cross-linguistically so common that central aspects of grammar such as definiteness marking and clause combining are crucially determined by this process (cf. Diessel 2006a).

5 Conclusion

This paper has surveyed deictic expressions in natural language and has considered the psychological mechanisms that underlie their use. Two basic types of deixis have been distinguished, participant deixis and object deixis, which serve different communicative functions expressed by different deictic terms. Participant deictics are primarily used to represent the speech participants in the state of affairs that is encoded in an utterance, whereas object deictics are used to orientate the interlocutors in the situational or discourse context. It has been argued that demonstratives constitute a special class of linguistic expressions that are essential for the communicative interaction between the speech participants and the organization of discourse and development of grammar.

6 References

Anderson, Stephen R. & Edward L. Keenan 1985. Deixis. In: T. Shopen (ed.). *Language Typology and Syntactic Description*, vol. 3. Cambridge: Cambridge University Press, 259–308.
Bammesberger, Alfred 1983. *Essentials of Modern Irish*. Heidelberg: Winter.
Barsalou, Lawrence W. 1999. Perceptual symbol systems. *Behavioral and Brain Sciences* 22, 577–609.
Boroditsky, Lera 2002. Metaphorical structuring: Understanding time through spatial metaphors. *Cognition* 75, 1–28.
Bruner, Jerome 1983. *Child's Talk: Learning to Use Language*. New York: W.W. Norton.
Bühler, Karl 1934. *Sprachtheorie: Die Darstellungsfunktion der Sprache*. Jena: Fischer.
Butterworth, George 1998. What is special about pointing in babies? In: F. Simion & G. Butterworth (eds.). *The Development of Sensory, Motor and Cognitive Capacities in Early Infancy. From Perception to Cognition*. Hove: Psychology Press, 171–190.
Carpenter, Malinda, Katherine Nagell & Michael Tomasello 1998. *Social Cognition, Joint Attention, and Communicative Competence from 9 to 15 Months of Age*. Chicago, IL: The University of Chicago Press.
Clark, Andy 1997. *Being there: Putting Brain, Body, and World together again*. Cambridge, MA: The MIT Press.

Clark, Eve V. 1978. From gesture to word: On the natural history of deixis in language acquisition. In: J. S. Bruner & A. Garton (eds.). *Human Growth and Development*. Oxford: Oxford University Press, 85–120.
Clark, Herbert H. 1996. *Using Language*. Cambridge: Cambridge University Press.
Comrie, Bernard 1998. Reference-tracking: Description and explanation. *Sprachtypologie und Universalienforschung* 51, 335–346.
Cooke, Joseph 1968. *Pronominal Reference in Thai, Burmese and Vietnamese*. Berkeley, CA: University of California Press.
Croft, William 2001. *Radical Construction Grammar. Syntactic Theory in Typological Perspective*. Oxford: Oxford University Press.
Cysouw, Michael 2003. *The Paradigmatic Structure of Person Marking*. Oxford: Oxford University Press.
Cyr, Danielle E. 1993. Definite articles and demonstratives in Plains Cree. In: C. Cowan (ed.). *Papers from the Twenty-Fourth Algonquian Conference*. Ottawa, ON: Carleton University, 64–80.
Cyr, Danielle E. 1996. Montagnais: An ethno-grammatical description. In: J. Maurais (ed.). *Québec's Aboriginal Languages: History, Planning and Development*. Clevedon: Multilingual Patterns, 174–203.
Davis, Steven (ed.) 1991. *Pragmatics: A Reader*. Oxford: Oxford University Press.
Dayley, John 1989. *Tümpisa (Panamint) Shoshone Grammar*. Berkeley, CA: Berkeley University Press.
Denny, Peter 1982. Semantics of the Inuktitut (Eskimo) spatial deictics. *International Journal of American Linguistics* 48, 359–384.
Diessel, Holger 1999. *Demonstratives. Form, Function, and Grammaticalization*. Amsterdam: Benjamins.
Diessel, Holger 2003. The relationship between demonstratives and interrogatives. *Studies in Language* 27, 581–602.
Diessel, Holger 2005a. Distance contrasts in demonstratives. In: M. Haspelmath et al. (eds.). *World Atlas of Linguistic Structures*. Oxford: Oxford University Press, 170–173.
Diessel, Holger 2005b. Demonstrative pronouns—demonstrative determiners. In: M. Haspelmath et al. (eds.). *World Atlas of Language Structures*. Oxford: Oxford University Press, 174–177.
Diessel, Holger 2006a. Demonstratives, joint attention, and the emergence of grammar. *Cognitive Linguistics* 17, 463–489.
Diessel, Holger 2006b. Demonstratives. In: K. Brown (ed.). *Encyclopedia of Language and Linguistics*. 2nd edn. Amsterdam: Elsevier, 430–435.
Dixon, Robert M. W. 2003. Demonstratives. A cross-linguistic typology. *Studies in Language* 27, 61–122.
Dunham, Philip J. & Chris Moore 1995. Current themes in research on joint attention. In: C. Moore & P. J. Dunham (eds.). *Joint Attention. Its Origin and Role in Development*. Hillsdale, NJ: Lawrence Erlbaum Associates, 15–28.
Dunn, Michael 2005. Plurality in independent personal pronouns. In: M. Haspelmath et al. (eds.). *World Atlas of Language Structures*. Oxford: Oxford University Press, 146–149.
Eilan, Naomi 2005. Joint attention, communication, and mind. In: N. Eilan et al. (eds.). *Joint Attention: Communication and Other Minds*. Oxford: Oxford University Press, 1–33.
Enfield, Nick 2002. 'Lip-pointing': A discussion of form and function and reference to data from Laos. *Gesture* 2, 185–211.

Enfield, Nick 2003. Demonstratives in space and interaction: Data from Lao speakers and implications for semantic analysis. *Language* 79, 82–117.

Evans, Vyvyan 2004. *The Structure of Time. Language, Meaning, and Temporal Cognition*. Amsterdam: Benjamins.

Fillmore, Charles J. 1982. Towards a descriptive framework for spatial deixis. In: R. J. Jarvella & W. Klein (eds.). *Speech, Place, and Action*. Chichester: John Wiley, 31–59.

Fillmore, Charles J. 1997. *Lectures on Deixis*. Stanford, CA: CSLI Publications.

Franco, F. 2005. Infant pointing: Harlequin, servant of two masters. In: N. Eilan et al. (eds.). *Joint Attention: Communication and Other Minds*. Oxford: Oxford University Press, 129–164.

Frei, Henri 1944. Systèmes de déictiques. *Acta Linguistica* 4, 111–129.

Gentner, Dedre 1982. Why nouns are learned before verbs: Linguistic relativity versus natural partioning. In: M. Bowerman & S. C. Levinson (eds.). *Language Acquisition and Conceptual Development*. Hillsdale, NJ: Lawrence Erlbaum Associates, 301–334.

Hagman, Roy S. 1977. *Nama Hottentot Grammar*. Bloomington, IN: Indiana University Press.

Hanks, William. 1990. *Referential Practice: Language and Lived Space in a Maya Community*. Chicago, IL: The University of Chicago Press.

Harrison, Sheldon P. 1976. *Mokilese Reference Grammar*. Honolulu, HI: University of Hawaii Press.

Heath, Jeffrey 1980. Nungguyu deixis, anaphora, and culture. In: J. Kreiman & A. E. Ojeda (eds.). *Papers from the Regional Meeting of the Chicago Linguistic Society (= CLS) 16, Part II: Papers form the Parasession on Pronouns and Anaphora*. Chicago, IL: Chicago Linguistic Society, 151–165.

Heine, Bernd, Ulrike Claudi & Frederike Hünnemeyer 1993. *Grammaticalization: A Conceptual Framework*. Chicago, IL: The University of Chicago Press.

Himmelmann, Nikolaus 1996. Demonstratives in narrative discourse: A taxonomy of universal uses. In: B. Fox (ed.). *Studies in Anaphora*. Amsterdam: Benjamins, 205–254.

Himmelmann, Nikolaus 1997. *Deiktikon, Artikel, Nominalphrase. Zur Emergenz syntaktischer Struktur*. Tübingen: Narr.

Hopper, Paul J. & Elizabeth C. Traugott 2003. *Grammaticalization*. 2nd edn. Cambridge: Cambridge University Press.

Jakobson, Roman 1957/1971. Shifter, verbal categories, and the Russian verb. In: R. Jakobson. *Selected Writings, vol. 2*. The Hague: Mouton, 1971, 130–147.

Kakumasu, James Y. 1986. Urubu-Kaapor. In: D.C. Derbyshire & G. K. Pullum (eds.). *Handbook of Amazonian Languages, vol. 1*. Berlin: de Gruyter, 326–403.

Kaplan, David 1989. Demonstratives. In: J. Almog, J. Perry & H. Wettstein (eds.). *Themes from Kaplan*. Oxford: Oxford University Press, 481–564.

Kasher, Asa 1998. *Pragmatics: Critical Concepts, vol. 3: Indexicals and Reference*. London: Routledge.

Kita, Sotaro 2003. Pointing. A foundational building block of human communication. In: S. Kita (ed.). *Pointing. Where Language, Culture, and Cognition Meet*. Hillsdale, NJ: Lawrence Erlbaum Associates, 1–8.

Krause, Mark A. 1997. Comparative perspectives on pointing and joint attention in children and apes. *International Journal of Comparative Psychology* 10, 137–157.

Kuno, Susumo 1973. *The Structure of the Japanese Language*. Cambridge, MA: The MIT Press.

Lakoff, George 1993. The contemporary theory of metaphor. In: A. Ortony (ed.). *Metaphor and Thought*. 2nd edn. Cambridge: Cambridge University Press.

Lakoff, George & Mark Johnson 1980. *Metaphors We Live by*. Chicago, IL: The University of Chicago Press.

Lakoff, George & Mark Johnson 1999. *Philosophy in the Flesh: The Embodied Mind and its Challenge to Western Thought.* New York: Basic Books.

Laycock, Don C. 1965. *The Ndu Language Family.* Canberra: Australian National University.

Levelt, William J. M. 1989. *Speaking: From Intention to Articulation.* Cambridge, MA: The MIT Press.

Levinson, Stephen C. 1983. *Pragmatics.* Cambridge: Cambridge University Press.

Levinson, Stephen C. 1996. Frames of reference and Molyneux' Question: Cross-linguistic evidence. In: P. Bloom et al. (eds.). *Language and Space.* Cambridge, MA: The MIT Press, 109–169.

Levinson, Stephen 2003. *Space in Language and Cognition. Explorations in Cognitive Psychology.* Cambridge: Cambridge University Press.

Levinson, Stephen C. 2004. Deixis and pragmatic. In: L. Horn & G. Ward (eds.). *The Handbook of Pragmatics.* Oxford: Blackwell, 97–121.

Lichtenberk, Frantisec 1996. Patterns of anaphora in To'aba'ita narrative discourse. In: B. Fox (ed.). *Studies in Anaphora.* Amsterdam: Benjamins, 379–411.

Linde, Charlotte & William Labov 1975. Spatial structure as a site for the study of language and thought. http://www.ingentaconnect.com/content/external-references?article = 0097-8507()51L.924%5baid = 1163816%5d*Language*http://www.ingentaconnect.com/content/external-references?article = 0097-8507()51L.924%5baid = 1163816%5d 51, 924–939.

Lockwood, Williams B. 1968. *Historical German Syntax.* Oxford: Clarendon.

Lyons, John 1977. *Semantics, vol. 1–2.* Cambridge: Cambridge University Press.

Lyons, John 1979. Deixis and anaphora. In: T. Myers (ed.). *The Development of Conversation and Discourse.* Edinburgh: Edinburgh University Press, 88–103.

Miller, George & Philip Johnson-Laird. 1976. *Language and Perception.* Cambridge, MA: Harvard University Press.

Montague, Richard 1974. *Formal Philosophy. Selected Papers of Richard Montague.* Edited and with an introduction by Richmond H. Thomason. New Haven, CT: Yale University Press.

Moore, Chris & Philip J. Dunham (eds.) 1995. *Joint Attention. Its Origin and Role in Development.* Hillsdale, NJ: Lawrence Erlbaum Associates.

Nunberg, Geoffrey 1998. Indexicality and deixis. In: A. Kasher (ed.). *Pragmatics. Critical Concepts.* London: Routledge, 145–184.

Peirce, Charles 1955. *Philosophical Writings of Peirce.* Edited by J. Buchler. New York: Dover Publications. Reprint of: J. Buchler (ed.). *The Philosophy of Peirce: Selected Writings.* New York: Dover Publications, 1940.

Pederson, Eric, Eve Danziger, David Wilkins, Stephen Levinson, Sotora Kita & Gunter Senft 1998. Semantic typology and spatial conceptualization. *Language* 74, 508–556.

Povinelli, Daniel J. & Jennifer Vonk 2003. Chimpanzee minds: Suspiciously human? *Trends in Cognitive Science* 7, 157–169.

Radden, Günter. 2004 The metaphor time as space across languages. In: N. Baumgarten et al. (eds.). *Übersetzen, interkulturelle Kommunikation, Spracherwerb und Sprachvermittlung – das Leben mit mehreren Sprachen.* Bochum: AKS-Verlag, 225–238.

Rauh, Gisa 1983. Aspects of deixis. In: G. Rauh (ed.). *Essays on Deixis.* Tübingen: Narr, 9–60.

Reesink, Ger P. 1987. *Structures and their Functions in Usan, a Papuan Language.* Amsterdam: Benjamins.

Reesink, Ger P. 1999. *A Grammar of Hatam. Bird's Head Peninsula, Irian Jaya.* Canberra: Australian National University.

Refsing, Kirsten 1986. *The Ainu Language*. Aarhus: Aarhus University Press.
Siewierska, Anna 2004. *Person*. Cambridge: Cambridge University Press.
Steels, Luc 1999. *The Talking Heads Experiment, vol. I. Words and Meanings*. Antwerpen: Laboratorium.
Talmy, Leonard 2000. *Towards a Cognitive Semantics, vol. 2*. Cambridge, MA: The MIT Press.
Tanz, Christine 1980. *Studies in the Acquisition of Deictic Terms*. Cambridge: Cambridge University Press.
Taylor, Holly A. & Barbara Tversky 1996. Perspective in spatial descriptions. *Journal of Memory and Language* 35, 371–391.
Tomasello, Michael 1999. *The Cultural Origins of Human Cognition*. Cambridge, MA: Harvard University Press.
Tomasello, Michael 2003. *Constructing a Language: A Usage-Based Theory of Language Acquisition*. Cambridge, MA: Harvard University Press.
Tomasello, Michael 2006. Why don't apes point? In: N. Enfield & S. Levinson (eds.). *The Roots of Human Sociality: Culture, Cognition, and Interaction*. Oxford: Berg, 506–524.
Topping, Donald M. 1973. *Chamorro Reference Grammar*. Honolulu, HI: The University of Hawaii Press.
Ullmer-Ehrich, Veronika 1982. The structure of living room descriptions. In: R. J. Jarvella & W. Klein (eds.) *Speech, Place and Action. Studies in Deixis and Related Topics*. New York: Wiley, 219–215.
Ulrich, Rolf & Claudia Maienborn 2010. Sentence processing and mental time line. Left-right coding of past and future in language: The mental timeline during sentence processing. *Cognition* 117, 126–138.
Wales, Roger 1986. Deixis. In: P. Fletcher & M. Garman (eds.). *Language Acquisition*. 2nd edn. Cambridge: Cambridge University Press.
Wilkins, David 2003. Why pointing with the index finger is not a universal (in socio-cultural and semiotic terms). In: S. Kita (ed.). *Pointing: Where Language, Culture, and Cognition Meet*. Hillsdale, NJ: Lawrence Erlbaum Associates, 171–216.
Wilson, Margaret 2002. Six views of embodied cognition. *Psychonomic Bulletin and Review* 9, 625–636.
Wolff, H. Ekkehard 1993. *Referenzgrammatik des Hausa* (Hamburger Beiträge zur Afrikanistik 2). Münster: LIT.
Yu, Ning 1998. *The Contemporary Theory of Metaphor: A Perspective from Chinese*. Amsterdam: Benjamins.

David Beaver and Bart Geurts
14 Presupposition

1 Introduction —— 494
2 Projection —— 497
3 Cancellability —— 498
4 Theories of presupposition —— 500
5 Current issues in presupposition theory —— 518
6 Concluding remarks —— 524
7 References —— 525

Abstract: We discuss presupposition, the phenomenon whereby speakers mark linguistically the information that is presupposed or taken for granted, rather than being part of the main propositional content of a speech act. Expressions and constructions carrying presuppositions are called "presupposition triggers", which is a large class including definites and factive verbs.

The article (an abridged and adapted version of Beaver & Geurts 2010), first introduces the range of triggers, the basic properties of presuppositions such as projection and cancellability, and the diagnostic tests used to identify them. The reader is then introduced to major models of presupposition from the last 50 years, separated into three classes: Frege-Strawson derived semantic models, pragmatic models such as that offered by Stalnaker, and dynamic models. Finally we discuss some of the main current issues in presupposition theory, including accommodation, which occurs when a hearer's knowledge state is adjusted to meet the speaker's presuppositions; presupposition failure, and the interaction between presuppositions and attitudes.

> Denial, projection, cancellation, satisfaction, accommodation:
> the five stages of presupposition theory.

1 Introduction

Speakers take a lot for granted. That is, they *presuppose* information. As we wrote this, we presupposed that readers would understand English. But we also presupposed, as we wrote the last sentence, repeated in (1), that there was a time when we wrote it, for otherwise the fronted phrase "as we wrote this" would not have identified a time interval.

David Beaver, Austin, TX, USA
Bart Geurts, Nijmegen, The Netherlands

https://doi.org/10.1515/9783110589849-014

(1) As we wrote this, we presupposed that readers would understand English.

We also presupposed that the sentence was jointly authored, for otherwise "we" would not have referred. And we presupposed that readers would be able to identify the reference of "this", i.e. the article itself. And we presupposed that there would be at least two readers, for otherwise the bare plural "readers" would have been inappropriate. And so on and on.

Here note a first distinction: the presupposition that an interlocutor would understand English corresponds to an assumption we made in using English words, but it has nothing to do with the meanings of any of those words. On the other hand, the existence of a time when we wrote the article is a requirement associated with our use of a specific word, "as". It is a requirement built into the meaning of the temporal preposition "as" that in a phrase "as X", the "X" has to hold at some time. We say that "as" is a *presupposition trigger*. Similarly, "this" is a presupposition trigger requiring something to refer to, the bare plural is a presupposition trigger requiring existence of multiple individuals, and "would" is a presupposition trigger requiring a salient future or hypothetical circumstance.

We can say that the presupposition that the interlocutor speaks English, like the presupposition that the interlocutor is interested in what the speaker (or writer) has to say, is a *conversational presupposition* or, following Stalnaker (1972, 1974), *speaker presupposition* or *pragmatic presupposition*. The presuppositions associated with specific triggers are said to be *conventional* or *semantic*. In fact, this terminological distinction is of theoretical import: as we will see later, some theorists regard it as an open question whether there are any purely conventional presuppositions. A halfway house, suggested for example by Karttunen (1973) and Soames (1982), is to define a notion of *utterance presupposition*, thus involving both a specific form that is uttered, and a speaker who utters it.

It is important to note that to call presuppositional expressions "conventional" or "semantic" is not necessarily to imply that the presuppositions they trigger don't depend on the context in any way. For example, although "this" may be viewed as a conventional/semantic presupposition trigger, its interpretation very much depends on the context, obviously.

What makes presuppositions special? That is, to the extent that presuppositions are just a part of the conventional meaning of some expressions, what makes them sufficiently distinctive that they merit their own entries in handbooks and encyclopedias, as well as many hundreds of other articles and book chapters elsewhere? First, presuppositions are ubiquitous. And second, there are various respects in which the behavior of presuppositions differs sharply from other aspects of meaning.

As regards the ubiquity of presuppositions, at least the following lexical classes and constructions are widely agreed to be presupposition triggers:

(2) Major classes of presupposition trigger
- *Factives* (Kiparsky & Kiparsky 1970)
  Berlusconi knows that he is signing the end of Berlusconism.
  ⤳ Berlusconi is signing the end of Berlusconism.
- *Aspectual verbs* ("stop, continue")
  China has stopped stockpiling metals.
  ⤳ China used to stockpile metals.
- *Temporal clauses headed by "before", "after", "since", etc.*
  The dude released this video before he went on a killing spree.
  ⤳ The dude went on a killing spree.
- *Manner adverbs*
  Jamie ducked quickly behind the wall.
  ⤳ Jamie ducked behind the wall.
- *Sortally restricted predicates of various categories* (e.g. "bachelor")
  Julius is bachelor.
  ⤳ Julius is an adult male.
- *Cleft sentences*
  It was Jesus who set me free.
  ⤳ Somebody set me free.
- *Quantifiers*
  I have written to every headmaster in Rochdale.
  ⤳ There are headmasters in Rochdale.
- *Definite descriptions* (see article 2 [Semantics: Noun Phrases and Verb Phrases] (Heim) *Definiteness and indefiniteness*)
  The Prime Minister of Trinidad and Tobago stood up and wagged his finger.
  ⤳ Trinidad and Tobago have a (unique) prime minister.
- *Names*
  The author is Julius Seidensticker.
  ⤳ Julius Seidensticker exists.
- *Intonation* (e.g., *focus, contrast*)
  HE set me free.
  ⤳ Somebody set me free.

And this is only a small sample of the words and syntactic constructions that have been classified as presupposition triggers, so even if in some cases there may be doubts about this diagnosis, it can hardly be doubted that presupposition triggers abound in everyday language. In the following sections we will discuss the behaviors which mark out presuppositions from ordinary entailments, and then introduce some of the theories that have been developed to account for those behaviors.

2 Projection

The hallmark of presuppositions, as well as the most thoroughly studied presuppositional phenomenon, is *projection* (Langendoen & Savin 1971). Consider (3). This has all the presuppositions in (3–a–c). These presuppositions all follow from utterances of the base sentence in (3), as do the regular entailments in (4): someone who sincerely uttered (3) would certainly be expected to accept the truth of (3–a–c) and (4–a–b), as well:

(3) It's the knave that stole the tarts.
   a. There is a (salient and identifiable) knave.
   b. There were (salient and identifiable) tarts.
   c. Somebody stole the tarts.

(4) a. The knave did something illegal.
   b. The knave took possession of the tarts.

Now consider the sentences in (5):

(5) a. It isn't the knave that stole the tarts. (*negation*)
   b. If it's the knave that stole the tarts, he will be punished. (*antecedent of a conditional*)
   c. Is it the knave that stole the tarts? (*question*)
   d. Maybe/It is possible that it's the knave that stole the tarts. (*possibility modal*)
   e. Presumably/probably it's the knave that stole the tarts. (*evidential modal probability adverb*)
   f. The king thinks it's the knave that stole the tarts. (*belief operator*)

In all these examples, sentence (3) is embedded under various operators. What is notable is that whereas the presuppositions in (4) do not follow from any of these embeddings (and would not be expected to follow according to classical logics), the presuppositions do follow. We say that the presuppositions are *projected*. Certainly, the inference is more robust in some cases than in others: while it is hard to imagine sincerely uttering (5-a) without believing some tarts to be salient, it is easier to imagine a circumstance in which (5-f) could be uttered when in fact the tarts were not eaten, but hidden. But in the absence of special factors, to which we will turn shortly, someone who sincerely uttered any of the sentences in (5) might be expected to believe all of the presuppositions in (3a–c).

Projection from embeddings, especially negation, is standardly used as a diagnostic for presupposition (hence the term "negation test"). It makes sense to try several such embeddings when testing for presupposition, because it is not always clear how to apply a given embedding diagnostic. Thus, for example, we might be specifically interested in the presuppositions of the cleft construction in (3), but doubt whether the sentence in (5-a) really involves the cleft being within the semantic scope of the negation. However, the other embeddings in (5) confirm that the it-cleft construction is a presupposition trigger. Similarly, although it is widely agreed that "too" is a presupposition-inducing expression, the negation test is awkward to apply in this case, too:

(6) a. Fred kissed BETTY, too.
    b. Fred didn't kiss BETTY, too.

If we embed (6-a), e.g., under a modal or in the antecedent of a conditional, it turns out that this sentence presupposes that someone other than Betty was kissed by Fred. However, as (6-b) shows, the negation test fails in this case, because "too" doesn't like being in a negative environment. These examples illustrate how important it is to consider several types of embedding when testing for presupposition.

3 Cancellability

What makes the "projection problem" problematic? If some part of the meaning of an expression α was never affected by the linguistic context in which α was embedded, that would be philosophically interesting, and would demand a theoretical explanation, but it would at least be trivial to completely describe the data: all presuppositional inferences would survive any embedding, end of story. But that isn't what happens. Presuppositions typically project, but often do not, and most of the empirical and theoretical work on presupposition since the 1970s was taken up with the task of describing and explaining when presuppositions project, and when they don't.

When a presupposition does not project, it is sometimes said to be "canceled". The classic cases of cancellation occur when the presupposition is directly denied, as in the following variants of some of the sentences in (5):

(7) a. In this court, it isn't the knave that steals the tarts: the king employs no knaves precisely because he suspects they are responsible for large-scale tart-loss across his kingdom.

b. If it's the knave that stole the tarts, then I'm a Dutchman: there is no knave here.
c. Is it the knave that stole the tarts? Certainly not: there is no knave here.
d. The king thinks it's the knave that stole the tarts, but he's obviously gone mad, since there is no knave here.

Presuppositional inferences are typically subject to cancellation by direct denial only when the presupposition trigger is embedded under some other operator. When the presupposition is not embedded, such cancelation (by the same speaker) is typically infelicitous, just as is cancelation of entailed content which is not embedded. Thus the denial of a presupposition in (8) and the denial of an ordinary entailment in (9) both lead to pragmatically infelicitous utterances (marked by a "#").

(8) #It's the knave that stole the tarts, but there is no knave.

(9) #It's the knave that stole the tarts, but he didn't do anything illegal.

The fact that presuppositions associated with unembedded triggers are not cancelable is one of the features that distinguishes most presuppositions from Gricean conversational implicatures (Grice 1989) (see article 15 [this volume] (Simons) *Implicature*). For example, an utterance of (10-a) might ordinarily lead to the so-called scalar implicature in (10-b). But while this implicature is cancelable, as in (10-c), the presupposition that there is a knave, once again, is not cancelable, as shown by the oddity of (10-d).

(10) a. The knave stole most of the tarts.
b. The knave did not steal all of the tarts.
c. The knave stole most of the tarts – in fact, he stole them all.
d. #The knave stole most of the tarts, but there was no knave.

We can summarize the typical behavior of entailments, presuppositions, and conversational implicatures as follows:

Tab. 14.1.

	entailments	presuppositions	implicatures
Project from embeddings	no	yes	no
Cancelable when embedded	–	yes	–
Cancelable when Unembedded	no	no	yes

Because presuppositions are typically only cancelable when embedded, Gazdar (1979a, 1979b) argued that presuppositions are usually entailed when the trigger is not embedded.

The literature is choc-a-bloc with examples of presuppositional inferences apparently disappearing. Whether such examples are appropriately described as involving *cancellation* is partly a theoretical decision, and, as we will see, many scholars avoid using the term "cancellation" for some or all such cases. One reason for this is that the term "cancellation" appears to suggest that an inference has been made, and then removed. But in many cases there are theoretical reasons not to regard this as an apt characterization, and we will now consider one class of such cases.

4 Theories of presupposition

4.1 The Frege-Strawson tradition

Strawson (1950) famously argued against Russell's (1905) theory of definite descriptions by proposing that when a definite description fails to refer, the result can be a sentence which lacks a truth value. Thus presuppositions are understood as definedness conditions, necessary requirements for an expression to have a meaning. Strawson's intuition, which can be traced back to Frege (1892), leads to the following definition (cf. Strawson 1952; see Beaver & Geurts 2010 for full references):

Definition 1 *(Strawsonian presupposition) One sentence presupposes another iff whenever the first is true or false, the second is true.*

Another definition that is often used is this:

Definition 2 *(Presupposition via negation) One sentence presupposes another iff whenever the first sentence is true, the second is true, and whenever the negation of the first sentence is true, the second sentence is true.*

These two definitions are equivalent if negation maps true onto false, false onto true, and is undefined when its argument is undefined. However, the second definition is notable in the context of the above discussion of projection, because it seems to directly encode the projection properties of at least one operator, negation. Specifically, it says that presuppositions are inferences that survive embedding under negation. It is clear that if the above assumptions about presupposition are made, then the presuppositions of a sentence will be the same as the presuppositions of the negation of the sentence. But what about projection from embeddings other than negation? A very simple account of projection is based on the *cumulative hypothesis*, first discussed by Morgan (1969) and Langendoen & Savin (1971). This is the idea that presuppositions always project from embedding, as if there were no effects like cancellation. A trivalent semantics that yields this behavior is obtained by using the *Weak Kleene* connectives (Kleene 1952). Assume (for all the partial/multivalued semantics given in this article) that for classically valued arguments, the connectives behave classically. Then Weak Kleene connectives (also known as the Bochvar Internal connectives) are defined as follows:

Definition 3 *(Weak Kleene)* *If any argument of a Weak Kleene connective lacks a classical truth value, then the sentence as a whole lacks a truth value.*

Weak Kleene fails as a theory of presupposition because it entails that presuppositions project uniformly, whereas in fact they do not. Another system of Kleene's, the Strong Kleene connectives, does not have this property:

Definition 4 *(Strong Kleene)* *If the classically-valued arguments of a Strong Kleene connective would suffice to determine a truth value in standard logic, then the sentence as a whole has that value; otherwise it doesn't have a classical value.*

For example, in classical logic a conjunction is bound to be false if one of its conjuncts is false, and therefore the same holds for Strong Kleene "and". Similarly, since in classical logic a disjunction must be true if one of its disjuncts is true, the same holds for Strong Kleene "or". We obtain the following truth tables for the main binary connectives:

Tab. 14.2.

$\phi \wedge \psi$	t	f	*	$\phi \vee \psi$	t	f	*	$\phi \rightarrow \psi$	t	f	*
t	t	f	*	t	t	t	t	t	t	f	*
f	f	f	f	f	t	f	*	f	t	t	t
*	*	f	*	*	t	*	*	*	t	*	*

Now consider the following example:

(11) If there is a knave, then the knave stole the tarts.

Let's ignore all presuppositions triggers in (11) save "the knave", and show that Strong Kleene predicts that the sentence as a whole does not presuppose that there is a knave. Using Definition 1, it suffices to find at least one model where (11) has a classical truth value, but there is no knave. This is easy: in such a model, the antecedent is false, and inspection of the above Strong Kleene table shows that when the antecedent of a conditional is false, the conditional is true, as would be the case classically. In fact, Strong Kleene predicts no presupposition for (11). This is in contradistinction to Weak Kleene, which would fail to give (11) a classical value in knave-less models, and hence predict that (11) presupposes the existence of a knave.

There are other cases where Strong Kleene does predict a presupposition, and the presupposition predicted is not what we might have expected. Thus Strong Kleene gives (12-a) a classical truth value in all models where there is a knave, and in all models where there was trouble. So while we might have expected the presupposition in (12-b), Strong Kleene predicts the presupposition in (12-c). We will return to this issue shortly.

(12)   a. If the knave stole the tarts, then there was trouble.
       b. There is a knave.
       c. If there was no trouble, then there is a knave.

Much of the discussion of partial and multivalent approaches to presupposition over the last three decades has centered on the treatment of negation. Specifically, the issue has been the treatment of cancellation examples like (13).

(13)   The tarts were not stolen by the knave: there is no knave.

A standard approach is to propose that negation is ambiguous between a presupposition-preserving negation and a presupposition-denying negation; see e.g. the discussion by Horn (1985, 1989). The presupposition-preserving negation (aka *choice* negation) we have already seen, and it is found in both the Weak and Strong Kleene systems. The presupposition-denying (or *exclusion*) negation is typically taken to map true to false and false to true, as usual, but also to map an argument lacking a classical value to true. Thus if (13) is interpreted in a model where there is no knave, but "not" is understood as a presupposition-denying negation, then "the tarts were stolen by the knave" would lack a classical value, but "The tarts were not stolen by the knave", and (13) as a whole, would be true.

Note that in this analysis the presupposition triggered by the "the knave" is not literally cancelled; rather, the negation is interpreted in such a way that the sentence as a whole doesn't inherit this presupposition. However, the idea that negation is ambiguous between a presupposition-preserving and a presupposition-denying sense is controversial, e.g. because thus far no language has been found in which presupposition affirming and presupposition-denying negations are realized by different lexical items.

4.2 Pragmatic presupposition

Probably the most significant philosophical counterpoint to the Frege-Strawson approach to presupposition, other than the original non-presuppositional work of Russell, is due to Stalnaker (1972, 1973, 1974), and later clarified in Stalnaker (1998) (cf. Simons 2003). Stalnaker suggests that a pragmatic notion of presupposition is needed, so that the proper object of philosophical study is not what words or sentences presuppose, but what people presuppose when they are speaking. A pragmatic presupposition associated with a sentence is a condition that a speaker would normally expect to hold in the common ground between discourse participants when that sentence is uttered.

One consequence of Stalnaker's view is that, *contra* semantic accounts of presupposition, presupposition failure need not produce a semantic catastrophe. There are, however, two weaker types of failure that can occur: (*i*) a speaker uttering some sentence S can fail to assume that some proposition P is in the common ground, even though most utterances of S would be accompanied by the presupposition that P; and (*ii*) a speaker can presuppose something that is not in the common ground. The former idea was used by Stalnaker to account for some tricky examples of Karttunen (1971b), involving a subclass of factive verbs that Karttunen referred to as "semifactives". The naturally occurring examples in (14-a) and (14-b), which involve the (semi-)factive verb "know", illustrate the point. The first sentence of (14-a) involves a first person, present tense use of "know", and there is clearly no presupposition that Mullah Omar is alive. On the other hand, (14-b) involves a past tense, third person use of "know", and in this case it does seem to be presupposed (at least in the fictional context of the story) that Luke was alive.

(14) a. I don't know that Mullah Omar is alive. I don't know if he's dead either. (General Dan McNeill, Reuters, 19 May 2008)
b. Vader didn't know that Luke was alive, so he had no intentions of converting Luke to the Sith. (Web example)

Examples like (14) led Karttunen to propose that "know" only triggers a presupposition in some person and tense forms; whence the term "semifactive". But, as Karttunen himself realized, such a stipulation is unmotivated. What Stalnaker noticed was that in the context of his pragmatic account of presupposition, these examples are not problematic. In the pragmatic account, the verb "know" need not presuppose that its complement is true. When an addressee hears the first sentence of (14-a), he will realize that if it were in the common ground that Mullah Omar was alive, then the speaker would know this, and so the speaker's claim would be false. Therefore the hearer can reason that the speaker is not presupposing the complement of "know" to be true. On the other hand, when a hearer is confronted by (14-b), it is consistent to assume that Luke was alive. Since speakers using "know" typically presuppose the truth of the complement, we can assume that this is the case here.

Stalnaker's work was part of an avalanche of pragmatic attacks on the semantic conception of presupposition. However, unlike Stalnaker's, many of these proposals had no distinctive role for a notion of presupposition. Working in the immediate aftermath of Grice's 1967 William James lectures (Grice 1989), many theorists attempted to reduce presupposition to various combinations of entailment and implicature. Thus Atlas & Levinson (1981), Wilson (1975), and Böer & Lycan (1976), among others, present detailed (and partly independent) arguments that presuppositions should be understood as something akin to conversational implicatures. Generally speaking, the approach is to justify presuppositional inferences using the maxims of relevance and quantity. Atlas (1976) suggests that an embedding of a definite under a negation will tend to produce a meaning that is ruled out as insufficiently strong to satisfy the maxim of quantity, unless it is strengthened by treating the definite as if it had wide scope and could act referentially. Contemporary descendants of this pragmatic tradition include Abbott (2000), Simons (2001, 2004), and Schlenker (2008). Both Abbott and Simons are at pains to distinguish between different presupposition triggers, rather than lumping them all together. Thus Simons, for example, makes a case for deriving presuppositional inferences associated with factives and aspectual adverbs using a combination of Stalnakerian and Gricean reasoning, but does not argue for making the same reduction in the case of typically anaphoric triggers like the additive "too". Schlenker does not make such fine-grained distinctions between presupposition triggers. Instead, he concentrates on deriving projection properties pragmatically, using both standard maxims and at least one rule specific to presuppositions. (Schlenker's special-purpose rule is: "Be Articulate". This exhorts speakers to assert content rather than presupposing it, but, because of interactions with other maxims, only forces them to do so when such an assertion would not yield redundancy. The net effect is much like that described for Karttunen's 1974 model, below.)

There is a contrast among pragmatic approaches to presupposition. Those discussed in the preceding paragraph attempt to derive presuppositional inferences from general conversational principles, thus explaining both the source of presuppositions, and the phenomenon of projection. But Stalnaker made no attempt whatsoever to explain where presuppositions came from, beyond indicating that they are inferential tendencies that might or might not be associated with semantic presuppositions. This emphasis on the projection of presuppositions rather than their source, which holds also of the contemporaneous work by Karttunen (1973, 1974), to which we shall turn shortly, lived on in much of the work influenced by these theories. It is particularly obvious in what we can collectively term *cancellation*-based theories of presupposition, led by Gazdar (1979a, 1979b), and including Soames (1979, 1982), Mercer (1987, 1992), Gunji (1981), Marcu (1994), Horton (1987), Horton & Hirst (1988), Bridge (1991), and, of particular note, van der Sandt (1982, 1988).

Cancellation accounts can be traced back in spirit to the Stalnaker account of semifactives discussed above, in which presuppositions are defeated by competing conversational inferences: the general idea is simply to make presuppositions into defaults, and wipe them out whenever they would cause pragmatic embarrassment. Gazdar's account provided a remarkably straightforward formalization of this account, as well as extending to many other projection phenomena, based on a general principle he characterizes as "All the news that fits". In Gazdar's model, the strategy for a hearer is first to identify sets of entailments, conversational implicatures, and presuppositions, and then to try adding them to the speaker's set of commitments.

Definition 5 (*Gazdar: cancellation*) *Implicatures and entailments defeat presuppositions, so a hearer adds to his or her commitments only those presuppositions that are compatible with both implicatures and entailments. All remaining presuppositions are cancelled.*

Consider (15-a), and assume there are no relevant pre-existing commitments:

(15) a. If the king is angry, then the knave stole the tarts.
b. If there is a knave, then the knave stole the tarts.

(15-a) entails is that if there is an angry king then there is a knave and he stole some set of tarts. (This much all theories agree on; some theories may predict stronger entailments.) The set of implicatures would include the implicature that the speaker doesn't know whether a king is angry, and doesn't know whether a knave stole tarts. The presuppositions (or "potential presuppositions", as Gazdar calls them at this stage) might be that there is a unique king, a unique knave, and a unique set of tarts. The hearer proceeds by adding the entailments to (his representation of) the speaker's commitment set, then adding whatever implicatures fit in, and then adding the presuppositions that fit after that. In this case, all the entailments, implicatures, and presuppositions are consistent, and all can be added without any being cancelled.

But now consider (15-b), repeated from (11). Here there is a implicature that the speaker doesn't know whether there is a knave. The hearer accepts this and other implicatures, and then considers the presuppositions that there is a knave and that there are some tarts. The presupposition that there are tarts is unproblematic, and is added, but the hearer cannot consistently add the presupposition that there is a knave. So this presupposition is canceled, and (15-b) does not presuppose that there is a knave. Hence, if Gazdar is right, presuppositions are sometimes blocked by conversational implicatures.

Within the space of cancellation-based accounts of presupposition, it is hard to beat Gazdar's for its conceptual and technical simplicity, and its empirical coverage. Some conceptual questions remain, however, such as why it should be that *presuppositions* are the last things to be added in the process of updating commitments. Van der Sandt's (1982, 1988) reformulation of the cancellation model gives us an alternative way to think about this, for in this model presuppositions are considered in terms of whether they could have come first.

Definition 6 *(Van der Sandt: cancellation) Project only those presuppositions that could be conjoined to the beginning of the sentence while leaving the utterance consistent with (neo-Gricean) conversational principles.*

The intuitive idea underlying van der Sandt's proposal is that presuppositions are *given* information, and in this sense "precede" their carrier sentences, if not *de facto* then at least *de jure*. In the case of (15-a,b), fronting the presupposition that there are some tarts yields the sentences in (16-a,b), respectively.

(16) a. There are some tarts and if the king is angry, then the knave stole the tarts.
b. There are some tarts and if there is a knave, then the knave stole the tarts.

These do not clash with any Gricean principles, so the presuppositions are predicted to project. Similarly, adding the presupposition that there is a knave to (15-a), as in (17-a), produces no clash, so (15-a) presupposes that there is a knave. But adding the presupposition that there is a knave to (15-b), as in (17-b), does result in a clash: since (17-b) is truth-conditionally equivalent to the simple conjunction "there is a knave and the knave stole the tarts", it is redundant. On van der Sandt's analysis, if fronting a presupposition would produce a redundant result, then that presupposition cannot project. So (15-b) is correctly predicted not to presuppose that there is a knave.

(17) a. There is a knave and if the king is angry, then the knave stole the tarts.
b. There is a knave and if there is a knave, then the knave stole the tarts.

It should be noted, however, that even if (17-b) is redundant, it is arguably a felicitous discourse, and therefore some subtlety is needed in applying van der Sandt's cancellation principle in the simplified form above. The issue is not simply whether a discourse is felicitous, but whether there is any clash with the maxims. And this will of course depend on how exactly the maxims are formulated. But for the purposes of understanding the intention of van der Sandt's analysis, we can take it that though an utterance of (17-b) could be felicitous, it would be a case of *flouting* (in Grice's sense), a case where a maxim is disobeyed in order to preserve some greater conversational goal.

4.3 Local contexts and the dynamic turn

For the last fifty years, the philosophical literature on presupposition has been primarily focused on definite descriptions. But by the early 1970s, more linguistically oriented work had expanded the empirical domain of presupposition theory from definite descriptions to other trigger types, including factives (Kiparsky & Kiparsky 1970), implicatives (Karttunen 1971a), focus particles (Horn 1969), verbs of judging (Fillmore 1971) and sortal constraints (Thomason 1972). Stalnaker's discussion of Karttunen's semifactives provides an early example of how this linguistic expansion of the empirical domain has impacted on philosophical work. Also by the early 1970s, linguists had expanded the empirical domain in another direction. The philosophical literature was largely oriented towards unembedded presupposition triggers and triggers under negation, but as we have already mentioned, Morgan (1969) and Langendoen & Savin (1971) generalized the issue by considering arbitrary embeddings. However, it was not until Karttunen (1973) that the full complexity of the projection problem became apparent. By methodically considering projection behavior construction by construction, Karttunen showed that there was more variation in projection behavior than had been previously described, making it quite clear that none of the extant Frege-Strawson derived systems could hope to cover every case.

4.3.1 Karttunen: first intimations of satisfaction

Karttunen (1973) presented a taxonomy of embedding constructions that divided them into three classes: *plugs*, *holes* and *filters*. Plugs comprise a class of predicates and operators which Karttunen claimed block the projection of presuppositions, while holes are a class of predicates and operators which allow presuppositions to project freely. So, since "told that" is a plug, according to Karttunen, (18) is predicted not to presuppose that there is a King of France. On the other hand, since "perhaps" is a hole, (19) is predicted to presuppose that there is a King of France.

(18) Mary told Jim that the King of France was bald.
(19) Perhaps the King of France is bald.

Karttunen's filters include the binary logical connectives "if then", "and", and "or". The intuition behind the filter metaphor is that these constructions allow only some presuppositions to project, and we have already seen examples of this phenomenon. Thus example (11) showed that sometimes a presupposition in the consequent of a conditional does not project: here the presupposition that there was a knave is, to use Karttunen's metaphor, filtered out. But the same example includes an occurrence of the definite "the tarts" in the consequent, and the presupposition that there are (or at least were) some tarts projects from the conditional. Karttunen concluded that the consequent of a conditional acts as a hole to some presuppositions, but filters out all those presuppositions which are entailed by the antecedent, or, more generally, by a combination of the antecedent and contextually supplied background information. (Here, of course, we simplify as regards the semantics of conditionals: see article 15 [Semantics: Noun Phrases and Verb Phrases] (von Fintel) *Conditionals*.)

Karttunen's key example showing the role of context bears repetition:

(20) Either Geraldine is not a mormon or she has given up wearing her holy underwear.

The second half of (20) contains (at least) two presupposition triggers: the definite description "her holy underwear" and the aspectual verb "give up", which trigger the presuppositions that Geraldine used to have and wear holy underwear, respectively. Karttunen's filtering condition for disjunctions removes from the right disjunct any presuppositions that are entailed by a combination of the context and the negation of the left disjunct. Now consider a context supporting the proposition that all mormons have holy underwear which they wear regularly. It follows from this proposition and the negation of the left disjunct, i.e. the proposition that Geraldine is a mormon, that Geraldine has holy underwear and has worn it regularly. But these are exactly the presuppositions triggered in the right disjunct, so they are filtered out. It follows that (20) has no presuppositions.

Karttunen's (1973) account is of interest not only for its triptych of plugs, holes and filters, but also because it sets the background for a crucial shift of perspective in Karttunen (1974), and thence to the dynamic approaches to presupposition that have been dominant in recent years. What remained completely unclear in the 1973 paper was why certain presuppositions should be filtered out if they were entailed by other material. Karttunen (1974) suggests an alternative conception based on the idea of *local contexts* of evaluation. The idea is that the parts of a sentence are not necessarily evaluated with respect to the same context as that in which the sentence as a whole is evaluated: a local context may contain more information than the global context. For example, when evaluating a conjunction, the second conjunct is evaluated in a local context which contains not only the information in the global context, but also whatever information was given by the first conjunct. Karttunen (1974) defined local contexts of evaluation for a range of constructions, and suggested the following requirement: presuppositions always need to be entailed (or "satisfied", as he puts it) in the local context in which the trigger is evaluated. Given this requirement, the overall presuppositions of a sentence will just be whatever propositions must be in a context of an utterance in order to guarantee that the presuppositions associated with presupposition triggers are satisfied in their local contexts of interpretation.

Karttunen spelled out how local satisfaction should be calculated separately for each connective and operator he considered. However, recent developments in Schlenker (2008) provide a general way of calculating what the local context should be. In the following reformulation of Karttunen's model we incorporate Schlenker's insights along the lines proposed by Beaver (2008).

Let us say that some clause in a complex sentence is redundant relative to some context of utterance if you can replace that clause by a tautology without affecting the amount of factual information conveyed by the sentence in that context. For example, in (21), the first conjunct is redundant in any context of utterance. Here, the same factual information would be conveyed by "Mary is Mary and Mary owns a sheep", where the first conjunct is replaced by the tautology "Mary is Mary".

(21) Mary owns an animal and Mary owns a sheep

Now let us say that a clause is left-redundant if it is possible to tell by looking at the material in the sentence to the left of the clause that the clause is redundant. So "Mary owns an animal" is not left-redundant in (21) (except if the context of utterance already entails that Mary owns an animal), because there is no material before that clause, implying that it is impossible to tell by looking at material to the left of the clause that the clause is redundant. On the other hand, "Mary owns an animal" is left-redundant in (22) and also in (23):

(22) Mary owns a sheep and Mary owns an animal.
(23) If Mary owns a sheep then Mary owns an animal.

Now we can put this to use to define the crucial notion in Karttunen's (1974) account.

Definition 7 *(Karttunen/Schlenker: Presupposition via satisfaction) A presupposition P is satisfied at point X in S iff P would be left-redundant if added at that point. A sentence presupposes whatever propositions must hold in global contexts of utterance such that each locally triggered presupposition is satisfied where its trigger occurs.*

As an example, let us consider the presuppositions predicted for (20), repeated below:

(20) Either Geraldine is not a mormon or she has given up wearing her holy underwear.

Note first that for all sentences of the form "A or B", the negation of A is satisfied within the right disjunct. So "Geraldine is a mormon" is satisfied in the right disjunct of (20). And more generally, anything entailed by a combination of propositions in the context and the negation of the left disjunct will be satisfied in the right disjunct. Now, let us consider the clause "she has given up wearing her holy underwear": we take this to trigger the presupposition that Geraldine has had holy underwear that she wore. This presupposition will be satisfied provided the global context of utterance, combined with the negation of the left disjunct, entails that she has had holy underwear that she wore. And classically this will be the case if and only if the context supports the conditional "if Geraldine is a mormon, then she has had holy underwear that she wore." Hence, this conditional is the presupposition Karttunen (1974) predicts for (20).

One notable property of the Karttunen (1974) treatment of examples like (20), a property not found in his 1973 model, is that the presupposition predicted is conditionalized. That is, (20) is not predicted to presuppose that Geraldine has had holy underwear that she wore, but that if she is a mormon then she has had such underwear. We already encountered such conditionalized presuppositions in our discussion of Strong Kleene; in fact, Strong Kleene predicts exactly the same conditionalized presupposition in this case. Karttunen's 1974 model also predicts conditionalized presuppositions when the presupposition trigger is in the right conjunct of a conjunction, or in the consequent of a conditional. Thus in (15-a), repeated below, the presuppositions predicted are that there is a king (since presuppositions triggered in the antecedent are not conditionalized), and that if the king is angry, then there is a knave. In (15-b), the conditional presupposition (that if there is a knave, then there is a knave) is trivial, so in effect there is no net presupposition. (Note that if in (15-b) we took the presupposition of the definite "the knave" to include a uniqueness or maximality requirement, i.e. that there was no more than one knave, then the overall presupposition of the example as predicted by the Karttunen (1974) model, and indeed by Strong Kleene, would no longer be trivial. The presupposition would be that if there was a knave then there was only one knave. More generally, the conditionalized presuppositions predicted by Karttunen came under withering attack by Gazdar 1979a, and have been a subject of controversy ever since.)

(15) a. If the king is angry then the knave stole the tarts.
b. If there is a knave, then the knave stole the tarts.

Although Karttunen's (1974) model seems quite distinct from any of its predecessors, we have already noted that it shares at least some predictions with Strong Kleene. An observation made by Peters (1979) showed that the 1974 model is surprisingly closely related to the semantic accounts of presupposition discussed above. In particular, Peters showed that Karttunen's way of calculating presuppositions for the truth conditional connectives is equivalent to what would be obtained within a three-valued logic, but with special non-symmetric connectives. Here is a general way of defining the Peters Connectives, inspired both by Schlenker (2008, 2009) and George (2008):

Definition 8 *(Middle Kleene/Peters connectives) Go from left to right through the sentence. For each argument X that takes a non-classical value, check whether on the basis of material on its left, assigning an arbitrary classical value to X could conceivably have an effect on the overall value. If so, the sentence as a whole lacks a classical truth value. If not, just assign X an arbitrary value, and carry on. If this procedure allows all non-classical values to be filled in classically, then the sentence can be assigned a classical value.*

For example, this procedure makes a conjunction classical if both its arguments are classical, false if the left conjunct is false, and undefined otherwise. Thus undefinedness of the left conjunct forces undefinedness of the entire conjunction, whereas undefinedness of the right conjunct only sometimes yields undefinedness of the entire conjunct, as seen in the following comparison of truth tables in various systems. The net effect is that presuppositions of the left conjunct project in the Middle Kleene system, just as in the Weak Kleene system, but presuppositions of the right conjunct are conditionalized, just as in the Strong Kleene system. The net effect is behavior that precisely mirrors that of the Karttunen (1974) model.

Definition 9 *(Trivalent truth tables for conjunction)*

Tab. 15.3.

Weak Kleene:				Middle Kleene/Peters:				Strong Kleene:			
$\phi \wedge \psi$	t	f	*	$\phi \wedge \psi$	t	f	*	$\phi \wedge \psi$	t	f	*
t	t	f	*	t	t	f	*	t	t	f	*
f	f	f	*	f	f	f	f	f	f	f	f
*	*	f	*	*	*	*	*	*	*	f	*

The equivalence between Peters' connectives and Karttunen's model paved the way for a more complete reformulation of the Karttunen model in Karttunen & Peters (1977, 1979), where certain types of presupposition (which Karttunen & Peters regard as conventional implicatures rather than presuppositions) are treated in a compositional grammar fragment. This fragment uses two dimensions of meaning, one for presupposition and one for assertion, and is effectively an implementation of the Peters connectives in a four-valued logic; see Krahmer (1994, 1998), Beaver (2001), and Beaver & Krahmer (2001) for discussion, and the latter for a fragment that mirrors that of Karttunen and Peters, but allows for a better treatment of the interaction between presuppositions and quantifiers.

4.3.2 Satisfaction theories

Although Karttunen's (1974) model turned out to be equivalent to a system which, from a purely technical point of view, is in the Frege-Strawson tradition, Karttunen (1974) was one of the seminal papers of the dynamic zeitgeist that swept through semantics and pragmatics in the last decades of the twentieth century. Also relevant here are Hamblin (1970), Stalnaker (1972, 1974) and Lewis (1979), all of whom advanced dynamic models of pragmatics in which the (joint) commitments of speakers and hearers evolve as new assertions are made and their content becomes part of the linguistic context available for future utterances (see also article 11 [this volume] (Jaszczolt) *Semantics and pragmatics*). It is against this background that Heim (1982, 1983) offered the first dynamic semantic account of presupposition. Heim's model utilizes Stalnaker's notion of a context as a set of all possible worlds compatible with what has been established at that point in a conversation, but involves a crucial twist adapted from Karttunen. In Stalnaker's model, a single *global* context is updated each time new information is asserted, but in Heim's model the context is updated *locally* in the process of computing the meanings of subparts of a complex expression. We can define a simplified version of Heim's system as follows:

Definition 10 *(Dynamic Semantics)* *Assuming that the context set C is a set of possible worlds and S and S' are sentences:*

i. $C + S$ = *the subset of worlds in C that are compatible with S, but this is defined iff S's presuppositions (if any) are true in all worlds in C.*
ii. $C + \neg S = C - (C + S)$
iii. $C + S \wedge S' = (C + S) + S'$
iv. $C + S \circ S'$, *where* $\circ$ *is some truth functional operator, is given by the simplest classical definition of* $\circ$ *in terms of* $\neg$ *and* $\wedge$ *that preserves the order of the two sub-clauses.*
v. *S is satisfied in a context C iff* $C + S = C$ *(i.e., updating C with S has no effect).*
vi. *S presupposes S' iff S' is satisfied in all contexts where update with S is defined.*

Clause (*iv*) entails that update with a conditional is defined via the equivalence $A \rightarrow B \equiv \neg(A \wedge \neg B)$. To see how this will work, let's reconsider (15-a), repeated once again below:

(15) a. If the king is angry, then the knave stole the tarts.

(24) a. It's not the case that [the king is angry and the knave didn't steal the tarts].
b. The king is angry and the knave didn't steal the tarts.
c. The king is angry.
d. The knave didn't steal the tarts.
e. The knave stole the tarts.

In order to update a context with (23), we must do the equivalent of updating with (24-a). Now clause (*ii*) says that to update a context with (24-a), we must first try updating with (24-b), and subtract the result from the original context (so as to leave behind whichever worlds are *not* compatible with (24-a)). But (24-b) is a conjunction, so we must first update with the left conjunct (24-c), and then with the right (24-d). Updating with (24-c) is only defined if the presupposition that there is a king is satisfied in all worlds in the context set. We immediately see that (24-c), (24-b), (24-a), and (23) all have this requirement, i.e. they presuppose that there is a king. Provided this presupposition is satisfied, updating with

(24-c) produces a subset of worlds where the king is angry. We use this reduced context set for update with (24-d). But update with (24-d) again uses the negation clause (*ii*) of the above definition. So we started off with a set of worlds where there is a king, we reduced it to a set of worlds where the king is angry, and now we must update that context with (24-e). But this update will only be defined if there is a knave. So it turns out that update of a context with (23) is only defined for contexts where (a) there is a king, and (b) where all the worlds where the king is angry are worlds where there is a knave. Following the definitions through, it turns out that, once again, the original sentence carries both a non-conditionalized presupposition, that there is a king, and the conditionalized presupposition that if the king is angry, then there is a knave.

The satisfaction based model has seen considerable further development – see e.g. Beaver (1992, 2001), Chierchia (1995), Heim (1992), Zeevat (1992), and, for a rather different formalization of a dynamic semantic approach, van Eijck (1993). (See also article 12 [Semantics: Theories] (Dekker) *Dynamic semantics*. Note that Definition 10 does not cover modals or attitude verbs: for discussion see the Beaver, Heim and Zeevat references, and section 5., below.)

The most important feature of the satisfaction model not covered in the description above is *accommodation*. For Heim (1982), following Lewis (1979), this is a process whereby contexts are adjusted so as to make update possible when presuppositions are not satisfied. In terms of her treatment of accommodation, Heim's major innovation over Lewis was to allow this process to take place not only in the global context of utterance, but also on local contexts found midway through an update. However, Heim (1982) was not explicit about exactly how accommodation should work and what should be accommodated.

Beaver's model of accommodation, first published in Beaver (1992), was the first to make explicit how accommodation might operate in the satisfaction framework, and on this model accommodation is a type of filtering operation. Beaver suggests that due to uncertainty about what the speaker takes the common ground to be, the hearer has to entertain multiple alternative context sets, with some ranking of which is the most plausible. All these alternative contexts are updated simultaneously. Accommodation is then what happens when the update is not defined on what was previously considered to be the most plausible context, in which case the hearer drops that context from contention. What remains is a new set of contexts in which the most plausible one is a context that has been successfully updated. For example, a hearer who was not certain about whether the speaker took there to be a king would represent contexts where there was a king, and contexts where there was not. Regardless of which the hearer took initially to be more plausible, updating with (23) would then cause contexts in which there was no king to be thrown out, leaving only contexts in which there was a king.

Though we will not go into detail here, we should note that Beaver's proposal is one of several attempts to deal with the conditionalized presuppositions that arise in satisfaction accounts and other theories (such as Strong and Middle Kleene). See the discussion in Beaver (2001), the earlier solution to the problem of conditionalized presuppositions offered by Karttunen & Peters (1979), the criticisms by Geurts (1996,1999a), and recent discussion of van Rooij (2007), Singh (2007) and Rothschild (2008).

4.3.3 Presupposition and anaphora

While a number of authors have noted that presuppositions behave in some respects like anaphors (e.g. Kripke 2009 and Soames 1989), it was van der Sandt (1989, 1992) who brought out the connection the most forcefully. He noted that for every case where a pronoun is interpreted anaphorically (see article 14 [Semantics: Sentence and Information Structure] (Geurts) *Accessibility and anaphora*), but is not interpretable as a bound variable, a similar configuration is possible with presuppositions. Thus in each of the following pairs, the (a) example includes an anaphoric pronoun ("it"), and the (b) example includes the factive verb "knows", triggering a presupposition that its propositional complement is true (i.e. that Fred left).

(25) *Inter-sentential (discourse) anaphora*
 a. There was a storm. It was fierce.
 b. Fred left. Mary knows that Fred left.

(26) *Donkey anaphora*
 a. If a farmer owns a donkey then he beats it.
 b. If Fred left then Mary knows that Fred left.

(27) *Modal subordination*
 a. A wolf might come to the door. It would eat you.
 b. Fred might leave. Mary would know that Fred left.

(28) *Bathroom anaphora*
 a. Either there's no bathroom in this house, or else it's in a funny place.
 b. Either Fred didn't leave, or else Mary knows that he left.

In order to account for these parallels, van der Sandt proposed a unified treatment of presupposition and anaphora, extending Discourse Representation

Theory so as to deal with both phenomena (see article 11 [Semantics: Theories] (Kamp & Reyle) *Discourse Representation Theory*). Presupposed information is information that is presented as given, and in van der Sandt's theory this means that presuppositions want to have discourse referents to bind to. However, whereas anaphoric pronouns are rarely interpretable in the absence of a suitable antecedent, the same does not hold for all presupposition-inducing expressions. For instance, a speaker may felicitously assert that he met "Fred's sister" even if he knows full well that his audience wasn't aware that Fred has a sister. In such cases, Stalnaker (1974) suggested, presuppositions are generally accommodated, which is to say that the hearer accepts the information as given, and revises his representation of the context accordingly. Accommodation, thus understood, is a form of exploitation in Grice's sense: the purpose of presuppositional expressions is to signal that this or that information is given, and if some information is new but not particularly interesting or controversial (like the fact that somebody has a sister) the speaker may choose to "get it out of the way" by presuppositional means.

Van der Sandt's theory incorporates the notion of accommodation as follows. Presuppositions, according van der Sandt, introduce information that prefers to be linked to discourse referents that are already available in the hearer's representation of the discourse, and in this respect they are like pronouns. Van der Sandt in fact uses the term *binding* to refer to configurations in which presuppositions have antecedents in the Discourse Representation Structure, thus generalizing the standard notion of a *bound pronoun* to cases involving multiple discourse referents. However, if a suitable discourse antecedent is not available, a new one will be accommodated, and the presupposition is linked to that. Generally speaking, accommodation is not an option in the interpretation of pronouns, and one reason that has been suggested for this is that a pronoun's descriptive content is relatively poor (see Section 5.1 for discussion). Being told that "she" is wonderful is not particularly helpful if it isn't clear who the pronoun is meant to refer to. By contrast, if the speaker refers to "Pedro's sister" there is more to go on, and accommodation becomes feasible. Hence, van der Sandt hypothesizes that pronouns are a special class of presuppositional expressions: while all presupposition triggers prefer to be linked to antecedents, pronouns almost always must be linked to antecedents, because they are descriptively attenuate, and therefore cannot be construed by way of accommodation (see below for further discussion of the last point).

To get a better idea how this is supposed to work, let us consider an example with several presupposition triggers:

(29) If Fred is gay, then his son is gay, too.

This sentence contains the definite NP "his son", which in its turn contains the pronoun "his", and the focus particle "too". Assuming the pronoun's antecedent is "Fred", the definite NP triggers the presupposition that Fred has a son, while the focus particle triggers the presupposition that someone other than Fred's son is gay. Note that in this example the presupposition triggered by the definite NP is "inherited" by the sentence as a whole, while the one triggered by "too" is not: normally speaking, an utterance of (29) would license the inference that (according to the speaker) Fred has a son, but not that someone else besides Fred's son is gay.

Van der Sandt's theory accounts for these observations as follows. We suppose that the grammar assigns (29) the intermediate semantic representation in (30-a). Here $[u_1, \ldots, u_m: \phi_1, \ldots, \phi_n]$ is a simple Discourse Representation Structure in linear form, with $u_1, \ldots, u_m$ a list of discourse markers, and $\phi_1, \ldots, \phi_n$ a list of conditions on those markers; connectives like ⇒ are used to build up complex conditions. We assume for convenience that most interpretative problems have been cleared out of the way already, and that the only thing that remains to be done is resolve the presuppositions triggered by "his", "his son" and "too", which are flagged by Beaver's (1992) trigger symbol, ∂.

(30) a. [x: Fred(x),
    [: gay(x)] ⇒[: ∂[z: ∂[y:], z is y's son], gay(z), ∂[u: u ≠ z, gay(u)]]]
  b. [x: Fred(x),   *(binding y to x)*
    [: gay(x)] ⇒ [: ∂[z: z is x's son], gay(z), ∂[u: u ≠ z, gay(u)]]]
  c. [x, z: Fred(x), z is x's son,   *(accommodating z)*
    [: gay(x)] ⇒ [: gay(z), ∂[u: u ≠ z, gay(u)]]]
  d. [x, z: Fred(x), z is x's son,   *(binding u to x)*
    [: gay(x)] ⇒ [: gay(z), x ≠ z]]

(30-a) is the initial semantic representation associated with (29), in which three presuppositions remain to be resolved. The first of these, triggered by the pronoun "his", is bound to the discourse referent representing Fred, which results in (30-b). The second presupposition, that Fred has a son, cannot be bound, and therefore must be interpreted by way of accommodation. Van der Sandt's theory, like Heim's (1983), stipulates that accommodation at the global level, as shown in (30-c), is preferred to accommodation at other sites, as will be discussed in section 5, below. Finally, the presupposition triggered by the focus particle can be bound in the antecedent of the conditional; after simplification, this results in (30-d), which represents the most natural way of interpreting (29).

5 Current issues in presupposition theory

5.1 Accommodation

Accommodation was first discussed by Karttunen (1974) and Stalnaker (1974), though only named as such by Lewis (1979). Karttunen introduces the concept as follows:

> [...] ordinary conversation does not always proceed in the ideal orderly fashion described earlier. People do make leaps and shortcuts by using sentences whose presuppositions are not satisfied in the conversational context. This is the rule rather than the exception [...] I think we can maintain that a sentence is always taken to be an increment to a context that satisfies its presuppositions. If the current conversational context does not suffice, the listener is entitled and expected to extend it as required. (Karttunen 1974: 191)

If this looks reasonably straightforward, the reader should be warned that accommodation is among the more contentious topics in presupposition theory.

To begin with, there are various notions of accommodation, some of which are stricter than others. To explain, consider the following example by Heim (1982):

(31) John read a book about Schubert and wrote to the author.

In order to determine the intended meaning of "the author", the hearer has to infer (*i*) that there is an author and (*ii*) that the said author wrote the book read by John. Whereas on a broad understanding of accommodation, all of this is accommodated, on a strict construal only (*i*) is, and (*ii*) is a bridging inference. This is not just a matter of terminology. If we choose to be strict, we can argue that there is something like an "accommodation module", which as such has nothing to do with world knowledge; whereas if the notion is construed more broadly, accommodation is of a piece with bridging. To facilitate the following discussion, we will adopt a strict notion of accommodation, and take the naive view that what is accommodated is the presupposition as triggered by, e.g., a definite NP or factive verb.

With these preliminaries out of the way, we turn to the first major question: *Where* are presuppositions accommodated? Though it may seem odd at first, this question is inescapable if we assume, as is standard in dynamic semantics, that an expression may occur in several contexts at the same time (cf. Section 4.3.2.). To illustrate, consider the following:

(32) a. (c_0) Maybe (c_1) Betty is trying to give up drinking.
   b. (c_0) Maybe (c_1) Wilma thinks that (c_2) her husband is having an affair.

Here c_0 refers to the global context in which a given sentence is uttered, and c_1 and c_2 are auxiliary, or local, contexts. In (32-a), the modal "maybe" creates an auxiliary context of possible states of affairs in which Betty is trying to give up drinking; the same, mutatis mutandis, for (32-b). Now, the presupposition triggered in (32-a), that Betty used to drink, can be accommodated *globally*, i.e. in c_0, or *locally*, in c_1. In the former case, the utterance is construed as meaning that Betty used to drink and may be trying to kick the habit; in the latter, it conveys that, possibly, Betty used to drink and is trying to give up drinking. Likewise, in (32-b), the presupposition that Wilma is married may be accommodated globally, or locally in the most deeply embedded context. But here there is a third option, as well: if the presupposition is accommodated in c_1, the sentence is read as "Maybe Wilma is married and she thinks that her husband is having an affair", and we speak of *intermediate* accommodation.

It is widely agreed that the following empirical generalization, made explicit by Heim (1983), is correct:

(PGA) Global accommodation is preferred to non-global accommodation.

In the examples in (32) the PGA clearly holds: non-global interpretations may be possible, but they require special contexts. One such context may be that the presupposition contains a variable which is bound by a quantifier:

(33) Most Germans wash their cars on Saturday.

The most natural interpretation of this sentence surely is that most Germans who own a car wash it on Saturday. So in this case intermediate accommodation seems to be the preferred option, and this might be explained, following van der Sandt (1992), by supposing that the possessive pronoun contains a variable bound by the quantifier.

There are other cases where intermediate accommodation is virtually impossible:

(34) If Fred is coming to the reception, he may bring his wife.

It is quite unlikely that this may be construed as, "If Fred is married and is coming to the reception, he may bring his wife." More generally, we don't know of any clear-cut cases (i.e. cases in which accommodation is not forced by independent contextual factors) in which a presupposition triggered in the consequent of a conditional is accommodated in the antecedent.

The picture is rather confusing. While in some cases, e.g. (32-b) or (33), intermediate accommodation seems possible and sometimes even preferred, in other cases it doesn't seem possible at all. And things get even more confused than this. Thus far, we have taken our examples at face value, but some authors have argued that we shouldn't because, as a matter of fact, intermediate accommodation doesn't exist. For instance, according to Beaver (2001), the presupposition in (33) is taken as evidence that the topic of conversation is car-owning Germans, and it is this topic that restricts the domain of the quantifier, making intermediate accommodation redundant. See von Fintel (1995), Geurts & van der Sandt (1999) and the full version of this article (Beaver & Geurts 2010), and article 11 [Semantics: Sentence and Information Structure] (Roberts) *Topics* for related issues.

5.2 Presupposition failure

What happens when a presupposition is false? The textbook story goes as follows. According to Frege (1892), if an expression A suffers from presupposition failure, then any sentence containing A will lack a truth value; Russell (1905) famously denied this, holding that such a sentence will always be true or false; and then Strawson (1950) reaffirmed Frege's position, more or less. What is less well known is that in subsequent work, Strawson partly recanted his initial view and came to doubt that presupposition failure invariably entails lack of truth value.

Taking a closer look at how speakers actually assess a sentence, Strawson's 1964 paper argues that presupposition failure may but need not cause a sentence to be infelicitous. Two of his examples are the following:

(35) a. Jones spent the morning at the local swimming pool.
 b. The exhibition was visited yesterday by the king of France.

If there is no swimming pool locally, it is "natural enough", according to Strawson, to say that (35-a) is false, and since the king of France doesn't exist, the same applies to (35-b). And if these sentences are false, their negations must be true. So, if these subtle judgments are accepted, then these are cases in which presupposition failure does not prevent us from saying that a sentence is true or false. But Strawson hasn't changed his mind about Russell's example:

> Confronted with the classical example, "The king of France is bald", we may well feel it natural to say, straight off, that the question whether the statement is true or false doesn't arise because there is no king of France. (Strawson 1964: 90)

Strawson goes on to observe, however, that speakers who subscribe to this judgment may want to reconsider their verdict if the context is set up the right way. For instance, if Russell's sentence is used to answer the question, "What examples, if any, are there of famous contemporary figures who are bald?", we may be more inclined to say that the answer is simply false.

Strawson's explanation for these facts is given in terms of topicality. The most likely purpose of a sentence like (35-a) is to describe what Jones has been doing in the morning, rather than, say, who the local swimming pool was visited by. That is, in the absence of further information about the context in which this sentence is uttered, its topic will be Jones's exploits. Similarly, a sentence like (35-b) will normally be used to convey information about the exhibition. If so, although the sentence purports to refer to the king of France, it is not about him; the king of France is not the topic of discourse, nor part of it. Strawson's suggestion is that this circumstance influences the way presupposition failure is dealt with. Not to put too fine a point on it, presupposition failure results in infelicity only if it affects the topic of a sentence; otherwise the sentence will be judged true or false, as appropriate.

One of the appealing features of this analysis is that it takes into account the context dependence of speakers' intuitions. As Strawson notes, Russell's sentence (36) will by default be construed as being about the king of France, whence a strong tendency to judge the sentence infelicitous.

(36) The king of France is bald.

If, however, the discourse is about royal baldness in general, for instance, the grammatical subject of (36) is used to say something about that topic, and Strawson's account predicts that the sentence is more likely to be judged false, which seems correct. Another observation that neatly falls into place is that word order may have an effect on speakers' intuitions about presupposition failure. As Strawson observes, if we compare (35-b) with (37), where the defective description is in subject position, we would be "a shade more squeamish" to say that the sentence is simply false (p. 91). This is precisely what one should expect if speakers' intuitions were topic-dependent.

(37) The king of France visited the exhibition yesterday.

Assuming that Strawson's observations are correct, should we say (a) that non-topical definites are non-presuppositional, or (b) that they do have presuppositions, whose failure happens not to affect speakers' truth-value judgments? Some authors argue for the former (e.g. Reinhart 1982, Horn 1989); this is Strawson's view, as well. Von Fintel (2004) argues for the latter: topical or non-topical, "the king of France" always triggers the presupposition that there is a king of France; it's just our truth-value judgments that fluctuate.

5.3 Presuppositions and attitudes

For nearly four decades, the Holy Grail of presupposition research has been to explain the behavior of presuppositional expressions occurring in embedded positions. Given that the theoretically most challenging mode of embedding is within the scope of an attitude verb, one might expect that the interaction between presuppositions and attitude verbs should have received a lot of attention. But it hasn't. And it can't be because this topic doesn't pose any problems – on the contrary.

Already the data are problematic. If we embed a presupposition trigger under, e.g., "believe", we observe two types of inference. This is seen in the following examples, where "~" indicates that there is an inference, but of unspecified type:

(38) Barney believes that *his sister* is drunk.
 ~ (a) Barney has a sister.
 ~ (b) Barney believes he has a sister.

(39) Wilma believes that Barney *knows* that his sister is drunk.
 ~ (a) Barney's sister is drunk.
 ~ (b) Wilma believes that Barney's sister is drunk.

Both inferences are fairly robust, and both seem to exhibit projection behavior, as we illustrate here by applying various embedding tests to (38):

(40) a. Barney doesn't believe that his sister is drunk.
 b. Perhaps Barney believes that his sister is drunk.

(41) a. If Barney has a sister, then he believes that his sister is drunk.
 b. If Barney believes that he has a sister, then he also believes that his sister is drunk.

It is natural to infer from both sentences in (40-a) that Barney has a sister and that he believes that he has a sister, and these inferences can be blocked in sentences such as those in (41), where "his sister" occurs in the consequent of conditional whose antecedent makes one or the other inference explicit. It may seem odd at first that (41-a) should block the inference that Barney believes that he has a sister, while (41-b) blocks the inference that Barney has a sister. Note however that, generally speaking, Barney has a sister *iff* he believes that he has a sister. We'll return to this theme below.

Interestingly, literally the same pattern of observations holds for other attitude verbs, like "want" for example:

(42) Barney wants to phone his sister.
  ⤳ (a) Barney has a sister.
  ⤳ (b) Barney believes he has a sister.

The puzzling thing is that (42) does not license the inference that Barney *wants* to have a sister, but rather that he believes that he has one.

So, in many cases at least, a presupposition ϕ triggered within the scope of "$x\ V_A \ldots$", where V_A is an attitude verb, gives rise to two inferences with a candidature for presuppositional status: (a) that ϕ and (b) that x believes ϕ. Hence, we have three possible ways of proceeding, all of which have been defended in the literature:

i. Both inferences are presuppositions (Zeevat 1992, at least for certain triggers).
ii. Only ϕ is a presupposition (Gazdar 1979a, van der Sandt 1988, Geurts 1998).
iii. Only "x believes that ϕ" is a presupposition (Karttunen 1974, Heim 1992).

The first strategy seems to require a stipulation that certain presuppositions have to be accommodated twice, once inside a belief context, and once outside, and such a strategy is difficult to motivate. On the other hand, for *(ii)* and *(iii)*, there is the obvious problem that if we adopt either one of them, we only account for half of the observed inferences. How to explain the other half? Three possible answers to this question have been discussed in the literature, mainly by Heim (1992):

i. *De re construal* (Heim 1992) What at first looks like a presupposition projecting to the global context may in fact be due to a *de re* construal of the presupposition trigger. This solution has several serious drawbacks. In particular, it hard to see how this proposal can give us both inferences at the same time, rather than one (*de re*) or the other (presupposition). For this and other reasons (see Geurts 1998), we will not consider it any further.
ii. *Exportation* (Karttunen 1974, Heim 1992, Kay 1992) If Barney believes that he has a sister, then it may plausibly be inferred that he has a sister. Therefore, if it is presupposed that Barney believes that he has a sister, then it may plausibly be inferred that he has a sister.
iii. *Importation* (Heim 1992, Geurts 1998) If Barney has a sister, then it may plausibly be inferred that he believes that he has a sister. Therefore, if it is

presupposed that Barney has a sister, then it may plausibly be inferred that he believes that he has a sister.

If our presupposition theory predicts that the inferences projected from "$x\ V_A \ldots$" are of the form "x believes that ϕ", then we can appeal to exportation to explain why ϕ is inferable, as well. Vice versa, a theory which predicts that ϕ is presupposed can use importation for deriving "x believes that ϕ". So we have two options:

Tab. 14.4

	x believes that ϕ	ϕ
Option A	importation	presupposition
Option B	presupposition	exportation

Which is it going to be? That's a hard question, which raises various issues, only some of which we can mention here. It should be noted that, whereas for theories of the satisfaction family it is hard, if not impossible, to *avoid* making the prediction that presuppositions projected from attitude contexts are of the form "x believes that ϕ", DRT-style theories are more flexible, and can predict either this or that the presupposition is simply ϕ. In other words, satisfaction theories are more constrained (which is good), but therefore practically forced to resort to Option B. (See Beaver & Geurts 2010 for further discussion of these issues, and article 16 [Semantics: Noun Phrases and Verb Phrases] (Swanson) *Propositional attitudes* for general discussion.)

6 Concluding remarks

We have presented an overview of the major strands of work on presupposition. But we have not considered the question of whether presupposition triggers form a natural class in the first place: maybe all presupposition triggers are not alike. Like the topics discussed in the last section, this is a possibility that has only just begun to be explored in detail, with several authors proposing to dichotomize presupposition triggers in some way or other (e.g. Zeevat 1992, Geurts 1999b, Abusch 2002).

Our own suspicion, if we may end on an opinionated note, is that these first attempts to separate presupposition types from each other may turn out to be too cautious. There are several philosophically and linguistically interesting dimensions along which the set of presupposition triggers can be partitioned, such as referentiality, anaphoricity, ease of accommodation, ease of cancellation, and maintenance of truth under presupposition failure. So perhaps what will eventually emerge is not a straightforward dichotomy, but a more complex taxonomy of different types of trigger. And at that point, perhaps we may re-ask the question of whether the things that the different so-called "presupposition triggers" are triggering are in fact presuppositions, in any of the theoretical senses of the term "presupposition" that we have considered in this article.

(Note: this article is an abridged version of Beaver & Geurts 2010, which includes more extensive references. We wish to thank the reviewers and editors at both the Stanford Encyclopedia of Philosophy and The Handbook of Semantics, and Noor van Leusen for commentary and for assistance in helping us meet the publisher's exacting specifications.)

7 References

Abbott, Barbara 2000. Presuppositions as nonassertions. *Journal of Pragmatics* 32, 1419–1437.
Abusch, Dorit 2002. Lexical alternatives as a source of pragmatic presuppositions. In: B. Jackson (ed.). *Proceedings of Semantics and Linguistic Theory (= SALT) XII*. Ithaca, NY: Cornell University, 1–20.
Atlas, Jay 1976. *On the Semantics of Presupposition and Negation. An Essay in Philosophical Logic and the Foundations of Linguistics*. Ph.D. dissertation. Princeton University, Princeton, NJ.
Atlas, Jay & Stephen Levinson 1981. It-Clefts, informativeness and logical form: Radical pragmatics. In: P. Cole (ed.). *Radical Pragmatics*. New York: Academic Press, 1–61.
Beaver, David 1992. The kinematics of presupposition. In: P. Dekker & M. Stokhof (eds.). *Proceedings of the Eighth Amsterdam Colloquium*. Amsterdam: ILLC, 17–36.
Beaver, David 2001. *Presupposition and Assertion in Dynamic Semantics*. Stanford, CA: CSLI Publications.
Beaver, David 2008. As brief as possible (but no briefer). *Theoretical Linguistics* 34, 213–228.
Beaver, David & Bart Geurts 2010. Presupposition. In: E. N. Zalta (ed.). *The Stanford Encyclopedia of Philosophy*. Stanford University. http://plato.stanford.edu/entries/presupposition/. May 6, 2011.
Beaver, David & Emiel Krahmer 2001. A partial account of presupposition projection. *Journal of Logic, Language and Information* 10, 147–182.
Boër, Steven E. & William G. Lycan 1976. The myth of semantic presupposition. In: A. Zwicky (ed.). *Papers in Nonphonology* (Working Papers in Linguistics 21). Columbus, OH: Ohio State University, 1–90.
Bridge, Derek 1991. *Computing Presuppositions in an Incremental Natural Language Processing System*. Ph.D. dissertation. University of Cambridge.
Chierchia, Gennaro 1995. *Dynamics of Meaning*. Chicago, IL: The University of Chicago Press.
van Eijck, Jan 1993. The dynamics of description. *Journal of Semantics* 10, 239–267.

Fillmore, Charles 1971. Verbs of judging. An exercise in semantic description. In: Ch. Fillmore & D. T. Langendoen (eds.). *Studies in Linguistic Semantics*. New York: Holt, Reinhardt & Winston, 272–289.

von Fintel, Kai 1995. *Restrictions on Quantifier Domains*. Ph.D. dissertation. University of Massachussetts, Amherst, MA.

von Fintel, Kai 2004. Would you believe it? The king of France is back! Presuppositions and truth-value intuitions. In: M. Reimer & A. Bezuidenhout (eds.). *Descriptions and Beyond*. Oxford: Oxford University Press, 269–296.

Frege, Gottlob 1892/1984. Über Sinn und Bedeutung. *Zeitschrift für Philosophie und philosophische Kritik* 100, 25–50. English translation in: B. McGuinness (ed.). *Frege. Collected Papers on Mathematics, Logic, and Philosophy*. Oxford: Blackwell, 1984, 157–177.

Gazdar, Gerald 1979a. *Pragmatics. Implicature, Presupposition and Logical Form*. New York: Academic Press.

Gazdar, Gerald 1979b. A solution to the projection problem. In: C.-K. Oh & D. Dineen (eds.). *Syntax and Semantics 11: Presupposition*. New York: Academic Press, 57–89.

George, Benjamin R. 2008. *Presupposition Repairs. A Static, Trivalent Approach to Predicting Projection*. MA thesis. University of California, Los Angeles, CA.

Geurts, Bart 1996. Local satisfaction guaranteed. *Linguistics & Philosophy* 19, 259–294.

Geurts, Bart 1998. Presuppositions and anaphors in attitude contexts. *Linguistics & Philosophy* 21, 545–601.

Geurts, Bart 1999a. *Presuppositions and Pronouns*. Amsterdam: Elsevier.

Geurts, Bart 1999b. Specifics. In: B. Geurts, M. Krifka & R. van der Sandt (eds.). *Focus and Presupposition in Multi-speaker Discourse*. Utrecht: ESSLLI 99, 99–129.

Geurts, Bart & Rob van der Sandt 1999. Domain Restriction. In: P. Bosch & R. van der Sandt (eds.). *Focus. Linguistic, Cognitive, and Computational Perspectives*. Cambridge: Cambridge University Press, 268–292.

Grice, H. Paul 1989. *Studies in the Way of Words*. Cambridge, MA: Harvard University Press.

Gunji, Takao 1981. *Towards a Computational Theory of Pragmatics. Discourse, Presupposition and Implicature*. Ph.D. dissertation. Ohio State University, Columbus, OH.

Hamblin, Charles L. 1970. *Fallacies*. London: Methuen.

Heim, Irene 1982. *On the Semantics of Definite and Indefinite Noun Phrases*. Ph.D. dissertation. University of Massachusetts, Amherst, MA. Reprinted: Ann Arbor, MI: University Microfilms.

Heim, Irene 1983. On the projection problem for presuppositions. In: M. Barlow, D. Flickinger & M. Wescoat (eds.). *Proceedings of the Second Annual West Coast Conference on Formal Linguistics (= WCCFL)*. Stanford, CA: Stanford University, 114–126.

Heim, Irene 1992. Presupposition projection and the semantics of attitude verbs. *Journal of Semantics* 9, 183–221.

Horn, Laurence 1969. A presuppositional analysis of only and even. In: R. Binnick et al. (eds.). *Papers from the Fifth Regional Meeting of the Chicago Linguistic Society*. Chicago, IL: Chicago Linguistic Society, 98–107.

Horn, Laurence 1985. Metalinguistic negation and pragmatic ambiguity. *Language* 61, 121–174.

Horn, Laurence 1989. *A Natural History of Negation*. Chicago, IL: The University of Chicago Press. Reissued with new introduction: Stanford, CA: CSLI Publications, 2001.

Horton, Diane 1987. *Incorporating Agents Beliefs in a Model of Presupposition*. Technical Report CSRI-201. Toronto, ON, Computer Systems Research Institute, University of Toronto.

Horton, Diane & Graeme Hirst 1988. Presuppositions as beliefs. In: D. Vargha (ed.). *Proceedings of the 12th International Conference on Computational Linguistics (= COLING)*. Budapest: ACL, 255–260.
Karttunen, Lauri 1971a. Implicative verbs. *Language* 47, 340–358.
Karttunen, Lauri 1971b. Some observations on factivity. *Papers in Linguistics* 5, 55–69.
Karttunen, Lauri 1973. Presuppositions of compound sentences. *Linguistic Inquiry* 4, 167–193.
Karttunen, Lauri 1974. Presuppositions and linguistic context. *Theoretical Linguistics* 1, 181–194.
Karttunen, Lauri & Stanley Peters 1977. Requiem for presupposition. In: K. Whistler et al. (eds.). *Proceedings of the Third Annual Meeting of the Berkeley Linguistics Society (= BLS)*. Berkeley, CA: Berkeley Linguistics Society, 363–371.
Karttunen, Lauri & Stanley Peters 1979. Conventional implicatures in Montague grammar. In: C.-K. Oh & D. Dineen (eds.). *Syntax and Semantics 11: Presupposition*. New York: Academic Press, 1–56.
Kay, Paul 1992. The inheritance of presuppositions. *Linguistics & Philosophy* 15, 333–381.
Kiparsky, Paul & Carol Kiparsky 1970. Fact. In: M. Bierwisch & K. Heidolph (eds.). *Progress in Linguistics*. The Hague: Mouton, 143–173.
Kleene, Stephen 1952. *Introduction to Metamathematics*. Amsterdam: North-Holland.
Krahmer, Emiel 1994. Partiality and dynamics. In: P. Dekker & M. Stokhof (eds.). *Proceedings of the Ninth Amsterdam Colloquium, volume 2*. Amsterdam: ILLC, 391–410.
Krahmer, Emiel 1998. *Presupposition and Anaphora*. Stanford, CA: CSLI Publications.
Kripke, Saul 2009. Presupposition and anaphora. Remarks on the formulation of the projection problem. *Linguistic Inquiry* 40, 367–386.
Langendoen, D. Terence & Harris Savin 1971. The projection problem for presuppositions. In: Ch. Fillmore & D. T. Langendoen (eds.). *Studies in Linguistic Semantics*. New York: Holt, Reinhardt & Winston, 373–388.
Lewis, David 1979. Scorekeeping in a language game. *Journal of Philosophical Logic* 8, 339–359.
Marcu, Daniel 1994. *A Formalisation and an Algorithm for Computing Pragmatic Inferences and Detecting Infelicities*. Ph.D. dissertation. University of Toronto, Toronto, ON.
Mercer, Robert 1987. *A Default Logic Approach to the Derivation of Natural Language Presuppositions*. Ph.D. dissertation. University of British Columbia, Vancouver, BC.
Mercer, Robert 1992. Default logic. Towards a common logical semantics for presupposition and entailment. *Journal of Semantics* 9, 223–250.
Morgan, Jerry 1969. On the treatment of presupposition in transformational grammar. In: R. Binnick et al. (eds.). *Papers from the Fifth Regional Meeting of the Chicago Linguistic Society (= CLS)*. Chicago, IL: Chicago Linguistic Society, 167–177.
Peters, Stanley 1979. A truth-conditional formulation of Karttunens account of presupposition. *Synthese* 40, 301–316.
Reinhart, Tanya 1982. Pragmatics and linguistics. An analysis of sentence topics. *Philosophica* 27, 53–94.
van Rooij, Robert 2007. Strengthening conditional presuppositions. *Journal of Semantics* 24, 289–304.
Rothschild, Daniel 2008. Presupposition projection and logical equivalence. *Philosophical Perspectives* 22, 473–497.
Russell, Bertrand 1905. On denoting. *Mind* 14, 479–493.
van der Sandt, Rob 1982. *Kontekst en Presuppositie. Een Studie van het Projektieprobleem en de Presuppositionele Eigenschappen van de Logische Konnektieven*. Ph.D. dissertation. Radboud University Nijmegen.

van der Sandt, Rob 1988. *Context and Presupposition*. London: Croom Helm.
van der Sandt, Rob 1989. Presupposition and discourse structure. In: R. Bartsch, J. van Benthem & P. van Emde Boas (eds.). *Semantics and Contextual Expression*. Dordrecht: Foris, 287–294.
van der Sandt, Rob 1992. Presupposition projection as anaphora resolution. *Journal of Semantics* 9, 333–377.
Schlenker, Philippe 2008. Be articulate. A pragmatic theory of presupposition. *Theoretical Linguistics* 34, 157–212.
Schlenker, Philippe 2009. Local contexts. *Semantics and Pragmatics* 2, 1–78.
Simons, Mandy 2001. On the conversational basis of some presuppositions. In: R. Hastings, B. Jackson & Z. Zvolensky (eds.). *Proceedings of Semantics and Linguistic Theory (= SALT) XI*. Ithaca, NY: Cornell University, 431–448.
Simons, Mandy 2003. Presupposition and accommodation. Understanding the Stalnakerian picture. *Philosophical Studies* 112, 251–278.
Simons, Mandy 2004. Presupposition and relevance. In: Z. Szabó (ed.). *Semantics vs. Pragmatics*. Oxford: Oxford University Press, 329–355.
Singh, Raj 2007. Formal alternatives as a solution to the proviso problem. In: M. Gibson & T. Friedman (eds.). *Proceedings of Semantics and Linguistic Theory (= SALT) XVII*. Ithaca, NY: Cornell University, 264–281.
Soames, Scott 1979. A projection problem for speaker presuppositions. *Linguistic Inquiry* 10, 623–666.
Soames, Scott 1982. How presuppositions are inherited. A solution to the projection problem. *Linguistic Inquiry* 13, 483–545.
Soames, Scott 1989. Presupposition. In: D. Gabbay & F. Guenthner (eds.). *Handbook of Philosophical Logic, volume 4*. Dordrecht: Reidel, 553–616.
Stalnaker, Robert 1972. Pragmatics. In: D. Davidson & G. Harman (eds.). *Semantics of Natural Language*. Dordrecht: Reidel, 389–408.
Stalnaker, Robert 1973. Presuppositions. *The Journal of Philosophical Logic* 2, 447–457.
Stalnaker, Robert 1974. Pragmatic presuppositions. In: M. Munitz & P. Unger (eds.). *Semantics and Philosophy*. New York: New York University Press, 197–214.
Stalnaker, Robert 1998. On the representation of context. *Journal of Logic, Language and Information* 7, 3–19.
Strawson, Peter F. 1950. On referring. *Mind* 59, 320–344.
Strawson, Peter F. 1952. *Introduction to Logical Theory*. London: Methuen.
Strawson, Peter F. 1964. Identifying reference and truth-values. *Theoria* 30, 96–118. Reprinted in: P. Strawson. *Logico-Linguistic Papers*. London: Methuen, 1974, 75–95.
Thomason, Richmond 1972. A semantic theory of sortal incorrectness. *Journal of Philosophical Logic* 1, 209–258.
Wilson, Deirdre 1975. *Presupposition and Non-Truth-Conditional Semantics*. New York: Academic Press.
Zeevat, Henk 1992. Presupposition and accommodation in update semantics. *Journal of Semantics* 9, 379–412.

Mandy Simons

15 Implicature

1 Introduction —— 529
2 The Gricean conception of conversational implicature —— 530
3 A case study: scalar implicature —— 541
4 Embedded implicature —— 549
5 Alternate models and competing conceptions —— 551
6 Formal and experimental approaches —— 556
7 References —— 559

Abstract: This article reviews in detail Grice's conception of conversational implicature, then surveys the major literature on scalar implicature from early work to the present. Embedded implicature is illustrated, and it is explained why this phenomenon poses a challenge to the Gricean view. Some alternate views of conversational implicature are then presented. The article concludes with a brief look at formal appraches to the study of implicature.

1 Introduction

Conversational implicature is the phenomenon whereby a speaker says one thing and thereby conveys (typically, in addition) something else. For example, in (1) below, Harold *says* that Sally should bring her umbrella, but further conveys that (he believes that) it is likely to rain. This is a standard case of the phenomenon under examination.

(1) Sally: What's the weather going to be like today?
    Harold: You should bring your umbrella.

Conversational implicature was identified and named by the philosopher Paul Grice in his paper "Logic and Conversation", originally presented at Harvard in 1969. Much of today's linguistic pragmatics has its origins in the insights of that paper, and concerns itself in some fashion with some aspect of conversational implicature.

Mandy Simons, Pittsburgh, PA, USA

https://doi.org/10.1515/9783110589849-015

2 The Gricean conception of conversational implicature

2.1 Implicature as part of what is meant

For Grice, what a speaker *means* by an utterance is the total content which she thereby intends to communicate (see also article 2 [Semantics: Foundations, History and Methods] (Jacob) *Meaning, intentionality and communication* and article 5 [Semantics: Foundations, History and Methods] (Green) *Meaning in language use*). One component of what is *meant* is what is *said*: roughly, the truth conditional content linguistically encoded in the utterance. The remainder – what is meant but not said – is what Grice calls *implicature*. Implicature itself subdivides into two major categories: conventional and conversational. Conventional implicature is content which is conventionally encoded but non-truth-conditional (cf. article 17 [this volume] (Potts) *Conventional implicature and expressive content*). In this article, we will be concerned with *conversational implicature*: implicatures that arise by virtue of general principles governing linguistic behavior. In "Logic and Conversation" (henceforward, *L&C*; Grice 1975) and "Further Notes on Logic and Conversation" (hence, *FN*; Grice 1978), Grice introduces the phenomenon of conversational implicature and lays out the principles which allow speakers to systematically mean more than they say.

2.2 The theory of conversational implicature

To account for the phenomenon of conversational implicature, Grice proposes that there are certain norms of conversational behavior, norms which are mutually known and typically adhered to by conversational participants. These norms prevent conversation from consisting of "a succession of disconnected remarks," and, at each stage in a conversation, render certain possible conversational contributions "unsuitable" (*L&C*; Grice 1975: 26). Grice summarizes the effect of these norms as a single overarching principle, which he calls the Cooperative Principle:

> Make your conversational contribution such as is required, at the stage at which it occurs, by the accepted purpose or direction of the talk exchange in which you are engaged.

This principle has little force without further clarification of what is in fact required of conversational contributions. Grice specifies this further in what he calls *Maxims of Conversation*, formulated as rules governing allowable conversational moves. Grice organizes these maxims into four categories: Quality, Quantity, Relation and Manner. In current usage, these terms are used to designate the specific maxims Grice proposed. Grice himself, however, gives these specifically as *categories* of maxims "under one or another of which will fall certain more specific maxims and submaxims" (Grice 1975: 26), apparently envisaging the possibility of substantial lists of conversational rules. The maxims which Grice proposes are listed below, in some cases slightly reformulated from the original:

Conversational Maxims

Quality

Supermaxim: Try to make your contribution one that is true

1. Do not say what you believe to be false.
2. Do not say that for which you lack adequate evidence.

Quantity

1. Make your contribution as informative as is required (for the current purposes of the exchange).
2. Do not make your contribution more informative than is required.

Relation

Be relevant

Manner

Supermaxim: Be perspicuous
1. Avoid obscurity of expression
2. Avoid ambiguity
3. Be brief (avoid unnecessary prolixity)
4. Be orderly

The view that conversation is a norm-governed activity provides the basis for Grice's account of how conversational implicatures arise. The general structure of the account is this: There is a standing presumption that speakers produce utterances which are in accord with the Cooperative Principle and its maxims. Interpreters will assign to an utterance an interpretation in accord with this presumption. In some cases, this will require the interpreter to attribute to the speaker the intention to communicate something more than, or different from, what she has actually said. In identifying what the speaker intends, the interpreter will rely on three things: first, her observation about what the speaker *said* (i.e., the truth conditional content expressed) and the form in which it was expressed; second, the presumption of cooperativity; and third, any world knowledge that might be relevant. Speakers can anticipate this behavior of interpreters, and thus can predict that particular utterances will be understood as conveying something more than or different from what is literally said. The fact that it is common knowledge that the CP is in effect thus allows speakers to implicate, and interpreters to identify implicatures.

Grice characterizes conversational implicature in the following way (slightly simplified from the original):

> A man who, by saying ... that p has implicated that q, may be said to have conversationally implicated that q, provided that:
>
> 1. he is to be presumed to be observing the conversational maxims or at least the Cooperative Principle
> 2. the supposition that he thinks that q is required in order to make his saying p (or doing so in *those* terms) consistent with this presumption and
> 3. the speaker thinks (and would expect the hearer to think that the speaker thinks) that it is within the competence of the hearer to work out, or grasp intuitively, that the supposition mentioned in 2. is required.

Grice's presumption here is that such suppositions of the speaker, when recognized by the hearer, will be understood to be meant.

Clause 2 of this definition is quite problematic, as it makes it a condition on implicature that the implicature (the "required supposition") be uniquely adequate to maintain the presumption of cooperativity. This is typically too strong: in almost any case of conversational implicature, there are multiple candidate suppositions, any of which might render the utterance cooperative. This point is noted by Grice (see the final paragraph of *L&C;* Grice 1975). Davis (1998) considers this (along with some other difficulties) to completely undermine the Gricean construction. The issue is worth further exploration, but I will not attempt it here.

Let's now make things clearer by examining some specific cases. Consider again the sample discourse from above, repeated here as (2):

(2) Sally: What's the weather going to be like today?
    Harold: You should bring your umbrella.

Observation: Sally is likely to conclude that Harold means to inform her that it is likely to rain. How so? First, Sally presumes that Harold is speaking in accord with the CP. Among other things, this means that she presumes that he intends his answer to be relevant. Now, strictly speaking, Harold's instruction is not an answer to the question Sally has asked: it says nothing about the weather. But *because* of her presumption, Sally presumes that what Harold says *is* relevant in some way to her question. It immediately occurs to her that one uses an umbrella when it rains; and that Harold is likely to tell her to bring an umbrella if he believes that it is going to rain. If she attributes this belief to Harold, and assumes that he intends, via his utterance, to communicate this belief to her, then she has successfully interpreted his utterance in a way which renders his behavior consistent with her presumption of his cooperativity. As Harold can, moreover, plausibly assume that Sally will reason in this way, he implicates that (he believes that) it is going to rain.

Note that this case illustrates the failure of the uniqueness condition on implicature (Clause 2 of the definition above). Suppose it is common knowledge between Sally and Harold that Sally uses her umbrella as a sunshade when the weather is hot. Then Sally might just as well have attributed to Harold the belief that it would be hot and sunny, and take him to intend to communicate this. So there are (at least) two candidate suppositions that would render Harold's utterance cooperative. On the other hand, contextual factors (such as the interlocutors' common knowledge of recent weather) might well render one of these suppositions far more likely or reasonable. This line of thought might offer a resolution of the difficulty.

The example in (2) involves a Relevance implicature. Implicatures can be generated via any of the maxims (or combinations thereof). Here is one which relies on the first Maxim of Quantity:

(3) Harold: Which of Bobby's teachers did you talk to at the picnic?
    Sally: Mrs. Smith and Mr. Jones.

Here, Sally implicates that Mrs. Smith and Mr. Jones were the *only* teachers that she talked to. This is by virtue of the first Maxim of Quantity. Given the assumption that Sally is abiding by this maxim, Harold must assume that she will provide all the information relevant to his question. If (she believed that) she had talked to additional teachers, then it would constitute a violation of the maxim to fail to mention them. So, to maintain the premise that Sally *is* abiding by the maxim, Harold must assume that Sally (believes that she) spoke to no other teachers. As Sally, moreover, can assume that Harold will recognize the required assumption, she implicates that she talked to no other of Bobby's teachers.

2.2.1 Characteristics of conversational implicature

In the final pages of *L&C* (Grice 1975: 57–58), Grice identifies certain characteristic features of conversational implicatures. The central ones are these:

1. Calculability: if some element of content is a conversational implicature, then it should be possible to provide an account of how it is calculated on the basis of what is said plus the maxims.
2. Nondetachability: On Grice's view, implicatures other than Manner implicatures are calculated on the basis of what is said – roughly, on the basis of the truth conditional content expressed. Hence, other ways of expressing the same truth conditional content in the given context should give rise to the same implicature. That is, implicatures are *nondetachable* from a particular truth conditional content.
3. Cancelability (of generalized conversational implicature): Because conversational implicatures are not part of the encoded or conventional content of any linguistic item, and because their presence is dependent on (more or less) specific assumptions, including the assumption of the cooperativity of the speaker, then it should be possible for an expected implicature to be contextually canceled.

These features, particularly cancelability, are sometimes taken as diagnostics of conversational implicature. However, Grice did not intend them this way, as he clarifies in *FN* (Grice 1978: 43). Sadock (1976) provides thorough arguments showing that none of these features, either separately or together, can serve as robust diagnostics of conversational implicature, as none are either necessary or sufficient conditions. The arguments are too lengthy to rehearse here in detail, but a couple of points are worth mentioning. With respect to calculability, Grice and Sadock agree that it is not sufficient to establish the presence of a conversational implicature, because what starts life as a conversational implicature may become conventionalized. Nondetachability is neither a necessary nor a sufficient condition. It is not necessary, because it is not a feature of Manner implicatures. It is not sufficient for the identification of conversational implicatures, because it is also a feature of entailments.

Sadock gives a second argument against the necessity of nondetachability, observing that there are cases of truth conditionally equivalent sentences whose utterance does not give rise to the same implicatures. Consider sentences (4) and (5) as answers to the question: *Did you eat any of the cake?*

(4) I ate some of the cake.
(5) I ate some and possibly all of the cake.

Obviously, (4) implicates that the speaker did not eat all of the cake, while (5) just as obviously does not so implicate. Yet the two sentences (by assumption) have the same truth conditional content i.e., in both cases the same thing is said. Hence, the implicature is *not* nondetachable: utterances of truth conditionally identical S and S' do not both produce the implicature.

One possible response to this argument is simply that the definition of non-detachability requires refinement: it should exclude candidates which are truth conditionally equivalent to the original but include an explicit denial of the potential implicature. Other reformulations of (4) do preserve the implicature. Consider *I ate part of the cake* or *I ate a bit of the cake*.

A second response is that the input to conversational implicature calculation is not simple truth conditional content, but some more structured entity. Arguments for this position are given by Gazdar (1979) and Atlas & Levinson (1981).

Finally, we turn to cancelability. First, note that the type of cancelability Grice has in mind involves the speaker being explicit that she is opting out of the observation of the CP, or the context being one which makes clear that the speaker is opting out. In *FN* (Grice 1978), he gives the example of a speaker who is giving a clue in the course of a treasure hunt saying:

(6) The prize is either in the garden or the attic, but I'm not telling you which.

In this context, the typical implication from a disjunction, that the speaker does not know which disjunct is true, is suppressed.

Sadock discusses a different type of cancelation, where the speaker explicitly denies the usual implicature, as in:

(7) Some philosophers are crabby, and I don't mean to say that some aren't.

In the current literature, when people discuss implicature cancelation, the latter is usually what is intended.

Grice seems to consider that cancelability can only apply to *generalized* conversational implicatures. What he seems to have in mind is that we make observations about what is normally or typically implicated by the use of a particular expression, and compare it with what (if anything) is actually implicated by the use of that expression in some specific situation. We clearly cannot make the same sort of comparison in the case of *particularized* implicatures. For example, no-one would claim that the sentence *I have to cook dinner* normally or typically implicates *I am not going to read you a story*, but certainly an utterance of that sentence might well so implicate if I say it in response to my six year old's request in easily imaginable circumstances. Nonetheless, we sometimes find cases like these:

(8) C: Mommy, will you read to me?
M: I have to cook dinner. So if I read to you now, will you play by yourself for a while afterwards, so I can get dinner done?

The first sentence, if uttered alone in this context, might well be used to implicate "no". The entire string, however, makes clear that this is intended to launch a "yes, but . . ." response. So, there is some temptation to say that the second sentence cancels the implicature arising from the first. This is similar to a second way of understanding implicature cancelation in the generalized case. In cases like (7), one might say that the use of the first clause *does* generate the implicature, but that the implicature is canceled – that is, the initial clause is reinterpreted – in light of the content of the second.

Which way we should see it depends in part on our assumptions about when implicature calculation takes place. It is clear that Grice assumes throughout most of his writing on the subject that the input is at least a complete proposition. The examples used typically involve a single sentence generating an implicature. But it is perfectly consistent with the Gricean model that the semantic content of a multi-sentence conversational contribution – presumed to be several propositions – could be the basis for a process of implicature calculation. If implicatures are calculated in this way, example (7) could only be said to involve cancelation in the sense that an implicature that typically arises fails to do so; and in the case of (8) it would not be sensible to talk about cancelation at all.

Cancelability remains an important diagnostic for distinguishing between conventional content and inferred content (although see again Sadock's arguments concerning ambiguity). However, it is important, in making use of this notion, to be clear just what we mean by it in any particular case.

2.2.2 Subtypes of conversational implicature

The Quantity implicature in (3) above straightforwardly fits Grice's own characterization of conversational implicature. But the Relevance implicature in (2) fits it rather awkwardly. Although I formulated it this way above, it is somewhat odd to say that Sally recognizes that Harold *presumes* that it will rain, and therefore takes him to intend to communicate this. It seems more natural to say that Sally recognizes that Harold *presumes* that she would want to have her umbrella with her if it rains, and thus infers, from his recommendation that she bring her umbrella, his intention to communicate that it might rain. Let's call the identified presumption a *background implicature*, and the communicated proposition, that it might rain, a *foreground implicature*.

Sally's recognition of the background implicature seems to make use of standard Gricean reasoning: searching for a way to interpret Harold's utterance as cooperative, she looks for a presumption he might be making which would render what he said relevant to her question. However, the background implicature is nonetheless not a true implicature in Grice's sense; for recall that for Grice, implicature is a subcategory of speaker meaning; and what a speaker means is what he intends to communicate. In the kind of conversation we are imagining between Sally and Harold, it would not typically be Harold's intention to communicate that Sally likes to have her umbrella with her when it rains.

Here we reach the first of many choice points, where we will have to decide: is our goal to follow Grice's conception as closely as possible? Or to use his proposal as a jumping off point from which to develop an empirically adequate and explanatory theory of pragmatics? For linguists, the answer is typically the latter. As a first departure from Grice, we might propose using the term *conversational implicature* for any inference the speaker intends the addressee to make on the basis of the assumption that he is being cooperative. The distinction made above between background and foreground implicature can be further explicated by distinguishing between implicatures which are not meant (in Grice's sense) and those that are. (For further discussion, and identification of background implicatures with presuppositions, see Simons 2004, 2008.)

One additional Gricean distinction remains to be made: that between *particularized* and *generalized* conversational implicature. Example (2) involves a particularized implicature. Here the implicature relies to a high degree on the conversational context and on specific background assumptions attributed to the interlocutors. Changes in the context or in these assumptions easily change the implicature or eliminate it. For example, if Harold had uttered the same sentence in a conversation in which the interlocutors we trying to figure out how to knock a ball out of a tree, it would give rise to no implicatures at all about the weather. There is thus "no room for the idea" (to use Grice's phrase) that the implicature is associated with this particular form of words or with the expression of this content.

In contrast, in the case of Generalized Conversational Implicatures, exactly this claim is warranted. GCIs are implicatures which normally arise when a particular form of words is used. The only example Grice gives of a GCI in *L&C* (Grice 1975) involves the interpretation of indefinite NPs, which turns out to be a rather complex case. In *FN* (Grice 1978), he discusses the implicature associated with the use of *or* that the speaker does not know which disjunct is true. Grice notes that "noncontroversial examples [of GCIs] are perhaps hard to find, since it is all too easy to treat a generalized conversational implicature as if it were a conventional implicature" (*L&C*; Grice 1975: 37).

In the post-Gricean literature, an element of content is identified as a GCI if, on the one hand, it can be explained as a Gricean implicature and is cancelable; but, on the other hand, its occurrence is not dependent on irregular features of context, but only on the basic assumption that the speaker is speaking in accord with the CP. Some authors deny that there is any theoretically significant distinction between generalized and particularized implicatures (e.g., Hirschberg 1991); while others hold the opposite view (see Levinson 2000, discussed below in section 5).

Presuppositions are also considered by some authors to be a subtype of implicature, although this view is far from widespread. The bulk of linguistic work on presupposition since the 1970's has focused on the projection problem: assuming the association of presuppositions with particular atomic sentences, how do we account properly for the presuppositions of complex sentences in which the atomic sentences are embedded? The possible relationship between implicature and presupposition becomes salient when we focus on a different question, namely, how do presuppositions arise in the first place? Many authors have suggested that some or all presuppositions arise via the workings of Gricean conversational principles: see among others Stalnaker (1974), Kempson (1975), Wilson (1975), Boër & Lycan (1976), Atlas (1977, 1978, 2005), Atlas & Levinson (1981), Grice (1981), Simons (2001, 2004). The idea underlying all of these proposals is formulated succinctly by Stalnaker: "one can explain many presupposition constraints in terms of general conversational rules without building anything about presuppositions into the meanings of particular words or constructions" (1974: 212). For a discussion of this issue in the broader context of the literature on presupposition, see article 14 [this volume] (Beaver & Geurts) *Presupposition*.

2.2.3 Rational underpinnings of the Maxims

After laying out the CP and the maxims in *L&C*, Grice (1975: 28) raises "a fundamental question about the Cooperative Principle and its attendant maxims, namely, what the basis is for the assumption which we seem to make, that talkers will in general . . . proceed in the manner that these principles prescribe." He goes on to say: "I would like to be able to think of the standard type of conversational practice . . . as something that it is *reasonable* for us to follow," and sets out the following as a set of claims to be explored:

1. There are certain goals that are fundamental to conversational exchange.
2. These goals can be accomplished only in conversational exchanges conducted in accordance with the CP.
3. Therefore rational speakers will behave in accord with the CP.

Claim 2 in this list seems unnecessarily strong. We might do better with 2':

2'. These goals can be best accomplished (i.e., most efficiently, with least effort of both speaker and hearer) in conversational exchanges conducted in accordance with the CP.

As part of the effort to establish these rationalist foundations for the account, Grice demonstrates that each of the Maxims has an analog in the non-linguistic domain, in other types of goal-oriented interactions. The effort, however, does not go much beyond this, and Grice leaves as an open question whether his conversational principles can be independently motivated. But this proposal sets a particular foundational project for pragmatics, namely, to determine the rational underpinnings of pragmatic principles.

Perhaps because of the label *Cooperative Principle*, it is standard to suppose that observation of the CP and maxims is tied to a certain amount of explicit cooperativity between the discourse participants. What is clearly not required is alignment of practical goals: Grice was clear that the CP must be construed as in effect even in cases like quarreling. The degree of cooperativity envisioned by Grice seems to go no further than a mutual desire on the part of the interlocutors to use language in a way that facilitates communication between them.

Nonetheless, there are some difficult cases: what account is to be given of apparent implicatures in cases where the misaligned goals of interlocutors should lead them to expect their discourse partners to be, for example, intentionally underinformative? (For discussion within a game theoretic framework, see Franke, de Jager & van Rooij 2009.) Both empirical and theoretical questions concerning such issues remain open.

2.3 A friendly amendment: Horn's Q- and R-principles

As noted, Grice seems to envision a long, open ended list of specific submaxims falling under each of his four categories. Horn (1984) develops Grice's view in a different direction. Setting aside Quality as having a special status, Horn proposes a reduction of the remaining Gricean principles to just two: Q ("to evoke Quantity") and R (Relation).

Horn's Principles

(Q) Make your contribution sufficient; say as much as you can (given R).
(R) Make your contribution necessary; say no more than you must (given Q).

The Q-principle corresponds to the first maxim of Quantity. R is intended to encompass Relation, the second maxim of Quantity, and Manner.

The precise wording of the principles is perhaps less important than the underlying idea, which Horn attributes to Zipf (1949) and Martinet (1962). The idea is that there are two basic and conflicting forces at work in the linguistic domain, representing the interests of the speaker and the distinct interests of the hearer. It is in the interest of the hearer/interpreter to receive maximum (relevant) information and to receive it in the clearest formulation available. The Q-principle encapsulates this as a hearer-oriented requirement imposed on the speaker. However, it is in the interest of the speaker to minimise the effort involved in producing her message; this interest underlies the R principle.

Horn emphasizes two points: first, that his two principles together do the work of Grice's categories of Quantity, Relation and Manner; second, that the two principles are in conflict. This latter observation provides the basis of an explanation of certain cases of miscommunication, where different parties may be exploiting or emphasizing different principles. But it also raises an empirical question, namely, in cases of successful communication involving implicature, on what grounds do speakers/hearers determine which principle takes precedence? Consider for example the following cases discussed by Horn:

(9) I broke a finger last week.
(10) I slept on a boat last night.

At issue is the natural interpretation of the indefinite. We are inclined to understand the speaker of (9) as saying that she broke one of her own fingers. This would be, in Horn's view, an application of the R-principle: what is meant is something informationally richer than what is said; the speaker has provided the minimum information necessary to convey the total intended message. In contrast, it is natural to understand the speaker of (10) as saying that she slept on a boat not belonging to her. This, Horn takes to involve an application of the Q-principle: as the speaker has provided no more specific information about the boat, we take it that no additional information is available or relevant. (It is not entirely transparent how the principles are to apply in each case to produce the specific interpretations. What is important here is that interpretation goes in two different directions with two superficially similar sentences.)

Horn's brief discussion suggests that there may be many different, and differently weighted, considerations involved in resolving a maxim-clash. The considerations may be specific to the construction involved, and hence it is likely that there is no global answer to the question of which maxim or principle applies; the question may well require a case-by-case answer.

The problem of clashes between maxims had received prior attention in Atlas & Levinson (1981). They offer a Principle of Informativeness to account for example (9) and a host of additional cases where the speaker is understood as conveying something more specific than what is literally said, noting that in many cases, a conflict exists between this principle and Grice's maxim of Quantity.

3 A case study: scalar implicature

So far, we have reviewed Grice's foundational proposal and some proposed extensions. In this section, we look in detail at one particular linguistic phenomenon – scalar implicature – which has commonly been analyzed in Gricean terms.

3.1 The basic phenomenon and the Gricean account

The following are standard examples of scalar implicature. In each case, the b. sentence represents an implication that would normally arise if the a. sentence was uttered in ordinary discourse:

(11) a. Some of my friends are Jewish. ⤳
     b. It is not the case that more than some of my friends are Jewish.

(12) a. Their new house is large. ⤳
     b. Their new house is not enormous.

(13) a. It's possible that I'll get funding for next year. ⤳
     b. It's not probable that I'll get funding for next year.

That the content of the b. sentences is an implication and not an entailment can be demonstrated by the possibility of cancelation, as in:

(14) Some of my friends are Jewish; in fact, most of them are.
(15) Their new house is large; indeed, it's enormous.

We will assume for now without argument that these implications are implicatures.
    The implicatures in question are clearly generalized, not particularized. This is evident, first, from the fact that we can identify them in the absence of any particular information about a context of utterance. Second, the implicatures seem to arise by virtue of the presence of particular expressions, or at least, expressions

with particular content: *some, large* and *possible*. It does indeed seem that it is the content that is relevant and not the particular lexical item: the same implicatures would arise from utterances of the sentences below:

(16) A few of my friends are Jewish.
(17) Their new house is big.
(18) I might get funding for next year.

These implicatures are amenable to what seems a very straightforward Gricean explanation, based on the first Maxim of Quantity. Recall that this Maxim says:

> Make your contribution as informative as is required (for the current purposes of the exchange).

It is crucial for the analysis we are about to give to remember that Quantity is circumscribed not only by Relevance but also by Quality: while you should give all the information that is required, you should only give reliable information.

Now, consider a speaker who utters (11a). Assume that it is relevant to the current conversation roughly what proportion of her friends are Jewish. Then Quantity1 enjoins her to be fully informative with respect to this question.

One natural way (although by no means the only way) to quantify informativity is in terms of entailment: If p asymmetrically entails q, then p is more informative than q. Now consider again the speaker who utters (11a), and assume that she is being fully informative in the sense just described. With respect to the (presumed) question at hand, her utterance rules out the possibility that none of her friends are Jewish, but leaves open the possibility that some, many, most or all of her friends are. She could have ruled out these possibilities by making a more informative statement, e.g., by saying:

(19) Many/most/all of my friends are Jewish.

But we presume that the speaker has made the most informative utterance she can given the requirements of Quality. So this leads to the conclusion that she is not in a position to utter any of the variants of (19). But she is presumably in a position to know (more or less) what proportion of her friends are Jewish. Therefore, we conclude further that she is not in a position to make the stronger assertions because they are not true. That is, we conclude that (11a) was the most informative true sentence the speaker could utter relative to the question at hand, and thus conclude from the utterance that some of the speaker's friends are Jewish, and no more than some are.

Parallel derivations can be given for the implicatures in (12) and (13). In each case, the implicature is the negation of a sentence (proposition) which entails (i.e., is informationally stronger than) the actual utterance. The negated proposition in each case represents a stronger alternative which (in some sense) the speaker "could have said" instead of what she actually said.

3.2 The scalar solution

In the account just sketched, I carefully avoided any reference to the presence of particular expressions. The account makes reference only to propositions ordered by entailment. But it is not really feasible to maintain so pure an account. Reference to expressions seems necessary to identify the alternative "possible utterances" relative to which these implicatures are calculated. For there are of course all sorts of other, stronger utterances which the speaker could have made whose content is potentially relevant to the same conversation. The speaker of (11a) could have said:

(20) Some of my friends are Jewish and they eat kosher.
(21) Some of my friends are Jewish and some of my friends are Muslim.

or any of an infinity of other possibilities.

In fact, there are imaginable conversational contexts in which utterance of (11a) *would* implicate the negation of some such other stronger sentence. For example, suppose that (11a) were uttered in response to the question:

(22) Do you know anyone who isn't a Christian?

In this context, utterance of (11a) would plausibly give rise to the implicature that the speaker has no friends who are neither Christian nor Jewish e.g., has no Muslim friends; and this could be explained by reference to the speaker's failure to utter this particular stronger alternative to her actual utterance. So it is not that random stronger alternatives do not give rise to implicatures based on the same kind of reasoning. Rather, they only do so when licensed by special features of the context, that is, they are particularized implicatures. What this tells us is that to fully explain the cases in (11)–(13), we need to say what allows for a context *independent* judgment about the relevant alternatives.

The solution offered by Horn (1972), now the standard account, invokes the notion of a scalar term. These are terms which cluster with other semantically related terms on a scale of informational strength, with relative informativity being measured, as above, in terms of entailment relations. The standard formalization of such Horn scales comes from Gazdar (1979): If Q is a Horn scale of form $<\alpha_1, \alpha_2, \alpha_3 \ldots \alpha_n>$, then each element in Q is logically weaker than any element to its left in the following sense: given a pair of sentences S, S' identical except that where S contains α_i, S' contains α_j and i>j, then, if α_i/α_j are not embedded under any operator, S entails S'. Let's call the relation between elements in such a scale *asymmetric lexical entailment*.

The basic Horn/Gazdar account of generalized scalar implicatures then runs like this: Utterance of a sentence containing an element in a Horn scale renders salient the set of stronger scalar alternatives to the original utterance (i.e., for the unembedded case, sentences identical to the original but with the scalar term replaced by a scale-mate to its left in the scale), regardless of the particular conversational context. A Quantity-based inference generates scalar implicatures based on these alternatives.

We'll see shortly that entailment-based scales do not give us a complete account of scalar implicature. But first, let's review two questions that arise even given this fairly simple model. First question: how many implicatures do scales generate? For example, given the scale <*all, most, many, some*>, does utterance of sentence S containing *some* implicate the negations of all of the scalar alternatives to S based on this scale? Does it implicate just the negation of the next strongest, which in turn entails the negations of the remainder? Does it implicate just the strongest? Hirschberg (1985) argues that the answer may depend on the context. Consider for example the pair of discourses below:

(23) a. A: Are all mushrooms poisonous?
B: Some are.

b. A: Are many mushrooms poisonous?
B: Some are.

Each question makes salient a different sub-part of the relevant scale, changing the implicature generated.

A second question raised by scalar implicatures concerns what Hirschberg calls their epistemic force. (In fact this question arises for all cases of Quantity implicature, but has been discussed in particular in the context of scalar implicatures.). This issue is discussed in almost all of the early research on scalar implicature (Horn 1972, 1989; Gazdar 1979; Hirschberg 1985; see also Soames 1982: 520–521 Levinson 1983: 135; Groenendijk & Stokhof 1984; Sauerland 2004).

Soames, Horn (1989) and Sauerland each adopt more or less the following position: Consider again example (11a) above. The Maxim of Quantity, bounded as it is by the maxim of Quality, supports only the weak inference that the speaker *does not know* any stronger assertion to be true. However, in some cases, like that of (11a), we can assume that the speaker has complete knowledge of the situation she is describing. In such cases, the weak inference supported by the Maxim can be strengthened: the interpreter can infer that the speaker *knows* the stronger alternative *not* to be true. In our example, the interpreter can infer that the speaker knows that it is not the case that many, most or all of her friends are Jewish. Then, by the factivity of knowledge, it is inferrable that it is not the case that many, most or all of her friends are Jewish.

This Gricean prediction does not, though, quite match up to intuition. Weak scalar implicatures are rather unusual, typically arising only when the speaker has explicitly acknowledged the incompleteness of her information, as in:

(24) I've only looked at a few pages of the manuscript, but I can already tell you that some of the pages require corrections.

It is much more typical for scalar implicatures to be epistemically unmodified, even in circumstances where, on reflection, the interpreter might have less than complete confidence in the speaker's authority or evidence. (For more detailed discussion of this topic, see Sauerland 2004 and van Rooij & Schultz 2004.)

Now we come to two questions much more central to the notion of scale. The first: what precisely are the elements of the scale? The discussion so far suggests that scales consist of lexical items. But Gazdar (1979) proposes that the elements should be semantic values or expressions in a formal language used to represent the semantic content of sentences. Gazdar argues for this on the basis of simplicity. For one thing, a language might contain multiple lexical items with similar content (e.g., *large* and *big*) which occupy the same location in a scale (e.g., relative to *huge*).

The second core question raised by scales themselves is this: Where do scales come from? Or where do they reside? The ideal answer (from a Gricean perspective) would be that scales are merely a formal construct capturing relations between lexical items (or semantic values of items) which are fully reconstructible just on the basis of lexical content. That is, we do not need to stipulate that, for example, <*all, most, many, some*> is a scale, and a language user does not need to learn that it is. Any speaker who knows the meanings of these terms will recognize that they form a scale by virtue of the lexical entailment relations which hold between them.

But additional observations have led many to conclude that such an answer is not available. The additional observation is that not every entailment scale is a

Horn scale i.e., a scale supporting scalar implicature. Gazdar (1979) gives a simple example to illustrate this: *regret* asymmetrically entails *know*, but use of *know* does not implicate *not regret*. The example shows that asymmetric lexical entailment is not a sufficient property to qualify a pair of words (or their meanings) as Horn scale-mates.

There is a second type of case where asymmetric lexical entailment is insufficient for Horn scale membership, giving rise to what has recently been dubbed the Symmetry Problem. Consider the pair: *some but not all, some*. The first asymmetrically entails the latter; but clearly, an utterance of (25a) does not implicate (25b):

(25) a. I ate some of the cookies.
 b. It is not the case that I ate some but not all of the cookies

for the conjunction of a. and b. is equivalent to "I ate all of the cookies" – and this is the negation of what (25a) is actually observed to implicate!

Horn (1972) addresses problem cases of this sort by positing a requirement that elements in scales have the same degree of lexicalization. As English contains no single word which means "some but not all," the semantic content of this expression cannot be a scale-mate with the content of *some*. This constraint can perhaps be given a Gricean motivation in terms of the Maxim of Manner, the idea being that the alternatives to be considered should only be those which do not increase the complexity of the utterance. (See also Matsumoto 1995; Katzir 2007.)

In light of these difficulties, many researchers adopt the position that Horn scales are linguistically given. So, although we can make certain general observations about the relations which hold between members of a Horn scale, we cannot predict merely on the basis of the linguistic properties of an item whether or not it will occur on a scale, or what its scale-mates will be. It is simply a contingent fact about a language what scales it contains, and what the members of those scales are.

3.3 Beyond scales

So, we reach the following position: We posit Horn scales as linguistic elements. Because of the existence of these scales, an utterance U of sentence S containing a scalar term makes salient a set of alternative sentences. We can then apply basic Gricean reasoning utilizing Quantity1 to give an account of scalar implicatures.

But that basic Gricean reasoning relied on cashing out informativity in terms of asymmetric entailment. Yet there appear to be cases of scalar implicature which don't rely on scales ordered by this relation. Horn (1989) observes several cases where lexical items within a particular domain are intuitively rankable (to borrow a term from Hirschberg 1985), but are not related by lexical entailment. Horn's examples include military rank (*private, corporal, sergeant*...), life stages (*newborn, infant, toddler, preschooler*...), and legal violations (*tort, misdemeanor, felony, capital crime*). These, Horn suggests, give rise to implicatures following the same pattern as entailment based scalar implicatures, as illustrated by the examples below:

(26) A: Do they have any pre-schoolers in the program?
      B: They have toddlers. [~ toddlers but no older pre-schoolers]

(27) A: Have you worked on any capital cases?
      B: I've worked on several felony cases. [~ felony cases but no capital cases]

Hirschberg (1985) goes further in her observations. She points out that scalar implicature-like phenomena arise with a variety of non-linear rankings including whole/part relationships, type/subtype, and prerequisite orderings. Examples of implicatures based on these relations (all borrowed from Hirschberg 1985: Ch. 5) are given below:

(28) A: Did you read that section I gave you?
      B: I read the first few pages.

(29) A: Do you have a pet?
      B: We have a turtle.

(30) A: Is she married?
      B: She's engaged.

Similarly, scalar implicatures can be produced wherever context makes salient some set of alternatives. Here, affirmation of one alternative gives rise to an implicature that no other alternative can be affirmed. So consider:

(31) A: Do you have apple juice?
      B: I have grape or tomato or bloody mary mix.

On the basis of such observations, Hirschberg (1985: 125) concludes that scalar implicatures are supported by the class of partially ordered sets, i.e., any relation which is reflexive, antisymmetric and transitive. Any set of lexical items referring to entities or processes which stand in such a relation may provide the basis for a scalar implicature.

In order for a scalar implicature to be generated, the ordering which underlies it must be somehow salient. But context can render all kinds of ad-hoc orderings salient, given adequate background. If the Hirschberg-type examples really are cases of scalar implicature, then an account of this phenomenon in terms of conventional, linguistically pre-given scales seems highly implausible. On the other hand, one might argue that these examples are simply cases of particularized quantity implicatures, whose explanation requires reference to the conversational context and goals.

What makes it unlikely that the Hirschberg-type cases are unrelated to standard cases of generalized scalar implicature is that both cases clearly involve the construction of alternative possible utterances. It seems likely that an account of the construction or identification of the alternatives in these context dependent cases will be extendable to the classic scalar cases.

A promising candidate for a more general account comes from work on exhaustivity, originating in Groenendijk & Stokhof (1984). These authors were concerned with the derivation of exhaustive answers to questions, as in the following case:

(32) A: Which students were late today?
      B: Francine was late.

It is natural to understand the question as requiring, and the response as providing, an exhaustive answer. That is, the response is taken as indicating that, of the relevant set of students, *only* Francine was late (for the event in question). The example is much like many of Hirschberg's, which typically involve question/answer pairs, and could similarly be accounted for on the basis of Quantity. Groenendijk & Stokhof, however, take exhaustification to be a semantic effect, the result of applying to the semantic content of the answer an exhaustivization operator, roughly equivalent to *only* in meaning. This account nonetheless requires, like Hirschberg's, positing a salient set of students who are potential alternatives to Francine.

G&S's proposal is extended and applied directly to the scalar case in van Rooij & Schulz (2004, 2006). The 2006 paper offers several revisions to G&S's original formalization of the semantics of exhaustivization, extending the scope of the account and improving on some of the original predictions. More importantly for our interests, van Rooij & Schulz attempt to derive exhaustivization explicitly as a Gricean effect, and explicitly connect exhaustivity to scalar implicature, suggesting (van Rooij & Schulz 2006: 245) that many scalar implicatures simply involve exhaustive interpretation. By extension, this suggests that the notion of scale may be dispensible for a large class of cases.

For Groenendijk & Stokhof, exhaustivization is a semantic effect. For van Rooij & Schulz, it is a pragmatic one. Fox (2007) argues for exhaustivization as a syntactic effect, resulting from the interpretation of a covert syntactic element. In terms of its interpretation, Fox's *exh* operator is essentially the same as G&S's, although its occurrence is much less constrained than in their theory. Fox uses his operator specifically to derive scalar implicature effects, unmooring these effects from their Gricean foundations and transplanting them into the grammatical system.

Fox's proposal is one of several in which scalar implicature is derived as a grammatical effect. Landman (1998, 2000) and Chierchia (2004, 2006) propose treatments in which scalar implicature is calculated by the compositional semantic component of the grammar, while remaining sensitive to general contextual factors in some ways. The primary motivation for this "grammatical turn" in the treatment of scalars comes from the phenomenon of embedded implicature, to be discussed briefly in the next section; but is further motivated by the apparent robustness of these implicatures. (But see Geurts 2009 and work cited therein for a challenge to the robustness claim.) What is of particular interest from a foundational perspective is that this one phenomenon is amenable to analysis in such widely differing ways, facing us with a paradox observed by Grice in *Further Notes*:

> If we, as speakers, have the requisite knowledge of the conventional meaning of sentences we employ to implicate, when uttering them, something the implication of which depends on the conventional meaning in question, how can we, as theorists, have difficulty with respect to just those cases in deciding where conventional meaning ends and implicature begins?

4 Embedded implicature

Cohen (1971) is one of the earliest published critiques of Grice's theory of conversational implicature. Cohen raises a number of problems for Grice, but his paper is best known for this pair of examples:

(33) The old king has died of a heart attack and a republic has been declared.
(34) If the old king has died of a heart attack and a republic has been declared, then Tom will be quite content.

Sentence (33) implies that the king died first, and the republic was subsequently declared. Cohen (1971: 58) points out that this ordering implication is present also when the conjunction occurs in the antecedent of the conditional in (34). In fact, this implication seems to be part of the *content* of the antecedent; for it is natural to judge the conditional true even if we believe that Tom would be unhappy if the republic had been declared first, and the king had subsequently died. But this implication, according to Grice, is supposed to be a conversational implicature. This thus appears to be a case where a purported conversational implicature falls under the scope of a semantic operator, a phenomenon now dubbed *embedded implicature*. (See also article 10 [this volume] (Chierchia, Fox & Spector) *Grammatical view of scalar implicatures*.)

Since Cohen's work, many additional types of embedded implicature have been identified. So why exactly are these examples problematic for Grice? They are problematic for two reasons, which I call *the calculation problem* and *the compositionality problem* (see Simons 2011).

The calculation problem is this: Grice's account of the calculation of conversational implicatures does not provide a means for the calculation of implicatures from non-asserted clauses. Anscrombe & Ducrot (cited by Recanati 2003) provide a succinct argument to this conclusion:

(a) Conversational implicatures are pragmatic consequences of an act of saying something.
(b) An act of saying something can be performed only by means of a complete utterance, not by means of an unasserted clause such as a disjunct or the antecedent of a conditional.
(c) Hence, no implicature can be generated at the level of an unasserted clause.

Now, perhaps it is to be expected that exceptions will be found for the case of Manner implicatures, which involve attention to the form in which something has been said. But apparent implicatures attaching to embedded clauses are of all kinds. Consider the examples in (35) and (36) below, both involving scalar implicatures:

(35) Either Kai ate the broccoli or he ate some of the peas. (Sauerland 2004)
 ⤳ Either Kai ate the broccoli or he ate **some but not all** of the peas.

(36) Bill thinks that Harriet wants to read some of his papers. (Cf. Chierchia 2004)
 ⤳ Bill thinks that Harriet wants to read **some but not all** of his papers.

In neither case can the observed implicatures be derived via standard Gricean reasoning from the entire asserted content. (For details, see the cited papers). Suppose then that we want to allow the implicatures to be generated *in situ*. The standard Gricean machinery simply does not provide a means to do this, as the clauses which give rise to the implicatures are not themselves said. The calculation problem, then, is the problem that the Gricean picture provides no means for calculating implicatures on the basis of content which is not said; but intuitively, syntactically embedded clauses do sometimes seem to give rise to implicatures in their own right.

The second problem, the compositionality problem, can be characterized in two different ways, depending on whether one is interested solely in the consequences of embedded implicatures for Grice's views, or for the theory of interpretation more generally. (For a more general discussion of compositionality, see article 6 [Semantics: Foundations, History and Methods] (Pagin & Westerståhl) *Compositionality*.) Starting with the Gricean perspective, the compositionality problem is this: According to Grice, what is said is supposed to be determined by conventional content (in addition to reference fixing and disambiguation). But in examples like (34)–(36), the implicatures apparently generated by embedded clauses seem to fall under the scope of the embedding operators, and thus to contribute to the truth conditional content expressed: that is, to what is said. But the compositionality problem is not merely a problem for Grice's conception of what is said. It is more broadly a problem for standard models of the interaction between conventionally encoded content and inferentially derived content. Translated into the language of current semantic theory, Grice's model of what we now call the semantics/pragmatics interface tells us that processes of semantic composition are independent of (and are analytically prior to) processes of pragmatic inferencing. But cases of embedded implicature suggest that the correct model is one in which, for example, a linguistic operator can apply to a proposition consisting of both encoded and inferentially derived content.

It is for this reason that local pragmatic effects are viewed by non-Gricean pragmaticists as being of central importance (see Sperber & Wilson 1986; Bach 1994; Recanati 1989, 2004; Levinson 2000). These effects do not merely require a rethinking of the mechanism whereby pragmatic effects are derived, but of the entire model of interpretation. The authors just mentioned all hold that such effects – what Levinson (2000) calls *pragmatic intrusion* – are ubiquitous, going well beyond the types of examples illustrated here. For such theorists, a central goal of any theory of pragmatic inference should be to provide an account of local effects, and on this ground the standard Gricean model is rejected.

5 Alternate models and competing conceptions

In this section, we will discuss the views of theorists who, while fully embracing the idea that what is conveyed by an utterance includes both encoded content and inferentially derived content, differ from Grice in various ways. There are three principal parameters of difference:

(i) the rules or principles involved in inference
(ii) the nature of the input to inference and the interaction between encoded content and inferential content
(iii) the appropriate analysis of "what is said" or "literal meaning"

5.1 Explicature and implicature in Relevance Theory

Relevance Theory (RT), first formulated in Sperber & Wilson (1986), is billed as a cognitive theory of communication. Conversational inference is a central feature of this theory. But Sperber & Wilson differ from the Gricean conception along all three of the parameters set out above.

On the RT view, inference is driven by a deep cognitive principle: the impulse to extract maximal useful information from a stimulus, balanced by the impulse to expend no more effort than seems justified by the anticipated benefits. (Here, we hear echoes of the Zipfian principles underlying Horn's Q- and R-principles.) RT uses the term *Relevance* (rather non-standardly) to characterize this balance between effort and pay-off: the more cognitive benefits – that is, useful information – a stimulus provides, the more Relevant it is; but this is offset by the processing effort required to derive the information. A stimulus has *optimal Relevance* just in case the cognitive benefits derived fully justify the cognitive effort required to derive them.

According to RT, linguistic communication is governed by the following principle:

Communicative Principle of Relevance
Every utterance conveys a presumption of its own optimal relevance.

The goal of interpretation is to identify a speaker meaning consistent with this presumption. This one over-arching principle is argued to do all the work which, in Grice's theory, is done by all the maxims combined.

So, one major difference between Grice and RT is the conception of what underlies conversational inference. A second is the specific principle which launches the process. The third major difference concerns the input to conversational inference and the interaction between encoded and inferential content.

On the RT conception, linguistic decoding produces an impoverished semantic object, a propositional radical or propositionally incomplete logical form. The first task of Relevance-driven inference is to fill out this skeletal object into a complete proposition. As noted above, Grice recognized that in order to identify the proposition expressed, an interpreter must fix the referents of referential expressions and resolve ambiguities, but said nothing as to the nature of the processes involved. RT argues, first, that what is required to construct a complete proposition from what is linguistically encoded goes well beyond reference fixing and disambiguation. Second, RT argues that there is no principled distinction to be made between processes involved in "filling out" a proposition and processes involved in deriving further inferences from the proposition so retrieved. All are driven by the same presumption of Relevance.

Inferentially derived content which goes towards "filling out" encoded content into a complete proposition is called *explicature*. Some aspects of content which Griceans treat as generalized conversational implicatures are analyzed in RT as explicatures, with a corresponding shift in the semantic analysis of the items in question. The interpretation of scalars is a central case.

Once all necessary explicatures have been derived, and the utterance has been associated with a proposition, Relevance-driven inference may continue. RT preserves the term *implicature* for these additional inferences, but makes a further subdivision within this class. In RT, the interpretation of an utterance is taken to proceed relative to a context, a context being simply some set of propositions retrievable by the addressee. The relevance of an utterance is partially determined by the number and utility of conclusions which can be deductively drawn from the context in conjunction with the proposition derived from the utterance. Part of the process of interpretation is the construction of an appropriate context. In RT, the term *implicature* is used both for propositions which are infered to be part of the context for interpretation, and for deductive conclusions drawn on the basis of the constructed context. The former type of implicature is called an *implicated assumption* or *implicated premise*, the latter, an *implicated conclusion*. This distinction (not coincidentally) maps onto the distinction made above between background and foreground implicature.

In introducing the background/foreground distinction, we noted that the extension of the term *implicature* to background implicatures involved a departure from the Gricean conception of implicatures as part of speaker meaning. RT's implicated conclusions are also not necessarily part of Gricean speaker meaning. Suppose a speaker produces an utterance U, knowing that there are multiple contexts relative to which the interpreter might find U relevant, and knowing that U would give rise to different implicated conclusions in different contexts. Then there is no *particular* implicature which the speaker intends to be drawn, and perhaps not even a determinate set of candidates. For Grice, these inferences could not count as implicatures; for RT, they do. In fact, RT recognizes a continuum of implicatures, from those clearly meant by the speaker, to cases where the speaker expects *some* implicated conclusions to be drawn but does not know what they will be. However, inferences drawn by the interpreter but not driven by the requirements of Relevance lie beyond the limits of implicature.

5.2 Bach's Conversational Impliciture

Kent Bach's (1994) "Conversational Impliciture" does not present any revised theory of what underlies implicature derivation. The purpose of the paper is to demonstrate that "the distinction between what is said and what is implicated is not exhaustive" (Bach 1994: 124). Between the two lies a level which Bach calls *impliciture*.

Like the Relevance theorists, Bach takes it that the output of semantic decoding may be propositionally incomplete. Propositional incompleteness drives a process which he calls *completion*: the filling in of "conceptual gaps" in a "semantically underdeterminate" sentence content. Completion is semantically or conceptually mandated. An interpreter, merely by virtue of their knowledge of the language, will be able to identify semantic incompleteness; and linguistic rules or forms will determine what sorts of completions are required.

But even after completion, we may not have arrived at the level of impliciture. In some cases, a further process called *expansion* takes place. This is best explained by illustration. Consider one of Bach's central examples: A mother says (unsympathetically) to her child who is complaining of a cut finger:

(37) You're not going to die.

She is not telling her son that he is immortal – the literal meaning of the sentence – but merely that he will not die from the cut on his finger. A proper understanding of her utterance requires expanding the proposition literally expressed to one which is "conceptually more elaborate than the one that is strictly expressed." (Bach 1994: 135) This process of expansion is driven by the interpreter's recognition that the speaker could not reasonably mean what she has literally said. So, like ordinary implicature, expansion is driven by the assumption of the general cooperativity of the speaker.

So, why are these not simply cases of implicature? Here is how Bach distinguishes the two notions:

> In implicature one says and communicates one thing and thereby communicates something else in addition. Impliciture, however, is a matter of saying something but communicating something else instead, something closely related to what is said (Bach 1994: 126) . . .

> Implicitures are, as the name suggests, implicit in what is said, whereas implicatures are implied by (the saying of) what is said. (Bach 1994: 140)

Recanati (1989, 2004 and elsewhere) offers a model of linguistic interpretation similar in many respects to that of Bach. Like Bach, Recanati distinguishes conversational implicature from other types of pragmatic inference which operate locally and which do not utilize "full blown" Gricean reasoning. Like Bach, Recanati recognizes two distinct sub-types of lower-level pragmatic processes, which he calls *saturation* and *modulation*: these are roughly equivalent to Bach's *completion* and *expansion*. Only after these are completed can anythig akin to Gricean implicature generation begin.

5.3 Levinson: Generalized conversational implicature as default interpretation

Like Bach, Levinson is essentially a Gricean, but considers that Gricean theory requires modification to allow for the fact of "pragmatic intrusion:" inferential contributions to what is said. These contributions are what he identifies as Generalized Conversational Implicatures in Levinson (2000). The specific aspects of interpretation which he identifies as GCIs more or less overlap with those identified by Relevance theorists, Bach and Recanati as local pragmatic effects. Unlike them, Levinson proposes that GCIs can be derived on the basis of (elaborated versions of) the standard Gricean maxims of Quantity, Relation and Manner. In his formulation, these become the Q-, I-, and M-Maxims, respectively ("I" for informativity: Cf. Atlas & Levinson 1981).

Two aspects of the revised maxims are noteworthy. First, for each principle, Levinson gives both a Speaker's Maxim and a Recipient's Corollary. The latter articulates in some detail what sort of inferences are derivable given the interpretation rule. This detail is the second noteworthy aspect of the formulation. Unlike Horn's proposal, discussed above, which aims for maximum generality, Levinson incorporates into the speaker corollaries specific inference rules which produce the central GCI types with which he is concerned. Readers are referred to the original for the full principles.

As presented so far, Levinson's view looks like nothing more than a reformulation of Grice's. What distinguishes his position is his view as to how his principles apply. The central notion for Levinson is that of a *default*: the principles are claimed to be default "inferential heuristics" (Atlas & Levinson 1981: 35) which produce default interpretations. Levinson proposes that the GCI-generating principles apply automatically in the interpretation of any utterance, unless some contextual factor over-rides their application. The inference underlying GCIs is supposed to be "based *not* on direct computations about speaker-intentions but rather on general expectations about how language is normally used" (Atlas & Levinson 1981: 22). Application of default interpretation principles thus lies somewhere in between decoding of linguistically encoded content and the calculation of true implicatures.

The notion of default occurs in two ways in Levinson's view. First, there is the claim that the interpretative principles apply by default. Second, Levinson describes the output of these principles as "default interpretations". Yet as pointed out by Bezuidenhout & Morris (2004), the interpretations which arise are not defaults in the sense that their selection requires no choice among alternatives. Levinson himself, throughout the book, presents multiple options for GCIs which may be associated with particular words or constructions. And it is clear, as emphasized by Bezuidenhout (2002), that the choice among these options often requires reference to wide context – and very likely, reference to considerations of speaker intention and standard Gricean principles.

As noted, a major motivation for Levinson's theory of GCIs is that these implicatures can attach to subordinate clauses, and contribute to what is said. Levinson claims that the nature of his rules is such that "the inference can be made without complete access to the logical form of the whole utterance . . . Procedurally, the expression *some of the boys G'd* can be immediately associated with the default assumption *some but not all of the boys G'd* even when some indeterminate aspect of the predicate G has not yet been resolved" (Levinson 2000: 259). Applications of the I-principle, which for Levinson include enrichment of lexical content, might similarly be triggered as soon as a particular word is encountered e.g., the interpretation of "drink" as "alcoholic drink" in *I went out for a drink last night.* This local triggering of GCIs is crucial to Levinson's account of pragmatic intrusion. However, Bezuidenhout 2002 argues rather convincingly against this view of GCIs.

Levinson clearly holds that standard Gricean implicatures also arise, but gives no indication as to whether they are generated by the same principles which produce GCIs, applying in a global, non-default manner; or whether PCIs are assumed to be generated by the standard (but almost identical) Gricean principles.

6 Formal and experimental approaches

In this article, we have reviewed the foundations of the analysis of conversational implicature. To conclude, I will briefly introduce two formal approaches to the study of implicature: Optimality Theoretic Pragmatics, and Game Theoretic approaches.

The Optimality Theoretic approach to interpretation is presented as a new take on the Radical Pragmatics program, adopting the view that linguistic form underdetermines the propositional content of utterances. In this respect, OT pragmatics shares underlying assumptions with Relevance Theory, which is cited in some presentations. It is proposed that OT can provide a framework both for the processes involved in filling out a full propositional content (e.g., pronoun resolution, fixing domain restrictions for quantifiers) and in further elaboration of the content expressed, that is, the generation of implicatures. OT pragmatics has so far focussed principally on generalized implicatures involving standard but defeasible interpretations of particular forms: for example, scalar implicatures, and the association of stereotypical situations with unmarked syntactic forms (e.g., the interpretation of *stop the car* vs. *cause the car to stop*) – Horn's "division of pragmatic labor". So far, highly particularized implicatures lie outside of the purview of the theory.

OT pragmatics take much of its inspiration from Horn's (1984) pragmatic taxonomy (see section 2.3 above), which posits the two conflicting principles, Q and R. Horn's proposal is interpreted within OT pragmatics as claiming that pragmatic interpretation is a matter of achieving an optimal balance in the pairing of forms and interpretations: a given form f' should be assigned an interpretation m which enriches the linguistic content of f, but not so much that some alternate form f' would be a better candidate for the expression of m; while a desired meaning m should be expressed in a form f which is adequately economical, but not so much so that some other meaning m' would be a better candidate to be expressed by it. This balancing of competing requirements is captured by a modification of standard OT called Bidirectional OT (Blutner 2000).

Clearly what this conception requires is a theory of what renders one candidate form-interpretation pair better than another. Identifying a set of pragmatic constraints relative to which to formulate a metric for evaluating the "goodness" of such pairs is one of the central tasks of OT pragmatics. (For some contributions to this project, see Blutner & Zeevat (2004). The introduction to that volume gives a useful overview of the framework.) A second task of the theory is to fix the definition of optimization, i.e., what counts as an "adequately good" pairing. See again the aforementioned volume, and also Blutner (2000). For a book length presentation of the OT approach to interpretation, integrating syntax, semantics and pragmatics, see Blutner, de Hoop & Hendriks (2006).

Decision theory is a mathematical framework used to model rational decision making, in particular in situations of incomplete knowledge about the world. The decisions in question are typically choices among some fixed set of options. Game theory, an extension of decision theory utilizing the same set of formal tools, is used to model decisions in situations where two agents interact, and where each agent's choices impact on the decision of the other, a so-called *game*. Decision theory and, more extensively, game theory have been applied to various aspects of linguistic analysis since Lewis's pioneering (1969) work. More recently, some theorists have begun to use game theory to model pragmatic inference, including the calculation of some types of implicature. (For a useful introduction to the basic mathematical machinery and its application to pragmatics, see chapter one of Benz, Jäger & van Rooij (2006); the rest of the book provides a good survey of central topics in the application of game theory to pragmatics. See also article 16 [this volume] (Jäger) *Game theory*.)

There are two (not entirely distinct) lines of work in this domain. One line of work attempts to formalize fundamental pragmatic concepts or principles using game theoretic tools. Particular attention has been given to the concept of Relevance (see e.g., Merin 1999; van Rooij 2001 and elsewhere). A second line of work attempts to replicate the effects of particular Gricean or neo-Gricean principles using Game Theory. Work in this line is generally presented as friendly to the Gricean framework, intended as a precise formulation of it rather than as an alternative.

Like OT, game theory is set up to model choices among a fixed set of alternative utterances/interpretations, and hence finds applications in attempts to model generalized implicatures involving choices among competing expressions. As with OT, particularized implicatures lie (at least so far) outside of the domain of the theory. Again, scalar implicature and Horn's "division of pragmatic labor" have been targeted for analysis (see van Rooij 2008 and article 16 [this volume] (Jäger) *Game theory*). The overlap between game theory and OT is not accidental. Dekker & van Rooij (2000) demonstrate that optimality theoretic models can be given a game theoretic interpretation, and that optimal interpretations represent Nash equilibria.

These are only samples of the formal approaches that have been utilized to develop robust accounts of conversational inference in general and conversational implicature in particular. A very different line of work, mainly pursued by computer scientists modelling discourse utilizes Planning Theory (for a starting point, see Grosz & Sidner 1986).

The developing area of experimental pragmatics offers another kind of enrichment of traditional Gricean pragmatics, applying the methods of experimental cognitive psychology to derive data for pragmatic theorizing. Some work in this area simply tries to apply proper methodology to elicit judgments from untutored informants, rather than using the standard informal (and, it is argued, often misleading) methods traditional in pragmatics: see for example

Geurts & Pouscoulous (2009). Other work is aimed at testing the adequacy of particular pragmatic theories or claims by evaluating their implications for processing. The approach is to formulate a specific claim about processing which is implied by the pragmatic theory under investigation, and then to test that claim empirically. This approach has been applied recently to the debate about the status of generalized conversational implicatures, with a variety of experimental techniques being applied to the question of whether or not these implicatures are "defaults" of some kind. Techniques range from the use of measures of reading or response time (e.g., Breheny, Katsos & Williams 2005), eye-tracking over visually presented examples (e.g., Bezuidenhout & Morris 2004) and even over real world tasks (e.g., Grodner & Sedivy 2004; Storto & Tanenhaus 2005). Noveck & Sperber (2004) offers a useful introduction to this area of research.

While an understanding of the conceptual foundations of the theory of implicature is crucial for meaningful work in this domain, it is only through the development of formal models that a substantive, predictive theory of conversational implicature can be provided.

7 References

Atlas, Jay 1977. Negation, ambiguity and presupposition. *Linguistics & Philosophy* 1, 321–336.
Atlas, Jay 1978. On presupposing. *Mind* 87, 396–411.
Atlas, Jay 2005. *Logic, Meaning and Conversation*. Oxford: Oxford University Press.
Atlas, Jay & Stephen Levinson 1981. *It*-clefts, informativeness and logical form: Radical pragmatics (revised standard version). In: P. Cole (ed.). *Radical Pragmatics*. New York: Academic Press, 1–61.
Bach, Kent 1994. Conversational impliciture. *Mind & Language* 9, l24–162.
Benz, Anton, Gerhard Jäger & Robert van Rooij 2006. *Game Theory and Pragmatics*. Basingstoke: Palgrave Macmillan.
Bezuidenhout, Anne 2002. Generalized conversational implicatures and default pragmatic inferences. In: J. Campbell, M. O'Rourke & D. Shier (eds.). *Meaning and Truth: Investigations in Philosophical Semantics*. New York: Seven Bridges Press, 257–283.
Bezuidenhout, Anne & Robin Morris 2004. Implicature, relevance and default inferences. In: D. Sperber & I. Noveck (eds.). *Experimental Pragmatics*. Basingstoke: Palgrave Macmillan, 257–282.
Blutner, Reinhard 2000. Some aspects of optimality in natural language interpretation. *Journal of Semantics* 17, 189–216.
Blutner, Reinhard & Henk Zeevat 2004. *Optimality Theory and Pragmatics*. Basingstoke: Palgrave Macmillan.
Blutner, Reinhard, Helen de Hoop & Petra Hendriks 2006. *Optimal Communication*. Stanford, CA: CSLI Publications.

Boër, Steven E. & William G. Lycan 1976. The myth of semantic presupposition. In: A. Zwicky (ed.). *Papers in Nonphonology* (Working Papers in Linguistics 21). Columbus, OH: Ohio State University, 1–90.

Breheny, Richard, Napoleon Katsos & John Williams 2005. Are generalised scalar implicatures generated by default? An on-line investigation into the role of context in generating pragmatic inferences. *Cognition* 100, 434–463.

Chierchia, Gennaro 2004. Scalar implicatures, polarity phenomena and the syntax/pragmatics interface. In: A. Belletti (ed.). *Structures and Beyond*. Oxford: Oxford University Press, 39–103.

Chierchia, Gennaro 2006. Broaden your views: Implicatures of domain widening and the 'logicality' of language. *Linguistic Inquiry* 37, 535–590.

Cohen, Jonathan L. 1971. Some remarks on Grice's views about the logical particles of natural language. In: Y. Bar-Hillel (ed.). *Pragmatics of Natural Languages*. Dordrecht: Reidel, 50–68.

Davis, Wayne 1998. *Implicature: Intention, Convention and Principle in the Failure of Gricean Theory*. Cambridge: Cambridge University Press.

Fox, Danny 2007. Free choice and the theory of scalar implicatures. In: U. Sauerland & P. Stateva (eds.). *Presupposition and Implicature in Compositional Semantics*. Basingstoke: Palgrave Macmillan, 71–120.

Franke, Michael, Tikitu de Jager & Robert van Rooij 2009. Relevance in cooperation and conflict. *Journal of Logic and Computation*. doi: 10.1093/logcom/exp070.

Gazdar, Gerald 1979. *Pragmatics: Implicature, Presupposition and Logical Form*. New York: Academic Press.

Geurts, Bart 2009. Scalar implicature and local pragmatics. *Mind & Language* 24, 51–79.

Geurts, Bart & Nausicaa Pouscoulous 2009. Embedded implicatures ?!? *Semantics and Pragmatics* 2, 1–34.

Grice, H. Paul 1975. Logic and conversation. In: D. Davidson & G. Harman (eds.). *The Logic of Grammar*. Encino, CA: Dickenson, 64–75. Reprinted in: H. P. Grice. *Studies in the Way of Words*. Cambridge, MA: Harvard University Press, 1989, 22–40.

Grice, H. Paul 1978. Further notes on logic and conversation. In: P. Cole (ed.). *Syntax and Semantics 9: Pragmatics*. New York: Academic Press, 183–97. Reprinted in: H. P. Grice. *Studies in the Way of Words*. Cambridge, MA: Harvard University Press, 1989, 41–57.

Grice, H. Paul 1981. Presupposition and conversational implicature. In: P. Cole (ed.). *Radical Pragmatics*. New York: Academic Press, 183–198.

Grice, H. Paul 1989. *Studies in the Way of Words*. Cambridge, MA: Harvard University Press.

Groenendijk, Jeroen & Martin Stokhof 1984. *Studies on the Semantics of Questions and the Pragmatics of Answers*. Ph.D. dissertation. University of Amsterdam.

Grodner, Daniel & Julie C. Sedivy 2004. The effect of speaker-specific information on pragmatic inferences. In: N. Pearlmutter & E. Gibson (eds.). *The Processing and Acquisition of Reference*. Cambridge, MA: The MIT Press.

Grosz, Barbara J. & Candace Sidner 1986. Attention, intentions and the structure of discourse. *Computational Linguistics* 12, 175–204.

Hirschberg, Julia 1985. *A Theory of Scalar Implicature*. Ph.D. dissertation. University of Pennsylvania, Philadelphia, PA. Reprinted: New York: Garland, 1991.

Horn, Laurence R. 1972. *On the Semantic Properties of the Logical Operators in English*. Ph.D. dissertation, University of California, Los Angeles, CA.

Horn, Laurence R. 1984. Toward a new taxonomy for pragmatic inference: Q-based and r-based implicature. In: D. Schiffrin (ed.). *Meaning, Form and Use in Context: Linguistic Applications*. Washington, DC: Georgetown University Press, 11–42.
Horn, Laurence R. 1989. *A Natural History of Negation*. Chicago, IL: The University of Chicago Press.
Katzir, Roni 2007. Structurally-defined alternatives. *Linguistics & Philosophy* 30, 669–690.
Kempson, Ruth 1975. *Presupposition and the Delimitation of Semantics*. Cambridge: Cambridge University Press.
Landman, Fred 1998. Plurals and maximalization. In: S. Rothstein (ed.). *Events and Grammar*. Dordrecht: Kluwer, 237–271.
Landman, Fred 2000. *Events and Plurality*. Dordrecht: Kluwer.
Levinson, Stephen 2000. *Presumptive Meanings: The Theory of Generalized Conversational Implicature*. Cambridge, MA: The MIT Press.
Lewis, David K. 1969. *Convention: A Philosophical Study*. Cambridge, MA: Harvard University Press.
Martinet, Antoine 1962. *A Functional View of Language*. Oxford: Clarendon Press.
Matsumoto, Yo 1995. The conversational condition on Horn scales. *Linguistics & Philosophy* 18, 21–60.
Merin, Arthur 1999. Information, relevance and social decision making: Some principles and results of decision-theoretic semantics. In: L. Moss, J. Ginzburg & M. de Rijke (eds.). *Logic, Language and Information, vol. 2*. Stanford, CA: CSLI Publications, 179–221.
Noveck, Ira & Dan Sperber (eds.) 2004. *Experimental Pragmatics*. Basingstoke: Palgrave Macmillan.
Recanati, François 1989. The pragmatics of what is said. *Mind & Language* 4, 295–329.
Recanati, François 2003. Embedded implicatures. *Philosophical Perspectives* 17, 299–332.
Recanati, François 2004. *Literal Meaning*. Cambridge: Cambridge University Press.
van Rooij, Robert 2001. Relevance of communicative acts. In: J. van Bentham (ed.). *Proceedings of the 8th Conference on Theoretical Aspects of Rationality and Knowledge (= TARK'01)*. San Francisco, CA: Morgan Kaufmann, 88–96.
van Rooij, Robert 2008. Games and quantity implicatures. *Journal of Economic Methodology* 15, 261–274.
van Rooij, Robert & Katrin Schulz 2004. Exhaustive interpretation of complex sentences. *Journal of Logic, Language and Information* 13, 491–519.
Sadock, Jerry M. 1976. On testing for conversational implicature. In: P. Cole (ed.). *Syntax and Semantics 9: Pragmatics*. New York: Academic Press, 281–297.
Sauerland, Uli 2004. Scalar implicatures in complex sentences. *Linguistics & Philosophy* 27, 367–391.
Simons, Mandy 2001. On the conversational basis of some presuppositions. In: R. Hastings, B. Jackson & Z. Zvolensky (eds.). *Proceedings of Semantics and Linguistic Theory (= SALT) XI*. Ithaca, NY: Cornell University, 431–448.
Simons, Mandy 2004. Presupposition and relevance. In: Z. Szabó (ed.). *Semantics vs. Pragmatics*. Oxford: Oxford University Press, 329–355.
Simons, Mandy 2008. *Presupposition and Cooperation*. Ms. Pittsburgh, PA, Carnegie Mellon University.
Simons, Mandy 2011. A Gricean view on intrusive implicature. In: K. Petrus (ed.). *Meaning and Analysis: New Essays on Grice*. Basingstoke: Palgrave Macmillan, 138–169.

Soames, Scott 1982. How presuppositions are inherited: A solution to the projection problem. *Linguistic Inquiry* 13, 483–545.
Sperber, Dan & Deirdre Wilson 1986. *Relevance: Communication and Cognition*. Oxford: Blackwell.
Stalnaker, Robert 1974. Pragmatic presuppositions. In: M. K. Munitz & P. K. Unger (eds.). *Semantics and Philosophy*. New York: New York University Press, 197–213.
Storto, Gianluca & Michael K. Tanenhaus 2005. Are scalar implicatures computed online? In: E. Maier, C. Bary & J. Huitink (eds.). *Proceedings of Sinn und Bedeutung (= SuB) 9*. Nijmegen: Nijmegen Center for Semantics, 431–445.
Wilson, Deirdre 1975. *Presupposition and Non-Truth-Conditional Semantics*. New York: Academic Press.
Zipf, George K. 1949. *Human Behavior and the Principle of Least Effort*. Cambridge, MA: Addison-Wesley.

Gerhard Jäger
16 Game theory in semantics and pragmatics

1 Introduction —— 563
2 Game construction I: Interpretation games —— 565
3 Strategies and best responses —— 570
4 Iterated Best Response —— 574
5 Examples —— 576
6 Game construction II: Lifted games —— 581
7 Embedded implicatures —— 587
8 Beyond nominal costs —— 590
9 Conclusion —— 593
10 Appendix —— 594
11 References —— 595

Abstract: Game theory is a mathematical framework that is being used in economics and biology, but also in philosophy, political science and computer science, to study the behavior of multiple agents that are engaged in strategic interaction. It has manifold applications in linguistics as well. In particular, it has been utilized to investigate stability conditions of linguistic features in a large speech community, and to explore the strategic aspects of single speech acts.

The following chapter gives an introduction into a particular incarnation of this research paradigm, the Iterated Best Response model of game-theoretic pragmatics. It can be seen as a formalization of the neo-Gricean program of pragmatics. Empirical issues touched upon include exhaustivication, free choice readings, ignorance implicatures, embedded implicatures and the pragmatics of measure terms.

1 Introduction

The interpretation of linguistic utterances is determined by the words involved and the way they are combined, but not exclusively so. Establishing the content that is communicated by an utterance is inextricably intertwined with

Gerhard Jäger, Tübingen, Germany

https://doi.org/10.1515/9783110589849-016

the communicative context where the utterance is made, including the expectations of the interlocutors about each other. Clark & Marshall (1981) make a good case that even the reference of a definite description depends on the reasoning of the speaker and hearer about each other's knowledge state. Likewise, computing the implicatures of a sentence requires reasoning about the knowledge states and intentions of the communication partners. To use a worn-out example, Grice (1975) points out that a sentence such as (1b), if uttered to the owner of an immobilized car by a passerby, carries much more information than what is literally said.

(1) a. *car owner*: I am out of petrol.
    b. *passerby*: There is a garage round the corner.

The listener will legitimately infer from this exchange that the garage is open and sells petrol (or at least so the passerby believes). This follows from his expectations that the passerby understands his situation and is cooperative. But this is not sufficient. The passerby must be aware of these expectations, and he must believe that the car owner is capable to make the required inference, the car owner must be able to assign these epistemic qualities to the passerby etc.

The standard tool to model this kind of inferences about mutual belief states is epistemic logic, and it has been extensively used to model the interface between semantics and pragmatics (see for instance Stone 1998; Gerbrandy 1999). *Game Theory* is another intellectual tradition that aims at a mathematical model of the inferences that are involved in the interaction of rational agents. Unlike epistemic logic, game theory puts its focus on the decisions and preferences of the interacting agents, rather than on explicit models of their internal states and reasoning processes. As communicative goals and decisions play a crucial role for pragmatics, the use of game theoretic methods in pragmatics suggests itself.

The application of game theory to linguistic issues traces back to David Lewis' dissertation (Lewis 1969), where he showed that the game theoretic notion of a *Nash equilibrium* is apt to explain how a linguistic convention can be self-sustaining in a community. While the game theoretic investigation of communication was mostly pursued by economists and biologists in the quarter century after Lewis' work (see for instance Spence 1973; Crawford & Sobel 1982; Maynard Smith 1991), since the mid-nineties formal linguists and philosophers of language have paid increasing attention to the potential of game theory to the analysis of language use and language evolution (see for instance Dekker & van Rooij 2000; Parikh 2001; van Rooij 2004; Skyrms 2010 or the papers in Benz, Jäger & vanRooij 2005; Pietarinen 2007).

In this article, I will not even attempt to give a comprehensive overview on the various applications of game theory to semantics and pragmatics that have emerged in recent years. Rather, I will describe a particular approach in some detail. The *Iterated Best Response* Model (IBR Model for short) of game theoretic pragmatics is an implementation of the neo-Gricean program of pragmatics to derive the mapping from *what is said* to *what is meant* from first principles of rational communication. Various incarnations of it have been proposed in recent years (cf. Jäger 2007c; Franke 2008; Jäger & Ebert 2009; Franke 2009; see also Benz & van Rooij 2007 for a related approach), drawing on earlier work in economics such as Rabin (1990) that was not specifically directed at the analysis of natural language. In this article I will largely follow the version from Franke (2009). In particular, the analyses of disjunction, free choice permissions and embedded implicatures given below are taken from there.

2 Game construction I: Interpretation games

Following the lead of Lewis (1969), the present approach models linguistic communication as a *signaling game*. This is a class of dynamic games involving two players, a *sender* and a *receiver*. The game proceeds in three stages:
1. The sender is assigned some piece of private information, its *type*, that is not revealed to the receiver.
2. The sender transmits a *signal* to the receiver. The choice of the signal may depend on the type.
3. The receiver chooses a certain *action*, possibly dependent on the observed signal.

To keep the mathematical analysis manageable, I will assume that the number of possible types, signals and actions are finite. The type of the sender is assigned according to a certain *prior* probability distribution that is common knowledge between the players.

A *history* of such a game is a type-signal-action triple. Both players have certain preferences over histories. These preferences are modeled as numerical *utilities*. It is important to keep in mind that the numerical values used are to some degree arbitrary. What is important is only the relative preferences between histories (or probability distributions over histories) that are captured by such a utility function. Unless otherwise noted, it is always tacitly assumed that both players are *rational*. This entails that they have a consistent epistemic state, and that they make their choices in a way that maximizes their *expected utilities*, given their epistemic state.

Unlike Lewis (1969) and much subsequent work, the IBR model is not concerned with the question how signals acquire meaning in a signaling game. Instead it is presupposed that signals already have a conventionalized meaning that is common knowledge between the players, and the model serves to study how the conventionalized meaning affects the way signals are used in particular strategic situations. Therefore we augment signaling games with a relation of truth that holds between types and signals.

Let us make the model formally precise. A signaling games consists of the following components:
- a finite set S of *signals* that the sender has at her disposal,
- a finite set T of *types* (information states) the sender might be in,
- a *prior probability distribution* p^* over T,
- a *truth* relation $\models$ between T and S,
- a set A of *actions* that the receiver may take, and
- utility functions u_s and u_r for the sender and the receiver respectively that both map triples from $T \times S \times A$ to real numbers.

Intuitively, a type $t \in T$ specifies the information that the sender wants to communicate in a given situation, and S is the set of linguistic expressions that she could, in principle, utter. It would be unwieldy though to identify S with all well-formed expressions of English (or some other natural language), and to pin down the set of possible information states of the sender seems to be outright hopeless. To analyze a particular linguistic example, we have to construct a local game that captures the relevant alternatives that the interlocutors take into consideration. In the sequel, I will present a recipe how to construct such a game. It closely follows the proposal from Franke (2009).

To illustrate the recipe, I will use the standard example for a scalar implicature:

(2) Some boys came to the party.

If the listener is interested in the question how many boys came to the party, (2.) carries the implicature that not all boys came to the party. Neo-Gricean pragmaticists usually assume (cf. for instance Horn 1984) that this effect arises because the word *some* in (2.) is element of a scale *{no, some, all}*. When interpreting (2.), the listener takes into consideration that the speaker could have uttered (3a) or (b):

(3) a. No boy came to the party.
     b. All boys came to the party.

When constructing a game for a particular expression s that is uttered in a particular context c, the set of signals S is simply $ALT_c(s)$, the set of expression alternatives to s in c. This set may be determined by lexical properties of the linguistic material involved (as in the case of scalar expressions), by information structure (cf. Rooth 1985; Büring 1995), by an explicit or implicit question and perhaps by other factors. The issue has been discussed extensively in the literature and I will not dwell further on it here – see for instance Fox (2007); Katzir (2007) for some recent discussion. For the running example, $S = \{(2.), (3a), (3b)\}$, mnemonically named {SOME, NO, ALL} in the sequel.

The set of T of *types* or information states that the sender may have can be identified with the set of answers to the current *question under discussion* that – according to the listener – the speaker might know. For the time being, I will assume the *strong competence assumption*, i.e. the idea that the speaker is perfectly informed about the issue at hand. (The name "competence assumption" is due to van Rooij & Schulz 2004, but the notion has been used by many neo-Gricean researchers under varying names. I call it "strong competence assumption" here because I will later introduce a weaker variant thereof.) This means that the speaker is assumed to know the truth value of all elements of S. (It is actually sufficient to assume that the speaker has a definite opinion about these truth values. I will continue to pretend that the speaker only has correct information, but nothing hinges on this.) The consequences of lifting this assumptions are explored in Section 6.

If the speaker is also rational, we can identify her possible information states with the set of maximally consistent sets of the elements of S and their negations that are consistent with the context and contain at least one non-negated element. To avoid the formal complication of defining an appropriate negation for whatever representation language we use, information states are defined as non-empty sets of sentences that are deductively closed within S, with the implicit assumption that a sentence which is not a member of an information state is false in this state (the so-called *closed world assumption*).

In the example at hand, these would be (under the assumptions that {NO, SOME} is inconsistent and ALL $\vdash$ SOME, where $\vdash$ indicates entailment):

$$T = \{\{\text{NO}\}, \{\text{SOME}\}, \{\text{SOME}, \text{ALL}\}\}.$$

Types are thus essentially *possible worlds* (provided the competence assumption holds). In our running example, I will denote the three types with $w_{\neg \exists}, w_{\exists \neg \forall}$, and $w_\forall$ respectively.

The *prior probability distribution p^** over T captures the subjective probabilities that the receiver assigns to the possible states of the sender. It has no obvious counterparts in the epistemic models that are commonly used in formal semantics and pragmatics. Unless any specific information is given, we have no reason to assume that the receiver considers a certain type as being more likely than any other type. In such a situation the *principle of insufficient reason* (cf. Jaynes 2003) applies: If two possibilities a and b are indistinguishable except for their names, they have the same subjective probability. This entails that $p^*(t) = 1/|T|$ for all types t. In our example, this means:

$$p^\star(w_{\neg\exists}) = p^\star(w_{\exists\neg\forall}) = p^\star(w_\forall) = \frac{1}{3}.$$

A signal s is *true* in a type t if $s \in t$. We thus have:

$$w_{\neg\exists} \models \text{NO}$$
$$w_{\exists\neg\forall} \models \text{SOME}$$
$$w_\forall \models \text{SOME, ALL}$$

In an interpretation game, the receiver's task is to figure out which type the sender has. The set $\mathcal{A}$ of receiver *actions* can thus be identified with $\mathcal{T}$. (I will continue to use the letters a and $\mathcal{A}$ when talking about receiver's options, and t/T when referring to information states.)

It is furthermore assumed that both players have an overarching interest in succesful communication. Formally this cashes out as the postulate that

$$t' \neq t \Rightarrow \forall s. u_{s/r}(t, s, t) > u_{s/r}(t, s, t').$$

Players have a secondary interest in avoiding complexity. For the sender this means that she prefers short or otherwise unmarked expressions over long and marked ones. I will refrain from spelling this out in more detail. The fact that there is differential signal complexity should be uncontroversial; it underlies Grice's Maxim of Manner as well as more recent implementations such as Bidirectional Optimality Theory (cf. Blutner 2001). Pinning it down in a general way is not trivial, but I will confine myself to clear examples. Formally this is captured by a cost function c_s that maps type-signal pairs to real numbers. The assumption to make signal costs dependent on types is motivated by regularities such as TOPIC PRECEDES COMMENT that indicate that preferences over expressions may depend on the meaning that the speaker wants to express.

Likewise, the receiver may have, *ceteris paribus*, differential preferences between different interpretations of an expression – such as a dispreference for coercion or type shift, a preference for presupposition binding over accommodation etc. (cf. van der Sandt 1992). This is implemented by a cost function c_r that maps signal-action pairs to real numbers. (To my knowledge, receiver's costs as well as type-dependent sender's costs were first introduced in Franke &

Jäger 2012.) In all examples discussed in this chapter, receiver costs do not properly depend on signals but only on actions.

These assumptions are implemented by the following utility functions:

$$u_s(t,s,a) = -c_s(t,s) + \begin{cases} 1 & \text{if } t = a, \\ 0 & \text{else}, \end{cases}$$

$$u_s(t,s,a) = -c_r(s,a) + \begin{cases} 1 & \text{if } t = a, \\ 0 & \text{else}. \end{cases}$$

Unless otherwise noted, it is always assumed that costs are *nominal*. This means that costs are extremely low in comparison to the payoff that is to be gained from getting the type across correctly. They only ever play a role when comparing options that are otherwise equally successful for communication. Formally this can be ensured by the following postulate (The reason for this particular definition is the following: It will be motivated in the next section that we only need to consider strategies where the probability that a sender has to achieve succesful information transmission with a certain signal s is either 0 or $1/n$, for some positive integer $n \leq |\mathcal{A}|$. The latter occurs if the receiver maps s to one out of n different actions. The minimal difference between the success chance of two different signals is thus $1/n - 1/(n-1)$, which is always larger than $|\mathcal{A}|^{-2}$. The argument for the receiver is analogous.):

(4) NOMINAL COSTS

$$0 \leq c_s(t,s) < |\mathcal{A}|^{-2},$$

$$0 \leq c_r(s,a) < |S|^{-2}.$$

In our running example differential costs play no role, and we thus assume that all costs are 0.

The game construction for an example sentence, represented as signal s, is summarized in the following definition. (An inference relation is assumed to be given, and a set of sentences is consistent if not everything can be inferred from it.)

Definition 1 ((Strong) Interpretation Game) *Let s be an expression that is uttered in a context ct (where a context is a set of sentences the truth of which is common knowledge between the interlocutors), and that has a set of alternatives ALT(s) such that each element thereof is consistent with ct. The strong interpretation game $G_s^* = (T, p^*, S, \mathcal{A}, u_s, u_r)$ for s is constructed as follows, where c_s and c_r are nominal cost functions:*

$$T = \{t \subseteq S \mid t \neq \emptyset \wedge t \cap ct \text{ is consistent} \wedge$$
$$\forall s' \in S.t \vdash s \Rightarrow s \in t\},$$
$$p^*(t) = \frac{1}{|T|},$$
$$S = ALT(s),$$
$$t \models s' \Leftrightarrow s' \in t,$$
$$A = T,$$
$$u_s(t,s',a) = -c_s(t,s') + \begin{cases} 1 & \text{if } t = a, \\ 0 & \text{else}, \end{cases}$$
$$u_s(t,s',a) = -c_r(s',a) + \begin{cases} 1 & \text{if } t = a, \\ 0 & \text{else}. \end{cases}$$

3 Strategies and best responses

A (behavioral) strategy for the sender is a probabilistic function from types to signals. Formally, the set of sender strategies Σ is defined as

$$\Sigma = T \mapsto \Delta(S),$$

(where $\Delta(X)$ is the set of probability distributions over the set X, i.e. $p \in \Delta(X) \Leftrightarrow p \in X \mapsto [0, 1] \wedge \sum_{x \in X} p(x) = 1$). We write $\sigma(s|t)$ rather than $\sigma(t, s)$ to stress the intuition that this is the probability that the sender uses signal s provided she is in type t.

Likewise, the set P (speak: *Rho*) of receiver strategies consists of the probabilistic functions from S to A:

$$P = S \mapsto \Delta(A)$$

where $\rho(a|s)$ is the probability that, upon observing signal s, the receiver will perform action a.

It is important to note that these probabilities are again subjective probabilities. $\sigma \in \Sigma$ does not model the plan of the sender, but rather the expectations the receiver has about the sender's behavioral dispositions (and likewise for $\rho \in P$).

If the sender is in type t and has a model ρ of the receiver, she can estimate the utility that she can expect for each signal. This is captured by the notion of *expected utility*:

$$EU_s(s \mid t; \rho) = \sum_{a \in A} \rho(a \mid s) u_s(t, s, a).$$

For the utility function defined above, this simplifies to

$$EU_s(s\,|\,t;\rho) = \rho(t|s) - c_s(t,s).$$

To estimate the receiver's expected utility upon observing a signal s given a model σ of the sender, one needs the probability of the types in T conditional on observing s. σ provides the exact opposite, the conditional probability of signals given types. These two conditional probabilities are related via *Bayes' Rule*:

$$\sigma(t|s) = \frac{\sigma(t|s)\,p^*(t)}{\sum_{t'\in T}\sigma(s|t')\,p^*(t')}.$$

If p^* is a uniform distribution, this simplifies to

$$\sigma(t|s) = \frac{\sigma(s|t)}{\sum_{t'\in T}\sigma(s|t')}.$$

This is only defined if the denominator is > 0. If it does equal 0, σ assigns probability 0 to the signal s in all types t'. This would be a scenario where the receiver observes a signal that contradicts his model of the sender's behavior. Such signals are called *surprise signals*. They force the receiver to *revise his beliefs* in a way that accommodates the unexpected observation. The issue of the appropriate belief revision policy is a major issue in epistemic game theory, and I will not discuss it here at any length (see for instance Batigalli & Siniscalchi 2002). In the context of this chapter, I will adopt a rather simple version. If the receiver observes a surprise signal, he gives up all his assumptions about the sender's behavior and about costs of signals. He does preserve his knowledge about the literal interpretation of signals and about prior probabilities though. This is implemented in the following way:

$$\sigma(t|s) = \begin{cases} \dfrac{\sigma(s|t)}{\sum_{t'\in T}\sigma(s|t')} & \text{if } \sum_{t'\in T}\sigma(s|t') > 0 \\ \text{undefined} & \text{else.} \end{cases}$$

The receiver's expected utility given a model σ of the sender thus comes out as

$$EU_r(a|s;\sigma) = \begin{cases} \sum_{t\in T}\sigma(t|s)u_r(t,s,a) & \text{if defined} \\ \text{undefined} & \text{else.} \end{cases}$$

For the utility function given above, this simplifies to

$$EU_r(a|s;\sigma) = \begin{cases} \sigma(a|s) - c_r(s,a) & \text{if defined} \\ \text{undefined} & \text{else.} \end{cases}$$

Rational players will play a *best response* to their model of the other player, i.e. they will always choose an option that maximizes their expected utility. If the expected utility is not defined (i.e. if the receiver observes a surprise signal), the receiver takes resort to hypothesizing that the observed signal is true. This taken into account, best responses are defined as:

$$br_r(t,\rho) = \{s \mid EU_s(s|t;\rho) = \max_{s' \in S} EU_s(s'|t;\rho)\}$$

$$br_r(s,\sigma) = \begin{cases} a \mid EU_r(a|s;\sigma) = \max_{a' \in A} EU_r(a'|s;\sigma)\} & \text{if } EU_r(\cdot|s;\sigma) \text{ is defined,} \\ \{a \mid a \models s\} & \text{else.} \end{cases}$$

The *best response* (singular definite) of a player to a model of the other player is the behavioral strategy that assigns equal probabilities to all best responses (due to the principle of insufficient reason), and 0 to all sub-optimal responses.

$$BR_s(\rho) = \sigma \text{ iff } \sigma(s|t) = \begin{cases} \frac{1}{|br_s(t,\rho)|} & \text{if } s \in br_s(t,\rho), \\ 0 & \text{else} \end{cases}$$

$$BR_r(\sigma) = \rho \text{ iff } \rho(a|s) = \begin{cases} \frac{1}{|br_r(s,\sigma)|} & \text{if } a \in br_s(s,\sigma), \\ 0 & \text{else} \end{cases}$$

Let me illustrate these notions with the running example. Suppose the receiver assumes the sender to be absolutely honest, and this is the only assumption he makes about her. A model of such a sender would be σ_0, who sends some true signal in each state. Applying the principle of insufficient reason again, a receiver who expects the sender to be honest but makes no further assumptions about her will assign her the following strategy:

$$\sigma_0(s|t) = \begin{cases} \frac{1}{|\{s|t \models s\}|} & \text{if } t \models s, \\ 0 & \text{else.} \end{cases}$$

In our little example, σ_0 would look as in tab. 16.1.

Tab. 16.1: Honest sender σ_0

	NO	SOME	ALL
$w_{\neg\exists}$	1	0	0
$w_{\exists\neg\forall}$	0	1	0
$w_\forall$	0	$\frac{1}{2}$	$\frac{1}{2}$

The *expected utilities* of the receiver against the honest sender's strategy σ_0 come out as given in tab. 16.2 (which is the result of flipping tab. 16.1 along the diagonal and normalizing rowwise).

Tab. 16.2: $EU_r(\cdot\,|\,\cdot\,;\sigma_0)$

	$w_{\neg\exists}$	$w_{\exists\neg\forall}$	$w_\forall$
NO	1	0	0
SOME	0	$\frac{2}{3}$	$\frac{1}{3}$
ALL	0	0	1

Consider $\rho_0 = BR_r(\sigma_0)$, the best response of the receiver against σ_0 from tab. 17.1. In each type, the receiver will maximize his expected utility. So in each row in tab. 16.2, he will choose a cell that is maximal within this row. If there were several such cells, ρ_0 would put equal probability to each of it. In the example, the maxima are unique and thus receive a probability 1, as shown in tab. 16.3.

Tab. 16.3: $\rho_0 = BR_r(\sigma_0)$

	$w_{\neg\exists}$	$w_{\exists\neg\forall}$	$w_\forall$
NO	1	0	0
SOME	0	1	0
ALL	0	0	1

Computing the sender's expected utility against ρ_0 also amounts to simply flipping the tab. along the diagonal, and the best response to ρ_0 puts all probability mass into the cells with a maximal expected utility within its row (see tab. 16.4).

It is easy to see that $BR_r(BR_s(\rho_0)) = \rho_0$, so iterating the best response operation will not alter the strategies anymore.

Tab. 16.4: $EU_s(\cdot|\cdot; \rho_0), BR_s(\rho_0)$

	NO	SOME	ALL
$w_{\neg\exists}$	1	0	0
$w_{\exists\neg\forall}$	0	1	0
$w_\forall$	0	0	1

	NO	SOME	ALL
$w_{\neg\exists}$	1	0	0
$w_{\exists\neg\forall}$	0	1	0
$w_\forall$	0	0	1

4 Iterated Best Response

The notion of a best response models the behavior of rational players, given certain (perhaps probabilistic) assumptions about the behavior of the other player. But how are these assumptions formed? It might seem reasonable to assume that one's opponents are also rational. This means that they play a best response to their model of one's own behavior. This answer apparently only shifts the problem one step further, and this could be repeated *ad infinitum*.

The standard solution concept in classical game theory is agnostic with regard to the question where beliefs about other players come from. It is only required that beliefs are consistent with the assumption that everybody is rational (and that this fact is common knowledge). If I believe that my opponent has a correct model of my behavior and is rational, I will ascribe to them a best response to my behavior and they ascribe to me a best response to my behavior. Such a state is self-reinforcing. It is called a *Nash equilibrium*. There is no simple answer to the question though how players find such an equilibrium in the first place. This problem is aggravated by the fact that many games have many equilibria. In our example, the 1–1 map between types and signals from tab. 17.3 (together with the best response to it) constitutes an equilibrium, but so do the other five 1–1 maps, plus an infinity of properly stochastic strategy pairs.

In the present context the equilibrium concept is thus problematic because it disregards the literal meaning of signals – any 1–1 map between meanings and signals is as good as any other. Also, results from behavioral experiments suggest that people are actually not very good at finding Nash equilibria, even if there is only one. This can be illustrated with the game "p-beauty contest". In this game, each of n test persons is asked to pick a (real) number between 0 and 100. The winner is the one whose choice is closest to p times the average of all numbers from the group, where p is some number that is announced in advance. Suppose $p = 0.7$. Then the only Nash equilibrium of the game is that everybody picks 0 (because for any other average, one could benefit by undercutting this average). This game has been tested experimentally many times, with very revealing results. For instance, Camerer & Fehr (2006) report that participants chose numbers from the entire interval [0, 100], with peaks around 50, 35 and 25. Their interpretation is that the participants fall into three groups. The irrational players simply choose a random number without any strategic thinking. (The authors do not interpret the peak at 50, but it seems to me that this is just a variant of irrational behavior were 50 is chosen because it is located nicely in the center of the interval.) Then there are *level-1 players*. They anticipate that many people are irrational, and that their average choice is 50. The best response to this is to pick $50 \times 0.7 = 35$. Finally, *level-2 players* expect there to be level-1 players and play a best response to their choice. This would be $35 \times 0.7 = 24.5$ and corresponds to the peak at 25.

Similar results have been found time and again by other researchers. (See Camerer 2003 for further information and references.) It is also interesting that the average choice quickly converges towards 0 if the game is repeated and the players get feedback about the average outcome after each round (as reported in Slonim 2005). So repeated playing seems to foster level-k thinking for levels > 2.

These considerations lead to the following model: There is a default strategy that people follow if they do not deliberate. In the beauty contest game, this is the strategy to pick randomly from the available numbers. Furthermore, there is a *cognitive hierarchy* of rational player types of ever higher sophistication. *Level-1* players play a best response to the default strategy, *level-2* players a best response to *level-1* players and so on. (Note that the level of a player does not necessarily measure their ability to perform nested reasoning. It is also bounded by their assumption about the level of their opponent.)

This architecture is readily applicable to interpretation games. The default strategy of a non-deliberating player is the honest sender σ_0 that sends each true signal with the same probability in each type. (Jäger & Ebert 2009 and Franke 2009 also consider a default strategy for the receiver where each signal is assigned a uniform distribution over types where this signal is true. This version of the model leads to unwelcome predictions in connection with I-implicatures though. In example (7), starting with the receiver would lead to a fixed point where the I-implicature does not emerge.) A *level-0 receiver* plays the best response ρ_0 to σ_0, a *level-1 sender* plays the best response to ρ_0 and so on. This is captured by the notion of an *IBR sequence* (where *IBR* abbreviates *Iterated Best Response*).

Definition 2 (IBR sequence)

$$\sigma_0(s|t) = \begin{cases} \dfrac{1}{|\{s\,|\,t\models s\}|} & \text{if } t \models s, \\ 0 & \text{else,} \end{cases}$$

$$\rho_n = BR_r(\sigma_n),$$
$$\sigma_{n+1} = BR_s(\rho_n)$$

In the running example σ_1 is given in the left panel of tab. 17.4. For all $n > 1$, $\sigma_n = \sigma_1$ and $\rho_n = \rho_0$. The strategy pair (σ_1, ρ_0) is a fixed point of the IBR sequence and thus a Nash equilibrium. It can be shown that with a utility function as given in Equation (1) and nominal costs, the IBR sequence always reaches a fixed point (see Appendix).

Let s be an expression and $\mathcal{G}(s)$ the interpretation game constructed for s. Let (σ^*, ρ^*) be the fixed point of the IBR sequence. The IBR model then predicts that s receives as possible readings the set $\{a\,|\,\rho^*(a|s) > 0\}$. For the running example, the prediction is thus that *Some boys came to the party* will be interpreted as entailing that not all boys came to the party. As this game is constructed from expression (2.), it does not serve to make predictions about the interpretation of the alternative expressions (even though in this example these predictions would be correct). Also, the model is not designed to make predictions about speaker behavior, so it is not claimed that a speaker who wants to express that some but not all boys came will use expression (2.).

5 Examples

The previous example illustrated how scalar implicatures are derived in the IBR model. Here is another example of a quantitity implicature:

(5) (Who of Ann and Bert came to the party?) Ann came to the party.

The question defines a set of alternative answers:

(6) a. Ann came to the party. (= ANN)
    b. Bert came to the party. (= BERT)
    c. Neither came to the party. (= NEITHER)
    d. Both came to the party. (= BOTH)

They define four possible worlds (i.e. maximally consistent sets of alternatives or their negations): Only Ann came (w_a), only Bert came (w_b), neither came ($w_\emptyset$) or both came ($w_{a,b}$).

σ_0 is constructed in the following way:
- Draw a table with types as rows and expressions as columns.
- Put a 1 in each cell where the column-expression is true in the row-world, and 0 everywhere else.
- Divide each row by its sum.

The result is shown in tab. 16.5.

Tab. 16.5: σ_0

	ANN	BERT	NEITHER	BOTH
w_a	1	0	0	0
w_b	0	1	0	0
$w_\emptyset$	0	0	1	0
w_{ab}	$\frac{1}{3}$	$\frac{1}{3}$	0	$\frac{1}{3}$

The table for the best response $BR_r(\sigma)$ to some sender strategy σ can be constructed by the following operations:
- Flip the table for σ along the main diagonal.
- If a row consists only of 0s, replace each cell corresponding to a true type-signal association with 1.
- Otherwise subtract receiver costs from each cell, replace each cell that is maximal within its row by 1, and every other cell by 0.
- Divide each row by its sum.

Note that the best response to a surprise signal (a column with only 0s in a receiver strategy) only makes use of the literal meaning of that signal and disregards costs. This reflects the fact that surprise signals enforce belief revision. In the present model, speakers only preserve their knowledge about the literal meanings of signals under belief revision and delete all other information.

The table for the best response $BR_s(\rho)$ to some receiver strategy ρ can be computed by the following steps:
- Flip the table for ρ along the main diagonal.
- Subtract sender costs from each cell.
- Replace each cell that is maximal within its row by 1, and all other cells by 0.
- Divide each row by its sum.

The strategy $\sigma_1 = BR_s(\rho_0)$ is given in tab. 16.6.

Tab. 16.6:

p_0	w_a	w_b	$w_\emptyset$	w_{ab}	σ_1	ANN	BERT	NEITHER	BOTH
ANN	1	0	0	0	w_a	1	0	0	0
BERT	0	1	0	0	w_a	0	1	0	0
NEITHER	0	0	1	0	$w_\emptyset$	0	0	1	0
BOTH	0	0	0	1	w_{ab}	0	0	0	1

(σ_1, ρ_0) form a fixed point. Hence the model predicts that (5.) is interpreted exhaustively, i.e. in the sense that Ann but not Bert came to the party.

The two examples illustrate the general pattern of *quantity implicatures*. If an expression A has an alternative B that is logically stronger than A, then in the fixed point A will be interpreted exhaustively, i.e. as entailing "A and not B".

This inference may be blocked though if the alternative set already contains an expression which literally denotes "A and not B". This may be illustrated with the next example.

(7) a. John opened the door. (= OPEN)
   b. John opened the door using the handle. (= OPEN-H)
   c. John opened the door with an axe. (= OPEN-A)

Normally (7a) will be interpreted as meaing (7b) rather than (c). This is an instance of an inference type that Levinson (2000) calls *I-implicatures* – underspecified expressions tend to be interpreted as the prototypical elements of their literal denotation.

Suppose (b) and (c) are expression alternatives in the interpretation game for (a), and suppose that the only ways to open a door is with the handle or with an axe. (This example is a bit more abstract than the previous two, first because the set of alternatives along the lines of (7c) is actually open-ended, and second because these alternatives are arguably not activated in the same way when interpreting (a) as for instance the scalar alternatives are in the first example. Nevertheless the example is instructive to illustrate the logic of the IBR model.) Under these assumptions, there are just two possible worlds: w_h where John opens the door with the handle, and w_a where he uses an axe. (Recall that the possible worlds are maximally consistent sets of alternatives or negations thereof *that contain at least one non-negated expression*. Therefore the alternatives do not generate a world where John does not open the door at all.)

In this example costs play a role. The implicature arises because (7a) is shorter than both (b) and (c), and because w_h is more prototypical than w_a. Let us thus say that the costs are as given in tab. 16.7, where the first number in each cell give the sender's cost and the second the receiver's. The actual choice of numbers is inessential for the IBR sequence. As long as costs are sufficiently small, only the relative ranking of the different alternative types and expressions according to their costs matters.

The construction of σ_0 follows the same procedure as explained above.

Tab. 16.7: Cost functions

c_s, c_r	OPEN	OPEN-H	OPEN-A
w_h	0, 0	$\frac{1}{20}$, 0	$\frac{1}{20}$, 0
w_a	0, $\frac{1}{20}$	$\frac{1}{20}, \frac{1}{20}$	$\frac{1}{20}, \frac{1}{20}$

The IBR sequence for example (7) is given in tab. 17.8. The fixed point is (σ_1, ρ_1). The signal OPEN is interpreted as the proposition $\{w_h\}$, i.e. as expressing that John opened the door using the handle.

Note that this outcome depends both on differential costs between the different signals and the fact that the more specific signals jointly exhaust the meaning of the more general signal. If OPEN would not entail OPEN-H ∨ OPEN-A,

Tab. 16.8: IBR sequence

σ_0	OPEN	OPEN-H	OPEN-A
w_h	$\frac{1}{2}$	$\frac{1}{2}$	0
w_a	$\frac{1}{2}$	0	$\frac{1}{2}$
σ_1	OPEN	OPEN-H	OPEN-A
w_h	1	0	0
w_a	0	0	1

ρ_0	w_h	w_a
OPEN	1	0
OPEN-H	1	0
OPEN-A	0	1
ρ_1	w_h	w_a
OPEN	1	0
OPEN-H	1	0
OPEN-A	0	1

there would be a third type w^* where John opened the door, but neither with the handle nor with an axe, and OPEN would be interpreted as $\{w^*\}$, i.e. we would observe a quantity implicature rather than an I-implicature.

A similar but slightly more complex inference pattern has been called *M-implicature* or *division of pragmatic labor* (Horn 1984). An example is given in (8).

(8) a. John stopped the car. (= STOP)
    b. John made the car stop. (= MAKE-STOP)

Normally (8a) is interpreted a referring to an event where John stopped the car in the usual way, i.e. using the foot brake, while (b) rather conveys that he stopped it in a less conventional way, such as using the hand brake or driving into the ditch.

The following game is again more of an illustration of the working of the IBR model than a serious attempt to analyze this particular linguistic example. Suppose there are two possible worlds: in w_1 John stops the car using the foot brake, and in w_2 he drives it into the ditch. These are the only ways to stop the car. Both STOP and MAKE-STOP are true in both worlds. The receiver has, *ceteris paribus*, a preference for w_1 over w_2, which is mirrored by the fact the latter has higher receiver costs than the former. Likewise, the sender has a preference for STOP over MAKE-STOP, which ich mirrored in the cost function. The cost functions are given in tab. 16.9.

Tab. 16.9: Cost functions

c_s, c_r	STOP	MAKE-STOP
w_1	0, 0	$\frac{1}{10}$, 0
w_2	0, $\frac{1}{10}$	$\frac{1}{10}$, $\frac{1}{10}$

Tab. 16.10 shows the IBR sequence for this game. In the fixed point (σ_2, ρ_2), STOP is interpreted as $\{w_1\}$ and make-stop as $\{w_2\}$.

Tab. 16.10: IBR sequence

σ_0	STOP	MAKE-STOP
w_1	$\frac{1}{2}$	$\frac{1}{2}$
w_2	$\frac{1}{2}$	$\frac{1}{2}$
σ_1	STOP	MAKE-STOP
w_1	1	0
w_2	1	0
σ_2	STOP	MAKE-STOP
w_1	1	0
w_2	0	1

ρ_0	w_1	w_2
STOP	1	0
MAKE-STOP	1	0
ρ_1	w_1	w_2
STOP	1	0
MAKE-STOP	$\frac{1}{2}$	$\frac{1}{2}$
ρ_2	w_1	w_2
STOP	1	0
MAKE-STOP	0	1

6 Game construction II: Lifted games

In its present version, our model assumes a very strong version of the competence assumption: it is hard-wired into the model that the speaker knows the complete answer to the question under discussion. This is not just unrealistic, it also leads to unwarranted predictions. Consider (9), the standard example for a quantity implicature.

(9) a. Ann or Bert showed up. (= OR)
    b. Ann showed up. (= A)
    c. Bert showed up. (= B)
    d. Ann and Bert showed up. (= AND)

Since Grice (1975) it is a common assumption that *or* literally denotes inclusive disjunction, and that the exclusive interpretation is due to a quantity implicature, arising from the competition with *and*. If we assume that the alternative set to (9) is (9a–d), we end up with a game that is represented by σ_0 in tab. 16.11.

In the fixed point (σ_1, ρ_1), OR receives the inclusive interpretation. What is even more odd is that OR is a surprise signal, because it is never used in σ_1. This is a consequence of the strong competence assumption. For each of the three maximally informative information states assumed here, there is a more specific signal, so OR is in fact superfluous in this game.

To adequately deal with examples like this, we have to take the possibility into account that the sender is underinformed. This can be accommodated if we

Tab. 16.11: IBR sequence

σ_0	OR	A	B	AND
w_a	$\frac{1}{2}$	$\frac{1}{2}$	0	0
w_b	$\frac{1}{2}$	0	$\frac{1}{2}$	0
w_{ab}	$\frac{1}{4}$	$\frac{1}{4}$	$\frac{1}{4}$	$\frac{1}{4}$

σ_1	OR	A	B	AND
w_a	0	1	0	0
w_b	0	0	1	0
w_{ab}	0	0	0	1

ρ_0	w_a	w_b	w_{ab}
OR	$\frac{1}{2}$	$\frac{1}{2}$	0
A	1	0	0
B	0	1	0
AND	0	0	1

ρ_1	w_a	w_b	w_{ab}
OR	$\frac{1}{3}$	$\frac{1}{3}$	$\frac{1}{3}$
A	1	0	0
B	0	1	0
AND	0	0	0

identify information states, i.e. types, with non-empty *sets* of possible worlds (as it is standard practice since Stalnaker 1978). Franke (2009) calls this kind of game *epistemically lifted games*. So if W is the set of worlds that is constructed from a set of alternative expressions,

$$T = POW(W) - \{\phi\}.$$

An expression is considered true in a state if it is true in all possible worlds in this state, i.e.

$$t \models s \text{ iff } \forall w \in t. w \models s.$$

The competence assumption is not completely given up though. A weaker version of it is implemented via the receiver's cost function. Everything else being equal, the receiver has a preference for more specific interpretations (cf. Dalrymple et al.'s 1994 *Strongest Meaning Hypothesis*). This corresponds to the *weak competence assumption*

$$a_1 \subseteq a_2 \Rightarrow \forall s. c_r(s, a_1) < c_r(s, a_2).$$

For concreteness' sake, let us say that

$$\forall s. c(s, a) \propto |a|.$$

Applied to example (9), this leads to the following cost functions (It is assumed that AND and OR are more complex than A and B for the sender, but nothing hinges on this in this example.):

$$\forall t. c_s(t, A) = c_s(t, B) = 0,$$
$$\forall t. c_s(t, AND) = c_s(t, OR) = \frac{1}{100},$$
$$\forall s. c_r(s, a) = \frac{|a|}{1000}.$$

The IBR sequence is given in tab. 16.12.

The fixed point here is (σ_1, ρ_0). Two things are noteworthy in this example. First, the construction correctly predicts that OR receives an exclusive interpretation. Second, the usage of OR triggers an ignorance implicature. In the fixed point strategy, the receiver infers from observing OR that the sender does not know a for sure, and she doesn't know b for sure either.

The game construction for lifted interpretation games is summarized in the following definition. These games are called *weak interpretation games* because they implement the *weak competence assumption*. Strong interpretation games emerge as the special case when the context contains the assumption that the speaker knows the complete answer to the question under discussion.

Tab. 16.12: IBR sequence in the epistemically lifted game

σ_0	OR	A	B	AND
$\{w_a\}$	$\frac{1}{2}$	$\frac{1}{2}$	0	0
$\{w_b\}$	$\frac{1}{2}$	0	$\frac{1}{2}$	0
$\{w_{ab}\}$	$\frac{1}{2}$	0	0	$\frac{1}{2}$
$\{w_a, w_b\}$	$\frac{1}{4}$	$\frac{1}{4}$	$\frac{1}{4}$	$\frac{1}{4}$
$\{w_a, w_{ab}\}$	$\frac{1}{2}$	$\frac{1}{2}$	0	0
$\{w_b, w_{ab}\}$	$\frac{1}{2}$	0	$\frac{1}{2}$	0
$\{w_a, w_b, w_{ab}\}$	1	0	0	0

σ_0	$\{w_a\}$	$\{w_b\}$	$\{w_{ab}\}$	$\{w_a, w_b\}$	$\{w_a, w_{ab}\}$	$\{w_b, w_{ab}\}$	$\{w_a, w_b, w_{ab}\}$
OR	0	0	0	1	0	0	0
A	1	0	0	0	0	0	0
B	0	1	0	0	0	0	0
AND	0	0	1	0	0	0	0

σ_0	OR	A	B	AND
$\{w_a\}$	0	1	0	0
$\{w_b\}$	0	0	1	0
$\{w_{ab}\}$	0	0	0	1
$\{w_a, w_b\}$	1	0	0	0
$\{w_a, w_{ab}\}$	0	$\frac{1}{2}$	$\frac{1}{2}$	0
$\{w_b, w_{ab}\}$	0	$\frac{1}{2}$	$\frac{1}{2}$	0
$\{w_a, w_b, w_{ab}\}$	0	$\frac{1}{2}$	$\frac{1}{2}$	0

Definition 3 (Weak Interpretation Game) *Let s be an expression that is uttered in a context ct and that has a set of alternatives ALT(s) such that each element thereof is consistent with ct. The weak interpretation game $\mathcal{G}_s = (\mathcal{T}, p^*, S, \mathcal{A}, u_s, u_r)$ for s is constructed as follows, where c_s and c_r are nominal cost functions:*

$$\mathcal{W} = \{w \subseteq S \mid w \neq \emptyset \land w \cap ct \text{ is consistent} \land$$
$$\forall s' \in S. w \vdash s \Rightarrow s \in w\},$$
$$\mathcal{T} = POW(\mathcal{W}) - \{\emptyset\}$$

$$p^*(t) = \frac{1}{|\mathcal{T}|},$$

$$S = ALT(s),$$
$$t \vdash s' \Leftrightarrow \forall w \in t. s' \in w,$$
$$\mathcal{A} = \mathcal{T}$$

$$u_s(t, s', a) = -c_s(t, s') + \begin{cases} 1 & \text{if } t = a, \\ 0 & \text{else,} \end{cases}$$

$$u_s(t, s', a) = -c_r(s', a) + \begin{cases} 1 & \text{if } t = a, \\ 0 & \text{else,} \end{cases}$$

$$a_1 \subseteq a_1 \Rightarrow \forall s'. c_r(s', a_1) < c_r(s', a_2).$$

The difference between the strong and the weak competence assumption may be significant. This applies for instance to *free choice permission* sentences such as (10a) (cf. Kamp 1973):

(10) a You may take an apple or a banana. (= $\Diamond(A \lor B)$)
  b. You may take an apple. (= $\Diamond A$)
  c. You may take a banana. (= $\Diamond B$)
  d. You may take and apple and a banana. (= $\Diamond(A \land B)$)

Sentence (a) normally receives a *free choice* interpretation: You may take an apple, and you may take a banana. Furthermore the sentence implicates that the adressee is not allowed to take both an apple and a banana.

The free choice interpretation rests on the background assumption that the speaker is the one who grants the permission. This of course entails that the speaker is maximally competent about the permission state of the adressee. If the speaker simply reports the permission that somebody else granted (enforced for instance by the continuation *but I don't know which*), the free choice inference does not emerge. The disjunction still preferably receives an exhaustive interpretation – the adressee is not allowed to take both kinds of fruit simultaneously.

Let us construct an interpretation game for (10a). It seems reasonable to assume that the alternatives to (10a) are (10b-d), which are taken to have the logical forms which are given in brackets. If we assume the standard inference relation for modal logic (system K), we have four possible worlds here:
- $w_a = \{\Diamond A, \Diamond(A \vee B)\}$: You may take an apple but not a banana.
- $w_b = \{\Diamond B, \Diamond(A \vee B)\}$: You may take a banana but not an apple.
- $w_{a;b} = \{\Diamond A, \Diamond B, \Diamond(A \vee B)\}$: You may take an apple and you may take a banana, but not both.
- $w_{ab} = \{\Diamond A, \Diamond B, \Diamond(A \vee B), \Diamond(A \wedge B)\}$: You may take both an apple and a banana.

(10a,d) are longer than (b,c), so it is reasonable to assume that they have higher costs. Let us say that $c(t, \Diamond(A)) = c(t, \Diamond(B)) = 0$ and $c(t, \Diamond(A \vee B)) = c(t, \Diamond(A \wedge B)) = \frac{1}{1000}$). Under the strong competence assumption, the IBR sequence comes out as in tab. 16.13.

In the fixed point (σ_2, ρ_2), (10a) correctly comes out as having the exhaustive free choice interpretation "You may take an apple and you may take a banana, but not both."

Tab. 16.13: IBR sequence

σ_0	$\Diamond (A \vee B)$	$\Diamond A$	$\Diamond A$	$\Diamond (A \vee B)$	ρ_0	w_a	w_b	$w_{a:b}$	w_{ab}
w_a	$\frac{1}{2}$	$\frac{1}{2}$	0	0	$\Diamond (A \vee B)$	$\frac{1}{2}$	$\frac{1}{2}$	0	0
w_a	$\frac{1}{2}$	0	$\frac{1}{2}$	0	$\Diamond A$	1	0	0	0
$w_{a:b}$	$\frac{1}{3}$	$\frac{1}{3}$	$\frac{1}{3}$	0	$\Diamond B$	0	1	0	0
w_{ab}	$\frac{1}{3}$	$\frac{1}{4}$	$\frac{1}{4}$	$\frac{1}{4}$	$\Diamond (A \wedge B)$	0	0	0	1

σ_1	$\Diamond (A \vee B)$	$\Diamond A$	$\Diamond B$	$\Diamond (A \vee B)$	ρ_1	w_a	w_b	$w_{a:b}$	w_{ab}
w_a	0	1	0	0	$\Diamond (A \vee B)$	$\frac{1}{4}$	$\frac{1}{4}$	$\frac{1}{4}$	$\frac{1}{4}$
w_b	0	0	1	0	$\Diamond A$	1	0	0	0
$w_{a:b}$	0	$\frac{1}{2}$	$\frac{1}{2}$	0	$\Diamond B$	0	1	0	0
w_{ab}	0	0	1	1	$\Diamond (A \wedge B)$	0	0	0	1

Tab. 16.13: *(Continued)*

σ_2	$\Diamond (A \vee B)$	$\Diamond A$	$\Diamond B$	$\Diamond (A \vee B)$
w_a	0	1	0	0
w_b	0	0	1	0
$w_{a:b}$	1	0	0	0
w_{ab}	0	0	0	1

ρ_1	w_a	w_b	$w_{a:b}$	w_{ab}
$\Diamond (A \vee B)$	0	0	1	0
$\Diamond A$	1	0	0	0
$\Diamond B$	0	1	0	0
$\Diamond (A \wedge B)$	0	0	0	1

Now suppose the strong competence assumption is replaced by its weak counterpart. This would be a scenario where the sender is not the person granting the permission, but just somebody who has information about the addressee's permission state. Then we end up with fifteen information states. For reasons of space, I will only show the the five of them which are relevant (see tab. 16.14). Here

Tab. 16.14: IBR sequence

σ_0	$\Diamond (A \vee B)$	$\Diamond A$	$\Diamond B$	$\Diamond (A \vee B)$
$\{w_a\}$	$\frac{1}{2}$	$\frac{1}{2}$	0	0
$\{w_b\}$	$\frac{1}{2}$	0	$\frac{1}{2}$	0
$\{w_{a;b}\}$	$\frac{1}{3}$	$\frac{1}{3}$	$\frac{1}{3}$	0
$\{w_{ab}\}$	$\frac{1}{4}$	$\frac{1}{4}$	$\frac{1}{4}$	$\frac{1}{4}$
$\{w_a, w_a\}$	0	0	0	0
⋮	⋮	⋮	⋮	⋮

ρ_0	$\{w_a\}$	$\{w_b\}$	$\{w_{a;b}\}$	$\{w_{ab}\}$	$\{w_a, w_b\}$	...
$\Diamond (A \vee B)$	0	0	0	0	1	...
$\Diamond A$	1	0	0	0	0	...
$\Diamond B$	0	1	0	0	0	...
$\Diamond (A \wedge B)$	0	0	0	1	0	...

σ_1	$\Diamond (A \vee B)$	$\Diamond A$	$\Diamond B$	$\Diamond (A \vee B)$
$\{w_a\}$	0	1	0	0
$\{w_b\}$	0	0	1	0
$\{w_{a;b}\}$	0	$\frac{1}{2}$	$\frac{1}{2}$	0
$\{w_{ab}\}$	0	0	0	1
$\{w_a, w_a\}$	1	0	0	0
⋮	⋮	⋮	⋮	⋮

a fixed point is already reached at (σ_1, ρ_0). In this fixed point, (10a) is interpreted as $\Diamond A \leftrightarrow \neg \Diamond B$, i.e. we get an ordinary exclusive wide scope interpretation for the disjunction plus an ignorance implicature (the speaker does not know whether the addresse may take an apple or whether he may take a banana), rather than a free choice reading.

7 Embedded implicatures

Chierchia (2004) makes a case that scalar implicatures are actually not the outcome of a Gricean reasoning procedure that is based on rationality assumptions. Rather, he proposes that these inferences are strictly speaking not implicatures at all, but rather part of the literal meaning of the sentence in question. He motivates this, among other arguments, with examples such as (11).

(11) a. Kai had broccoli or some of the peas. (B ∨ ∃xPx)
     b. Kai had broccoli or all of the peas. (B ∨ ∀xPx)

The argument runs as follows. Let A be an expression which competes with a logically stronger scalar alternative B. According to the Gricean view, if the speaker would believe that B, he would have said said so. Since she didn't say it, she doesn't believe it. If she is also competent, we can conclude that she does not believe that B, and thus B is false. If this is applied to (11a), we have a scalar alternative (11b), which is logically stronger. Hence there should be an implicature to the effect that (11b) is false, i.e. that Kai didn't have broccoli and didn't eat all of the peas.

However, the (a)-sentence does not implicate that Kai didn't have broccoli. What is implicated is much weaker, namely that Kai had broccoli or he had some *but not all* of the peas. The strengthing of *some* to *some but not all* happens within the scope of the disjunction. Chierchia and his followers conclude from this that the information *he did not eat all of the peas* is part of the truth conditions of the second disjunct.

This is not the place to explore the issue whether or not implicatures are computed locally. (An extensive discussion from a neo-Gricean point of view can be found in Geurts 2010.) I will confine myself to showing why Chierchia's argument does not apply to the kind of pragmatic reasoning that is formalized by the IBR model.

As pointed out by Sauerland (2004), the alternatives that have to be taken into consideration when evaluating (11a) also include the sentences in (12).

(12) a. Kai had broccoli. (= B)
    b. Kai had some of the peas. (= $\exists x P x$)
    c. Kai had all of the peas. (= $\forall x P x$)
    d. Kai had broccoli and some of the peas. (= $B \wedge \exists x P x$)
    e. Kai had broccoli and all of the peas. (= $B \wedge \forall x P x$)

These seven alternatives give rise to five different possible worlds:

- $w_{B\neg\exists} = \{B, B \vee \exists x P x, B \vee \forall x P x\}$,
- $w_{\neg B \exists \neg \forall} = \{\exists x P x, B \vee \exists x P x\}$,
- $w_{\neg B \forall} = \{\exists x P x, \forall x P x, B \vee \exists x P x, B \vee \forall x P x\}$,
- $w_{B \exists \neg \forall} = \{B, \exists x P x, B \vee \exists x P x, B \vee \forall x P x, B \wedge \exists x P x\}$,
- $w_{B \forall} = \{B, \exists x P x, B \vee \exists x P x, B \vee \forall x P x, B \wedge \exists x P x, B \wedge \forall x P x\}$.

As the strong competence assumption is not warranted in this example, we have to construct a weak interpretation game, which has 31 different types. For reasons of space I will only present the IBR reasoning for the relevant subset thereof, which are seven types in this case. These are the five maximally informative types, plus two types consisting of two possible worlds each. These seven types are the only relevant ones in the sense that all other types have probability 0 for each signal under each ρ_n in the IBR sequence. The first two steps of the IBR sequence are given in tab. 16.15. The relevant part of σ_1 is simply the transpose of the displayed part of ρ_0, and (σ_1, ρ_0) form a fixed point.

Tab. 16.15: IBR sequence

σ_0	B	$\exists x P x$	$\forall x P x$	$B \vee \exists x P x$	$B \wedge \exists x P x$	$B \vee \forall x P x$	$B \wedge \forall x P x$
$\{w_{B\neg\exists}\}$	$\frac{1}{3}$	0	0	$\frac{1}{3}$	0	$\frac{1}{3}$	0
$\{w_{\neg B \exists \neg \forall}\}$	0	$\frac{1}{2}$	0	$\frac{1}{2}$	0	0	0

Tab. 16.15: (Continued)

σ_0	B	∃xPx	∀xPx	B ∨ ∃xPx	B ∧ ∃xPx	B ∨ ∀xPx	B ∧ ∀xPx
$\{w_{\neg B\lor}\}$	0	$\frac{1}{4}$	$\frac{1}{4}$	$\frac{1}{4}$	0	$\frac{1}{4}$	0
$\{w_{B\exists\neg\forall}\}$	$\frac{1}{5}$	$\frac{1}{5}$	0	$\frac{1}{5}$	$\frac{1}{5}$	$\frac{1}{5}$	0
$\{w_{B\lor}\}$	$\frac{1}{7}$	$\frac{1}{7}$	$\frac{1}{7}$	$\frac{1}{7}$	$\frac{1}{7}$	$\frac{1}{7}$	$\frac{1}{7}$
$\{w_{B\neg\forall}, w_{\neg B\exists\neg\forall}\}$	0	0	0	1	0	0	0
$\{w_{B\neg\exists}, w_{\neg B\lor}\}$	0	0	0	$\frac{1}{2}$	0	$\frac{1}{2}$	0

ρ_0	$\{w_{B\neg\exists}\}$	$\{w_{\neg B\exists\neg\forall}\}$	$\{w_{\neg B\lor}\}$	$\{w_{B\exists\neg\forall}\}$	$\{w_{B\lor}\}$	$\{w_{B\neg\forall}, w_{\neg B\exists\neg\forall}\}$	$\{w_{B\neg\exists}, w_{\neg B\lor}\}$
B	1	0	0	0	0	0	0
∃ x Px	0	1	0	0	0	0	0
∀ x Px	0	0	1	0	0	0	0
B ∨ ∃xPx	0	0	0	0	0	1	0
B ∧ ∃xPx	0	0	0	1	0	0	0
B ∨ ∀xPx	0	0	0	0	0	0	1
B ∧ ∀xPx	0	0	0	0	1	0	0

As can be seen from the fourth row of ρ_0, (11a) is interpreted as $\{w_{B\neg\exists}, w_{\neg B\exists\neg\forall}\}$. This means that either Kai ate broccoli or some but not all of the peas, but not both, and the speaker does not know which. The IBR model thus predicts a narrow scope exhaustive interpretation of *some*, an exclusive interpration of *or* and an ignorance implicature, which is empirically correct.

It is illuminating to explore why Chierchia's problem does not apply here. It is true that the sender could have uttered B ∨ ∀xPx, but she did not do so. There may be more than one reason though why she avoided that signal. In $w_{B\neg\exists}$ she believes it to be true but prefers to utter B, because it is more informative. In $w_{\neg B\forall}$ she prefers ∀xPx, for the same reason. In $w_{B\exists\neg\forall}$ she prefers B ∧ ∃xPx, again for the same reason. In $w_{B\lor}$, finally, she prefers the more informative B ∧ ∀xPx. So if the speaker is maximally competent, she would never utter (11b). The most plausible explanation for her using that signal would be that she is in state $\{w_{B\neg\exists}, w_{\neg B\lor}\}$, i.e. she believes that Kai either had broccoli but no peas or all peas but no broccoli, but not both. The fact that she refrained from using this signal thus only entails that she doesn't hold this belief state, which is consistent with the intuitive interpretation of (11a).

8 Beyond nominal costs

In the model presented so far, the main objective of the players is to achieve correct information transmission. If the receiver guesses the sender's type correctly, both score a utility close to 1; otherwise their utility is close to 0. There are various domains where the degree of communicative success is not binary. If the sender wants to communicate that the temperature is 21 degree and the receiver guesses that the temperature is 20 degree, information transmission was not perfect, but much better than in a scenario where the receiver guesses 10 degree. Quite generally, there may be a graded notion of *similarity* between types, and the goal of communication is to maximize the similarity between the sender's type and receiver's action. (This idea has been explored in detail in Jäger & van Rooij 2007; Jäger 2007a; Jäger, Koch-Metzger & Riedel 2011.) If the degree of similarity between types is continuous, there may be scenarios where the expected gain in communicative success for choosing a more costly signal is lower than the increase in costs. This means that costs are not always nominal anymore. The consequences of this approach are explored in the final example of this article.

Krifka (2002) observes that the pragmatic interpretation of number words follows an interesting pattern:

"RN/RI principle:

a. Short, simple numbers suggest low precision levels.
b. Long, complex numbers suggest high precision levels."

(Krifka 2002: 433)

This can be illustrated with the following contrast:

(13) a. The distance is one hundred meters. (= 100)
b. The distance is one hundred and one meter. (= 101)

The sentence (13b) suggests a rather precise interpretation (with a slack of at most 50 cm), while (13a) can be more vague. It may perhaps mean something between 90 and 110 meter. Actually, (13a) is pragmatically ambiguous; depending on context, it can be rather precise or rather vague. The crucial observation here is: A shorter number term such as "one hundred" allows for a larger degree of vagueness than a more complex term such as "one hundred and one."

Krifka also observes that the degree of vagueness of a short term can be reduced by making it more complex – for instance by modifying it with "exactly":

(14) The distance is exactly one hundred meter. (= EX-100)

Krifka (2002) accounts for these facts in terms of bidirectional OT, assuming a general preference for vague over precise interpretation. Krifka (2007) contains a revised analysis which employs game theoretic pragmatics. Space does not permit a detailed discussion of Krifka's proposals; in the following I will just briefly sketch how the IBR model accounts for Krifka's observations.

We use (13a,b) and (14) as expression alternatives. If we assume that the literal denotation of 100 and EXACTLY-100 is identical – 100 meter sharp – , we end up with two possible worlds. However, the scenario potentially contains another source of uncertainty of the receiver about the sender's information state. The sender may or may not consider precision important for the task at hand. (Like in the examples relating to I- and M-implicatures, this game cannot be constructed according to the recipe given above. For the time being, I simply stipulate the parameters of the game and leave the issue how the game is to be extracted from the linguistic information for further research.) This gives us four possible worlds:

- w_1: length is 100 meter; precision is important.
- w_2: length is 101 meter; precision is important.
- w_3: length is 100 meter; precision is not important.
- w_4: length is 101 meter; precision is not important.

If $[\![\cdot]\!]$ is the function that maps a signal to the set of types where it is true, we assume

$$[\![100]\!] = [\![\text{EXACTLY-100}]\!] = \{w_1, w_3\}$$

$$[\![101]\!] = \{w_2, w_4\}$$

The utility functions now depend on the similarity between types. Formally, they are defined as:

$$u_s(t, s, a) = \text{sim}(t, a) - c_s(t, s)$$
$$u_r(t, s, a) = \text{sim}(t, a) - c_r(s, a)$$

The similarity function sim is given in tab. 16.16.

Furthermore, I assume that $c_s(t, 100) = 0$ and $c_s(t, 101) = c_s(t, \text{EXACTLY-100}) = 0.15$. The IBR sequence then comes out as shown in tab. 16.17.

Tab. 16.16: Similarity function

sim	w_1	w_2	w_3	w_4
w_1	1	0.5	1	0.5
w_2	0.5	1	0.5	1
w_3	1	0.9	1	0.9
w_4	0.9	1	0.9	1

Tab. 16.17: IBR sequence

σ_0	100	101	EXACTLY-100
w_1	$\frac{1}{2}$	0	$\frac{1}{2}$
w_2	0	1	0
w_3	$\frac{1}{2}$	0	$\frac{1}{2}$
w_4	0	1	0

ρ_1	100	101	EXACTLY-100
w_1	1	0	0
w_2	0	1	0
w_3	1	0	0
w_4	1	0	0

ρ_2	100	101	EXACTLY-100
w_1	0	0	1
w_2	0	1	0
w_3	1	0	0
w_4	1	0	0

ρ_0	w_1	w_2	w_3	w_4
100	$\frac{1}{2}$	0	$\frac{1}{2}$	0
101	0	$\frac{1}{2}$	0	$\frac{1}{2}$
EXACTLY-100	$\frac{1}{2}$	0	$\frac{1}{2}$	0

ρ_1	w_1	w_2	w_3	w_4
100	$\frac{1}{2}$	0	$\frac{1}{2}$	$\frac{1}{2}$
101	0	1	0	0
EXACTLY-100	$\frac{1}{2}$	0	$\frac{1}{2}$	0

ρ_2	w_1	w_2	w_3	w_4
100	0	0	$\frac{1}{2}$	$\frac{1}{2}$
101	0	1	0	0
EXACTLY-100	1	0	0	0

In σ_0 and ρ_0 all signals are used/interpreted according to their literal meaning. In σ_1 the sender of type w_4 decides that it is better to use the imprecise but more economical expression 100 rather than 101. Note that in type w_2, σ_1 still uses 101 because for this type precision is sufficiently important to justify the higher expression costs.

As a consequence, 100 receives a vague interpretation in ρ_1. To avoid this vagueness, type w_1 in σ_2 prefers the more costly but also more precise expression EXACTLY-100. As a consequence, the expression 100 does not carry any information anymore about the distinction between the two possible lengths in ρ_2. It still does convey information though, namely the pragmatic information that the sender is in a state where precision is not important. The two complex expressions only receive a precise information in ρ_2. (σ_2, ρ_2) are a fixed point.

9 Conclusion

Game theoretic methods have received a good deal of attention in the linguistics commmunity in recent years. The aim of this chapter is to illustrate the potential of this approach by showing how the neo-Gricean program of pragmatics can be spelled out in this framework. It is thus representative of one major line of research, which uses rationalistic game theory to model the decision making of language users in specific communicative situations. This is mostly applied to problems of pragmatic interpretation (such as the work by Benz, Parikh, van Rooij and others that has aleary been mentioned above), but there is also some interest in NLP circles to apply these concepts to language generation (see for instance Golland, Liang & Klein 2010; Klabunde 2009).

Even though game theory has originally been conceived as a tool to make prescriptive claims about the behavior of fully rational agents, since the seminal work of Maynard Smith (1982) it has also become a standard tool in biomathematics. There it is used to model Darwinian evolution in situations where replicative success depends on interactions between different organisms. In this context, evolutionary game theory has been used extensively to study the evolution of animal communication systems, including human language (see for instance Maynard Smith 1991; Nowak & Krakauer 1999).

Since the 1990s is has been recognized by economists that the evolutionary logic can be fruitfully applied to study cultural phenomena in situations where the behavior of humans is governed by imitation and learning. This perspective has been applied to natural language as well to explain the emergence and stability of linguistic conventions in various domains of grammar (see for instance van Rooij 2004; Huttegger 2007; Jäger 2007b).

Thanks to Michael Franke and Roger Levy for pointing out several mistakes in a draft version of this article, and to Jason Quinley for correcting my English.

10 Appendix

Theorem 1 (Fixed Point of IBR sequence) *For each Strong or Weak Interpretation Game, there is a number $n \geq 0$ such that for all $m > n$: $\sigma_m = \sigma_n$ and $\rho_m = \rho_n$.*

Proof: All strategies that are considered in an IBR sequence assign a uniform distribution over a subset of S to each type (sender) or a uniform distribution over a subset of $\mathcal{A}$ to each signal (receiver). Since the games are finite, there are only finitely many such strategies.

Consider a strategy profile $\langle \sigma, \rho \rangle$. We define five measures over profiles (average sender utility, measure of entropy of σ, average receiver utility, negative of the number of false interpretations assigned to surprise signals, measure of entropy of ρ):

- $m_1(\sigma, \rho) = \sum_{t \in T} p^*(t) \sum_s \sigma(s|t) \sum_{a \in \mathcal{A}} \rho(a|s) u_s(t, s, a)$,

- $m_2(\sigma, \rho) = \sum_{t \in T} |\{s | \sigma(s|t) > 0\}|$,

- $m_3(\sigma, \rho) = \sum_{t \in T} p^*(t) \sum_s \sigma(s|t) \sum_{a \in \mathcal{A}} \rho(a|s) u_r(t, s, a)$,

- $m_4(\sigma, \rho) = \sum_{s: \forall t \sigma(s|t)=0} |\{a | \rho(a|s) > 0 \land a \neq s\}|$,

- $m_5(\sigma, \rho) = \sum_{s \in S} |\{a | \rho(a|s) > 0\}|$.

Next we define a partial order over profiles via a lexicographic order of their $m_1 - m_5$-values:

$$(\sigma_1, \rho_1) > (\sigma_2, \rho_2) \text{ iff } \exists i. m_i(\sigma_1, \rho_1) > m_i(\sigma_2, \rho_2) \land \forall j < i : m_j(\sigma_1, \rho_1) = m_j(\sigma_2, \rho_2).$$

It is obvious that $>$ must be acyclic.

Let (σ_n, ρ_n) be an element of an IBR sequence, and let $\sigma_{n+1} \neq \sigma_n$. As $\sigma_{n+1} = BR_s(\rho_n)$, for each t and each s with $\sigma_{n+1}(s|t) > 0$, $EU_s(s|t; \rho_n) = \max_{s'} EU_s(s'|t; \rho_n)$. Hence $m_1(\sigma_{n+1}, \rho_n) = \max_\sigma m_1(\sigma, \rho_n)$. The usage of the principle of insufficient reason in the definition of BR_s ensures that within the set of sender strategies having this property, σ_{n+1} is the unique strategy that maximizes $m_2(\cdot, \rho_n)$. Hence $\forall \sigma \neq \sigma_{n+1}. \langle \sigma_{n+1}, \rho_n \rangle > \langle \sigma, \rho_n \rangle$. In particular, $\langle \sigma_{n+1}, \rho_n \rangle > \langle \sigma_n, \rho_n \rangle$.

Now suppose $\rho_{n+1} \neq \rho_n$. Note that for any t, s, a_1, a_2, if $u_r(t, s, a_1) \geq u_r(t, s, a_2)$, then $u_s(t, s, a_1) \geq u_s(t, s, a_2)$. To see why this is so, suppose $a_1 \neq a_2$. If $u_r(t, s, a_1) \geq u_r(t, s, a_2)$, then either $a_1 = t$ and $a_2 \neq t$, or $a_1, a_2 \neq t$ and $c_r(s, a_1) \leq c_r(s, a_2)$. In both cases, $u_s(t, s, a_1) \geq u_s(t, s, a_2)$.

Since $br_r(s,\sigma)$ gives the set of actions that maximize the expected value of u_r given s and σ, it only contains actions that also maximize the expected value of u_s given s and σ. Hence $BR_r(\sigma)$ is a strategy that maximizes $m_1(\sigma,\cdot)$. m_2 only depends on σ. Hence $BR_r(\sigma)$ maximizes $m_1(\sigma,\cdot)$ and $m_2(\sigma|\cdot)$. By definition, it also maximizes $m_3(\sigma,\cdot)$. By the belief revision policy that is implemented via the best response to surprise signals in the definition of BR_r, $BR_r(\sigma)$ also maximizes $m_4(\sigma,\cdot)$. Finally, the definition of BR_r ensures that $BR_r(\sigma)$ is the unique strategy among all strategies that maximize $m_1, \cdots, m_4$ that maximizes m_5. Therefore $\langle \sigma_{n+1}, \rho_{n+1} \rangle > \langle \sigma_n, \rho_n \rangle$.

The relation > is acyclic. All elements of the IBR sequence are strategies that map types (signals) to uniform distributions over subsets of $S(\mathcal{A})$. There are only finitely many such strategies. Therefore the IBR sequence must have a fixed point. -|

11 References

Battigalli, Pierpaolo & Marciano Siniscalchi 2002. Strong belief and forward induction reasoning. *Journal of Economic Theory* 106, 356–391.
Benz, Anton, Gerhard Jäger & Robert van Rooij (eds.) 2005. *Game Theory and Pragmatics*. Basingstoke: Palgrave Macmillan.
Benz, Anton & Robert van Rooij 2007. Optimal assertions and what they implicate. *Topoi – An International Review of Philosophy* 27, 63–78.
Blutner, Reinhard 2001. Some aspects of optimality in natural language interpretation. *Journal of Semantics* 17, 189–216.
Büring, Daniel 1995. *The 59th Street Bridge Accent*. Doctoral dissertation. University of Tübingen.
Camerer, Colin F. 2003. *Behavioral Game Theory: Experiments in Strategic Interaction*. Princeton, NJ: Princeton University Press.
Camerer, Colin F. & Ernst Fehr 2006. When does "economic man" dominate social behavior? *Science* 311(5757), 47–52.
Chierchia, Gennaro 2004. Scalar implicatures, polarity phenomena and the syntax/pragmatics interface. In: A. Beletti (ed.). *Structures and Beyond*. Oxford: Oxford University Press, 39–103.
Clark, Herbert & Catherine Marshall 1981. Definite reference and mutual knowledge. In: A. Joshi, B. Webber & I. Sag (eds.). *Elements of Discourse Understanding*. Cambridge: Cambridge University Press, 10–63.
Crawford, Vincent P. & Joel Sobel 1982. Strategic Information Transmission. *Econometrica* 50, 1431–1451.
Dalrymple, Mary, Makotoa Kanazawa, Sam Mchombo & Stanley Peters 1994. What do reciprocals mean. In: M. Harvey & L. Santelmann (eds.). *Proceedings from Semantics and Linguistic Theory* (= *SALT*) *IV*. Ithaca, NY: Cornell University, 61–78.
Dekker, Paul & Robert van Rooij 2000. Bi-directional optimality theory: An application of game theory. *Journal of Semantics* 17, 217–242.
Fox, Danny 2007. Free choice and the theory of scalar implicature. In: U. Sauerland & P. Stateva (eds.). *Presupposition and Implicature in Compositional Semantics*. Basingstoke: Palgrave McMillan, 71–120.

Franke, Michael 2008. Interpretation of optimal signals. In: K. Apt & R. van Rooij (eds.). *New Perspectives on Games and Interaction*. Amsterdam: Amsterdam University Press, 297–310.

Franke, Michael 2009. *Signal to Act: Game Theory in Pragmatics*. Ph.D. dissertation. University of Amsterdam.

Franke, Michael & Gerhard Jäger 2012, Bidirectional optimization from reasoning and learning in games, Journal of Logic, Language and Information, 21, 117–139.

Gerbrandy, Jelle 1999. *Bisimulations on Planet Kripke*. Ph.D. dissertation. University of Amsterdam.

Geurts, Bart 2010. *Quantity Implicatures*. Cambridge: Cambridge University Press.

Golland, Dave, Percy Liang & Dan Klein 2010. A game-theoretic approach to generating spatial descriptions. In: H. Li & L. M'arquez (eds.). *Proceedings of Empirical Methods in Natural Language Processing (= EMNLP) 2010*. Stroudsburg, PA: Association for Computational Linguistics, 410–419.

Grice, H. Paul 1975. Logic and conversation. In: P. Cole & J. Morgan (eds.). *Syntax and Semantics 3: Speech Acts*. New York: Academic Press, 41–58.

Horn, Laurence 1984. Towards a new taxonomy for pragmatic inference: Q-based and R-based implicatures. In: D. Schiffrin (ed.). *Meaning, Form, and Use in Context*. Washington, DC: Georgetown University Press, 11–42.

Huttegger, Simon H. 2007. Evolution and the explanation of meaning. *Philosophy of Science* 74, 1–27.

Jäger, Gerhard 2007a. The evolution of convex categories. *Linguistics & Philosophy* 30, 551–564.

Jäger, Gerhard 2007b. Evolutionary Game Theory and typology: A case study. *Language* 83, 74–109.

Jäger, Gerhard 2007c. Game dynamics connects semantics and pragmatics. In: A.-V. Pietarinen (ed.). *Game Theory and Linguistic Meaning*. Amsterdam: Elsevier, 89–102.

Jäger, Gerhard & Christian Ebert 2009. Pragmatic rationalizability. In: A. Riester & T. Solstad (eds.). *Proceedings of Sinn und Bedeutung (= SuB) 13* (SinSpeC 5). Stuttgart: University of Stuttgart, 1–15.

Jäger, Gerhard, Lars Koch-Metzger & Frank Riedel 2009. *Voronoi Languages*. Jäger, Gerhard, Lars Koch-Metzger & Frank Riedel 2011. Voronoi Languages. Games and Economic Behavior 73, 517–537.

Jäger, Gerhard & Robert van Rooij 2007. Language stucture: Psychological and social constraints. *Synthese* 159, 99–130.

Jaynes, Edwin Thompson 2003. *Probability Theory: The Logic of Science*. Cambridge: Cambridge University Press.

Kamp, Hans 1973. Free choice permission. *Proceedings of the Aristotelian Society 74*, 57–74.

Katzir, Roni 2007. Structurally-defined alternatives. *Linguistics & Philosophy* 30, 669–690.

Klabunde, Ralf 2009. Towards a game-theoretic approach to content determination. In: E. Krahmer & M. Theune (eds.). *Proceedings of the 12th European Workshop on Natural Language Generation (= ENLG-09)*. Stroudsburg, PA: Association for Computational Linguistics, 102–105.

Krifka, Manfred 2002. Be brief and vague! and how bidirectional optimality theory allows for verbosity and precision. In: D. Restle & D. Zaefferer (eds.). *Sounds and Systems. Studies*

in Structure and Change. A Festschrift for Theo Vennemann. Berlin: Mouton de Gruyter, 439–358.
Krifka, Manfred 2007. Approximate interpretation of number words: A case for strategic communication. In: G. Bouma, I. Krämer & J. Zwarts (eds.). *Cognitive Foundations of Interpretation*. Amsterdam: Koninklijke Nederlandse Akademie van Wetenschapen, 111–126.
Levinson, Stephen C. 2000. *Presumptive Meanings*. Cambridge, MA: The MIT Press.
Lewis, David 1969. *Convention*. Cambridge, MA: Harvard University Press.
Maynard Smith, John 1982. *Evolution and the Theory of Games*. Cambridge: Cambridge University Press.
Maynard Smith, John 1991. Honest signalling: The Philip Sidney game. *Animal Behaviour* 42, 1034–1035.
Nowak, Martin A. & David C. Krakauer 1999. The evolution of language. *Proceedings of the National Academy of Sciences* 96, 8028–8033.
Parikh, Prashant 2001. *The Use of Language*. Stanford, CA: CSLI Publications.
Pietarinen, Ahti-Veikko (ed.) 2007. *Game Theory and Linguistic Meaning*. Amsterdam: Elsevier.
Rabin, Matthew 1990. Communication between rational agents. *Journal of Economic Theory* 51, 144–170.
van Rooij, Robert 2004. Signalling games select Horn strategies. *Linguistics & Philosophy* 27, 493–527.
van Rooij, Robert & Katrin Schulz 2004. Exhaustive interpretation of complex sentences. *Journal of Logic, Language and Information* 13, 491–519.
Rooth, Mats 1985. *Association with Focus*. Ph.D. dissertation. University of Massachusetts, Amherst, MA.
van der Sandt, Rob 1992. Presupposition projection as anaphora resolution. *Journal of Semantics* 9, 333–377.
Sauerland, Uli 2004. Scalar implicatures in complex sentences. *Linguistics & Philosophy* 27, 367–391.
Skyrms, Brian 2010. *Signals: Evolution, Learning, and Information*. Oxford: Oxford University Press.
Slonim, Robert L. 2005. Competing against experienced and inexperienced players. *Experimental Economics* 8, 55–75.
Spence, Michael 1973. Job market signaling. *The Quarterly Journal of Economics* 87, 355–374.
Stalnaker, Robert 1978. Assertion. In: P. Cole (ed.). *Syntax and Semantics 9: Pragmatics*. New York: Academic Press, 315–332.
Stone, Matthew 1998. *Modality in Dialogue: Planning, Pragmatics and Computation*. Ph.D. dissertation. Rutgers University, New Brunswick, NJ.

Christopher Potts

17 Conventional implicature and expressive content

1   Introduction —— 598
2   Dimensions of meaning —— 600
3   Pragmatic enrichment —— 613
4   Conclusion —— 619
5   References —— 620

Abstract: This article presents evidence that individual words and phrases can contribute multiple independent pieces of meaning simultaneously. Such multi-dimensionality is a unifying theme of the literature on conventional implicatures and expressives. I use phenomena from discourse, semantic composition, and morphosyntax to detect and explore various dimensions of meaning. I also argue that, while the meanings involved are semantically independent, they interact pragmatically to reduce underspecification and fuel pragmatic enrichment. In this article, the central case studies are appositives like *Falk, the CEO*, and the taboo intensive *damn*, though discourse particles and connectives like *but*, *even*, and *still* play supporting roles. The primary evidence, both quantitative and qualitative, is drawn from large interview and product-review corpora, which harbor a wealth of information about the importance of these items to discourse.

1 Introduction

Natural language meanings are multifaceted. Even the simplest words, phrases, and sentences can, when uttered, convey a variety of distinct messages. Some derive solely from the conventions of language, others from rich interactions between language and context. Important examples include presuppositions, conversational implicatures, conventional implicatures, connotations, and at-issue (truth-conditional, entailed) content, as well as blends of these. Many of the central issues of semantic and pragmatic theory revolve around how to manage this complex network of interdependent meanings.

Christopher Potts, Stanford, CA, USA

https://doi.org/10.1515/9783110589849-017

The present article focuses on secondary meanings that (i) derive from the conventions of language, albeit with extreme context dependency in many cases, and (ii) are semantically separate from the at-issue content but interact with it pragmatically. Appositives and expressives typify this multidimensionality:

(1) a. Charlie, *an infamous axe murderer,* is at the door!
    b. Charlie is at the door.

(2) a. The *damn* dog is on the couch.
    b. The dog is on the couch.

These sentences are information-rich even without contextualization; if uttered, they convey even more. My focus is on the meanings that we can trace, in whole or in part, to the highlighted (italicized) elements.

For example, both (1a) and (1b) convey that Charlie is at the door. However, the appositive in (1a) contributes a second meaning, by ascribing the property of being an infamous axe murderer to Charlie. These two meanings are, in a sense to be made clear below, independent of one another, but they interact pragmatically. In this case, each supports the other's relevance to guide us towards the speaker's intended message. The interaction is quite different if we replace this appositive clause with *the pizza delivery guy*. Thus, we'd like a semantic theory that allows this sentence to denote two propositions, and we'd like a pragmatic theory that explains how those propositions interact to produce a pragmatically-enriched message.

Something similar happens in (2). Whereas (2b) can be a neutral report, (2a) encodes charged information about the speaker's emotional state. The nature of this contribution is context dependent and challenging to specify, but it nonetheless leaps out, helping us to understand why the speaker is offering the content of (2b) at this point in the conversation. Once again, we have semantic independence—we can identify (2b) in (2a), both semantically and morphosyntactically—and once again we have rich pragmatic interactions between the two meanings.

Grice (1975) sketched the notion of conventional implicature (CI) for roughly this class of phenomena, and Bach (1999), Neale (1999), and Horn (2007) find the seeds of that classification in Frege's writings. Both Frege and Grice used expressions like these to probe the limits of their theories of meaning. Ever since, the study of CIs has branched off in numerous directions. The resulting picture appears fragmented; as Horn (2007: 39) says, CIs have had "a long and sometimes difficult history". I've argued, though, that multidimensionality of the sort seen in (1)–(2) unites this research (Potts 2007b). Here, I argue for a unifying pragmatic concept as well: CI items are primarily devices for situating the main clause in the web of information that comprises the discourse. This seems a fitting characterization not only of the above examples, but also of items more standardly regarded as contributing CIs, as in (3)–(5).

(3) Alfie is a baby, *but* he is quiet.
    a. At-issue = Alfie is a baby, and he is quiet
    b. CI ≈ Babies are not usually quiet

(4) Isak is *still* swimming.
    a. At-issue = Isak is swimming
    b. CI ≈ Isak was swimming earlier

(5) *Even* Bart passed the test.
    a. At-issue = Bart passed the test
    b. CI ≈ Bart was among the least likely to pass

The CI paraphrases are very rough, as indicated by the approximation signs. A recurrent theme of CI meanings is that they are hard to specify in propositional terms. I return to this in section 3..

In the next section, I take a closer look at the semantic multidimensionality of these examples, providing diagnostics for identifying secondary dimensions of meaning and isolating them compositionally and pragmatically. Following that, I address how CIs feed pragmatic enrichment. The overall picture reconciles the lexical and constructional origins of CIs with the usual assumption that they belong, in some sense, to pragmatics.

2 Dimensions of meaning

Grice (1975) calls upon multiple dimensions of meaning to resolve conflicting intuitions about speaker commitments. The definition proceeds by way of example:

> If I say (smugly), *He is an Englishman; he is, therefore, brave*, I have certainly committed myself, by virtue of the meaning of my words, to its being the case that his being brave is a consequence of (follows from) his being an Englishman. But while I have said that he is an Englishman and said that he is brave, I do not want to say that I have *said* (in the favored sense) that it follows from his being an Englishman that he is brave, though I have certainly indicated, and so implicated, that this is so.

On Grice's proposal, the conventional implicature is the proposition denoted by 'its being the case that his being brave is a consequence of (follows from) his being an Englishman', and the at-issue content ('what is said') is the proposition denoted by the conjunction 'he is an Englishman and brave'. One sentence, two propositions. One might dispute whether Grice's analysis of *therefore* is correct, but the logical and linguistic idea is compelling.

Karttunen & Peters (1979) brought this idea to life by fitting it into a standard model-theoretic package. The essence of their idea is captured by the four truth-value combinations in (6).

(6) ⟨T,T⟩ ⟨F,T⟩
    ⟨T, F⟩ ⟨F, F⟩

Suppose we treat the first value in each pair as modeling at-issue content and the second as modeling CI content. Then we have a nuanced system that includes absolute truth (upper left), absolute falsity (lower right) and blends of the two with an intermediate status. Appositives provide an easy illustration of the promise of this idea:

(7) Falk, the CEO of Acme Products, gave the keynote address.

Here, we have two propositions expressed. Let's connect them with the meaning tuples in (6) by assuming that the at-issue dimension (that Falk gave the keynote address) is the first coordinate, with the appositive content (that Falk is the CEO of Acme) given by the second coordinate. If both propositions are true, the value is ⟨**T, T**⟩. If Falk merely consults for Acme, but he did give the keynote, then the value is ⟨**T, F**⟩. And so forth. This seems to be very close to Grice's (1975) original proposal; the quotation at the start of this section continues with its analysis of *therefore* by saying, "I do not want to say that my utterance of this sentence would be, *strictly speaking*, false should the consequence in question fail to hold." Presumably, it wouldn't be, strictly speaking, true in this situation either: ⟨**T, F**⟩.

There is no reason to limit ourselves to truth values when dealing with multiple dimensions of meaning. We certainly want to enrich the coordinates to be propositional, for example. If W is the space of possible worlds, then this gives us all the meanings in $\wp(W) \times \wp(W)$ to work with. However, if appositives are to be a test case, then mere pairs won't suffice. A single sentence could have multiple appositives hanging off of it, each contributing in its own way. This might lead us to conclude that the meaning space is $\wp(W)^n$, the set of all n-tuples of propositions, again with the first member corresponding to the at-issue content and the rest corresponding to secondary meanings of whatever kind we discover.

However, the phenomena in question are compositional: they trace to particular words and constructions. This is central to Karttunen & Peters' theory. For them, not only sentences, but also individual words and phrases, can have multidimensional meanings. Pursuing this idea, we can identify *Falk, the CEO of Acme Products* as a phrase that has two meaning components. Its first dimension picks out Falk, and is thus indistinguishable from the unadorned proper name *Falk*. Its second dimension is the proposition that Falk is the CEO of Acme Products. Since appositives can affix to sentences *(It's raining, which is unexpected)*, verb phrases *(Joan jogs, which Jed does too)*, and a host of other constituents, it looks like the space of meanings is at least as broad as $M \times \wp(W)^n$, the set of all pairs in which the first coordinate is a member of the set M of all meanings (whatever that space is like) and the rest of the coordinates are propositional.

I think we want to generalize even more than that to deal with expressive content. Here is Kaplan (1999) drawing a distinction that bears a family resemblance to Grice's above, but that more directly links semantics and pragmatics:

> When I think about my own understanding of the words and phrases of my native language, I find that in some cases I am inclined to say that I know what they *mean*, and in other cases it seems more natural to say that I know how to *use* them.

Kaplan goes on to define *descriptive correctness* and *expressive correctness*, two very different measures of a sentence's status when uttered in context. The two are independent. If I utter *The damn dog is on the couch*, my utterance is descriptively incorrect if I'm wrong in my claim about the dog, but it's expressively correct if my emotions are heightened in the way that *damn* indicates. Conversely, my utterance is descriptively correct if I am right about the dog, but it is expressively incorrect if I am, for example, simply confused about the use conditions of this item and thus send an inaccurate or unintended signal about my emotional state. We can reconnect with Karttunen & Peters' (1979) semantic multidimensionality by treating sentences as denoting n-tuples of meanings, where our notion of meaning is left broad enough to encompass not only the propositional stuff of appositives but also the more elusive emotionality of expressives.

The above very general logical ideas form the backbone of this article, and versions of them are evident in the quite varied formal approaches of Hawkins (1991), Asher (2000), Barker (2003), Potts (2005), and Corazza (2005), and see Heim (1983), Dekker (2002), Beaver (1997), Simons (2006) for critical discussion of whether presuppositions should be handled in similar terms. I introduce these technical concepts first largely to shift the emphasis off of what I or others believe about how to define 'conventional implicature' and 'expressive', or how to interpret others' definitions of these terms. Instead, I'd like to focus on the formal and empirical issues that arise when we move to a theory in which individual words and phrases denote n-tuples of meanings. There is a great deal of space, in such a setting, for new empirical investigation and formal innovation. I turn now to the task of identifying dimensions of meaning, using phenomena from discourse (section 2.1.), semantic composition (section 2.2.), and morphosyntax (section 2.3.).

2.1 Dimensions in discourse

In the previous section, I used truth-value judgments to acquaint us with the idea that some sentences denote tuples of meanings. If these values are truly independent, then we should expect to see the effects in discourse as well. The present section reviews evidence that this is what we find.

Let's start with simple, straightforward denials, again using appositives as a test case. In (8), from the Larry King Live TV show (August 9, 2005), King is finishing his show by passing control of the airwaves to Aaron Brown. Brown disputes just the appositive relative's content; the at-issue content concerns an uncontroversial fact about the network's schedule.

(8) King: Right now, it's time to turn it over to our man in New York, the host of "NEWSNIGHT," Aaron Brown, who carries on, as all great newsmen do, in that great tradition of, the show must go on.
Brown: No, that's what show business people do. [. . .] That's what you do. I do something else.

We also, of course, find cases in which the target of a denial is just the at-issue content of the preceding utterance, with the appositive left unaddressed. This is the dynamic in the following exchange from the TV show The Situation Room (September 26, 2008):

(9) Blitzer: You're with the House Republicans, who say you know what, not so fast.
Dobbs: No, no, no, no, no. I'm with the American people [. . .]

In both (8)–(9), the first statement is semantically multidimensional, and the reply exploits this fact.

Assent and denial are not the only phenomena that can tease meaning dimensions apart. In the following Switchboard corpus (Godfrey & Holliman 1993) exchange, for example, Speaker A55 acknowledges the truth of the at-issue content of Speaker B54's assertion but queries the appositive content:

(10) Speaker B54: Actually I just, put a, uh, little fence around my yard, uh, um, which is I suppose, technically illegal, but I had so many groundhogs last year that I think they'll let me get by with it, and it, it's got this one inch mesh and what I've noticed it's kept the cats out and I love it.
Speaker A55: Um, yeah, yeah, because they, they like to get in and fertilize things too. But, uh, why would it be illegal?

The reverse—querying the at-issue content while accepting the appositive content—is also robustly attested in naturally-occurring dialogue.

It is easy to accumulate additional evidence for the multidimensionality of appositive-containing sentences. For example, sometimes the appositive and at-issue dimensions fuel different speech acts (e.g., *Is Sam, who was in the hospital recently, feeling well enough to attend?*), and they can host distinct speech-act modifiers (e.g., *Please visit Sam, who could, quite frankly, use some cheering up!*). For further discussion, data, and references see Potts (2005: §4) and Horn (2007).

I think the situation does not differ in kind for other CI and expressive items, though many of them contribute in ways that are harder to characterize precisely, which makes them inherently less open to negotiation in dialogue and which can lead to what Horn (2002) calls *assertoric inertia*. However, there are some identifiable techniques for accessing even these more ineffable dimensions. For example, all of the phrases in (11) are robustly attested on the Internet. (Examples marked with 'G' were found using Google.)

(11) a. But? What do you mean, *But?* [G]
 b. *Again?* What do you mean, *Again?* [G]
 c. *Still?* What do you mean, *Still?* [G]
 d. *Even?* What do you mean, *Even?* [G]

More generally, the template *W? What do you mean W?* (i) highlights an element *W* that arguably makes multiple meaning contributions, (ii) homes in on the non-at-issue part of that meaning, and (iii) challenges it. This resembles the 'Hey, wait a minute!' strategy discussed by Shanon (1976) and von Fintel (2004) in the context of identifying and negotiating presuppositions. Example (12), from a CNN interview between Anderson Cooper and As'ad AbuKhalil (May 14, 2003), illustrates with a very clear case of presupposition-challenging, tracing ultimately to the presuppositions of *make* in the intended sense.

(12) AbuKhalil: Well, it's an extremely organized party. And I worry that we may inevitably or willingly make them an enemy of the United States. I did an interview with (CROSSTALK)

Cooper: Wait a minute. Wait a minute. You're saying they're not an enemy of the United States already?

This strategy is also widely used for other kinds of non-at-issue meaning. In (13), for example, basketball coach Bobby Knight recounts an incident in which he hurled a chair onto the court. King calls him on the surprise conversational implicature that the outburst was merely a performance (Larry King Live, March 26, 2001).

(13) Knight: Yeah. Somebody said, you know, you are really good actor, and — like the chair, I didn't hit anybody with the chair, pretty good aim, I thought.
King: Wait a minute! Are you telling me you knew what you were doing there?

Thus, the 'Hey, wait a minute' test is useful for identifying a wide range of non-at-issue meanings, especially those that are difficult to articulate and thus difficult to unambiguously query or challenge.

Expressive content is the most reticent of all. It is common for speakers to call upon the 'Hey, wait a minute!' strategy to object to the appropriateness of another speaker's swears, honorifics, and exclamations. This is effective, but it is limiting from an analytic standpoint, since it is rarely clear which aspects of the meaning are being challenged. It makes sense, then, to turn to subsentential discourse phenomena, where questions about what is asserted and what is accepted are less pressing. Ellipsis is especially useful here (article 9 [Semantics: Sentence and Information Structure] (Reich) *Ellipsis*). Example (14) shows that verb-phrase ellipsis can reuse an expressive-laden phrase without thereby incorporating the expressivity (Potts et al. 2007):

(14) Speaker A: I saw your fucking dog in the park.
Speaker B: No, you didn't. You couldn't have. The poor thing passed away last week.

In using the strong expressive *fucking*, Speaker A evinces hostility towards Speaker B's dog. Speaker B reuses the verb phrase *see your fucking dog in the park*, but clearly without the expressive coloring. Although indexicals easily shift under ellipsis (Fiengo & May 1994; article 17 [Semantics: Noun Phrases and Verb Phrases] (Schlenker) *Indexicality and de se*), as we see with the pronoun *you* in this example, the expressive does not shift for B's utterance. Rather, it is simply factored out. Multidimensionality provides a straightforward analysis of this case: Speaker A's verb phrase denotes a pair consisting of (i) the property of seeing B's dog in the park, and (ii) the expressive associated with *fucking*. Speaker B's ellipsis reuses only (i).

2.2 Dimensions in semantic composition

In the previous section, I argued that individual meaning dimensions can lead different lives in discourse. The present section shows that this multidimensionality is felt throughout semantic composition as well. Indeed, the case for dimensions of meaning is even easier to make at the subsentential level; once we move to the discourse level, there is a tendency for all discourse meanings to enter the swirl of the common ground. Karttunen's (1973) *presupposition* holes are a straightforward place to start this investigation. The standard holes are negation, modalization, conditionalization, and questioning (article 14 [this volume] (Beaver & Geurts) Presupposition). They are united in the following sense: if a hole H combines semantically with an at-issue proposition p, then the result of that combination, Hp, does not entail p. For example, let's suppose that p is the proposition expressed by the sentence in (15a). If this is left unembedded, it yields a commitment to p when uttered. However, if embedded as in (15b–e), this commitment disappears.

(15) a. Sam fed the dog.
 b. Sam didn't feed the dog.
 c. We don't have to stop by the house if Sam fed the dog.
 d. Sam might feed the dog.
 e. Did Sam feed the dog?

The presupposition holes earn their name because they do not have these expected modulating effects on *presuppositions* that are expressed by constituents in their scope. This is evident already in (15): the basic example (15a) presupposes the existence of a unique, salient dog, in virtue of the phrase *the dog*. Thus, let's say that the content of (15a) is better given by p_q, where q is the proposition that there is a unique, salient dog. Evidently, the values of $\neg p_q$, $(p_q \rightarrow r)$, $might(p_q)$, and $?p_q$ all still have q as a commitment; the presupposition slips past all these operators.

All the meanings discussed in the previous section—appositives, expressives, particles, and so forth—uniformly project out of hole environments, with embedded interpretations typically requiring special discourse conditions or special intonational tunes (Boër & Lycan 1976; Horn 1989). In (16), for example, Pelosi's answer does not target the content of King's appositive; the two are discussing Pelosi's public criticism of the Bush administration's handling of the Iraq War, which Pelosi goes on to defend (Larry King Live, February 27, 2007).

(16) King: And you don't think at all they have a point when they say you and others like you, who speak out forcefully against it, help al Qaeda?
 Pelosi: No.

Thus, despite being embedded in an interrogative, the appositive itself becomes a commitment of King's (admittedly somewhat biased) question. Conditional antecedents like (17), from the Switchboard corpus, also make the point. Here, if the appositive were interpreted as part of the antecedent, then the antecedent as a whole would be semantically contradictory, which is clearly not the speaker's intent.

(17) I think it would concern me even more if I had children, which I don't, [...]

Karttunen's *plugs* are less uniform in their handling of these meanings. The plugs are non-factive attitude predicates (article 16 [Semantics: Noun Phrases and Verb Phrases] (Swanson) *Propositional attitudes)*, and perhaps also tense operators. Plugs contrast with holes in that they typically do force presuppositions to be interpreted in their scope: if P is a plug and p_q is the meaning of a presupposition-laden sentence, then Pp_q typically does not presuppose q.

In the case of appositives, projection out of plug environments is routine. Example (18), from the widely available 20_newsgroups corpus, is a clear illustration, here centering around the non-factive attitude predicate *report*.

(18) ESPN *report*ed on Sunday, April 11, that *the Lightning, who have been playing in 10,400-seat Expo Hall, are exploring opportunities to move to either Atlanta or Minneapolis*. But Esposito [Lightning general manager— CP] said there was no truth to the report.

The sentential complement of *report*, the constituent we would expect to determine the content of the *report*, is the clause *the Lightning, who have been playing in 10,400-seat Expo Hall, are exploring opportunities to move to either Atlanta or Minneapolis*. This contains the appositive. Yet it is evident from the second sentence that the appositive content must be factored out—it is not part of the argument to *report*, despite its syntactic position.

We expect the embedded constituent to denote the pair of propositions in (19). The first is modified by *report*, whereas the second goes on to become an unqualified discourse-level commitment in this case.

(19) a. The Lightning are exploring opportunities to move to either Atlanta or Minneapolis
      b. The Lightening have been playing in 10,400-seat Expo Hall

Thus, this example indicates that it needs to be possible for the two dimensions to interact differently with plugs. Similar behavior is widely attested for expressives.

In (20), for example, the complaint in question was written by the lawyers for "the idiot"; the attitude that this referential device conveys is clearly that of the author, not part of what the complaint says.

(20) The complaint says that the idiot filled in a box labeled "default CPC bid" but left blank the box labeled "content CPC bid (optional)". [G]

These examples show that appositives and other CIs *can* be interpreted outside of syntactically embedding holes and plugs. Whether they *must* be interpreted in this way is controversial. The issues surrounding expressives nicely illustrate the general empirical and theoretical issues that complicate things. Amaral, Roberts & Smith (2007) present examples like (21) as evidence that some expressives do receive embedded readings.

(21) [Context: We know that Bob loves to do yard work and is very proud of his lawn, but also that he has a son Monty who hates to do yard chores. So Bob could say (perhaps in response to his partner's suggestion that Monty be asked to mow the lawn while he is away on business):]
Well, in fact Monty said to me this very morning that he hates to mow the friggin' lawn.

However, Potts (2007a) argues that examples like this do not involve true embedding, but rather an independently attested form of perspective shifting that is not tied to syntactic configurations or semantic binding and that is closely connected with discourse-bound logophoric reflexives (Kuno 1987; Büring 2005). Such shifting is facilitated by embedded attitude predications (they supply a salient perspective), but it is not dependent upon it. Example (22) illustrates well. The text, from the July 1995 issue of Harper's Magazine, is by Lewis Lapham, the populist author and editor. The adjective *idiotic* used in the final sentence is not one that Lapham would endorse himself. Rather, he means to connect it with the group he characterizes in the preceding sentence. The perspective involved in this expressive modifier (indeed, in the entire rhetorical question) is thus shifted, not via interaction with other parts of the sentence, but rather as a matter of pragmatics.

(22) I was struck by the willingness of almost everybody in the room—the senators as eagerly as the witnesses—to exchange their civil liberties for an illusory state of perfect security. They seemed to think that democracy was just a fancy word for corporate capitalism, and that the society would be a lot better off if it stopped its futile and unremunerative dithering about

constitutional rights. Why humor people, especially poor people, by listening to their idiotic theories of social justice?

For further discussion of these issues, as they relate not only to expressives, but also to appositives and other CI items, see Schlenker (2003); Potts (2005, 2007a); Wang, Reese & McCready (2005); Amaral, Roberts & Smith (2007); Harris & Potts (2009).

For the more typical CI items exemplified in (3)–(5) above, the facts pertaining to presupposition plugs are clearer: they generally take scope inside plug environments. The most extended, detailed case for this position is due to Bach (1999), whose Indirect Quotation (IQ) Test is designed specifically to see where and how items like *but* take scope with respect to plugs. Bach's central examples have the form of (23).

(23) Marv: Shaq is huge and agile.
 a. Marv said that Shaq is huge but agile.
 b. Marv said that Shaq is huge and agile

The IQ Test concerns what it takes to give a complete and accurate indirect report of Marv's utterance (23). If the contrastive non-at-issue meaning of *but* could take scope out of an embedded speech report, then we might expect (23a) to be fine. However, (23a) seems to imbue Marv's claim with extra content not evident in his original utterance. While Marv might endorse such content, it seems not to be conveyed by (23) alone. Thus, the IQ Test suggests that *but* is plugged by *say*. We can also work in the reverse direction: if Marv had uttered (24), then (23a) would satisfy the demand for a complete paraphrase, because we could freely interpret all aspects of *but*'s content inside the attitude predicate.

(24) Marv: Shaq is huge but agile.

The projection of meaning from hole and plug environments remains an active area of research. As new lexical items are found and explored, the picture grows ever more complex. In my view, facts like the above suggest that projection patterns are highly lexical and subject to many pragmatic influences. The best strategy, then, seems to be to approach each item with an open mind about how it will project, rather than assuming that an existing classification of it (as a presupposition trigger, CI item, discourse particle, etc.) will determine its meaning contribution in complex sentences. The main conclusion of this section is therefore quite general: multidimensional phenomena provide a window into the semantic composition process, and they also pose deep challenges for how to characterize that process.

2.3 Morphosyntactic parochialism

Testing with presupposition holes, plugs, and other complex semantic operators often involves delicate judgments about scope and discourse commitments. Modern semantic theories hew tight to the morphosyntax (Partee 1984; Barker & Jacobson 2007; articles 6 [Semantics: Foundations, History and Methods] (Pagin & Westerståhl) *Compositionality* and 9 [this volume] (Kay & Michaelis) *Constructional meaning*), though, so we expect those phenomena to correlate with generalizations concerning forms. This section describes some instances in which meaning dimensions rise to the surface in this way. The general result is that many natural language meanings operate only internal to their own meaning dimensions.

A simple first example is provided by *both*, which modifies only binary coordinated phrases:

(25) a. * Jed lamented both that it was raining.
 b. Jed lamented both that it was raining and that the weather report had been wrong.

If an appositive is affixed to a sentence, the result denotes a pair of propositions, so we might expect *both* to combine with such sentences. This is not the case, though:

(26) Jed lamented (*both) that it was raining, which the weather report had gotten wrong.

Example (26) involves a sentential appositive relative clause, adjoined sentence-finally so that it looks superficially very much like a coordinate structure. However, as far as *both* is concerned, its content is not there; *both* is unable to reach beyond the at-issue dimension, even when circumstances would seem to favor that.

The *both* test is useful for detecting that a given meaning is not in the at-issue dimension, but it doesn't tell us much about what kind of non-at-issue meaning we have on our hands. For example, presuppositions are also invisible to *both*; in (27), the predicate *stop* arguably presupposes that Ali ran the marathon before, so we have two propositions expressed, and yet inserting *both* results in ungrammaticality:

(27) Ali (*both) ran the marathon again.

However, there are morphosyntactic phenomena that allow us to diagnose CI and expressive content in particular. Potts et al. (2007) report on a number of such phenomena, in English, Hindi, and Japanese, and they reference related cases in

Arabic (Aoun & Choueiri 2000) and German (Schwarz 2009). There isn't space to review all that evidence here, but it is worth looking at one case in detail, to convey a sense for how the arguments work. The example builds on Pullum & Rawlins' (2007) findings for the matching construction *X or no X* (e.g., *War or no war*).

The English *as AP as AP can be* construction, illustrated in (28) with examples found using Google, requires matching, in some sense, between the two APs:

(28) a. as sure as sure can be [G]
 b. as gun nut as gun nut can be [G]
 c. as washed up as washed up can be [G]
 d. as average and vanilla as average and vanilla can be [G]

If the two APs don't match, the result is often ungrammatical:

(29) a. * I'm as sure as certain can be.
 b. * I'm as sure as absolutely sure can be.

This might lead one to conclude that the two APs need to be string-identical. However, examples like (30) show that this is incorrect:

(30) their society is as *secular and religiously neutral* as neutral and secular can be [G]

Here, the APs are *secular and religiously neutral* and *neutral and secular*, which obviously do not match. Once we sort out the ellipsis and arrive at a meaning for these phrases, though, we find that they match in their *at-issue* meanings. This seems, in fact, to be the right level at which to state the matching requirement: the construction demands identity of at-issue content. This matching requirement encompasses string-identity cases like (28), it properly rules out mismatches like (29), and it leaves enough leeway for (30).

It is important to emphasize, as part of this generalization, that we are restricting attention to *at-issue* content. Mismatches arising from the expressive dimension do not result in ungrammaticality:

(31) a. I'm as sure as fucking sure can be.
 b. I'm as fucking sure as sure can be.
 c. He's as fucking crazy as motherfucking crazy can be.

Let φ be the meaning contribution of *fucking* in expressive uses like (31), and let [[*sure*]] be the at-issue content of *sure*. The multidimensional theory of expressives allows us to say that *sure* and *fucking sure* denote [[*sure*]] and ⟨[[*sure*]], φ⟩, respectively, which match in the relevant semantic sense.

Expressives are unique among modifiers in creating a permissible imbalance of this sort. Even emotive items like *absolutely* have at-issue content that violates the matching requirement. Thus, the correct generalization about the form of the *as AP as AP can be* construction crucially depends on a distinct expressive dimension.

This multidimensionality is the key to understanding the famous infixing properties of expressives as well (McCarthy 1982):

(32) a. o-fucking-kay, fan-friggin-tastic
     b. *o-surely-kay, *fan-stunning-tastic

The infixed expressive cannot possibly combine with, or modify, its syntactic sister, which seems not even to be morphemic. Rather, the expressive operates on a more general level, contributing something about the speaker's emotional state at the time of utterance. Even very emotive at-issue modifiers do not achieve the required independence, as we see in (32b).

2.4 Summary of findings

We've now seen a variety of different pieces of evidence that a single constituent can simultaneously contribute multiple independent meanings. It is worth pausing to recap before moving to the pragmatic interactions.

At the discourse level (section 2.1.), we saw speakers responding to individual parts of these multifaceted meanings. Some meanings in secondary dimensions seem less accessible, in this sense, than others. However, we were able to identify techniques (falling broadly under the rubric of 'Hey, wait a minute!' responses) that isolate even these.

In semantic composition (section 2.2.), we leaned on the presupposition holes and plugs to understand how various meanings project, i.e., how they are, or are not, semantically modified by the operators that embed them syntactically. The picture was again one of complex variability. All the items we looked at routinely project out of presupposition hole environments. Presupposition plugs evince more complex behavior, and they are difficult to separate from more discourse-oriented facts concerning perspective.

The morphosyntax is also revealing of the multidimensional semantic foundation (section 2.3.). There, we were able to correlate judgments about grammaticality with semantic generalizations that hinge on being able to have more than one dimension of meaning. This evidence is reassuring, since the semantic and pragmatic facts of section 2.2. can be rather subtle and variable. I turn now to studying how the various dimensions interact to produce rich, coherent pragmatic interpretations.

3 Pragmatic enrichment

All the secondary meanings that we've seen so far trace to specific lexical items and constructions. This is not an accident; the 'conventional' part of 'conventional implicature' captures the arbitrary, encoded source of these meanings, contrasting them with those that derive from pragmatic interactions (article 15 [this volume] (Simons) *Implicature*). Nonetheless, there is an important pragmatic angle on both CIs and expressives; it is arguably the case that the value of having multifaceted meanings is that they deliver richer, more nuanced messages than one could obtain with just a single dimension.

The goal of the present section is to identify and explore some of these pragmatic interactions. We have already seen that individual CI and expressive items differ markedly in their morphosyntax and their semantics, making it hard (or unsatisfying) to study them en masse. The variability is even greater at the pragmatic level. Thus, I do not attempt to provide sweeping generalizations. Instead, I focus on the two items that I opened with and that play a significant role in the preceding discussion: nominal appositives and the expressive *damn*. I take each in turn, beginning with appositives (section 3.1.), then applying those lessons to the trickier case of *damn* (section 3.2.).

3.1 Nominal appositives

Appositives of the sort considered here are prototypically used to *comment* upon the main-clause's content (Asher 2000; Huddleston & Pullum 2002; Potts 2005). They are excellent vehicles for side remarks that would badly interrupt the narrative if expressed as free-standing sentences. For example, (33a) is more natural than (33b) because the digression into the speaker's relationship with Edna intrudes less when expressed appositively than when given the prominence of a free-standing sentence.

(33) a. I had lunch with Edna, whom I've known since high school. She now works for a design firm.
b. I had lunch with Edna. I've known her since high school. She now works for a design firm.

Similarly, in (34), from the Penn Treebank (Marcus et al. 1999), the appositive essentially just satisfies the presupposition of the antecedent verb phrase headed by *cool off*.

(34) Recovery could be hampered if Britain's major trading partners in Europe, which are enjoying robust economic activity, cool off as expected in late 1990 and 1991.

However, appositives are vital to the overall import of the clauses to which they affix, often in ways that go beyond commentary (Ifantidou-Trouki 1993; Blakemore 1996). The most telling indication of their potential is that that they can answer the immediate question under discussion, pushing the at-issue content into the background, as in (35), from Larry King Live, June 10, 2003:

(35) King: Maybe the Harry Potter line was—Michael Beschloss, why are people rushing to buy this book?
Beschloss: I think it's exactly what I was sort of saying earlier, which is they watched her for all those years and wondered what was in her mind and they want to get some idea of what it was.

Can we reconcile the commentary insight with the observation that appositives are often central to the flow of the discourse? I think we can. The crucial insight lies in the fact that natural language sentences are, quite generally, wildly underspecified representations of the meanings that they convey in context (Bach 1994; Levinson 2000; articles 9 [Semantics: Lexical Structures and Adjectives] (Egg) *Semantic underspecification* and 14 [this volume] (Pinkal & Koller) *Semantics in computational linguistics*). Appositives allow speakers to strategically resolve this underspecification and thus increase the overall communicative value of the sentences that contain them. Most lexical items have context-dependent aspects of their meanings (article 12 [this volume] (Zimmermann) *Context dependency),* and appositives often serve to help resolve this. For example, the primary function of the appositive in (36) is to provide information about the scale that is relevant for understanding *even* in this situation.

(36) Even Gary Kasparov, a world chess champion for 15 years, lost to Deep Blue.

Because the appositive can be niched (Ross 1973) right next to *even Gary Kasparov*, it is superior to a sequence of sentences when it comes to resolving the context dependency. This is also likely a primary function of the appositive in (33a), which helps the listener to contextualize the proper name *Edna*. Indeed, the primary function of definite nominal appositives like the ones in (37), taken from the CNN show Lou Dobbs Tonight (July 14 and February 15, 2008) is to help the listener fix the referents of the proper name they adjoin to (Elbourne 2005: §3.3; Potts 2005: §4.5.5):

(37) a. OTS, the regulator, was asleep at the switch and allowed things to happen without restraint.
b. Bush, the elder, was not wholly committed [. . .]

Even if a sentence's context-dependent features are resolved, an appositive can still play an essential role, by helping the listener to understand why that particular content is being offered at all. My simple example (1b), repeated here, is a good illustration:

(38) Charlie is at the door.

Even if we know exactly what proposition this expresses, we might still be at a loss to understand *why* it was uttered. Inserting an appositive can help reveal the speaker's intentions:

(39) a. Charlie, a pizza delivery person, is at the door!
b. Charlie, an infamous axe murderer, is at the door!

Thinking of discourse as structured by abstract *questions under discussion* or *decision problems* (Roberts 1996; Büring 1999; van Rooy 2004) is revealing of the differences between (38) and (39). With focal prominence on the subject, (38) simply answers the question of who is at the door. The speaker might have richer issues in mind, but whether or not his audience detects this is left to purely pragmatic inferences. In contrast, (39a) and (39b), which naturally make the subject prominent, effectively force enriched interpretations. The question (or decision problem) they address is not merely who is at the door, but rather also, What should we *do* in light of that fact?

Many appositive elements function in similar ways in discourse, including appositive relatives, As-parentheticals (*Ed, as we now know, is a spy*), and speech-act modifiers like *frankly*. While more could be said, both about the ways in which appositives differ from separate main clauses and the ways in which they interact with the at-issue content, I think the above suffices to make the point that, despite separation at the compositional level, at-issue and appositive content interact to flesh out underspecified meanings and enrich them.

3.2 The taboo intensive *damn*

The meanings contributed by expressive elements like *damn* are, of course, quite different from those of appositives, but both feed pragmatic enrichment in similar ways. The goal of this section is to begin to build a refined pragmatics for *damn* that relates it, in an abstract sense, to apposition.

One is inclined to start by asking what *damn* means and then build a pragmatic theory from that foundation. However, asking for a traditional semantics here seems to miss the point; the interest of this item lies in its *use conditions*, in Kaplan's (1999) terms (as summarized near the start of section 2.). We want to get a grip on the expectations that *damn* creates in the hearer, and the ways in which a speaker can exploit those expectations when talking.

So, what expectations does *damn* set up? In answering this question, we are apt to think first of negative uses—those that convey agitation, frustration, and the like. These are essential uses of this item, but they tell only part of the story, as we see when we look to naturally occurring cases. The examples in (40)–(41) are drawn from one of the large collections of online product reviews that Constant et al. (2009) use to study a wide variety of expressives. These examples range from the truly negative, as in (40), to the exclamatively positive, as in (41).

(40) a. About time someone took a wrecking ball to the whole damn rotten structure.
 b. Trouble is Steyn doesn't know a damn thing about Americans.

(41) a. I couldn't put the damn thing down.
 b. Chelsea is delightful and so damn funny.
 c. I've read about 3/4th of it ... and I just can't get the damn thing done.

What unifies these uses is *heightened emotion*. Constant et al. (2009) quantify this perspective by studying the distribution of *damn* and other expressives in the corpus from which the above are drawn, which consists of 53,557 reviews by over 40,000 authors, for a total of about 8.1 million words. Each review in the collection is tagged with a star-rating, one through five stars. Authors writing one or five star reviews are in more heightened emotional states than authors writing reviews in the middle of the rating scale. This emotionality is reflected in their language, which is rich in intensive, exclamatives, and the like. Constant et al. (2009) argue, on the basis of this language and our intuitions about what it conveys, that the star-ratings provide a rough but nonetheless useful approximation of the speaker's emotional state: the extreme ratings (one and five stars) correlate with heightened emotion, and the middle ratings (two to four stars) correlate with more measured outlooks.

The distribution of *damn* in this collection is depicted, on a log-odds scale, in figure 17.1. The empirical points are the black dots; for each rating category R, we calculate

(42) $$\ln\left(\frac{\text{count}(damn, R)}{\text{count}(R) - \text{count}(damn, R)}\right)$$

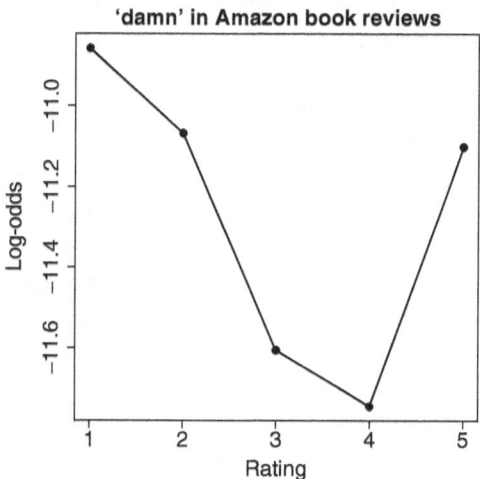

Fig 17.1: The frequency distribution of the taboo intensive *damn* in a large corpus of online product reviews with star ratings attached to them. The empirical points are black. The lines are included to bring out the U shape. The distribution reveals that *damn* is used primarily in the extreme rating categories, where the authors either loved or loathed the product they are writing about.

where ln is the natural logarithm, count(*damn*, R) is the number of occurrences of *damn* in reviews in category R, and count(R) is the total number of words in reviews in category R. This calculation is similar to a basic frequency distribution obtained by calculating count(*damn*, R)/ count(R), but it affords a more powerful and reliable statistical perspective on these distributions.

The distribution is noteworthy for its U shape with respect to the rating categories: *damn* is significantly more frequent at the extreme ends of the rating scale than it is in the middle. Indeed, it is about 66% more likely to appear in a five-star review than in a three-star review. Thus, it is an excellent indicator of an extreme review and, in turn, of heightened emotion. In contrast, by itself, it is a poor signal of the polarity of that emotion: it is just 27% more likely to appear in a one-star review than in a five-star one. This is the same profile that Constant et al. (2009) report for intensives like *absolutely* (Beaver & Clark 2008) and exclamatives like *wow*. Setting the mildly taboo qualities of *damn* aside, we can say that it is, like intensives and exclamatives, a reliable indicator that the speaker is in a heightened emotional state (or at least intends to create such an impression).

The frequency distribution is a rich source of information about what *damn* does to utterances containing it. The subjective/objective corpus of Pang & Lee (2004) is another piece of the puzzle. Pang & Lee classified sentences according to whether they were objective or subjective. The resulting corpus has 5,000 sentences in each of the two categories, and each has around 650,000 words in it. The corpus contains 24 occurrences of *damn*, and 23 of them occur in the subjective corpus. What's more, the single *damn* in the objective corpus is used in the context of objectively describing the subjective mental state of a character in a movie. Thus, we have suggestive evidence that *damn* correlates strongly with subjectivity, and we might even go so far as to say that it can move otherwise objective statements into a subjective realm, an ability that seems in keeping with the perspective dependence of expressives in general (Potts 2007a).

All this corpus evidence paints a rich picture of the contribution of *damn*. The associations between this word and the conceptual categories (the rating scale, the subjective/objective distinction) are representative of our linguistic experiences. As speakers, we have strong expectations that uses of *damn* will correlate with the speaker's being in a heightened emotional state (or wishing to create that impression). In turn, we use it only when we are in such a state (or wish to create that impression). The total effect of these assumptions is that *damn* is a *reliable* signal of emotionality. Knowing its use conditions, in the Kaplanian sense, largely involves being attuned to this information. As a result, whereas an utterance of (43a) might leave you unsure of how the speaker views the situation being described, (43b) creates a window into his underlying emotional state at the time of utterance.

(43) a. Sam bought that bike.
 b. Sam bought that damn bike.

Even (43b) is indeterminate, though. I noted above that *damn* is about as frequent in positive reviews as it is in negative ones. As Constant et al. (2009) observe, this means that we look to the context to understand the polarity of the emotionality it signals. If Sam's new bike is going to ensure that he beats us in every race, then you'll perceive a resigned solidarity in my utterance of (43b). In contrast, if I'm simply eager to try out his fancy new ride, then exuberance will shine through.

The immediate linguistic environment often provides the strongest indicators of what a given expressive utterance means. Looking back at (40)–(41), we see that the predicates surrounding *damn* guide the emotional polarity of *damn* itself. Predicates like *rotten* tend to take us to negative parts of the emotional spectrum; predicates like *funny* tend to take us to positive parts of it. When Constant et al. (2009) restrict attention to tokens of *damn* that immediately precede positive adjectives, the U shape seen in figure 17.1 becomes a pronounced Reverse L, i.e., a dramatic bias for positivity emerges.

Thus, the expressive imbues the at-issue content with new meaning and importance, and the at-issue content clarifies the meaning of the expressive. The two dimensions shape each other.

3.3 Unifying themes

Appositives and expressives are very different in form and content, and this is reflected in the ways in which they contribute to utterance interpretation. However, both often play the role of contextualizing the at-issue content that surrounds them. Appositives resolve underspecification and enhace relevance; expressives color with subjectivity and emotionality.

4 Conclusion

This article builds a case for a theory of meaning in which individual words and phrases denote tuples of independent meanings. Section 2. describes a framework for modeling such meanings and goes on to present evidence that the effects of multidimensionality are felt in discourse (section 2.1.), in semantic composition (section 2.2.), and in morphosyntax (section 2.3.).

Appositives and expressives provide the primary empirical evidence in this article, with various connectives and particles playing supporting roles. Though multidimensionality arguably unities these morphosyntactically disparate items, we should take care not to overstate the unity; many differences emerge, suggesting that we need to study each item on its own terms, with the known diagnostics and generalizations guiding investigation rather pressuring us to pack phenomena into rigid categories.

In section 3, the emphasis shifts from semantic denotations to the role that conventional implicatures and expressives play in pragmatic inference. The case studies are appositives and the taboo intensive *damn*. These investigations highlight a few ways in which secondary dimensions of meaning can play primary roles in shaping the overall message of an utterance.

My thanks to Christopher Davis, Jesse Harris, and Florian Schwarz for their comments on an earlier draft of this paper. Thanks also to Ash Asudeh, David Beaver, Craige Roberts, Aynat Rubinstein, and the participants in LSA.314 at the 2007 Linguistic Institute, Stanford University, for stimulating these ideas.

5 References

Amaral, Patricia, Craige Roberts & E. Allyn Smith 2007. Review of *The logic of conventional implicatures* by Chris Potts. *Linguistics & Philosophy* 30, 707–749.
Aoun, Joseph & Lina Choueiri 2000. Epithets. *Natural Language and Linguistic Theory* 18, 1–39.
Asher, Nicholas 2000. Truth conditional discourse semantics for parentheticals. *Journal of Semantics* 17, 31–50.
Bach, Kent 1994. Conversational implicature. *Mind & Language* 9, 124–162.
Bach, Kent 1999. The myth of conventional implicature. *Linguistics & Philosophy* 22, 367–421.
Barker, Chris & Pauline Jacobson (eds.) 2007. *Direct Compositionality*. Oxford: Oxford University Press.
Barker, Stephen 2003. Truth and conventional implicature. *Mind* 112, 1–33.
Beaver, David 1997. Presupposition. In: J. van Benthem & A. ter Meulen (eds.). *Handbook of Logic and Language*. Cambridge, MA: The MIT Press, 939–1008.
Beaver, David & Brady Zack Clark 2008. *Sense and Sensitivity. How Focus Determines Meaning*. Oxford: Wiley-Blackwell.
Blakemore, Diane 1996. Are apposition markers discourse markers? *Journal of Linguistics* 32, 325–347.
Boër, Steven E. & William G. Lycan 1976. *The Myth of Semantic Presupposition*. Bloomington, IN: Indiana University Linguistics Club.
Büring, Daniel 1999. Topic. In: P. Bosch & R. van der Sandt (eds.). *Focus. Linguistic, Cognitive, and Computational Perspectives*. Cambridge: Cambridge University Press, 142–165.
Büring, Daniel 2005. *Binding Theory*. Cambridge: Cambridge University Press.
Constant, Noah, Christopher Davis, Christopher Potts & Florian Schwarz 2009. The pragmatics of expressive content. Evidence from large corpora. *Sprache und Datenverarbeitung* 33, 5–21.
Corazza, Eros 2005. On epithets qua attributive anaphors. *Journal of Linguistics* 41, 1–32.
Dekker, Paul 2002. *A Proper Architecture for Presupposition and Quantification*. Ms. Amsterdam, University of Amsterdam.
Elbourne, Paul 2005. *Situations and Attitudes*. Cambridge, MA: The MIT Press.
Fiengo, Robert & Robert May 1994. *Indices and Identity*. Cambridge, MA: The MIT Press.
von Fintel, Kai 2004. Would you believe it? The King of France is back! (Presuppositions and truth-value intuitions). In: A. Bezuidenhout & M. Reimer (eds.). *Descriptions and Beyond*. Oxford: Oxford University Press, 315–341.
Frege, Gottlob 1892/1980. Über Sinn und Bedeutung. *Zeitschrift für Philosophie und philosophische Kritik* 100, 25–50. English translation in: P. Geach & M. Black (eds.). *Translations from the Philosophical Writings of Gottlob Frege*. Oxford: Blackwell, 1980, 56–78.
Godfrey, John J. & Ed Holliman 1993. *Switchboard-1 transcripts*. Philadelphia, PA: Linguistic Data Consortium.
Grice, H. Paul 1975. Logic and conversation. In: P. Cole & J. Morgan (eds.). *Syntax and Semantics 3: Speech Acts*. New York: Academic Press, 43–58.
Harris, Jesse A. & Christopher Potts 2009. Predicting perspectival orientation for appositives. In: *Papers from the Regional Meeting of the Chicago Linguistic Society (= CLS)* 45. Chicago, IL: Chicago Linguistic Society.
Hawkins, John A. 1991. On (in)definite articles. Implicatures and (un)grammaticality prediction. *Journal of Linguistics* 27, 405–442.

Heim, Irene 1983. On the projection problem for presuppositions. In: M. Barlow, D. P. Flickinger & M. T. Wescoat (eds.). *Proceedings of the 2nd West Coast Conference on Formal Linguistics*. Stanford, CA: Stanford Linguistics Association, 114–125.

Horn, Laurence R. 1989. *A Natural History of Negation*. Chicago, IL: The University of Chicago Press. Reprinted: Stanford, CA: CSLI Publications, 2001.

Horn, Laurence R. 2002. Assertoric inertia and NPI licensing. In: M. Andronis et al. (eds.). *Papers from the Regional Meeting of the Chicago Linguistic Society (= CLS) 38: The Panels*. Chicago, IL: Chicago Linguistic Society, 55–82.

Horn, Laurence R. 2007. Towards a Fregean pragmatics: Voraussetzung, Nebengedanke, Andeutung. In: I. Kecskes & L. R. Horn (eds.). *Explorations in Pragmatics. Linguistic, Cognitive and Intercultural Aspects*. Berlin: Mouton de Gruyter, 39–69.

Huddleston, Rodney & Geoffrey K. Pullum 2002. *The Cambridge Grammar of the English Language*. Cambridge: Cambridge University Press.

Ifantidou-Trouki, Elly 1993. Sentential adverbs and relevance. *Lingua* 90, 69–90.

Kaplan, David 1999. *What is Meaning? Explorations in the Theory of Meaning as Use. Brief version—draft 1*. Ms. Los Angeles, CA, University of California.

Karttunen, Lauri 1973. Presuppositions and compound sentences. *Linguistic Inquiry* 4, 169–193.

Karttunen, Lauri & Stanley Peters 1979. Conventional implicature. In: C.-K. Oh & D. A. Dinneen (eds.). *Syntax and Semantics 11: Presupposition*. New York: Academic Press, 1–56.

Kuno, Susumo 1987. *Functional Syntax. Anaphora, Discourse, and Empathy*. Chicago, IL: The University of Chicago Press.

Levinson, Stephen C. 2000. *Presumptive Meanings. The Theory of Generalized Conversational Implicature*. Cambridge, MA: The MIT Press.

Marcus, Mitchell P., Beatrice Santorini, Mary A. Marcinkiewicz & Ann Taylor 1999. *Treebank-3*. Philadelphia, PA: Linguistic Data Consortium.

McCarthy, John J. 1982. Prosodic structure and expletive infixation. *Language* 58, 574–590.

Neale, Stephen 1999. Coloring and composition. In: R. Stainton (ed.). *Philosophy and Linguistics*. Boulder, CO: Westview Press, 35–82.

Pang, Bo & Lillian Lee 2004. A sentimental education. Sentiment analysis using subjectivity summarization based on minimum cuts. In: *Proceedings of the 42nd Annual Meeting of the Association for Computational Linguistics (= ACL)*. Barcelona: Association for Computational Linguistics 271–278.

Partee, Barbara H. 1984. Compositionality. In: F. Landman & F. Veltman (eds.). *Varieties of Formal Semantics*. Dordrecht: Foris, 281–311. Reprinted in: Barbara H. Partee. *Compositionality in Formal Semantics*. Oxford: Blackwell, 2004, 153–181.

Potts, Christopher 2005. *The Logic of Conventional Implicatures*. Oxford: Oxford University Press.

Potts, Christopher 2007a. The expressive dimension. *Theoretical Linguistics* 33, 165–197.

Potts, Christopher 2007b. Into the conventional-implicature dimension. *Philosophy Compass* 4, 665–679.

Potts, Christopher, Luis Alonso-Ovalle, Ash Asudeh, Rajesh Bhatt, Seth Cable, Christopher Davis, Yurie Hara, Angelika Kratzer, Eric McCready, Tom Roeper & Martin Walkow 2007. Expressives and identity conditions. *Linguistic Inquiry* 40, 356–366.

Pullum, Geoffrey K. & Kyle Rawlins 2007. Argument or no argument? *Linguistics & Philosophy* 30, 277–287.

Roberts, Craige 1996. Information structure. Towards an integrated formal theory of pragmatics. In: J. H. Yoon & A. Kathol (eds.). *OSU Working Papers in Linguistics, vol. 49: Papers in Semantics*. Columbus, OH: The Ohio State University Department of Linguistics, 91–136.

van Rooy, Robert 2004. Signalling games select Horn strategies. *Linguistics & Philosophy* 27, 493–527.

Ross, John Robert 1973. Slifting. In: M. Gross, M. Halle & M.-P. Schützenberger (eds.). *The Formal Analysis of Natural Languages*. The Hague: Mouton, 133–169.

Schlenker, Philippe 2003. A plea for monsters. *Linguistics & Philosophy* 26, 29–120.

Schwarz, Florian 2009. *Two Types of Definites in Natural Language*. Ph.D. dissertation. University of Massachusetts, Amherst, MA.

Shanon, Benny 1976. On the two kinds of presupposition in natural language. *Foundations of Language* 14, 247–249.

Simons, Mandy 2006. Foundational issues in presupposition. *Philosophy Compass* 1, 357–372.

Wang, Linton, Brian Reese & Eric McCready 2005. The projection problem of nominal appositives. *Snippets* 10, 13–14.

Index

A-bar movement 174, 202, 203
accommodation 15–20, 25–27, 33, 36, 122, 137, 164, 320, 494, 514–520, 524, 568
affixation 75–77, 80, 88, 92, 100, 152, 239
alternative question 15, 19–24, 32, 36
A-movement 174, 197, 201–203
analogy and linguistic templates 116, 117
antipassive 240, 241, 244–248, 260–264, 284
applicative 77, 80, 81, 156, 157, 233, 240, 249, 250, 253–259, 262–269
appositives 139, 598–610, 613–616, 619
argument
– alternation 155, 233, 269–272
– extension 193, 196, 250–257, 264, 280
– hierarchy 233–239, 251, 259, 271, 272
– reduction 241–250, 264
– structure 79–83, 95, 128, 155–157, 233–272, 279, 297, 301, 304–308, 317, 321
assertion 5–9, 12–20, 25, 27, 32–36, 67, 327–331, 337, 345, 387, 504, 512, 542, 545, 603
attitude reports 432–445, 448

Bach's Conversational Impliciture 388–390, 554, 555, 559
Best Response 563, 565, 570–577, 595
bracketing paradox 143, 144, 152

cancelability 350, 494, 498, 534–536
cancelation 313, 343, 346, 348, 494, 498–502, 505–507, 524, 535, 536, 541
case 19–21, 41, 61–66, 94, 98, 127, 182, 201, 202, 237–239, 248, 279–286, 317, 330, 352, 435, 443, 453, 504, 507, 536, 541, 550
– alternations 247, 279, 284
causative 77, 80, 81, 92, 155, 156, 159, 160, 233, 234, 240, 245, 250–267
characters 171, 179, 413–419, 422–434, 438, 440, 443, 447, 452–454, 457, 458
common ground 1, 6, 9–14, 17–20, 25–30, 35, 36, 503, 504, 514, 606
comparative operator 207, 208
complex words vs. syntactic phrases 124–126
compositional(ity) 170, 293–322, 326, 393, 551

compositional/postcompositional divide 326, 327
compounding 75–79, 84, 93, 103–109, 121–123, 134, 136
compounds 76, 83, 103–117, 121–139
compound template 103, 126, 128, 132, 133, 139
concept combination 117–121
constraint 134–138, 239, 266, 267, 279, 287–290, 319, 340–350, 361–363
construction 130, 131, 201, 207, 211, 214, 245, 246, 271, 272, 281, 296–322, 431, 445, 447, 453, 455, 565–570, 581–587, 611
context 17, 19, 56, 112, 225, 309–311, 327, 336–352, 360, 370, 374, 382, 392–397, 403–458, 464, 507–521, 543, 544, 548, 553, 614
– dependence 403, 408, 409, 418, 440, 521
contextualism/minimalism debate 368, 388, 390, 394–397
conventional implicature 12, 19, 297, 301, 308–311, 326, 375, 512, 530, 537, 598–602, 613, 619
conversational implicature 296, 371, 374, 375, 387, 391, 499, 504–506, 529–541, 549, 550, 553–559, 598, 605
– generalized 374, 391, 534–537, 553, 555, 556, 559
Conversational Maxims 531, 532
Cooperative Principle 372, 373, 530–532, 538, 539

dative shift 233, 270
deictic centre 466–470, 477–486
deictic projection 470
deixis 404–407, 458, 463–466, 471–476, 481–486, 489
– participant 464, 472–475, 489
demonstratives 246, 249, 300, 321, 370, 374, 405, 407, 427, 447, 451, 463, 464, 475–489
denial 310, 494, 499, 535, 603
de re / de dicto 196–200, 285, 435–444, 523

derivation 42, 75–101, 147–151, 164, 165, 264–269, 288
determinative compounds 104, 138
diagonals 383, 415, 421–430, 439, 440, 443, 446–449, 456–458, 573, 577
dimensions in discourse 603–605
discourse 111–115, 318, 471, 475, 486–489, 516, 603–615
– deixis 471, 475, 486
Distributed Morphology 98, 143–146, 155, 159, 162–165, 269
– Model 146
dynamic semantics 223–229, 513, 514, 518

echo question 1, 28, 29
echo wh-questions 28
ellipsis 5, 15, 16, 36, 205–210, 605, 611
emotion 64, 616, 617
encapsulation 353
evaluative derivation 87, 88
evidentials 43, 67, 68
exhaustification 329–336, 339–349, 36–363, 548
explicature 384–386, 393, 552, 553
explicit/implicit boundary 384–387
expressives 598, 599, 602, 606–613, 616–619
extension 97, 179, 190–196, 200, 216, 250–258, 279, 280, 382, 409, 415–418, 428–435, 443–445, 452, 458
extensionality 430
Extensional Language 179, 200

frame of reference 468, 469
free choice 358–360, 363, 563, 565, 584–587
functor vs. incorporation 257–259

game construction 565–570, 581–587
game theoretic pragmatics 556–558, 563–565, 591–593
game theory 539, 556, 558, 563–595
gender 41–45, 54, 57–60, 129, 160, 164, 165, 449, 472–474, 481
Generative Grammar 2, 107, 170, 173, 178, 200, 218, 297
Grice 313, 326, 328, 335, 355, 370–376, 379, 391, 499, 504, 529–539, 549–553, 564, 581, 599, 600

head 45, 58, 104–114, 117–124, 127–139, 147–150, 154–159, 162, 174–177, 182, 189, 190, 204–207, 259, 297, 303, 304
Horn's division of pragmatic labor 557, 558, 579
Horn's Q- and R-principles 391, 539–541, 552
Hurford's constraint 340–342, 363

idiom(aticity) 162, 163, 295–300, 305, 321
illocutionary force 171, 295, 297, 301–304, 312
implicature 308–311, 325–364, 383–394, 499, 529–559, 587–591, 598–619
– conversational 296, 371, 374, 375, 387, 391, 499, 504–506, 529–541, 549, 550, 553–559, 598, 605
– embedded 333–350, 361, 529, 549–551, 563, 565, 587–589
– generalized 375, 557, 558
– particularized 375, 535–538, 543, 557, 558
– scalar 51, 325–364, 374, 382, 392, 499, 529, 541, 544–550, 557, 558, 566, 576, 587
– I- 575, 578, 579
– M- 579, 591
impliciture 388–390, 394, 554, 555
indexical 383, 396, 465
individuation hierarchy 47
inferred stereotypic and basic relations 110, 111
inflection 41–68, 77, 78, 85, 89–90, 121
information flow 316
inheritance 62, 302, 307, 321
intension 169, 170, 179, 183, 190–196, 199, 200, 205, 206, 285, 286, 290, 383, 414, 417–424, 427–437, 441–448, 453–458
intensionality 190, 446, 447
intervention effects 353, 356–358
intonation 1, 2, 5–7, 10–23, 26–35, 352, 496
– in declaratives 6–14
– in interrogatives 14–33
Iterated Best Response 565, 574–595

joint attention 463, 475–477, 483, 488

knowledge structures and discourse 111–115

left-headed compounds 128–134, 139
lexical classes/categories 41, 60, 92, 496
lexicalist approach 143, 144, 152
lexical marking 233, 239, 240, 269, 270
lexical semantic classes 92, 98
lexical system of grammar 123
lifted games 581–587
logical form 58, 144, 145, 178, 327, 334, 342–346, 360, 362, 378–387, 391, 393, 552, 556

markedness 41, 42, 45, 53–57, 65, 238, 264, 287, 325
Maxims of Conversation 333, 372–375, 391, 530
measure terms 162, 563
merge 145–148, 153, 176–178, 181, 182, 186, 198
metalinguistic 56, 173, 297, 301, 313–316, 336, 362
– constructions 313, 316
minimalism 145, 177, 205, 229, 390, 394–397
mirror principle 143, 152, 267, 268
modification template 124–128, 139
modifier 118–124, 127–138, 189, 278, 281–284, 608
monotonicity 42, 144, 261, 331, 332, 382
monsters 443, 447–449, 452, 457, 458
morphology 52, 58, 75, 78, 85–88, 94, 97–101, 121, 123, 143–146, 152–165, 169, 205–217, 234, 241, 268, 269, 351–353, 450
morphology/syntax interface 154

Negative Polarity Items 56, 271, 314, 353, 356–358, 448
nominal appositives 613–615
nondetachability 534, 535
number 41–61, 85, 162, 355, 380, 381, 481, 575, 590

object deixis 463, 464, 472, 475, 489
Optimality Theory 243, 261, 288–290, 557, 558, 568, 591

parameterization 440, 452–457
participant oriented 42, 81, 82
passive 81, 94, 159, 201, 234, 239–245, 251, 253, 261–267, 270, 281, 299

passive/antipassive 240–250, 261–264
person 18, 41–61, 131, 137, 161, 187, 191, 202, 220, 272, 404, 405, 409, 438, 439, 448–451, 468–474, 487, 488, 503
Phonetic Form 2, 6, 58, 124, 145, 148–152, 169, 174–177, 184, 205–209, 214, 215, 227, 228, 261, 267
place deixis 471, 475, 481–483
plural 45–61, 85,161, 210, 215–218, 228, 351–353, 437, 473–475
– expressions 47, 50, 54, 162
polyfunctional affix 260–264
polysemy vs. homophony 93–97
post-Gricean pragmatics 370, 371, 383, 384, 387, 395
pragmatic enrichment 326, 328, 377, 381, 383, 386, 388, 397, 598, 600, 613–619
pragmatic presupposition 301, 308–311, 495, 503
pragmatics 326, 368–397, 512, 557, 558, 563–595
pragmatic wastebasket 370–376
presumptive meanings 390–392
presupposition 15–20, 26, 27, 33, 36, 57, 216, 308–311, 319–321, 495–525, 538, 606, 612
– accommodation 15–20, 26, 29, 36, 320, 494, 514–520
– and anaphora 327, 515–517
– failure 19, 494, 503, 520–522, 525
– trigger 57, 319, 335, 494–504, 507–511, 515–525, 609
presuppositions and attitudes 522–524, 607
Principle of Full Interpretation [FI] 183–190, 194, 197, 198, 203, 206–209, 228
productive compounding process 104, 134–138
projection 64, 147, 153–159, 176, 235, 315–318, 470, 497–501, 504–508, 538, 607, 609
PRO-movement 182, 199, 203–205
propositional attitudes 434, 524, 607
prosody 1–5, 317, 321
protolanguage 121–124, 128

Quantifier Raising [QR] 154, 169, 174, 182–190, 197–229
question operator 205–207
questions under discussion 615

radical contextualism 382, 392–394, 397
reflexive 57, 59, 159, 226, 234, 241, 248, 262, 263, 271, 308, 442, 547
relation 43, 62–66, 83, 95, 103–120, 125–139, 197, 205, 234, 248–253, 268, 279–284, 297, 310, 318, 369, 372, 386, 406, 410, 422, 434, 437, 442–450, 454, 531, 539–540, 544–547, 555, 566, 569, 585, 595
relevance 9, 15, 16, 19, 24, 36, 110, 132, 310, 316, 328–331, 334, 371, 385, 387, 390–393, 504, 533, 536, 542, 552–558, 599, 619
Relevance Theory 328, 393, 552, 557
resultative 159, 250, 256, 259, 268, 282
root 75–77, 86, 88, 104, 139, 144, 146, 150, 153–156, 162, 164, 326, 335, 482, 485

salient propositions 9–25, 32, 33, 36, 37
satisfaction 18, 26, 27, 58, 112–115, 151, 494, 507–515, 524
scalar implicature 51, 25–364, 374, 382, 392, 499, 529, 541–550, 557, 558, 566, 576, 587
scales 309, 331–335, 374, 544–548
semantic composition 143–146, 152, 194, 227, 233, 266, 267, 280, 284, 285, 294, 299, 551, 598, 603, 606–609, 612, 619
semantics/pragmatics interface 363, 370, 371, 383, 397, 551, 564
semantic underdetermination 368, 376–381, 389, 390, 394, 397
signaling game 565, 566
speaker's intention 27, 326, 328, 333–335, 371, 372, 384, 385, 389–397, 405, 407, 556, 615
speech act 6, 15–18, 24–32, 36, 37, 43–46, 67, 243, 300, 335, 336, 394–397, 487, 494, 563, 604
speech errors 143, 144, 163–165
Spell-Put / surface structure (SS) 107, 169, 174–178, 183, 184, 187–190, 194–199, 202–214, 218, 220, 223–229

structural and inherent case 62–64, 104, 127, 238
syntax 57–60, 169–225, 298, 315
syntax/semantics interface 41, 57–60, 147, 170, 173–178, 200, 201, 205, 227, 277

tense 41, 43, 61, 68, 121, 149–152, 165, 169, 183, 201, 208, 211–214, 228, 235, 246, 247, 453, 463, 464, 477, 503, 607
theory-of-mind 463, 465, 476
time deixis 471, 483–486
traces 150, 200, 201, 221, 224, 564
transitivity 64, 261–264, 277, 279, 282, 286, 291
transposition 75, 78–81, 89, 91
truth condition 326, 337, 368–370, 379, 383, 384, 389–397, 410, 421, 534, 535
– intuitive 383, 384, 393, 396
two-dimensional semantics 382, 383, 394
type shifting 169, 190, 218, 219, 227, 277–279, 286–288, 291

underspecification 144, 158, 378, 598, 614, 619
unmarked number 53–57
utterance 18, 28, 29, 310, 344, 354, 368–370, 372, 379, 384, 390–395, 403–417, 428–430, 458, 486, 509, 533, 542–546, 553, 618

valency-decreasing operations 240, 241
variable free syntax/semantics 173, 221, 222, 227, 228
vocatives 1, 9–12, 37, 464

what is said and what is implicated 370–376, 388, 389, 532. 535, 554, 587
word order 237, 277, 280, 286–291, 521
– variation 286–290

yes/no-question 15, 16, 18, 20, 35

zero morphemes 158

www.ingramcontent.com/pod-product-compliance
Lightning Source LLC
Chambersburg PA
CBHW031538300426
44111CB00006BA/95